$2495C

# Contemporary Psychology and Effective Behavior

**Fifth Edition**

# Contemporary Psychology and Effective Behavior

**Fifth Edition**

**James C. Coleman**

University of California at Los Angeles

**Alan G. Glaros**

Wayne State University

**Scott, Foresman and Company**
Glenview, Illinois
Dallas, Tex.   Oakland, N.J.   Palo Alto, Cal.
Tucker, Ga.   London, England

**Library of Congress Cataloging in Publication Data**
Coleman, James Covington.
   Contemporary psychology and effective behavior.

   Bibliography: p.
   Includes indexes.
   1. Psychology.   2.   Adjustment (Psychology)   I.   Glaros,
Alan G., 1948–    .   II.   Title.
BF121.C58   1983          158          82-20536
ISBN 0-673-15640-0

# Preface

## TO THE INSTRUCTOR

The preparation of a fifth edition of *Contemporary Psychology and Effective Behavior* is a time for reflection and a time for celebration. The senior author is most encouraged by the continuing acceptance of this text by instructors and students alike. He would like to believe that this acceptance bears testimony to the quality and relevance of *CPEB*. It is also time to welcome a co-author, Alan G. Glaros, who is primarily responsible for the many modifications in the fifth edition.

It seems only a short time since the fourth edition of *CPEB* was published. Yet during these few brief years, the world has undergone major crises and changes. At the same time, we have seen marked advances in science—including psychology—advances which we have tried to incorporate in this new edition. As earlier editions have done, this fifth edition of *Contemporary Psychology and Effective Behavior* continues to focus on self-direction, personal growth, and the challenges of coping and building a fulfilling life in our changing and sometimes troubled world.

Previous editions of *CPEB* have reflected the tenor of their times, and this edition is no different in that regard. In this context, we have attempted to prepare a text that would be helpful and meaningful to the increasingly heterogeneous mix of students enrolled in our colleges and universities of the 1980s. As we see it, the "traditional" college student is changing. The idealism of the sixties remains, but it has been tempered by an increased understanding of the difficulties and costs of rapid social and economic change. The self-centered concerns of the seventies are also present, but they are softened by an increased appreciation of friendships, family life, and other interpersonal concerns. This edition addresses those concerns and changes.

Additionally, we see an increased number of part-time and older students entering our institutions of higher learning. This "new" student may be an individual who, having worked for a few years, decides to return to school for further study. Or, pressing economic issues may cause this "new" student to attend school part-time or take night classes. Or, the "new" student may be a person of middle age or older—often a woman who, having raised a family, now wishes to resume her formal education, perhaps in preparation for a particular occupation. This edition also addresses the needs and concerns of these students.

Our goals for this text have been several. First, we wanted to maintain the personal tone of the text. We hope that our readers will feel as though we are addressing them directly. At the same time, we have also had the goal of maintaining (and when possible, improving) the scholarship of the text. This edition contains more than 500 references, a substantial proportion of which are new to this edition or which reflect the most recent scholarship. As before, our selection of topics reflects our concerns that issues be presented in a fair, balanced, and eclectic manner.

Our third goal has been to improve the pedagogy of the text. Important terms are clearly marked in boldface and are defined in the margins. The use of a marginal glossary should facilitate students' understanding of technical terms and improve their performance on examinations. We have also streamlined the presentation of many topics and more clearly specified important concepts. Instructors should, as a result, find it easier to prepare examinations from this edition.

Finally, we wanted to increase the practicality, helpfulness, and meaningfulness of the text. A new feature—Psychology in Action—presents interesting case studies, activities, or information in an attempt to involve students in the text. Readers will find, for example, specific instructions for relaxation exercises, a scale to measure college life-stress, and a case study on prejudice.

The organization of the text has also been changed somewhat. In Part 1, we identify the major problems of adjustment and emphasize the contributions that psychoanalytic, social-learning, and humanistic-existential perspectives make to understanding the problems of human adjustment. We also stress the concept of adjustment as an active process in which each of us is influenced by and in turn influences our selves, our experiences, and our environments.

Part 2 focuses on the personal aspects of adjustment. Included here are discussions of personality development, motivation, and emotions. We have also added a new chapter on adjustment in the life span, stressing the continuing nature of the challenges to developing identity, intimacy, generativity, and ego integrity as well as the changes and opportunities for personal growth that occur throughout life.

Part 3 focuses on stress, its effects and its management. Chapter 10 on maladaptive behavior has been reorganized to include the concept of an adaptive-maladaptive continuum, new material on life-style problems, and DSM-III terminology. The chapter on psychotherapy and counseling (Chapter 11) contains new material on the therapeutic process and setting and more clearly relates the three perspectives introduced earlier in the book to the counseling process.

Part 4 concerns interpersonal and social aspects of adjustment. Covered in this section are issues in interpersonal relationships, marriage (and its alternatives), work and leisure, and group and individual processes. A new chapter on human sexuality (Chapter 13) integrates biological material with the psychological aspects of sexuality. Receiving increased emphasis or appearing for the first time are discussions of love, work, leisure, and issues in social facilitation, conformity, obedience, helping, crowding, and prejudice. The closing Epilogue emphasizes the importance of values to human life and adjustment.

The text is adaptable to both semester and quarter systems. Since most of the chapters are relatively self-contained, instructors can assign chapters to fit their needs. Also available are an Instructor's Manual and Student Study Guide, prepared by Professor Kenneth L. Thompson. We also wish to alert instructors to the materials on effective study techniques, contained in student preface.

We wish to thank the many distinguished writers and scientists who gave permission to quote from their works. We are also indebted to Elaine Thomas, Ann Edwards, Walt Tarrow, and Paula Canfield for their assistance. Our thanks also go to our reviewers: William J. Gnagey, Illinois State University; Nancy Dixon, Tennessee Technological University; Dale D. Simmons, Oregon State University; Kenneth L. Thompson, Central Missouri State University; Louis J. King, California State Polytechnic University, Pomona; and Renee L. Harrangue, Loyola Marymount University, Los Angeles. Their comments have been most helpful, providing both needed guidance and welcomed encouragement.

Our special thanks go to Betty Slack of Scott, Foresman whose thorough and painstaking editorial assistance and sense of humor helped in innumerable ways. We would also like to express our appreciation to Katie Steele, psychology editor at Scott, Foresman, for her many valuable contributions to this project. Finally, the senior author wishes to thank his wife Azalea for her unfailing assistance and understanding; and co-author Alan Glaros extends a special thank-you to his spouse, Eileen L. Spony, whose gentle encouragement, patience, and understanding were much appreciated during the often hectic months of preparation of this edition. Special thanks also to Joe Fitzgerald for his assistance with the preparation of chapter 4.

At the close of his journeys, Tennyson's Ulysses says, "I am a part of all that I have met." It is our hope that those who read this book will feel a part of the people and ideas they encounter and that they will experience the joy, challenge, and pleasure in reading this book that we have had in preparing it.

James C. Coleman

Alan G. Glaros

# To the Student

This book has been written with you in mind. It is a book about the psychology of adjustment—the personal meanings of psychology. In it you will find information relating the findings of psychology and other disciplines to your life.

Several objectives have guided our preparation of the fifth edition of *Contemporary Psychology and Effective Behavior*. First, we wanted this book to be scholarly and up-to-date but not dry. We also wanted this text to be helpful without being a rigid and inflexible "how-to" book. We have attempted to make explicit the idea that adjustment is an active process that extends throughout the life span. For us, adjustment is not simply a matter of adapting to one's environment once and for all, but a continuing endeavor through which we shape our lives and our selves. Finally, we have tried to make you feel as though we are addressing you directly and personally. And it is our hope you will use material from this book to increase the understanding and satisfaction you get from life.

## EFFECTIVE STUDY TECHNIQUES

" . . . *Much study is a weariness of the flesh.*"
*ECCLESIASTES XII, 12*

Effective study is an active process. It does not mean passively reading some material; it does not mean cramming for exams; and it does not mean endless hours spent in a frustrated search for understanding. Rather, effective study involves actively "digging in" and mastering course material; it involves steady progress; it involves more efficient use of your study time and, possibly, a reduction in the time you devote to study. In short, effective study can reduce the "weariness of the flesh" and replace it with an exhilarating sense of competence, pleasure, and mastery.

## Where to Study

Choosing appropriate study areas is the first step in an effective study program. Ideally, a study area should be free from distractions, well lit, and quiet.

Eliminating distractions is both a subtle and an obvious process. Some of the obvious distractors include telephone calls, friends or family stopping to chat, and so forth. The subtle distractors are often more numerous, but they can just as easily interrupt a study session. These subtle distractors can be a newspaper or magazine within easy reach, hobby materials such as records, photographs, and piles of unfinished projects in the study area. Even a textbook from another course can be a distractor. As you study for a particular course, the sight of another textbook reminds you how far behind you are in another course, and you begin to worry and daydream and become distracted. Once you become attuned to these distractions, you can eliminate them and improve your study skills.

Seeking a quiet and well-lit study area is equally important. A radio blaring in the background, a stereo playing next door, and the sounds of an interesting conversation are but a few of the factors that can disturb a study area.

Many students erroneously believe that a radio playing softly in the background improves their study skills. Unfortunately, this belief is *not* supported by scientific data. If anything, the use of a radio *increases* the time spent in a study session because of the distracting, noise-producing characteristics of the radio.

Finally, a study area should be used only for studying, not for any other activity. This implies that you should not study while lying in bed. If you choose a desk to be your study area, you should only study while at the desk. Socializing should be conducted elsewhere. Talking on the telephone or listening to the stereo should be performed away from the desk. And when you find yourself daydreaming, you should get up and move away from the desk. In short, establishing a specific study area ensures that you will be mentally attuned to study when you sit in your study area.

## When to Study

Two principles govern suggestions for deciding when to study. The first principle is that, for learning textual material, *continuous practice is better than massed practice.* We retain more information when we attempt to learn it in small, manageable packets than when we attempt to learn a great deal of material all at once. This implies that all-night study sessions just prior to an exam are less effective (and more exhausting!) than continuous, regular study sessions.

The second principle is an old one, repeatedly confirmed by research—*practice improves retention.* Reviewing course material on a regular basis facilitates the learning process. Adhering to a regularly scheduled study program has major benefits for remembering and retaining course material.

## How to Study: The SQ3R Approach

The SQ3R method was devised to increase your involvement with text material. Although the SQ3R system appears to be somewhat involved and complex, it can significantly increase your comprehension and understanding of the material.

The SQ3R method has five parts: Survey, Question, Read, Recite, and Review. Let us examine how to use each of these steps to help you increase your study efficiency.

**Survey.**   Briefly survey the chapter; look at the chapter title, section headings, and so forth. Your aim here is not to go into detail but to develop a general idea of the structure and focus of the chapter.

The text is designed to help you with this step. You will notice that a chapter outline is placed at the beginning of each chapter. Look over this outline as you survey the chapter. Also, examine the chapter summary to get some idea of the material presented in the chapter. Remember, your goal in this part of your study is to become acquainted with the material to come.

**Question.** As you survey the chapter, write down several questions about the material you are about to learn. These questions should be relatively detailed and should cover the chapter. Portions of the outline may be written as questions.

The purpose of asking questions is to increase your involvement with the material and to give some purpose to your studying. By formulating questions, you are not simply reading the material, but you are trying to find answers to important issues. Also, you will focus on the more important material without becoming overwhelmed by details.

The text can help you formulate questions. The major and minor headings of the chapter are printed in color and are excellent sources for generating questions. Additionally, key terms are printed in **boldface type,** and definitions for these terms can be found in the page margins.

**Read.** Now that you have formulated some questions, read the material in order to answer the questions. Write down the answers to the questions you have posed. It is important to read actively and with involvement, for this increases your understanding of the material. If you become tired or distracted, stop reading until you can devote your entire energies and attention to reading. Remember, your job here is not just to cover a number of pages but to "dig in" while you read.

**Recite.** Recitation is the part of the SQ3R method that most people find difficult (or embarrassing) to carry out. Look at your questions and try to answer your questions *aloud.* Listen to your responses. Are they complete? Are they correct? If not, reread the appropriate section and try again to answer your question. This form of rehearsal increases the likelihood that you will retain the material.

If you find it difficult to carry out this portion of the SQ3R method by yourself, enlist the cooperation of other members of your class. Form a small group and meet on a regular basis. Ask questions of each other, and answer these questions. Prepare short lectures on the material. (Be sure to stay on target and not let extraneous material enter into your study sessions.) If you make a mistake, briefly review the material and state aloud your corrected answer.

**Review.** On a regular basis, look over your notes. Answer the questions you have posed to yourself. Try to summarize the major points in the chapter. By making this rehearsal an active and a regular process, you again increase your chances of retaining the material.

In closing, we hope that you will benefit from our suggestions on improving your study skills. And we also hope that reading this book will be as exciting, challenging, stimulating, and rewarding for you as preparing this new edition has been for us.

# Overview

# Contents

# Contemporary
# Psychology
# and
# Effective Behavior
## Fifth Edition

*"I am a human being, whatever that may be. I speak for all of us who move and think and feel and whom time consumes. I speak as an individual unique in a universe beyond my understanding, and I speak for all people. I am hemmed in by limitations of sense and mind and body, of place and time and circumstances, some of which I know but most of which I do not. I am like a person journeying through a forest, aware of occasional glints of light overhead with recollections of the long trail I have already traveled, and conscious of wider spaces ahead. I want to see more clearly where I have been and where I am going, and above all I want to know why I am where I am and why I am traveling at all."*

*(BERRILL, 1955)*

# Part One

# The Individual in Today's World

The Human Dilemma

The Quest for Answers

# Chapter 1

# The Human Dilemma

*"It was the best of times, it was the worst of times, it was the age of wisdom, it was the age of foolishness, it was the epoch of belief, it was the epoch of incredulity, it was the season of Light, it was the season of Darkness, it was the spring of hope, it was the winter of despair, we had everything before us, we had nothing before us . . . in short, the period was . . . like the present period . . ."*
*A TALE OF TWO CITIES (DICKENS, 1859)*

The human dilemma of progress and hope vs. anxiety and despair has existed throughout history. It characterized the period of the French Revolution so vividly portrayed in the opening lines of *A Tale of Two Cities;* it characterized the civilizations of Greece and Rome; and it characterizes the world today.

The accelerating advances of modern science and technology have led to unprecedented social progress and to unprecedented social problems. On the one hand, we can point to an increasing mastery of the secrets of nature, to the conquest of disease, and to spectacular cultural advances. On the other, we can point to the dangers of ecological violations and the problems of toxic waste, to grinding poverty existing side-by-side with affluence, and to the specter of thermonuclear war. These problems must be solved if the human race is to survive and progress. And the solutions appear to depend less upon increased technological know-how and more upon a better understanding of ourselves and our social systems.

## PROGRESS AND ANXIETY

Despite the high cost of food, fuel, and housing and other "inconveniences," we live in an affluent society. The average person in the United States is better fed, housed, clothed, and educated than anyone else in history. Myriad slaves—powered by electricity instead of human labor—remove much of the drudgery from everyday living, giving us more time for creative pursuits. We can enjoy the finest literature, music, and art. We can experience the stimulating rewards of travel. We can participate in sports and other leisure-time activities once available only to the very rich. Through motion pictures, television, cable networks, and other video systems, we are entertained by spectacles that would have taxed the imagination of ancient kings. Modern achievements in medicine have made us among the healthiest people of all time and have greatly increased our life expectancy. Most of us have many options and opportunities for educational and creative pursuits and freedom for self-development. We live in an exciting age of scientific wonders where humans have walked on the moon, and we are on the threshold of still greater wonders in the fields of electronics and computers. In fact, most people have never before possessed such opportunities for enjoying life to its fullest. Indeed, it might seem that we have entered upon a Golden Age.

Yet it is apparent that all is not going exactly as we might hope and expect. Certain problems endure and new ones arise. Paradoxically, the same scientific and technological advances that have made this a Golden Age have created many

# Insight

## THE PARADOXES OF OUR TIME

*The paradox of technology*—While modern technology has enabled us to land people on the moon and return them safely to earth, it has not enabled us to solve many critical problems on earth, some of which have been caused or aggravated by technology itself.

*The paradox of communication*—Via communication satellites and mass media, we have developed highly advanced communication facilities and techniques; yet "communication gaps" prevent or distort our understanding of each others' ideas and motives.

*The paradox of affluence*—The United States is the most affluent nation in the world and in history; yet we have more than 25 million people living below the government-set poverty line, are curtailing school programs and urban renewal programs for lack of funds, and are adding each year to an already mammoth national debt.

*The paradox of equality*—In a society based on the principle of freedom, equality, and justice for all, we find widespread group prejudice and discrimination with limited opportunities and unequal justice for the poor and the "different."

*The paradox of defense*—The security our costly military defense system should provide is offset by the spiraling arms race, the proliferation of nuclear weapons, and the increase in the number of "superpowers."

*The paradox of values*—In a society founded on principles which have brought unprecedented well-being and opportunity to a majority of its citizens, we find a sizable number of youth and adults feeling alienated and dehumanized and rejecting an achievement orientation.

problems which also make this an Age of Anxiety. We have squandered the earth's resources, polluted our air and water, and caused the extinction of thousands of plant and animal species. National and international tensions proliferate, while new weapons for mastery and destruction are being placed in uncertain hands. The world birthrate has slowed but continues to strain our abilities to grow and distribute food and other resources. Illiteracy, poverty, and disease remain widespread problems.

The impact of the scientific age upon our hopes and fears for the future has been forcefully described by psychologist Hadley Cantril (1958).

*As more and more people throughout the world become more and more enmeshed in a scientific age, its psychological consequences on their thought and behavior become increasingly complicated. The impact comes in a variety of ways: people begin to feel the potentialities for a more abundant life that modern technology can provide; they become aware of the inadequacies of many present political, social, and religious institutions and practices; they discern the threat which existing power and status relationships may hold to their own development; they vaguely sense the inadequacy of many of the beliefs and codes accepted by their forefathers and perhaps by themselves at an earlier age.*

*The upshot is that more and more people are acquiring both a hope for a "better life" and a feeling of frustration and anxiety that they themselves may not experience the potentially better life they feel should be available to them. They search for new anchorages, for new guidelines, for plans of action which hold a promise of making some of the dreams come true. (pp. vii–viii)*

This description, written more than two decades ago, seems even more applicable today.

In an attempt to ascertain what the world will be like in the last quarter of the twentieth century, the National Education Association sought the views of fifty distinguished leaders and world citizens. In summarizing their findings, Shane (1976) reported that: "Without exception, the respondents recognized that not only the U.S. but the world as a whole is passing through the greatest tidal wave of transition in history" (p. 253).

Wherever we look, we see the world changing with incredible rapidity—and established customs, traditions, and values are changing with it. There are few places in the world today where children follow, as a matter of course, the lifestyles of their parents. Indeed, one of today's major problems is the continuing adjustment individuals and groups must make to rapid social and technological change. Whether we like it or not, we are members of a society that has become interdependent with other societies of the world. This means learning to understand and deal with over four billion people, most of whom have different languages, different beliefs, and different customs from ours. We have difficulty enough understanding ourselves and those closest to us, and our problems are only magnified when we attempt to understand other cultures and societies. Often, our misunderstandings about other people lead to conflict, and our conflicts can range from puzzlement or dislike on the personal level to the propaganda battles of the cold war and armed conflict on the global level. The possibility of worldwide destruction through biological, chemical, and thermonuclear war only aggravates our anxieties about ourselves and our futures.

Thus, global unrest, conflict, and change form the background against which we function as we try to find our way in an increasingly complex, bureaucratic, and impersonal mass society. The stress this causes is indicated by the incredible amounts of tranquilizing drugs, the tons of sleeping pills, and the billions of dollars worth of alcoholic beverages Americans consume each year. It is indicated by the difficulties that people have in establishing and maintaining satisfactory long-term relationships with others, by the marked increase in suicide among our youth, and by the alarming increase in crimes of violence.

In pointing to the problems of our "Golden Age of Anxiety" we are not advocating a return to the "good old days." We have come far toward realizing the dream of a great and creative society, and few would care to exchange the benefits of modern civilization for the allegedly greater stability of an earlier age. In any case, we have set out upon a path of change and there is no road back. We recognize both the necessity and the utility of change. Our hope lies not in reversing change or in trying to hold the line but in guiding change and developing new values and modes of adaptation which are appropriate to the problems and challenges of our contemporary world. In this process we must constantly guard against the danger of discarding the essential for that which is new but trivial or unsound. For change in and of itself is no guarantee of progress.

Traditional patterns of sex-typed activities are one area of modern life in which changes are occurring. Today many men share in child care responsibilities and perform household chores, tasks once considered "women's work."

As Haskins (1968) has pointed out, we must be continually aware of the danger that "in embracing new and experimental courses on myriad fronts of movement with the ardor that we must, we do not at the same time discard long-tested values and long-tried adaptive courses which, if they are lost, will only have, one day, to be rewon—and probably at enormous cost."

## THE PROBLEM OF SELF-DIRECTION

*"From now on, everything in our environment, in our physical makeup and behavior, and in our future development is subject to human meddling, interference, and 'control.' But we lack the appropriate guiding ethic and institutions for making the momentous choices which face us."*
*(HARMAN, 1977, P. 8)*

A unique problem which greatly intensifies the human dilemma is that of **self-direction.** Like other species, we have been forced thoughout our history to pit our abilities against the world in the struggle to survive. All living things strive to maintain themselves, to resist destruction, and to grow and function in accordance with their inner natures. The process by which an organism (1) attempts to meet the demands placed upon it by its own nature and by the environment and (2) attempts to structure its environment and experience to enhance survival,

**self-direction:** using intellectual powers, rather than instinct, to devise effective methods of adjustment

**adjustment: the outcome of our efforts to meet personal and environmental demands and to structure our environment and experience**

**adaptive behavior: effective adjustive behavior**

**maladaptive behavior: ineffective adjustive behavior**

understanding, and growth is called **adjustment.** Our definition of adjustment thus has two aspects: one aspect is *reactive*—we respond and adapt to events in the world; the second aspect describes a *proactive* process—the actions that we take to alter and modify our personal, social, and physical environments to help ensure growth and the fulfillment of potentials. Adjustment is therefore an *interactive* process in which we influence our lives, experiences, and environments and are, in turn, influenced by these factors.

Adjustive behavior may or may not be effective, depending on how well it meets proactive and reactive demands and satisfies the needs of the organism. When it is effective, the behavior is considered **adaptive.** When it is ineffective, it is considered **maladaptive.** Effective or ineffective, adaptive or maladaptive,

Like this athlete, whose wheelchair didn't stop him from competing in the New York City Marathon, well-adjusted individuals not only learn to meet the demands placed upon them but strive to reach the goals they set for themselves.

adjustment goes on continuously, whether it means adjusting to a change in economic status or a change in temperature, actively improving study habits, or developing a sense of humor.

In the universal struggle for survival, many different adjustive patterns have emerged in the animal world. Some species manage to survive by sheer number of offspring. Others rely heavily upon defensive armaments such as poisons, camouflage, or speed. Though widely different, these various patterns have one thing in common: they rely largely upon "built-in" adjustive know-how. While most animals are capable of some learning, much of their behavior is determined primarily by adjustive patterns that are instinctive. We might say that most animals come factory-equipped with adjustive know-how. As Branden (1965) has put it: "Given the appropriate conditions, the appropriate physical environment, all living organisms—with one exception—are set by their nature to originate automatically the actions required to sustain their survival. The exception is man" (p. 2).

Human beings have few, if any, instinctive behavior patterns beyond the level of the simplest reflex. We are, however, endowed with superior mental abilities. We must rely on our ability to learn and reason in working out the most satisfactory mode of adjustment and in continually modifying our behavior to meet the demands of new situations. These superior mental gifts—and the superior adaptability that goes with them—have helped us go far toward controlling our physical environment. We can hope that our intelligence will enable us to achieve a brighter future for all people.

Ironically enough, the dinosaur—considered to be much less intelligent than we are—endured for more than 150 million years, while the human race appears to be in danger of extinction after only some 2 million years on Earth. But unlike the dinosaur, our capacity for self-direction gives us a choice—and herein lies the source of our greatest strength and our greatest weakness. Unlike the other animals, we can choose our course in life and history. In theory, our options are unlimited. But, will we make the right choices? As the futurist Hubbard (1981) put it: "We can create new worlds . . . or self-destruct" (p. 31). Thus, self-direction can be a source of anxiety and despair as well as one of hope and challenge.

## The Problem of "Know-How"

Our unique problem of self-direction brings with it the responsibility for acquiring suitable amounts of information about ourselves and our environment. In trying to learn about ourselves, however, we have encountered some basic problems. As Overstreet and Overstreet (1956) have pointed out: "We have been as confused about ourselves, often—as uncertain about what our human nature is and what it requires of us—as an acorn would be if it were not sure whether its proper destiny was to be an oak or a cabbage" (p. 240). But if we are to direct our behavior in appropriate ways, we must clear up this confusion and gain an accurate view of what and who we are—as human beings and as individuals.

Each of us must also learn about the world in which we live. We must learn about the ways in which our environment influences our behavior, its potentials for meeting our needs, its pitfalls and dangers, and the skills we will need for coping. And as socialized human beings, we will need comparable information about the groups to which we belong and how we can contribute to their well-being and progress.

The ways in which we view ourselves and the world, whether accurate or inaccurate, are key determinants of our behavior. The goals we strive for and the methods we select for trying to achieve them are heavily influenced by what we conceive ourselves to be, by what we think we can become, and by the ways we picture the opportunities and limitations of the world around us. Thus the problem of self-direction places a heavy demand upon us to acquire information about ourselves and our world as a basis for effective coping behavior. And with accelerating technological and social change, acquiring the "know-how" for living becomes an increasingly difficult and time-consuming task.

## The Problem of "Know-Why"

*"Thus we envision the possibility of an evolutionary leap to a transindustrial society that not only has know-how, but also has a deep inner knowledge of what is worth doing."*
*(HARMAN, 1976, P. 112)*

Coping with personal and social problems and achieving a good future for humanity is not simply a matter of acquiring information. We must also solve the problem of "know-why." We must find a comprehensive value system to guide our choices and adjustive behavior. From among the many goals and ways of living available to us, we must identify and choose those we think will best meet our needs and assure our greatest well-being and progress. Thus we are engaged in a continual process of evaluating good and bad, desirable and undesirable. While information is concerned with what *is* or what *could be,* values are concerned with what *ought* to be.

The problem of values also involves a consideration of *meaning*—of what human existence is all about. This concern with meaning, so basic to thought and action, is probably unique to our species. We are concerned with our proper roles in life and with the meaning of our existence. We are also concerned with our finite existence here on earth, an awareness which adds a crucial note of urgency to the human situation. As psychoanalyst Erich Fromm (1955) has pointed out: "Man is the only animal who finds his own existence a problem which he has to solve and from which he cannot escape" (pp. 23–24).

Widespread feelings of disillusionment, apathy, and alienation offer eloquent testimony to the need for know-why and the difficulty of finding it. Often people are repulsed by what they perceive to be the superficiality, hypocrisy, and gross materialism which seem to permeate our way of life. Yet alternative values are not always easy to find or agree upon—particularly when we consider the bewildering array of conflicting and changing values offered by contemporary society.

Surprisingly, it is only recently that we have come to realize that our social structures are of our own making and are therefore subject to change. As McCall and Simmons (1966) have pointed out: "Most people, throughout most of history, have reflected the cultures they grew up in in the important sense that they have taken the culturally defined patterns and meanings of life for granted, even though they may have balked and quibbled about specifics" (p. 254). However, the systematic study of different cultures, carried out mainly in the last hundred years, has made us aware of how many different answers human beings have worked out to the problems of existence. Today we are much more critical of our existing value patterns and social structures and also much more aware of the possibilities for planned change.

Deciding among these possibilities, however, requires value judgments, and the soundness of these judgments is crucial to our well-being. If we choose values which are not in keeping with either the needs of our own nature or the realities of the world, they will work against us. Although we are free to act against the requirements of our nature and our world, we are not free to escape the consequences.

## THREE KEY QUESTIONS

We have spoken of the problem of self-direction, our need to solve the uniquely human problems of acquiring both "know-how" and "know-why." For the individual, this means trying to find the answers to three key questions: *Who am I? Where am I going? How do I get there?* These questions deal with one's self-concept, one's life plans and value patterns, and the skills necessary to achieve one's needs and goals—in essence, with the self-knowledge, goals and value judgments, and competencies involved in self-direction.

The meaningfulness of these questions varies, of course, depending upon a person's opportunities. In many parts of the world, freedom for self-direction is severely curtailed by a struggle for physical survival or by authoritarian forms of social organization. Even in affluent societies, personal limitations or stressful socioeconomic circumstances may shift the emphasis from these questions to simply "How can I cope?" Nevertheless, most people in our society have unprecedented opportunities for shaping their own lives.

### Who Am I?

By delineating the characteristics common to all men and women, we can understand much about ourselves, for we are all members of the human species. We can fill in more details by studying the patterns and values of the culture and family setting in which we have grown up. And, we can get some general in-

The traditions and values we receive from our families are important components of our self-identity, as is our cultural heritage. Formal education and study of the experiences of others may also help us know and understand ourselves.

sights into others by learning about the details of their past and their experience. But each individual is unique and therefore has the problem of getting to know and understand himself or herself.

Adequate self-knowledge can prove very beneficial. Knowledge about bodily functioning and the maintenance of health can lead us to follow life-styles that prevent bodily damage and ensure greater energy and vigor. Knowledge of psychological makeup can help us to understand the irrational forces in our personality, to gain an accurate appreciation of our own capabilities and aptitudes, and to plan appropriate courses of action and make good decisions. Ironically, our educational system may impede our quest for self-knowledge by having us study almost everything else before we get around to studying ourselves.

With an adequate sense of self-knowledge and self-identity, we can learn to understand ourselves and use our resources to make our lives productive and satisfying. On the other hand, a blurred sense of self-identity may make it difficult for us to plan and decide effectively. Our lack of knowledge and its effects on our behavior may bewilder us. Rebecca McCann (1932/1960) makes the latter point in a little poem called "Inconsistency":

*I'm sure I have a noble mind*
*And honesty and tact*
*And no one's more surprised than I*
*To see the way I act!*

The need for a clear-cut and realistic sense of who we are has become particularly crucial in modern society. We may feel we are puppets in the hands of a vast, impersonal bureaucracy. As a result, we may lose faith in our identity or in our ability to find a place for ourselves.

## Where Am I Going?

As we acquire knowledge about ourselves and our world, we are in a better position to delineate our goals. The question "Where am I going?" centers around our *life plans*—our **goals.** Goals focus our energy and effort, help to determine what competencies we need to develop, and provide a basis for deciding between alternative courses of action.

**goal: object or condition for which an individual strives**

The choice of long-range goals is particularly important to the individual since they dictate appropriate subgoals as well. It is the long-range goals that give coherence and continuity to one's life. Some goals, of course, are more appropriate than others in relation to the individual's personal resources and opportunities, and some goals are superior to others in the satisfactions which they afford. Pursuit of unrealistically high goals leads to failure and frustration. Pursuit of goals that are too low leads to wasted opportunities and lost satisfactions. Pursuit of "false" goals leads to disillusionment and discouragement.

The inability to formulate meaningful life plans also leads to serious difficulties. Here one is reminded of the poignant lines of Biff in Arthur Miller's *Death of a Salesman:* "I just can't take hold, Mom. I can't take hold of some kind of a life." Many individuals appear to drift along with little or no sense of direction and usually experience a sense of dissatisfaction, aimlessness, and being lost.

Whether or not we find adequate answers, most of us are searching—sometimes desperately—for information and values that will provide purpose and meaning in our lives. We do not easily accept the doctrine of despair so dramatically portrayed in the lines of Shakespeare that life "is a tale/Told by an idiot, full of sound and fury,/Signifying nothing."

Developing a life plan also involves a series of choices and decisions, many of which involve values: "Why this life plan rather than another?" "What kind of life is good or bad for human beings in general and for me as an individual?" "What makes this goal good and that one bad?" From among the options we see open to us, we make choices in terms of what we consider most desirable and most likely to be satisfying to us. Hadley Cantril has compared values to a "compass" which shows us the direction—how we should act and why. Whether or not we have thought through our values or are even clearly aware of them, our life plans reflect our value patterns. Even if we forfeit the chance to plan for ourselves and instead "take life as it comes," we are making a choice and in this sense living out a value decision.

Finding adequate values is not an easy task in a rapidly changing world. Old values daily give way to new ones and value conflicts seem to be the order of the day. And the values that prove satisfying and fulfilling to one person may not appeal to another.

# Insight

Sometimes the most troubling questions can be the most basic. This is especially true of the seemingly simple question "Why?" In the brief quote that follows, Charles Burke and Robert Cummins (1970) describe the many problems we encounter in trying to answer this question and the problems we find if we try to avoid it.

*Each of us is faced with the fact that we are here, alive in the twentieth century. We had no choice in the matter of our coming and we are not sure about exercising our right to end it all. Nor are we sure just why we are here or where we are going. Some of us have come to fear life as much as we do death because of our uncertainty with regard to both.*

*We are amazed at our own powers as human beings, our creativity, our insight, and our adaptability. Yet we are shocked by our history of inhumanity—our cruelty, greed, and prejudice. The struggle between good and evil goes on in each of us and is a constant source of confusion for every human being.*

*How often we wish we had some simple answer to the meaning of life. If only we could find a definite pattern to follow. In our frustration we strike out at the world around us and often hurt the ones we most love. In fear we attempt to run from our responsibilities and suffer the uneasiness of one who seeks to cut himself off from life without paying the price of death itself.*

*The question of why each of us exists is indeed a troubling one, but we cannot afford to avoid it and still presume to live a full life. (p. 1)*

## How Do I Get There?

**competence: having adequate skills in a given area**

The third question involves skills and **competencies**—the means by which we hope to answer the first two questions. Although the specific skills required will vary with the circumstances, certain general competencies appear basic for reaching one's goals.

1. *Physical competencies:* the practice of good physical health measures and the use of medical resources to keep one's body functioning efficiently.

2. *Intellectual competencies:* the acquisition of essential information about one's self and one's world and the achievement of efficiency in learning, problem solving, and decision making.

3. *Emotional competencies:* the ability to love and be loved and to deal with fears, anxieties, anger, and other problem emotions that we all experience.

4. *Social competencies:* the ability to deal effectively with other people and to build satisfying interpersonal relationships.

Failing to develop these competencies can prevent us from "getting where we want to go," even when our goals are potentially within our reach. Fortunately, our understanding and knowledge of human emotions and behavior have advanced to the point where we can suggest solutions to everyday problems.

Concerned about their physical well-being, many people exercise regularly to maintain health and vigor. An understanding of psychological functioning is also important for effective adjustment in today's world.

Besides such general competencies, we also need to equip ourselves to meet specific hazards and responsibilities that we can anticipate along the way. Although we cannot foresee all the problems we will have to face during our lifetime, there are certain adjustments—such as obtaining an education, preparing for rewarding life work, building a fulfilling marriage, bringing up children, finding a personalized philosophy of life, and growing old gracefully—which most of us will want to make. We can increase the probability of success if we know what difficulties may be involved and what information and competencies we will need in dealing with them.

## THE ORIENTATION OF THIS BOOK

It is apparent that psychology and allied sciences have helped us to understand many facets of human nature and human behavior, but the answers they can give to the crucial questions "Who?" "Where?" and "How?" are far from complete. We still have to deal with the increasing stresses of everyday life.

## The High Cost of "Muddling Through"

Most people would consider it sheer folly to attempt to climb a high mountain peak without studying the possible routes, obtaining a clear understanding of the hazards, and procuring the necessary equipment. Yet many of these same people expect inadequate information, competencies, and values to carry them successfully through the journey of life—a far more difficult undertaking than the conquest of a mountain peak.

For many of us, living is a matter of muddling through. Instead of using the information and resources which human history and modern science have put at our disposal, we go through life making many costly and needless mistakes and wasting much of our potential for self-fulfillment. Literally millions of people in our society guide their lives by blind custom, superstition, and "common-sense" notions which science has proven to be false. They prepare for the wrong occupations, choose incompatible mates, and bring up children with the naive hope that good intentions will be sufficient. But behind the brave front of confidence they may present to the world are apt to lie deep-seated feelings of bewilderment, inadequacy, and unhappiness. The price of muddling through is a high one.

## A Scientific and Humanistic Approach

Today the findings of modern science are reducing our "ignorance of the law." As people become increasingly aware of the fallibility of custom, superstition, and common sense in guiding their lives, they look increasingly to modern science—particularly to psychology—for dependable sources of information. While psychology cannot fully answer the questions of "Who?" "Where?" and "How?" it can provide us with some information and it can reduce the probability of our getting inaccurate answers.

Although still a young science, psychology has acquired a substantial body of information concerning human learning, problem solving, decision making, motivation, interpersonal relations, coping with stress, and many other aspects of our behavior. Yet it has become apparent that we cannot expect science to give us all of the answers. In fact, science often presents us with new and difficult problems rather than answers. An example is the truly amazing progress science is making in understanding the functioning of DNA, the molecular basis of heredity. Experiments have successfully created new forms of life, and some predict that we will eventually be able to control human heredity as well. But, the question truly is "should we?"

Thus, in taking the view that a sound approach to human behavior should be based on scientific findings, we shall not assume that science is infallible, although it does have built-in corrective tendencies. Nor shall we assume that science can solve all human problems. While science can supply the means for space exploration, for example, the decision to use these means is a matter of values. So we will use scientific findings as far as we can, but we will not expect the impossible of them. And while we will view science as a dependable source of information about human beings, we will remain free to utilize information from other sources as well.

Psychology and allied sciences have no monopoly on understanding human behavior. In fact, there is little scientific information about such vital experiences as hope, faith, concern, love, alienation, and despair. In literature, art, religion, philosophy, and autobiographical accounts, we often find poignant and authentic descriptions of experiences meaningful to all of us. In fact, over the centuries we have accumulated a vast store of "nonscientific" information about the nature, behavior, mistakes, and grandeur of human beings. To ignore this information concerning our experiencing and existential problems would be to run the risk of dehumanizing ourselves. No description and explanation of human behavior would be complete that does not encompass the intimate experiences which characterize our existence. So, in subsequent pages we shall not hesitate to draw upon the humanities—literature, art, history, religion—and related fields for insights into human behavior.

## Belief in the Individual's Dignity and Growth Potential

The preamble of the Ethical Standards of Psychologists (1977), as formulated by the American Psychological Association, begins as follows: "Psychologists respect the dignity and worth of the individual and honor the preservation and protection of fundamental human rights. They are committed to increase knowledge of human behavior and of people's increasing understanding of themselves and

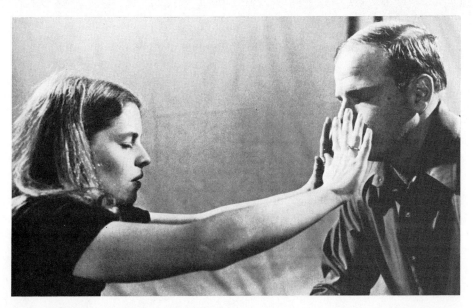

Through our study of psychology we hope to gain a better understanding of ourselves and an insight into the behavior of others.

others and to the utilization of such knowledge for the promotion of human welfare'' (p. 22). Implicit in this statement is a belief in the growth potential of each of us and in our ability to play an active role in building the kind of life we choose and a better future world for humankind.

This does not mean that personal effectiveness and growth can be achieved by simply reading a book. Nor does exposure to research findings about human behavior and well-being ensure that we can or will utilize such information in our own lives. Despite widely publicized research findings pointing to the harmful effects of smoking cigarettes, for example, they are still widely used in our society. Modern psychology can provide dependable information about ourselves and our world, but the mastery and effective use of this knowledge is up to the individual.

In the remainder of this book, we shall attempt to show how the findings of contemporary psychology—in conjunction with other relevant sources of information—can help us to better understand ourselves and others, to improve personal and career competence, and to develop our resources for effective living.

This effort will lead to an inquiry into our basic nature and potentials; our intellectual, emotional, and social development throughout the life span; our ways of coping with life stress and what happens when things go wrong, plus the psychological resources available to us for help and personal growth. We shall also examine the social context of our behavior, including interpersonal relationships, sexual behavior, marriage and intimate relationships, work and leisure, and group interactions. We shall conclude with an examination of our quest for values and our role in building a good future for ourselves and for our world.

The search for personally relevant values sometimes leads to a rejection of traditionally prized goals. During the 1960s and 1970s many persons, disillusioned with modern society, sought a simpler life through communal living.

## SUMMARY

1. The accelerating advances of modern science and technology have led to unprecedented progress and problems. While we live in an affluent society with seemingly endless opportunities for personal growth, we are also beset by seemingly endless problems. We live in the best of times and the worst of times, in a time of progress and of panic, in a "Golden Age of Anxiety."

2. Adjustment is the process by which an organism attempts to meet the demands placed upon it by its own nature and by the environment and by which an organism attempts to structure and alter its environment and experience to enhance survival, understanding, and growth. Adjustment is an interactive process in which the individual influences and is influenced by his or her environment, experiences, and self.

3. Since we have few instinctive behaviors, we must rely on self-direction and the ability to learn and reason in helping us work out effective modes of adjustment and achieve meaningful and fulfilling lives. We must also deal with the question of values in making the choices that guide our behavior. Answers to the questions, "Who am I?" "Where am I going?" and "How do I get there?" can help each of us avoid the high cost of "muddling through."

4. In the quest for answers, we shall rely heavily upon the findings of modern psychology and allied behavior sciences. At the same time, we shall take a humanistic approach coupled with a firm belief in the dignity and growth potential of the individual.

# Chapter 2

# The Quest for Answers

If the crew of a spacecraft were to report finding intelligent beings on another planet, our first question to the crew would probably be "What sort of creatures are they?" Through the centuries members of the human race have asked the same question about themselves without finding a satisfactory answer.

One reason for the difficulty in getting a clear answer is that there are so many differences to be accounted for. Human beings come in many colors and sizes and behave in many different ways. The vast differences among us make it hard to identify what we all share in common as human beings. Contrast, for example, the hired killer and the kindly priest, the hermit and the socialite, the child abuser and the loving parent. It is difficult to see what "human nature" these people have in common. And when we expand our horizons to include the people of other cultures, we find even greater differences in values, goals, and ways of life.

Is there a hidden order beneath this diversity, comparable to the order that scientists have found in the rest of nature? Just what sort of creatures are we "down underneath"? This question is not an idle one, for on its answer hinges the type of life we should lead and the kind of world we should try to construct for ourselves.

In the present chapter we shall examine some of the conflicting historical views of human nature, survey the major psychosocial models of human behavior, and try to gain a broader perspective of ourselves as human beings by noting what we share in common with—and how we differ from—other living things.

## CONFLICTING VIEWS OF HUMAN NATURE

**human nature: the basic makeup of human beings**

Long before modern science entered the arena, philosophers, theologians, and politicians argued over the problem of **human nature.** From a welter of conflicting views, several questions kept recurring: Are human beings basically *good,* or *evil,* or *neutral?* Are we basically *rational* or *irrational?* Is our behavior the result of *determinism* or *free will?*

### Good, Evil, or Neutral

Some people have asserted that human beings are basically selfish and self-seeking. Others have denied it. Some have seen us as competitive by nature, others as cooperative. Some have maintained that our "real" nature is hostile and cruel, others that it is friendly and kind. All of these assertions become involved in the larger issue of whether human nature is basically good, or evil, or neutral.

**Human nature as evil.**  The view that human beings are basically "sinful" has received substantial support from both history and human experience. The Christian doctrine of original sin teaches that the entire human race was corrupted by the Fall and that its members are incapable of resisting temptation and living a good life without divine intervention.

The theories and writings of Sigmund Freud, which have had a pervasive impact on psychological thought, emphasized the negative side of human nature. In *Civilization and Its Discontents* (1930/1955), Freud depicted our basic nature as predatory, cruel, and destructive.

*men are not gentle, friendly creatures wishing for love, who simply defend themselves if they are attacked, . . . a powerful measure of desire for aggressiveness has to be reckoned as part of their instinctual endowment. The result is that their neighbor is to them not only a possible helper or sexual object, but also a temptation to them to gratify their aggressiveness . . . to seize his possessions, to humiliate him, to cause him pain, to torture and to kill him. . . .*

*. . . Anyone who calls to mind the atrocities of the early migrations, of the invasion of the Huns or by the so-called Mongols under Jenghiz Kahn and Tamurlane, of the sack of Jerusalem by the pious crusaders, even indeed the horrors of the last world-war, will have to bow his head humbly before the truth of this view of man. (pp. 85–86)*

This essentially negative view has been supported by contemporary ethologists, scientists who study the adaptive evolution of particular behavior patterns. One such ethologist, Konrad Lorenz (1966), argues for the essentially aggressive nature of humanity:

*It is hard to believe that aggression is anything but the pathological product of our disjointed cultural and social life. And one could only wish it were no more than that! [But] it is more than probable that the destructive intensity of the aggression [is] . . . a hereditary evil of mankind. (pp. 49, 42)*

Other social scientists and historians have also championed the view that humans are basically cruel and violent. In his *African Genesis,* Robert Ardrey (1961) concluded that "Man emerged and triumphed over his rival primates for this single reason—he was a killer." And from a historical perspective, Toynbee (1970) has emphasized the violent side of human nature and the thin veneer that separates civilization from savagery: "There is a persistent vein of violence and cruelty in human nature" (p. 3).

The view of human nature as evil has been well summarized by Ghiselin (1974): "Where it is in his own interest, every organism [human being] may reasonably be expected to aid his fellows. Where he has no alternative, he submits to the yoke of communal servitude. Yet given a full chance to act in his own interest, nothing but expedience will restrain him from brutalizing, from maiming, from murdering—his brother, his mate, his parent, or his child. Scratch an 'altruist,' and watch a 'hypocrite' bleed" (p. 247).

Indeed, the chain of war, violence, assassination, and cruelty evidenced by the human race reaches from the most ancient times to today's headlines. It is not surprising that the view of human nature as basically evil has greatly influenced much of Western thought.

**Human nature as neutral.**   Despite humanity's deplorable record of pillage, rape, betrayal, torture, and destruction of our fellow human beings—often on a large scale—there is another side to the picture, a picture characterized by startling diversity and contrasts.

Studies of different cultures have shown that there are many people in the world who as a group are friendly and kind. Anthropologist Margaret Mead (1939) found that the Arapesh, a primitive tribe living in the mountains of New Guinea, were a peaceful people who thought that all human beings were naturally co-operative, unaggressive, self-denying, and primarily concerned with growing food to feed growing children. In contrast, a neighboring tribe, the Mungudumor, were highly aggressive, warlike, and cruel. Early studies of American Indians also indicate the peaceful nature of some tribes, such as the Hopi, Zuni, and Pueblo; while other studies emphasized the aggressive and warlike characteristics of tribes such as the Apaches and Comanches.

Evidence of the diversity of human behavior is not limited to studies carried out many years ago or to "primitive" groups. In more technologically sophisticated societies, there are also marked differences in behavior. For example, crimes of violence—such as murder, assault to kill, armed robbery, and forcible rape—are relatively rare in countries such as England, Iceland, and Sweden, while they are common in other countries, such as Argentina, Brazil, and the United States.

Such contrasts have led many social scientists to conclude that human beings are highly educable creatures who are neither good nor bad by nature. Instead, we have the potential to develop in either direction. Whether we become selfish, cruel, and warlike or self-sacrificing, kindly, and peaceful will depend largely upon the sociocultural conditions in which we grow up. While we admittedly have the capacity for selfish and cruel behavior, we clearly have the capacity for love and goodness as well.

**Human nature as good.**  Going a step further, an increasing number of psychologists have come to view human nature as essentially good. They believe that our basic tendencies are toward friendly, cooperative, and loving behavior. These psychologists view aggression and cruelty as pathological behavior resulting from the distortion of our essential nature.

Although it emphasizes that people tend to "innate depravity" if left to their own resources, the Judeo-Christian tradition also teaches that human beings were created in the likeness of God. There is a divine spark in each of us. As Jesus said, "The kingdom of God is within you."

A belief in essential human goodness, particularly strong during the late eighteenth and nineteenth centuries, was forcefully expressed in the writings of many poets and philosophers of the romantic period. They believed that if people were allowed to live "naturally" much of the evil in the world would disappear. For example, in *Èmile*, a treatise on education published in 1762, the philosopher Jean Jacques Rousseau maintained that the aim of education should be self-expression rather than the suppression of natural tendencies. The chief function of the school should be to provide children with opportunities to develop their natural gifts, unhampered by the corrupting influence of society.

And, nearly two hundred years later, psychologist Gordon Allport (1954) concluded: "Normal men everywhere reject, in principle and by preference, the path of war and destruction. They like to live in peace and friendship with their neighbors; they prefer to love and be loved rather than to hate and be hated. . . .

Violent crimes, aggression and cruelty, and the frequency of war throughout the world seem to illustrate that human nature is basically evil. On the other hand, we often read of an individual performing some selfless and heroic act to assist another or of many people working together to achieve some common good. For example, the cooperative effort to work for world peace can be cited as evidence of the positive side of human nature.

While wars rage, yet our desire is for peace and while animosity prevails, the weight of mankind's approval is on the side of affiliation" (p. xiv).

These diverse views of human nature as evil, neutral, or good have important social implications. All agree that human beings are highly educable creatures and that their development for good or evil can be markedly influenced or even controlled by cultural conditions. But here the agreement ends. If people are by nature selfish, predatory, and evil, society must shape them into social creatures by stringent discipline and social control. If, on the other hand, their tendencies are toward friendly, cooperative, and constructive behavior, then society can best achieve its purposes by encouraging spontaneity, naturalness, and self-direction. And if human nature tends to be neutral, we can try to push the balance toward "good" by encouraging and rewarding "good" behavior.

## Rational or Irrational

The human race has not only been indicted for being selfish and cruel, it has also been characterized as irrational and irresponsible. In every age there have been those who scoffed at the much-celebrated gift of reason. Even Alexander Hamilton spoke with contempt of "the impudence of democracy, where the people seldom judge or determine right." The ordinary person is governed by emotion, he insisted, and is changeable and unpredictable.

**Early faith in human rationality.**   But from earliest times reason has also had its champions. The ancient Greeks exalted reason as the highest human virtue. The Roman aristocrats emphasized human rationality and prided themselves on their pragmatic approach to social problems. Although belief in reason had its setbacks during medieval times, it emerged again as the basic fabric on which the democratic social organization of Western culture is based—the belief that, given sufficient information and opportunity, human beings can direct their own affairs and those of their society with wisdom and responsibility.

Thomas Jefferson, an aristocrat by birth, maintained that the average person could reason and judge rightly if given access to the facts: "I know of no safe depository of the ultimate powers of society but the people themselves; and if we think them not enlightened enough to exercise their control with a wholesome discretion, the remedy is not to take it from them, but to inform their discretion." In his first inaugural address Abraham Lincoln expressed a similar faith when he asked: "Why should there not be patient confidence in the ultimate justice of the people? Is there any better or equal hope in the world?"

**Depreciation of rationality in modern times.**    During our own age, our faith in the innate nature of human rationality has been repeatedly questioned and devaluated.

The psychoanalytic viewpoint has been particularly influential in the downgrading of human rationality. In *Psychopathology of Everyday Life* (1901/1954), Sigmund Freud emphasized the unconscious and irrational influences that are evident in much of our thinking and behavior. Reading of "repressed sex drives," of "unconscious hostility," and of "rationalization" and "projection," many came to the seemingly obvious conclusion that human behavior is inherently and inevitably self-deceptive and irrational.

To further complicate matters, modern psychology has found a number of sociocultural factors such as propaganda, misleading information, and outright deceit on the part of leaders and groups, which can distort our thinking and lead to irrational beliefs and solutions to problems. Thus, it is not surprising that many psychologists tend to view human beings as rather malleable creatures whose thinking is shaped primarily by the environment. We may think rationally if we are trained and rewarded for doing so, but the existence of any inherently rational force in our makeup is denied or minimized.

Unquestionably, too, rapid social change and the uprooting of many cherished beliefs and values has led both to confusion and to a questioning of our vaunted rationality. If men and women once believed so firmly in things which we now consider false, how much faith can we place in the rationality of newer ideas and convictions?

**Continuing evidence of human rationality.**    Although faith in human rationality has been substantially weakened in recent times, it has by no means been destroyed. Many modern statesmen, philosophers, and scientists believe in natural tendencies toward common sense and reason.

Of course, our rational tendencies can readily be distorted by environmental influences. We can be misled by false information, all but stupefied by repetitious stimuli from mass communication media, restricted by cultural deprivation, handicapped by lack of training in learning and problem solving, and overwhelmed by the number and complexity of issues demanding our attention.

The achievements of modern science, nevertheless, indicate the human capacity and inclination for dealing with problems in rational ways. Our unremitting efforts to probe the secrets of the universe and to make sense of our world, to obtain accurate information and sound values for dealing with our problems, and to establish order in both our physical surroundings and our social relationships all indicate a potential for rational behavior and, perhaps, a basic propensity for it.

## Free or Determined

In our everyday lives we operate on the assumption that we are free to make decisions and choose our course of action, at least within certain limits. We see ourselves as continually weighing alternatives and choosing among them. Yet many philosophers, theologians, and scientists have raised the question of whether this freedom of action is real or illusory—whether we are active and responsible agents with some measure of free will or puppets whose behavior is actually determined by forces beyond our control.

**The assumption of determinism.**   Various kinds and degrees of **determinism** have been argued since ancient times. The great dramatic tragedies of Aeschylus and Sophocles, for example, are pervaded by the ancient Greek belief that men and women are, in the last analysis, the pawns of fate. There is an inevitability to their actions, an end from which they cannot escape. This fatalism is clearly illustrated in the well-known legend of Oedipus. In trying to avoid fulfilling the oracle's prophecy that he would kill his father and marry his mother, Oedipus turned headlong into fate's trap and unwittingly did as prophesied. A later example is the Calvinist doctrine of predestination, which holds that at birth every individual has already been elected to salvation or condemned to damnation.

determinism: the belief that all events have a prior cause

Another kind of determinism is the cornerstone of modern science. This is the assumption that the universe is an orderly place where all events occur in keeping with natural laws. Everything follows cause-and-effect relationships. In essence, the universe is a giant "machine" which functions according to certain built-in principles. If we had complete information about the machine, we could understand and predict its functioning in every detail.

Applied to human behavior, the doctrine of determinism holds that human behavior is lawful—that cause must precede effect. Given a complete knowledge of the past experiences of an individual, we would be able to predict with great accuracy how he or she will act. As B. F. Skinner (1953) has so succinctly put it: "The hypothesis that man is not free is essential to the application of the scientific method to the study of human behavior."

For evidence, psychologists adhering to this "strict" determinism have pointed to the diverse customs and beliefs of people throughout the world, all shaped by cultural forces. They have emphasized the experimental finding that people's beliefs and values can be influenced through punishment and reward, and that suggestion and imitation are important forces in shaping a person's assumptions and behavior. Despite the "illusion" of freedom, the individual is at the mercy of past experiences and present environmental conditions.

**The assumption of freedom.**   In our personal lives, probably none of us believes in a strict determinism. The psychologist Shibutani (1964) expressed it this way: "Each person believes that he is able to exercise some measure of control over his own destiny. He is capable of making decisions and of selecting among alternative lines of action. It is this widespread belief that provides the basis for the doctrine of 'free will' and for the concept of moral responsibility" (p. 233).

Our way of life, with its freedom of discussion, ballot boxes, democratic institutions, and assumptions of personal responsibility, is based heavily on the assumption that we are capable of self-determination.

The apparently irreconcilable paradox of determinism vs. **freedom** has been well described by Carl Rogers (1969) in relation to the situation in psychotherapy.

*In the therapeutic relationship some of the most compelling subjective experiences are those in which the client feels within himself the power of naked choice. He is free—to become himself or to hide behind a facade; to move forward or to retrogress; to behave in ways which are destructive of self and others, or in ways which are enhancing; quite literally free to live or die, in both the physiological and psychological meaning of those terms. Yet as we enter this field of psychotherapy with objective research methods, we are, like any other scientist, committed to a complete determinism. From this point of view every thought, feeling, and action of the client is determined by what preceded it. There can be no such thing as freedom. The dilemma I am trying to describe is no different than that found in other fields—it is simply brought to sharper focus, and appears more insoluble. (p. 294)*

**The assumption of "reciprocal determinism."**   The paradox of free will vs. determinism has by no means been resolved and may never be resolved. However, many psychologists have adopted a position of **reciprocal determinism** that emphasizes the interaction of the individual and the environment. This viewpoint has been well summarized by Craighead, Kazdin, and Mahoney (1981):

*The existing psychological evidence does strongly support the notion that environmental events exert control over behavior. However, there is equally strong evidence illustrating that behaviors exert control over environments. . . The influence process is reciprocal in that it works both ways. Environments influence behavior; behaviors influence environments.*

*This reciprocal determinism between behavior and environment has tremendous significance for human performance and the issues of personal freedom, responsibility, and choice. Since environments are a function of behavior, the individual can take an active role in self-determination. (pp. 186–87)*

While they acknowledge that human behavior is heavily influenced—and often dominated—by the individual's background of experience, scientists adhering to this viewpoint are impressed with our self-awareness, our ability to reflect upon and reinterpret past experience, and our ability to imagine new possibilities different from anything previously experienced. In short, they see us as capable of modifying our environment and thus capable of taking an active role in shaping our destiny (Bandura, 1977, 1982a).

What conclusions can we draw from our examination of these conflicting views of human nature? It seems evident that we are capable of both good and

**freedom:** view that human beings have some control over their behavior and destiny

**reciprocal determinism:** view that an individual can affect the environment, just as the environment can affect the individual!

# Insight

## FROM NATURAL SELECTION TO HUMAN SELECTION

*In the last two decades or so, we have . . . come to the end of the era of evolution—I mean the era of evolution as Darwin interpreted it, that is, evolution by natural selection. It is rather shocking to say this about a vast period in the earth's history—a period that we now believe has lasted for about 3.6 billion years on the earth's surface. Nevertheless, it is over; and the reason it is over is not that things will not change any further (in fact, they may change more rapidly than ever!) but that we are now at the beginning of the era of evolution by human selection. It is now our human activity, intentional or not, which determines the numbers and species of all the plants and animals on the earth's surface. . . .*

*In short, the whole human race, the whole planet, is passing through a kind of watershed. It is the end of the era of innocence; it is the end of adolescence. It is a sudden incredible change. And beyond it, we will be, if we survive, a different kind of human race, and a different kind of species, on a different kind of planet. For we will be different from the past in the food we eat, in our methods of hunting and fishing and gathering and communicating, and in our methods of living and managing the world—more different than two species of animals are from each other. . . .*

*If we survive this sudden electric jump, we will move into a totally new kind of society. . . .*

*This potential transformation through which we are passing today, a transformation to an integrated worldwide human organism, is what I call The Step to Man, because the new man (or woman) will look back and see us as the old, incompetent, unstable pre-men of the past. (Platt, 1972, pp. 3, 6)*

---

evil, of both rationality and irrationality, of being both active and reactive. These are not mutually exclusive types of behavior but poles of a continuum. Though we may operate closer to one pole at a given time, we retain the potential for both. None of us is always rational or irrational, selfish or altruistic, active or reactive. However, the patterns of a given society or the life-style of a given individual may push us towards one or another of the extremes.

In the section which follows, we shall attempt to broaden our perspective of human nature by reviewing some of the major models of behavior used by psychologists and other social scientists.

## MODELS OF HUMAN BEHAVIOR

A **model** is essentially an analogy which can help a scientist to see important relationships. Consider, for example, a child who builds a model car. The model may be built of plastic or wood or metal. It may be small or large. It may be very detailed, or it may suggest only indirectly the specific characteristics of the car. It may have working parts, or it may be totally nonfunctional. The model of the car

**model: a representation of reality or analogy that helps an individual see important relationships among data**

need not be physical in nature; it can be represented on a television or computer screen as colored lines against a dark background, or as a series of mathematical expressions describing the relationship of some parts of the car to other parts.

In essence, a model is a *representation of reality,* a way of understanding a complicated object or process. Models are useful because they keep scientists and other individuals from being overwhelmed by masses of unwieldly factual information. And, they provide a framework for understanding and interpreting new pieces of information.

Just as a car can be represented by a small metal object, lines on a television screen, and mathematical formulas, so too can the models of human behavior differ significantly. Indeed, the models that we shall discuss below seem so utterly different from each other, that we may at times doubt that we are talking about the same phenomenon, human behavior.

Models also influence the importance that we attach to certain observations. Although we may agree on a particular observation, such as a child's love for a parent, our interpretation of the meaningfulness and importance of those observations will be strongly influenced by the model of human behavior that we adopt.

We shall discuss three models of human behavior: the psychoanalytic model, the social-learning model, and the humanistic-existential model. To aid your understanding of these models, we have presented a case study on page 31. Later in this chapter, we shall return to this case and examine the ways in which the three models view and interpret the information presented in the case.

## The Psychoanalytic Model

**psychoanalytic model: view that human behavior is basically irrational and results from the interaction of the id, ego, and superego**

The **psychoanalytic model** is based on the observations and writings of Sigmund Freud, whose pioneering work extended over a period of fifty years. The major principles of his model are based on the clinical study of patients undergoing psychoanalysis. This approach relies heavily on the method of free association in which the patient is asked to provide an unrestricted account of whatever comes to mind, leaving nothing out.

The psychoanalytic model is a complex one, but its outlines can be sketched as follows.

**id: a completely unconscious portion of the personality, characterized by instinctual cravings and unrestrained pleasure seeking**

**libido: basic energy of life**

**Id, ego, and superego.**　The psychoanalytic model is based on the concept that behavior results from the interaction of three key subsystems within the personality: the *id,* the *ego,* and the *superego.*

The **id** contains our primitive, instinctual drives—such as hunger, thirst, aggression, and sex. These instinctual drives are seen as being of two types: (1) constructive drives, primarily of a sexual nature, which provide the basic energy of life, called **libido;** and (2) destructive and aggressive drives, which are more obscure but tend toward self-destruction and death. In essence, *life* instincts are opposed by *death* instincts. It should be pointed out that Freud used the term

# Psychology in Action

**THE CASE OF ROBERT W.**

Here we introduce you to Robert W. Robert W. is a fairly typical student—he is not exceptionally well-adjusted, nor is he exceptionally poorly adjusted. He is, in other words, average in his psychological makeup. Later in this chapter (pp. 44–45), we will examine and interpret Robert W. from the perspectives of three models of human behavior—the psychoanalytic model, the social-learning model, and the humanistic-existential model. Our task here is simply to describe him to you.

*Robert W. is the oldest of three children. He has a brother two years younger than he and a sister five years younger. Robert's mother and father both graduated from high school. Robert's father holds a fairly responsible white-collar position with a large manufacturing firm; Robert's mother was a housewife until three years ago, when she took a clerking job in a lawyer's office to help pay for Robert's college expenses and the upcoming expenses of his brother and sister.*

*At age nineteen, Robert is a college sophomore. Although he has not yet declared a major, he is leaning toward business and accounting because it is "practical" and because he feels he can easily get a job following graduation.*

*Robert feels relatively close to his mother, whom he describes as warm and affectionate. On the other hand, he describes his father as somewhat formal and cold, although he is certain that his father loves him. Robert notes that his father is the disciplinarian in the family; he also notes that his father sets very high standards for the children. When the standards are not met, the children receive a stern lecture on the importance of achievement.*

*As a result, Robert's performance in high school and college is routinely above average. However, he often experiences severe stomach pains prior to exams. In grade school and high school, these pains would become so intense that his mother would take him to the doctor for a checkup. However, each checkup revealed that he suffered from no physical illness.*

*Robert has a small number of friends whose company he enjoys. He dates relatively frequently, but he has no steady girlfriend. His hobbies include jogging, listening to music, and reading. On the whole, Robert regards himself as "relatively normal and relatively well-adjusted."*

"sexual" to refer to practically anything of a pleasurable nature—from eating to bathing.

The id operates upon the **pleasure principle** and is concerned only with immediate gratification. It is completely selfish and unconcerned with reality or moral considerations. The id generates images and wishes related to need grati-

**pleasure principle: the demand that an instinctual need be immediately gratified, regardless of reality**

**primary process:** gratification of an instinctual need by fantasy

**ego:** the rational subsystem of the personality that mediates between the demands of the id, superego, and reality

**secondary process:** reality-oriented rational processes of the ego

**reality principle:** awareness of environmental constraints and adjustment of behavior to meet these constraints

**superego:** portion of the personality in which conscience, ethics, and moral standards are located

**inhibition:** restraint of a desire or impulse

**psychosexual development:** theory of personality development emphasizing pleasure derived from various areas of the body during the early years of life

fication of such needs as hunger or sex, and these images and wishes are referred to as the **primary process.**

A second key subsystem—the **ego**—develops to mediate between the demands of the id and the realities of the external world. Although the primary purpose of the ego is that of meeting id demands, it must do so in a way that will ensure the individual's survival. This requires the use of reason and other intellectual resources—the **secondary process**—in dealing with the realities of the external world as well as in exercising control over id demands. Hence the ego operates in terms of the **reality principle.**

The third key system—the **superego**—is the outgrowth of learning the taboos and moral values of society. In essence, the superego is what we refer to as *conscience* and is concerned with good and bad, right and wrong. The superego, like the id, operates through the ego system. Thus the superego strives to compel the ego to **inhibit** desires which are considered immoral.

The interplay of these intrapsychic forces of id, ego, and superego is of crucial significance. Often the instinctual desires and demands of the id are in conflict with superego demands or with the demands of the external world. The adequate resolution of such conflicts by the ego is considered essential to a healthy personality. People who cannot resolve these inner conflicts were called *neurotic* by Freud.

**Psychosexual development.** Freud described the development of the three psychic structures in his celebrated theory of **psychosexual development.** According to Freud, certain areas of the body become particular sources of pleasure and gratification at various points in life. For example, the area around the mouth is especially important during the first year of a child's life. Much of the child's gratification at this point comes from eating, thumb sucking, and putting things into the mouth. Because of the special importance of the mouth region during a child's first year, Freud termed this period the *oral* stage of psychosexual development.

During the first year, the child learns to differentiate "me" from "not-me," self from others. The child also begins to grapple with reality issues. For example, the hungry child learns that crying does not always result in the breast or the bottle. Similarly, the id-inspired wishes for food do not immediately result in the desired outcome. This contact with reality demands begins the development of the ego.

The process of ego development is accelerated during the second year of life, characterized by the *anal* stage of psychosexual development. During this time, the child discovers pleasure centering around the anus and in withholding and releasing feces. The child's pleasure, however, is not shared with his or her parents, who hope that the child will quickly learn to use toilets in an appropriate manner.

Beginning in the third year, the child enters the *phallic* stage of psychosexual development. Freud believed that the center of physical pleasure moved from the anal region to the genital area. At the same time, the child develops an intense attraction for the opposite-sexed parent and hopes to replace the same-sexed

In psychoanalytic theory, thumb sucking is an activity associated with the oral stage of psychosexual development. According to this theory, deprivation or overindulgence of gratification at any one stage of development can result in fixation at that stage. For instance, an adult's smoking behavior may be interpreted as an indication of an oral fixation.

parent. For example, boys may develop a "sexual" attraction to their mothers and hope to replace their fathers in the mother's affection and attention.

However, fear of reprisal from the same-sexed parent produces anxiety in the child. This anxiety is resolved when the child adopts the moral standards of the same-sexed parent, and in the process, develops a superego as well. Freud noted that the Greek legend of Oedipus had elements very similar to the process that he was describing. In the legend, Oedipus unknowingly kills his father and marries his mother. Because of its similarity to this legend, Freud named the psychological process that occurs during the phallic stage the **Oedipal conflict.**

Freud believed that the Oedipal conflict applied equally to males and females. However, some later psychoanalytic theorists proposed that the Oedipal myth applied only to males and that a related myth, that of Electra, applied only to females. In the Greek legend, Electra goads her brother, Orestes, into killing her mother, Clytemnestra. While there are some similarities between the two legends, Freud specifically rejected the notion of an **Electra complex,** preferring instead the Oedipal conflict for both sexes (Freud, 1931/1961; Rychlak, 1981). Nonetheless, the term *Electra complex* has become a part of later psychoanalytic tradition, and it is a term that we too shall employ.

Following the resolution of the Oedipal (or Electra) conflict, the child enters a period of *latency* during which social and educational skills are learned. This period lasts until puberty, when physical maturity and the ability to reproduce ushers in the final, *genital* stage of psychosexual development.

Freud placed great emphasis on early development, arguing that an individual's personality was essentially fixed by age seven. In the psychoanalytic view, the problems of adult life are a reflection of events that took place at an early age. For example, an adult's difficulty expressing affection and love toward others probably has its genesis in the earliest years of life.

**Oedipal conflict:** fear and anxiety experienced by a child as a result of the child's desire for the opposite-sexed parent

**Electra complex:** Oedipal conflict occurring in females

**The unconscious.**  We often believe that our actions result from logical, rational approaches to a problem. For example, the choice of one college major over another may be explained by job prospects in the future, salary considerations, job security and benefits, and similar reasons. However, psychoanalysts argue that much of our behavior springs from a source within ourselves that is unknown to us. This unknown source of wishes, desires, and preferences is called the **unconscious.**

**unconscious: an area of the mind marked by a total lack of awareness**

Freud believed that the conscious represented only a small area of the mind, while the unconscious, like the submerged part of an iceberg, was much the larger portion. Between the conscious and the unconscious is an area of knowledge and memory that, while not conscious, can be brought into conscious awareness. This area is called the **preconscious.** Its operation is illustrated by our ability to recall information after a moment's reflection. Freud believed that all of the id and much of the ego and superego were located in the unconscious.

**preconscious: a region of the mind that can be brought into conscious awareness after a moment's reflection**

Many of our unconscious desires cause us anxiety and discomfort. While we are normally unaware of these desires, we can get a glimpse at the unconscious through indirect means. For example, dreams are often indirect expressions of unconscious desires. Similarly, the embarrassing slip of the tongue—"Mr. McCarthy, how sorry I am to see you!"—may reveal our hidden, innermost feelings.

On most occasions, these unconscious impulses, often from the id or superego, can be managed effectively by the ego. However, rational measures do not always suffice, and in these situations, the ego resorts to irrational protective measures called **ego-defense mechanisms.** Some examples of ego-defense mechanisms are rationalization and repression. We shall deal with these mechanisms in greater detail in Chapter 8.

**ego-defense mechanisms: irrational reactions designed to avoid anxiety and maintain feelings of adequacy and worth under conditions of stress**

Essentially, then, the psychoanalytic model describes an individual dominated by instinctual biological drives and by unconscious desires and motives. While there is the constructive libidinal side to human nature, there are also the darker forces pushing toward destruction and death. The ego tends toward rationality, while other processes of the mind push the individual toward a high degree of irrationality.

## The Social-Learning Model

**social-learning model: view that human behavior, whether adaptive or maladaptive, is essentially learned**

The general format of the modern **social-learning model** stems from the early work of John B. Watson (1919). Watson insisted that if psychology were to become a science of behavior, it must limit itself to the study of events that could be observed objectively. He rejected the introspective study of conscious states or processes as being essentially mentalistic and prescientific, since such observations were not open to verification by other investigators.

Starting with this basic assumption, Watson changed the focus of psychology from inner psychic processes to outer behavior which could be objectively observed. Only through the objective observation of such behavior and the stimulus conditions which brought it about could psychologists learn to predict and control human behavior.

# Insight

### THE COMPONENTS OF PERSONALITY IN PSYCHOANALYTIC THEORY

The subsystems of the personality, according to psychoanalytic theory, can be depicted as an iceberg, of which only the tip rises above the water. Similarly, only a small part of the mind—the very tip of the iceberg—is conscious. The largest part of the mind, including all of the id (the largest subsystem of the personality) remains unconscious.

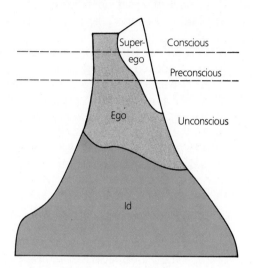

In achieving this change in focus, Watson depended heavily upon the concept of classical conditioning discovered some years earlier by the Russian physiologist Pavlov in his experiments with dogs. Watson suggested that Pavlov's findings could be applied to humans—and in so doing opened up a new and valuable approach to the study of human behavior.

This viewpoint has been greatly expanded by B. F. Skinner (1953, 1971, 1974, 1977), Albert Bandura (1969, 1977b, 1982b), and a number of other theorists who are interested in cognitive approaches to behavior (e.g., Ellis & Harper, 1961; Mahoney, 1975; Mahoney & Arnkoff, 1978; Meichenbaum, 1977). Largely as a result of its scientific study of learning and its success in formulating and applying the principles of learning to the modification of human behavior, social-learning approaches have become a dominant theme in contemporary psychology.

Social-learning approaches are generally characterized by the hypothesis that virtually all behavior, whether adaptive or maladaptive, is learned. To the social-learning theorist, our dislike for one individual is as much a function of a learning process as our love for another.

Secondly, social-learning approaches emphasize the importance of the environment to the learning process. According to the theorists, the social and environmental context in which learning takes place is an important determinant of behavior. For example, we may learn to wear funny hats, become intoxicated, and sing "Auld Lang Syne" at New Year's Eve parties, but we would also quickly learn that similar behavior in a worship setting would be frowned upon.

Since most behavior is learned, social-learning theorists have concentrated on the question of how learning comes about. In trying to answer this question, they have focused on three different types of learning: classical conditioning, operant conditioning, and observational learning.

**classical (respondent, Pavlovian) conditioning: a learning process in which a neutral stimulus comes to elicit a response after multiple pairings with another stimulus**

**stimulus: a physical or environmental event that excites a receptor or sense organ**

**respondent learning: another term for classical conditioning**

**Classical conditioning.**     **Classical conditioning,** sometimes called Pavlovian or respondent conditioning, teaches an individual a new type of reaction to a previously neutral environmental **stimulus.** For example, prior to conditioning, a very mild puff of air will produce a blink of the eye, while the sound of a bell will typically have no effect on eye blinking. In this situation, the puff of air is the *unconditioned stimulus,* the eye blink is the *unconditioned response,* and the sound of the bell is the *conditioned stimulus.* During conditioning, the bell is sounded just before the puff of air is delivered to the eye. This pairing of the conditioned stimulus (sound of the bell) and the unconditioned stimulus (puff of air) continues for a number of learning trials.

If, after the learning trials, the bell sounds but is *not* followed by the puff of air, the eye blink will still occur (the *conditioned response*). In other words, the bell is no longer a neutral stimulus since it is now capable of eliciting an eye blink. When the previously neutral stimulus has the power to elicit a response, we can say that **respondent learning** has occurred. Of course, if the bell is repeatedly presented without the puff of air, the individual will soon stop blinking in response to the bell.

In a now classic experiment, Watson and Rayner (1920) used respondent conditioning to demonstrate the role of learning in maladaptive behavior. Using little Albert—an eleven-month-old boy who was fond of animals—as a subject, they showed how an irrational fear or phobia could be readily learned through conditioning. Their procedure was simple. The experimenter stood behind little Albert while the boy was playing with a white rat. Whenever Albert reached for the animal, (conditioned stimulus), the experimenter struck a steel bar with a hammer (unconditioned stimulus). The sudden loud noise elicited a fearful reaction from Albert and made Albert cry (unconditioned response). After several repetitions of this procedure, Albert became greatly disturbed at the sight of the rat even when the loud noise was not made. His fear (conditioned response) generalized to include other furry animals and objects as well. This dramatic demonstration of the development and generalization of an irrational fear suggested that other types of maladaptive behavior might also be the result of learning.

Watson and Rayner's experiment with little Albert is an example of classical or respondent conditioning, in which a simple response comes to be elicited by a wide range of other stimuli. Many of our emotional reactions appear to be based on this kind of learning. This type of learning can be adaptive, as when we learn to avoid aversive stimuli, or it can be maladaptive, as when we learn irrational fears and phobias.

As our final example suggests, respondent learning need not be limited to mechanical eye blinks or negative emotional states but can also involve humorous elements as well:

*Dear Abby:*

*My friend fixed me up with a blind date and I should have known the minute he showed up in a bow tie that he couldn't be trusted. I fell for him like a rock. He got me to love him on purpose and then lied to me and cheated on me. Every time I go with a man who wears a bow tie, the same thing happens. I think girls should be warned about men who wear them. (Taken from the* Dear Abby *column. Copyright © 1982 by Universal Press Syndicate. Reprinted with permission. All rights reserved. Cited in Bandura, 1968, pp. 306–7)*

**Operant conditioning.**   A second type of learning is called **operant conditioning.** Operant conditioning is based on the deceptively simple premise that learning is controlled by its consequences. Behaviors that are followed by positive events will be maintained and strengthened, while behaviors that are followed by negative events will be weakened or eliminated (Thorndike, 1898).

The term *operant* suggests that the individual operates upon or changes the environment to meet his or her goals. For example, students may arrange their study techniques in ways to reduce distraction and improve concentration. The hope is that these behaviors, which "operate" upon and influence the environment, will improve study habits to the degree that the desired consequence, improved grades, will be the outcome.

Among the most important consequences to behavior are **reinforcers,** consequences which strengthen or maintain behavior. When a positive stimulus is added to a situation and when the stimulus strengthens behavior, we speak of **positive reinforcement.** Some positive reinforcers are quite obvious: when our parents wanted us to finish our vegetables, they would offer us dessert. In this situation, the dessert is the positive stimulus that is added to the situation following the action of eating the vegetables. In a more subtle example, a smile or an embrace from a loved one can act as positive reinforcers for our behavior.

Some consequences weaken rather than strengthen behavior. These types of consequences are termed **punishments.** Perhaps the most common type of punishment involves the addition of a negative stimulus to a situation. For example, we may yell at a friend or acquaintance who damages a prized possession of ours. The negative consequence, yelling, is added to the situation so that the undesired behavior, destruction of property, is weakened or suppressed.

Punishment can also occur when a positive stimulus is taken away from an environment. For example, individuals who violate certain laws may have their freedom taken away by being placed in prison. Similarly, a child may have television privileges suspended as punishment for some undesired act.

A fourth kind of consequence involves the removal of a negative stimulus from the environment. Like other reinforcers, negative reinforcers are consequences that strengthen or maintain behavior. The difference between positive and negative reinforcers lies in whether something is added to or removed from the situation. In positive reinforcement, a stimulus is added to the situation, while

**operant conditioning: a learning process that emphasizes the rewarding consequences of some activity**

**reinforcer: a consequence that strengthens or maintains some behavior**

**positive reinforcement: process of strengthening or maintaining behavior by adding a stimulus to the environment**

**punishment: process of weakening or suppressing a behavior by adding a stimulus to the environment**

**negative reinforcement: a consequence that strengthens or maintains behavior by removing a stimulus from the environment**

in **negative reinforcement,** something is taken *away* from the situation. Both positive and negative reinforcers strengthen behavior. Negative reinforcers should not be confused with punishment, which decreases behavior.

The concept of negative reinforcers is somewhat difficult to understand, but it describes a relatively common chain of events in our lives. For example, if a parent or roommate nags us to clean up the kitchen, we will often comply solely to stop the constant nagging. In this example, cleaning the kitchen is strengthened by the removal of a negative stimulus, the nagging.

**extinction: gradual disappearance of a learned behavior when reinforcement is withheld**

Finally, behavior can be weakened if it is followed by no consequence whatsoever. This procedure, called **extinction,** is embedded in the popular instruction, "Just ignore her and she'll stop." Since the individual receives no reinforcers for the act, the behavior is gradually weakened and disappears.

Interestingly, reinforcement need not be consistent or continuous to be effective. In some situations, *intermittent* or *partial reinforcement* can be particularly powerful in strengthening and maintaining behavior. For example, a gambler may win at cards or the slot machines very irregularly and inconsistently. Nonetheless, these intermittent reinforcers can strengthen gambling tendencies to the degree that the individual may become a compulsive gambler.

**generalization: tendency to respond to similar, but not identical, stimuli**

**Generalization and discrimination.**    **Generalization** is the tendency for a response which has been conditioned to one stimulus to become associated with other, similar stimuli. For example, in Watson and Rayner's experiment, we noted that little Albert's fear generalized from white rats to other furry animals.

**discrimination: tendency to respond differently to similar stimuli**

A complementary process is **discrimination,** which occurs when the individual learns to distinguish between similar stimuli and to respond differently to each. The ability to discriminate may be brought about through selective reinforcement. For example, since red strawberries taste good and green ones do not, a discrimination will be learned if the individual has experience with both.

According to the social-learning model, complex processes such as attention, perception, concept formation, and decision making are based on an elaboration of this basic discriminative process.

**observational learning (modeling): form of learning in which an individual learns by watching someone else**

**Observational learning and cognitive behaviorism.**    The third type of learning is called **observational learning** or **modeling.** In this type of learning, individuals observe others and, when the conditions are appropriate, imitate or perform similar behaviors.

Observational learning is a very powerful kind of learning. As Bandura (1977b) notes:

*Learning would be exceedingly laborious, not to mention hazardous, if people had to rely solely on the effects of their own actions to inform them what to do. Fortunately, most human behavior is learned observationally . . . : from observing others one forms an idea of how new behaviors are performed, and on later occasions this . . . information serves as a guide for action. Because people can learn from example what to do, at least in approximate form, before performing any behavior, they are spared needless errors. (p. 22)*

Consider the danger involved in learning a complex skill such as driving a car.

Modeling is one of the most powerful methods of learning in the view of social-learning theorists. We learn by observing the behavior of others, paying attention to the behavior, understanding and remembering it, then reproducing the modeled behavior. Although parents may be the most influential models for children, other models may include teachers, older children, peers, even television.

Without observational learning, much of our trial and error learning would result in heaps of metal on the highways. Fortunately, our observations of both good and poor driving skills help teach us what our actions should be once we start to drive. Similarly, we learn long, complicated, and sophisticated sequences of social actions through observing others.

Observational learning is not simply imitation or "monkey see, monkey do." Rather, a complex series of internal processes accompanies this type of learning. For example, individuals must pay attention to the modeled behavior, they must encode and retain the information that was observed, they must reproduce the observed behavior, and they must be motivated to perform (or refrain from performing) the observed act (Posner, 1982; Woodward, 1982).

This emphasis on internal processes is strikingly different from more traditional social-learning approaches. Neither respondent nor operant learning procedures consider internal processes important. Indeed, according to these approaches, only those aspects of behavior that can be directly recorded and monitored should be considered. Because of their emphasis on overt behavior, traditional social-learning approaches are sometimes called *behavioral* approaches as well.

More recently, investigators have begun to examine internal processes with increased interest. Researchers such as Ellis, Mahoney, Beck, and Meichenbaum are focusing on such internal processes as thoughts, emotions, and feelings. For example, Beck (1972) feels that irrational or incorrect thought processes are primarily responsible for a variety of neurotic and depressive disorders.

This "new look" in the social-learning perspective, with its emphasis on internal processes, should be differentiated from the psychoanalytic model, which also uses inferred concepts such as the ego and superego extensively. Essentially, the major difference between the two approaches rests primarily on the social-learning model's insistence that all processes be related to recordable, observable actions. For example, our liking for food may be considered an expression of an oral phase personality by psychoanalytic theorists. In contrast, social-learning theorists would examine our observable patterns of overeating, determine whether others have modeled overeating for us, consider the social and environmental events that precede, accompany, and follow overeating, and ask about the emotional states that are related to overeating.

The incorporation of cognitive principles has markedly expanded the principles and applications of the traditional social-learning approaches. As a result, therapeutic techniques inspired by this expanded social-learning model are being applied with increasing sophistication to problems in many fields, including education, industry, and mental health.

In Chapter 11, we shall discuss social-learning approaches to therapy and note its practical implications for self-direction and personal growth. Social-learning approaches have made a major contribution to the development of psychological thought. As this approach continues to develop, it will probably play an increasingly important role in contemporary psychology.

## The Humanistic-Existential Model

**humanistic-existential (phenomenological) model:** view of human behavior emphasizing the self, self-direction, and the maintenance and actualization needs of the self

The **humanistic-existential model,** also known as the **phenomenological model,** is characterized by its emphasis on *perception,* or how the individual views and interprets his or her experience. This approach is also characterized by its positive view of our basic nature and potential for self-direction and growth rather than by any coherent set of principles of personality development and functioning.

**The humanistic approach: "Self" as a unifying theme.**    Although William James made extensive use of the self-concept in his *Principles of Psychology* (1890), the concept of self was later dropped by behaviorists and other psychologists because of its "internal" and hence unobservable nature. Eventually, however, the need for some kind of unifying principle of personality—as well as for some way of taking cognizance of the subjective experience of each individual—led to its reemphasis in the humanistic model.

Psychologist Carl Rogers (1951, 1969, 1977) has played a major role in delineating the self-concept in the phenomenological model. His views may be summarized as follows:

1. Each of us exists in a private world of experience in which the *I, me,* or *myself* is the center.

2. Our most basic striving is toward the maintenance, enhancement, and actualization of the self.

# Insight

**HUMAN NATURE AS SEEN BY
DIFFERING MODELS OF BEHAVIOR**

| Model | Good/Evil | Rational/Irrational | Free/Determined |
|---|---|---|---|
| Psychoanalytic | Evil | Irrational | Determined |
| Social-Learning | Neutral | Depends on learning | Reciprocal determinism |
| Humanistic-<br>Existential | Good | Rational | Free |

3. We react to situations in terms of our unique perception of ourselves and our world. We react to "reality" as we perceive it and in ways consistent with our self-concept.

4. A perceived threat to the self is followed by defense, including the narrowing and rigidification of perception and coping behavior and the introduction of self-defense mechanisms such as rationalization.

5. Our inner tendencies are toward health and wholeness. Under normal conditions we behave in rational and constructive ways and choose pathways toward personal growth and self-actualization or fulfillment.

Although this concept of self is similar to the psychoanalytic concept of ego, the humanistic model extends the concept to include tendencies toward personal growth and self-actualization or fulfillment.

In this context, great importance is given to the uniqueness of the individual. Not only is the human species unique, but each of us, by virtue of our own particular learning and experience, is unique. This uniqueness makes it our duty to gain a clear sense of our identity. We must discover who we are, what sort of person we want to become, and why. Only in this way can we fully develop our potential as self-directing human beings.

**Positive view of human potential.** Humanistic psychologists also emphasize the essentially positive and rational propensities of human beings and view us as having some measure of freedom for self-direction. As Allport (1955) puts it, "[people] possess a measure of rationality, a portion of freedom, a generic conscience, [personal] ideals, and unique value" (p. 100).

Another humanistic psychologist, Abraham Maslow, not only believes in the positive aspects of human nature, he also believes that psychology and the behavioral sciences should focus their attentions on the positive facets of individuals. According to Maslow (1968), the social and behavioral sciences have focused almost exclusively on the negative or pathological, when the focus should instead be on the healthy and well-adjusted:

*Perhaps we shall soon be able to use as our guide and model the fully growing and self-fulfilling human being, the one in whom all his potentialities are coming to full development, the one whose inner nature expresses itself freely, rather than being warped, sup-*

*pressed, or denied. . . It is as if Freud supplied to us the sick half of psychology and we must now fill it out with the healthy half. Perhaps this health psychology will give us more possibilities for controlling and improving our lives and for making ourselves better people. Perhaps this will be more fruitful than asking "how to get* unsick." *(p. 5)*

We shall return to the ideas of Maslow in our discussion of motivation in Chapter 5.

While the humanistic model attributes importance to learning, it also emphasizes reflection, reasoning, and creative imagination. Although unconscious and irrational motives exist, there is also a strong propensity for conscious planning and rational choosing. Human beings are self-aware, evaluative, and future oriented.

The strongly humanistic outlook taken by Carl Rogers and other theorists has had a major influence on contemporary thought about human nature and behavior. This approach's emphasis on the **self-concept,** the uniqueness of the individual, and the human potential for self-direction and personal growth has struck a responsive chord both with psychologists and with the general public.

**self-concept: an individual's sense of his or her identity, worth, capabilities, and limitations**

**Existentialism.**     Although it is similar in many respects to the humanistically oriented phenomenological model of Carl Rogers, the *existential* approach represents a somewhat less optimistic view of human nature. There is more emphasis on irrational trends and the difficulties inherent in self-fulfillment.

Existentialists emphasize the breakdown of traditional faith, the depersonalization of the individual in a standardized mass culture, and the loss of meaning in human existence. In such a situation, it becomes the task of each of us to stand on our own, to shape our identity, and to make our existence meaningful—to make our life count for something—not on the basis of philosophical or scientific abstractions, but through our personal experience of being.

A basic theme in existentialism is that our existence is given, but what we make of it—our essence—is up to us. The individual who defiantly blurts out, "I didn't ask to be born!" is stating a profound but irrelevant truth. For whether any of us asked to be born or not, here we are in the world and answerable for one human life—our own. What each of us makes of our existence is up to us. It is our responsibility to shape the kind of person we are to become and to live a meaningful life.

Finding a meaningful and fulfilling way of life, however, is not an easy task. In an age of profound cultural change and conflict, traditional beliefs and values no longer provide adequate guides for the good life or for finding meaning in human existence. In our bureaucratic mass society the individual tends to be depersonalized and submerged in the group.

Yet, the alienation that results from this predicament can be viewed as a challenge to make something worthwhile of our lives. In striving for increased self-definition in the *experience of being,* each will travel the perilous path of self-fulfillment. "Being" is a commitment to increased self-awareness and self-definition, to true communication with others, to concern with values and evaluation, and an acceptance of the responsibility for making choices and directing our own destiny.

**Freedom, choice, courage, and obligation.**   Our essence is created by our *choices,* for our choices reflect the values on which we order our lives. As Sartre put it, ''I am my choices.'' In choosing what to become, each of us has absolute freedom; even refusing to choose represents a choice.

Despite the high value placed on this freedom, the problems of choice and responsibility often become an agonizing burden, for finding satisfying values is a lonely and highly individual matter. Each of us must have the courage to break away from old patterns, to stand on our own, and to seek new and more fulfilling pathways. In a sense, the freedom to shape our essence is both our agony and our glory.

Often people lack ''the courage to be''—to follow the path to greater self-definition and actualization—and so they cut themselves off from new possibilities for being. Many individuals want some outside authority like religion or society to advise them on how to act and what to believe. But if blind conformity and immersion in the group lead to a wasted life, these individuals cannot blame anyone else or evade the consequences. To flee from their freedom and obligation to life is to be unauthentic, to show bad faith, and to live in despair.

Existentialism also places strong emphasis upon the individual's *obligation* to his or her fellow human beings. The most important consideration is not what one can get out of life but what one can contribute to it. One's life can be fulfilling only if it involves socially constructive values and choices.

Although there are many variations on the three major models we have reviewed, the basic models remain relatively distinct and are to some extent contradictory viewpoints. Like the blind men feeling different parts of the elephant and describing it as a different animal, each model makes a contribution to the part of the puzzle of human experience and behavior that it has tackled but does not seem to be adequate for some of the parts it has not tackled.

In this book we shall not limit ourselves to any one model but shall maintain an eclectic approach, utilizing concepts from differing theoretical orientations, including that of a fourth model—systems theory. This model takes cognizance in an orderly way of the continuity of all living systems and the uniqueness of the human race. It takes into account both inner experiencing and outer behaving, both actions and transactions (Buckley, 1968; Laszlo, 1972, 1975; Miller, 1965a, 1965b, 1977; von Bertalanffy, 1968). We will explore this model in the next section.

## TOWARD A UNIFIED VIEWPOINT: GENERAL SYSTEMS THEORY

All living **systems** have certain characteristics in common. For example, living systems contain genetic material (DNA)—indicating the common origin of all living things. Similarly, living systems contain a central ''decider'' and other subsystems, integrated in a way that makes the total system capable of self-regulation, development, and reproduction.

system: an assemblage of interdependent parts, living or nonliving

# Psychology in Action

## ROBERT W. AS SEEN BY THE MODELS OF HUMAN BEHAVIOR

The models of human behavior that we have described greatly affect the ways in which we view people, the questions that we ask, and the importance that we attach to various pieces of information.

We return here to the case of Robert W. to see how the various models view him. As we shall see, each model interprets Robert W. quite differently. But, despite the differences in the interpretations, each is describing the same individual.

Presented below are the views of Robert W. as seen by the psychoanalytic, social-learning, and humanistic-existential perspectives. To aid your understanding of these various perspectives, we have also listed the distinguishing characteristics of each of the models beneath each interpretation.

### Psychoanalytic View of Robert W.

There are some elements of an unresolved Oedipal conflict in Robert's personality. His closeness to his mother and his distance from his father suggest that his conflict with his father has not been fully resolved. However, there are also some elements in Robert's personality that suggest some identification with his father. In particular, Robert's apparently high motivation and achievement orientation comes from identification with his father. Unfortunately, his superego, the aspect of his personality that sets these high standards in Robert, cannot tolerate the possibility of less than excellent performance. Thus, in a situation where Robert's performance might be less than perfect, the anxiety that is aroused results in a "deflection" or "conversion" of his anxiety to physical symptoms.

*Distinguishing characteristics of the psychoanalytic model:*
  1. focus on early childhood events;
  2. importance of unconscious processes;
  3. key role of personality structures in behavior.

Depending on their level on the evolutionary scale, living systems can be simple or complex, but all have certain properties in common: *structural, integrative,* and *field* properties.

1. *Structural properties.* Each living system contains parts or subsystems which are interdependent and whose combined action enables the system to function as an integrated unit. Some of these subsystems, such as the nervous system, can be observed; others, such as the self-system, are inferred on the basis of the functioning of the system. Structural properties—and hence potentials for behavior—vary greatly from one type of living system to another. The behavior potentials of a fish are obviously not those of a human being. That is why it is important to understand the structure of a system if we are to understand its behavior.

### Social-Learning View of Robert W.

Many of Robert's behavior patterns appear to be learned. For example, his high achievement motivation appears to be related to the model set by his father through observational learning. Also, his father has emphasized the importance of achievement through his many talks about achievement. While there may be some anxiety associated with difficult test situations, Robert's response in these situations seems to be related to past learning experiences. That is, he appears to have been reinforced in the past for complaints of stomach pains through his mother's attention to his complaints. Robert's focus on business and accounting seems to be related to his expectation that important sources of reinforcement (well-paying job, security, etc.) will become available once he finishes his college program.

*Distinguishing characteristics of the social-learning model:*
1. key role of the effects of learning;
2. importance of environmental events in shaping behavior;
3. focus on observable behavior with some interest in cognitive events.

### Humanistic-Existential View of Robert W.

Robert's opinion of himself as "relatively well-adjusted" is an important piece of information, for it gives us the impression that he is in no apparent distress. And, his hobbies and social activities help confirm that his tendencies for self-fulfillment and growth are present and are an important part of his life. However, Robert's goals in life seem to be related more to parental wishes and training and less to his own desires and capabilities. His desire to complete a business and accounting program may be more related to his father's emphasis on success and achievement than to Robert's own desires in this area. Robert's mother seems to like him for what he is, but his father may like him only in the context of his performance in school. This failure to choose a course of life for himself and make his own decisions may ultimately give him difficulties.

*Distinguishing characteristics of the humanistic-existential model:*
1. importance of self-report and self-perception;
2. focus on present events and experiences;
3. key role of choice, growth, and self-actualization.

2. *Integrative properties.* Living systems have built-in tendencies to maintain their organization and functional integrity. If a system's equilibrium is disturbed beyond a certain point, it automatically takes action to restore its balance. This integration is achieved by means of transactions with the surrounding environment as well as by the inner organizational properties of the system itself. In both instances, these transactions involve *matter-energy processing,* as in the assimilation of food, and *information processing,* as in the recognition of danger.

3. *Field properties.* Each lower-level system is part of a higher-level system. For example, an organ is a subsystem of an individual, an individual of a group, and a group of society. The total field, of course, includes the physical as well as the sociocultural environment. Living systems are "open systems"—that is, they

are not self-sufficient but continue to exist only if they maintain favorable transactions with their surroundings. Thus each living system is in continual transaction with its field, and this constant interaction modifies both system and field.

## Special Characteristics of the Human System

As we go up the scale from simple to complex living systems we find that new structural and functional properties begin to appear. Often properties present in rudimentary form at lower levels of life become refined and more influential at higher levels. The evolution of the nervous system, for example, can be traced from a very simple segmental apparatus in a worm to the highly complex human brain.

While we share many characteristics with lower-level systems, human beings reveal many characteristics that are different and some that are unique. We shall note a few of the most significant of these.

1. *Self-awareness.* The human race alone seems to have evolved to a high level of reflective consciousness or self-awareness. We are able not only to be aware of ourselves as unique individuals but also to reflect upon, review, and reevaluate aspects of our own experiences.

2. *Ability to modify action.* Our highly refined mental ability provides a tremendous capacity for learning, reasoning, and imagining, giving us almost unlimited flexibility for coping with new and changing situations. This flexibility is further extended by the ability to evaluate the effects of our actions and to make indicated corrections.

3. *Use of symbols.* Our unique mental endowment also enables us to deal with ideas—symbols of absent or even imaginary objects, events, and concepts. This has made possible the development of written language and scientific procedures for understanding and making predictions about the order in the world. This helps us to base our behavior on sound assumptions about past, present, and future conditions.

4. *Concern with information, values, and meaning.* Since human beings have the fewest "built-in" coping patterns of all living creatures, we must choose our goals and the means for achieving them. This requires not only that we obtain information about ourselves and the world but also that we make value judgments about what is good and bad. And, ultimately, we must come to grips with the meaning of our existence in the universe.

5. *Complexity of transactions with field.* Whereas animals must rely on instinctual responses for feeding and coping with environmental hazards, human beings are not so limited. In fact, there seems to be almost no limit to the ways in which we can modify the environment for our own ends. As a result, our transactions with the environment are far more complex than those of other species. In fact, we are witnessing the decreasing importance of "natural selection of species" and the increasing importance of "human selection." This is the result of our fantastic ability to control the survival or extinction of other species and to shape the world around us.

6. *Self-direction.* These various properties of human beings—reflective self-

awareness, the ability to modify action, the use of symbols, concern with information, values, and meaning, and the complexity of our transactions with the environment—make possible a high degree of self-direction.

## Changes in the System with Time

Despite the special characteristics of the human system, we have much in common with other living things. The most prominent is the fact that all systems change with time. Living organisms develop in accordance with their inherited potentials throughout a life cycle that is characteristic for their species. Human beings, like other living creatures, change substantially between the early and late phases of the life cycle. We shall note some of these developmental changes in various sections of this book.

The general systems approach gives us a tool that is equally useful whether the system we are considering is an individual or a group and whether it is functioning effectively or ineffectively. In each case, we look for structural and integrative characteristics of the system itself as well as for properties in its field—and in its field interactions—that may be responsible for the system's adaptive or maladaptive functioning. Only with such a broad approach are we likely to understand, accurately predict, and constructively modify the behavior of living systems.

## SUMMARY

1. We addressed but did not resolve the question of the basic nature of human beings. As humans, we can be evil, neutral, or basically good. We can act in rational and irrational ways. And, our behavior can appear to be influenced by external factors (i.e., our behavior is determined) or appear to be totally free from external control (i.e., our behavior is free).

2. Human behavior can also be examined with the use of models or representations of reality. In the field of adjustment, three models of human behavior, the psychoanalytic, the social-learning, and the humanistic-existential, are the primary ways in which human behavior and emotion have been viewed. Human behavior can also be examined through the use of general systems theory, a framework that encompasses both our uniqueness as human beings and our continuity with other living creatures.

3. Each model makes different assumptions about human beings and emphasizes different aspects. The psychoanalytic model, for example, emphasizes the contribution of early childhood experience and the influences from unconscious processes. The social-learning model emphasizes the learned nature of human adjustment and the contribution of environmental influences in shaping behavior. Finally, the humanistic-existential model emphasizes the role of the self and the importance of inherent tendencies toward growth and self-actualization. All three models, however, attempt to describe human behavior.

# Part Two

# Personal Aspects of Adjustment

**Personality Development**

**Adjustment in the Life Span**

**Motivation: Our Needs and Goals**

**Effective Emotional Experiencing**

# Chapter 3

# Personality Development

*"How did it come about that a man born poor, losing his mother at birth and soon deserted by his father, afflicted with a painful and humiliating disease, left to wander for twelve years among alien cities and conflicting faiths, repudiated by society . . . and driven from place to place as a dangerous rebel, suspected of crime and insanity, and seeing, in his last months, the apotheosis of his greatest enemy—how did it come about that this man, after his death . . . transformed education . . . inspired the Romantic movement and the French Revolution, influenced the philosophy of Kant and Schopenhauer, the poems of Wordsworth, Byron and Shelley, the socialism of Marx, the ethics of Tolstoi, and, altogether, had more effect on posterity than any other writer or thinker of that eighteenth century in which writers were more influential than they had ever been before?"*

This puzzling question is posed by Will and Ariel Durant (1967, p. 3) as an introduction to their book *Rousseau and Revolution.* Although others might not evaluate the influence of Rousseau so highly, there is no question that it has been far-reaching. Yet the conditions of his life would have been expected to prevent the development of a person capable of making such a major impact on history.

This dramatic illustration highlights the enormous complexity of the forces that shape human development and behavior. Although we cannot yet provide a complete answer to the Durants' question "How did it come about . . . ?" we can describe the many influences that shape our growth as human beings.

In this chapter, we shall initially discuss the general patterns of development, including general trends toward personal maturity. After a brief assessment of the role of heredity and sociocultural influences, we shall examine the ways in which the three perspectives that we introduced in Chapter 2 deal with the issue of personality development. Finally, we shall discuss both healthy and faulty development and discuss development as a lifelong process of becoming.

## THE PATTERNS OF DEVELOPMENT

In contrast to other animals who have "built-in" patterns of behavior and who mature rapidly, the human infant begins life as a helpless creature with few built-in patterns. A key characteristic of the human life cycle is the relatively long period of infancy and childhood, during which the body grows toward maturity and the individual begins to acquire the information and competencies needed for adult functioning. This process is called **development.** In this section we shall focus on development during infancy and childhood; in the next chapter our primary focus will be on adjustment from adolescence to late adulthood.

**development: the predictable process of growth and change throughout the life span**

### Developmental Stages and Tasks

The process of development can be thought of as a series of stages through which each of us pass or as a set of tasks that must be satisfactorily completed.

**Developmental stages.**    Intensive studies of infants and children by Gesell (1956), Piaget (1952, 1970), and other investigators (e.g., Freeman, 1980; Knobloch & Pasamanick, 1974) have shown that human development follows a definite sequence, not only in physical and motor development but also in intellectual, emotional, moral, and social development. Crawling and sitting up come before walking. Early diffuse emotional reactions become differentiated into love, humor, grief, and other specific patterns. Language behavior progresses from random vocalizations to the words that eventually become the vehicles for thinking.

The work of Jean Piaget exemplifies the concept of developmental stages. Piaget studied **cognition**—our learning, understanding, knowing, thinking, imagining, reasoning, and creative processes (Flavell, 1977)—and described several stages of cognitive development in infants and children.

In the first stage, called the **sensorimotor** phase, a child learns by doing and gradually develops the ability to represent objects and events mentally and symbolically. Early in this stage, an object that is "out of sight" is also "out of mind." Later, a child learns that an object which is no longer physically present continues to exist nonetheless—that objects exist independently of perception. Children also learn to think ahead and plan during this phase and to develop a rudimentary sense of cause and effect.

From about ages two to seven, the child enters the **preoperational** period in which he or she shows great cognitive and language development. However, the pattern of thought that emerges in this period may seem strange to an adult. For example, a child may notice adults carrying umbrellas during a rainstorm. Later, when the child sees an adult carrying an umbrella on a sunny day, he or she may insist that it will rain. For a child in the preoperational period, carrying an umbrella causes rain.

Some of Piaget's most fascinating studies have concentrated on this period. For example, a child in the preoperational stage of development may exhibit seemingly illogical thought when faced with a **conservation** problem. A typical conservation problem might involve two balls of clay, both the same size. As the child watches, one of the balls of clay is rolled into a long, thin rope. The child is then asked, "Which of these has more clay?" Typically, he or she will select one of the two as having more clay, even though the initial amounts of clay were identical.

**Egocentrism** also occurs in the preoperational stage. The egocentric child is incapable of understanding another individual's point of view and is, in a sense, very self-centered. Of course, adults sometimes insist on their perspectives and points of view. In the adult, however, this insistence may not be related to preoperational thought but to other psychological processes.

Following this period, children enter the stage of **concrete operational** thought. This period typically exists during the early school years (ages seven to eleven), and is characterized by an increasing, though limited, ability to understand logical relationships. A child in this phase would have little difficulty solving the clay problem described above.

However, abstract ideas and relationships are difficult for the concrete operations child to grasp. For example, understanding the abstract idea of "adjust-

cognition: mental processes associated with learning, understanding, knowing, thinking, imagining, reasoning, and creativity

sensorimotor stage: first stage of Piaget's theory in which children learn a rudimentary sense of cause and effect

preoperational stage: second stage of Piaget's theory in which a child exhibits egocentrism and has difficulties with conservation problems

conservation: the ability to understand that an object retains properties such as mass or volume despite alterations of physical appearance

egocentrism: preoccupation with one's concerns or beliefs

concrete operational stage: third stage of Piaget's theory, characterized by a child's limited ability to understand cause and effect relationships

ment" would be very difficult for this child unless some explanation could be provided in terms of the child's actual experience in the world.

Developmental stages need not be limited to cognitive processes alone but can be extended to other areas of personality development. One such area is **moral development.** As described by psychologist Lawrence Kohlberg (1976), three levels of moral development can be distinguished:

*Stage I. Preconventional level.* While the preconventional child may be well behaved and even sensitive to labels such as "good" and "bad," behavior is interpreted in terms of physical consequences such as reward and punishment. Essentially, there is no real standard of morality at this level.

*Stage II. Conventional level.* This level is characterized by conformity to existing social norms and a desire to maintain that order. "Good" and "bad" behaviors are those so labeled by others, particularly people in authority.

*Stage III. Postconventional level.* This level is characterized by the morality of contract, of mutual rights, and of universal principles that are independent of the authority of specific groups that may hold power. Eventually, ethical principles are self-chosen and based on abstract concepts, such as the Golden Rule.

According to Kohlberg, most adult Americans operate at the level of conventional morality or relatively "blind" conformity to existing social norms and authority. We should note that the progression through developmental stages occurs in a gradual fashion. In moral development, for example, our movement from Stage I to Stage II levels is characterized by an increasing preponderance of Stage II over Stage I moral judgment.

**Developmental tasks.** It appears that certain tasks or competencies must be mastered at each stage of development if the individual is to maintain a normal schedule of development. For example, learning to walk and talk are major tasks of infancy, while establishing a mature sense of identity and acquiring the intellectual, emotional, and social competencies needed for adulthood are key tasks of adolescence.

If these **developmental tasks** are not mastered at the appropriate stage, the individual's immaturities and incompetencies will make it harder to master later developmental tasks. For example, a young child who has not learned to walk or talk would be at a serious disadvantage in entering nursery school or kindergarten. And the adolescent who does not date misses a major opportunity to acquire the experience and skill in interpersonal relations that will be needed to establish a satisfactory marriage. The demands of a given developmental period may be relatively easy or difficult to meet, depending on how well the tasks of prior developmental stages have been mastered and the kind of guidance the individual receives.

## The Crucial Roles of Maturation and Learning

**Maturation** refers to the growth of an organism that is determined primarily by genetic factors and occurs more or less independently of learning. These built-in maturational processes provide the potentials for the orderly progression of de-

moral development: changes in an individual's understanding of and ability to make judgments about right and wrong behavior

developmental tasks: competencies to be mastered during a particular stage of development

maturation: growth of an organism that is determined primarily by genetic factors

**Learning to walk is one of the key developmental tasks of infancy.**

velopment, but these potentials can be realized only under favorable environmental conditions.

During **critical periods** certain types of stimulation and learning are essential for normal development. For example, Hunt (1961) showed that if chicks were kept in darkness for up to five days after hatching, they showed no apparent defects in their pecking response; but if the perceptual restriction lasted eight or more days, they were unable to learn to peck. Similarly, Harlow and Harlow (1966) found that infant monkeys reared in isolation during the first six months after birth later showed serious inadequacies in social and sexual behavior.

**critical periods:** periods of development when an organism most needs certain inputs or is most ready for the acquisition of a given response

We know less about critical periods in human development. However, mental retardation, the inability to form warm interpersonal relationships, and antisocial behavior have been shown to be associated with extreme emotional, social, and intellectual deprivation in infancy.

If the opportunities for needed stimulation and learning are lacking during early critical periods, the functions expected to develop at these times may not appear, may appear more slowly, or may be only partially adequate. And, once the critical period has passed, it may be difficult or impossible to correct the physiological and/or psychological deficiencies that have occurred.

## Trends Toward Personal Maturity

Although a child's growth will be shaped in different ways in different cultures, certain characteristic trends can be seen in any society, primitive or advanced. These trends lead the individual toward responsible self-direction and the ability to participate in and contribute to society. Here we briefly note these specific but interrelated trends toward personal maturity.

1. *Dependence to self-direction.* One of the most obvious progressions toward maturity is from the dependency of the fetus, infant, and child to the independence of adulthood. Associated with self-direction is the development of a clear sense of personal identity and the acquisition of information, competencies, and values. In our society, this includes enough freedom from family and other social groups to be a person in one's own right.

2. *Pleasure to reality (self-control).* As we have seen, Freud thought the *pleasure principle*—the tendency to seek pleasure and avoid pain—was fundamental in governing early behavior. However, he thought this principle was in time subordinated to the *reality principle*—the realization that the individual must learn to perceive and face reality in order to meet his or her needs. This means distinguishing between fantasy and reality, controlling impulse and desire, delaying immediate gratification in the interest of long-range goals, and learning to cope with the inevitable hurts, disappointments, and frustrations of living.

3. *Ignorance to knowledge.* Although human infants are born in an apparent state of ignorance, they rapidly begin to acquire information about themselves and their world. With time, this information is organized into a stable **frame of reference** for guiding behavior. To be adequate, this frame of reference must be realistic, relevant to the kinds of problems the individual will face, and one in which the individual has faith. Also, it needs to be flexible, so that it can be modified by new experiences.

4. *Incompetence to competence.* The entire preadult period from infancy through adolescence is directed toward the mastery of the intellectual, emotional, and social competencies needed for adulthood. The individual acquires skills in problem solving and decision making, and learns to control and use his or her emotions, deal with others, and establish satisfying relationships. These competencies help prepare the individual for the various sexual, marital, occupational, and parental roles of adulthood.

frame of reference: assumptions concerning reality, value, and possibility that form an individual's "cognitive map" for interpreting and coping with his or her world

5. *Self-centered to other-centered.* Infants are concerned almost exclusively with their own needs and wants. But, with time, they normally develop an expanding understanding and concern for the needs of others as well. This includes the ability to give love to significant others and to be concerned about and involved with people in their community and society.

6. *Similarity to dissimilarity.* Most infants are relatively similar, while most older adults are exceedingly different from one another. As individuals grow and develop, their experiences set them increasingly apart from their peers.

7. *Amoral to moral.* The newborn infant is amoral, in the sense that he or she has no concept of "right" or "wrong." Very early, however, the infant learns that certain forms of behavior are approved or "good," while others are disapproved or "bad." With time, the growing individual gradually learns a pattern of value assumptions that operate as inner guides of behavior—the conscience or superego. Initially, the individual may accept these values blindly. But, with increasing maturity, he or she learns to appraise them and work out a personalized set of values.

## MAJOR DETERMINANTS OF PERSONALITY

Both heredity and the environment provided by our culture and by our society are among the major determinants of personality. These two major determinants do not influence personality development in independent ways. Rather, they interact in both obvious and subtle ways to influence our growth and development as human beings.

### Heredity

Each of us is born with a set of genetically determined characteristics that are given to us by our parents. This genetic inheritance provides the potentials for our development and our behavior. We will consider two aspects of our genetic endowment which are of particular interest: constitutional reaction tendencies and the unique human brain.

**Constitutional reaction tendencies.** **Heredity** influences the determination of some traits more than others. Its influence is perhaps most noticeable in physical features such as eye color, sex, and physique. Of equal if not greater importance, however, is the role our genetic inheritance plays in determining our "primary reaction tendencies" such as activity level, sensitivity, and adaptability. Even young babies reveal differences in how they react to particular stimuli. Some cry if their faces are exposed to sunlight; others are seemingly insensitive to such stimulation. Thus, conditions that one baby can tolerate may be quite upsetting to another.

One of the most striking things about these constitutional reaction tendencies is their unique patterning for each individual and their tendency to remain

**heredity: genetically determined characteristics given by parents and ancestors**

stable from infancy through young adulthood. Their special significance lies in their effect on the way the individual reacts to and is influenced by the environment—on his or her characteristic *coping style.*

Psychologist Hans Eysenck (1967) has further suggested that many aspects of human personality and development are genetically based. According to Eysenck, introverts and extroverts develop their distinctive interaction patterns because of their differing abilities to learn or condition. Introverts condition very readily and must protect themselves from too much physiological arousal. Extroverts, on the other hand, condition less readily and therefore seek out the company of others for needed stimulation.

**The unique human brain.**    Probably the most unique aspect of our genetic endowment is the human brain. It has been aptly described as the most highly organized apparatus in the universe. It consists of over 10 billion neurons with countless interconnecting pathways as well as myriad connections with other parts of the body. Even when we are asleep, more than 50 million nerve mes-

Identical twins Jim Springer and Jim Lewis were separated as infants and reared apart. Tests conducted on the two, after their reunion at age 39, revealed striking similarities in physical appearance, medical history, intelligence, interests, mannerisms, and mental abilities.

sages are being relayed between the brain and different parts of the body every second. Thus the human brain provides a fantastic communications and computing network with tremendous capabilities for learning, "storing" experience, reasoning, imagining, and integrating the overall functioning of the human organism. Not only do we have greater capacity for learning and modifying our behavior, but we must also deal with the "complications" presented by these competencies—the task of choice and values.

Available evidence indicates that the essential characteristics of our genetic inheritance are basically the same for all racial and ethnic groups. However, the specific features of this endowment may vary considerably from one person to another. Thus heredity not only provides common potentials for development and behavior typical of the human species but is also an important source of individual differences.

## Society and Culture

Our physical and sociocultural environments both heavily influence the way and the extent to which our genetic potentials are realized. The sociocultural environment is of importance to behavior and personality development.

In much the same sense that each person receives a genetic inheritance which is the end product of millions of years of biological evolution, he or she also receives a sociocultural inheritance which is the end product of thousands of years of social evolution. The significance of this inheritance has been well described by Aldous Huxley (1965):

*The native or genetic capacities of today's bright city child are no better than the native capacities of a bright child born into a family of Upper Paleolithic cave-dwellers. But whereas the contemporary bright baby may grow up to become almost anything—a Presbyterian engineer, for example, a piano-playing Marxist, a professor of biochemistry who is a mystical agnostic and likes to paint in water-colours—the paleolithic baby could not possibly have grown into anything except a hunter or food-gatherer, using the crudest of stone tools and thinking about his narrow world of trees and swamps in terms of some hazy system of magic. Ancient and modern, the two babies are indistinguishable. . . . But the adults into whom the babies will grow are profoundly dissimilar; and they are dissimilar because in one of them very few, and in the other a good many, of the baby's inborn potentialities have been actualized. (p. 69)*

Let us briefly note two specific aspects of our sociocultural inheritance and the way in which it is transmitted: culture and subculture, and socialization.

**Culture and subculture.**   A complex society such as ours has both an overall **culture**—a way of life shared by most members—and many subcultures. As Americans we share the same language, live under the same form of government, follow the same customs and laws, are exposed to television and other technological innovations, and have a mass of accumulated knowledge available to us.

**culture: the sum total of way of living built up by a given group, including technological innovations and manufactured objects**

We receive our socio-cultural legacy from our culture, from the subcultures to which we belong, and from our interactions and relationships with significant others, including parents and peers.

**subculture: an identifiable ethnic, regional, economic, or social group existing within the context of a culture**

At the same time, various **subcultures** exist in our society—such as those defined by regional boundaries and by ethnic, religious, and social class. While sharing the same general culture, these subgroups may vary markedly in certain specific beliefs, customs, values, and ways of life. To cite an extreme example, some juvenile gangs in our society espouse a "subculture of violence"—shared beliefs, values, and responses that make violence socially acceptable. In contrast, belonging to a Boy Scout or Girl Scout troop will probably have a quite different effect on development.

**Socialization.**   Each society fosters its own cultural patterns by systematically teaching the young. As a result, its members tend to be somewhat alike—to conform to certain basic personality types. Thus individuals reared among headhunters will become headhunters; individuals reared in societies that do not sanction violence will learn to settle their differences in nonviolent ways. Through the process of **socialization,** each of us accepts the values, beliefs, and acceptable behavior patterns of the group as our own (Levinson & Malone, 1980).

**socialization: process by which individuals come to accept the values, beliefs, and acceptable behavior patterns of a society as their own**

The more uniform and thorough the education of the younger members of a group, the more alike they will become. Thus, a society characterized by a limited and consistent point of view will not show the wide individual differences typical of a society like ours, where children have contact with many divergent beliefs. Even in our society, however, there are certain core values that we attempt to perpetuate—including the beliefs and values upon which our society is founded.

# Insight

## CULTURAL DIFFERENCES IN SEX ROLES

The strikingly different sex roles that develop in different societies have been described by Margaret Mead (1939) in her studies of New Guinea tribes. The contrasts she found among the three tribes she studied highlight the extremes that are possible—and the extent to which the "human nature" a child will develop is dependent on his or her early experiences.

1. *The Arapesh.* In this tribe both sexes showed characteristics and behavior that would be considered feminine in our own society. Both men and women were encouraged to be unaggressive, mild, cooperative, and responsive to the needs of others. Neither sex took an aggressive role in courtship. The ideal marriage consisted of a mild, responsive man married to a mild, responsive woman.

2. *The Mundungumor.* In this tribe both sexes would be characterized as masculine by our traditional standards. Both men and women were encouraged to be aggressive, violent, and ruthless; gentleness and tender behavior were at a minimum. The ideal marriage was that of a violent, aggressive male married to a violent, aggressive female.

3. *The Tchambuli.* While neither the Arapesh nor the Mundungumor had clearly defined roles which distinguished the behavior of the sexes, the Tchambuli did have such roles. But they were reversed by our standards. The women were characteristically dominant, impersonal, and businesslike and took the initiative in courtship and sexual behavior. By contrast, the men were irresponsible, emotionally dependent on the women, relatively passive, concerned about their physical appearance, and interested in arts and home activities.

In this study, then, we see three societies in which sex roles differ considerably from our own. In two, the roles are social rather than specifically sexual; there is very little distinction between the norms for the two sexes but a striking difference between the norms of the two societies. In the third, there is a reversal of sex roles as compared with ours.

During the past decade, there has been a trend in our society toward the convergence of conventional sex roles. That is, behaviors which were formerly considered either masculine or feminine—such as knitting, running for political office, and military service—are now considered appropriate for both sexes. Many men are now taking an active part in caring for children and performing household duties, while women are taking on responsibilities and duties in the business world that were once considered exclusively "men's work."

One interesting indication of this trend is the toys that are given to children. At one time, little boys got fire trucks and erector sets and doctor's kits, while little girls were given dolls and toy kitchens and nurse's kits. Some parents who were not following traditional sex roles objected. As a result, some companies began designing toys that do not observe traditional sex roles. Many parents are quite determined that their male and female children will both grow up with the idea that they can be whatever they want to be, regardless of traditional sex roles.

# PERSPECTIVES ON PERSONALITY DEVELOPMENT

In Chapter 2 we described three models of human behavior that can be used to help us understand the nature of human beings. Each of these three models can also help us understand personality development. In this section, we shall examine personality development from the perspective of the psychoanalytic, social-learning, and humanistic-existential viewpoints. As with our earlier discussions, we shall note how these perspectives focus on different aspects of the individual in their attempt to help explain the same phenomenon—personality development.

## The Psychoanalytic Perspective: Psychosexual and Psychosocial Stages

In Chapter 2, we briefly discussed psychoanalytic theory and outlined its approach to personality development. Here we shall expand that presentation as well as present Erik Erikson's psychosocial theory of personality development.

**Psychosexual development.**  As we noted earlier, psychosexual development is intricately related to three psychic structures: the id, the ego, and the superego, and we noted that the sequence of the psychosexual stages was: oral, anal, phallic, latency, and genital.

Freud termed his approach *psychosexual* because of his belief that sexual/pleasurable issues had a marked influence on the psychological functioning and development of an individual. In each of the psychosexual stages, the child experiences some sexual "tension" that can only be reduced through the gratification of the need. In the anal stage, for example, the tensions center in the region of the anus, and children experience both tension reduction and pleasure in the withholding and expelling of feces.

Assuming that no major problems arise in any of the stages, children progress more or less smoothly through the stages and ultimately become healthy, well-adjusted adults. However, a number of factors can inhibit progress through the psychosexual stages. One of these is **deprivation** in which the child does not receive enough satisfaction of personal needs. For example, the child in the oral stage who is rejected by her mother will suffer the loss of parental contact, affection, and love, especially in the context of feeding. Another factor that can impede progress through the psychosexual stages is **overindulgence** in which the child receives too much gratification and is therefore unwilling to continue to the next stage of development. An example of this might be the child who is overprotected and overfed.

Both deprivation and overindulgence result in the psychological consequence of **fixation.** The fixated child invests a great deal of mental energy in the psychological processes and behaviors characteristic of that stage and, as a result, has less energy to progress successfully through later stages. We would see the adult consequences of childhood fixation in the oral stage in an adult who was

**deprivation: failure to gratify needs**

**overindulgence: giving into needs in an excessive fashion**

**fixation: concentration of psychic energy in a pregenital period**

obese, dependent, and passive. Or, if fixation occurred in the anal phase, the adult consequences might be the stinginess and miserliness well-exemplified by the Charles Dickens character, Scrooge. As these examples suggest, the consequences of fixation are lifelong, and, as Freud maintained, may be changed only through intensive psychoanalysis.

The psychosexual phallic stage and its associated Oedipal conflict is particularly important for personality development. The child's growing attachment to the opposite-sexed parent and the anxiety that is associated with this attachment provides an ideal opportunity for the development of *sexual identity.* A boy who is attached to his mother but fears his father resolves this conflict by identifying with his father. Similarly, a girl who is attracted to her father reduces her anxiety concerning retribution from her mother by identifying with the mother.

Not only does the resolution of the phallic phase help establish the child's sense of him- or herself as male or female, but it also has important implications for adult psychological development. Freud believed that a consequence of the Oedipal conflict was the establishment of strong tendencies toward activity in the male and toward passivity in the female. Freud also maintained that the greater degree of castration anxiety in the male ultimately produced a stronger conscience in the male as compared with the female. As a result, males are the "prime mover[s] of civilization," while women are "undoubtedly painted as lesser human creatures" (Rychlak, 1981, p. 69).

More contemporary psychoanalysts, however, dispute this aspect of Freud's work. The neo-Freudians, for example, emphasize the functioning of the ego and downplay the sex-typed outcome of the Oedipal conflict. Robert White (1960), for example, emphasizes the development of competence in the phallic period, while Heinz Kohut (1977) views the Oedipal conflict as an opportunity to learn the joy of living.

As we noted earlier, Freud placed great emphasis on the early years. According to Freud, personality development was essentially complete by the end of the phallic phase, ages five to seven. In his view, everything that is of significance to an adult's behavior is a reflection of these very early experiences. Thus, the psychoanalytic view proposes that personality development essentially ended in childhood.

**The psychosocial stages.** An extension of Freudian psychoanalysis has been developed by Erick Erikson (1963, 1968). Erikson's approach emphasizes personality development throughout the course of an individual's life, including childhood, adolescence, and early to late adulthood.

Erikson's approach has been termed **psychosocial** because of its emphasis on the social relationships and interactions of the person—functions that Erikson considered characteristic of ego functioning. In contrast, Freud's approach emphasized sexual instinct and desires as the basic motivating force in personality development. That is, Freud emphasized the functioning of the id.

Erickson's psychosocial stages are eight in number, and each centers on a **crisis** or *conflict* that must be resolved. According to Erikson, as the individual matures biologically, certain capacities emerge. These changes are recognized by

**psychosocial development:** Erikson's theory of development, emphasizing personal and social aspects of development

**crisis:** a crucial time whose outcome will make an important difference for better or worse

the individual's community, and new social demands are made. This coming together of biological changes and social demands produces a conflict that must be resolved. The resolution of the conflict can be favorable—one that enhances personal growth and development—or it can be negative. Successful resolution of each conflict must occur before a person can fully prepare for the next conflict. However, successful resolution is not an all-or-nothing event, but a predominance of adaptive outcomes over maladaptive outcomes.

1. *Trust vs. mistrust.* This stage begins at birth and lasts until the child is about one year old. In this stage, which corresponds to Freud's oral phase, a child is helpless and totally dependent on parents for food, affection, and warmth. If a parent is responsive to the infant's needs, the infant begins to trust the world. In a sense, the infant learns that the world is consistent, predictable, and an interesting, secure place. The favorable outcome of this stage is thus the development of basic trust and optimism and the capacity to become psychologically attached to another person.

**Sensitive meeting of the infant's physical needs as well as needs for warmth and affection helps the infant acquire a sense of basic trust in the world and fosters healthy development of the child's personality.**

However, if children are not provided affection and care, they learn that they cannot trust the world to respond to their needs. Not only do they mistrust the world, but they also do not trust others and will themselves become suspicious and anxious.

2. *Autonomy vs. doubt and shame.* During this stage, a child must learn a variety of physical and mental skills. During ages one to three (corresponding to Freud's anal phase), a child learns to do things and think independently. The successful outcome of this conflict engenders a sense of control over oneself and the environment. Additionally, the capacity for a sense of self is also developed in this stage. Parents can help their toddlers develop a sense of autonomy by providing safe limits for their children to develop these skills. However, should parents be too restrictive, children may come to feel that they do not have skills for dealing with the environment and themselves (doubt) or that they do not have skills for dealing with others (shame).

3. *Initiative vs. guilt.* This period ranges from ages three to five and corresponds to Freud's phallic phase. In this stage, a child begins to show independent thought and independent action in daily life in the form of fantasy. As with the Oedipal conflict, the fantasy often focuses on the opposite-sexed parent. Since a child cannot ultimately possess the parent, the fantasies fail. On a more overt level, children may involve themselves in creative play, in the care of their siblings, or in risk-taking. However, without the knowledge of the consequences of their actions, children can become engaged in personally destructive or socially disapproved acts. However, loving and concerned parents can help show their children which thoughts and behaviors are acceptable and which are unacceptable and thus help their children develop a sense of purpose and goal-directedness. If children are instead taught that all their behaviors are unacceptable, they may develop a sense of guilt.

4. *Industry vs. inferiority.* This period lasts from about six to eleven years of age and corresponds to Freud's latency phase. During this time, children enjoy developing and demonstrating skills that will provide them a place in adult society. Some of the skills may be academic, some may be athletic, and some may be practical. But all may be related to valued adult skills. A child who receives praise and encouragement for his or her efforts may develop a sense of industry—a sense that he or she is competent and will be able to find a place in the adult world. If, however, children's efforts are ridiculed, they may develop a sense of inferiority in which they believe that all they attempt is worthless.

5. *Identity vs. role confusion.* Erikson thought that this period, which lasts from about ages twelve to eighteen, was especially important. During this phase, adolescents must develop a self-image (that is recognized by others as well) and a sense of their essential sameness through time and in their community. If they succeed in developing an identity, they will be able to decide what kind of life they will build for themselves in their society.

However, some people do not resolve this **identity crisis.** Those who do not may suffer from **role confusion** (also known as *identity diffusion*) in which they are aimless and uncertain. These individuals have a chameleonlike pattern in which they adopt whatever role they think is suited to the particular setting in which they find themselves.

**identity crisis: a stage in Erikson's theory in which individuals face the difficulties of developing a personal sense of self**

**role confusion: the lack of a sense of self; also known as *identity diffusion***

6. *Intimacy vs. isolation.* The attainment of intimacy is the task of the young adult, aged nineteen to thirty-five. During this phase, the young adult comes to love another adult for the other person's real qualities, not for the personal satisfactions that can be obtained from the relationship. If the young adult is able to establish this type of relationship without fear or defensiveness, he or she has begun to resolve the intimacy vs. isolation conflict. However, the failure to establish intimate relationships may result in the development of isolation in which an individual prefers being alone to being with others.

7. *Generativity vs. stagnation.* The need to teach and direct the next generation is the hallmark of the adult who has successfully solved the generativity vs. stagnation crisis. During this period, which typically lasts from ages thirty-five to fifty, the individual becomes concerned with giving younger generations guidance and training. This may involve raising one's own children or it may be a more universal concern with youth organizations, schools, or such broader issues as pollution and nuclear war. Those who do not successfully resolve this conflict may instead stagnate and become very self-indulgent and absorbed in their own wishes and desires.

8. *Ego integrity vs. despair.* From age fifty, the individual increasingly looks back upon his or her life and tries to evaluate its purpose and meaning. Those who are satisfied with the pattern and structure of their lives experience ego integrity—a sense that "It's my life, the only one I could have lived." Those who are dissatisfied with their lives develop despair and may plunge themselves into denial of physical decline.

## The Social-Learning Perspective: Reinforcement, Observational Learning, and Expectancies

The social-learning perspective tends to be more concerned with current behavior and its modification than with its development. Also, the social-learning perspective focuses more on observable or measurable behavior rather than discussing personality or developmental processes. However, research in the social-learning area has dramatically shown that the processes of reinforcement, observational learning, and expectancies may have a significant influence on the development of our patterns of behavior.

**Reinforcement: The early years.**   In the early years of a child's life, reinforcers tend to be *primary* in nature. That is, reinforcers during infancy and childhood are often related to the biological processes of eating, drinking, and avoiding pain. For example, parents often reinforce an infant's first attempts at talking with food or juice. The child may point to a water fountain and say, "wah-wah." The parent, in turn, interprets this request correctly and provides the asked-for water to the child.

Even at an early age, though, social forms of reinforcement are used to shape a child's development. For example, the artistic endeavors of a child may be reinforced by a parent's expression of delight when he or she is presented with a "portrait" of the parent consisting of a circle and some extraneous marks.

Reinforcement in the form of a blue ribbon encourages these young sheep-raisers.

Encouraged by the parent's response, the child may return to a drawing pad and continue his or her efforts.

At the same time, through the use of reinforcers or punishers, the parent is also guiding the areas in which artistic effort may be channeled. A child who colors in coloring books is likely to be praised for his or her work, while a child who decides to be artistic on living room walls is likely to provoke a much different reaction from a parent.

Thus, reinforcers in the early years can be *primary reinforcers* (food, water, etc.) or they can be *secondary reinforcers* (praise, disapproval, etc.). Additionally, reinforcers can be used to help guide skills and talents, including those creative abilities often thought to be "inborn."

**Reinforcement: The later years.**  The effects of reinforcement are not limited to the young. Adolescents and adults also tend to be responsive to its effects, although the type of reinforcement may differ somewhat.

Reinforcement in the later years tends to be primarily social in nature. That is, adolescents and adults are more responsive to praise, a pat on the back, and recognition from self, peers, and family. For example, a stained-glass artisan may have a feeling of pride in completing a window for a church or temple. This pride may result in the self-spoken praise, "You did a beautiful job." Or, neighbors' expressions of thanks to us for watering their plants while they were away on vacation may increase the chances that we will be equally helpful in the future. And, of course, the reinforcers for effective studying may involve a mark of "A" on a grade sheet.

Each of these reinforcers is learned, and the value of each may depend on an individual's life conditions. Thus, a grade of "A" on a course may not be relevant to a forty-five-year-old police officer, while a student may be indifferent to a promotion in the police force. Reinforcers (and punishers) are thus quite individualized and become even more individualized as the person ages.

**Observational learning.**    In considering observational learning on personality development, we must make a distinction between acquisition and performance. In observational learning, **acquisition** refers to the covert learning of some new skill, while **performance** refers to the production or performance of that skill. Obviously, if an individual can perform the behavior, he or she has also acquired it as well. However, the opposite is not true; that is, an individual can acquire a new skill but need not perform it.

Observing the actions of others and noting the consequences that their actions produce can increase or decrease our own behavior. For example, a clerical worker may notice a co-worker's particular friendliness to a supervisor. Should that co-worker get a raise or promotion, the clerical worker may decide to be more friendly to the supervisor as well. Or, if an adolescent male observes the ridicule and derision a peer receives for being emotionally expressive, he may decide to decrease his efforts to express his emotions.

Perhaps the most important models in an individual's life, at least initially, are parents. However, a child learns from other models as well, including siblings, peers, and media figures. Research has shown that the most effective models are those who are (1) nurturant and rewarding, (2) powerful, and (3) similar to the observer (Bandura, 1977b). However, we should point out that children and adults can learn from models who are highly dissimilar from them.

**Expectancies and self-regulatory systems.**    An individual's behavior in a situation is not simply a function of environmental contingencies. Rather, we make an active attempt to predict outcomes and thereby guide our behavior.

In general, expectancies take the form of "If . . . , then . . . " (Mischel, 1981; Rotter, 1954). That is, an individual examines a given situation, compares it to similar, previous situations, and estimates the probability of a given outcome. For example, a man may be driving down a deserted road, far exceeding the speed limit. He then compares his present situation to similar situations and makes an estimate of the chances of being caught by the police. This estimate will then be used to alter the man's behavior. If he was given a speeding ticket on prior, similar occasions, he may slow down to the legal limit. On the other hand, if he has never received a ticket for speeding, he may maintain his current speed. Of course, guesses about the outcome are not always correct, and the individual who continues to speed may be surprised to see flashing red lights in the rear-view mirror.

Another way in which expectancies operate is through our sensitivity to certain cues that others give us. A friend who nods understandingly when we start talking about our personal problems gives us information that further disclosure of difficulties will be accepted. On the other hand, if the friend stares out the

**acquisition:** in observational learning, gaining a new skill or knowledge

**performance:** demonstration of learned competencies through behavior

window, does not pay attention to us, or drums her fingers across the table, the cues suggest that further disclosure will not be eagerly received (Mischel, 1981).

Finally, people can have **self-efficacy** expectations in which they make a prediction about their ability to perform a task. Self-efficacy expectations are based primarily on self-evaluation of one's abilities (Bandura, 1982a). Research has suggested that individuals whose self-efficacy is raised often function and develop more effectively in a variety of situations (Bandura, 1978).

**self-efficacy: belief of an individual in his or her ability to perform a task**

These expectancies can be combined into larger self-regulatory systems. If we believe that certain kinds of study behaviors help improve grades, we can use our beliefs to help us structure and regulate our own behavior. Similarly, we can regulate our interpersonal relationships based upon our desires for the structure of the relationship. If we wish to end the relationship, we can, based upon our expectancies, alter our behavior to produce this result. And if we wish to improve the relationship, we can regulate our actions to help achieve that outcome.

## The Humanistic-Existential Perspective: The Self

*"If a public opinion poll were to ask the question 'What is the most interesting topic on earth?' most people would probably answer, 'My own self.' No one else, even those nearest to us, can share in the same intimate way this center of centers where all life and mental activity take place. Every waking hour is filled with one's own personal thoughts and with emotions that only he can experience firsthand. They may, of course, be communicated to others or inferred from external behavior, but nonetheless they are uniquely one's own."*
*(SEVERIN, 1973, P. 1)*

In the humanistic-existential perspective, the **self** develops via the interaction of heredity and environment. As the self-structure develops, it becomes the integrating core of the personality—the reference point around which the individual's experiences and coping patterns are organized. As new situations arise, they are perceived, thought about, and acted upon in relation to the self. Thus the self becomes a crucial force in shaping further development and behavior.

**self: the central reference point in the personality around which experience and actions are organized**

The humanistic-existential perspective not only emphasizes the concept of the self, but it also emphasizes an individual's inherent tendency to grow, develop, and fulfill his or her potentials. This positive view of personality development is one of the unique contributions of investigators such as Carl Rogers and Abraham Maslow.

When psychologists refer to the self, they are not thinking of some "little person" sitting in the brain. Rather, self is a useful concept for understanding and predicting many aspects of our perceiving, thinking, feeling, and behavior. Like gravity, the self cannot be observed directly but is inferred from various behaviors that can be observed. In this section, we shall view the self as a complex psychological process which has a developmental course, is influenced by learning, and can be studied by means of scientific procedures (Suls, 1982).

**self-concept: an individual's sense of his or her identity, worth, capabilities, and limitations**

**Development of our self-concept.** Our **self-concept** is the picture or image we have of ourself. This self-image incorporates our perception of what we are really like *(self-identity)*, of our worth as a person *(self-evaluation)*, and our aspirations for growth and accomplishment *(self-ideal)*.

1. *Self-identity.* We are not born with a sense of self (Rogers, 1959). In fact, newborn infants apparently do not know where their own bodies leave off and the environment begins. But gradually we discover the boundary lines of our body and learn to distinguish between the *me* and the *not-me*. This perception of the physical self is called the **body-image** and appears to form the primitive core of our self-concept. Since others perceive and react to us—at least partially—in terms of our physical appearance, it is not surprising that our body image continues to be an important component of our self-identity throughout our life.

**body image: an individual's perception of his or her body**

We play a variety of social roles, and sometimes we feel as though we have several different "selves." Thus a young mother who teaches school may play the role of wife, parent, and teacher—each with its different role expectations and demands. When such roles are in conflict or cannot be integrated into a coherent "master role" of some sort, the individual may have difficulty in establishing a

**Our self-image includes not only how we perceive ourselves but how others see us as well.**

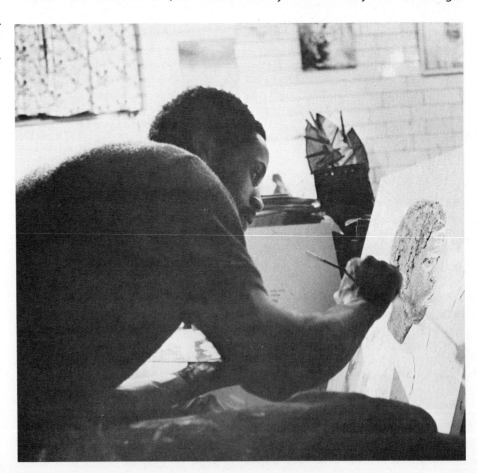

stable sense of identity. This is often a problem during adolescence in our society, when social roles are unclear and conflicting. With time, however, such role problems are usually resolved into a reasonably coherent **self-identity,** which shows considerable consistency across a wide range of situations and behaviors (Erikson, 1968).

> self-identity: an individual's perception of "who I am"

Each of us sets goals, hopes, prays, and makes decisions in terms of this awareness of ourselves as unique people. Each of us exists in the center of a changing world of experience, and most events in the world are perceived and dealt with in relation to the individual's self-identity.

2. *Self-evaluation.* As we achieve a sense of self-identity, we begin to make value judgments about ourselves. Thus, we may evaluate ourselves as superior or inferior, worthy or unworthy, adequate or inadequate.

During early life, our **self-evaluation** is heavily dependent upon the way we are viewed by significant others, such as our parents. In these early years, we have few standards for measuring our adequacy and worth other than those supplied by the people around us. If their words and behavior label us as inadequate and unworthy of love and respect, we have little choice but to accept their negative evaluation. If, on the other hand, we are warmly accepted and respected as adequate and capable persons, our self-evaluation will probably be positive (Rogers, 1959). We will have a high level of **self-esteem.**

> self-evaluation: ways in which an individual views him- or herself in terms of worth and adequacy

> self-esteem: feeling of personal worth

As we grow older, culturally defined standards of desirability—such as peer group standards concerning physical appearance and so on—increasingly provide the yardstick against which we compare ourselves. Since these standards may vary considerably from one group to another, our particular group memberships may influence our level of self-esteem. However, the evaluations of our adequacy and worth learned during childhood tend to have a continuing effect on our personality development. Later experiences can change them but never quickly or easily.

Obviously there is no one-to-one relationship between people's actual assets and liabilities and the way they evaluate themselves. A highly talented person may have deep feelings of inferiority and unworthiness, while a person with mediocre or even inferior ability may be convinced of his or her superior capability and worth. These inconsistencies between our self-evaluation and others' evaluation of us are typically reduced through social interaction and other interactions with the environment. For example, the high-school student who regards herself as immensely musically talented may find her evaluation of herself changing as a result of interactions with other music students.

3. *Self-ideal.* Besides a sense of personal identity and worth, our self-concept includes our aspirations for accomplishment and growth. Our image of the person we would like to be and think we should be is called our **self-ideal** (Rogers, 1959).

> self-ideal: the self that an individual thinks he or she should be or become

Our self-ideal is closely related to the identification we make with various models—parents, friends, prominent personalities, national heroes, and other people we admire. Depending upon whether our aspirations are difficult or easy to achieve in relation to our abilities and environmental opportunities, we are said to have a high or low *level of aspiration.* If our level of aspiration is too high, we will suffer inevitable failure and self-devaluation no matter how hard we try or how well we actually perform. If it is too low, we will waste our personal resources and opportunities for growth and fulfillment. Realistic levels of aspiration thus offer the greatest opportunities for personal development.

It seems likely that some discrepancy between a person's existing self-image and self-ideal is necessary to foster personal growth, but we do not know how wide a discrepancy is desirable. We know, however, that a marked discrepancy between one's real and ideal self can lead to serious inner conflict and self-devaluation.

4. *Self-actualization.* Both Rogers and Maslow agree that a central tendency of the self is the movement toward the fulfillment of potentials and the actualization of possibilities. In essence, both theorists hypothesize that we are generally motivated to seek out those experiences that enhance us as individuals while we avoid those experiences that are unpleasant or which devalue us. The self-actualizing process can not only provide us with the means by which we maintain and enhance the self, but it can also help us seek out and experience special moments of joy and wholeness (Maslow, 1968). We will consider self-actualization in greater detail in our discussion of motivation in Chapter 5.

**Maintenance, continuity, and differentiation of the self.**    Because the self is at the very core of our existence, its maintenance becomes a matter of special concern. Serious disorganization or devaluation of the self, such as occurs in severe depression, can disable us just as surely as a serious physical illness. Thus we tend to develop a system of *self-* or *ego-defense mechanisms,* such as denial, rationalization, and projection, to help maintain the adequacy and worth of the self. We will discuss these mechanisms in greater detail in Chapter 8.

Despite changes in physical appearance, competencies, roles, and other aspects of the self, we maintain a feeling of continuity over time. That is, we tend to think of ourselves as pretty much the same persons we were yesterday and will be tomorrow. Our sense of continuity between past, present, and future contributes further to our sense of identity and self-direction—but it does not prevent personal change and growth.

self-differentiation: development of the self into increasingly more complex structures

The influence of the self will depend heavily upon the extent of **self-differentiation.** In some societies, people are assigned a position and role, often dependent upon their sex and the status of their family. These assigned roles largely determine their self-identity and behavior, and people in these societies may be submerged in the group and develop very little sense of individuality. They may not perceive themselves as having a high degree of choice or freedom for self-direction. In contrast, our society encourages each of us to develop our potentials. Though there are many pressures toward conformity, we tend to value the individual as a unique person with the right to a high degree of individuality and self-determination.

As we develop a clear-cut sense of selfhood, we tend to become an increasingly important force in directing our behavior. Each new experience is evaluated and dealt with in terms of its meaning and significance to the self. And because the ongoing activities of the human system are organized in relation to the self, each of us tends to develop a relatively consistent **life-style**—a characteristic way of thinking, doing, and growing that distinguishes us from other people. We put our personal stamp on each role we play and on each situation we encounter.

**life-style:** general pattern of assumptions, motives, cognitive styles, and coping techniques that characterize the behavior of an individual and give it consistency

# HEALTHY AND FAULTY DEVELOPMENT

Researchers are increasingly impressed with the uniqueness of each person they study. Though scientists search for order, uniformities, and predictable patterns, they keep reminding us that generalizations never fully encompass any particular person. Despite the characteristics we share in common as human beings, each of us is also a unique individual.

In studying differences in development, questions arise concerning: *(a)* the problem of defining "healthy" development, *(b)* the nature or forms of "faulty" development, and *(c)* the conditions conducive to healthy development.

## The Problem of Defining Healthy Development

Defining and describing healthy development is a more difficult task than it might initially appear. We can describe two general approaches that researchers have employed in trying to solve the problem of defining healthy development.

1. *"Normal" as healthy.* This view considers development as healthy when there is no apparent physical or psychological **pathology** and no marked deviation from the group average. In essence, healthy development is development that does not deviate from the norm.

**pathology:** abnormal mental or physical condition

This approach, however, is not always adequate in dealing with personality development. Take the case of an adolescent, for example, who is making passing grades at school, getting along well with classmates and teachers, and, while showing no indications of delinquency or maladjustment, is just drifting along, using only a fraction of a superior intellectual ability. This may not be "sick," but is it healthy?

2. *"Optimal" as healthy.* According to this approach, healthy development can be defined as a process leading to complete physical, mental, and social well-being. As the example above suggests, people who do not use the abilities they possess to fullest advantage are not utilizing their skills in an optimal fashion. Healthy development goes beyond the average or norm in the direction of the maximal utilization of talents and the fulfillment of potentials.

The concept of optimal development is a meaningful one, but we are a long way from agreeing on just what pattern of traits or behaviors constitutes optimal development. What people regard as desirable and optimal inevitably reflects the customs, demands, beliefs, and values of the larger society as well as the personal beliefs and values of the person making the judgment. Thus, optimal development is a general principle and not something we can define and measure precisely and universally.

The problem of defining healthy development is further complicated by the fact that, as we learn more about human development, we keep changing the criteria we use to make judgments. The quiet, polite little boy who never expressed anger was admired in the Victorian era. Today, he would be regarded as inhibited. Similarly, as educational procedures improve, the intellectual development that is normal for a six-year-old today may be considered indicative of mental retardation fifty years from now.

Hence, we will need much more information about human potentials and needs before we can establish adequate standards for evaluating an individual's psychological development.

## Forms of Faulty Development

Our tendencies toward health and normality do not guarantee healthy development. Three common types of unhealthy psychological development have been delineated: arrested development, special vulnerability, and distorted development. These may appear singly or in combination. In one way or another, each impairs the individual's coping ability and adaptation.

**Arrested development.**  In speaking of arrested development, we are concerned with the immaturities that seriously impair an individual's adjustive resources. For example, adolescents who remain emotionally dependent on their parents and avoid interaction with their peers show arrested development. People who never learn to delay gratification of their impulses lack a prerequisite for mature planning and choice.

Immaturities may be pervasive or limited to certain facets of a person's development. For example, an individual may show a high degree of intellectual development but be immature in emotional and social development. On a more restricted level we might cite the case of a young adult who throws temper tantrums when frustrated or a middle-aged Don Juan who is unable to form a stable or meaningful intimate relationship. In some cases immaturities may pervade an individual's development, but the more common pattern involves our carrying a residue of immature attitudes and behavior patterns into later developmental stages.

**Special vulnerabilities.**  Life experiences, especially during early stages of development, sometimes leave a lowered resistance to certain types of stress. On a biological level, a severe case of influenza may lead to increased **vulnerability** to other respiratory disorders. On a psychological level, early traumatic experiences may create "psychic wounds" or "weak spots" which never completely heal, leaving the individual vulnerable to certain types of stressful situations. For example, an individual who has been deserted by his or her partner may have unusual difficulty in coping with rejection by others in later life. Similarly, a child who has shared a parent's intense feelings of devaluation and hurt during a traumatic divorce may be particularly stressed when his or her own marriage is

**vulnerability: increased susceptibility to damage or disease**

# Insight

## MALADAPTIVE FAMILY PATTERNS

Recent research on families as group systems has revealed that a child's maladaptive behavior may be fostered by the general family environment as well as by the child's relationships with one or both parents. Although we have no model of the "ideal" family, four family patterns have been distinguished which typically have a detrimental effect on child development.

1. *The inadequate family.* This type of family is characterized by an inability to cope with the ordinary problems of living. It lacks the resources, physical and/or psychological, for meeting demands with which most families can cope satisfactorily. Such a family cannot provide its children with needed feelings of safety and security, nor can it guide the children in the development of essential competencies.

2. *The disturbed family.* Disturbed homes may involve many pathological patterns, but such homes appear to have certain characteristics in common: *(a)* the presence of parents who are fighting to maintain their own equilibrium and who are unable to give the child needed love and guidance; *(b)* the child's involvement in the emotional problems of the parents to the detriment of his or her development; and *(c)* the child's exposure to constant emo-

tional turmoil, irrationality, and faulty parental models.

3. *The antisocial family.* Here the family holds values that are not accepted by the wider community. In some families, the parents are overtly or covertly engaged in behavior that violates the standards and interests of society and may be chronically in trouble with the law. Antisocial values, such as dishonesty, deceit, and lack of concern for others, provide undesirable behavioral models for the child.

4. *The disrupted family.* The most common form of disrupted family is the family without a father. Due to a number of circumstances, including divorce, separation, and desertion, more and more children are being reared in homes with only one parent present. The departure of one parent often causes severe stress and economic hardship for the remaining family members. If the family cannot be reorganized into an effectively functioning group, the result may be an undesirable environment for the children.

It may be emphasized, however, that the long-range effects of family disruption can vary greatly. In some cases, a relatively peaceful home with one caring parent can be better than a two-parent home filled with marital conflict and tension.

---

threatened. As hypothesized by the psychoanalytic perspective, traumas occurring during any life period may increase vulnerability, particularly if they are experienced as acutely threatening and self-devaluating. Probably most of us have a vulnerable **Achilles' heel** as a result of some earlier trauma.

**Distorted development.**   Sometimes development proceeds in grossly undesirable forms or directions. Such distortions are readily apparent on biological as well as psychological levels. People born without lower limbs or with a cleft palate are examples of distortions on a biological level. On a psychological level,

"Achilles' heel": special vulnerability to a specific type of stress

distorted development can be seen in the individual who murders for "kicks," the adult who abuses children, and the adolescent who refuses to cope with day-to-day living by turning to heavy and consistent drug use. In all these cases, development has proceeded in a fashion that is not conducive to the individual's or society's well-being and growth.

## Psychological Conditions Fostering Healthy Development

We shall summarize several family conditions which seem to be essential for healthy development.

**Emotional warmth and acceptance.**   As predicted by the humanistic-existential approach, an atmosphere of love and acceptance is an important factor in healthy personality development. In one of the first comprehensive studies of child-rearing practices, Sears, Maccoby, and Levin (1957) concluded that the most crucial and pervasive of all the influences exerted in the home were the love and warmth expressed by the parents.

Later studies have supported this conclusion, demonstrating a close relationship between parental love and acceptance and the development of such traits as self-esteem, self-reliance, independence, and self-control. In addition, love and acceptance help infants develop a basic sense of trust toward their parents and the world around them. This sense of trust becomes a major safeguard against fear and anxiety, giving the infant the feeling of security needed to explore the environment and master developmental tasks. Furthermore, many conditions that might otherwise impair development—such as a physical handicap, poverty, or harsh discipline—may be neutralized for the child who feels loved and accepted.

Love and acceptance usually form part of a broader pattern of positive family interrelationships. For example, love and acceptance tend to be accompanied by an interest in the child and what he or she is doing, by respect for the child as a person, and by displays of warmth and affection (Coopersmith, 1967). Children are typically encouraged to interact with their world—within limits essential for their protection—and are subjected to firm but not coercive controls. Often, too, the parents encourage the child to meet high but realistic standards. Thus a whole cluster of attitudes and actions is usually involved in "love and acceptance." Farnsworth (1966) made this point very well in discussing the child's broader needs:

*Every child needs affection, the feeling of belonging and being wanted, respect as an individual in his own right, a favorable setting for growth and the development of security, freedom from excessive domination, firm discipline from a respected source, and privacy enough to allow his active imagination to develop. (p. 44)*

**Effective structure and discipline.**   A clearly structured environment—one which is orderly and consistent and in which the child knows what is expected and acceptable and what will be disapproved or punished—appears to foster healthy development. As described by the social-learning perspective, this involves both inducing and shaping desired responses and eliminating undesirable ones—an overall process which goes under the general term **discipline.**

**discipline:** methods used to teach children acceptable and unacceptable behavior

Three elements of structuring seem particularly important: *(a)* clearly defined standards and limits, so that children understand what goals, procedures, and conduct are approved, *(b)* adequately defined roles for both older and younger members of the family, so that children know what is expected of both themselves and others, and *(c)* established methods of handling children that encourage desired behavior, discourage misbehavior, and deal with infractions when they occur. The limits, roles, and methods of dealing with an individual child should of course be realistic and appropriate to his or her age, needs, and abilities. Approaches that help one child develop and maintain desirable behavior patterns may make another child resentful and rebellious and still another insecure and withdrawn.

Flexibility in rearing children is not the same as permissiveness, however. A child can be handicapped by a lack of structure and discipline. Too much permissiveness tends to produce a spoiled, demanding, and inconsiderate child—and often an insecure and unhappy one. Overly severe restraints and punishment, on the other hand, tend to foster fear of the punisher, reduced initiative and spontaneity, and a lack of trust in authority figures.

In general, it appears that freedom should be commensurate with maturity—the child's ability to use freedom wisely—and that parents need to love their children enough to discipline them. And, the best discipline occurs when parents make it clear that, in disapproving a child's behavior, they are not disapproving or rejecting the child as a person (Ginott, 1966). It is also important to make clear the response that is expected and acceptable rather than just saying in effect, "You misbehaved."

**Encouragement of competence and self-confidence.** **Guidance** is closely related to discipline. Usually we take it for granted that a child needs help in learning to read, but we may not realize that a child also needs guidance in learning nonacademic skills. Today children are exposed to many ideas, situations, and points of view before they are mature enough to evaluate them critically. Thus, they need guidance in deciding what is true and real, what is right, and what is worth striving for—decisions that will form the foundation for an adequate frame of reference. At the same time, children need help in acquiring the intellectual, emotional, and social competencies needed to anticipate and meet the demands that will be made upon them.

**guidance:** helping children make value judgments

Children also need to succeed and to have their successes recognized. One need only observe a child's eager request to "Watch me!" as he or she demonstrates some new achievement to understand the importance of success and recognition in the development of competence and self-confidence.

Although it would be imprudent as well as impossible to protect a child from every failure, healthy development requires that the balance be kept on the side of success. All children experience setbacks, rejections, and disappointments—experiences that challenge their feelings of capability and worth. But if, as the humanistic-existential theorists suggest, the child, on balance, has more experi-

Through effective guidance, parents can teach their children both skills and values. These boys are not only learning how to set the table but may also be learning the value of contributing to the family and assisting parents.

ences adding to self-esteem than detracting from it, he or she usually continues to grow in competence and self-confidence.

**Helping children meet challenges.**   While parents strive to protect their children from unnecessary hurt and trauma, they may handicap their children if they keep them from seeking out and coping with new experiences. In studies of infant, child, and adolescent development, Lois Murphy (1962) and her associates (Murphy & Moriarity, 1976) emphasized the need for such experiences:

*Over and over again we saw how the impact of a new challenge intensified the child's awareness of himself; his capacity to meet such a challenge enhances his pleasure, his sense of adequacy, and his pride. Through the successive experiences of spontaneous mastery of new demands and utilizing new opportunities for gratification the child extends and verifies his identity as one who can manage certain aspects of the environment. Through his coping experiences the child discovers and measures himself, and develops his own perception of who and what he is and in time may become. We can say that the child creates his identity through his efforts in coming to terms with the environment in his own personal way. (Murphy, 1962, p. 374)*

Inevitably, learning to cope with new experiences leads to occasional failures. In addition, children are likely to encounter life crises—as when they require hospitalization, their parents divorce, or a pet dies. As the psychosocial approach might predict, Murphy and her colleagues found parental support and encouragement to be of crucial importance in helping the child cope with failures and crises and maintain healthy development.

Parental support and assistance do not always take the form of direct instruction. Parents may also render assistance by restructuring their children's environment to provide certain kinds of experiences and reinforcements. For example, parents may take children to zoos and museums, or they may take children to visit different people, cities, and areas of the country to expand their knowledge and horizons.

**Appropriate role models.**    Research in the social-learning tradition has shown that much of our learning occurs through the observation of models. Thus, children are likely to adopt many of the beliefs, feelings, and coping patterns of those around them. In their efforts at explicit instruction, parents often fail to realize how much guidance they are unwittingly providing through their own behavior. This applies to fairly simple skills, like table manners, and to more complex behaviors, like handling frustration.

The presence of a parent-model who is a satisfactory example of appropriate, adaptive behavior can make a positive contribution to the child's healthy development. Unfortunately, children may also learn the behavior of parents who are seriously maladjusted. For example, children and teen-agers who become alcoholics have often grown up with at least one parent who drinks excessively. Similarly, studies of delinquent youth reveal a disproportionate number of parents who have committed destructive antisocial or criminal acts. And, adults who abuse children have often been themselves the victims of parental abuse.

Fortunately, there is nothing inevitable in the effects of parental pathology on a child's development. The pathology of one parent may be compensated for by the wisdom and concern of the other. Or an alcoholic parent may serve as a "negative model," showing the child what he or she does *not* want to be like. In their book *Cradles of Eminence,* Victor and Mildred Goertzel (1962) looked back over the lives of 400 famous people and found that only 58 had come from warm, supportive, and relatively untroubled homes. The remainder had come from homes that demonstrated considerable pathology.

In an attempt to understand children who seem to thrive despite pathogenic family and environmental conditions, Norman Garmezy (1976) and his associates began the study of a group of children they called the *invulnerables.* An example is Todd, age eleven. His mother died when he was three and he lives with an alcoholic father, who is usually unemployed, in an environment of poverty and unrelieved grimness. Yet Todd is bright, cheerful, does well in school, is a natural leader, and is well liked by peers and school officials. Preliminary findings indicate that these invulnerables tend to find solutions rather than blame others, to make the best of very little, and to show an unusual capacity to "bounce back" after severe setbacks and traumas. In addition, these investigators suspected the children had a desirable role model somewhere in their lives.

**A stimulating and responsive environment.**  Infants do not have to learn to be curious. They are constantly exploring—touching, tasting, listening, and looking. As nerves and muscles mature and mental capacities develop, the scope of their explorations widen. Soon they learn to talk and ask questions. Good parents will provide an environment conducive to new but not overwhelming experiences, making learning a pleasurable experience. Even though the infant's tendencies toward curiosity, exploration, and learning are built-in, they can be blocked either by lack of opportunity and stimulation or by early experiences that teach the child that curiosity is dangerous and unrewarding.

Children not only need a stimulating environment but also a responsive one in which they receive immediate and adequate feedback. Their inevitable questions of "who," "what," "where," and "why" must be both answered and encouraged. Children need to acquire a vast amount of information about themselves and their world, which will enable them to assess problems accurately and learn to predict the results of their actions. Like adults, children experience feelings and problems that they need to talk about and explore. Thus, they need parents who are willing to listen and communicate in meaningful ways—rather than parents who answer their questions with "Can't you see I'm busy?"

## Development as Becoming

Living a life is neither simple nor easy. Opportunity, chance, personal resources, values, and many other conditions enter in. It is largely through our choices and actions, however, that we shape the kind of person we will become and the kind

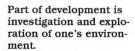

Part of development is investigation and exploration of one's environment.

of personal world we will live in. These are the decisions we make every day of our life—not just at certain times and certain places. Thus, development is a lifelong process of *becoming*—a process that profoundly affects our thoughts, emotions, and behavior.

Our efforts to become autonomous—to increase our self-reliance, self-regard, and self-direction—can assist this general process. So, too, can the related processes of improving our competencies in our intellectual, social, and emotional lives, increasing our awareness and openness to experience, and increasing our understanding of ourselves and our world. In essence, these guidelines can help people better understand who they are and who they can realistically become, how to expand the awareness and depth of their experience, how to build warm and loving relationships with others, and how to gain confidence in their ability to shape their own lives. While we may not have total control over our lives, each of us plays a key role in shaping ourselves and our existence and in achieving a truly meaningful and fulfilling life.

## SUMMARY

1. Development follows a pattern that can be characterized by stages or tasks. The effects of learning and maturation are important to development, but of equal importance are psychological trends toward personal maturity. Heredity and environment also contribute to personality development.

2. Personality development can be studied from the psychoanalytic, social-learning, and humanistic-existential perspectives. In the psychoanalytic perspective, the psychosexual and psychosocial stages are of importance. In the social-learning perspective, reinforcement, modeling, and expectancies and other self-control systems are important. In the humanistic-existential perspective, the self is of greatest importance.

3. Psychologists are also interested in healthy and faulty forms of development. Defining healthy development is a difficult task, in comparison to describing the factors that lead to faulty development.

4. Finally, several conditions seem conducive to healthy development. Although these factors do not necessarily lead to healthy development, researchers feel that healthy development can be attained in a warm, loving, and supportive environment.

# Chapter 4

# Adjustment in the Life Span

*"To every thing there is a season, a time to every purpose under the heaven:*
*A time to be born, and a time to die; a time to plant, and a time to pluck up that which is planted;*
*A time to kill, and a time to heal; a time to break down and a time to build up;*
*A time to weep, and a time to laugh; a time to mourn, and a time to dance;*
*A time to cast away stones, and a time to gather stones together; a time to embrace, and a time to refrain from embracing;*
*A time to get, and a time to lose; a time to keep, and a time to cast away;*
*A time to rend, and a time to sew; a time to keep silence, and a time to speak;*
*A time to love, and a time to hate; a time of war, and a time of peace."*
*(ECCLESIASTES 3:1—9)*

In this chapter, we will be concerned with the normal adjustive changes that occur during an individual's life. Life, growth, and personal adjustment do not end at age seven, age thirty, or age sixty-five. Rather, the events that occur during our lives form the backdrop of experiences through which we learn to grow and develop. Adjustment is, in other words, a lifelong process.

Our focus will be on the physical, cognitive, and emotional changes that occur during late adolescence, early adulthood, middle adulthood, and late adulthood. In our discussion of late adolescence, we will concentrate on the topic of identity. Our focus in early adult life will be on the development of intimacy and the establishment of family and occupational life. In middle adulthood, we will concentrate on the "predictable crises" of adult life. We shall also focus on generativity—the issue of how to assist the next generation. And, in late adulthood, we will discuss how people age and examine the ways in which individuals and society react to aging. In our discussion of these topics, we shall employ Erikson's concepts of psychosocial stages and crises—concepts that were briefly described in Chapter 3.

We will end our discussion of the challenges of adjustment in the life span with a discussion of death, dying, and loss. As we shall see, the experience of death can be an occasion for personal growth in both the individual who dies and in those who are left behind.

We begin our discussion with some topics of special interest to young adults— the establishment of personal identity, and the development of independence in both social and occupational settings.

## LATE ADOLESCENCE AND YOUNG ADULTHOOD

The transition between adolescence and adulthood begins about the time individuals graduate from high school. For most people, that time occurs around ages seventeen to nineteen—a time when we become increasingly independent of our immediate family. No longer are we "Daddy's little girl" or "the Jones kid." We become individuals in our own right, individuals with an identity and purpose of our own choosing. In essence, we "become ourselves" and are no longer appendages to our family or subject to some parental plan. At the same time, we also start to make our own choices in life, including choices in the occupational, educational, and social spheres.

During the early parts of the young adult phase, we typically make several important life decisions. We become psychologically and financially independent of our parents. We may end our occupational training and education. Deep interpersonal commitments may occur and result in our marriage and the beginnings of a new family. Many of our dreams and aspirations, hopes and desires, will get an opportunity for expression during these years.

## Biological Changes in Early Adult Life

The period of late adolescence and young adulthood is typically considered to be the biological prime of life. During the early twenties, individuals are generally at the peak of biological capabilities. Muscles are strong; skin is smooth; senses are sharp; and minds are keen. However, aging is occurring even during these peak times. Just as we have been developing from the moment of conception, we have been aging as well.

The muscular system continues its development during late adolescence and the first part of the early adult phase. Individuals can grow taller through the late twenties. During the twenties, strength and agility are at their peaks. Young adults can work longer and harder at physical tasks than adults in the middle or late phases. Similarly, there are greater reserves in the cardiovascular and respiratory systems of young adults, who are less likely to reach their physical limits while exercising and working.

Perceptual abilities are also most sensitive during these years. The amount of light or sound energy needed to trigger receptors becomes increasingly greater as the individual ages. Thus, a young adult may be able to see and hear better under conditions of low light or sound.

Individuals are most fertile during the late adolescent and young adult years. Sperm count in men is highest in these years as compared with later years, and the ability of women to conceive and bear children is correspondingly high. Most women who have children will bear them during the young adult years, particularly the late teens and early twenties. And, the chances for birth defects in children, particularly for Down's syndrome (mongolism), are small but increase as parents grow older.

Matching reproductive capabilities are the young adult's sexual desires and needs. Sexual activity is highest in the young adult, particularly if he or she is married, declining progressively in later years. For example, data from the Kinsey studies (Kinsey, Pomeroy, & Martin, 1948; Kinsey, Pomeroy, Martin, & Gebhard, 1953) suggest that couples in their twenties and thirties engage in intercourse two to three times per week, but the incidence of intercourse declines to once a week or less when the couple is in their fifties.

Finally, the causes of death during the late adolescent and early adult years are very different than the causes of death in later years. During late adolescence and early adulthood, the major causes of death are accidents and suicide, while later in life, cardiovascular disease and cancer claim the majority of lives. Most fatal accidents in this age group involve driving under the influence of alcohol or unnecessary risk-taking. And death by suicide is, of course, self-induced. Thus, death in late adolescence and early adulthood is largely a controllable and preventable phenomenon. In other words, the "biological" causes of death in young adults are not as important as the "social" or "emotional" causes of death.

## Cognitive Changes in Early Adult Life

**formal operations stage: fourth stage of Piaget's theory characterized by an individual's ability to think and reason abstractly**

In Chapter 3, we noted that infants and children progress through the cognitive developmental stages of sensorimotor, preoperational, and concrete operational thought. Beginning in mid-adolescence, individuals become increasingly able to understand and deal with abstract ideas and possibilities. That is, they enter the fourth stage of cognitive development, the stage of **formal operations.** Not only can they begin to successfully manage abstract ideas about the physical world—as seen in the ability to understand and apply the laws of physics, for example—but they can also understand abstract social and interpersonal ideas.

In one test of formal operational thought in adolescents, Peel (1971) gave a group of children and adolescents of above-average intelligence the following problem:

*Only brave pilots are allowed to fly over high mountains. This summer a fighter pilot flying over the Alps collided with an aerial cable railway, and cut a main cable causing some cars to fall to the glacier below. Several people were killed and many others had to spend the night suspended above the glacier. Was the pilot a careful airman? Why do you think so?*

Children under the ages of fourteen or fifteen provided responses that were either irrelevant ("No, he was a show-off") or were concerned only with the situation described in the problem ("No, because if he were careful he would not have cut the cable"). However, the older group was able to give much more imaginative answers, considering a variety of possibilities that were not directly presented in the problem. For example, some mentioned bad weather, a mechanical problem in the plane, and so forth.

The opening up of the world of the possible can lead to some difficulties, however. The application of general ethical principles such as fairness and justice to an imperfect world may provoke strong feelings of distress or uneasiness in the adolescent. Taught that all should be treated fairly, the adolescent may become very upset when adults or others in authority act in an arbitrary fashion.

Of course, these adolescent fires may become less intense as a person learns additional abstract possibilities. In later years, the arbitrary act may be evaluated differently as other considerations, such as group effectiveness or efficiency, come into play.

Thus, the attainment of formal operations marks the beginning of adult patterns of thought in an individual. Reality and possibility are now separate, and abstract ideas can be employed in dealing with the physical world, the social world, and the emotional world. In essence, a person can become self-reflective.

## Emotional Changes in Early Adult Life

A number of events occur in the social and emotional spheres during the late adolescent and early adult years. As Erikson suggested, we may develop a sense of identity and move toward intimacy and marriage and bearing and raising children. We may also face the challenges of occupational choices and decisions during this period.

**Identity and independence.**    **Identity** refers to our sense of ourselves as unique persons. As Whitbourne and Weinstock (1979) have put it, "Adult identity is the integration of the physical characteristics, abilities, motives, goals, attitudes, values, and social roles that are attributed by the individual to his or her self. Identity organizes the adult's interpretation of experiences and is in turn further

**identity: our sense of ourselves as unique individuals**

High school dropout Fred Demara, often known as the "Great Imposter," adopted several identities throughout his life. He posed convincingly as a Trappist monk, a Latin teacher, a cancer researcher, a military surgeon, and a psychology professor but decided against becoming an actor, commenting that acting seemed "too artificial."

modified by experiences'' (p. 93). Identity is also related to our desire to maintain some connection with and understanding of past experiences. In other words, we seek a sense of continuity with the past and with past experiences. A good analogy of this aspect of identity is to consider the events in our lives as frames of a motion picture. As individual frames, they may have no meaning. But, when they are projected onto a screen, we get a sense of flow and meaning as each frame blends imperceptibly with another. Finally, identity is concerned with our acceptance of group values. Development of identity thus marks the psychological passage from adolescence to young adulthood.

In developing this sense of identity, each individual must select and reject various elements of his or her past experiences and training. Parental values, for example, will be examined and some elements will be incorporated into one's sense of identity, while others will be discarded. Parental hopes and dreams for the individual will also undergo examination.

Erikson (1968) has suggested that the development of identity is preceded by a crisis of some sort. The form that the crisis takes may be quite varied, but elements of the crisis typically involve the individual's peers, parents, and society. In general, an identity crisis involves a conflict between our perception of ourselves and the experience of reality. For example, an athlete may have the perception that he does not need much practice or training. However, this perception may clash with real-world experiences in which his athletic performance was not as good as he had hoped.

The crisis need not involve negative perceptions. For example, a woman who believes that her talents center around homemaking skills and abilities may find that perception contradicted by evidence that she is very capable of managerial and executive tasks that were developed in community and volunteer settings.

**foreclosure: premature attainment of identity, typically not preceded by a crisis**

In some cases, adoption of an identity may occur too quickly, as when a woman accepts her parents' pressure to seek a teaching career instead of a career in business. This is the process of **foreclosure,** in which an individual takes on an identity, but in which the acquisition of identity is not preceded by a crisis. The consequence of failing to ''be your own person'' is that the crisis is often delayed until a later point in life. In our example, the young woman may teach for several years but find the task increasingly difficult and unsatisfying.

**negative identity: selection of an identity opposite that preferred by parents or society**

In other cases, an individual adopts a role opposite that which might be expected of them. In these cases of **negative identity,** the son of a police officer may develop a drug- and crime-oriented way of life. Or the daughter of a minister may become a member of a religious cult opposed to the family's religion.

**commitment: pledging oneself to some goals, persons, or values**

In attaining an identity, an individual makes a **commitment** to adult goals and values. However, not all people make a commitment to the issues that are important to adult identity (Marcia, 1966). For example, an individual may have made no commitment to adult values and may not have experienced a crisis. In this case, **identity diffusion** may occur. In identity diffusion, a person has no motivation to develop an identity, and no commitment to larger goals and values. The apathetic and uninvolved adult ''dropout'' may exemplify identity diffusion.

**identity diffusion: a lack of a sense of self; role confusion**

# Insight

**THE DEVELOPMENT OF IDENTITY**

|  | Crisis | |
|---|---|---|
|  | Yes | No |
| Commitment **Yes** | Identity | Foreclosure |
| **No** | Moratorium | Diffusion |

Finally, some people may declare a **moratorium** in which they "try on" a variety of identities. In a sense, the individual is in the midst of a crisis but has not yet resolved it. This trying on of identities can be very helpful and useful, particularly since our society presents an almost unlimited series of choices and possibilities for achieving identity. Higher education and military service are two of the ways in which a moratorium can be declared. A moratorium may be beneficial as it allows a person some "breathing room" to experiment. But, when it lasts too long, it becomes destructive, as in the individual who has not "made adult commitments, such as choosing an ideology, a life style, a vocation, or a spouse" (Berger, 1980, p. 508). A failure to commit one's self fully to the task of developing an identity only prolongs the period of psychological adolescence.

Societies can aid the development of identity by providing **rites of passage** and by maintaining stable and useful values. In less technologically oriented societies, the rites of passage can involve elaborate rituals in which an individual must undergo special tests of readiness and learn special adult social codes. The **initiation rites** of many societies can help provide this function. For example, Australian aborigines initiate males into adult status through an elaborate system of instruction, terminated by a painful circumcision. The person who entered the rite as a child leaves as an adult in the eyes of the community.

Our society, however, has very few initiation rites that signify entrance into the adult world. For some, religious rituals such as baptism, confirmation, and Bar Mitzvah may help mark adult status. Other markers of adult status may include getting a driver's license, graduation from high school, voting, or sexual activity. Unfortunately, our society has no consistent rules for determining when an individual is an adult. For example, many people can drive a car at age sixteen, but they cannot vote until age eighteen. And, while they are allowed to vote at

**moratorium:** a "pause" in identity formation in which an individual explores alternatives

**rites of passage:** rituals used by societies to mark the passage from one stage of life to another

**initiation rites:** rituals used by societies to signify entrance to the adult world or to other special groups

eighteen, they may not be permitted to purchase liquor legally until age twenty-one. Attainment of adult status in our society may thus be more uncertain and confusing than in other societies.

Good societal values can also make the achievement of a personal identity easier. Many youth in the 1960s found that they could not accept a society that assassinated its leaders. However, more recent studies have suggested that most adolescents and young adults value our society. That is, democracy, a loving family life, a decent education, and a challenging job appear to be values that most young adults are willing to accept (Berger, 1980).

Finally, a stable society appears to be beneficial to the development of a personal identity. When societies change rapidly, values may also change rapidly, resulting in an increased readiness to accept totalitarian principles. German youth of the 1920s and 1930s, for example, lived in a time of postwar defeat, monetary inflation, and economic depression. By offering them an identity that society was not able to provide, Hitler and Nazism captured the minds of adolescents and young adults throughout Germany (Erikson, 1968). Erikson's message for our rapidly changing technological times appears to be that identity may be difficult to achieve—and become increasingly more difficult—as young adults in our society are exposed to multiple and contradictory models and values.

With the achievement of identity comes psychological independence and an increasing confidence in our ability to think and plan for ourselves. Accompanying this psychological independence may be financial and occupational independence. We may move from our parents' home to establish our own residence. Additionally, we may take steps toward the attainment of an occupation.

Having developed identity, we now strive to master the next developmental challenge, the crisis of young adulthood—intimacy vs. isolation.

**The development of intimacy.**    The next challenge for the young adult is the establishment of a deep, caring relationship with another person—the establishment of **intimacy.** Having "found" ourselves in the formation of identity, we are now free to "find" others to share a life with. In practical terms, this means that we may fall in love, marry, and have children.

**intimacy: establishment of a deep, caring relationship with another person**

The process by which intimacy develops involves several factors. One is mutual self-disclosure in which we reveal ourselves to another person, and the other person responds in kind. Intimate relationships can also develop out of a sharing of personal ideals and values and a similarity of interests and goals. Meaningful communication is another aspect of intimacy, and physical and mental attraction can also play a role in the development of intimacy.

Like the development of identity, the development of intimacy does not necessarily occur all at once. And, intimacy can develop more than once. The young adult may therefore fall in and out of love several times, marry, become divorced, remarry, and so forth.

Since so much sexual activity occurs among adolescents and young adults, it may be tempting to suggest that the development of intimacy occurs before the development of identity. That is, some individuals may attempt to develop a sense of identity through sexual activity. The gratifying nature of sexual contact may lead people to feel that they have found themselves as individuals in sexual activity with others.

However, research supports Erikson's contention that a strong sense of identity is a prerequisite to the formation of intimacy. A weak sense of self cannot easily tolerate the sharing that occurs in a truly intimate relationship. Without a strong sense of identity, an individual may seek praise and adulation from the other—a condition that prevents the shared commitment and honest communication that are so necessary for an intimate relationship (Stevens-Long, 1979).

According to Erikson, only the person who has developed a strong and secure sense of self will be able to establish an intimate relationship with another individual.

We shall return to the topic of intimacy in greater detail in a number of other chapters. In particular, we will discuss interpersonal relationships, sexuality, and marriage and intimate relationships in greater detail in Chapters 12, 13, and 14, respectively.

**Work and vocations in early adult life.** Sigmund Freud maintained that the key to successful adulthood was *Lieben und arbeiten*—"to love and to work." Just as the establishment of intimate relationships is a crucial task for the young adult, so too is the development of a satisfactory work life.

Much of the guidance we receive in selecting an occupation comes from adult models, prior work experiences, and training received in high school and college or universities. For some, military service can also be a valuable tool in helping find satisfactory work.

The process of establishing an occupational identity is substantially more involved than the simple process of finding a job and collecting a paycheck. Basically, we can divide the process of establishing an occupational identity into two separate, but parallel, streams of development (Van Maanen & Schein, 1977). One stream, the **external career,** deals primarily with observable events, while the second stream, the **internal career,** deals primarily with the hopes, aspirations, and emotions that accompany the attainment of an occupational identity.

external career: observable events that occur during development of an occupational identity

internal career: hopes, aspirations, and emotions that accompany development of an occupational identity

exploration stage: first stage in the development of an occupational identity, characterized by tentative first steps in the selection of an occupation

We may also divide occupational development into a number of stages. According to the model devised by Van Maanen and Schein (1977), the process of occupational development consists of four stages: *exploration, establishment, maintenance,* and *later career.* We shall also add *retirement* as a factor in our discussions.

The stages of exploration and establishment seem to characterize the young adult. In the external career, **exploration** involves getting advice from friends, counselors, and parents regarding occupational selection. Much of this information will be tested against evidence of the individual's competence for the occupation. For example, recommendations to pursue a medical career will be tested against performance in biology and chemistry courses and against performance on admissions tests. An additional consideration may involve our personal, financial, and historical resources to seek this occupation. For some, the cost of a medical school education may be prohibitive. Or there may be a family history of seeking training in business or education rather than in medicine. Thus, individuals seeking a medical career under these circumstances may find that their families are not supportive of their occupational goals.

The internal career during the exploration stage involves different aspects of occupational identity. We seek work that is fun, playful, and enjoyable to do, and we may consciously try to model ourselves after successful practitioners of a given occupation. For example, the person who wishes to become a nurse may deliberately try to develop the social and attitudinal skills that are "nurselike." For this individual, a sense of commitment to helping others may be consciously cultivated. Or an individual may try to emulate the aggressive and hard-driving characteristics of a successful executive. Of course, these images are only tenta-

# Insight

**THE STAGES OF OCCUPATIONAL DEVELOPMENT**

tive, and they need to be tested in the real world. But the images help form and shape behavior and attitudes.

In the next stage comes the initial **establishment** of an occupational identity. Externally, the process appears to be quite direct: we seek and are offered employment. Next, we receive some orientation and training to mark our entrance into the new job. We are given assignments to perform. If we master or accomplish the tasks quickly, we may be given a new assignment. Or, if we master the tasks slowly (or not at all), we may remain at an initial level or may be asked to seek employment elsewhere. Periodically, our performance will be reviewed, and we may ultimately be given a promotion. Not incidentally, we also meet bosses and co-workers and learn to interact successfully with others in the work setting.

Internally, however, the process is somewhat more complex during the establishment stage. Emotionally, we may suffer from ''reality shock'' as the actualities of the work situation confront the often idealized picture that we may have had of work. We may experience fear, anxiety, and insecurities: Will I be able to keep up? Will I be fired? What if I make a mistake? These are some of the issues that the young adult must deal with during the initial phases of the new occupation.

Another internal issue that must be addressed during the early phases of

**establishment stage:** second stage in the development of an occupational identity, occurring in the first months and years of employment in a chosen occupation

**dream: idealized life plan developed during the early adult years**

work concerns the development of a theme or **dream** (Levinson, Darrow, Klein, Levinson, & McKee, 1978). The dream is the idealized life plan that we develop during the young adult years. In the dream, we specify, to a greater or lesser extent, our goals for the future. The dream can consist of occupational achievement, personal achievement, family goals, and emotional goals. For example, the dream may specify our level of achievement in work (including issues of position, power, and salary) by age thirty or age forty. Or the dream may specify that we will be married by age twenty-five, have three children by age thirty-five, and be well-respected as a community leader by age forty-five. On the other hand, the dream may simply indicate a desire for increased self-satisfaction and happiness as we grow older.

In the occupational sphere, the dream helps shape our behavior and goals. However, we may find conflict between our hopes in a work setting and our hopes for a particular type of family life. Or, we may find that our aspirations were too high and need to be revised. And if we fail on the job and are fired, we must also adjust to this change and plan accordingly.

Our brief discussion of the late adolescent and early adult phases has suggested several recurring ideas: Late adolescence and early adulthood are periods of time marked by substantial, visible change. We leave parental homes, complete our educations and occupational training, establish our own homes, and develop intimate relationships with others. We may marry and have children. Accompanying these overt changes are some interesting internal events as well. From the experience of a personal crisis, we may develop a sense of identity. Later, we may also develop a sense of intimacy with others.

In our next section, we shall see that many of the changes initiated during the early adult phase continue in middle adulthood.

## MIDDLE ADULT LIFE

*"Thou hast nor youth nor age."*
*(SHAKESPEARE)*

The middle adult years typically range from about age forty to age sixty. Surprisingly, little is known about these years. Developmental psychologists have traditionally focused their attentions on the early years, including infancy, childhood, and adolescence. Later, psychologists began some intensive investigations of the late adult years. But the middle adult years have only recently begun to claim the attention of researchers.

This lack of inquiry is surprising, since recent evidence indicates that "the years between forty and sixty may be second only to the teen-age years in the degree of biological, psychological, and social change experienced by most individuals" (Stevens-Long, 1979, p. 214). The stereotype of the middle-aged adult as stodgy, conservative, predictable, and dull is giving way to a portrait that portrays the middle-aged adult as undergoing a variety of changes during these years, particularly in the social and emotional spheres of experience.

## Biological Changes in Middle Adult Life

During the middle adult years, the first signs of aging appear. The first wrinkles appear, as does gray or thinning hair. Another change during the middle adult years is weight gain and redistribution. The svelte shape of early adult life gradually gives way to body proportions that emphasize the middle part of the body. At the same time, middle-aged people are very likely to weigh more during these years than at any other time in their lives. The combination of weight gain and redistribution gives men "beer bellies" and women a thicker appearance around the waist.

One reaction to these obvious changes is a rush to hair dyes and reducing parlors. Advertisements extol the positive benefits that occur when the hair has a youthful appearance: men are told they will receive new, well-paying jobs when their gray hair is eliminated. Women are promised they will feel better about themselves if they exercise regularly and keep a trim figure. Fortunately, most middle-aged adults accept these biological changes with equanimity and incorporate the changes into their sense of identity.

An important biological change that occurs during the middle years is the development of cardiovascular disease, particularly in men. During these years, fatty materials called **plaques** build up in the arteries. Additionally, the cardiovascular system becomes less flexible and elastic. These changes, which can also be associated with high blood pressure or hypertension, high levels of fatty acids in the blood, and disturbances in the kidneys, are significantly associated with "premature" death in the middle years. That is, the person who appears to be quite healthy one day may suddenly and unexpectedly die of a heart attack on the next. Since many of these biological changes are subtle, monitoring of blood pressure, cholesterol levels, and other physiological indices can help us identify problem areas early and change those aspects of our life styles, particularly Type A personality styles (see Chapter 7), that may contribute to these processes. For most men, however, these biological changes have very little, if any, effect on the day-to-day behavioral or emotional functioning of the individual.

**plaques: (pronounced PLAKS) build-ups of fatty materials in the arteries**

For women, the most dramatic biological change is **menopause,** the cessation of reproductive functioning. Menopause typically occurs between the ages of forty-five and fifty-five and is marked by the end of menstrual periods. The normal reactions to menopause, sometimes called the *change,* include hot flashes, increased irritability, and depression. Most women report only mild symptoms, typically hot flashes and headaches, which appear to be due to changes in the woman's hormonal balance.

**menopause: cessation of menstrual functioning**

Psychologically, menopause can have a number of meanings. For the woman whose sense of self-esteem is directly tied to her ability to bear children, menopause can be unsettling. Some women, on the other hand, are relieved:

# Psychology in Action

## MAINTAINING VITALITY THROUGHOUT LIFE: SLOWING THE BIOLOGICAL CLOCK

An issue of concern to all of us is how to slow or prevent the degenerative changes of aging. All of us, for example, wish to keep our cardiovascular system as young as possible, and all of us wish for an active and productive old age. Although the desire for a useful and healthy old age is virtually a universal one, the evidence on how to structure one's life at the moment to insure this type of old age is a matter of controversy.

Part of the reason for the controversy is that there is little agreement on what constitutes the process of aging. Some researchers believe that aging is a consequence of wear and tear on the biological system (Stevens-Long, 1979). Others (Bierman & Hazzard, 1973) believe that aging is a consequence of "disease." According to this approach, air pollution, poor diet, alcohol, and other factors produce diseaselike states that ultimately result in our aging and in our death.

Another set of theories (Sinclair, 1969; Timiras, 1972) focuses on the cellular level. Since human cells seem to have a limit to their abilities to divide, aging may be related to our reaching the end of cellular reproduction. Once the normal end is reached, abnormal growth and mutation may occur, placing the individual in jeopardy of aging. Yet another theory (Comfort, 1963) suggests aging is the result of the body's turning against itself. That is, aging may be due to a self-destructive *autoimmune* response in which bodily defenses do not recognize tissues as part of the body but regard them as foreign substances to be destroyed. Other approaches (Hershey, 1974) have emphasized the lack of flexible proteins in the body and the availability of "free-radical" molecules as potential sources of aging. None of these approaches, however, gives much useful advice for maintaining health and vitality in late adulthood.

---

*I felt physically in better shape—in my prime—unencumbered by the cycle of pain, swelling, discomfort, nuisance, etc.*

*I felt better and freer since menopause. I threw that diaphragm away. I love being free of possible pregnancy and birth control. It makes my sex life better. (Boston Women's Health Book Collective, 1976, p. 328)*

As sociologist Bernice Neugarten and her colleagues (Neugarten, Wood, Kraines, & Loomis, 1963) have shown in studies of menopause, most women of middle-adult age do not anticipate or experience menopause in any "special" way. That is, most of the women in Neugarten's study saw menopause as simply another life event of no overwhelming importance. The women in Neugarten's study reported greater fears of cancer and of losing their husbands than of menopause. And, most middle-adult women did not find that menopause altered their sexual desires.

Of course, we do in fact age. But the chronological years during which we show degeneration and decay differ from individual to individual. For example, some people show very little deterioration of the cardiovascular system well into old age, while some persons in their thirties and forties are extremely "old" as measured by cardiovascular status. A comparison of a group of seventy-year-olds may reveal that some are very active and involved in what is going on around them, while others fit the stereotype of an inactive, sedentary, elderly invalid.

Obviously, some of these differences are due to genetic factors. But, some may be due to life-styles. We know, for example, that those who sit and work out in the sun show much greater aging of the skin than those who avoid the sun. Thus, some steps can be taken to alter one's life-style to control the effects of aging—to push back the biological clock of decay and degeneration.

Many of the approaches that have been suggested for slowing the biological clock are also related to suggestions for maintaining health. Some of the methods suggested for maintaining health and vitality are:

- Eat a balanced diet
- Maintain your weight within normal limits
- Exercise often and vigorously
- Limit alcohol, caffeine, and nicotine intake
- Develop a wide circle of friends
- Stay involved with everyday affairs
- Develop interesting and absorbing hobbies

Of course, we cannot guarantee that adoption of these healthier life-styles will increase life span significantly. However, research evidence clearly points out that life-styles that emphasize the opposite of our suggestions are associated with decreases in life expectancy. Thus, it may be possible to alter the biological functioning through the psychological processes associated with healthy and productive life styles (Hancock, 1982).

## Cognitive Changes in Middle Adult Life

Continued cognitive growth in the middle adult years is greatly dependent on our environments and on our activities. In contrast to children whose cognitive development may be linked to biological and environmental events, learning in the adult seems to be primarily dependent on experience. While children and adolescents may receive educational and cognitive training that is more or less the same for all of them, adult experiences may differ from person to person. For example, we normally expect that high-school students will enroll in English, social studies, and science courses. Because of the similarity of their educational experiences, adolescents may be quite similar in their cognitive abilities and structures.

Adults, on the other hand, have increasingly different experiences. Some will marry and raise children at a relatively early age, while some may delay or bypass marriage and child rearing. Some will enter professions, while some will take jobs requiring little skill. And, some will interact with a wide circle of acquaintances and friends, while others will become increasingly isolated. The end result of these many different experiences is that the cognitive development of the adult is probably more variable than that of the adolescent (Flavell, 1970).

Some theorizing has, in addition, suggested the possibility that a fifth stage of cognitive development occurs in adults (Riegel, 1976). Although the characteristics of this stage are not well-defined, Arlin (1975) has suggested that the fifth stage may consist of **problem-finding**—a tendency to discover questions, not answers. This problem-finding stage may be characterized by a creative tendency to view the world in different ways. Thus, rather than solve problems that others have posed, we may increasingly generate questions that need solution.

The evidence thus suggests that we show no decline in our abilities to learn or solve problems during the middle-adult years. Instead, our abilities to help generate questions may grow during this period.

**problem-finding: proposed fifth stage of cognitive development, characterized by the tendency to discover questions rather than solve problems**

## Emotional Changes in Middle Adult Life

The patterns, attitudes, and behaviors that were prevalent during the young adult years continue into the middle adult years. In this section, we shall deal with both the continuity and change that is characteristic of the middle adult years. Our focus will be on the "predictable crises" of adult life, including those involving the individual directly, as well as family, work and occupational satisfaction.

**Identity in the middle adult years.**　Studies of the middle adult years have suggested that the early forties represent a difficult period of adjustment, equaling or exceeding the adolescent years in their effect on us. Studies by Gould (1972), Levinson and his colleagues (1978), and Vaillant and Milofsky (1980) point to a major shift in the individual's perception of him- or herself in relation to the world at about age forty. As Levinson et al. (1978) note, the "mid-life transition" is characterized by the first signs of aging and by the recognition of one's own mortality. Realizing that time is not unlimited may help initiate this **mid-life crisis.** Often the recognition of mortality occurs when a peer dies.

Our perception of ourselves comes into conflict with reality during the middle adult years. As we noted earlier, the first gray hairs no longer allow us the opportunity to see ourselves as young. Our failure to achieve all that we had hoped for in our jobs comes into conflict with the dream developed during the young adult years. Our hopes for our families may be shattered by divorce or separation; our bright, charming, achieving, and loving children of the dream may in fact be more human and fallible than the dream allowed.

Since perception is in conflict with reality, middle adults, like their adolescent and young adult counterparts, must also struggle with the problem of identity. Perception must be adjusted to correspond better with reality (Sheehy, 1976).

However, this portrait of the mid-life crisis should not be exaggerated. Men do not suddenly empty their bank accounts, purchase flashy clothes and expensive sports cars, and run away with their blond twenty year-old secretaries. And,

**mid-life crisis: an identity crisis of middle adult life brought about by recognition of one's aging and mortality**

middle-aged women do not become embittered, narrow-minded people whose interests and friendships become increasingly conservative. Rather, the portrait of middle-aged person that develops from research findings is that the personality characteristics that were present in the young adult years tend to continue into the middle adult years.

Thus, the challenge of identity continues in the middle adult years. Identity is not "solved" once and for all during the adolescent and early adult years. Rather, the conflict between reality and perception continues throughout life. The quest for identity is thus a never-ending process.

**Intimacy in middle adult life.**   Just as the search for identity is never fully resolved in adult life, so too is the quest for intimacy never complete.

Researchers Orlofsky, Marcia, and Lesser (1973) have proposed that the intimacy we share with another can be one of five types:

1. *Intimate.* In an intimate relationship, the sharing and mutuality that we discussed earlier are present. Typically an individual has several close friends and a more intense, often sexual, relationship with one or more persons.

2. *Preintimate.* In a preintimate relationship, an individual may have several close friends, but is not deeply involved with another.

3. *Stereotyped.* In a stereotyped relationship, an individual may have several acquaintances of both sexes. However, the relationships lack depth and meaning. This intimacy type is "stereotyped" because the person has taken on the apparent, external aspects of an intimate relationship, but has not made the internal commitment to the relationship. A male of this type would be considered a "playboy" by others, for example.

4. *Pseudointimate.* In this style, an individual may have shallow relationships with others, including those of the opposite sex. In a pseudointimate relationship with someone of the opposite sex, the relationship is established primarily for convenience, rather than for mutuality of interests and values.

5. *Isolate.* The isolate has no close relationships with others and may be threatened by such relationships.

The characterization of an individual's intimacy status should not be considered permanent. Intimacy, like identity, is a process that shifts and changes over time. For example, we may become involved in an intimate relationship with a member of the opposite sex. This relationship may result in marriage and children. However, the intimacy may become reduced over time, resulting in separation and divorce. At this point, we may become involved in stereotyped relationships. Fearful of intimacy but still desiring it, we may move to a preintimate set of relationships, out of which ultimately develops another intimate relationship. Thus, we can move from one type of relationship to another as conditions and circumstances warrant.

**Work and generativity in the middle adult years.**   In the mid-life years, both the external and internal careers pass through the **maintenance** and **later career** stages. Externally, the middle adult is less concerned with establishing him- or herself in work. Rather, concerns now turn to productivity and teaching.

**maintenance stage:** third stage in the development of an occupational identity, characterized by a well-learned ability to perform work tasks

**later career stage:** fourth stage in the development of an occupational identity in which an individual attempts to pass on work skills and knowledge to younger generations

That is, the middle adult's work life is characterized by a firm ability to perform work tasks and a desire to help others through a teaching or mentor role. Often, as an individual nears the end of a working career, he or she becomes increasingly concerned with teaching younger workers the "tricks of the trade."

Internally, the maintenance and later career stages are somewhat more complex. The mid-life crisis of the early forties may eventually lead us to a reappraisal of work and its relationship to other areas of our lives. While work, whatever its definition, may have occupied a substantial proportion of our energies and commitments in early adult life, work in middle adulthood may be given an important though not controlling position in the middle years. Work may continue to be important, and we may find a renewed sense of pleasure and satisfaction in our work. For those people who do not find work satisfying, a desire to start a new or second career may appear during this stage.

For virtually everyone, the appearance of ambitious and capable younger co-workers may prove to be a source of concern and anxiety. Many middle-aged workers, however, solve this problem in productive ways by establishing a mentor relationship with a younger co-worker.

**mentor: an older individual who helps guide the occupational development of a younger person**

A **mentor** is an older worker who guides the occupational development of a younger worker. In a business setting, the mentor may be an immediate supervisor or an executive. To the young teacher in a school, the mentor may be an older teacher who helps the younger teacher to "learn the ropes." The mentor is not necessarily a parental figure, nor is the mentor a peer. Rather, the mentor is a guiding figure who helps a young adult establish an occupational identity (Levinson et al., 1978).

**generativity: activities and interests intended to aid future generations**

**stagnation: the self-indulgence, inactivity, and lack of personal growth characteristic of the individual who has not successfully resolved the generativity vs. stagnation crisis**

As we noted in Chapter 3, the major task of the middle adult years is, according to Erikson, the resolution of the crisis of generativity vs. stagnation. **Generativity** involves an expansion of one's interests with a view to the future. In essence, we structure our lives around tasks and attitudes that will leave a lasting mark on generations to come. Failure to achieve generativity results in **stagnation**—self-indulgence, inactivity, and a lack of personal growth. An example of generativity might involve an individual who serves as mentor to some younger co-workers. It might involve a commitment to community and family affairs. In the family, generativity can be expressed as increased concern with giving children and grandchildren a sense of family history, an appreciation for society and values, or an involvement with those who need assistance. Generativity involves leaving behind some kind of legacy by which future generations can remember us (Stevens-Long, 1979).

During this phase, the middle-aged individual must alter his or her relationship with older and increasingly independent children. Since parents no longer need to tend to scraped knees and broken dolls, they can now concentrate on relating to their offspring as mature, independent people.

Just as their relationships with their children change during the mid-life years, middle-aged adults must also change their relationships with their own parents. Elderly parents may require greater assistance, both financially and emotionally. And, the middle-aged adult may find him- or herself in the awkward position of acting in a protective, parental role toward parents.

A middle-aged adult may act as a mentor to a younger worker, teaching the younger person the skills of the trade and giving him or her both personal and professional advice.

Finally, the middle-aged adult may also need to adjust to the label "in-law" or "grandparent." Middle-aged adults are not only taking on more responsibility for their parents, they may be becoming grandparents themselves. Not only do these changes alter the middle adult's sense of identity, but they provide a challenge—a challenge of how to adapt readily to these changes and yet provide the guidance that is the mark of the productive and emotionally healthy middle adult.

## LATE ADULTHOOD

*"Grow old along with me!*
*The best is yet to be,*
*The last of life, for which the first was made."*
*(ROBERT BROWNING)*

More people than ever before are reaching late adulthood. In 1920, the average life expectancy of a woman was 54.6 years, while the average life expectancy of a man was 53.6 years. In contrast, a child born in this decade can expect to live to about his or her mid-seventies. These are, obviously, dramatic changes.

The steadily increasing life expectancy and the declining birth rate will cause the proportion of the population aged sixty and over to rise steadily in the next few decades. With this increase will come some significant social changes. In the past, society's need to accommodate to older adults was not a pressing issue. However, the future will probably bring changes in the ways older adults are treated in their work, in their social settings, in their housing, and in their family relationships.

In this section we shall focus on the personal changes that accompany life in the late adult years. Following the structure we have already employed, we will focus our discussion on the physical, cognitive, and emotional changes of late adult life.

## Biological Changes in Late Adult Life

Most of the biological changes of late adult life are associated with degenerative processes. Some men, for example, suffer from hereditary baldness, a pattern that can be altered only by hair transplants. Women also suffer from thinning hair, but the pattern is not as pronounced. Late adulthood is also associated with thinning of the bones (osteoporosis), leaving older adults, particularly women, vulnerable to fractures. Partially as a result of these skeletal changes, both sexes become increasingly stooped with age.

The internal organs also show decline. Muscular strength and agility decrease. The heart, a muscular organ, becomes less efficient, as do the lungs and kidneys (Stevens-Long, 1979).

Vision and audition (hearing) are also affected in old age. The older adult may lose visual *acuity,* the ability to discriminate fine details. The ability to hear also undergoes some changes, particularly in the high frequency ranges. Since much of our social interaction is dependent on our ability to hear and understand what other people are saying, the loss of some hearing abilities can negatively affect us. For example, if an older adult asks a younger person to repeat what he or she had said, the younger person may react with exasperation to the request. The older person, sensing the impatience of the younger person, may not make the request in the future, thereby limiting the older adult's understanding of and interaction with the world, and removing the older person from the mainstream of social conversation.

Of course, the effect that these biological changes have on an older adult may depend heavily on how they affect the individual's day-to-day functioning. Reductions in muscular strength and agility may be important to the man whose work involves heavy manual labor. On the other hand, such reductions may have little impact on the ability and performance of a secretary nearing retirement. Similarly, the changes in vision and audition do not typically deprive the older adult of the pleasures associated with a child's smile or mighty orchestral works.

Sexuality can also pose some adjustive demands for the older adult. Males take longer to develop an erection, and females may not produce as much vaginal lubrication as in younger years. On the positive side, older males are better able to control their orgasmic responding than younger men. Older men also do

For some people, a high degree of activity is the key to successful aging; others may be content with a less active life-style.

not have as great a need or desire to experience orgasm with each sexual contact. As long as his partner is comfortable with this change, the lack of desire to ejaculate can be accommodated with ease by the older couple.

Additionally, older adults may not be as able to resume sexual activity as readily as young adults following a period of inactivity. For example, a woman who was sexually inactive during a serious illness may find that she does not show as much vaginal lubrication as she had prior to the illness. Similarly, a man who was sexually inactive following his spouse's death may not achieve an erection as readily with a new partner.

Of potentially greater significance is the availability of partners, particularly for widows. Since men die at an earlier age than women, there are more older women than men. The unmarried older male may thus have greater opportunities to find partners than his female peers.

As many older adults have discovered, the maintenance of sexual activity into old age is both possible and desirable. The need to be held and caressed does not diminish with age, nor does age reduce the pleasure that the older adult derives from sexual activity.

## Cognitive Changes in Late Adult Life

Until recently, it had been assumed that the cognitive changes of late adulthood followed the pattern of degeneration that is generally typical of biological changes. However, more recent evidence has suggested that our hypotheses regarding the learning and memory abilities of older adults are in need of revision.

**verbal learning:** a learning task in which individuals are asked to memorize words or pairs of words

Most studies of learning in older adults focus on **verbal learning.** In verbal learning, an individual is asked to memorize a list of words or is asked to memorize pairs of words. Studies using these tasks have consistently shown that older adults perform more poorly than younger adults. The problem, as Irene Hulicka (1967) has pointed out, is that tasks such as these typically do not hold any meaning for an older adult. In other words, older adults may regard these tasks as nonsensical. And, given their unwillingness to participate in these tasks, their performance, as compared with that of younger adults, may be lower because they are bored and uninterested, poorly motivated to perform well, distrustful of the experimenter, and so forth.

When the conditions are optimal, older adults show very little decline in their ability to master these verbal tasks. However, when the speed of presentation is increased, when extraneous noise is introduced, and when other distracting factors are presented, performance in the older adult declines—as it does in younger adults.

Not surprisingly, older adults do not perform as well as younger adults in tasks that emphasize speed or agility. For example, one task on an intelligence test pairs the numbers 1 through 9 with symbols associated with each number. Thus, the number 3 might be paired with the symbol †, while the number 8 might be associated with the symbol ⊥. The person is then given nearly a hundred digits in random order and asked to provide the proper symbol for each number within a limited period of time.

The relatively better performance of younger adults on tasks such as these does *not* imply that older adults suffer from declining intelligence. Fortunately, the originators of intelligence tests are aware that motor speed decreases with age and have taken this fact into account in determining intelligence scores.

**fluid intelligence:** a basic ability to learn, unrelated to formal education or experience

These differences in performance may be related to differences in the structure of intelligence. Psychologist Raymond Cattell (1971) has proposed that intelligence is comprised of two factors: *fluid* and *crystallized* intelligence. **Fluid intelligence** is "a basic capacity for learning and problem solving, independent of education and experience" (Sattler, 1974, p. 11). As seen by Cattell, fluid intelligence is related to the integrity of the nervous system, and fluid intelligence declines with age because of repeated, though small, traumas, damages, and insults to the nervous system as the individual ages. In contrast, crystallized intelligence is related to formal education and training. **Crystallized intelligence,** in other words, consists of "learned knowledge and skills" (Sattler, 1974, p. 11).

**crystallized intelligence:** learned skills and knowledge related to education and experience

If we try to stay informed and keep up with daily events and remain actively involved with others, crystallized intelligence may show an increase during the later years (Baltes & Schaie, 1976). When careful studies are conducted, the results suggest that, with the exception of tasks that involve fine motor agility and speed, intelligence tends to remain at the same level throughout the late adult years (Schaie, Labouvie, & Buech, 1973).

Finally, the role that illness and psychological processes have on the cognitive functioning of an older adult must also be taken into account. An older person who becomes ill may have to use more adaptive resources than a younger person would. Each of us has probably had the experience of being tired, dis-

# Insight

## SOME MYTHS ABOUT OLD AGE

1. *The myth of senility.* There is a common stereotype that older people are forgetful and in their "second childhood." In actual fact, like young people, old people represent a heterogeneous group. Some people are old at twenty and others are young at eighty.

2. *The myth of unproductivity.* Another common stereotype is that a person's work efficiency falls dramatically after the age of sixty-five. Of course this is true at a much younger age in some occupations, such as that of professional athletes. But in general, older workers can be efficient and productive.

3. *The myth of available jobs for the elderly.* Despite overwhelming odds, about a third of the elderly find jobs, but these are usually of a menial nature and often far below their level of education and prior work experience. A classic example here is that of the babysitter.

4. *The myth of adequate Social Security.* While Social Security is a great help for many older people, it falls far short of providing an adequate income for living in a semblance of comfort and dignity. In and of itself, it often fails even to keep people above the officially defined poverty line.

5. *The myth of serenity.* While there are adults of all ages in our society who do find serenity, it is no more characteristic of the old than of the young. Like other life periods, the late adult years have their share of stresses—and in many instances more than their share (Butler, 1975).

tracted, and irritable when we are sick. In the older person with a chronic illness, these outcomes have the appearance of altering cognitive functioning. Similarly, depression in the older adult, a relatively common response to personal and societal devaluation of the individual's worth as well as a common response to illness (Kastenbaum, 1979), may appear to alter cognitive functioning. Thus, cognitive functioning shows little real change during the later years, although the older person may be more sensitive to the effects of chronic illness and depression.

## Emotional Changes in Late Adult Life

For many, old age is the least exciting and valued part of life. In a youth-oriented society, it is not surprising that young adults regard old age negatively. Interestingly, the old also regard the later years negatively. Part of these negative feelings comes from declining health, declining income, and declining self-esteem. But, for some, the later years provide a sense of satisfaction that had never been present in the younger years.

**Identity, intimacy, and generativity in the late adult years.** The late adult years do not end the quest for a successful identity, for fulfilling intimate relationships, or for the need to help and assist younger generations.

Age does not diminish the need for intimacy nor the satisfactions derived from an intimate relationship.

For the older adult, the major issue in identity is the accommodation to an altered biological and social status. A look in the mirror provides insistent information that we are no longer the youthful individuals of our photo albums and our memories. And yet, as we noted earlier, one of the major tasks of identity is the development of a sense of continuation with the past. To the older individual, this may not be easy. How is it that the wrinkled face of today developed from the smooth, supple skin of yesterday? How is it that the individual who had energy for young children, work, hobbies, and home repair is now exhausted if grandchildren visit for a few hours? How is it that death seems so near and personal now?

Social changes also provide challenges to identity. Retirement brings a loss of a major definition of the self. Society may no longer view older adults as potentially productive individuals but as a drain on health, housing, and governmental resources. Fixed retirement incomes reduce the standard of living, and inflation brings with it worries about the adequacy of financial resources.

There is also the fear that independence will be taken away, that retirement incomes will dwindle into poverty, that health will deteriorate. All these concerns may contribute to an identity crisis in later years.

Intimacy issues can also be important to older adults. People continue to strive for intimacy during late adulthood. However, intimacy may not be as easy to achieve in our later years. Spouses die; close friends die. Older adults may move to a retirement home far from friends and family.

Societal stereotypes do not aid the development of intimacy in the older adult. An older couple walking through a park hand-in-hand may be "cute" and somewhat laughable—as though older adults did not deserve and did not derive pleasure from intimate contact with others. And, adult children are upset when a widowed parent wishes to remarry, thinking that love and sexuality are the sole province of the young.

The attainment of generativity can also pose challenges for the older adult. Our youth-oriented society is eager for older workers to step aside and let younger, more "knowledgeable" workers take over. Thus, older workers cannot give others the wisdom and skills they have developed over the years. Our emphasis on mobile, nuclear families also deprives older adults of the time they could spend providing guidance and assistance to children and grandchildren.

Despite these problems, many older adults do find ways to maintain successful identity, intimacy, and generativity. For example, rather than focus on what cannot be done, the older individual may focus on the possible and attainable. If a woman's identity was that of a mother, she can now turn her energies to other crafts she can perform or emphasize other skills such as gardening or traveling. When spouses or friends die, we need not withdraw from intimate contact with others but seek the comfort and company of those the same age or younger. And when we cannot transmit our knowledge and skills to younger co-workers and family, we can become involved in programs such as Foster Grandparents. In essence, the attainment of late adult status does not end the quest for a satisfying and fulfilling life.

**Ego integrity in late adult life.** Successful aging seems to be related to the older adult's ability to master Erikson's last crisis of life, the crisis of ego integrity vs. despair. As we noted earlier, **ego integrity** involves the development of a sense of satisfaction and acceptance over the course of one's life. As we review our lives, we may come to feel that all that had transpired was useful and valuable. Since death may be a real, though unseen, presence in the experience of the late adult, our review of life is thus a way for us to find value and meaning. We cannot go back and relive parts of our lives; we cannot return and make corrections. The major part of life has been lived, and the crisis of integrity involves an examination of that life and our evaluation of whether that life, with all of its triumphs and errors, its pleasures and pains, was valuable. In contrast, **despair** involves bitter feelings of opportunities lost, the sense that all of life has been meaningless and empty.

Some theorists have proposed that the life review we undergo in our attempt to resolve the integrity vs. despair crisis is part of a more general process of **disengagement.** Disengagement theory (Cumming & Henry, 1961) is based on the assumption that we become more focused on inner thoughts and feelings as we grow older. As people become more involved in internal processes and less involved in external, social events, their investment in others and in the external world decreases.

However, disengagement is not the only model of aging that has been developed. For example, successful aging can be accomplished by the individual who is deeply involved in the world. Successful aging can also occur in the person who is moderately active and who concentrates on a few role areas, such as the older adult who focuses his or her energies on grandchildren, spouses, or church (Havighurst, 1969). In essence, those who make the best transition to old age are those whose personality integration was successful earlier in life (Neugarten & Hagestad, 1977). The active, engaged individual of middle age is likely

ego integrity: sense of satisfaction over the course of one's life

despair: despondency over the course of one's life

disengagement: increasing focus on inner thoughts and feelings as one ages

Many older adults maintain their sense of self-worth by imparting the knowledge and skills they have developed over the years to younger generations.

to be the active and engaged individual of the later years. And, those with high self-esteem as young adults are likely to have high self-esteem in later years.

**The effects of retirement.**    It has been said that next to dying, the recognition that we are aging may be the most profound shock of our lifetime. Each day this shock is brought home to the 1500 or so persons who cross the invisible barrier of age and by custom and law are forced into **retirement.**

retirement: formal cessation of work

Although retirement at some arbitrary age may have some advantages and humanitarian consequences, it also has serious implications for many older workers who are both able and eager to continue working and playing a productive role in society. Not only does it deprive them of a feeling of being needed and useful, but it tends to provide them with an image of being outmoded. Of equal importance, it leads to financial problems and loss of independence during a highly stressful transition period in life. As Robert Butler (1975) has expressed it: "The right to work is basic to the right to survive. Work, denied to older people by practice and by attitudes, is often needed to earn a living and provide personal satisfaction" (p. 64).

The magnitude of the problem of older workers and retirement is indicated by the fact that in 1980 there were more than 25 million Americans aged sixty-five or older. By the year 2000, this number is expected to increase to well over 30 million. Although recent legislation has eliminated mandatory retirement for most workers before the age of seventy, the issues are complex and the problems of older workers are by no means resolved.

**The importance of families.**   Since the older person no longer has an opportunity to work, families and social contacts may assume greater importance in the older person's life. Those individuals who have maintained their marriages into late adulthood report an increased sense of satisfaction in the marital relationship, particularly as children leave home. And, as the children leave home and retirement occurs, the need for fixed sex-roles diminishes. It is no longer necessary for males to focus predominately on their instrumental roles. In late adulthood, men can allow themselves an opportunity to develop their emotional and dependent aspects. Women, on the other hand, often become more independent, seeking new skills and friends. Although these trends have been identified in other cultures as well as our own (Neugarten, 1968), these marriages were initially characterized by a high degree of sex-role separation. Whether newer relationships among young people that emphasize the equalitarian aspects of the relationships will show similar sex-role reversals in old age must, of course, await the passage of years.

The availability of a supportive network of friends and family can be of great assistance to the older adult. Even though children are generally independent of their older parents, adult children can be a source of aid and comfort.

In summary, the findings on older adults suggest a complex picture. On the biological level, many changes are degenerative in nature. On the cognitive level, a more subtle picture emerges. On some skills, older adults are at a disadvantage as compared with younger adults. However, skills that reflect learning and experience remain stable or may, in fact, climb during the later years. On a social and emotional level, late adulthood is associated with a variety of changes. In general, life satisfaction appears to be related to personality functioning in the earlier years. People whose lives were well-integrated socially and emotionally tend to adjust to the changes of late adulthood best. Although there may be some tendency for older adults to withdraw from the world and focus on inner thoughts and emotions, it appears that at least a moderate level of interaction with the world is an aid to the older adult. Finally, friends and family assume greater importance in the later years.

In our next section, we examine death, the final stage of life, and examine the ways in which death can be an experience for growth.

## DEATH, DYING, AND LOSS

Each of us during our lifetimes will experience death. Each of us will experience the death of others, and each of us will die. For some, death will come quickly and virtually without warning, as with accident or heart attack victims. Others will learn that death is imminent for them, as with those who learn they have a chronic or terminal illness.

Our ability to deal with loss and with death places enormous demands upon us. The death of others is a personal loss to us, a loss that we must learn to cope with, and a loss that we must ultimately recover from and continue with our lives. Our own death is both easier to think about and more difficult to imagine. On the one hand, we cannot dream of there not being another tomorrow, another sunrise, another horizon to seek. And yet, death is a certainty—a certainty that we must plan for in both ourselves and our loved ones. Although death is for many a terrifying possibility, it is also an occasion for learning, an occasion for personal growth. Thus, Lipton (1979) has emphasized that death, as the final stage of growth, can both illuminate and show the continuity of life.

In this section we will discuss various concepts of loss, the process of dying, and the effects of death on those who continue to live. We begin with a discussion of loss.

## Loss

When we were children, we cried when a favorite toy was damaged beyond repair. We grieved when a pet died. In later life, we felt empty when an important relationship ended, when we moved from one town to another, or when a parent or spouse died. These are examples of **loss,** and they help illustrate our definition of loss as a state of being deprived of or being without something we once had (Schoenberg, Carr, Pereta, & Kutscher, 1970).

**loss: a state of being deprived of or being without something one once had**

**Types of loss.**   Many different experiences and events can produce a sensation of loss in us. Some types of loss identified by Schoenberg et al. (1970) are:

1. *Loss of a significant loved or valued person.* This type of loss can occur through the death of a loved one, divorce or separation, or a broken relationship. Additional examples can include entrance of a valued person into the military or placement of a loved one into a jail or other correctional institution. Valued and loved individuals can also be lost to serious or incapacitating illness. For example, an illness that keeps an individual bedridden may deprive us of that person's skills at home or at work. Additionally, their contribution to the social functioning of the home or work place will also be missed, as in a bedridden woman who may not be able to care for her young children.

2. *Loss of some aspect of the self.* In this type of loss, we experience some deprivation or reduction of our positive feelings about our worth, attractiveness, competencies, physical appearance, and esteem. For example, not only does an illness affect others, it affects us as well. If we are unable to perform the normal, day-to-day tasks that we are accustomed to, we may experience some loss.

Loss of function can also be perceived as a loss to the self. As we grow older, we may find that our physical and perceptual abilities are not as acute as when we were younger. Our strength and coordination may decrease; our ability to see and hear clearly may diminish. If these aspects of our selves are important to us, their diminution will negatively affect us.

The loss of positive self-attitudes can also pose difficulties for young and old alike. Rape, military induction, and hospitalization may cause self-attitudes to become more negative. Our sense of attractiveness, pride, independence, and control can decrease, causing us to perceive a loss.

Finally, we may lose self-definition. In our society, we often inform people that they are no longer useful members of society by asking them to retire. And, older adults may not command the respect and attention from their families and co-workers that they once had.

3. *Loss of external objects.* Natural disasters, crime, and political and economic forces may induce a profound sense of loss in us. When a house goes up in flames, or when a family is the victim of theft or robbery, significant loss can occur. While some of the possessions can be replaced, and while some money may be restored, the loss of special possessions may be a significant event to us. We cannot, for example, replace photographs taken on special, memorable occasions. The pin that was given to us by a parent or grandparent had a sentimental value that far outweighed its nominal worth.

Social and political forces also can produce significant losses. In many parts of the world, people who live in the rural and undeveloped areas of a country seek out and move to urban centers in a search for a better way to live. In making this move, they leave behind the comforts of family and an established way of life. Political forces also produce loss through wars, refugees, and resettlements.

4. *Developmental loss.* Developmental loss occurs during the normal process of human growth and development. A child may lose gratifications associated with being the "only" child in the family when a sibling is born. We end our education in high school or college. Our children grow up, leave home, and marry. We age. These processes continue throughout our lives, but they may produce loss.

**The experience of loss.**     Loss is something that cannot be avoided. In the normal course of living, each of us will experience loss. In other words, loss can be a result of growth. Some losses, for example, are predictable, as in the loss of a job at retirement, or the loss of close family support when we first move from our parents' home. Some losses, on the other hand, are haphazard and unpredictable. For example, we may lose a car in an auto accident, or a worker may lose the respect of his or her peers as the result of failure to perform a job adequately.

Losses may also be sudden or gradual. A parent who dies suddenly from a stroke is an example of a sudden loss, while the loss of strength and coordination in the elderly is an example of a gradual loss. Some losses may be traumatic, while others may be nontraumatic. A man may be devastated at the loss of a home due to fire, while the loss of the reproductive capability in a woman who is undergoing menopause may not be at all bothersome.

Obviously, the factor that determines whether we have experienced a loss is not *what* is lost, but our *perception* of and reaction to the loss. It is thus possible for two individuals to experience exactly the same degree of deprivation but react to it in very different ways. One person may react to the end of a relationship with a shrug of the shoulders and an almost carefree "Oh, well," while another may find the same set of circumstances devastating.

As we have seen, loss is a broad concept, involving many aspects of our normal experience. However, probably the greatest loss is death, the subject to which we now turn.

## Death and Dying

*"We make the dead look as if they were asleep, we ship children off to protect them from the anxiety and turmoil [telling them] . . . "Mother has gone on a long trip." . . . We don't allow children to visit their dying parents in the hospital, we have long and controversial discussions about whether patients should be told the truth . . . Dying nowadays is more gruesome in many ways, namely, more lonely, mechanical, and dehumanized."*
*(KÜBLER-ROSS, 1969, PP. 6–7)*

Death is a frightening experience both to those who die and to those who continue to live. Both today and in the past, death was a fearful event. However, in the past hundred years, modern science has given us the tools to increase life dramatically. Advances in nutrition, sanitation, control of infection, and modern diagnostic and treatment practices in medicine have advanced our life spans sufficiently so that we can reasonably expect to live well past age sixty-five.

Despite these advances, we seem to fear and deny the reality of death even more than in the past. Our society is focused on youth and life. Advertisements in newspapers, magazines, and television inform us about the joys of young life. And, should a dreaded wrinkle appear on our skin, or, even worse, a gray hair appear on our heads, a variety of products is ready and available to help us recapture that important, elusive characteristic of youth. Except for some insurance advertisements, very little in our culture addresses the issue of dying.

**Issues in the societal reaction to death.**    Elisabeth Kübler-Ross (1969) has made an intensive study of death in our society and the process of death. She, as well as a number of social scientists, e.g., Robertson (1981), has pointed to several reasons for our refusal as a society to deal with death.

One important factor is the decreased importance of religion. In many traditional approaches to religion, especially in Christianity, the promise of death was an afterlife in which suffering, pain, and want would be eliminated. Death was therefore not something to be feared, but a force to be welcomed. Nowadays, fewer people believe, or believe less strongly, in the concept that there are rewards after death for an individual's suffering on earth. In the past, painful diseases or disabilities had a purpose, a purpose that fewer people see today.

A second issue involves the development of weapons of mass destruction. A number of nations are capable of destroying themselves and others many times over through nuclear weapons. Nerve gasses and biological weapons enable an individual nation to exterminate systematically huge sections of the population. These weapons further feed our fear of death by increasing our fear of a violent, catastrophic death.

A third issue involves medical education. Physicians are, not surprisingly, trained to focus on the prolongation of life. Treatment that focuses on diminishing human suffering is, to many physicians, an admission that life cannot be significantly lengthened or improved. It is, in other words, an admission that traditional care has failed and that no reasonable hope remains. This is, of course, a difficult admission for many physicians to make. And, patients' sudden realization that physicians cannot successfully treat all diseases also increases the fear of death.

The final issue deals with the separation of death from the mainstream of life and experience. In the past, death was a normal part of living, and people learned or developed ways of coping with the process of death. The extended family structure characteristic of our society earlier in this century provided an excellent background for learning about death. Grandparents often shared the same house with their grandchildren, and grandchildren eventually learned first-hand about death by experiencing the death of their grandparents, parents, or siblings. Additionally, people tended to die earlier. In essence, people learned that death was a natural part of life.

In our present society, death is sanitized. We go into hospitals to die. News reports of the latest catastrophes, disasters, murders, and accidents desensitize us to death. And, movies and action dramas make killing a simple, easy sport. All these conditions make death somewhat unreal. Since we have no real understanding about death, it is alien and frightening to us.

**Some recent changes.**   Our reaction as a society to death appears to be undergoing some change. Both the hospice movement and the enactment of "death with dignity" laws are increasing our abilities to deal with death in a more accepting fashion.

A **hospice** is a center for the care of the terminally ill. A hospice operates under the premise that when medical science can offer no hope for cure or remission, a reasonable alternative to further treatment is **palliative care**—care that attempts to keep a patient as comfortable as possible without undue sedation or drug-induced mental cloudiness. At the same time, hospices typically try to achieve a very homelike atmosphere in which patients are encouraged to surround themselves with meaningful possessions and in which visitors, including young children, are welcomed.

**hospice: center for the care of the terminally ill**

**palliative care: care that attempts to reduce physical suffering without inducing mental cloudiness**

The staff of hospice centers are usually given special training to help them deal with the emotional aspects of caring for the dying. Additionally, hospice centers may try to aid families in dealing with the death of loved ones.

Death with dignity laws are another way to reduce the institutional and impersonal aspects of death. Typically, death with dignity laws allow an individual to set up a "living will" that gives a particular family member or physician permission to discontinue extraordinary medical treatment when hope for recovery has gone. In this way, a person can be spared the dehumanizing experience of having life sustained only by machines and can reduce the financial burden on their family for costly medical care.

Hospices encourage terminally ill patients to remain in their own homes whenever possible while members of the hospice staff make home visits to provide care and counseling for the dying person and his or her family. Here a hospice patient, center, talks with a hospice nurse, left, and a nurse volunteer, right, in the kitchen of the patient's home. The patient's son is at the back.

## Stages of Dying

In her extraordinary study of dying patients, Kübler-Ross (1969) described five stages through which dying individuals seem to pass. As she observed, these stages need not occur in a fixed, one-after-another sequence. Not all dying patients experience all stages, and some stages can be experienced simultaneously. While there is some controversy regarding the concept of stages of dying (Kastenbaum, 1977), these five stages are well worth reviewing, for this analysis gives us a revealing glimpse at the feelings and emotions that the dying individual may experience.

**First stage: Denial.**   The first reaction of the person who learns or "figures out" that he or she is dying is denial: "No, it can't be me. It isn't true." At this point, we are unwilling to accept our condition. We seek out second opinions from other physicians. We hope that the Xrays were wrong or that the pathologist made a mistake.

For most people, denial is a useful defense mechanism. It is difficult to go from a basic assumption of health and life to a realization of impending death.

By denying the possibility that he or she will die, an individual makes it somewhat easier to accept this new knowledge in smaller and more manageable doses. Thus, denial helps the individual cope with some new and terrifying information.

**Second stage: Anger.**  At some point, the reaction of, "This can't be me," gives way to the painful realization, "It is me. It wasn't a mistake." With the understanding that our lives are indeed limited in time comes anger, rage, and envy. "Why me?" we ask. Other people, we think, are more "deserving" of death— the old, incapacitated man, the abusive alcoholic woman of our acquaintance— these are more deserving of death.

In this stage, we may wonder why this "punishment" has been inflicted upon us. We may regard our lives as exemplary and feel that death is inappropriate for us. We may have plans that we wish to carry out. There are dreams yet to be fulfilled. But, the imminence of death and the frustration of knowing that we will die without getting the opportunity to accomplish all that we want to or that control over our lives will transfer inexorably to the disease and to the physicians and hospitals produces great anger.

This anger is focused indiscriminately, and it may strike without warning. It may be directed at loved ones, at medical personnel, at co-workers. It appears when we are reminded that tomorrows to come will not be available to us. Overhearing co-workers planning a weekend trip may, for example, produce anger and envy because we may not be able to enjoy such trips anymore and may not even have the option of planning for such "frivolities."

**Third stage: Bargaining.**  In the bargaining stage, people seek to increase their time by bargaining with physicians, themselves, their families, and God. When denial and anger have not worked, a more conciliatory approach may succeed. By behaving more "correctly," these individuals seek to win the prize of longer life. One woman engaged in bargaining was described as follows.

*Another patient was in utmost pain and discomfort, unable to go home because of her dependence on injections for pain relief. She had a son who proceeded with his plans to get married, as the patient had wished. She was very sad to think that she would be unable to attend this big day, for he was her oldest and favorite child. With combined efforts, we were able to teach her self-hypnosis which enabled her to be quite comfortable for several hours. She had made all sorts of promises if she could only live long enough to attend this marriage. The day preceding the wedding she left the hospital as an elegant lady. Nobody would have believed her real condition. She was "the happiest person in the whole world" and looked radiant. I wondered what her reaction would be when the time was up for which she had bargained.*

*I will never forget the moment when she returned to the hospital. She looked tired and somewhat exhausted and—before I could say hello—said, "Now don't forget I have another son!" (p. 73)*

Of course, not all people bargain. However, the promise of good behavior in exchange for longer life may motivate a significant portion of the dying individual's behavior.

**Fourth stage: Depression.**   As the disease progresses and as we experience a variety of losses, depression can occur. The weakness and disability from the disease can no longer be ignored, and we experience a loss of functioning. The sums of money spent in treatment and the time spent in hospitals are another source of loss. Jobs may be lost, and the normal functioning of the family may be disrupted. All these losses can result in depression.

An important source of depression results from our impending separation from the world and loss of all that is loved and dear to us. We may never see the colorful leaves of autumn again. Wrongs may never have the chance to be righted. We will be separated from loved ones forever. And the bright promise of tomorrow will never be experienced.

**Fifth stage: Acceptance.**   Assuming that death has not come quickly and that we have had an opportunity to express denial, anger, bargaining, and depression in constructive forms, a stage of acceptance may occur. Acceptance is not a cheery wish for death, but a final rest before that long journey into "the dark night." In this stage, we may be quite weak and fatigued. It may be difficult to stay awake and to talk. And, we may not wish to be bothered by visitors, telephone calls, and other unimportant details. In essence, we have said goodbye to the world and to our families and loved ones and now wish to die. Having detached ourselves from the world and from our important relationships, death becomes a great relief.

It is important to emphasize that the sequence proposed by Kübler-Ross is not fixed, nor do all people experience these various stages. Rather, her model is a description of the changes that may take place in the dying individual.

## Dealing with the Death of a Loved One

Dealing with the impending death of a loved one is a difficult task, as is the task of dealing with the grief, anger, and depression that occur in us following a loved one's death. These tasks are a vital part of living, but they are also tasks for which we receive little training. We can, however, offer some general guidelines for dealing with the deaths of those close to us:

1. *Treat a person, not a disease.* Dying people are typically treated in hospitals, and the dying person may have little control over the care he or she receives. As Kastenbaum (1979) notes:

*In taking away the responsibility, credibility and control of the old person himself, we also set up a situation in which much of his life has become the property of others long before the process of dying begins. The terminally ill old person deserves to live and die as he himself would choose. Simple though it may seem, this concept runs counter to much in our social and health care network. It is easier to treat "diseases" and to look after "geriatric patients" than to work intimately with each person's individual needs as a person. (p. 110)*

# Insight

## ARE THERE TARGET DATES FOR DEATH?

Many people seem determined to live until a given target date. In fact, there are reports that older persons are more likely to die after a holiday or birthday than before. Cases have even been recorded of terminally ill patients who managed to stay alive until an important event took place, such as a wedding anniversary or the birth of a grandchild.

Apparently the setting of such "target dates" for living is relatively common. Many middle-aged persons, when asked, will state that they want to live until New Year's Day of the year 2000—to see the dawning of the twenty-first century.

In somewhat similar fashion, some persons also set what amount to "target dates for death." For example, the prospect of life without the companionship of one's mate

has caused many happily married older people to say they want to die when their mates do. So powerful is the loss of the will to live in some cases that the bereavement may actually precipitate the spouse's own death.

An interesting case with respect to target dates for death is that of Mark Twain (Samuel Clemens). He was born on November 30, 1835, when Halley's comet made its spectacular appearance in the sky; and he died—as he had predicted—on April 21, 1910, when Halley's comet returned. Death was attributed to a heart attack, but the question still remains about the underlying cause: Was it the excitement surrounding the fiery comet's return, or the conviction that the incontrovertible date for death had arrived?

---

2. *Be open with the dying person.* Dying people have the right to know what is happening to them. Being "protected" from the knowledge of one's condition does not help the person—but it does protect family members and friends from discussing the issue of death with the dying individual. Acknowledging the impending death of the person can help both the sick and the well cope more readily.

3. *Ask what is needed.* Dying people often feel a need to "put their affairs in order." We can aid this process by asking what they need and by following their instructions and wishes. Some of their requests can be very structured: "I want Jean to get my jewelry after I'm gone." Some may be interpersonal: "Take care of your Uncle Rick. He needs to be looked after." And some may be more general: "Come sit with me." In carrying out these tasks, we can aid the dying person and confront our own, often mixed, emotions about death and dying.

The death of a loved one often brings with it an intense sense of grief. If the death was unexpected, we may be shocked and horrified. Or if the death had been expected for some time, we still feel a loss, even if we think that the death was "for the best."

Our grief can consist of feelings of guilt, distress, and hostility, and the grieving process can be as short as a few weeks or as long as two years. We shall deal with grief and associated emotions in greater detail in Chapter 6.

The point we wish to make here is that grief should not be denied. Although it can be an unpleasant experience, the expression of grief is part of the healing process. In time, our feelings of grief will begin to dissipate, and we will begin to resume the normal pattern of our lives. We never return to our "old selves," since loss and grief change us. But, we can become stronger and deeper people, better able to help others because of our experience (Caplan, 1981). We can, in other words, use the experience of death, loss, and grief to help us to grow as individuals.

## A Closing Note

Learning and talking about aging, loss, and death is a sobering experience. We greatly value life, and we wonder what the future holds for us. As young children, we wondered what life would be like as young adults. And, we feared the future, thinking of all the potentially negative things that could happen to us. Now that we have reached those adult years, we continue to worry about our later years. Again we think of all the potentially negative events that may befall us. However, just as our current years hold fewer negatives than our childhood imaginations had generated, so too will our future years be more positive and hopeful than our fears suggest. As Robert Kastenbaum (1979) has stated:

*There was a time in my own life when I wondered about the value of growing and being old. No more. I do not want to miss my old age any more than I would choose to have skipped childhood or adolescence. But I do feel an increased sense of responsibility to this future self and to all those whose lives may cross my path. What kind of old man will I be, given the chance? The answer to that question largely depends on the kind of person I am right now. For growing old is an ongoing project of self-actualisation through the life-span. (p. 121)*

## SUMMARY

1. Adjustment is a lifelong process. During our lives, many changes will occur, and the effect that these changes will have on us depend on our previous ways of dealing with and managing changes in our lives.

2. Late adolescence and early adulthood are often considered a peak time of life. Our biological capacities are at their greatest, and we begin to use and understand abstract ideas. Emotionally, the task of late adolescence and early adult life is the challenge of achieving identity and intimacy. The formation of identity may be associated with a crisis, but the attainment of identity may result in our commitment to adult goals and patterns. The young adult also strives for intimacy in his or her relationships with others.

3. Middle adult life is something of a mystery to researchers. There may be slight biological declines, but there may also be continued cognitive develop-

ment. The major emotional challenge for this period is the development of generativity—achieving a productive life and assisting others. The first signs of aging may provoke a "mid-life crisis" of identity.

4. Substantial biological change occurs during late adulthood. Cognitively, the older adult may show strengths in areas related to academic training and experience but may show declines in tasks requiring agility and speed. The major emotional challenge of the late adult years involves the review of one's life. During this time, we examine our lives and either accept our lives and achieve ego integrity or find our lives wanting and thereby experience despair.

5. Death and loss are a normal part of life, and it is possible that personal growth can occur even in dying. The five-stage model proposed by Kübler-Ross is a useful way to approach the issue of death and understand its process.

# Chapter 5

# Motivation: Our Needs and Goals

*"Kilimanjaro is a snow covered mountain 19,710 feet high . . . the highest mountain in Africa . . . Close to the western summit there is the dried and frozen carcass of a leopard. No one has explained what the leopard was seeking at that altitude."*
(HEMINGWAY, 1955, P. 52)

This dramatic introduction to Hemingway's well-known story, ''The Snows of Kilimanjaro,'' makes two interesting assumptions: (1) that the behavior of the leopard was motivated—that the leopard was seeking something by climbing to the top of a snow-covered mountain, and (2) that to understand the leopard's behavior we would have to understand what the animal was seeking and why.

**motivation: inner conditions that activate behavior and influence its direction**

The term **motivation** refers to any condition of the organism that leads to goal-directed behavior. Although no concept of motivation seems necessary to explain the actions of atoms or planets, this concept is useful in understanding and predicting the behavior of living creatures—particularly human beings. *Motives* and *goals* focus our energy and effort, help determine the competencies we need, and provide a basis for deciding between alternative courses of actions.

In this chapter, we shall address several issues in motivation. First, we shall present some basic concepts of motivation, followed by a discussion of areas in which our maintenance and actualization strivings seem particularly important. We shall also note some social forces in motivation. Finally, we shall indicate how motive patterns can influence our behavior.

## CONCEPTS OF MOTIVATION

Here we shall briefly present some basic concepts of motivation and describe a number of dimensions along which theories of motivation differ. In particular, we shall discuss *(a)* basic concepts in motivation, *(b)* similarities and differences in motive patterns, *(c)* push vs. pull models of motivation, *(d)* hierarchy of motives, and *(e)* deficiency vs. growth motivation. As we shall see, each of these concepts may be used in understanding more specific behavioral patterns.

**need: biological or psychological condition whose gratification is necessary for the maintenance of homeostasis**

### Basic Concepts in Motivation

**drive: internal condition that pushes the individual to seek some goal**

**goal: object or condition for which an individual strives**

**motive: psychological condition whose gratification is necessary for the maintenance of homeostasis**

Many psychologists describe motivation as having three aspects: (1) bodily **needs,** environmental stimuli, or cognitive events generate a **drive** within the organism; (2) these drives help initiate and direct behavior; and (3) the behavior, in turn, helps the organism reach a **goal,** producing relief and a reduction of the drive (Morgan, King, & Robinson, 1979). According to this approach, needs are typically biological necessities—food, air, and water. Drives, on the other hand, are the psychological states aroused by the needs. Some psychologists believe that drives need not be aroused simply by biological needs. These researchers contend that broad psychological **motives** can help direct behavior toward a goal. In either case, motivation includes not only the internal states of the individual but the actions and goals of the individual as well.

We cannot observe motivation directly; we can only infer it from the individual's actions. Although unseen, it is nonetheless a powerful concept that allows us greater understanding of human behavior. Psychologists use the concept of motivation to explain the needs, drives, beliefs, attitudes, values, and other factors that influence goal-directed behavior (Howe & Flowers, 1981; Howe & Page, 1980). Motivation accounts for the energies and forces that give rise to and influence our behavior. A knowledge of motivation helps us understand how the **primary drives** such as hunger and thirst exert marked influences on our actions and how **secondary** (learned) **drives** are present in our strivings for money and prestige, curiosity, and self-actualization.

As we can see, motivation is a broad concept which includes the needs, goals, and strivings of the individual. In this context, it is important to emphasize the key role which our thoughts (cognitions) and the environment play in shaping our motives. Thus, it is not surprising that motives and behavior differ markedly from one individual to another as well as from one social group to another.

**primary drive: drive generated by basic biological need such as food or water**

**secondary (learned) drive: drive generated by nonbiological factor such as desire for money or self-actualization**

## Similarities and Differences in Motive Patterns

Sometimes we are motivated by powerful built-in drives, like hunger and thirst. Other motives, such as a belief in the importance of financial success or of fighting poverty, may be entirely learned. Since we can acquire almost any motive as a consequence of learning, it is inevitable that our motivational patterns show almost infinite variety.

**Maintenance vs. actualization motives.** At first glance, human motives appear to defy classification. Yet, if we look closer, we can distinguish between *maintenance* and *actualization motives.* Strivings toward self-maintenance are primarily concerned with survival and with meeting primary psychological needs. Our strivings for curiosity and sensation combined with our needs for biological necessities are examples of strivings toward self-maintenance. Strivings for the actualization of potentials are concerned with meeting "higher," more difficult, or more challenging psychological needs.

The strivings that satisfy maintenance often seem less important to us than do the strivings that lead to actualization. A scientist completing an exciting experiment may be much more concerned about its outcome than about eating or sleeping; a mountain climber may undergo great hardship and danger in climbing a high mountain peak; and an astronaut may risk his or her life on a space mission. In fact, it is in our voluntary attempts at creative expression, at coping with great challenges, and in our quest for values and meaning that we reveal ourselves as human and distinct from other species.

**Key motives.** **Key motives**—the motives of greatest importance to us—are particularly important in determining our life-style. For some, key motives may

**key motives: important and continuing motives that exert a profound influence on a person's life**

Mountain climber Don Bennett twice reached the top of Mt. Rainier, Washington's highest peak—once in 1970 before he lost his leg in an accident and again in 1982 when he made the climb to encourage other handicapped persons to participate in sports activities.

center around love and belonging; for others, around social approval and security; for others, around competence and actualization; and for still others, around achievement and power. Since our key motives tend to be relatively enduring, they contribute to the continuity and consistency of our behavior.

Our key motives largely determine our *level of aspiration*—our reach for easy or difficult goals. Well-adjusted persons generally have a reasonably accurate picture of themselves and their world. They will strive toward relatively realistic goals, while maladjusted persons will tend to set their goals too low or too high in relation to their personal resources and the limitations and opportunities presented by their environment.

## Push vs. Pull Models of Motivation

Most approaches to motivation can be viewed as either "push" or "pull" models. The push models emphasize our inner needs and cognitions. In these models, the individual is a purposeful agent who deals with the environment in accordance with his or her needs, motives, and values. As Bandura (1977b) has noted, our motives and values are heavily based on learning and other cognitive processes. "Past experiences create expectancies that certain actions will bring valued benefits, that others will have not appreciable effects, and that still others will avert future trouble. By representing forseeable outcomes symbolically, people can convert future consequences into current motivators of behavior" (p. 18).

The pull models, on the other hand, emphasize environmental stimuli as the forces that induce and channel behavior. Behavior is a reaction to demands and pressures, rewards and punishments—in essence, as the result of the patterning of stimuli in the environment. By manipulating the rewards and punishments for given behaviors, society can shape and channel the behavior of the individual in the directions which the given society deems desirable. While the push models emphasize the internal strivings of the individual, the pull models emphasize the incentives and stimuli that are most potent in the environment.

Neither a push nor a pull model is sufficient by itself. Human beings are both active and reactive. Our behavior, like that of other living systems, is the result of both our inner structural and integrative properties and the conditions and forces in the environment. Some things we do primarily because of inner demands or conditions; others primarily because of environmental incentives and demands. Both the instigation of behavior and the form it takes result from our own makeup and the environmental setting in which our behavior takes place.

Intellectual pursuits are one way through which we can fulfill our needs for personal growth.

## Hierarchy of Motives

Maslow (1954) suggested that our needs arrange themselves in a **hierarchy** from the basic biological needs to the need for self-fulfillment or actualization, representing the highest development of the human personality. Maslow's hierarchy has five levels of needs:

1. *Physiological needs*—basic bodily needs including the needs for food, sleep, stimulation, and activity.

2. *Safety needs*—needs for protection from bodily harm or injury and for security from threat.

3. *Love and belongingness needs*—including needs for acceptance, warmth, affection, and approval.

4. *Esteem needs*—including needs for adequacy, worth, status, and self-respect.

5. *Self-actualization (fulfillment) needs*—needs for personal growth and the realization of potentialities.

According to Maslow, the lowest level of unmet need is prepotent—the one that commands the individual's attention and efforts. For example, unless the needs for food and safety are reasonably well met, behavior will be dominated by these needs. Once these needs are gratified, however, the individual will be free to devote his or her energies to meeting needs on higher levels. This concept of a built-in prepotency of needs has been supported by observations of behavior in extreme situations. In both the Nazi concentration camps and Japanese prisoner-of-war camps in World War II, it was not unusual for prisoners subjected to prolonged deprivation and torture to lower their moral standards, take food from each other, and in other ways surrender the loyalties and values they had held under more normal conditions (Bettelheim, 1943; Nardini, 1952). Similar patterns, although involving a far lower percentage of American POWs, were observed in the Korean and Vietnam wars.

Under conditions of extreme deprivation or torture, many individuals sacrifice their higher-level actualization needs to meet their more basic needs for personal safety and survival. This pattern does not always hold, however, particularly with people who believe in their cause. Many creative people have pursued their special talents despite serious handicaps and social ridicule. Social reformers have continued their struggles despite harassment, jail sentences, and other punishment. Every age has had its heroes and martyrs who remained faithful to their principles and beliefs despite social ostracism, physical deprivation, torture, and sometimes death. Through learning and experience, our beliefs, values, and self-esteem may become more important to us than our needs for social approval and security or even our need for safety. The extent to which safety and physiological needs dominate our behavior even under extreme conditions is an individual decision.

# Insight

According to the findings of Maslow (1969, 1971) so-called lower level needs—such as needs for food and security—tend to dominate our behavior. When lower level needs are met, however, our behavior tends to be dominated by "higher" level needs, such as various forms of actualization strivings.

**HIERARCHY OF NEEDS**

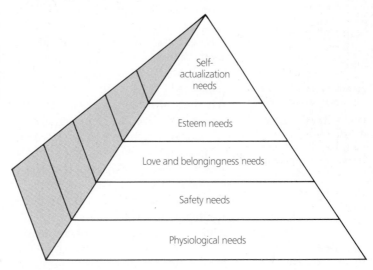

## Deficiency vs. Growth Motivation

Maslow has emphasized the distinction between **deficiency** and **growth motivation.** Behavior motivated primarily by maintenance needs—hunger, safety, social approval, and so on—is deficiency motivated. That is, it is motivated by the lack of something the individual needs for stability. In contrast, growth motivation is aimed at increasing our long-term capabilities. Gratifying our deficiency needs releases us from their domination and frees us for self-actualization.

**deficiency motivation:** domination of behavior by maintenance needs and strivings

**growth motivation:** domination of behavior by actualization needs and strivings

People who are dominated by deficiency needs despite adequate resources or who have not found anything else worth striving for tend to be maladjusted and unhappy. Maslow (1954) has summarized it this way: "I should say simply that a healthy man is primarily motivated by his needs to develop and actualize his fullest potentialities and capacities. If a man has any other basic needs in any active, chronic sense, he is simply an unhealthy man." In a comparison of deficiency-motivated and growth-motivated people, Maslow discovered that the latter showed more efficient perception of reality, could tolerate uncertainty better, were more spontaneous and creative, were more accepting of themselves and others, were more problem-centered and less ego-centered, had deeper than average relationships with other people, had a philosophical, unhostile sense of humor, and felt kinship with and concern for all humanity.

# STRIVINGS TOWARD MAINTENANCE AND ACTUALIZATION

Digestion, circulation, and other bodily functions operate to maintain the physiological equilibrium of the body. While we may go several hours with no food, the concentration of sugar and other chemicals in the blood must remain relatively constant; a slight increase in acidity, for example, would result in coma and death. Similarly, body temperature must remain within a very limited range even though the temperature in the environment may go above a hundred degrees or below zero. Thus living systems endeavor to maintain **steady states**—to maintain their physiological variables within a range essential for survival—an endeavor referred to as **homeostasis.**

On the psychological level, we understand less about the processes involved in maintenance. However, they appear to be an extension of the strivings we see operating on the biological level. Damage to the self, through severe guilt feelings or excessive stress, can disable a person just as surely as can the failure of homeostatic mechanisms on the biological level. Thus we also strive to maintain the steady states essential to psychological integration—for thinking, feeling, and acting in organized and coherent ways.

In an attempt to understand our **maintenance strivings,** we shall review some of the generally agreed-upon requirements—biological and psychological needs—that must be met for normal functioning. Then we shall attempt to deal with the even more complex problem of actualization strivings—particularly the forms such strivings take on the psychological level as we attempt to fulfill ourselves as human beings.

**steady state: state of physiological equilibrium**

**homeostasis: the tendency to keep internal body conditions within a certain range, maintaining "steady states"**

**maintenance strivings: strivings toward maintenance of biological or psychological equilibrium and integration**

## Biological Needs

For normal functioning the human body has many needs, ranging from food and vitamins to sleep. In our present discussion, we shall not attempt to cover the gamut of biological needs. Rather, we will briefly summarize those requirements which seem particularly relevant to understanding our behavior—that is, those bodily needs essential for normal bodily functioning and survival.

**hypothalamus: area of the brain that helps regulate biological functions such as eating and drinking**

**stimulus-binding theory: theory suggesting that certain individuals, particularly the obese, are much more responsive to environmental cues than are typical persons**

**Hunger and thirst.**   The biological factors that control hunger appear to be related to the workings of the **hypothalamus** in the brain. Other biological factors are also important in the control of hunger. These factors include the functioning of the hypothalamus, stomach contractions, glucose levels in the blood, and the presence in the body of specialized hormones. However, biological factors are not the only regulators of hunger motivation. Other research has suggested that situational factors may also be of importance, particularly in the obese individual.

One major approach, called the **stimulus-binding theory**, suggests that the obese are much more affected by external, situational cues than by internal cues for hunger. In a fascinating study conducted by Schachter and Gross (1968), obese and normal-weight subjects participated in a sham "experiment" on physiological responses. During the course of the experiment, food was made available to the subjects. Unknown to the subjects, however, was the fact that the speed of the room clock was under the control of the experimenter. When the clock was running faster than normal, obese subjects ate more than the normal-weight subjects when the clock indicated dinner time. In essence, the obese said to themselves, "It's time to eat! I must be hungry." Normal-weight subjects, on the other hand, waited until their internal hunger mechanisms indicated that it was time to eat. They seemed to say, "It's time to eat, but I'm not hungry." When the clock was running slower than normal (i.e., the actual time was later than the room clock indicated), the obese ate *less* than normal-weight subjects. In both the slow-time and the fast-time conditions, the obese were strongly affected by external environmental stimuli.

Biological mechanisms are also important in the regulation of thirst. Receptors in the hypothalamus help trigger drinking. Additionally, a complicated homeostatic mechanism involving blood volume, blood pressure, kidneys, and various hormones also helps motivate drinking behavior.

As with hunger, the motivation for thirst is also controlled by situational factors. In a study conducted by Decke (1971), obese and normal-weight subjects were given access to bad- or good-tasting drinks. As seen in Figure 5.1, both groups drank less of the bad-tasting liquid than the good-tasting liquid. However, obese drank substantially less of the bad-tasting drink than normals, and significantly more of the good-tasting drink than normals. These findings illustrate the importance of considering both biological and psychological forces in motivations as primary as hunger and thirst.

**Sex.**    Sexual motivation is probably second only to the hunger motive in its far-reaching implications for social living. The family is based upon a sexual union as well as upon enduring emotional ties. And sex is a dominant theme in much of our lives, including our music, art, drama, and literature.

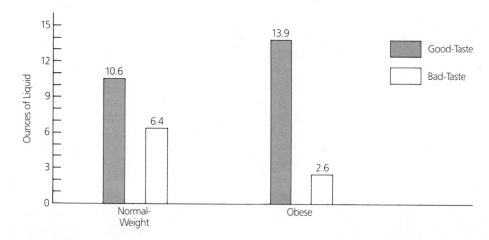

**FIGURE 5.1**

Unlike hunger and thirst, the sexual drive does not appear to be related to cyclic variations in bodily chemistry in humans. For example, the *androgens,* which appear to be primarily responsible for the sex drive in both men and women, are relatively constant in humans. In contrast, lower mammals show periods of sexual desire and receptivity only when particular hormones are at a high point in the body. For example, a female dog is sexually receptive only when she is in "heat," a condition brought about by profound changes in the animal's hormones.

Another significant difference between humans and other mammals is that sexual activity in humans appears to be primarily a learned phenomenon, not an instinctual one. Humans can react sexually to other persons, to themselves, and to objects in the environment (as in the various fetishes). Humans can also voluntarily deny or limit their sexual activities or pleasures. For example, a youth who is indoctrinated with the view that sex is evil and dirty may develop little sexual motivation and as an adult may even find sexual intercourse unpleasant or repugnant.

As a consequence of differing cultural viewpoints and individual life experiences, there are widespread differences in the strength and perceived significance of the sex drive among adolescents and adults. Approved patterns of sexual gratification also vary considerably from one society to another although sexual codes seem generally to be becoming more liberalized. In any event, the great variety of sexual activities and preferences among human beings attests to the importance of learning in humans.

Although the meaning and importance of sex vary greatly from one person to another, sexual tensions, fantasies, and experiences, as well as problems centering around sexual gratification, are usually important facets of most people's lives in our society. Depending on our attitude toward sexual behavior and the part we assign it in our overall life plan, sex can be an important channel for self-actualization and intimacy or a source of anxiety and self-devaluation.

**Sleep.**   Jouvet (1967) has estimated that: "At sixty years of age a man has spent more than twenty years in sleep. Fifteen of these years are passed in the subjective emptiness of dreamless sleep, and about five in the imaginary and prodigiously rich life of dream activity. We thus spend more than a third of our life unconscious of the universe which surrounds us" (p. 105).

Research has shown that both the amount and the kinds of sleep we get are important. Laboratory studies have demonstrated that with prolonged deprivation of sleep, individuals become uneven in their adaptive responses. They may respond accurately to stimulation at one moment but miss it completely the next. This may explain some highway accidents in which people fail to respond to signs or other visual cues. What apparently happens is "microsleep," when, for a split second, their brain waves are those of sleep. Sleep deprivation is also associated with increased irritability and impaired judgment as well as with a marked decline in performance on complex learning and problem-solving tasks.

**Warmth and cold.**   Human beings have built-in homeostatic mechanisms which enable them to adjust to minor variations in heat and cold. For example, at a signal that the body is overheating, blood vessels on the surface of the skin dilate

# Insight

## STAGES OF SLEEP, SLEEP NEEDS, AND SLEEP PROBLEMS

Research has shown that there are four stages of sleep, ranging from light sleep through progressively deeper stages. The normal adult spends about 20 percent of his or her sleeping time in Stage 1—the main stage for vivid, active dreaming, as evidenced by the presence of rapid eye movements (REM). The type of sleep associated with Stage 1 is termed **REM sleep**. About 60 percent of sleeping time is spent in intermediary Stages 2 and 3, and about 20 percent in the deep sleep of Stage 4. Stages 2, 3, and 4 are referred to as **non-REM** or **NREM sleep** and may be associated with less vivid forms of dreaming. Typically, all four stages occur in cycles of about ninety minutes, from light through deep sleep and back again to light sleep.

Although we do not understand the precise role of REM and deep sleep in maintaining normal physiological and psychological functioning, a number of studies have pointed to the significance of normal sleep patterns for mental health—particularly adequate REM and deep sleep. For example, Dement (1960) deprived five normal subjects of most of their REM sleep for five consecutive nights by awakening the subjects whenever their brain waves and eye movements indicated that they were entering a REM period. This procedure reduced REM time some 80 to 90 percent. Among the many interesting findings reported by Dement were: (1) An increasing number of awakenings were required to keep the subjects from having REM periods—from four to five the first night to twenty to thirty the fifth night. (2) In the daytime, during the deprivation period, the subjects were unusually tense and irritable; although they had slept six to seven hours, they behaved as if they had been deprived of a great deal of sleep. (3) During the recovery period, the subjects showed a marked increase in REM time which often took up to 30 to 40 per-

cent of their total sleeping time. These findings have implications for people who have trouble sleeping.

Many people occasionally have difficulty falling asleep or staying asleep, and some of these may resort to some sleep medication. However, many of the common sleep medications disrupt REM or deep sleep. The lack of REM or deep sleep produced by sleep medications has the same effect on psychological functioning as does REM deprivation by experimental awakening. That is, people become irritable, tense, and tired.

Unfortunately, many patients blame weak sleep medications for their sleep difficulties and seek out stronger medications from their physicians. The stronger medications, however, continue the REM deprivation, and the individual eventually becomes caught up in a cycle of medication that makes the problem even worse. And, when these drugs are combined with alcohol and other tranquilizing or sleep-inducing drugs, the results can be fatal.

Withdrawal from sleep medications, while ultimately the best course, presents some difficulties of its own. Too rapid withdrawal from some classes of drugs, such as the barbiturates, is quite dangerous and should not be attempted except under the supervision of a physician. Additionally, withdrawal from sleep medications can produce intense REM rebound, in which the proportion of time spent in the vivid imagery of REM sleep is greatly increased. Some people experience these periods of REM rebound as unpleasant and nightmarish.

Perhaps the best solution to sleep difficulties is to recognize that sleep, like other bodily functions, should not be rushed or planned. If people find it difficult to relax and feel sleepy, self-control procedures such as relaxation (Chapter 9) may prove to be a safe and effective alternative to sleep-inducing drugs.

**REM sleep:** stage of sleep involving rapid eye movements and associated with vivid, intense dreaming

**NREM sleep:** stages of sleep not characterized by rapid eye movements

and circulation of the blood increases, thus exposing a greater amount of the blood to the outer surfaces of the body for cooling. At the same time, activities of the sweat glands are increased, and perspiration helps cool the surface of the body. Such homeostatic mechanisms maintain body temperature at the fairly constant ninety-eight to ninety-nine degrees necessary for normal functioning.

**negative feedback: information about the operation of a system that is used to help regulate the system**

The regulation of bodily heat is an excellent example of the homeostatic mechanism of **negative feedback**. In negative feedback, information about the operation of a system is used to help control the system and keep its operation within narrow limits. In the example noted above, too much body heat results in sweating. When body temperature drops into the normal range, the body's ''thermostat'' shuts off the peripheral blood flow, thereby reducing sweating. And, when body temperature again rises, the physical ''thermostat'' again calls for sweating. Negative feedback cycles operate throughout the body. For example, negative feedback loops are involved in temperature regulation, thirst, and menstrual cycles. Additionally, we can find examples of negative feedback in the operation of home furnaces, air conditioners, and stereo amplifiers. In all cases, negative feedback is an important mechanism for maintaining homeostasis.

**positive feedback: information about the operation of a system that is used to help accelerate the ongoing process**

In contrast, a **positive feedback** process does not maintain homeostasis but enhances the ongoing processes. Positive feedback can be useful when a desirable outcome is to be increased. For example, the feedback that we receive about our good study habits may encourage us to continue or even intensify our study habits. In a sense, positive feedback is similar to positive reinforcement (recall Chapter 2).

**Avoidance of pain and injury.**   Even a very young infant will withdraw from painful experiences or try to avoid objects that have brought pain or discomfort in the past. The threat or experience of pain is unpleasant and highly motivating, since it serves as a warning of bodily harm. Since it is usually produced by situations that are harmful to the organism, pain is crucial to survival.

**pain: physical or mental suffering**

Pain differs from other biological drives, such as hunger and thirst, in that it does not involve a cyclic pattern of occurrence and gratification. **Pain** is an episodic condition of the organism that can be produced at any time by pain-inducing stimuli. Most forms of intense stimulation, such as light, sound, heat, cold, or pressure, as well as tissue inflammation and damage can produce pain.

The tendency to avoid pain is so strong that it can override other needs that are necessary for survival. Delivering a moderately painful shock to an animal while it is eating can induce the animal to stop eating. Such suppression can be permanent, leading to self-starvation. In male dogs and cats, sexual behavior can be suppressed by administering mildly painful electric shocks to the animals.

## Psychological Needs

Despite the almost unlimited differences in motive patterns, there seems to be a common core of psychological needs which must be met for normal development and functioning. These needs appear to represent a common psychological substratum comparable to our basic biological needs.

**Stimulation and activity.** Research studies have shown that a certain level of meaningful sensory input (information) is essential for the maintenance of physiological functioning and psychological integration. When sensory input falls below the minimal level, the individual strives to increase it. If the information input increases to the point of overloading the system, the individual will strive to decrease the input. Students who have attempted too many courses at once or who have left studying for their final exams until the last moment are well aware of the detrimental effects of information input overloading on learning and problem-solving.

Similarly, lowered input—in terms of a marked reduction in the quantity and variation of information input—may also have seriously detrimental effects. In a study of the psychological strains engendered when small groups are isolated from others and confined to a limited space, as in undersea stations and space capsules, Haythorn and Altman (1967) concluded:

> People confined to dark, quiet chambers—the traditional "solitary confinement" of the prisoner, or the sound-proof room used for training astronauts—often display bizarre stress and anxiety symptoms, including hallucinations, delusions, apathy, and the fear of losing sanity. Their performance deteriorates. In fact, recent evidence suggests that important changes may actually occur in the nervous system that will persist for some time after the isolate comes back to the normal world. Men in lonely military stations have shown similar reactions, if to a lesser degree. Men simply may not be built to adapt well to a world with too little stimulus or variety. (p. 19)

Of course, individuals in astronaut training and in submarines do not necessarily suffer from **sensory deprivation** but from **social isolation**. Thus, it is important to separate these two sources of psychological stimulation. In a series of studies by Zuckerman, Albright, Marks, and Miller (1962), and Zuckerman, Persky, Link, and Basu (1968), individuals were exposed to social isolation or to sensory deprivation. Socially isolated subjects were allowed to hear music and see slides, but they were not able to contact other people during the course of the experiment. Subjects in the sensory deprivation condition were devoid of

**sensory deprivation:** lack of environmental stimulation needed to help maintain homeostasis

**social isolation:** deprivation of contact with others

The problem of social isolation may be especially acute for older persons, many of whom have lost close friends, companions, and spouses to death.

social contact and perceptual stimulation. In the typical sensory deprivation condition, subjects rested in a comfortable bed and had their hands wrapped and forearms cuffed so that they could not inadvertently touch themselves and thereby increase sensory stimulation. To eliminate further stimulation, subjects wore translucent masks and rested in a soundproof room.

The results of the Zuckerman studies suggest that social isolation produces depression and worry and also reduces cognitive efficiency. However, subjects in the sensory deprivation group showed more markedly negative effects (Zuckerman et al., 1962; Zuckerman et al., 1968). Social isolation produces negative effects, but the effects of sensory deprivation are much more severe. We thus need the presence of environmental stimuli to help meet our need for psychological stimulation. Of course, these needs vary with the individual and with time.

**Curiosity.**   An early and unmistakable characteristic of healthy infants is their preoccupation with exploring the sights, sounds, tastes, and feel of objects around them. As parents are quick to testify, as soon as infants become mobile, they are "all over the house" and "get into everything."

Experiments done with monkeys verify the importance of curiosity. In one series of studies (Butler, 1953, 1954), monkeys were allowed to look outside their cages if they correctly solved a simple discrimination problem. The results indicated that the monkeys easily learned this task. Not surprisingly, the monkeys' curiosity waned if what they viewed from the cage remained the same. However, if the view changed, their interest in examining the world outside the cage again increased. These results demonstrate that the curiosity motive is strong—even for monkeys.

Since a child's curiosity may be punished or positively reinforced, it is not surprising that there are wide differences among adults in the strength of this need and the ways it is met. In general, however, human beings are inherently curious and strive to understand and to gain a coherent picture of the world.

**Order and predictability.**   Our striving to achieve an orderly and coherent picture of our world is shown in our dislike of ambiguity, lack of structuring, chaos, and events which seem beyond our understanding. People in even the most primitive societies develop explanations for lightning, thunder, death, and other events which they do not understand. Accurate or not, such explanations provide order and meaning and a sense of potential prediction and control. Modern science is simply a more sophisticated attempt to meet the same need.

On occasion, however, our desires for consistency and order are rudely upset by thoughts and actions that do not appear to be in agreement with one another. These discordant thoughts and actions produce a state of **cognitive dissonance** in us. Like other motivational states, cognitive dissonance produces a drive that we attempt to reduce.

In one interesting examination of the motivating effects of cognitive dissonance, Cohen (1962) contacted university students after an altercation with the police in which the students charged that the police had acted with undue force. The students who were recruited into this study were asked to write an essay

**cognitive dissonance:** motivating condition brought about by discrepancy in thoughts, beliefs, attitudes, or actions

A child whose curiosity is positively reinforced is likely to have a strong need to explore and understand the world as an adult.

supporting the police. Following completion of the essay, most of the students were paid between fifty cents and ten dollars for their work. The students' attitudes toward the police were then measured.

If discrepant cognitions are motivators for change, the students who received the ten-dollar payment for their essays would probably be expected to show the *least* dissonance. Their explanation to themselves for writing an essay in support of the police (despite their original feelings about the police) was clear for all to see—ten dollars. On the other hand, why would anyone write a strongly supportive essay for only fifty cents? One possible explanation is that their attitudes toward the police really were supportive, and the essays they wrote simply gave them the chance to express their feelings. Following this line of reasoning, it is not surprising to learn that those who received the smallest payment for their efforts rated their feelings toward the police as more favorable than students who were paid ten dollars.

In essence, research on cognitive dissonance shows us that when the incentive for resolving dissonant cognitions is small, we will work to change our attitudes and cognitions to make them consistent with our actions. In this way, we attempt to maintain a sense of order and predictability in our attitudes and behavior.

To say that we strive for order and meaning in our world does not mean that we always act rationally. But curiously enough, we strive to prove to ourselves and others that our actions are rational. To face the fact that one's behavior may be irrational arouses anxiety, for it implies a lack of order and dependability in oneself, comparable to what one would experience in a world lacking in order and stability.

**Adequacy, competence, and security.**   Each of us needs to feel basically capable of dealing with our problems. When our resources are inadequate for coping with a stressful situation, we may become anxious and disorganized, for we anticipate failure and painful consequences.

The development of competencies for dealing with life's problems can help increase our feelings of adequacy. Strivings for competence are evident even in the behavior of children. Through exploration and play, the child tries out different kinds of interactions with the environment and practices many basic skills. Later, these early foundations of knowledge and competence are greatly expanded by the processes of formal education. In a broad sense, it appears that our strivings toward competence are part of our human tendency to grow toward autonomy, independence, and self-direction.

The need for security develops with and is closely related to our need for adequacy. Security is our assurance of adequacy in the future. Because the failure to meet our needs is acutely unpleasant, we strive to establish and maintain conditions that will ensure future as well as present need gratification. Our need for security is reflected in our preference for jobs with tenure, in social security legislation, in insurance policies, and in the maintenance of law and order.

**Love, belonging, and approval.**   Both loving and being loved appear to be crucial for healthy functioning and normal personality development. Human beings need and strive to achieve warm, loving relationships with others. Our longing to be with others remains with us throughout our lives, and separation from or loss of loved ones usually presents a difficult problem of adjustment. In fact, Lynch (1977), after a review of the medical evidence, has concluded that there is a direct connection between loss of love, loneliness, and premature death. In essence, we must learn to love and live together or we shall die, prematurely and alone.

Often the need for love and affiliation is thought of simply as a need to receive love and affection from others, but our need to love is fully as great. We need to relate to and care about other people if we are to grow and function properly as human beings. Although we ordinarily meet our needs for love in marriage, family, and other intimate relationships, we are capable of "brotherly love" which goes beyond the love of family and particular individuals to a basic concern for all people.

Our need for social belonging and affiliation was well brought out many years ago by William James (1890): "No more fiendish punishment could be devised . . . than that one should be turned loose in society and remain absolutely unnoticed by all the members thereof. If no one turned around when we entered, answered when we spoke, or minded what we did, but if every person we met 'cut us dead,' and acted as if we were non-existing things, a kind of rage and impotent despair would ere long well up in us, from which the cruelest bodily tortures would be a relief . . ." (pp. 293–94).

**Self-esteem and worth.**    As we learn society's values and standards concerning education, physical appearance, economic status, and moral behavior, we begin to use these standards in evaluating ourselves. When we measure up to the standards we have accepted, we feel good about ourselves and worthy of the respect of others. If we see ourselves as falling short, we may feel worthless and anxious. Thus we place a high value on the situations and activities that bring us evidence of our own worth.

Self-esteem has its early grounding in parental affirmation of our worth and in our mastery of early developmental tasks. It receives continued nourishment from the development of new competencies and from our achievement in areas we think are important. Being a football star, earning a Phi Beta Kappa key, or carrying out work assignments competently can contribute to our self-esteem. We also depend on others for continuing confirmation of our worth. Most of us try to ensure such esteem by making ourselves attractive to others, conforming to their norms, and seeking acceptance in groups we respect. We may have difficulty maintaining a conviction of our own worth when those we admire look down on or don't accept us.

As might be expected, our feelings of self-esteem and worth are closely linked to our feelings of adequacy and competence. It is difficult to maintain feelings of self-esteem and worth if one feels incompetent and inadequate.

## Forms of Actualization Strivings

The concept of motivation, as we have seen, is dominated by the concept of maintaining steady states—on overcoming deficits, reducing tension, and returning to a state of equilibrium. But maintenance strivings do not explain the behavior of the explorer, the scientist, the artist, the composer, or the dramatist. We strive to grow, to improve, to become more capable, to express ourselves—to actualize our potentialities and fulfill ourselves as human beings. Huxley (1953) has made this point with dramatic clarity: "Human life is a struggle—against frustration, ignorance, suffering, evil, the maddening inertia of things in general; but it is also a struggle for something. . . . And fulfillment seems to describe better than any other single word the positive side of human development and human evolution—the realization of inherent capacities by the individual and of new possibilities by the race; the satisfaction of needs, spiritual as well as material; the emergence of new qualities of experience to be enjoyed; the building of personalities" (pp. 162–63).

Our **actualization strivings**, like our maintenance strivings, seem to be initiated from within. That is, they apparently do not need to be learned and are characteristic of human beings in different cultures. Yet, the motivation for growth,

**actualization strivings: strivings directed toward growth and fulfillment of potential**

prevalent as it is, does not always result in growth. The person who must struggle hard for mere survival may have little time or energy left for personal growth, just as the neurotic is too busy with self-defense to grow.

**Finding increased satisfactions.**    The norms that we use in evaluating new experiences as "worthwhile" or "disappointing" are based on our standards and expectations. We use such standards in deciding which new experiences to choose and which ones to avoid. We plan a trip because we expect certain values from it. We avoid a party, a television program, or a lecture if we think it will not be worth our time.

But this is not all. We seem to suffer from what the poets call "divine discontent." What was perfectly satisfying yesterday seems a little flat today. We are constantly trying to improve the quality of our experience. We wait in line to see the movie that the critics have given a top rating, watch championship football games, read interesting new novels, and attend outstanding art exhibits. The increased satisfaction that we find in any new experience becomes a part of our new standard for judging the value of subsequent experiences.

As our standards become higher, increments of satisfaction may become increasingly hard to achieve. Yet one of our most persistent urges seems to be to build, to improve, to go beyond previous achievements and understandings, to reach just a little higher and farther than we did before.

**Developing and using potentials.**    The development and use of potentials may take the form of developing new competencies and improving old ones, and of expressing our capabilities in creative and constructive ways. Even though many of us do not have special talents in athletics, art, writing, or music, we may experience fulfillment by developing and using the potentials we do have.

Increasing our supply of information and our understanding of ourselves and our world are other ways in which our potentials may be fulfilled. We listen and read to find out what is going on and what others have thought about it. We try to broaden our viewpoint, to get a more complete picture, to expand our assumptions and generalizations about what is true, what is possible, and what is important. We may also try to improve our understanding by redefining and reorganizing the ideas and assumptions we already have, trying to reconcile contradictory elements.

**Building rich associations with the world.**    One of the ways we seek to grow is through the associations we form with our world, especially with other people. We have a deep capacity for caring for others, for protecting, encouraging, and teaching others, and for helping them grow and find meaning and satisfaction in their lives. Unless we use this capacity, we feel incomplete and unsatisfied. Caring deeply for someone else is one of the most gratifying and self-fulfilling of human experiences.

Sharing valuable experiences with others close to us can also be satisfying. Sharing a crisis or joy or even just an hour of silence with those dear to us is an enriching experience. We treasure our family anecdotes, triumphs, and traditions.

Very often a person finds great satisfaction through service to and caring for others. For example, a teen-aged volunteer and a nursing home resident may share a relationship that both find fulfilling.

Louise Rich (1946), in her autobiographical novel, *Happy the Land,* said: "Of Plymouth Rock, I may tell my children: 'This is where the Pilgrims landed.' Of the rock by the side of the road, halfway up Wangan Hill, I say 'Right here is where your father found the little deer that time' " (p. 19). Throughout our lives we build landmarks of this kind which enrich our lives and add to their meaning and value by increasing our sense of relatedness to the world around us.

*"For this is the journey that men make: to find themselves. If they fail in this, it doesn't matter much else what they find."*
*(MICHENER, 1949, P. 488)*

**The search for significant selfhood.**   Closely allied with the striving to develop one's potentials is the striving to become a person—to achieve a clear-cut sense of one's identity. As Rogers (1958) has put it: "As I follow the experience of many clients in the therapeutic relationship which we endeavor to create for them, it seems to me that each one has the same problem. Below the level of the problem situation about which the individual is complaining—behind the trouble with studies, or wife, or employer, or with his own uncontrollable or bizarre behavior, or with his frightening feelings lies one central search. It seems to me that at bottom each person is asking: 'Who am I, *really?* How can I get in touch with this real self, underlying all my surface behavior? How can I become myself?' '' (pp. 9–10).

The Danish philosopher Kierkegaard described this search for self more than a century ago. He pointed out that the most common despair is in being unwilling to be one's self, but that the deepest form of despair is choosing to be other than one's self. Becoming a person seems to be bound up with a striving toward wholeness, toward integration and self-direction.

## SOCIAL FORCES IN MOTIVATION

Thus far we have viewed motivation primarily in terms of the needs and strivings of the individual. But just as individuals have needs, so do groups. Families and other groups have to maintain themselves and actualize their potentials if they are to survive and prosper. In some cases, group needs take precedence over those of individuals.

Social forces shape and channel our motives in important ways, just as they shape our overall development. Social rewards and punishments, for example, are of great importance in facilitating or inhibiting needs, in formulating our goals, and in determining the extent to which our needs are met.

### Needs of Groups and of Society

Like individuals, social groups have basic needs. And like individuals, groups have developed a variety of "homeostatic" mechanisms, such as **social norms** and laws, as a means for meeting those needs.

**social norms: group standards concerning behavior**

When their organization and functioning are disrupted, groups strive to re-establish a state of equilibrium. This applies to small groups as well as larger ones. If a general is killed in combat, another officer moves up to take over that place. If the head of a household dies, the relationships and responsibilities of other family members change in an attempt to establish a new pattern of effective functioning.

In most cases, meeting family and group needs and the needs of society promotes the well-being of individual members. However, group needs may conflict with and take precedence over the needs of the individual—as when a woman must work long hours at a monotonous job to support her family.

### Social Inhibition and Facilitation of Motives

By its system of norms and values and by the manipulation of rewards and punishments, society encourages some methods of need gratification while it discourages other methods. Most societies, for example, strictly regulate patterns of sexual gratification.

Since social conditions and standards vary markedly from one group to another, the goals that are highly valued in one group may have little or no value in another. Charms to protect a person from witchcraft would be considered of little value in our society, while the financial goals that are important to many Americans would inspire little effort among the members of a monastic order. Western societies, for example, strongly approve of sexual gratification through marriage, while they strongly discourage sexual gratification through homosexual activity. In contrast, another society might approve of homosexual activity during adolescence, but strongly discourage this activity after marriage or official attainment of adult status.

Some groups and societies offer rich opportunities for the satisfaction of basic needs and the actualization of potentials. Others are extremely repressive and rigid, and others simply lack essential resources. But in any group, an individual's goals and the likelihood of achieving them are dependent upon the opportunities and limitations, norms and rules, and rewards and punishments provided by the group.

## Achievement Motivation

One of the best understood social motives is the need for achievement (Atkinson, 1981; Fyans, 1980; McClelland, Atkinson, Clark, & Lowell, 1953). As developed by Atkinson, **achievement motivation** addresses a basic issue in our society: how can we understand the direction, persistence, and magnitude of behavior in situations in which a person's performance will be evaluated, knowing that the consequence of the individual's actions will be regarded favorably (success) or unfavorably (failure) (Geiwitz, 1969). In essence, achievement motivation examines the complex interrelationships among performance, internal and external evaluations, incentive and risk, and success and failure.

**achievement motivation: desire to excel or perform well according to some standard of excellence**

For example, a premedical student, who knows that a particular biology course is especially difficult, must nonetheless take the course in order to enter medical school. The risk for taking the course is high, and the incentive for taking the course is also high. Assuming that the student received a grade of "B" for the course, we can guess that the student's performance in laboratory experiments and examinations was somewhat better than average, resulting in the external evaluation given by the instructor—the grade of "B". However, the student may be dissatisfied with her performance, and her internal, self-evaluation might be lower than the external evaluation supplied by the instructor.

There appear to be two variables in the situation which are important to achievement motivation. The two situational aspects are *incentive* and *expectancy*. Incentive deals with the question of the value of the outcome to the individual. In other words, is it "worth it" for the person to undertake the task? The second situational aspect, expectancy, deals with the probability of success—will the individual succeed or fail?

Some internal motive patterns also play an important role in achievement motivation. In the motive to succeed, individuals show a "drive" to take moderate risks and engage themselves fully in the situation. In contrast, the motive to avoid failure results in "unusual" behavior, in which there is an equal tendency to engage in those acts which have the least likelihood of failure or, surprisingly, in the act which has the *greatest* likelihood of failure. Under the motive to avoid failure, selection of the easiest task minimizes risk. Selection of the riskiest task, on the other hand, virtually guarantees failure. In either case, the emotional outcome of the motive to avoid failure is likely to be dissatisfaction or despair.

Achievement motivation has a strong basis in learning and experience. Research has suggested that the highest levels of achievement motivation are found in individuals who were encouraged to be independent at an early age. Maehr and Kleiber (1981) note that "more extrinsic, competitive patterns of achievement may give way with age to more intrinsic, task-oriented patterns and that, with an aging population, this shift may be reflected in the culture as a whole" (p. 787). Given the differing socialization practices for males and females in our society, it is possible that part of the apparently greater achievement motivation in males may be due to the earlier training in independence they received from their parents (Winterbottom, 1958).

The findings from this field have also been used to help understand social motives in society at large. For example, some research has suggested that increases in achievement motivation are correlated with later increases in economic activity (Bradburn & Berlew, 1961). If these findings are reliable, it may be possible to examine our society's current achievement motivation and estimate its future economic pattern. In this context, Feshbach and Weiner (1982) have pointed to indicators suggesting that achievement motivation as an economic stimulant has shown a steady decline in our society since the early years of this century.

## MOTIVE PATTERNS AND BEHAVIOR

We have been talking about various needs and motives as if they were independent of each other and of other psychological processes, but they are not. Nor are they independent of the social field in which they develop and are expressed.

In this section we will briefly examine: *(a)* the influence of motives on perception and other psychological processes, *(b)* the extent to which we are aware of our motives, and *(c)* how our motive patterns change over time.

### Motivational Selectivity

Just as our various motives are related to each other, so are our motivational processes interrelated with other psychological functions. Our motives influence what we attend to, the way we perceive, what we learn, our feelings and emotions, our reasoning and problem solving, and our fantasies and dreams.

1. *Attention and perception.* Attention and perception are active processes in which we select, organize, and give meaning to the information we receive

The need for social acceptance and approval often leads individuals to conform to group norms of behavior and dress, even to wear similar hair styles.

from external and internal sources. Our attention and perception may be influenced in three ways by the motive states which predominate at the moment.

First, we are more sensitive to information related to our motives. A student scanning a bibliography to find studies on role expectations in marriage typically ignores titles dealing with other topics. On a more dramatic level, a person lost in the desert and suffering from intense thirst would be searching for some indication of water and probably never notice the beauty of the sunset. In such situations the stimuli that are relevant to the active motive tend to stand out, while irrelevant stimuli tend to fade away. This tendency to single out what we consider most relevant to our purposes is called **selective vigilance.**

Second, we try to screen out information that would make us uncomfortable. Thus we see only the aspects of a situation that are consistent with our expectations, assumptions, and wishes. Proud parents may selectively perceive the desirable traits of their children while not recognizing undesirable ones. Or they may use the same process in evaluating themselves. This form of selectivity, in which one actively resists certain perceptions, is termed **perceptual defense**.

Third, we perceive things as we would like them to be rather than as they are. It has been shown, for example, that many people perceive their leaders as noble and strong—not so much on the basis of their actual qualities but because their own security and future depend upon having leaders with such qualities. When we encounter information that does not fit in with what we have already accepted, our need for an orderly, meaningful, predictable view of the world leads us to change the new information to achieve greater consistency.

selective vigilance: tendency to single out perceptions considered most relevant to one's purposes

perceptual defense: type of selective vigilance used to screen out potentially troublesome perceptions

2. *Thinking and learning.* We prize our ability to reason and solve problems, and we also use this ability to justify what we want to do or believe. It is notoriously difficult to think objectively about a situation when our own needs and purposes are directly involved. A marriage counselor can be more objective about the problems of other couples than about his or her own marital problems, just as a mother can reason more objectively about the child-rearing problems of other mothers than she can about her own. When research first began to link smoking to lung cancer, heavy smokers, as a group, were slower to accept the findings and readier to argue that a causal relationship had not been proved.

Learning underlies our motivational requirements. It is difficult to learn things that appear unrelated to our key motives, whereas we willingly devote time and energy to learning things that seem important and useful to us. As our effort pays off and we experience satisfaction from learning, our incentive for similar learning is increased. Where learning requires changing what we have already learned, motivation also plays an important role. We tend to resist learning new information contradictory to our existing assumptions. Thus, what we learn, how rapidly, and how much are influenced by our motivation.

3. *Remembering and forgetting.* Psychoanalytic models of forgetting have emphasized the relationship between the unpleasantness of a memory and the inability to recall it. Numerous experiments have shown that pleasant memories, particularly those favorable to the individual's self-concept, are more likely to be recalled than unpleasant memories. In the same way, incidents which reflect poorly upon the self's adequacy and worth are less likely to be remembered.

4. *Fantasy and dreams.* The thoughts and images which occur when we are not busy responding to current demands can reflect our concerns and motives. Children who live in orphanages commonly dream—both in daydreams and during sleep—about being adopted into a happy family. Men and women in prison commonly dream of being free.

We have probably all experienced both fantasies and dreams concerning sexual activities, revenge, self-enhancement, and other matters in which we could readily see the influence of motivational factors. In some forms of psychotherapy, a patient's dreams are often used in an attempt to better understand his or her motives and problems.

5. *Feelings and emotions.* How we perceive a situation—its significance in terms of our motives—directly influences the feelings and emotions which may be aroused. If we perceive a situation as a threat to our safety, self-esteem, love relationship, or any other important need or motive, we are likely to react with intense negative emotions typically involving a combination of fear, anxiety, and anger. On the other hand, if we perceive a situation as enhancing our self-esteem or fostering the meeting of other key motives, our perception is likely to be accompanied by positive feelings and emotions.

Thinking and other psychological processes are, of course, influenced by factors other than motivation. Our cognitive processes may also lead to changes in our motives, particularly when feedback concerning the achievement of given motives turns out to be disappointing and unsatisfying.

## To What Extent Are We Aware of Our Motives?

*"Sleepless questions*
*In the small hours;*
*Have I done right?*
*Why did I act*
*Just as I did?*
*Over and over again*
*The same steps,*
*The same words:*
*Never the answer."*
*(HAMMARSKJÖLD, 1964/1974, P. 209)*

Although writers and dramatists have long portrayed the influence of unconscious motives—motives of which we are unaware—on our behavior, Sigmund Freud was the first to study this phenomenon systematically. He noted that unconscious motives may express themselves in several forms of behavior: *(a)* dreams, in which "forbidden" desires may appear; *(b)* slips of the tongue and "forgetting" appointments that we do not want to remember; and *(c)* certain neurotic reactions, as when a person feels compelled to wash his or her hands many times during the day. Freud concluded that such motives were not admitted to consciousness because they are unacceptable to the individual.

Although there is considerable controversy among psychologists concerning the nature and importance of unconscious processes in human behavior, there is abundant evidence that we are often unaware or only partially aware of the motives underlying our behavior. Other people may be able to infer our motives more accurately from observing our behavior than we can from introspection. Thus it may be apparent to others—but not to us—that we continually lean on others or prevent people from getting too close to us or constantly try to build ourselves up by belittling other people. Similarly, we may show off, wear expensive clothes, even marry for reasons which are unclear to us. Of course, we may offer good reasons to justify our behavior, but these explanations may be only partially accurate.

Recent research has shown that often we are not only unaware of our motives but also of environmental factors that may elicit specific behaviors on our part (Mahoney & Thoresen, 1974; Nisbett & Wilson, 1977b). In fact, Mahoney and Thoresen (1974) have concluded that: "An individual's ability to regulate his own behavior is dependent on his knowledge of and control over current environmental factors . . . . In this sense, the Greek maxim 'Know thyself' can be translated to 'Know thy controlling variables' " (pp. 21–22).

It appears that awareness of the motives and the environmental cues that influence our behavior varies considerably from person to person. At one time or another, most of us may be puzzled by some of the things we do and think. An understanding of our motive patterns can help us achieve greater insight into our own behavior.

# Insight

The following now-classic demonstration has often been used to suggest the possibility that our behavior may be dominated by motives of which we are partially or totally unaware (Dembar, 1974).

*During profound hypnosis the subject was instructed to feel that smoking was a bad habit, that he both loved and hated it, that he wanted to get over the habit but he felt it was too strong a habit to break, that he would be very reluctant to smoke and would give anything not to smoke, but that he would find himself compelled to smoke; and that after he was awakened he would experience all of these feelings.*

*After he was awakened the subject was drawn into a casual conversation with the hypnotist who, lighting one himself, offered him a cigarette. The subject waved it aside with the explanation that he had his own and that he preferred Camels, and promptly began to reach for his own pack. Instead of looking in his customary pocket, however, he seemed to forget where he carried his cigarettes and searched fruitlessly through all of his other pockets with a gradually increasing concern. Finally, after having sought them repeatedly in all other pockets, he located his cigarettes in their usual place.*

## ARE WE OFTEN UNAWARE OF OUR REAL MOTIVES?

*He took them out, engaged in a brief conversation as he dallied with the pack, and then began to search for matches, which he failed to find. During his search for matches he replaced the cigarettes in his pocket and began using both hands, finally locating the matches too in their usual pocket. Having done this, he now began using both hands to search for his cigarettes. He finally located them but then found that he had once more misplaced his matches. This time however he kept his cigarettes in hand while attempting to locate the matches. He then placed a cigarette in his mouth and struck a match. As he struck it, however, he began a conversation which so engrossed him that he forgot the match and allowed it to burn his finger tips whereupon, with a grimace of pain, he tossed it in the ash tray. . . .*

*This behavior continued with numerous variations. He tried lighting a cigarette with a split match, burned his fingers, got both ends of one cigarette wet, demonstrated how he could roll a cigarette, kept stopping to converse or tell a joke, and so on. Several cigarettes were ruined and discarded. When he finally got one going successfully, he took only a few good puffs with long pauses in between and discarded it before it was used up. (Erickson, 1939, pp. 342–45)*

## Motive Change over Time

**"Each of us has a continuity. We are certain persons with certain names and fairly consistent physical and functional characteristics. . . . Indeed, there are consistencies. But change and variability are also ever present, more than we recognize, because we tend to be aware of the consistencies."**

**(FORDYCE, 1976, P. 7)**

Our motive patterns are of key importance in both continuity and variability. Although we may show a relatively consistent pattern of motives, this pattern can change over time. On a simple level we can see this in the short-term changes in our physiological needs and goals such as our need for food. With deprivation, the need increases; with satiation, it is replaced by other needs and goals. While a periodic rhythm is not apparent on the psychological level, the achievement of given goals usually leads to their replacement by others. This is often dramatically illustrated when we achieve some long-sought goal in life, such as college graduation or a promotion at work, only to find that instead of feeling contentment we become aware of new goals which have replaced the old ones now attained.

There are also predictable changes in motive patterns as we go through life. The key motives of a child are not those of an adult. Changes in the environment and in our life situation may lead to modification of our motive pattern. For example, the individual who becomes a parent may well show considerable shift in motives and behavior.

A classic example of changed motives with new environmental demands is that of young King Henry of England, as portrayed by Shakespeare in *Henry V*. Before he became king, he had been a fun-loving young man without apparent interest in anything but the next riotous party. After he became king, he developed a deep concern for the welfare of his country and disciplined himself for responsible service to it. Less dramatic but equally basic changes in motivation may occur in any one of us if we see our environment making new demands on us. Similarly we may reevaluate the worth of goals we have been avidly pursuing

According to Maslow's theory, when our basic biological and psychological needs are met, we strive for higher goals; we seek to know ourselves, to develop our potential, to become self-actualizing.

A significant change in motives may occur when an individual marries or becomes a parent.

if changes in our environment make more attractive ones available or lead to changes in our values.

To better understand their own motives and to make motive changes in a more systematic manner, many people participate in encounter groups and other programs directed toward personal change and growth. We shall examine some psychological resources for personal change and growth in Chapter 11.

While specific motives and goals may change during the course of our lives, the basic core of biological and psychological needs required for maintenance and actualization—needs that we share in common as human beings—remains essentially the same throughout our lives.

## SUMMARY

1. Motivation deals with needs and drives that help initiate and direct behavior toward a goal. Some drives are biologically based and others are psychologically based. Motivation can help us understand the goals we pursue, the effort we exert in pursuing our goals, and the similarities and differences in motive patterns.

2. Motivation can have both "push" and "pull" qualities, and our motivational energies can be directed toward meeting deficiencies or toward meeting growth and actualization needs. Maslow's five-step hierarchy of motives helps describe how the attainment of basic motives frees the individual to seek other, higher motives.

3. Among our primary, or biological, drives are hunger and thirst, sex, and sleep. These biological drives, however, are importantly influenced by learning and environmental variables. Our psychological needs must also be met for normal development and functioning. Among the psychological needs are the needs for stimulation, order and predictability, adequacy, love, and self-esteem.

4. Like individuals, groups attempt to maintain themselves and actualize their potentials. One way in which group needs are expressed in the individual is through achievement motivation.

5. Our motivations may affect many aspects of life, including attention and perception, thinking and learning, and feelings and emotions. Motivations have a significant influence on so many aspects of life that it may not be possible to be aware of all of them. Though our motive patterns may change over time as we experience changes in our environment and life situation, our basic biological and psychological needs remain the same throughout life.

# Chapter 6

# Effective Emotional Experiencing

Imagine that in our exploration of the universe, we were to land our spacecraft on a planet inhabited by intelligent beings who are similar in appearance to us and think and act much like we do. But they are different from us in one major way: They have no feelings and are incapable of experiencing fear, anger, love, or any other emotion. Could we relate to them in a warm and intimate way? Or would it be like trying to develop an intimate relationship with a computer? And while we might understand their behavior, could they really understand ours?

**affect: feelings and emotions**

The **affective** or emotional aspects of life are a dimension of human experiencing welcomed by many and ignored or regretted by others—an aspect capable of adding richness and meaning to life or capable of causing confusion and suffering. Successful, mature human functioning requires that we come to terms with the affective side of living. Because nearly all our activities and relationships, our thoughts, dreams, and actions elicit feelings, it is important that we find a balance between the richness and information imparted by feelings and the potential disruptions they may entail. Throughout our lives we must learn how to live with our emotions but not be ruled by them, to experience and express feelings appropriate in kind and degree to a situation, and to express and be receptive to a variety of feelings.

Needless to say, there are many kinds of dysfunctions in the emotional sphere of living, including feelings too strong or not strong enough, feelings too transitory or too persistent, and feelings of anxiety or guilt over the experiencing of certain emotions. In short, the achievement of adaptive and effective emotional experiencing can be a difficult and demanding task.

In this chapter we shall explore some psychological aspects of emotional life, including the contribution of feelings to full human functioning, some dimensions of affective experience, some theories of emotion, and a few particular emotions that many people discover are problems from time to time.

## EMOTIONS AND FULL HUMAN FUNCTIONING

**emotions: complex states of feeling involving conscious experience, internal and overt responses, and power to motivate an individual to action**

There are many facets of human **emotions.** On a biological level, our emotions may be viewed as states of arousal involving changes in heart rate, muscle tension, and other physiological functions. On a psychological level, we may talk about different feeling states, such as anger, fear, pain, and love, and the ways in which they influence our perception, thinking, and behavior. Finally, on a social level, we may view emotions as a universal language, such as smiling, which shows our kinship as human beings.

### The Language of Emotions

Our emotions can be measured physiologically, observed behaviorally, and studied cross-culturally. Yet the information that is obtained does not do justice to the wealth of meaning conveyed by our feelings. In many cases, emotions are a primary means of communication between individuals. For example, the sharing of feelings maintains and strengthens intimate relationships.

Awareness and healthy
expression of emotions
can add richness and
meaning to our lives.

**What our emotions tell us.** To be alive as a human being is to experience and be responsive to our feelings. As psychiatrist David Viscott (1976) has expressed it, "When we lose touch with our feelings, we lose touch with our most human qualities" (p. 14).

Our feelings also serve as indicators of our physical and psychological well-being. They provide information about whether a particular situation is threatening, sad, or joyous. They help determine our perceptions. In addition, our feelings serve as guides and motives in directing our behavior, as is illustrated by the tendency to flee when we feel fear.

And since we learn from experience, feelings are not only reactions to our present perception of events but will influence our perception of similar events in the future. This is illustrated in a dramatic way by phobias.

**What our emotions tell others.** Emotions provide a common reservoir of experience that makes possible the communication of meanings between individuals. For example, in marriage and other intimate relationships—we often rely on facial expressions rather than formal language to convey our feelings of affection, anger, or distress.

In a broader context, our emotional experiences and expressions constitute a universal language which most people understand and share. Psychologist Paul Ekman (1975) and his colleagues (Ekman, Friesen, & Ellsworth, 1973) have found that facial expressions of our primary emotions—anger, fear, disgust, surprise, sadness, and happiness—are recognized and given the same labels in cultures throughout the world. Preliterate New Guinea tribesmen, for example, and American and Japanese students express and interpret these emotions in comparable ways. As Ekman (1975) has pointed out: "If you meet a native in New Guinea or your old boss in a Manhattan bar, you will be able to interpret their facial expressions easily, knowing how they feel—or how they want you to think they feel" (p. 35).

## Patterns of Emotional Experience

Although we often assume that other people feel the same way we do, there is considerable evidence that this is not always the case. We seem to differ greatly in the depth and range of our feelings, in our moods, and in the proportion of our positive and negative emotions.

**Intensity of feeling.**   In terms of intensity, emotions may be described as mild, strong, or disintegrative. Each level of intensity is associated with different patterns of behavior.

1. *Mild emotions.* A mild level of emotional intensity is typically accompanied by increased alertness, a focusing of attention on meaningful factors in the situation, and a slight increase in tension, along with feelings of being "pepped up" and having increased vigor. Even negative emotions, such as fear and anger, may be pleasant when they occur in mild form and when the individual believes he or she has control over the situation and can terminate it at will. This is readily illustrated by the emotions we commonly experience in watching suspenseful television and movie dramas.

2. *Strong emotions.* In strong emotions, the increased intensity of the emotion leads to a quite different picture. In strong negative emotions, for example, there is an emergency mobilization of bodily resources for immediate action. Processes related to digestion are suspended and the mouth becomes dry, while heartbeat, blood pressure, respiration, and adrenaline production are increased.

The range of human emotional experience extends from the greatest joy . . .

The capillaries along the alimentary canal constrict, while those in the brain and the large muscles enlarge for better circulation. Red blood cells from the spleen and sugar from the liver are released into the blood. Even the factor that induces blood clotting in injuries is increased—just in case. In strong depressive emotions like grief, no action is usually called for, and action potentials are restricted accordingly. Pulse rate and respiration are typically reduced somewhat.

3. *Disintegrative emotions.* In addition to mild and strong emotions, both of which can be normal and healthy, we may experience **disintegrative emotions.** These are the outgrowth of normal emergency emotions continued too long, or they are emotions precipitated by overwhelming stress.

**disintegrative emotions: extremely intense emotions causing maladaptive functioning**

The intensity of disintegrative emotions is well illustrated by observations of soldiers who had suffered combat exhaustion in World War II and were later given sodium pentothal interviews. Under the influence of this drug, which produces effects somewhat similar to hypnosis, a soldier could "relive" his combat experience and reexperience some of his overwhelming fear and anxiety:

*The terror exhibited in the moments of supreme danger, such as at the imminent explosion of shells, the death of a friend before the patient's eyes, the absence of cover under a heavy dive bombing attack is electrifying to watch. The body becomes increasingly tense and rigid; the eyes widen and the pupils dilate, while the skin becomes covered with fine perspiration. The hands move about convulsively, seeking a weapon, or a friend to share the danger. The breathing becomes incredibly rapid and shallow. The intensity of the emotion sometimes becomes more than they can bear; and frequently at the height of the reaction, there is a collapse and the patient falls back in bed and remains quiet for a few minutes, usually to resume the story at a more neutral point.* (Grinker & Spiegel, 1945, p. 80)

Effective emotional experiencing seems to require sufficient depth of feeling to allow active, vigorous, healthy participation in living. Although wide differences in emotionalism seem to be within the normal range, the extremes at either end are not adaptive. Overreacting to every minor situation squanders a person's resources. Conversely, a very shallow reaction to a major situation usually indicates a lack of normal depth and richness in emotional experience.

. . . to the deepest grief and sorrow.

**Range of feeling.** Human beings have the potential for experiencing a tremendous variety of emotions, from the most intense elation to the depths of depression, from the greatest happiness to the greatest sorrow, from deep and enduring love to lasting hatred.

Despite this available range of feelings, some people experience only a limited range of emotions, often with a preponderance of negative emotions such as fear and anger or hostility. Conversely, others appear to experience a much wider range of emotions and sentiments—often with subtle nuances and fine shades of feeling. The failure to develop a full repertoire of emotions may result from a variety of factors, including personal immaturity and faulty attitudes.

Some individuals show no emotions whatsoever. Like robots, they go through life in a brisk, efficient manner without experiencing either the joys or sorrows that are so important to the human experience. In some situations, of course, absence of emotions can be an adaptive response to an intensely stressful situation. Individuals who have undergone a major **trauma** or loss often find that their initial reaction is one of numbness. Examples might include the person who learned that her family had been killed in an airplane crash, or the individual who lost a house to flood waters or tornadoes. However, the persistence of no emotional response may indicate a fear of experiencing emotions. This absence of feeling may occur because the individual fears going "out of control." Or, the absence of emotion can be self-protective, as in the case of the person who defends against emotional involvement—and the potential loss of a relationship. These failures to experience emotion may seriously limit the richness and meaningfulness of life.

**trauma: severe psychological or physiological injury**

## Expression and Control of Emotions

People vary not only in their patterns of emotional experience but also in their patterns of expression and control. Some people are effusive and demonstrative, freely expressing their feelings. Others hide their feelings—sometimes just from other people, sometimes from themselves as well.

Our culture views rationality and emotional control as a virtue, while emotional arousal and expression are often viewed as weakness. Hence, a key problem for the individual is to find a suitable balance between expression and control. In this section, we will examine (a) control and denial of emotions, (b) expression of emotions, and (c) cognitive factors in emotional control.

**Control and denial of emotions.** Most people were taught as children to keep their emotions under tight control. James Elliott (1976) has described this process: "Feelings made our parents uncomfortable, so they told us things like: 'Big boys don't cry.' 'You don't really hate your little sister, do you?' 'You shouldn't feel that way.' Pretty soon we learned that we'd better not express what we really felt" (p. 11). And, as children grow up, the requirement to keep emotions under control remains: "Don't get angry." "You're too sensitive." "Please don't cry." Eventually, only strong emotions may get through, and these may elicit anxiety and guilt since they seem to signify a loss of control.

In some cases, emotional control can be expressed as a denial of emotions. We all have had the experience of encountering a person whose verbal statements were in marked conflict with their nonverbal responses. For example, we may inquire, "Are you feeling all right?" but receive two conflicting responses: the verbal "I'm feeling just fine" contrasting with the clear signs of worry and concern evident in the individual's face. In more severe cases, the level of control becomes so intense that we can discern no evidence of emotion whatsoever.

Emotions that are denied some means of direct expression may find outlets in disguised ways. Anger and hostility, for example, can be expressed through teasing or nagging, while anxiety and fear may be expressed through chronic fatigue and somatic complaints. Such indirect expression often fails to relieve emotional tension.

The cost of such high emotional control may be inappropriate and unwanted emotional displays:

*When a person is living behind a front, a facade, his unexpressed feelings pile up to some explosion point, and are then apt to be triggered off by some specific incident. But the feelings which sweep over the person and are expressed at such a time—in a temper storm, in a deep depression, in a flood of self-pity, and the like—often have an unfortunate effect on all concerned because they are so inappropriate to the specific situation and hence seem so unreasonable. The angry flare-up over one annoyance in the relationship may actually be the pent-up or denied feelings resulting from dozens of such situations. But in the context in which it is expressed it is unreasonable and hence not understood. (Rogers, 1961, p. 318)*

**Healthy expression of emotions.**   Fritz Perls, the founder of Gestalt therapy, has argued that awareness of our truest, most honest feelings is essential for personal change, growth, and full human functioning. Our feelings act as guides in interpreting the world we are perceiving. Thus, to deny our feelings or "to be awash in confusing or dimly perceived feelings is to be overwhelmed by a confusing world" (Viscott, 1976, p. 11). People who are attuned to their feelings are more likely to perceive their world accurately and more capable of dealing with it effectively than are people who attempt to rely solely on intellect.

Thus, one goal of growth-oriented therapies, such as Gestalt therapy, is usually an increase in the spontaneous expression of emotion. Such **spontaneity** should not be confused with impulsiveness. Rather, it is an attempt to help individuals become aware of, understand, and express their emotions in constructive ways.

**spontaneity: natural and unrestrained behavior**

In a broader perspective, it is apparent that some degree of emotional control is necessary for effective personal functioning and civilized living. But control can be carried too far. As in the description by Rogers, such control may lead to inappropriate and unwanted emotional displays. Perhaps more important, the rigid control of feelings and emotions may deprive a person of the experiences that enrich human life.

Effectiveness in emotional expression and control, like effectiveness in other forms of behavior, means that both inner needs and outer demands are taken into account. Emotional competence is not achieved once and for all, however. Although we can develop more realistic expectations and greater ability to ac-

# Insight

**"RICHARD CORY"
BY E. A. ROBINSON**

Sometimes it is possible to control our emotions too tightly, as the poem below shows.

*Whenever Richard Cory went down town,
We people on the pavement looked at him:
He was a gentleman from sole to crown.
Clean favored and imperially slim.*

*And he was always quietly arrayed,
And he was always human when he talked;
But still he fluttered pulses when he said,
"Good morning,"—and he glittered when
he walked.*

*And he was rich—yes, richer than a king—
And admirably schooled in every grace:
In fine, we thought that he was everything
To make us wish that we were in his place.*

*So on we worked and waited for the light,
And went without the meat, and cursed
the bread;
And Richard Cory, one calm summer night,
Went home and put a bullet through his
head.*

knowledge our real feelings, we can expect that finding personally satisfying and constructive ways to express negative emotions such as anger or fear will be a continuing task.

**"Feelings are our reaction to what we perceive, and in turn they color and define our perception of the world."**
**(VISCOTT, 1976, P. 11)**

**Cognitive factors in emotional control.**   Consider the emotions of two young women who have sought marital counseling as a result of impending divorces. A. reports that she feels "terribly depressed." She feels that her husband is the only man for her, that she is not an attractive woman, and that she will be unable to find anyone else. B. reports that she feels "mildly depressed" but also "somewhat excited." While she is discouraged about the breakup of her marriage, she considers herself an attractive woman and believes there are plenty of other men from whom to select. And she feels rather excited about the prospect of meeting other men and "getting back into circulation." In actual fact, both A. and B. are attractive women. But their assumptions and perceptions of themselves and their world led to quite different emotional reactions.

If A.'s negative assumptions about herself can be changed to more positive and accurate ones, she is likely to find her divorce less traumatic. Her depression will probably be less severe and clear up sooner. Similarly, a laboratory study conducted by Goldfried and Sobocinski (1975) investigated the nature of emotional arousal among college students in relation to one specific irrational belief—the overriding importance of social approval. "When asked to imagine themselves in social situations that might be interpreted as involving rejection by others, subjects holding this belief reported feeling significantly more anxious and angry than those who did not" (p. 504). Thus, it appears that helping people correct inaccurate assumptions may have important implications for personal effectiveness and adjustment.

## "Working Through" Emotional Hurt

Many people have suffered deeply hurtful emotional experiences that temporarily shattered their feelings of security, adequacy, and worth, and influenced their later behavior. An illustration is the tragic case of a young wife and mother who had gone to visit a friend in the neighborhood and came back to find her home enveloped in flames and her two young children trapped inside. She was restrained from entering the burning structure by firefighters who risked their lives in a vain effort to save the children. A year later in therapy she made the following statement: "I know I must put it in the past, that life must go on . . . that somehow I must think of the present and future. But I can't seem to forget. I shouldn't have left my children alone . . . I can never really forgive myself. The memory of that awful night will haunt me as long as I live . . . and I can't bear the thought of having more children for fear something awful will happen to them too . . . maybe I will do something irresponsible and crazy again."

Such emotional experiences are likely to leave psychological wounds that never completely heal. As a result, the individual may find it particularly difficult to handle a later stress that reopens these early wounds.

Part of the reason that these emotional hurts last so long is that our emotional reactions may be conditioned to the situations that originally produced the hurt. For example, if we were hurt because of a rejection from a former lover, we may find that as we enter other intimate relationships, the similarity to the previous painful relationship may produce in us an increasing sense of wariness or discomfort. Similarly, if we were involved in an automobile accident at a particular intersection in a city, we may find our anxieties rising each time we approach the intersection.

The learning process involved in these emotional reactions is *classical conditioning* or *respondent learning*, a type of learning we discussed in Chapter 2. Unfortunately, these reactions are not easily amenable to rational analysis. In the example noted above, we may "know" that our distrust in the relationship is unfounded, but our knowledge does not prevent the distrust from occurring. Similarly, our fears of approaching the intersection may be based on past experience alone, but a rational evaluation of the facts still does not prevent the emotion from occurring. The automatic nature of these responses clearly limits the effectiveness of a rational appraisal of the situations and also limits the flexibility of response that might lead to more adaptive emotions and behavior.

There are several ways in which people can get over emotional hurt. One way is to do the necessary "grief work" over the loss or hurt. Once this is done, the individual can put the event into the perspective of the past and build anew. More direct means can also be taken, including some strategies used for coping with stress (Chapter 9) or counseling and psychotherapy (Chapter 11).

# THEORIES OF EMOTION

We have already described emotions as affective states that involve both physiological and psychological processes. We have also noted the important role emotions play in our lives. In order to understand emotional expression more fully and its importance to mature human functioning, we shall examine three approaches that physiologists and psychologists have developed to explain what determines emotions. In particular, we shall discuss the James-Lange theory, the Cannon-Bard theory, and the Schachter-Singer cognitive theory of emotions.

## James-Lange Theory

Imagine the following situation: you are walking in a forest when suddenly a huge and dangerous bear jumps out of the underbrush and starts running toward you. Your reaction to this situation is a natural one and quite unplanned: you too begin to run as quickly as possible away from the bear.

Our commonsense theory of emotions suggests that we see the bear, feel fear, and then run. In a similar fashion, the commonsense theory of emotions suggests that we first feel joy and then laugh, that feelings of despair precede our tears.

**James-Lange theory: theory of emotion suggesting that emotion follows specific bodily responses**

However, the **James-Lange theory** of emotions reverses commonsense theory. Instead of the look-fear-run sequence, the James-Lange theory, as developed by psychologist William James and Danish physiologist Karl Lange, postulates a look-run-fear sequence. That is, the James-Lange theory suggests that *emotion follows specific bodily responses.*

In the context of our example, the James-Lange theory suggests that we perceive the situation first and then react with particular bodily changes—in this case running and other signs of physiological arousal. Our perception of our bodily changes then leads us to the emotional state. In simplified terms: "I'm running fast and my heart is beating rapidly. Therefore, I am experiencing fear."

The James-Lange theory hypothesizes that each emotion is associated with a particular set of physiological reactions. Some research evidence supports this position. For example, Ax (1953) induced strong feelings of fear or anger in humans. Ax also monitored the physiological changes that accompanied these induced emotional states. As predicted by the James-Lange theory, Ax found that strong fear and anger were associated with different types of physiological changes.

## Cannon-Bard Theory

**Cannon-Bard theory: theory of emotion emphasizing the role of the brain in emotional experience**

The **Cannon-Bard theory** takes a position quite different from that proposed by the James-Lange theory. Essentially, the Cannon-Bard theory, proposed by American physiologist Walter B. Cannon and extended by physiologist Philip Bard, says that emotional states and physical arousal occur simultaneously, and both are triggered by changes in the activity of the lower areas of the brain.

According to the Cannon-Bard theory, we perceive a situation in the external world, and our perception produces changes in the lower areas of the brain, such as the hypothalamus. The changes in the lower parts of the brain result in messages being sent in two different directions. One set of electrical messages is sent to the higher areas of the brain, such as the cerebral cortex, and results in the perception of emotion. The other set of messages is sent to the internal organs and voluntary muscles and produces the gross physiological changes that are part of an emotional experience.

A great deal of research has supported the role of the brain in emotional arousal. In one study, for example, both men and women were shown a series of slides that earlier had been identified as being primarily of interest to one or the other sex. The slides that were rated as most interesting by women included pictures of babies and of male pinup models. On the other hand, men rated slides of female pinups as more interesting, and both sexes rated a landscape scene as relatively uninteresting.

These slides were then shown to men and women, and the reactions of their pupils were noted. The findings from this study showed that when women were shown the slides of the baby and the male pinup, their pupils dilated substantially more than the pupils of the male subjects. In contrast, male pupils dilated substantially in response to the female pinup, while women showed a much smaller reaction to this slide. Finally, both sexes showed little reaction to the bland, uninteresting, and unemotional landscape slide (Hess & Polt, 1960).

These and many other studies have shown the importance of the brain in producing and coordinating the many physiological changes that accompany emotional reactions.

## Schachter-Singer Cognitive Theory

The **Schachter-Singer theory** of emotion states that it is our *interpretation* of physical arousal and environmental cues that determines emotion.

In the original study conducted by Schachter and Singer (1962), male college students were given a shot of epinephrine (adrenaline). This particular drug produces a generalized state of physiological arousal. All the students were led to believe that the injection contained a vitamin, but some of them received accurate information about the effects of the "vitamin" they had received. That is, they were told to expect an increased heart rate, perspiration, and so forth. The remaining students were given misleading information about the drug.

At this point, the subjects were exposed to one of two experimental conditions. In one condition, a confederate of the experimenter entered the room where the subject was located and acted in a happy, euphoric manner. In the second condition, the experimental accomplice acted in an increasingly irritated and angry fashion as he and the subject filled out questionnaires asking for very personal information.

The results of this study showed that the people who received accurate information regarding the injection did not join in the euphoric or angry states

Schachter-Singer cognitive theory: a theory of emotion suggesting that environmental cues help give emotional labels to ambiguous physiological states

# Psychology in Action

### DOES THE RIGHT HEMISPHERE CONTROL EMOTIONS?

For many motor and intellectual functions, one side of the brain predominates over the other. For example, many language skills seem to be localized in the left hemisphere. Patients who receive damage to this side of the brain through disease or trauma typically have difficulty expressing or understanding oral speech.

The right hemisphere, on the other hand, seems to be somewhat more specialized for visual and spatial tasks. This specialization can be seen in patients whose *corpus callosum,* a major communication pathway between the two hemispheres of the brain, had been surgically severed to help prevent epileptic seizures. In these patients, information can be presented visually to one hemisphere through the use of a device called a tachistoscope. For example, if a picture of an apple was presented to the right hemisphere, the patient could not name the object. Interestingly, however, the patient could point to and select the apple from a number of fruits with his or her left hand. Since the right hemisphere controls the left side of the body, the ability of the left hand to pick up the apple from a number of fruits suggests that the right hemisphere "knew" what the form and shape of the object was, even though the patient could not name the object.

A number of intriguing findings have suggested that the right hemisphere is also specialized for emotional response. In one woman patient whose corpus callosum was severed, a picture of a voluptuous nude was presented tachistoscopically to the right hemisphere. Not surprisingly, she was unable to name what had been presented. But a few moments after the presentation, she began to giggle, remarking about "that funny machine" (Gazzaniga, 1970).

Since studies of an unusual patient group may not be representative of the population at large, some investigators have developed other means for studying the probable emotional specialization of the right hemisphere. One approach that was employed by Sackheim (1978) involved the construction of mirror-image composites of faces. A picture of an individual expressing an emotion was split in two. A composite photo made up of two "left" sides and a composite photo made up of two "right" sides were constructed. These photos were then given to judges who were asked to rate the intensity of emotion in each photo.

modeled by the experimental confederate. However, those subjects who received inaccurate, misleading information about the effects of the injection developed emotional states similar to the modeled emotional behavior. That is, those who were exposed to the euphoric model tended to become happy, while those subjects exposed to the angry model showed signs of irritation.

This study suggests that emotions are produced when three conditions are present. First, the individual must be physiologically aroused. Second, the source of the arousal must be ambiguous. Third, the individual uses environmental cues to help give an emotional label to the physiological arousal. The Schachter-Singer

The results of this study suggested that the left side of the face seemed to be more expressive of emotion than the right side. Since the left side of the face is largely controlled by the right hemisphere, we again have evidence of the somewhat greater involvement of the right hemisphere in emotional expression.

You can confirm Sackheim's findings by rating the three faces presented here. One of them is a composite of the left sides of the face, one is an original photo, and one is a composite of the right sides of the face. Which of the photos best illustrates an intense emotion? When you have made your choice, you can check page 164 and compare your results to Sackheim's results.

The finding that the right hemisphere is somewhat specialized for emotions raises some interesting questions. For example, are depression and other emotional disorders related to biochemical disorders in the right hemisphere (Tucker, 1981)? How do these hemispheric differences develop (Springer & Deutsch, 1981)? Do the different hemispheres "think" differently?

The mysteries of the human brain have only yet begun to be tapped. But researchers in this intensely active and exciting field of research are helping provide some answers in our quest for understanding the most human of functions—consciousness and emotion.

  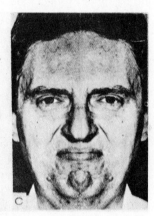

(From H. Sackheim, "Emotions Are Expressed More Intensely on the Left Side of the Face," *Science* 202, Oct. 1978, Fig. 1, p. 434. Copyright © 1978 by the American Association for the Advancement of Science.)

theory of emotion is thus a *cognitive* theory because it requires an individual to interpret the emotional cues present in the environment.

Let us return for a moment to the results of the Schachter and Singer (1962) study. The subjects who received incorrect information regarding the effects of the injection experienced physiological arousal but initially had no explanation for their increased heart rates and other bodily changes. To explain these changes, the subjects looked to the environment for help in interpreting their arousal. The accomplice, through the modeled emotions of anger or euphoria, provided the information that the subject was seeking. On the other hand, the subjects who were fully and correctly informed about the effects of the injection had no need of environmental cues to help explain the physiological arousal. In other words, they noticed the arousal and explained it to themselves by thinking, "The feelings that I have now are due to the injection, not to the person in the room with me."

These theories of emotion are not mutually contradictory and, in fact, illuminate different aspects of emotional response. For example, the Schachter-Singer theory is similar to the James-Lange theory in the physiological arousal-emotion sequence involved in emotional responses. However, the Schachter-Singer theory emphasizes the cognitive features of emotions. Similarly, the Cannon-Bard theory points out the importance of physiological arousal in emotions, a point made by both the James-Lange theory and the Schachter-Singer theory.

To summarize, the three theories of emotion make different predictions about the development of emotional states. James-Lange suggests that physiological arousal precedes emotion; Cannon-Bard suggests that the lower areas of the brain are critical for emotional response; Schachter-Singer emphasizes the importance of cognitive labels. Although there are some points of overlap in the theories, it is clear that no theory is comprehensive enough to account for the broad range and intensity of emotions that are so important to full and meaningful human functioning.

## DEALING WITH PROBLEM EMOTIONS

Up to this point, we have emphasized the role of emotions in conveying important information about ourselves and our environment and in providing meaning and depth to living. Additionally, we have described some general theories of emotion.

Our final task is to learn not to judge our emotions as good or bad but to learn to accept them and find appropriate ways of dealing with them. In this context, it is useful to briefly discuss some of the emotions that are potentially troublesome for us. While our focus will be on so-called negative emotions, we shall see that positive emotions, such as love, may also present problems.

### Fear and Anxiety

**fear: feeling of threat or danger related to a specific object or event**

**anxiety: generalized feelings of fear and apprehension**

The term **fear** is generally used to describe a response to a specific danger, while the term **anxiety** is used to describe a response to danger or threat that is less clearly perceived. According to this distinction, a frightened individual usually knows what he or she is afraid of and what can or cannot be done about it, whereas an anxious individual senses danger but is not certain about its exact nature or

Picture A is the composite of the left sides, Picture B is the original picture, while Picture C is the composite of the right sides. The judges in Sackheim's experiment rated Picture A as showing the most intense emotion.

what action he or she can take to deal with it. Often fear and anxiety go to-gether. Fear is elicited by the clearly perceived aspects of the dangerous or stress-ful situation and anxiety by its unpredictable or uncertain implication. For exam-ple, an individual approaching marriage may feel fear concerning financial prob-lems and new responsibilities and at the same time feel vaguely anxious and apprehensive about whether this is really the "right" person and whether the marriage will be a success.

**Worry** is the term commonly used to describe the simultaneous experiences of fear and anxiety. Typically, worry involves uncertainty about our ability either to prevent or to deal with an aversive situation. A certain amount of anxiety and worry is probably an inevitable by-product of modern living. Most of us feel vaguely apprehensive much of the time about possible accidents, failures, set-backs, losses, or other poorly defined future possibilities.

**worry: commonly used term to describe the si-multaneous experiences of fear and anxiety**

**Negative effects of anxiety and worry.** Chronic anxiety and worry can hamper us in three basic ways. First, anxiety beyond a minimal level leads to a defensive orientation, which makes us less able to face our problems objectively and work effectively toward their solution. Our perception narrows. We become more rigid and less inventive and try to protect ourselves through the use of defense mechanisms. Second, chronic anxiety keeps us physiologically mobilized for emergency action when no appropriate action is evident, leading to psycho-physiological disorders. Third, chronic worrying deprives us of much of the enjoy-ment of living. We are continually concerned with the negative and dangerous aspects of living rather than with the positive and enriching ones. Often a chronic worrier will worry about things that never happen and then be taken unawares by the stresses that do occur.

**Realistic and unrealistic fears and anxieties.** Fear and anxiety are normal experiences. Yet many people consider it a form of weakness or even cowardice to feel fear and anxiety—let alone express them. It is often especially difficult for males in our society to admit their fears and anxieties because the stereotyped role of the male is that of a strong, confident provider under whose protection his family can feel secure. Recognizing fear and anxiety as normal aspects of the human situation is a first step in dealing with these emotions.

A second step in dealing with these emotions is distinguishing between re-alistic and unrealistic fear, anxiety, and worry. Are our responses elicited by a real danger? Is it proportional to the actual degree of danger, or is it exaggerated? Is it rational or irrational? Is it an actual, present stress situation, or does it reflect a pervasive feeling of inadequacy and inferiority?

Of course, it is not always easy to distinguish between realistic and unreal-istic fears and anxieties or to determine whether a given individual is overly prone to fear and anxiety in dealing with the everyday problems of living. However, an awareness of this distinction and an approach to fear and anxiety as reactions to be recognized and understood rather than denied and hidden are important steps in dealing with these emotions.

**Knowing what to expect and what to do.**   Since fear and anxiety may stem from a feeling of inadequacy in the situation, one effective way for dealing with them is through the development of needed competencies. Obviously we cannot know all the demands we will face ahead of time, but we can foresee many common ones and prepare ourselves for them. With specific preparation for marriage, vocation, parenthood, and old age, for example, we are much more likely to maintain a constructive, task-oriented approach in meeting the problems they typically bring. Knowing what to expect and what to do about it can make us feel confident instead of fearful, even in a very demanding situation.

We can also modify our emotional responses to particular situations, and we can learn to carry on despite the fear. As we shall see in our discussion of systematic desensitization (Chapter 11), we can learn to function in fear-producing situations. As we do so, we may find our fear lessening with time.

Taking action in a fear-producing situation may also be effective. Fear often leads to a paralysis of action and paralysis to an intensification of the fear. Action—almost any action—can break this circle and lessen feelings of fear, even when it does not lessen the actual danger. The performer usually loses stage fright once the action begins, as does the athlete once the contest is under way.

## Anger and Hostility

**anger: strong feelings of displeasure or rage**

Anger may be viewed as a normal response to frustration and interference. Anger has a variety of forms, ranging from the intenseness of rage, to hostility, to hatred.

**hostility: angry feelings coupled with a desire to inflict harm**

Although **anger** and **hostility** can be normal aspects of adjustment, we differ greatly in the degree and frequency of the hostile feelings we experience, both as individuals and as groups. Some cultures value and encourage hostility

Preparing for retirement and old age by developing new skills and hobbies may relieve fears and anxieties about aging.

and aggressiveness, while others discourage such emotions. As individuals we may find that immature or unrealistic expectations lead to frequent or chronic hostilities and resentments.

**Understanding and expressing anger and hostility.**   As with other emotions, competence in dealing with anger and hostility begins with an understanding and acceptance of our feelings rather than denial or moral self-condemnation. When people view their hostile feelings as dangerous and immoral, they may resort to some defense mechanism to keep their feelings out of consciousness. Or they may turn their hostility inward and engage in self-recrimination for having such feelings. Either approach only aggravates the problem.

Unexpressed or indirectly expressed anger and hostility are common in our society and often lead to irrational behavior, psychosomatic disorders, and unhappiness. One "safety valve," which has been emphasized by Singer (1976), is fantasy: "Sometimes, for instance, it is more sensible in the long run just to think and fantasize about an activity than to go ahead and do it" (p. 32). Most of us probably have fantasy lives in which we act out our hostile feelings toward those we feel treat us unfairly. Repeated fantasies of this type may reduce our anger and hostility to a point where we can cope with it in rational and effective ways. Feshbach and Weiner (1982) have outlined several methods emphasizing the cognitive control of emotions which have proven helpful in regulating anger and aggressive behavior. These methods include reacting with a response which is incompatible with anger, empathizing with the person eliciting the anger, and downgrading the importance of the situation.

**Constructive vs. destructive hostility.**   In some situations anger and hostility can lead to constructive action. Anger and hostility aroused by autocratic and unjust treatment may be used constructively in working for social reforms. On a more personal level, our expression of anger may help another person realize that he or she is being inconsiderate.

However, this expression of anger is likely to be effective only if it can be delivered in a nonthreatening, constructive fashion. Anger that attacks another will likely generate a defensive reaction. Thus, if our expression of anger is to have a constructive effect, we must direct it toward the issues that need change. A response that respects the self-worth and dignity of the individual while pinpointing areas that need to be changed is often called an *assertive* response.

More commonly, however, anger and hostility take destructive forms. For example, we may let anger and hostility interfere with important interpersonal relationships. Or we may become unduly upset and angered by irritating situations that are relatively unimportant. Strong anger can lead to ill-considered action that may be regretted later. That is, poorly controlled anger can lead to *aggressive* responses.

Thus, it becomes important to distinguish between appropriate and constructive **assertion** and inappropriate and destructive **aggression**. Although many people can be aroused to inappropriate anger and hostility when unduly fatigued or under the influence of alcohol, drugs, or special stress, habitual overreaction to minor frustrations or frequent extremes of anger and hostility usually indicates unrealistic expectations or underlying feelings of immaturity and inferiority.

**assertion: behavior that produces positive outcomes while respecting the dignity and self-worth of another**

**aggression: pushing toward one's goals despite opposition or potentially negative effects upon another person**

**Expecting some hostility from others.**     Just as we learn to accept our own feelings of anger and hostility, it is important that we learn to accept such emotions in others—even when they are directed toward us. Perhaps the most essential aspect of dealing with overt anger and hostility from others is to be prepared for it and give up the notion that everyone should love and appreciate us at all times (Ellis & Harper, 1961; Goldfried & Sobocinski, 1975). Although there is a certain satisfaction in reacting angrily to the seemingly unjustified anger of another person, this is a form of self-indulgence that seldom pays off.

Two people preoccupied with anger against each other and with retaliation for past offenses only feed and perpetuate their feelings of hostility. In essence, they create a **vicious circle** of anger, retaliation, and more anger. It is often helpful to remember that anger can result from a variety of frustrating and self-devaluating conditions, including rejection. If we can pinpoint specific behavior on our part that is eliciting the other person's anger, it is often possible to make appropriate changes and establish a more harmonious relationship.

It is unlikely that we can interact with other people and not elicit anger and hostility from some of them—and occasionally this may include significant others. When it seems impossible to reason with or placate other people, however, it may be useful to view their anger as a problem for them rather than as a threat to our own self-esteem and worth.

**vicious circle: chain reaction in which an individual resorts to a defensive reaction in trying to cope with a problem, which only complicates the problem and makes it more difficult to cope with**

## Guilt

*"Of all the forms of mental suffering, perhaps none is as pervasive or as intense as the ache of guilt."*
**(GELVEN, 1973, P. 69)**

**guilt: unpleasant emotion arising from behavior or desires contrary to one's ethical principles**

Humans universally experience a sense of **guilt** when they violate ethical or moral principles in which they believe—either by doing something they consider wrong or by failing to do something they consider required. Guilt is characterized by a feeling of being bad, evil, and unworthy, usually intermixed with remorse, self-recrimination, and anxiety.

Of our various emotions, guilt is one of the most painful, complex, and difficult emotions to deal with. It is likely to be particularly stressful when it seems that nothing can be done to rectify the error.

**Understanding feelings of guilt.**     Acknowledging our responsibility when we fail to live up to our ethical and moral values is a necessary part of self-direction. Thus, guilt is potentially a normal and useful emotion that can lead to a correction of error. And since most of us probably feel guilty at times, one of the first steps in dealing constructively with guilt is understanding its nature.

To understand guilt feelings it is useful to remember that: *(a)* values concerning right and wrong are learned, *(b)* these values are then applied to one's own behavior, and *(c)* we also learn, often by hard experience, that wrong-doing leads to punishment. Thus, when we behave in ways that we consider unethical or immoral, we not only experience self-devaluation but some degree of anxiety as well. Since we feel responsible for the wrongful act, we blame ourselves— often engaging in severe self-recrimination. The intensity of our guilt feelings will depend in large part upon how serious we consider our misdeed to be and whether we can make amends for it.

In our society, many experiences of guilt center around feelings of hostility and sexual desires. Many people feel especially guilty over feeling hostility toward parents, mates, children, or other loved ones. When a person feels hostile toward his or her mother, for example, the question, "How can I possibly feel hostile toward her after all she's done for me?" is likely to arise. If the guilt-related answer is "Because you are a bad person," the result can be devastating to feelings of self-esteem and worth.

**Destructive vs. constructive ways of dealing with guilt.**   Some people attempt to cope with their guilt feelings by engaging in exaggerated self-condemnation and even self-hatred. The result is usually severe self-devaluation and depression (Murphy, 1978). Often such reactions reflect immature, rigid, and unrealistic moral standards, which may lead to a vicious circle of failure and self-recrimination. In other instances, people resort to self-defense mechanisms such as projection, placing the blame for their misdeeds on others and defending themselves from feelings of guilt and self-devaluation. Neither of these approaches is conducive to effective behavior or personal growth.

Normal guilt feelings can usually be dealt with more constructively through confession of guilt to one's self or others, a sincere effort at reparation, and a willingness to accept forgiveness. The individual must then look to the future instead of dwelling on the past. This sequence usually leaves the individual better equipped to avoid the same mistake on subsequent occasions. For some, the opportunity for confession, the provision for reparation, and the assurance of forgiveness are met through religious practices. For others, the resolution of guilt is a more individual matter.

## Grief, Depression, and Loneliness

In grief, depression, and loneliness, we suffer negative emotions primarily because important sources of interpersonal contacts or other pleasurable events in life are not available to us. We feel grief, for example, when friends or family members are taken from us by death. We become depressed when important relationships or other reinforcements are lost to us. And, we feel lonely when we are cut off from the joys of closeness and friendship that others can provide us.

*"Loss, separation, and the fear of loss are universal, lifelong experiences common to all peoples in all cultures and extending over every stage of the life cycle."*
*(SIMOS, 1977, P. 337)*

**grief: sad feelings produced by death or loss**

**grief work: the processes associated with mourning and the recovery from loss**

**ambivalence: simultaneous existence of contradictory emotions toward the same person**

**depression: emotional state of dejection, gloomy rumination, and feelings of worthlessness**

**Grief.** **Grief** is an emotion that is commonly associated with the discouragement, dejection, and gloomy thoughts characteristic of depression. It is also a universal reaction to bereavement, found even among animals. We experience grief when we suffer severe loss. Such grief is especially apparent with the death of one's spouse. Since women have a longer life expectancy than men in our society, three out of every four married women will some day experience the loss of their spouse. But whether it is the wife or husband who is bereaved, coping with grief presents an immediate and difficult problem.

In a study of women suffering bereavement due to loss of their husbands, Parkes (1972) found three stages involved in **grief work** or mourning: *(a)* an initial stage of shock or numbness accompanied by a strong tendency to deny or screen out the reality of what had happened, *(b)* a second stage involving anxiety, depression, and so-called pangs of grief, and *(c)* a final stage in which they gave up hope of recovering what they had lost and began to make the necessary readjustment to life.

The characteristics of the individual who is grieving are not always easy to spot. Right after the death, we may cry, feel depressed, and show other normal signs of grief. However, when the funeral or cremation is over, we may be left to our own devices. We must return to our homes and our lives, feeling empty, isolated, and lonely. Such feelings are particularly acute when we have lost a spouse, a parent, or a child. Many aspects of the home remind us of the deceased individual—a favorite chair, unfinished hobby materials, clothes, and other personal effects. These constant reminders increase our sensation of loss.

The process of grief work ordinarily lasts from a few weeks to several months, depending upon the individual and his or her method of coping. Using denial or tranquilizing drugs to avoid grief may offer some immediate, if temporary, relief. But their use tends to prolong the grief work that must be carried out if the person is to make an adequate adjustment to his or her new life situation. As Ramsay (1977) has pointed out, grief is an extremely stressful emotion and people often try to protect themselves from the unpleasantness of grief work. As a result "the 'normal' reactions of shock, despair, and recovery are often distorted, exaggerated, prolonged, inhibited, or delayed" (p. 132). Grief work may also be prolonged and complicated by feelings of guilt and depression, particularly when the bereaved person has **ambivalent** feelings toward the deceased.

**Depression.** **Depression,** the feeling of being dejected, discouraged, and "down in the dumps," is usually accompanied by lowered initiative, listlessness, and some degree of self-devaluation. Often the clinical picture also includes loss of appetite, sleep disturbances, and a lowered sex drive. Most of us have probably felt depressed at one time or another as a result of a disappointment in love, an accident, a failure, or the death of a loved one. In fact, there are literally hundreds of thousands of Americans who show mild depression. Even in mild form, depression can lead to thoughts of despair or suicide and can markedly reduce one's personal effectiveness and joy in living.

Depression usually occurs in response to life stress, and often seems to be based upon **learned helplessness** (Seligman, 1975). In learned helplessness, an individual learns as a result of past experience that there is no effective way of coping with the stress situation. In response, he or she stops fighting and gives up. In an experiment with animals, for example, dogs were given electric shock in a situation from which they could not escape. Later the dogs failed to escape even though the situation had been changed to allow for escape. Similarly, past experiences presumably lead people to perceive stress situations in a limited and habitual way. As a result, they fail to see the available and effective ways of coping with the situation.

According to this viewpoint, the most effective way of coping with depression is to realize that the stress situation can be dealt with effectively—that one is not helpless after all. Fortunately, feelings of helplessness and depression tend to dissipate in time. Perhaps the individual becomes somewhat desensitized to the stress situation or finds a feasible solution. Of course, obtaining professional assistance can often help to shorten the period of depression.

While we all lose control over some situations that are important to us— parents die, failures occur, loved ones disappoint us—we can prepare ourselves for coping with most of the stress situations that we are likely to encounter in living. And knowing what to expect and what to do can help to prevent needless feelings of helplessness and depression.

**Loneliness.**   **Loneliness** is a painful feeling of emptiness and deprivation that we cannot eliminate merely by making a choice. We experience loneliness when we are cut off from the pleasures of close interpersonal relationships. Widowed and aged persons are perhaps most likely to suffer acutely from loneliness, but loneliness is a problem that affects young and old alike. We can feel lonely even in the midst of a crowd.

**learned helplessness:** a depressed-like state in which an individual believes that he or she is helpless to cope with adjustive demands

**loneliness:** emotional state of feeling alone, solitary, or without perceived concern or care of others

Experiences of depression and loneliness often make us feel isolated, empty, and helpless.

We can distinguish between aloneness and loneliness (Ivanhoe, 1977). There are many occasions when we are subjected to short or long periods of aloneness. While such occasions may be unpleasant, aloneness can often be desirable. In fact, many individuals strive to preserve their periods of aloneness or solitude. It is important to realize, however, that these people choose aloneness and know that they can choose to end it.

Perhaps the first step in dealing with loneliness is to accept the reality that sometimes we are going to feel lonely. The second step, as Moustakas (1961) has pointed out, is to use this experience as an opportunity to get to know ourselves better and to draw upon potentials never before realized. Deeply lived loneliness can lead not only to greater self-acceptance but to increased compassion for and relatedness to others. This process has been referred to as "creative loneliness." The third and essential step in dealing with loneliness is to build truly meaningful, loving, and enduring relationships with others. And this often requires not only relating on an individual level but developing a concern for, involvement in, and commitment to the human enterprise.

## THE SPECIAL NATURE OF LOVE

*"Love alone is capable of uniting living beings in such a way as to complete and fulfill them, for it alone takes them and joins them by what is deepest in themselves."*
*(TEILHARD DE CHARDIN, 1961, P. 265)*

The ability to give and receive love is one of the most important of all emotional competencies. The evidence points to the necessity of loving and being loved for normal human development and functioning.

In this section, we shall look briefly at the nature of love and consider its importance to our emotional development. In our discussion of marriage and intimate relationships (Chapter 14), we shall again address the topic of love.

### The Nature and Forms of Love

**love: positive emotional state associated with strong or passionate affection for another person**

**Love** may take different forms and may have different meanings. For example, we can love humanity; parents can love and be loved by their children; we can experience love in its erotic, exciting, and romantic form; we can experience less passionate but usually more enduring companionate love; and we can experience love as a union with a supreme being (Fromm, 1956; Mathes, 1980; Walster & Walster, 1978). Central to all forms of love, however, appears to be an attitude of care, concern, and responsibility for the loved one, and a desire to promote his or her growth, well-being, and interests. An individual usually does not show only one form of love. More commonly, the ability to feel any of the particular forms of love is part of a broader orientation involving the valuing of other human beings and an eagerness to form close bonds with other people. As Fromm (1956) has put it: "If a person loves only one other person and is indifferent to the rest of his fellow men, his love is not love but symbiotic attachment, or an enlarged egotism" (p. 46).

## Infatuation

Often the question is raised about the distinction between love and infatuation. Lacking a clear understanding of either, we can make only a general distinction. **Infatuation** is usually an intense romantic relationship of short duration. As such, it is a purely emotional reaction and does not take into account the personalities involved and many other rational considerations. Often infatuation involves a high degree of wishful thinking in which the lover projects a halo over the head of the loved one and sees only what he or she wants to see instead of what is there. Once these perceptions become more realistic, the halo may disappear.

infatuation: an intense, usually brief, romantic relationship characterized by disregard of realistic considerations that will affect the quality or longevity of the relationship

Unfortunately, a person usually thinks of his or her current romantic experience as love rather than infatuation. Infatuation is usually recognized as such—at least by the person involved—only after it is over. But although infatuation may not last, it is a powerful force while it holds sway. It provides both rose-colored spectacles and a sense of urgency to its victims. When it leads to a hasty marriage, they may find themselves married to someone they scarcely know and whose weak points come to them as quite a shock.

Many other irrational elements may also make it difficult for a person to tell whether he or she is really in love. Relatively mature persons may convince themselves that they are truly in love and want to get married when actually what they want is someone to take care of them, to ensure their sexual satisfaction, or to protect them from loneliness. Often people are indoctrinated with the notion that there is only one person in the world who is "right for them." And in their eagerness to believe that they have found that person, it is easy to convince themselves that they are in love.

## The Ability to Love and Be Loved

*"One day a stranger entered my domain*
*and my solitude was transformed*
*into love."*
*(RINDER, 1970)*

Genuine love appears to grow out of shared experiences of many kinds. The climate of a happy marriage or other intimate relationships is not necessarily one of complete harmony at all times, but it is one in which the bonds of love are deepened by shared problems and experiences. Love also allows both partners to grow as individuals (Branden, 1980). The latter point is particularly important,

Genuine romantic love, like parental love and brotherly love, is nurturing and fulfilling for both partners.

for a love that feeds on dependency or domination tends to destroy itself. Romantic love, like brotherly love and parental love, nurtures the growth of the loved one as an individual.

In a pioneering study of self-actualizing people, Maslow (1954) found that in their love relationships his subjects were able to drop their defenses and be themselves without fear or pretense. Presumably this opened the way for and fostered personal growth: "One of the deepest satisfactions coming from the healthy love relationship reported by my subjects is that such a relationship permits the greatest spontaneity, the greatest naturalness, the greatest dropping of defenses and protection against threat. In such a relationship it is not necessary to be guarded, to conceal, to try to impress, to feel tense, to watch one's words or actions, to suppress or repress. My people reported that they can be themselves without feeling that there are demands or expectations upon them; they can feel psychologically (as well as physically) naked and still feel loved and wanted and secure'' (pp. 239–40).

People differ greatly in their ability to love and maintain a durable love relationship with another person. This ability, like other emotional competencies, appears to depend upon a number of factors, including early experiences with parents, extent of trust in others, degree of personal maturity and self-acceptance, and freedom from exaggerated self-defenses. At least a minimally favorable emotional climate in childhood seems essential if the individual is to give and receive love in later years. Yet, love is a powerful force, and long-held patterns of distrust, self-doubt, and defensiveness may be dissipated by the experience of genuinely loving and being loved by another human being.

## SUMMARY

1. The affective or emotional aspects of life are an important part of human existence. They give us information about ourselves, and they are capable of informing others about our feelings.

2. The patterns of emotion can range from mild to strong to disintegrative. Our awareness of and control over our emotional states is related to the degree of awareness and denial, spontaneity and control, and direct and disguised expression of our emotions. Cognitive factors also play a role in emotional control. Mechanisms for dealing with emotional hurts rely primarily on learning new approaches to our difficulties.

3. The three different theories of emotion make different predictions about the development of emotional states. However, all three stress the importance of physiological states and higher cortical and perceptual states in the recognition of emotion.

4. Strong emotions are a problem for many people. Although many of the problem emotions are negative, such as fear and anxiety, anger and hostility, guilt, grief, depression, and loneliness, some positive emotions such as love can also present adjustment difficulties. In dealing with the problems of strong emotions, several general approaches seem to be helpful. First, we must accept our emotions and neither ignore nor exaggerate them. Next, we must seek mechanisms for dealing with these emotions if they present problems for us. Finally, when our own resources fail, other mechanisms, including professional assistance, may prove useful.

# Part Three

# Stress:
# Its Nature,
# Effects, and
# Management

**Problems of Adjustment: Life Stress**

**Reactions to Stress**

**Effective Methods of Coping**

**Maladaptive Behavior**

**Psychotherapy and Counseling**

# Chapter 7

# Problems of Adjustment: Life Stress

*"Whether emotional or physical, natural or man-made, public or private, stress exerts an influence on our lives . . . [and] . . . more than any other factor . . . determines the point at which we find ourselves sliding down the slope from health. . . . Stress is not unique to Americans, but given our way of living, one would not be far off to call it the 'American disease.' "*

*(LAMOTT, 1975, PP. 8—9)*

**stress:** any adjustive demand, often resulting from situations or reactions to situations that are potentially harmful to the individual

**Stress** refers to adjustive demands which must be dealt with if an individual is to meet his or her needs. As our definition suggests, stress has three aspects: Stress can refer to some unpleasant, uncontrollable, or unpredictable aspect of the environment. For example, the loss of a home through fire, earthquake, or flood can be a source of stress. The loss of a job or a loving interpersonal relationship can also be a source of stress, as can be the taking on of new, increased responsibilities at home or at work. These environmental aspects of stress are often termed *stressors.*

Stress can also occur when the individual perceives stressors in the environment. The student who imagines dire consequences happening to him or her if the highest possible grades are not earned may experience the effects of stress. The athlete and businessperson who compete intensively may experience stress. And the teen-ager who would "die of embarrassment" if he or she did not wear the latest fashions might also experience stress. It is not critical that an environmental stressor actually exist. Rather, it is the *perception of threat* that may produce the stress reaction. Often, the perceived threat is to the individual's self-esteem.

Stress can also refer to the psychological and physiological responses to environmental and perceived stressors. Psychological responses can range from the virtually undetectable to a psychotic breakdown. Some individuals will develop mechanisms for effective coping, others will employ ego-defense mechanisms, while still others may develop severely maladaptive reactions. Physiological effects of stress can be seen in a number of reactions, including changes in hormonal function and changes in appetite.

All stress involves *demands for change or adaptation,* and there are many sources of stress in contemporary life. We are confronted by delays, losses, pressures, conflicts, and other conditions that place demands on us. The demands can come from within us, as in our personal desire to practice and become more accomplished musicians or athletes; they can also come from others and from the environment. Nonetheless, we must deal with and adapt to these demands.

From the time of infancy, through adolescence, adulthood, and old age, we are confronted by stress. As infants and toddlers, we may cry from a bruised knee or from the frustration of having a favorite toy taken away from us. As adolescents, we may rage against parents who grant us the independence we seek, but rarely at a pace we desire. In adulthood, we may feel constrained by marriages, occupations, and children. And, in old age, we may become frustrated by increasing physical disability and loss of self-esteem.

Some of the stressors we face are easy to cope with. If food is available and we are hungry, we eat. When we meet an individual who isn't friendly and outgoing, we may soon forget the unpleasant encounter. On the other hand, some stressors are difficult to cope with. Major surgery, divorce, and serious financial difficulties are examples of such stressful situations. For some people, the daily pressures and worries of modern life are a constant source of stress.

Capacities for dealing with stress differ as well. Some individuals appear to be able to tolerate markedly unpleasant situations with apparent equanimity. Others burst into tears at a cross look from a friend.

How we respond to stress also differs. Some individuals respond by developing physical reactions. Perhaps the reactions will be as severe as hypertension (high blood pressure) or ulcers. Others may show only some trouble sleeping or a decrease in sexual desires. Stress can also affect people's day-to-day activities. Perhaps they will function less well at work. Perhaps their ability to study and prepare for courses will be affected. Or, they may find that they become irritable and difficult toward others.

Stress is a multidimensional phenomenon. As we grow and develop, as our lives change, we will find that the factors that produce stress and our expressions and reactions to stress will change, as will our ability to cope with stress.

Much of our discussion and many of our examples will concentrate on the negative aspects of stress, often termed **distress.** As we shall see, change and adaptation are also necessary parts of life and can be joyous experiences as well. These positive aspects of stress, termed **eustress,** will also be examined in our discussion of stress.

> **distress: negative aspects of stress**
>
> **eustress: (pronounced YOU-stress) positive aspects of stress**

In this chapter, we shall discuss several basic issues related to stress. First, we will consider the types and sources of stress and the factors influencing the severity of stress. The measurement of stress will be considered briefly before we turn our attention to some general principles underlying stress reactions. We shall also discuss positive stress.

## TYPES AND SOURCES OF STRESS

Problems of adjustment can be classified as frustrations, conflicts, or pressures. Of course, elements of all three may be present in the same stressful situation, but for simplicity, we shall discuss them separately.

### Frustration

**Frustration** results from the blocking of needs and motives—either by something that prevents or hinders our achieving a desired goal or by the absence of a desired goal object. Overly restrictive parents would be a source of frustration to an adolescent who wanted to go to a school party, while a lack of water would be a source of frustration to a person lost in the desert. Frustrations may be minor and inconsequential or they may represent serious threats to our well-being and survival.

> **frustration: thwarting of a need or desire**

Environmental obstacles such as accidents, hurtful interpersonal relationships, and the deaths of loved ones can be sources of frustration. Personal characteristics such as physical handicaps, inadequate competencies, and lack of self-discipline can also be sources of frustration.

Some of the more common frustrations, which often cause us special difficulty, include delays, lack of resources, losses, failure, and loneliness and meaninglessness.

1. *Delays.* In our time-conscious culture, where we feel we must make every minute count, delays are especially galling. Yet, with our crowded urban centers and high degree of interdependence, delays are inevitable. Often it seems as if we are continually standing in line or waiting in traffic. Preparation for a career can take long years of intensive study. Many delays, especially those related to material possessions, are made especially difficult by the constant barrage of advertising that stimulates our desire for things we cannot presently afford—and perhaps never will be able to afford.

2. *Lack of resources.* Although most of us do not lack the basic necessities of life, probably few of us are satisfied with what we do have. We all might like to have more money to buy and do the things we want—perhaps to buy a new car or to buy the freedom to travel. Many people feel that they lack the educational, occupational, or social opportunities essential for realizing their potentials.

Personal limitations can also be highly stressful in our competitive society. Physical handicaps which limit our attractiveness or place serious limitations on our activities can be highly frustrating. Similarly, the inability to obtain outstanding grades in college may be severely frustrating to a student who wishes to pursue a professional career.

3. *Losses.* The loss of something we value is frustrating because it deprives us of a resource for meeting our needs. Loss of money or time may mean for-

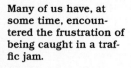

**Many of us have, at some time, encountered the frustration of being caught in a traffic jam.**

going a cherished dream. Loss of friendship or love may deprive us of satisfactions we have come to depend upon and may threaten our self-esteem. Losses are especially frustrating because they are often beyond our control; once they have occurred there is nothing we can do about them.

4. *Failure.* Even if we did not live in a highly competitive society, we would be bound to fail at some time. The competitive setting in which we operate merely increases the frequency of failure and frustration. Athletic teams do not win all the time, and those who have the desire to become movie or television stars or achieve high political office rarely achieve their dreams. Even when we do well in light of our own abilities, we may have a feeling of failure if we have not done as well as someone else.

5. *Loneliness and meaninglessness.* Probably most of us experience painful feelings of isolation and loneliness at some time in our lives, and these feelings appear to be key sources of frustration for people throughout the world (Chandler, 1976; Fidler, 1976). In examining the reasons for high suicide rates for female physicians, Southgate (1975) considered the stresses of singleness and loneliness to be of key importance. Being unloved and lonely has been called "the greatest poverty." For many people, the world is a lonely place.

Closely related to loneliness is the inability to find and lead a meaningful and fulfilling life. Apparently many people are repelled by the phoniness, hypocrisy, and materialistic status-seeking they see in the world around them. And those who have all the material satisfactions may feel a sense of emptiness. Yet both groups may have difficulty finding more satisfying goals and values. Emptiness, meaninglessness, and a sense of **alienation** are often the result.

**alienation: sense of detachment or separation from others**

## Conflict

In frustration, stress comes from a single obstacle. In **conflict,** multiple frustrations are involved. In a conflict of motives, selecting one option entails giving up another option. For example, an individual may find a job offer particularly attractive in terms of salary but may also find that accepting the job involves a less satisfying and unpleasant work situation. In this situation, selecting the job with the high salary involves the problem of the poor work situation, while not accepting the job involves giving up a good salary. No matter what the choice, stress is involved. We also experience conflicts in selecting which major in college is most suitable, in selecting the right person to share a life with, and in selecting the kind of life-style that will prove most fulfilling. It is not surprising that people in conflict often hesitate and vacillate while trying to make a decision.

**conflict: simultaneous arousal of two or more incompatible motives**

Conflicts are usually classified in terms of the reward or punishment value the alternatives have for the individual. The conflicts we meet can be conveniently classified as approach-approach, avoidance-avoidance, approach-avoidance, and double approach-avoidance conflicts.

1. *Approach-approach conflicts.* As the name implies, **approach-approach conflicts** involve competition between two or more desirable alternatives. On a simple level, a decision may have to be made between two courses of action—

**approach-approach conflict: conflict produced when a person must choose between two or more desirable alternatives**

for example, between two invitations for the same evening. To a large extent, these "plus-plus" conflicts result from the inevitable limitations in our time, space, energy, and personal resources. We cannot be in two places at once, nor do we have the time and energy to do all the things we would like.

Although even simple decisions—such as whether to have steak or fish for dinner—may be hard to make, they do not ordinarily upset us greatly because we are assured of reasonable gratification at the moment and because we are often able to obtain the other desired alternative at a later time. In more complex cases—as when a young person is torn between preparing for a career in law or medicine or between present and future satisfactions—decision making may be very difficult and stressful, since selecting one option may forever limit access to the second option.

2. *Avoidance-avoidance conflicts.* In an **avoidance-avoidance conflict** we are caught "between the devil and the deep blue sea" and must try to choose the lesser of two evils. The unskilled young person may have to choose between unemployment and a disagreeable job. A middle-aged person may have to choose between a loveless marriage and a life of loneliness. When such "minus-minus" conflicts are severe, they can bring about serious adjustment problems, because the resolution of the conflict will produce stress rather than relief.

3. *Approach-avoidance conflicts.* In an **approach-avoidance conflict,** there are strong tendencies both to approach and to avoid the same goal. A man may want to marry for social and security reasons, while at the same time he fears the responsibilities and loss of personal freedom that marriage would involve.

**avoidance-avoidance conflict: conflict produced when an individual must choose between two or more undesirable alternatives**

**approach-avoidance conflict: conflict produced when a goal has both positive and negative features**

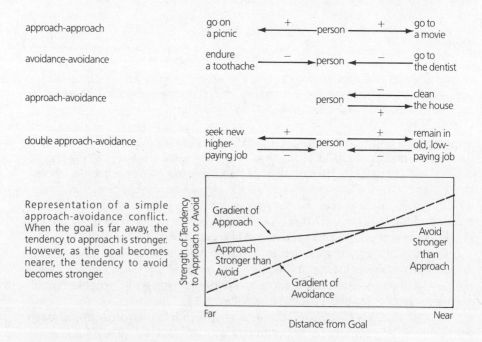

Representation of a simple approach-avoidance conflict. When the goal is far away, the tendency to approach is stronger. However, as the goal becomes nearer, the tendency to avoid becomes stronger.

**FIGURE 7.1 Types of Conflict**

Thus, the same goal, marriage, has positive as well as negative aspects.

4. *Double approach-avoidance conflicts.* While an approach-avoidance conflict involves a single goal, **double approach-avoidance conflicts** involve two or more goals, each of which has positive and negative attributes. For example, an athlete may receive a large scholarship to a small school and a small scholarship to a large school.

Dollard and Miller (1950), who have done extensive work on conflict, have noted that the approach and avoidance tendencies differ depending on our nearness to the goal. Approach tendencies are strongest when we are furthest from the goal, while avoidance tendencies are strongest when we are nearest to the goal. For example, the delight that accompanies the announcement of marriage in six months becomes uncertainty and anxiety one week before the event. These changes in the approach and avoidance tendencies may help explain many neurotic or other puzzling behaviors.

**double approach-avoidance conflict: conflict produced when an individual must choose between two or more goals, each of which has positive and negative features**

## Pressure

**Pressure** forces us to speed up, intensify, or change the direction of goal-oriented behavior. If our families have made sacrifices to send us to college, for example, we may feel great pressure not to let them down. Such pressure may force us to intensify our efforts to an uncomfortable degree.

**pressure: adjustive demand that requires an organism to speed up, intensify, or change the direction of goal-oriented behavior**

We shall discuss three sources of pressure: competition, change, and interpersonal relationships. In each category, both inner and outer sources of pressure may be present. Competition, for example, may come from others, or it may come from unrealistically high expectations that we have set for ourselves.

1. *Competition.* In our highly competitive society we compete for grades, athletic honors, jobs, marital partners, and almost everything else we want. Although we endorse certain rules for playing the game and may give grudging credit for effort, success gains the rewards. The losing football team does not attract crowds or gain plaudits for its performance. The company that fails to win customers is likely to go bankrupt. The strain of sustained effort may never cease. In school, we are expected to study hard and get good grades. At work, a person may be under pressure to advance and make more money. In general, we are encouraged to be ambitious and "think big." Yet not everyone can come in first, and striving to do the impossible invites frustration and self-devaluation.

2. *Change.* All life involves change. We grow up, marry, have children, face the death of parents, undergo illnesses, and adjust to innumerable other major and minor changes as we go through life. Up to a point, change *per se* need not cause difficulty.

The rate and pervasiveness of change today, however, are different from anything our ancestors ever experienced. Just trying to keep up with these adjustments can be a source of considerable pressure. And as change comes faster and more often, the pressure also increases. Too much pressure and we are in danger of "overloading" our adaptive circuits. When the change becomes too rapid, we may suffer from **"future shock"** (Toffler, 1970, 1980).

**future shock: stress produced by rapid, accelerating technological, social, and cultural change**

College life places many adjustive demands on a person. A student may have to adjust to the change of being on his or her own, perhaps for the first time; there may be pressure to study hard, perform well, and get good grades; meeting new people and forming new interpersonal relationships may be another source of stress.

3. *Interpersonal relationships.* Although many of our deepest needs are satisfied through interpersonal relationships, such relationships can also place difficult pressures upon us. Marriage calls on the individual to adjust to an intimate relationship with another person, to help work out a mutually satisfactory approach to problems, and to resolve conflicts.

Relationships with those outside our families can also be sources of pressure. We are constantly being called on by other individuals or groups to help advance their concerns. Our friends may need our help at inconvenient times. Organizations to which we belong may need long hours that we cannot easily spare. Community problems may make demands upon us as concerned citizens. All these demands add to the pressures that complicate our lives.

# FACTORS INFLUENCING THE SEVERITY OF STRESS

The **severity of stress** refers to the disruption or imbalance that occurs if the individual fails to cope with the stresses and demands of life. In mild stress, there is little disturbance, and adjustive action is usually relatively simple. In moderate and severe stress, proportionately greater demands are imposed on the organism, and adjustive action may be difficult. In excessive stress, the adaptive capacities of the organism are overtaxed, and breakdown may occur. Thus, we may think of the severity of stress as lying on a continuum from mild through moderate and severe to excessive stress.

> severity of stress: degree of adjustive demand made on an individual by stress

The severity of stress is determined primarily by three factors: *(a)* the characteristics of the adjustive demand; *(b)* the characteristics of the individual; and *(c)* the resources and supports available to the individual. Let us examine each of the factors in more detail.

## Characteristics of the Adjustive Demand

Several characteristics of the adjustive demand affect its severity regardless of the makeup of the individual or the situation in which it occurs. We will consider five characteristics of the adjustive demand that affect the severity of stress. These are intensity, number, duration, predictability, and imminence of the stress.

**Intensity.**   The severity of a stress is directly related to its *intensity.* Some stresses are intrinsically mild, while others are quite strong. Postponing a trip to the movies is probably less intense than breaking off an engagement. Similarly, failing the bar exams is likely to be more demanding of adjustive resources than performing poorly on a surprise quiz. The more intense the stress, the more likely it is to have a negative effect on us (Rabkin & Struening, 1976).

**Number.**   The *number* of demands can also influence the severity of a stress. As the number of demands increases, so does the severity of the stress (Holmes & Rahe, 1967). For example, consider the situation in which an individual must cope with a promotion, increased responsibilities at work, a soured interpersonal relationship, and a burglarized apartment. If these events occurred one at a time, the individual might have more adequate resources for dealing with them. However, should they occur all at once, the individual might not be able to cope effectively with these multiple demands.

**Duration.**   The length of time or *duration* of a stress clearly affects its severity. If we have a minor disagreement with a friend, the dispute usually lasts no more than a few hours or days. However, should the dispute go on months or even years, as in the case of bickering marital partners, the stress can become quite severe. Similarly, we might be able to function reasonably well in a short-term crisis situation at work or during exam weeks, but if the "crisis" becomes part of the normal routine, our ability to deal with these demands diminishes.

**Predictability.**   Our ability to deal successfully with stress is related to our ability to foresee or *predict* future events. For example, a natural catastrophe such as an earthquake strains our adjustive capacity because it is so unexpected. On a more individual level, unexpected and unpredictable events such as rape can have a devastating effect on the victim of the attack.

However, some demands can be predicted. Individuals who plan for future demands find themselves better able to cope with the changes that occur. Workers, for example, who plan for retirement through the development of hobbies, good health habits, and sound financial planning find retirement more enjoyable and less stressful than individuals who go from worker to retiree status without any advance preparation (O'Brien, 1981).

**Imminence.**   Anticipating stress is itself stressful, particularly as the event comes closer in time. Thinking about one's marriage or the arrival of a child is less stressful six months before the event than one week before the event. As the following passage illustrates, the same is true of students approaching exam time:

*As the examinations approached and as student anxiety increased, various changes occurred in behavior. Joking increased, and while students still sought social support and talked a great deal about examinations, they began specifically to avoid certain people who aroused their anxiety. Stomach aches, asthma, and a general feeling of weariness became common complaints, and other psychosomatic symptoms appeared. The use of tranquilizers and sleeping pills became more frequent.*

*When the examinations are nearly upon the student, anxiety is very high, even for those rated as low-anxiety persons, although students do fluctuate between confidence and anxiety. Since studying is difficult, the student questions his motivations, interest, and ability in the field. (Mechanic, 1962, pp. 142, 144)*

We may be able to cope successfully with stressful events that we know are approaching, such as graduating from school, taking on a new job, or retiring from work. Unexpected events, like tornadoes or other natural disasters, may be a much greater strain on our adjustive capacities.

## Characteristics of the Individual

Situations that one person finds very stressful may be only mildly stressful or even nonstressful for another. Some people relish the opportunity to talk with strangers at a party, while others might react with numb, tongue-tied panic in the same situation. The person's prior experience with the situation, his or her tolerance for stress, and his or her control over the situation all help determine the severity of the stress he or she will experience.

**Type A vs. Type B behavior.**  Friedman and Rosenman (1974) have described two different types of personality and life-style that appear to influence the severity of stress. One style, named **Type A**, is characteristic of the individual who is rushed and hurried. Speech is quick and abrupt. Walking and eating are done quickly. The Type A individual finds it difficult to relax and do nothing. The Type A person is competitive, even in noncompetitive situations, and is likely to become hostile and aggressive.

> **Type A behavior:** behavior pattern characterized by an emphasis on speed, competition, and hostility

The Type A individual also is concerned with not having enough time to complete tasks. Part of this feeling may result from the tendency to take on many responsibilities and perform more than one task at a time. For example, a Type A individual may try to write a letter, eat lunch, and carry on a conversation at the same time. Type A's are also occupied with things and numbers. They will report on the cost of their new home and inform the listener of its square footage, exterior dimensions, and gallons of paint needed to cover the interior. Or they may report on their grade point averages, the number of pages covered in the most recent study session, and the number of records in their record and tape collection. They are typically impatient with others and intolerant of slowness. The Type A individual thus corresponds to our image of the hard-driving, achievement-oriented, and status-conscious individual. The Type A individual is also likely to suffer from stress-related cardiovascular disease (Rosenman, Friedman, Strauss, Wurm, Jenkins, & Messinger, 1966; Yarnold & Grimm, 1982).

In contrast, the **Type B** individual is easy-going, relaxed, patient, and tolerant. The Type B individual does not boast about accomplishments and feels little time pressure. The Type B individual is also less likely to suffer from stress-related cardiovascular disease.

> **Type B behavior:** behavior pattern characterized by tolerance, relaxation, and lack of time pressure

Type A behavior seems to be related to stressful life-styles as well. The Type A personality may be associated with increased consumption of fatty foods, increased alcohol intake, and increased use of tobacco. All these are indicators of a stressful life-style.

**Prior experience.**  New situations are often more stressful than old situations. Faced with a familiar situation, the individual can call upon *prior experience* to help guide behavior in the situation. If his or her prior attempts at coping with the situation were successful, the individual is likely to choose the same strategy with perhaps only modest amounts of change. If his or her prior attempts were not successful, the individual will stay away from a "solution" that has already failed and try yet another approach to the problem.

Even an unsuccessful attempt at coping with an earlier situation is likely to be more successful than coping with an entirely new situation. In a new situation, the person has few guidelines for attempting to solve the problem. Consider the problems facing an individual who is taking a laboratory course in chemistry. If the individual has never taken chemistry before, or has never taken any laboratory-based course before, the lab problems will seem quite overwhelming. Not only will the person have difficulty with the course topic, but he or she will also have problems finding the proper materials, arranging for lab fees, knowing how to carry out the laboratory assignments, writing up the experiments, and so on. This individual is more likely to find the situation stressful than the individual who has already taken a chemistry course and who has already had experience in the lab.

**Stress tolerance: amount of stress an individual can tolerate before functioning is seriously impaired**

**Stress tolerance.**  By **stress tolerance** we mean the individual's capacity for withstanding stress, or operationally speaking, the amount of stress the individual can tolerate before his or her functioning is seriously impaired. Although tolerance for stress is relatively constant for a given individual, tolerance for stress can differ markedly among individuals.

Figure 7.2 illustrates the differences in stress tolerance. The horizontal line refers to the severity of the stress, while the vertical line refers to the proportion of individuals showing impaired functioning. As the graph illustrates, the proportion of people showing impaired functioning (the shaded area of the graph) increases as the severity of the stresses increases. However, even at the same level of stress (indicated by the arrow), there can be marked individual differences. The individual who falls into the shaded area is impaired by stress, while the person who is above the shaded area does not show impaired functioning. In other words, one individual has greater tolerance for stress than does another.

The factors that influence stress tolerance are not clearly understood. It appears that too much stress early in life, or conversely, no stress at all seems to predispose the individual to react to adjustive demands more strongly as an adult.

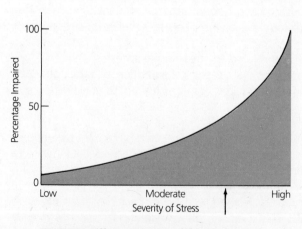

**FIGURE 7.2 Differences in Stress Tolerance**

**Control.**  A sense of *control* over a situation greatly reduces the severity of a stressor. In situations where we feel competent to act, the stress is less severe. When we feel that we are helpless to deal with a situation, our ability to cope effectively with the situation diminishes as well (Bandura, 1982b).

Interestingly, our actual ability to control the situation is not as important as our belief or *perception* that we have control over the situation. Individuals who believe that their successes and failures in life are under their personal control are more likely to cope effectively with stress than individuals who routinely attribute their successes and failures to luck or other factors outside their control (Geer, Davison, & Gatchel, 1970).

For example, an individual who feels that his or her poor performance on an exam is due to an unfair professor constructing an unfair exam is more likely to show a stress reaction than the student who believes that increased study (or more properly focused study) will result in an improved grade. Although attributing success and failure to an outside force or agent may seem to be an appealing defensive strategy, it has a very significant drawback, the **self-fulfilling prophecy.** A student who believes that he or she has no control over a grade is not very likely to study the material. And not studying the material is almost certain to result in a further stress-inducing low grade.

**self-fulfilling prophecy:** an individual's prediction about the future influencing behavior to ensure that the prediction will come true

## Resources and Supports Available to the Individual

Usually we are not alone when we meet severe stress situations. In many cases we can count on the emotional support of family and friends to help us deal with stressful situations. External resources generally come in two types: social support and material and financial support.

**Social support.**  Family and friends can often aid individuals to deal successfully with stress. Although some people prefer to be alone during a time of stress, the suggestions and encouragement of others can often provide the emotional strength needed to deal with a difficult situation. For example, the simple presence of friends at the funeral of a loved one can ease the pain of a loss.

Emotional support that realistically deals with the problem situation can also be helpful. That is, the information that others can provide during a time of stress can be useful in reducing the stress. The tactful and sympathetic advice of a friend on how to cope with the break-up of a long-term relationship can prove very beneficial.

When emotional support from friends or family is not sufficient, the helping professions can often provide assistance. Psychologists, ministers, and physicians and other health professionals can assist the individual through helpful, realistic solutions to the problems of stress.

**Material and financial support.**  Access to material and financial support can markedly reduce stress. A student who must prepare many papers is enor-

The emotional support of friends and family can be especially helpful during times of severe stress, as when a loved one dies.

mously aided by access to a typewriter. The ability to get away for a weekend or longer can give the stressed individual a break from adjustive demands and a chance to recuperate and renew his or her personal resources.

## THE MEASUREMENT OF STRESS

Until recently, the study of stress and its effects was handicapped by a lack of reliable methods for measuring this phenomenon in everyday life. True, the severity of an immediate stress could be measured in a controlled laboratory setting by various physiological and psychological measures, such as the level of muscle tension and changes in heart rate and by responses to psychological tests. But how do you ascertain the severity of stress to which an individual is exposed in real life—particularly over a period of time?

This question was answered with the development of the Social Readjustment Rating Scale (SRRS) by Holmes and his colleagues (Holmes & Rahe, 1967; Holmes & Holmes, 1970). The SRRS is a self-rating questionnaire made up of forty-two life changes to which a person may have been exposed. (The entire scale is shown on p. 193.) It is designed to estimate the amount of stress in a person's life over the past twelve months.

Each life change event is given a number designating its severity in terms of **Life Change Units** (LCUs). For example, death of a spouse is assigned 100, divorce 73, and personal illness or injury 53 LCUs. By simply adding up the num-

Life Change Unit: quantitative measure of the effects of stress

# Insight

## THE SOCIAL READJUSTMENT RATING SCALE

| Events | Scale of Impact (LCUs) | Events | Scale of Impact (LCUs) |
|---|---|---|---|
| Death of spouse | 100 | Son or daughter leaving home | 29 |
| Divorce | 73 | Trouble with in-laws | 29 |
| Marital separation | 65 | Outstanding personal achievement | 28 |
| Jail term | 63 | Spouse begins or stops work | 26 |
| Death of close family member | 63 | Begin or end school | 26 |
| Personal injury or illness | 53 | Change in living conditions | 25 |
| Marriage | 50 | Revision of personal habits | 24 |
| Fired at work | 47 | Trouble with boss | 23 |
| Marital reconciliation | 45 | Change in work hours or conditions | 20 |
| Retirement | 45 | Change in residence | 20 |
| Change in health of family member | 44 | Change in schools | 20 |
| Pregnancy | 40 | Change in recreation | 19 |
| Sex difficulties | 39 | Change in church activities | 19 |
| Business readjustment | 39 | Change in social activities | 18 |
| Change in financial state | 38 | Mortgage or loan less than $10,000 | 17 |
| Death of close friend | 37 | Change in sleeping habits | 16 |
| Change to different line of work | 36 | Change in number of family get-togethers | 15 |
| Change in number of arguments with spouse | 35 | Change in eating habits | 15 |
| Mortgage over $10,000 | 31 | Vacation | 13 |
| Foreclosure of mortgage or loan | 30 | Minor violations of the law | 11 |
| Gain of new family member | 30 | | |
| Change in responsibilities at work | 29 | (Holmes & Holmes, 1970) | |

ber of LCUs, the severity of stress a person has experienced over a given period can be assessed.

As might be expected, aversive events carry the highest number of LCUs, but many of the less heavily weighted items are positive in nature. For example, outstanding personal achievement is assigned twenty-eight LCUs; a vacation receives thirteen LCUs. Within limits, it is not the type of life change that is of key importance. Rather, it is the adjustive demand that life change places on the individual. As these adjustive demands increase in number and severity, there is a corresponding increase in life stress. For example, for persons who have been exposed to stress events that add up to an LCU score of 200 to 299 within recent months, the risk of developing a major illness in the next two years was about 50 percent. For those individuals with scores of 300 or greater, the risk is much higher, approximating 80 percent.

# GENERAL PRINCIPLES UNDERLYING STRESS REACTIONS

Up to this point, we have discussed the types and sources of stress in our lives, the factors that influence the severity of stress, and a method for measuring the severity of stress. In the next chapter, we shall examine reactions to stress, both the physiological components of the stress response and the psychological reactions to stress. Before we turn to that examination, however, we shall consider some general principles underlying our reactions to stress.

Whether our reactions to stress are wise or foolish, appropriate or inappropriate, effective or ineffective, some general principles underlie our reactions to stress. Understanding the following five principles will help us gain a better perspective on our coping behavior. As we shall see, stress reactions can be holistic, economical, and automatic or planned. In addition, stress reactions can involve emotions and have both inner and outer determinants.

## Stress Reactions Are Holistic

The human organism functions as a holistic or integrated unit. Just as our biological functioning is organized to help us accomplish some task, so too does our psychological functioning follow an integrated pattern.

In dealing with stress, both biological and psychological patterns work to meet adjustive demands. Although severe stress can impair the smooth functioning of our physiological and psychological processes, under normal conditions the organism functions as an integrated unit in coping with stress.

## Stress Reactions Are Economical

Although our adjustive resources are impressive, they are limited. We tend to respond to stress in an economical manner and in ways that will require a minimal expenditure of our adjustive resources. In essence, we tend to be thrifty in going about the business of living. We rely on our usual coping responses unless we have clear evidence that our normal coping responses are ineffective. When established methods of coping become ineffective, we resort to alternative methods of coping. Unfortunately, these alternatives are often less economical and more demanding of the individual's resources than the usual coping responses.

## Stress Reactions May Be Automatic or Planned

Reactions to stress situations may be undertaken with conscious planning, with only partial awareness, or with no conscious involvement at all. On a biological level, defensive and repair processes take place automatically. Some psychological coping processes—such as crying—also take place automatically. Even if the individual is aware of what he or she is doing, such responses are not usually planned or consciously thought out.

These **automatic responses** can be extremely helpful in dealing with routine stress situations, since they free our attentions for other matters. In all but routine situations, the ability to adapt depends on conscious effort and the flexibility to choose an appropriate response.

**automatic responses: habits and other responses that do not require conscious attention or decision making**

## Stress Reactions Involve Emotions

The particular emotional states that accompany our reactions to stress may vary greatly. Three emotional patterns are of special significance here: anger, fear, and anxiety.

Frustrating conditions often elicit anger. Anger may be employed to remove the obstacle to one's goals. If the frustration and resulting anger continue for a long time, the individual may develop an enduring attitude of hostility. Both anger and hostility may not be obvious. But, when anger is intense and when inner controls are lowered by alcohol or other drugs, the result may be impulsive behavior of a destructive nature. For example, newspapers and television stations all too often report on cases of family violence in which one individual, angered by financial problems, divorce, and the like, lashes out at family members in violent ways.

Fear is another common emotional reaction to stress. When we feel danger, we attempt to withdraw or flee from the dangerous situation or individual. In the face of extreme danger, we may panic or freeze and become unable to function in an organized manner. Such behavior is commonly observed in fires and other disasters.

When our goals are blocked, we may express our frustration with angry words and angry gestures.

# Psychology in Action

## THE COLLEGE LIFE-STRESS SCALE

The College Life-Stress Scale was specifically designed for use by college students. As used by Marx, Garrity, and Bowers (1975), the college life-stress scale can predict illness in college students.

 For each of the items below, put a value of "0" if you have not experienced this event in the past twelve months, a "1" if the event occurred once in the past twelve months, a "2" for twice, a "3" for three times, and a "4" for four or more times in the past twelve months. After you complete the scale, multiply the number of occurrences of each item by the value assigned to that item. For example, item 38—major change in social activities—has a value of 43. If you experienced two major changes in social activities, you would multiply the value of 43 by 2.

 Finally, add the results of your multiplications. You can then compare your score with those reported by other college students and estimate your chances of incurring some illness or experiencing some health problem.

|  |  |  |
|---|---|---|
| 1. Entered college | 50 | _____ |
| 2. Married | 77 | _____ |
| 3. Trouble with your boss | 38 | _____ |
| 4. Held a job while attending school | 43 | _____ |
| 5. Experienced the death of a spouse | 87 | _____ |
| 6. Major change in sleeping habits | 34 | _____ |
| 7. Experienced the death of a close family member | 77 | _____ |
| 8. Major change in eating habits | 30 | _____ |
| 9. Change in or choice of major field of study | 41 | _____ |
| 10. Revision of personal habits | 45 | _____ |
| 11. Experienced the death of a close friend | 68 | _____ |
| 12. Found guilty of minor violations of the law | 22 | _____ |
| 13. Had an outstanding personal achievement | 40 | _____ |
| 14. Experienced pregnancy or fathered a pregnancy | 68 | _____ |
| 15. Major change in health or behavior of family member | 56 | _____ |
| 16. Had sexual difficulties | 58 | _____ |
| 17. Had trouble with in-laws | 42 | _____ |
| 18. Major change in number of family get-togethers | 26 | _____ |
| 19. Major change in financial state | 53 | _____ |
| 20. Gained a new family member | 50 | _____ |

21. Change in residence or living conditions                     42 _____

22. Major conflict or change in values                           51 _____

23. Major change in church activities                            36 _____

24. Marital reconciliation with your mate                        58 _____

25. Fired from work                                              62 _____

26. Were divorced                                                76 _____

27. Changed to a different line of work                          50 _____

28. Major change in number of arguments with spouse              50 _____

29. Major change in responsibilities at work                     47 _____

30. Had your spouse begin or cease work outside the home         41 _____

31. Major change in working hours or conditions                  42 _____

32. Marital separation from mate                                 74 _____

33. Major change in type and/or amount of recreation             37 _____

34. Major change in use of drugs                                 52 _____

35. Took on a mortgage or loan of less than $10,000              52 _____

36. Major personal injury or illness                             65 _____

37. Major change in use of alcohol                               46 _____

38. Major change in social activities                            43 _____

39. Major change in amount of participation in school activities 38 _____

40. Major change in amount of independence and responsibility    49 _____

41. Took a trip or a vacation                                    33 _____

42. Engaged to be married                                        54 _____

43. Changed to a new school                                      50 _____

44. Changed dating habits                                        41 _____

45. Trouble with school administration                           44 _____

46. Broke or had broken marital engagement or a steady relationship  60 _____

47. Major change in self-concept or self-awareness               57 _____

## Association between amount of life change and number of health problems

| Amount of Life Change | Number of Health Problems |
|---|---|
| High (total score greater than 1434) | 3.6 |
| Medium (total score between 348 and 1434) | 2.9 |
| Low (total score less than 348) | 2.2 |

Anxiety is similar to fear. Stress situations inducing anxiety are often difficult to cope with, since the precise nature of the threat is usually unclear to the individual yet the anxiety calls for some sort of protective response. Anxiety is probably the most common response to severe stress.

All these emotions may be aroused singly or in various combinations, and these negative emotions can also be intermeshed with more positive ones, such as love. The specific emotions that occur, however, are heavily influenced by past learning.

## Stress Reactions Have Inner and Outer Determinants

As we have seen, behavior is determined by both personal and environmental factors. Sometimes personal or inner determinants, such as a person's motives, play the dominant role. At other times external factors, such as social demands, are of primary importance. But adjustive action reflects the interplay of both inner and outer determinants. Inner determinants of an individual's reactions to stress include his or her frame of reference, motive patterns, competencies, emotions, stress tolerance, and momentary physiological and psychological conditions. Environmental determinants of stress reactions include the nature of the physical environment, social demands and reinforcements, interpersonal and group resources, momentary events, and the general life situation of the individual.

## POSITIVE STRESS

As we suggested earlier, not all stress is harmful or negative. Some stress can be useful and beneficial. These positive forms of stress or eustress can take a variety of forms. For example, active participation in sports or exercise programs, vacations and trips, and mastery of new academic or practical skills can be sources of positive stress. Any demand can be a source of eustress as long as we approach it with a sense of zest and anticipation.

Naturally, eustress, like distress, is a personal matter. Getting an opportunity to meet new people can be eustress to some individuals and distress to others. Learning about oneself can be eustress or distress, depending on the personal characteristics of the individual involved.

Positive stress is not necessarily an unmitigated blessing. Too much positive stress can place significant adjustive demands upon the individual and lead to stress reactions (Evans & Bartolomé, 1980). As the Social Readjustment Rating Scale indicates, positive events such as outstanding personal achievement can place an adjustive demand upon the individual. When an individual experiences stress, whether eustress or distress, that exceeds the individual's capability for handling the stress, we speak of *overstress* or *hyperstress*. Clearly, overstress should be avoided.

On the other hand, too little adaptive demands can lead to *understress (hypostress)*. The individual who is not sufficiently challenged in life may suffer from a lack of self-realization and boredom (Selye, 1980). As Selye (1980) has put it, "Our goal should be to strike a balance between the equally destructive forces of hypo- and hyperstress, to find as much eustress as possible, and to minimize distress" (p. 141).

## SUMMARY

1.  Stress is a multidimensional phenomenon. Stress can be some aspect of the environment (stressors). Stress can involve our perceptions of threat and our physiological and psychological responses to stressors. All stress, however, involves demands for change and adaptation.

2.  In general, there are three sources of stress: frustration, conflict, and pressure. Frustration can be induced by delays, lack of resources, losses, failure, and loneliness and meaninglessness. Conflict may be of four types: approach-approach, avoidance-avoidance, approach-avoidance, and double approach-avoidance. Pressure can come from a number of sources, including competition, change, and interpersonal relationships.

3.  The factors that influence the severity of stress are similarly complex. The characteristics of the adjustive demand include intensity, number, duration, predictability, and imminence of the stress. The characteristics of the individual include Type A vs. Type B behavior, prior experience, stress tolerance, and control. Resources and supports available to the individual—including social support and material and financial support—are a third part of the formula that helps determine the severity of a response to stress.

4.  The use of rating scales such as the Social Readjustment Rating Scale has made the task of determining stress levels increasingly reliable and valid.

5.  Our reactions to stress follow some general principles. Stress reactions are holistic and economical. Stress reactions can be automatic or planned. They involve emotions, and they can have both inner and outer determinants.

6.  Some stress can be positive in nature. However, too much positive stress can tax the adaptive resources of the individual as can too much negative stress. Similarly, a lack of stress can lead to a failure to achieve self-realization.

# Chapter 8

# Reactions to Stress

All behavior is an attempt to meet the adjustive demands confronting us or which we perceive as confronting us. How we respond depends upon a host of factors, including the nature of the demand, the characteristics of the environment, and our frame of reference, our motives, and our competencies. Often we will meet the adjustive demand without undue difficulty. In other cases, we may be only partially successful, and in still other cases, the cost of the adjustive demand may be our physical and mental well-being. Whatever the outcome, coping with stress is a never-ending venture for each of us.

In this chapter we shall discuss our reactions to stress, both the physiological components of the stress response and the three general types of psychological reactions to stress. We shall also consider the costs of stress, its effects on our adaptive resources and its role in physical and mental disorders.

## PHYSIOLOGICAL COMPONENTS OF THE STRESS RESPONSE

**General Adaptation Syndrome: coordinated series of physical reactions in response to physical and psychological stress**

Anyone who has ever felt his or her face burn with embarrassment or anger knows that psychological states can affect the body. Although the ways in which stress can affect physical functioning are many and varied, there appears to be a model that summarizes the major effects of stress on the body. This model, called the **General Adaptation Syndrome,** was developed by Canadian physiologist Hans Selye (pronounced sell-yee) to identify the physical reactions a living organism goes through in coping with both physical and psychological stress (Selye, 1976). According to the General Adaptation Syndrome (GAS), stress produced by an infection is not substantially different from stress produced by an embarrassing failure. That is, the physical effects of stress are similar, even though the sources of the stress may differ.

The GAS is divided into three major stages: alarm and mobilization, resistance, and exhaustion and decompensation. Let us examine each in more detail.

### Alarm and Mobilization

**alarm and mobilization: first stage of the General Adaptation Syndrome, characterized by the mobilization of defenses to cope with stress**

During the *shock phase* of **alarm and mobilization,** the body begins to organize itself to cope with the adjustive demand. As Selye showed, an organism faced with an infection or maximal physical effort responds with a coordinated series of physical changes. Signals from the brain step up some body functions, quickening the heart rate and respiration and tensing muscles. Other parts of the nervous system slow down other body functions, so that energy can be concentrated on meeting the adjustive demand.

These changes also occur when the adjustive demand is psychological in nature. Faced with the demand to make a public speech, many people experience the pounding heart, dry mouth, and sweaty palms that characterize the initial stages of the GAS. Viewed from a physiological perspective, we may say that these changes are produced through the activation of the **sympathetic** branch of the **nervous system.** This portion of the nervous system increases or arouses a number of physical functions when an individual is under stress.

The *countershock phase* of the alarm reaction is marked by the mobilization of defenses (Selye, 1980). Physiologically, the adrenal glands enlarge and produce a variety of hormones. Psychologically, the defense mechanisms are brought into play.

**sympathetic nervous system: portion of the nervous system primarily responsible for physiological arousal**

## Resistance

If the stress situation continues, the individual attempts to find some way of dealing with it and resisting psychological or physical disorganization. In the case of infection, the individual develops a fever. Through the fever, the body attempts to fight off the infection by making the internal biological environment of the individual less hospitable to the germ or virus.

A psychological demand can also produce physical effects in the **resistance** stage. Very often, changes in the internal organs and workings of the body appear. Hypertension, ulcers, asthma, hives, and other psychophysiological ("psychosomatic") reactions may develop during this stage. These **diseases of adaptation,** as Selye has called them, are quite common and may be clearly related to stress.

**resistance: second stage of the General Adaptation Syndrome in which physical and psychological resources are used to combat continued stress**

People may function at this stage for months and years at a time. However, the physical cost may become increasingly greater. The woman who develops an ulcer may find the ulcer becoming progressively more severe, more painful, and more dangerous to her general health. The man with hypertension may find that his disease will continue until he takes the necessary steps to cope more effectively with the stress.

**diseases of adaptation: disorders that occur as a result of inadequately managed stress**

Sometimes the diseases of adaptation are more subtle and may not even be recognized as physical responses to stress. Some sexual dysfunctions that are reactions to adjustive demands may develop in both sexes. Changes in appetite or minor but annoying difficulties in sleep can also be responses to stress. In essence, the troublesome reactions of the alarm phase are brought under control—but at the cost of decreased resistance to other stimuli.

## Disorganization and Exhaustion

disorganization and exhaustion: last stage of the General Adaptation Syndrome, characterized by the use of extreme measures to cope with stress

In the face of continued exposure to severe stress, coping methods used during the stage of resistance may give way. At this point, the person must use more extreme measures to cope with the stress. These new measures greatly tax the resources of the individual. Severe and potentially dangerous changes accompany this last phase of **disorganization and exhaustion.** For example, the capsized sailor who must swim to stay alive may find him- or herself becoming delirious. Physical effort becomes immensely difficult, and only the barest attempts to breathe and stay alive become possible. At this point, quick intervention is imperative. Otherwise, the individual's condition may deteriorate further, and he or she may die.

## PSYCHOLOGICAL REACTIONS TO STRESS

Three general types of psychological reactions to stress can be delineated: *(1) "built-in"* coping and damage-repair mechanisms; *(2) learned task-oriented* reactions aimed primarily at coping directly with the stress situation; and *(3) defense-oriented* reactions aimed primarily at protecting the self from devaluation and disorganization.

An example of a "built-in" coping and damage-repair mechanism is crying in response to some hurtful stress situation. An example of a task-oriented reaction would be improving one's study habits in response to failing grades in college. An example of a defense-oriented reaction would be unjustly blaming one's partner for a disappointing love relationship. Many stress reactions involve components of two or even all three of these patterns, but it is usually possible to characterize an action as principally one or the other. Let us now turn to the first of the psychological reactions to stress, "built-in" coping and damage-repair mechanisms.

## "Built-in" Coping and Damage-Repair Mechanisms

built-in coping mechanisms: predominately unlearned patterns such as crying and discussion that an individual uses in reaction to stress

Certain coping reactions appear to come into operation automatically rather than as a result of deliberate choice. These **built-in coping mechanisms** are basically constructive in alleviating tension and anxiety, repairing psychological damage, and restoring psychological equilibrium.

# **Insight**

## ARE THERE "BUILT-IN" PATTERNS FOR COPING WITH TRAGEDY?

It appears that there may be "built-in" mechanisms for coping with severe personal loss that follow much the same pattern regardless of the specific nature of the loss.

In a pioneering study, Cholden (1954) delineated three typical stages in the coping pattern of newly blinded persons: (1) a period of shock; (2) a period of depression or mourning involving feelings of dejection, self-pity, and hopelessness; and (3) a period of readjustment involving changes in life plans designed to salvage what the person could from the tragedy.

In a more recent study, Parkes (1972) found a similar pattern in the reactions of two groups of subjects: amputees and

women suffering bereavement. The first stage was characterized by feelings of shock and numbness accompanied by a strong tendency to deny or screen out the reality of what had happened. This was followed by a second stage involving anxiety, depression, and the so-called pangs of grief. Finally, stage three emerged in which the persons gave up hope of recovering what they had lost and began to make the necessary readjustment to life.

These patterns appear to operate with a minimum of learning, to be characteristic of most people undergoing such personal tragedies, and to function as "damage-repair" mechanisms.

Among the more common and important of these mechanisms are the following:

1. *Crying.* A built-in mechanism which is useful in relieving emotional tension and pain is crying. This reaction is commonly seen in the behavior of children who have been frustrated or hurt. And although we are often taught that "grown-ups don't cry," crying is not uncommon among adults and may serve as an important means of relieving tension and hurt and restoring inner equilibrium. For example, crying appears to be an important part of the "grief work" that a person goes through in recovering from the loss of a loved one.

2. *Talking about it.* Another built-in way of relieving emotional tension is by discussing or talking out a problem. This mechanism is so simple and so widely used that we often overlook its great reparative value.

All of us have probably encountered individuals who enjoyed telling us in gory detail about their accidents, operations, or other traumatic experiences. Similarly, people who have survived catastrophes—such as major fires, floods, and earthquakes often show a compulsive need to tell others about their experiences. Apparently, repetitive talking about the experience helps the person to become desensitized to it and to cope more readily with it. Talking it out—gaining relief through putting one's feelings into words and gaining an understanding of one's situation—is also an important part of most psychotherapy.

3. *Humor.* Trying to view one's problems with a sense of humor and laughing off setbacks and hurts are widely used means of reducing tension. This mech-

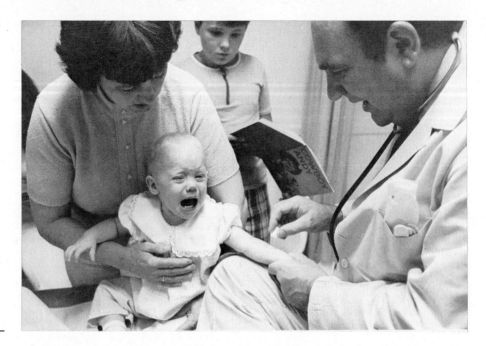

Crying is a common built-in coping mechanism that we begin to use very early in life to cope with many types of stress, whether it is the fear of unfamiliar surroundings or the pain of a vaccination.

anism seems to be directed toward keeping things in perspective, accepting inevitable hurts and setbacks, and not taking oneself too seriously. Humor is also used to reduce the tension associated with resenting others. Such humor tends to be hostile in nature, as in stories or jokes that put people down.

4. *Reflection.* After an emotional hurt, some people want to get away, to retreat and to think things through. A thoughtful review of the stressful situation helps individuals determine the sources of the stress, evaluate their responses to the stress, and develop different ways of dealing with future stresses. Reflection can also be used by individuals to evaluate the actual significance of the event and to review their assumptions about themselves and the stressful situation.

5. *Sleep and dreams.* Many people cannot sleep when they are under stress. However, when sleep is possible, it does appear to have a healing function. People who have undergone highly traumatic events—such as combat experiences—often have repeated nightmares in which they reenact their experiences and apparently are eventually desensitized to them. Here nightmares appear to serve somewhat the same function as repetitive talking in desensitizing individuals to a traumatic event and helping them understand and accept their experiences.

Sleep may also be used as a method of coping with less stressful situations. For example, researchers Mischel and Ebbesen (1970) placed children in a situation in which the children were required to wait for an adult's return before they could receive a reward. Although the rewards were tempting, some of these preschool children dealt with the frustration by attempting to fall asleep and succeeding. Sleep and dreams may indeed be a "built-in" response to stress.

# Task-Oriented Responses

**Task-oriented responses** are aimed at realistically coping with the adjustive demand. They tend to be based on an objective appraisal of the stress situation and on a conscious, rational, and constructive course of action.

**task-oriented response:** realistic approach to coping with stress, characterized by conscious, rational, and constructive courses of action

The task-oriented response may involve making changes in one's self or one's surroundings or both. The response may be overt—as in improving one's study habits—or covert—as in lowering one's level of aspirations or changing one's attitudes. And the responses may involve attacking the problem, withdrawing from it, or finding a workable compromise.

Although we shall consider attack, withdrawal, and compromise reactions separately, a given response may embody components of all these types. A student who is going to college to prepare for a career (attack) may drop courses which he or she finds too difficult (withdrawal) and take fewer units in order to participate in campus activities (compromise). These reactions are not "all-or-nothing" patterns but rather convenient categories for ordering our discussion.

**Attack.**  A hero in a western who sees the "bad guy" start to draw his gun may handle the situation by beating him to the draw. This is a simple attack response and it is the prototype of many of our responses. We size up the requirements of the situation and try to meet them by direct action.

Attack responses can usually take somewhat different forms, depending on the nature of the stress, the situation, and the individual's resources. For example, we may respond to stress through aggression. If we believe that we have a good case for getting a C raised to a B in an important course but meet with a blunt refusal from the instructor, we are likely to experience anger. A possible response is, of course, physical assault on the instructor, but physical attack would more likely aggravate than resolve our problem. Consequently we usually resort to more subtle and effective action responses, such as going beyond the instructor to the department head, dean, or ombudsman.

We can also resist pressures that are brought upon us. This resistance can take many forms: A child becomes defiant and rebellious in the presence of excessive pressure. Adults become inattentive, dawdling, helpless, and deliberately underachieving as a means to protect themselves from excessive demands and overloading. Resistance can be obvious, as when an individual responds with an emphatic "No!" to an unreasonable request. Resistance can also be passive, as in the early days of the civil rights movement.

Attack-oriented responses need not involve aggression or resistance. Long-range planning, increased effort, and restructuring one's view of the situation are a few of the ways in which people can deal with stress. Properly focused attack responses are among the most effective methods for dealing with stress.

**Withdrawal.**  Refusing to place oneself in a stressful situation is a second task-oriented response to stress. We can escape, vacillate, or avoid in our attempts to deal with stress.

If our goals are blocked, we may respond in an angry or aggressive fashion by lashing out at the person or object we perceive as the obstacle preventing us from reaching our goal.

**escape:** getting away from or avoiding a stressful situation

Sometimes, **escape** may be the best way to deal with a stressful situation. For example, we may handle a boring and unrewarding job by "escaping" to a more suitable one. Similarly, students sometimes complete most of the requirements for their college major—such as teaching—only to realize that this career field is not for them. One task-oriented response here may be to salvage what one can from the situation and switch to another major. Another task-oriented response may involve leaving school and taking a job that will provide the time and distance needed to make a rational decision.

**vacillation:** wavering or hesitating in making a choice

Another method of refusing involvement in a stressful situation involves **vacillation.** People in stressful situations tend to vacillate and to be indecisive in an effort to avoid making choices. For example, a woman who is trying to choose between two eligible suitors, one exciting and fun to be with but sometimes irresponsible and immature and the other steady and dependable but a bit dull, may find herself deciding on first one and then the other. The more equally matched the alternatives, the harder the decision. And when the choice involves serious consequences, we may try to delay and vacillate indefinitely. These delays allow us to keep our options open until we are better prepared to make a decision. Sooner or later, however, we will have to choose or resign ourselves to letting time and chance work for us.

**avoidance:** keeping away from stressful situations

We may also try to **avoid** many situations that we view as potentially dangerous or threatening. Such behavior is shown by students who avoid taking courses that they think may be too difficult or by business executives who refuse promotions because they prefer to avoid the increased responsibilities and pressures. And of course, most of us avoid emotional involvement in situations where we are afraid of being hurt.

Once again, we see that we are not passive recipients of stress. Often we can exercise considerable control over the nature of situations to which we are exposed and thus keep stress from becoming excessive.

**Compromise.**   Most task-oriented behavior does not involve direct action or withdrawal. Rather, it involves a compromise. While we may change what we can in the stress situation and in ourselves, we often have to live with what cannot be changed. This means we **compromise.**

One way in which compromise works is through **substitution.** In a situation of sustained or seemingly inescapable frustration, we often tend to reduce the stress by accepting whatever goals and satisfactions we can get. For example, a man who is consistently turned down by the woman he really wants to date may finally take out someone else. Or, a woman may compromise her dream image of a husband and marry the man who is actually available.

In more severe stress situations, compromises may be more extreme. For example, a prisoner of war may collaborate with hated captors in an effort to ensure better treatment or even survival. In a somewhat less dramatic case, the sexually frustrated person may find some satisfaction in erotic magazines or sexual fantasies.

A second method of compromise is **accommodation,** in which we settle for part of what we wanted. And since the resolution of so many of our problems is dependent on the action of others, we often need *mutual accommodation,* in which both parties give a little and get a little.

Negotiating, bargaining, and making concessions are compromise behaviors in which the participants accommodate their requirements and get part but not all of what they wanted. We see such patterns in labor-management disputes, student-faculty conflicts, and relationships between nations, as well as in our relationships with friends and family members. If a compromise reaction succeeds in meeting the essential requirements of a situation, the stress problem is satisfactorily resolved and a person's energies can be devoted to other matters.

**compromise: making concessions to help cope with stress**

**substitution: acceptance of alternative goals or satisfactions in place of those originally sought after or desired**

**accommodation: settlement for a portion of that which was originally desired**

**Sometimes compromise is the most successful way to deal with the stresses of an interpersonal relationship. The compromise may involve mutual accommodation or give-and-take on the part of both parties in the relationship.**

Although a task-oriented approach usually has the best chance of solving our problems, even a task-oriented approach can fail. If our choices are based on faulty values, for example, we may meet the immediate demand, only to lay the basis for more serious problems later. If, because of limited knowledge, we choose an unsuitable course of action, it may even compound our problem. And even when we choose well and act with skill, factors beyond our control may tip the balance in preventing our action from solving the problem. As Robert Burns put it so succinctly:

*The best-laid schemes o' mice an' men,*
  *Gang aft agley,*
*An' lea'e us nought but grief an' pain,*
  *For promis'd joy!*

## Defense-Oriented Responses

In **defense-oriented responses** to stress, the individual concentrates on self-protection through psychological means rather than relying on some "built-in" mechanism or engaging in some task-oriented behavior. Our focus here will be on the *ego-defense mechanisms*. These mechanisms were first formulated by psychoanalytic theory in an attempt to understand both normal and abnormal behavior. All of us make some use of such defenses. They are essential for softening failure, reducing cognitive dissonance, alleviating anxiety, repairing emotional hurt, and maintaining our feelings of adequacy and worth. They are normal coping mechanisms even though they involve some measure of self-deception and reality distortion. They become abnormal when they are used to such a degree that they impair an individual's ability to meet life's problems. These mechanisms are heavily dependent on learning, but they tend to operate on habitual and unconscious levels.

The ego-defense mechanisms we discuss below merit special attention. To aid your understanding of these mechanisms, a chart appears on page 211.

**Repression.**  **Repression** is a defense mechanism in which threatening or painful thoughts and desires are excluded from consciousness. Although the material that is repressed is denied admission to awareness, it is not really forgotten. Repression is the most important ego-defense mechanism, and many of the defense-oriented responses contain elements of repression.

Repression is illustrated in a dramatic way by the soldier who has undergone an extremely traumatic combat episode and is brought to an aid station suffering from amnesia. Although he may be nervous and depressed and show other signs of his ordeal, the intolerable combat situation is screened from consciousness—thus protecting him from overwhelming stress. The repressed experience is not forgotten, however, and may be brought into conscious awareness through psychotherapy or by means of hypnosis or a drug (like sodium pentothal). Such repressive defenses operate on a temporary basis until time and other conditions

# Insight

**SUMMARY CHART OF THE DEFENSE MECHANISMS**

| | |
|---|---|
| **Repression** | ● Preventing painful or dangerous thoughts from entering consciousness |
| **Denial** | ● Refusing to perceive or face unpleasant reality |
| **Fantasy** | ● Gratifying frustrated desires by imaginary achievements |
| **Rationalization** | ● Attempting to prove that one's behavior is "rational" and justifiable and thus worthy of the approval of oneself and others |
| **Projection** | ● Placing blame for difficulties upon others or attributing one's own unethical desires to others |
| **Displacement** | ● Discharging pent-up feelings, usually of hostility, on objects less dangerous than those which initially aroused the emotions |
| **Regression** | ● Retreating to earlier developmental level involving less mature responses and usually a lower level of aspiration |
| **Compensation** | ● Covering up weakness by emphasizing some desirable trait or making up for frustration in one area by overgratification in another |
| **Acting out** | ● Reducing the anxiety aroused by forbidden desires by permitting their expression |
| **Undoing** | ● Counteracting "immoral" desires or acts by some form of atonement |
| **Emotional insulation** | ● Reducing ego involvement and withdrawing into passivity to protect oneself from hurt |
| **Intellectualization** | ● Suppressing the emotional aspect of hurtful situations or separating incompatible attitudes by logic-tight compartments |

have desensitized him to the point where he can recall the event without serious psychological disorganization. In a less dramatic situation, sexual desires that a person considers immoral may be blocked from consciousness by means of repression.

Repression is an important means of helping the individual cope with the potentially disorganizing effects of painful experiences and desires regarded as dangerous and unacceptable. In fact, in varying degrees repression enters into most other defensive patterns. However, repression may screen out stressful experiences that could better be met by realistically facing and working through the situation. We cannot solve and learn from a problem that we do not see.

**Denial.** A primitive defense mechanism for restricting experience involves the **denial** of realities. We evade many disagreeable realities simply by ignoring or refusing to acknowledge them. Very few of us, for example, accept the full inevitability of death. Even if we act as if we were quite resigned to the idea, the

**denial:** ego-defense mechanism in which the individual protects the self from unpleasant aspects of reality by refusing to perceive them

vision of our own death is usually mercifully vague. We turn away from unpleasant sights, refuse to discuss unpleasant topics, ignore or deny criticism, and refuse to face many of our real problems.

Denial appears to protect the individual from the full impact of a traumatic experience. In a study of stroke, lung cancer, and heart disease patients, Levine and Zigler (1975) found that denial was commonly used as a means of coping with the threat of impaired functioning, disability, and, in some cases, impending death.

By ignoring or denying unpleasant reality, we protect ourselves from a great deal of stress, but we may fail to take cognizance of many realities that we need to know about for effective adjustment.

**Fantasy.**   Besides screening out unpleasant aspects of reality, we may use **fantasy** to picture things as we would like them to be.

Often, we fantasize being the "conquering hero" or the "suffering hero." In the first, people may picture themselves as great athletes, renowned soldiers, persons of immense wealth, or other remarkable figures who perform incredible feats and win the admiration and respect of all. James Thurber used this theme in his popular "Secret Life of Walter Mitty."

Another common fantasy pattern is the "suffering hero" type. Here people may imagine that they are suffering from some horrible affliction or handicap. When the rest of the world finds out about their difficulties, they will be accorded the respect due them. According to this fantasy, the suffering individuals have actually demonstrated remarkable courage and are highly successful, considering the handicaps under which they have labored. In short, they merit the sympathy and admiration of all.

**Rationalization.**   **Rationalization** is a defense mechanism in which we justify our behavior by imputing logical and admirable or at least acceptable motives to it. If we decide to go to a movie instead of studying for an examination, we can usually think up various reasons to justify our decision: we only live once; everyone needs a change of pace; the relaxation will help us think more clearly. Often people try to justify cheating by pointing out that others cheat, that there is no virtue in being a sucker, and that in real life society doesn't ask too many questions as long as you are successful. By rationalizing, we can usually justify almost everything we have done, are doing, or propose to do and hence can alleviate the devaluating effects of failure, guilt, and irrational behavior.

Rationalization is also used to soften the disappointment of thwarted desires. A common example of such rationalization is the "sour grapes" reaction. In Aesop's fable, the fox was unable to reach a cluster of delicious grapes and decided he did not want them anyway because they were probably sour. Similarly, if we are turned down for a date, we may decide the evening probably would have been dull anyway. The opposite of the sour grapes type of rationalization is the "sweet lemon" mechanism—not only is what we cannot have not worth having, but what we do have is remarkably satisfactory. It is better to be poor than rich because money is the root of all evil.

---

**fantasy:** ego-defense mechanism in which the individual escapes from the world of reality and gratifies his or her desires in fantasy achievements

**rationalization:** ego-defense mechanism in which the individual thinks up "good" reasons to justify what he or she has done, is doing, or is going to do

Rationalization is a very complex mechanism that is often difficult to detect, since it frequently contains some elements of truth. However, we may suspect that we are rationalizing when we: *(a)* hunt for reasons to justify our behavior or beliefs, *(b)* cannot recognize inconsistencies that others see, and *(c)* become emotional when others question our behavior.

**Projection.**   **Projection** is a mechanism in which we blame others for our mistakes and shortcomings or ascribe to others our unacceptable motivations. A husband who feels guilty about his extramarital affairs may place the blame on his unsympathetic wife or on "women who lead him on." The boy punished for fighting protests, "He hit me first—it was his fault." If an individual loses a job because of difficulties with other employees, he or she is quick to project the blame onto their former colleagues who "have it in for them." Similarly, an individual may experience sexual desires which are viewed as immoral and hence highly threatening and self-devaluating. As a consequence, these desires are projected onto others, who now become the offenders, while the individual remains conveniently "pure." Thus, projection serves as a means of defending the worth and adequacy of the self (Sherwood, 1981, 1982).

projection: ego-defense mechanism in which the individual attributes his or her unacceptable desires and impulses to others

**Displacement.**   **Displacement** discharges hostility toward a person or object other than the one actually eliciting it. A common subject for cartoons is that of the meek employee who has been mistreated by a domineering supervisor. Instead of expressing any hostility toward the supervisor—which would be dangerous—our hero goes home and snaps at his wife because dinner is a few minutes late. She, in turn, takes out her hostility on their young son, who displaces *his* anger by kicking the family dog.

displacement: ego-defense mechanism for redirection of emotions to objects less dangerous than those which initially aroused the emotions

Displaced hostility may also take other forms. One is blaming problems on a scapegoat who cannot fight back. Among the ancient Israelites, the priest symbolically heaped all the sins of the people upon an unblemished goat—the scapegoat. Then the goat was driven into the wilderness to die. In Hitler's Germany, the Jews were blamed for the country's ills, and pent-up feelings of frustration and hostility were discharged against this group.

In its milder forms, displacement may be of adjustive value as it provides a means of discharging dangerous emotions without risking retaliation. However, the cost of using this defense mechanism may be quite high: The man in the cartoon may preserve a good relationship with his boss, but his displaced emotions may threaten the peace and harmony of his marriage. In the long run, it is usually healthier and less painful to face and work through these stressful situations than to avoid them through displacement.

**Regression.**   In **regression,** one uses reaction patterns that have been long outgrown. For example, a five-year-old who feels threatened by the amount of attention shown to a new baby may revert to bed-wetting and other infantile behavior that once earned parental attention.

regression: ego-defense mechanism in which the individual retreats to the use of less mature responses in attempting to cope with stress and maintain self-integration

It is not surprising that, in the face of severe stress or new challenges, an individual may retreat to a less mature level of adjustment. We might expect something like regression to occur just because newly learned reactions frequently fail to bring satisfaction. In looking for other, more successful methods of adaptation, it is only natural to try out discarded patterns that had previously brought satisfaction.

**compensation: ego-defense mechanism in which an undesirable trait is covered up by emphasizing a desirable trait**

**Compensation.**   **Compensation** is used to defend the individual against feelings of inadequacy by disguising or counterbalancing a weak or undesirable trait by emphasizing or developing a desirable one. Compensatory reactions take many forms and may have considerable adjustive value. For example, a physically unattractive youth may develop a pleasing demeanor and become an interesting conversationalist. As a consequence, physical unattractiveness is no longer a major obstacle to social acceptance and success.

Unfortunately, not all compensatory reactions are desirable or useful. Children who feel insecure may show off to get more attention and increase their status. The boy who feels inferior and unpopular may become the local bully. The person who feels unloved and frustrated may eat too much. Some people build themselves up by bragging about their own accomplishments; others do it by criticism or innuendos in an attempt to cut other people down.

In general, compensatory reactions are ineffective because the activities engaged in are aimed not at a positive goal but at balancing a deficit. They tend not to be constructive—as in the case of eating too much as a reaction to frustration. Or they incur social disapproval—as in showing off—which only increases the person's sense of failure and inferiority.

**acting out: ego-defense mechanism in which the individual reduces anxiety, hostility, or other unpleasant emotions by permitting their expression in overt behavior**

**Acting out.**   One may reduce the tension and anxiety associated with forbidden desires by **acting out** and by permitting their expression. Instead of trying to deny, repress, change, or hold in check some strong desires, one simply engages in the behavior. For example, a person who has nursed a long history of grievances may finally lash out verbally or physically and may damage property associated with those held responsible for his or her frustration. Much acting out is to some degree antisocial or violent.

Under most circumstances acting out is not a good method for dealing with stress. Most people are deterred not only by their values but also by the likelihood of social disapproval or perhaps punishment. Although acting out may reduce emotional tension, it does not usually cope with the adjustive demand and often makes matters much worse.

**undoing: ego-defense mechanism in which the individual performs activities designed to atone for misdeeds**

**Undoing.**   **Undoing** is a mechanism designed to negate or atone for some disapproved thought, impulse, or act. It is as if the individual has spelled a word wrong and wants to use an eraser to clear the paper and start over. Apologizing for wrongs against others, penance, repentance, and undergoing punishment are some of the common forms that undoing may take. For example, an unfaithful husband may have a sudden impulse to bring his wife flowers; an unethical business executive may give unusually large sums of money to some charitable organization; and the rejecting mother may shower her child with material indications of her alleged care and concern.

PUBLIC SCHOOL 37

Destruction or deface-ment of property may be one method of ex-pressing pent-up feel-ings of anger and frus-tration. Such vandalism is often seen as an ex-ample of the defense mechanism of acting out.

Since undoing promotes ethical human relations and helps us maintain our feelings of self-esteem and worth, it is one of our most valuable defense mech-anisms. However, undoing does not always enable people to escape from the consequences of their actions. Even though an individual apologizes for lying to a friend on an important matter and attempts to atone for it, their relationship may never be the same again.

**Emotional insulation.** In **emotional insulation,** we reduce our degree of emotional involvement in potentially hurtful situations. Since we all undergo many disappointments in life, we usually learn to keep our hopes and anticipations within bounds until a hoped-for event actually occurs. We are careful to avoid premature celebrations or to let our hopes get too high. The student who is looking forward to a date with a very attractive man may not let herself get too emotionally involved for fear that something will go wrong or that he may not like her.

Under conditions of long-continued frustration, as in chronic unemploy-

emotional insulation: ego-defense mechanism in which the individual reduces his or her emo-tional involvement in potentially hurtful situ-ations

Through the defense mechanism of emotional insulation, a person attempts to defend him- or herself against pain and hurt by withdrawing into a protective shell.

ment, many people lose hope and become resigned and apathetic. Such individuals protect themselves from the hurt of sustained frustration by further reducing their involvement—they no longer care and hence deprive the stress situation of much of its power to hurt them.

Up to a point, emotional insulation is an important mechanism for defending ourselves from both unnecessary and unavoidable hurt. But life involves calculated risks, and most of us are willing to take our chances on active participation. Although we may get badly hurt on occasion, we have the resilience to recover and try again. Emotional insulation provides a protective shell that prevents a repetition of previous pain, but in so doing it also prevents the individual's healthy, vigorous participation in living.

**Intellectualization.** In **intellectualization,** the anxiety and emotions that would normally accompany a stressful event are avoided by treating the situation as an abstract problem to be analyzed. Grief over the death of one's mother may be softened by pointing out that she lived to be over seventy years of age. Failures and disappointments are softened by pointing out that "it could have been worse."

intellectualization: ego-defense mechanism by which the individual achieves some measure of insulation from emotional hurt by treating the situation as an abstract problem to be analyzed

Intellectualization may be utilized under extremely stressful conditions as well as in dealing with the milder stresses of everyday life. Bluestone and McGahee (1962) found that this defense was often used by prisoners awaiting execution. "So they'll kill me; and that's that'—this said with a shrug of the shoulders suggests that the affect appropriate to the thought has somehow been isolated." Or they may feel as though it is all happening to someone else, and they are watching impersonally from a distance.

In the preceding discussion we have examined the major defense mechanisms that we use in coping with the stresses of life. Although we have dealt with them singly, they are often used in combination. They may also be combined with more task-oriented behavior. Because they are essential for softening failure, alleviating tension and anxiety, and protecting one's feelings of adequacy and worth, we consider them to be normal adjustive reactions unless they seriously interfere with the effective resolution of stress situations.

## THE COST OF STRESS

Stress is a fact of life. Sometimes, we choose events that bring us stress. For example, no one forces us to become mountain climbers, race drivers, or hang gliders. Many other stresses, however, are so typical of our society that we tend to take them for granted. Most of us are accustomed to competing for grades in school, and later, for jobs and promotions. We can never be completely free of stress; to say "no" to all stress is equivalent to saying "no" to life. As Hans Selye (1980) puts it, "Complete freedom from stress is death" (p. 128).

Mental health and effective adjustment are largely the result of learning to cope effectively with stress, rather than avoiding it. Nonetheless, coping with stress involves some costs to the individual, usually in the form of reduction of adaptive resources or in its effects on physical and mental health.

### Reduction in Adaptive Resources

Severe stress may lead to a reduction in adaptive resources in three ways: a lowering of adaptive efficiency, a lowering of resistance to other stresses, and wear and tear on the entire system.

1. *Lowering of adaptive efficiency.* On a physiological level severe stress may result in alterations which impair the body's ability to function efficiently. We may become fatigued more easily. We may catch colds and the flu more readily.

Our adaptive efficiency may also be impaired by the emotions that typically accompany severe stress. For example, acute stage fright may disrupt the performance of a public speaker. Test anxiety may lead to poor performance despite adequate preparation. In a sudden catastrophe, intense fear may cause an individual to panic or freeze. As stress increases beyond a moderate level, the efficiency of problem solving and decision making tends to progressively decrease.

2. *Lowering of resistance to other stresses.* In using its resources to meet one severe stress, the organism may suffer a lowering of tolerance for other

stresses. Hans Selye (1976) has found that mice exposed to extremes of cold developed increased resistance to the cold but became unusually sensitive to X rays. Similarly, soldiers who develop resistance to combat may show a lowering of tolerance to other stresses, such as bad news from home. A woman who has learned to handle her difficult boss tactfully all day may find that she has no patience left for trying to cope with her thirteen-year-old son.

It appears that the coping resources of the system are limited; if they are already mobilized to capacity against one stress, they are not available for coping with others. This helps to explain how sustained psychological stress can lower biological resistance to disease, and how sustained bodily disease can lower resistance to psychological stress.

3. *Wear and tear on the system.* Probably many people believe that even after a very stressful experience, rest can completely restore them. In his pioneering studies of stress, Selye (1976) found evidence that this is a false assumption:

*Experiments on animals have clearly shown that each exposure leaves an indelible scar, in that it uses up reserves of adaptability which cannot be replaced. It is true that immediately after some harassing experience, rest can restore us almost to the original level of fitness by eliminating acute fatigue. But the emphasis is on* almost. *Since we constantly go through periods of stress and rest during life, just a little deficit of adaptation energy every day adds up—it adds up to what we call aging. (p. 429)*

Recent research on the role of stress in cardiovascular and other degenerative diseases has confirmed these earlier findings. Thus, stress can be expensive in terms of both short-term and long-term reduction of adaptive resources.

## Role of Stress in Physical and Mental Disorders

As we noted, early studies of stress were handicapped by the lack of a reliable method for measuring stress in everyday life. With the development of the Social Readjustment Rating Scale by Holmes and Rahe (1967), as well as the development of more recent scales to measure life stress (e.g., Fairbank & Hough, 1979), research studies have implicated stress in the risk of a person becoming physically and mentally ill.

A number of research studies have shown the role of stress in peptic ulcers, high blood pressure, and other psychophysiological (psychosomatic) disorders. The magnitude of the problem is great; over 25 million Americans suffer from high blood pressure and the majority of these people don't know they have it. Yet hypertension can lead to many other disorders.

Recently, stress has also been directly implicated in heart disease—the number one cause of death in the United States—and in a wide range of other disorders formerly thought to be strictly physical in nature. In a study of sudden cardiac death, Rahe and Lind (1971) gathered life-change data on thirty-nine subjects over the last three years of their lives prior to their sudden cardiac deaths. For both subjects with and those without histories of coronary disease, there was a significant increase in the number and intensity of life-changes during the final

A stress test is conducted to determine how well the heart functions under heavy exertion. In the test, the patient's heartbeat is checked while the patient performs strenuous exercises. Severe life stress also exacts a toll on our physical and mental well-being.

six months of their lives compared to identical time periods two and three years prior to death. The life-change increase was threefold in magnitude.

Finally, it may be noted that life stress has also been implicated as a causal factor in schizophrenia, depression, suicide, and a wide range of maladaptive behaviors (Grant, Sweetwood, Yager, & Grant, 1981). In essence, the role of stress in physical and mental disorders can cover the entire range of human behavior.

Although severe stress can be expensive, we can and do learn to cope ef-

# Insight

VOODOO DEATH

Most of our stresses are relatively mild, and most of our responses to stress are also correspondingly mild. However, in unusual cases, very stressful conditions can lead to death. Consider the following cases:

*A Brazilian Indian condemned and sentenced by a so-called medicine man is helpless against his own emotional response to this pronouncement—and dies within hours. In Africa a young Negro unknowingly eats the inviolably banned wild hen. On discovery of his "crime" he trembles, is overcome by fear, and dies in 24 hours. In New Zealand a Maori woman eats fruit that she only later learns has come from a tabooed place. Her chief has been profaned. By noon of the next day she is dead. In Australia a witch doctor points a bone at a man. Believing that nothing can save him, the man rapidly sinks in spirits and prepares to die. He is saved only at the last moment when the witch doctor is forced to remove the charm. (Richter, 1957, p. 191)*

As these reports show, stress can be so severe that it can lead to physical deteriora-

tion and death. The remarkable aspect of these studies is that these severe emotional states seem to be set off by such apparently "minor" factors as a bone pointed in the victim's direction.

From the perspective of the GAS model, we can hypothesize that the severe effects reported in these cases resulted from extreme autonomic arousal. That is, the physiological arousal was so intense that the individual rapidly entered the disorganization and exhaustion phase which, in turn, led to death.

Alternatively, we can hypothesize that the individuals "condemned" to die simply gave up hope. That is, believing that they were about to die, they developed a sense of helplessness and hopelessness (Seligman, 1975). And these feelings, in turn, helped produce some biological changes.

Of course, a piece of fruit or a bone is not in itself stressful. But these objects become stressful when we perceive them and react to them in negative ways. Thus, in examining the reactions to stress, we must also be aware of and pay close attention to the perceptions and experiences of the individual.

fectively and efficiently with the stresses of everyday living. In the next chapter we will look at some of the steps we take when we cope effectively. Then we will suggest some ways to use stress for your growth—not destruction.

## SUMMARY

1. The physiological components of the stress response are best understood through reference to the General Adaptation Syndrome. The GAS model proposes that the physiological components of the stress response can be divided into three major phases: alarm and mobilization, resistance, and disorganization and exhaustion.

2. Psychological reactions to stress can involve any combination of three patterns: "built-in" coping and damage-repair mechanisms, task-oriented responses, and defense-oriented responses.

3. Some of the "built-in" coping and damage-repair mechanisms are crying, discussion, reflection, humor, and sleep and dreams. These mechanisms are often used automatically, rather than by choice.

4. Task-oriented responses are based on a conscious, realistic, and deliberate appraisal of a situation and a specific, constructive course of action. In some cases, the task-oriented response may involve action, while other task-oriented responses may emphasize withdrawal.

5. The defense-oriented responses to stress attempt to protect the individual psychologically. They are sometimes called the ego-defense mechanisms. Among the more important of the defense-oriented responses are repression, denial, and rationalization.

6. Stress exacts a toll on the individual. Some of the costs of coping with stress are a reduction in adaptive resources and an increase in physical and mental disorders.

# Chapter 9

# Effective Methods of Coping

*"Sitting in a dentist's chair is stressful, but so is exchanging a passionate kiss with a lover—after all, your pulse races, your breathing quickens, your heartbeat soars, and yet, who in the world would forgo such a pleasurable pastime simply because of the stress involved? . . . Our aim shouldn't be to completely avoid stress . . . but to learn how to recognize our typical response to stress and then try to moderate our lives in accordance with it."*
**(SELYE, 1978, P. 60)**

In this chapter, we shall review some of the ways that individuals can successfully cope with stress. First, we shall examine some practical criteria for evaluating stress reactions. We shall then review some effective methods for coping with stress.

As we noted in Chapter 7, stress has three aspects: *(a)* unpleasant, uncontrollable, and unpredictable environmental stressors; *(b)* the perception of threat; and *(c)* the psychological and physiological responses to environmental or perceived stressors. Our discussion of effective methods of coping will follow the format suggested by our definition of stress. That is, we shall discuss *(a)* coping with stressors; *(b)* coping with one's perception of threat; and *(c)* coping with the psychological and physiological responses to stress. We shall conclude with an examination of the ways in which stress can be used for personal growth.

We begin with a discussion of some practical criteria for evaluating stress reactions.

## CRITERIA FOR EVALUATING STRESS REACTIONS

Our reactions to stress may be evaluated quite differently, depending upon both the situation and the group or person doing the evaluating. However, it seems possible to ask questions that apply to human behavior in most settings, from Madison Avenue to the Andes:

1. *Does the action meet the adjustive demand?* Some actions do not resolve the stress situation but merely provide temporary relief. For example, individuals who use tranquilizers to alleviate their tension and anxiety are probably not coping effectively with the adjustive demands which led to their difficulties. When defense-oriented behavior is relied on as the primary means of coping with stress, it usually only puts off the day of reckoning. Indeed, in the long run it may even increase stress and make it harder to meet adjustive demands successfully. For example, people who escape from unhappy home situations by resorting to alcohol not only fail to solve their problems—they usually make them worse. One criterion of effective adjustment, then, is that it meets the objective requirements of the situation, both immediate and long-range.

2. *Does the action meet the individual's needs?* Sometimes an action seems to meet the demands of a situation but fails to meet the needs of the individual. The woman who wants to be an engineer but gives in to her family's wish that she go into nursing may relieve the stress of parental pressures at the expense

Rescue workers, like these hospital attendants who are rushing the victim of an airplane crash to emergency treatment, must know how to deal immediately with unpredicted and often life-threatening events. A knowledge of what to do in a stressful situation is often an essential part of coping effectively with the stress.

of frustrating her need for self-fulfillment. Far from being an effective adjustment, such a decision is likely to create inner conflict and cause more difficult problems of adjustment later on.

Another factor to consider here is how much the stress reaction costs in relation to the satisfactions it yields. A promotion to a high level executive position may offer rich rewards in money, prestige, and increased occupational competence. But if unrelenting pressure and long hours of work make an executive, male or female, a stranger to spouse and children, the cost may be too great.

3. *Is the action compatible with the well-being of others?* Ideally, effective coping behavior is compatible with the well-being of others as well as with the integrity and well-being of the individual. If we attempt to meet our needs at the expense of other people, our coping behavior is likely to be self-defeating in the long run—to lead to the frustration of our needs as well. Admittedly this is a value judgment and assumes an environment in which the same action can contribute to both individual and group needs.

While our criteria do not completely resolve the problem of assessing stress reactions, they can serve as useful guidelines for assessing most coping behavior.

## COPING EFFECTIVELY WITH STRESSORS

Although some coping mechanisms are "built-in," most people *learn* a variety of coping techniques. People can learn both efficient and inefficient ways of dealing with stress. Our task in this section is to describe some of the methods that researchers in this field have developed to help people deal effectively with stressors. Our approach will involve a *general problem-solving strategy* developed by D'Zurilla and Goldfried (1971). As described by these psychologists, a problem-solving strategy not only helps solve the problem at hand, but gives an individual an experience at success and an increased feeling of self-efficacy. For our purposes, the problem-solving strategy will consist of four general steps: *(1)* evaluating the stress situation, including available resources for coping with it; *(2)* formulating alternatives and deciding on a course of action, *(3)* taking action; and *(4)* utilizing feedback and correcting possible problems.

## Evaluating the Stress Situation

We are continually scanning our environment to see what opportunities or difficulties may be present. When we become aware of a new adjustive demand, our first task is to define it and evaluate its degree of threat. Here it is important that we make an accurate evaluation of the problem, for an incomplete or distorted picture would place us at a disadvantage in coping with it.

**Define the situation accurately.**   One of our first acts when faced with a new demand for adjustment is to define the situation accurately. Often, the individual faced with an adjustive demand inaccurately assesses the situation and then makes plans for dealing with the stress based on the inaccurate assessment. In such a situation, we may find that any action taken will increase, not decrease, the stress. For example, a loved one may ask us for an opportunity to spend time alone or with close friends. If we define the situation accurately—she needs to have some time for herself—we can then plan an appropriate course of action. However, if our definition of the situation is inaccurate—she hates me and wants to get away from me—our responses probably will increase the stress that we feel. Since adjustive demands often reduce the accuracy of our perceptions, we must be particularly careful to define the stress situation accurately.

**Categorize the experience.**   Once we have appropriately assessed the situation, we can then categorize the experience. That is, we attempt to make some judgment about and classify the demand. Our evaluation of the demand will depend on our prior experience with similar (and different) demands. For example, we may classify a demand for adjustment as good if similar demands were also labeled as *good,* or if quite dissimilar demands were labeled *bad.* Consider what would happen if we had to categorize every experience we had as though it were a totally new phenomenon, unrelated to all our prior experience:

*The world of experience of any normal man is composed of a tremendous array of discriminably different objects, events, people, impressions. There are estimated to be more than 7 million discriminable colors alone; and in the course of a week or two we come in contact with a fair proportion of these. . . .*

*But were we to utilize fully our capacity for registering the differences in things and to respond to each event encountered as unique, we would soon be overwhelmed by*

*the complexity of our environment. Consider only the linguistic task of acquiring a vo-
cabulary fully adequate to cope with the world of color differences! The resolution of
the seeming paradox—the existence of discrimination capacities which, if fully used,
would make us slaves to the particular—is achieved by man's capacity to categorize. To
categorize is to render discriminably different things equivalent, to group the objects and
events and people around us into classes, and to respond to them in terms of their class
membership rather than their uniqueness. . . . In place of a color lexicon of 7 million
items, people in our society get along with a dozen or so commonly used color names.
(Bruner, Goodnow, & Austin, 1956, p. 1)*

It thus becomes apparent that our natural tendency to simplify by categorizing is a highly useful one, since it makes our environment simple enough to
evaluate. However, this tendency may be a source of error since our categorization of a new situation depends so heavily upon the characteristics it shares with
past situations of a similar nature rather than upon its unique characteristics. Too
often, simplification becomes oversimplification. This can be readily seen, for example, in overly simplified **stereotypes** that many people hold of liberals and
conservatives. All those labeled *liberals,* for example, are assumed to be unrealistic and naive, or idealistic and humanitarian, depending on the perceiver's political beliefs. As Miller (1962) has pointed out: "It makes the world a great deal
simpler when the good guys are always smart, honest, beautiful, and brave, while
the bad guys are always stupid, crooked, ugly cowards" (p. 274). Although we
are not usually as naive as Miller's statement might imply, our natural tendency
to simplify by categorizing makes it easy for us to see things in black and white
while ignoring the many shades of gray.

**stereotype: a generaliza-
tion of how people of a
given sex, religion, or
other group appear,
think, feel, and act**

**Minimize oversimplification.**   Psychologist George Kelly (1955) has pointed
out that **oversimplification** is a major cause of much personal unhappiness and
distress. In Kelly's view, the individual whose view of him- or herself and others
is narrow and restricted is more likely to exhibit maladaptive behaviors. The solution, says Kelly, is to increase both the accuracy and complexity of our views of
the world.

This complexity allows us to experience adjustive demands in less threatening ways. For example, if an individual is asked to take on more responsibility at
work or to take difficult courses in school, the first reaction might be one of
panic or anger. "I don't see how I could possibly take on this new responsibility."
"How dare they require me to take another foreign language or chemistry course!"
These responses may be based on the overly simplified views that the extra responsibility at work could *never* be successfully handled or that taking a chemistry course or an advanced foreign language course is guaranteed to result in
failure.

However, a more accurate view of the demand might result in a less stressful
or threatening evaluation: "In this work situation, I could successfully handle the
responsibility for supervising another person, but I might have some trouble learning
how to fill out all of these forms." "Taking an advanced chemistry course may
not be the most enjoyable thing I'll ever do, but I have successfully taken chemistry courses before, and if I study effectively, I'll probably do well."

**oversimplification: sim-
plifying concepts of situations to the point
where they are no
longer accurately de-
picted because key fac-
tors or dimensions are
left out**

Thus, our first step in dealing with stressors is to accurately define and categorize the demands being placed upon us. When our categorizing patterns are too simple or inaccurate, we are handicapped in dealing with stress problems. On the other hand, if our assessments are reasonably accurate and realistic, we are aided in defining the stress situation and have taken the first step to cope effectively with the stressor.

## Working Out an Appropriate Course of Action

Having defined the problem appropriately and accurately evaluated the degree of difficulty it presents to us, we must next decide what to do about it. This involves formulating alternative courses of action that might solve the problem and selecting the most promising one.

**Formulating the alternatives.** The process of formulating alternatives involves generating courses of action that might be used to deal with the stress-inducing problem. Sometimes, the whole process of definition, formulation of alternative actions, and choice of action may take place automatically with little or no conscious involvement. An example of this would be our almost instantaneous reaction to a car stopping suddenly ahead of us on a freeway. In this situation, our reactions occur quickly and with little thought.

However, many stress situations contain unfamiliar elements that do not lend themselves to immediate categorization and action. In these less familiar situations, our response may show some variability: some of us will avoid coming to grips with a difficult problem as long as we can, hoping that time will resolve the situation; some will seek advice or assistance from more knowledgeable or more experienced individuals; some may tackle a stress situation head-on as though they were knights slaying a dragon.

In more structured situations calling for a solution to the stress situation, we may act more carefully and deliberately than in situations where the demands are quite intense and must be immediately managed. Since well worked-out, constructive solutions offer long-term benefits over impulsive and poorly planned options, our emphasis will be on the more carefully considered approaches to coping with stressors.

Perhaps the easiest way to generate solutions is to "brainstorm" a variety of options. In **brainstorming,** an individual attempts to generate as many solutions to a problem as possible. During brainstorming, criticism and evaluation are postponed, and "killer" phrases that stop the flow of ideas are firmly suppressed. Some examples of "killer" phrases are:

- "Yes, but . . . "
- "It won't work. . . . "
- "I've never done it that way before. . . . "
- "Let me think it over and see what happens. . . . "

Brainstorming operates under the hypothesis that many potential solutions probably contain one or more excellent ideas. It does not matter how seemingly

**brainstorming: generation of many potential solutions to a problem while postponing criticism or evaluation of the suggestions**

unworkable or silly the solution may appear to be; rather, it is important to generate as many potential solutions as possible (Osborn, 1953). To remember all the ideas generated during this phase of the problem-solving situation, jot down the ideas as they occur to you.

**Balancing probability, desirability, and cost.**    Once we have formulated alternative solutions to a stress situation, the task remains of assessing the relative merits of these alternatives and making a choice. In so doing, we weigh the probabilities of success, the degree of satisfaction we will accept, and the cost we are willing to pay.

1. *Weighing the odds.* Each of the alternatives formulated in the earlier steps of the problem-solving situation has associated with it a *probability of success.* Some alternatives have a very high likelihood of success, while others are quite likely to end in failure. In figuring the odds, we examine the relevant information at our disposal, decide whether we need more information, and make some decision. Although we dislike uncertainty, our world offers us only probabilities, and we have to make the best of the situation that confronts us.

Being forced to bet on probabilities, however, does not mean that we always calculate the odds rationally. Wishful thinking may lead us to take unnecessary risks or disregard danger signs. Sometimes, our behavior resembles that of the gambler who continues to utilize a strategy that consistently fails.

Thus, it is important in this step to separate the probability of success from the desirability of the outcome. A student may find, for example, that he or she would greatly enjoy the option of not studying for exams; however, if the student's goal is to perform well in class, the desirable outcome has a very low probability of success.

Coping effectively with stressors sometimes resembles gambling strategy as we attempt to weigh the probable success of a particular coping method against the outcome we want to achieve.

2. *Deciding on an acceptable level of satisfaction.* Each of the alternative solutions formulated also has associated with it a level of satisfaction. Some alternatives will produce great satisfaction, while others will produce only modest amounts of satisfaction. There need not be any relationship between the probability of success, which was calculated earlier, and the satisfaction the alternative will produce. For example, one alternative may have a low probability of success but may also be associated with a bigger potential gain. On the other hand, an equally unlikely event may be associated with a relatively low level of satisfaction.

All other things being equal, we tend to select the course of action that seems to offer the greatest probability of success (Peterson & Beach, 1967). Naturally, what is satisfying and successful to one individual may not be to another. For example, one person may be willing to accept a good job offer rather than wait for a better one, while another would take the opposite course of action.

Most people find a course of action that is "good enough" and not necessarily perfect. Consider the situation of a person who is selling a used car. Although she or he would no doubt accept an offer to buy the car at the advertised price, the seller might be willing to accept a lower offer. The price that the seller would accept would depend on a number of factors: Are there many people interested in buying the car? How many times does he or she wish to explain the car's features to a potential buyer? How urgent is the seller's need for money? Depending on these and other individually determined factors, the price for which the car is eventually sold will likely seem fair and satisfactory to both seller and buyer.

Obviously, problems can occur when an individual's level of satisfaction is too low or too high. When the level of satisfaction is too low, we may be willing to accept an outcome that deprives us of important satisfactions. On the other hand, satisfaction levels that are too high can also result in an overall loss of satisfaction and would be just as self-defeating as accepting too low a level of satisfaction. Selecting a middle-of-the-road course seems to offer the best chance at effective coping, particularly when this course is realistic and achievable.

3. *Weighing the costs.* All behavior has its costs in effort, material resources, time, and the surrender of other possibilities. Some behavior also exacts costs in unpleasantness or loss. Thus, staying in school may require such long hours of study that a student must give up hobbies or social life, but dropping out of school might cost future opportunities for more advanced training.

In choosing between alternative courses of action, we balance the risks and the costs—the amount of effort or other costs—against the possible satisfactions. For high stakes and good odds we may be willing to work hard and undergo considerable sacrifice. But, if the returns look small and the risk of losing is considerable, we are usually reluctant to exert much effort. Although we often weigh the factors differently, we all look for what we regard as the best balance of probable gains and costs.

Thus, we must take each alternative, determine the benefits and costs associated with it, estimate its probability of success, and come to some reasonable conclusion about whether the alternative should be acted upon. Unfortunately, there are no hard and fast rules for weighing the alternatives. Each individual must take the information he or she has at hand and decide which is the best alternative. Clearly, the more information each person has, the more likely that the decision made will be a good one.

In balancing risk, satisfaction, and cost, we are also confronted with the problem of weighing the importance of a single decision. Some choices are likely to arise only once and may have a continuing influence on our lives—for example, the decision to go to college or marry a particular person. Other choices may be relatively unimportant in the long run—such as whether we buy a new or used car—although they may seem very important at the time.

It is also apparent that since we are dealing with probabilities and not certainties, we cannot expect to win every time. As Overstreet and Overstreet (1956) have pointed out: " . . . we live by batting averages, not by perfect scores. . . . We live by making plans and by making efforts that are, so far as we can see, in line with the results we want; by improving our plans and efforts as experience dictates; and by believing that a fair batting average constitutes enough success to justify our staying on the job" (p. 24).

## Taking Positive Action

Once a decision has been made, the next step is to implement it—to put the chosen alternative into action.

In this context we are focusing primarily upon task-oriented and rational rather than defense-oriented and often irrational coping responses. However, even the implementation of task-oriented reactions is not always a simple matter, particularly if we lack confidence in ourselves or in our decision. As a consequence, we may experience fear, anxiety, apprehension, and related feelings which can interfere with the effective implementation of our decision.

Often such emotions impair actual performance, whether it be intellectual or physical. Most of us have probably had the experience of speaking or performing before a group. When the time for action arrived, we may have been so fearful and anxious that our actual thought processes were partially blocked and our performance was impaired. Many trial lawyers experience excruciating stress during the first few times they address a jury. Typically, however, they discipline themselves to function effectively despite their inner feelings. We could cite similar instances of football players before and during the first few minutes of play in an important game.

Perhaps of more importance for effective coping is the delay in action that may result from such feelings. Often in dealing with serious conflicts, for example, we may vacillate, attempt to stall for time, and even get sick—despite the fact that we have already decided on the best probable course of action. Kaufman (1973) has referred to this as "decidophobia." When time permits, such diversionary tactics may prove constructive, since they enable us to postpone the action until we have more information, have had time to reconsider our alternatives, and feel more confident of our decision. In other instances, however, delay may be disastrous. Often, the timing of an action is of crucial importance. What might have been an effective response today may not be so tomorrow.

*George, a man who had gone through a rather painful divorce some four years previously, decided that he was very much in love with and wanted to marry Sharon, a very attractive woman whom he was dating. Since she had told him she loved him and wanted to marry him, he felt reasonably secure about taking his time. But he did not realize that underneath, Sharon was becoming resentful and withdrawing because of his unwillingness to tell her he loved her, let alone propose marriage. In fact, he had insisted that the relationship be on his terms, which were "no strings attached."*

*As a consequence, she accepted a date with Bill, a man who had also been divorced some time previously. She continued to see Bill each evening and during the ensuing weekend while George was away at a convention. They had really enjoyable times together, found that they had common interests, and before the week was over had established a very satisfactory relationship.*

*Sharon had told Bill about George and her relationship with him, which he understood and accepted. On Sunday, the day before George's return, Bill told Sharon that he loved her and wanted to marry her—a decision he said he had been seriously considering since their first date. Although Sharon felt that she had fallen in love with Bill, she was a little hesitant about marrying him because of the short period that she had known him. But Bill had been around enough to know what he wanted, and he convinced her. That Sunday evening they flew to Las Vegas and were married.*

*When George returned, Sharon went to see him to explain, but before she could say anything he told her how much he had missed her, that he did love her, and that he wanted to marry her. But his action came too late. Had he taken the same action before he left for the convention, the story might have had a different ending.*

Perhaps one might wonder whether Sharon had not made a somewhat impetuous decision, perhaps in part based on her resentment toward George. But she had also been divorced, was a mature person, and knew what she wanted. She decided that, while both men had much to offer, Bill was the more mature, had more interests and values in common with hers, and that she really did love him.

In some situations, the issue is not fear or anxiety, but poor or incomplete knowledge about how to carry out a chosen course of action. For example, we may have decided upon the appropriate way to handle a troublesome acquaintance but do not know precisely how to carry out the course of action. In those situations where our knowledge is poor or lacking, consultation with friends, family, or professionals can prove invaluable. If, for example, we find that our original choice of a college major is incorrect, we may drop that program of study and select another. However, our knowledge of other major programs may not be complete, and we may need to see a college adviser or counselor prior to making another choice. In a somewhat different vein, we may wish to end a relationship and have decided to accomplish this goal with as little distress as possible. Our skills at ending relationships may never have been utilized, and we may seek the advice of a more knowledgeable friend to learn how to end a relationship while preserving the integrity and self-esteem of the other individual.

Sometimes the best method of dealing with stress is seeking professional assistance. If a relationship is troubled, for example, the couple may consult a counselor for help in resolving their problems.

## Utilizing Feedback

As the action is proceeding, we can use available **feedback** to gauge the wisdom of our decision and the effectiveness with which we are carrying it out. Feedback enables us to make corrections in our actions when such corrections are indicated and feasible.

Feedback may indicate that we are either on or off the beam. **Convergent feedback** is information telling us that we are making satisfactory progress toward our goal or that the goal has been achieved. If the adjustment problem is highly stressful or if we are uncertain about the course of action we have chosen, convergent feedback usually alleviates anxiety, builds self-confidence, and leads to increased effort, for it is a signal that the stress will be resolved and our needs met.

Feedback is rarely altogether favorable. When an action is not progressing as satisfactorily as we had anticipated, we get **divergent feedback,** indicating that—perhaps because of unforeseen complications or a wrong choice of action—we are not progressing toward our goal as well as we might or perhaps that our action is ineffective or even making the stress situation worse. A young person who talks too much in an effort to gain attention and approval may be informed, through the negative actions of other people, that his or her efforts are not succeeding. Besides signaling the need to modify this behavior, divergent feedback indicates that stress is likely to be prolonged or intensified.

In some situations we receive relatively complete information concerning the progress and outcome of our actions. In other situations we may receive only

**feedback:** knowledge of the results of one's behavior, used in judging the appropriateness of one's responses and making corrections where indicated

**convergent feedback:** feedback indicating satisfactory progress toward or attainment of a goal

**divergent feedback:** feedback indicating unsatisfactory progress toward or inappropriate selection of a goal

# Insight

### THE IMPORTANCE OF FLEXIBILITY

It is all too easy to become "weighted down" by rigid beliefs and coping styles that lack the flexibility essential for dealing with changing conditions in a changing world. The importance of flexibility has been well expressed by tennis professional Pancho Gonzales, who was still competing successfully in his early forties—a feat considered virtually impossible in the fast-paced world of professional tennis: "Vary your game to the conditions. Shorten your strokes on a fast court, play more steadily on a slow court; hit harder when you are playing against the wind and softer when you are playing with it" (1972).

This advice, coming as it does from a professional who has learned to roll with the punches but not at the expense of becoming non-task-oriented or inauthentic, is applicable to many areas of our daily lives.

partial or even zero feedback. The amount of feedback is determined not only by the information available but also by our ability to perceive it. A child may not associate a stomachache with having eaten green apples; an adult may ignore or misinterpret frowns or other signs of social disapproval.

Zero feedback usually means that we receive no information until our action is complete. For example, students may not be given any grades on lab reports until several reports have been submitted. In general, the delay of feedback until after the completion of an important action tends to cause worry and anxiety.

Often we receive prompt but only partial feedback. A student who gets a low grade on a test may have little information about why he or she received such a low rating or what he or she is doing wrong. Or we may notice that people seem to be avoiding or reacting negatively to us but not have any clues about the reason. Limited feedback is often ambiguous and difficult to interpret; it makes us anxious and uncertain, especially in important situations.

In some situations we receive relatively complete feedback and can modify our action to make it more effective. A football player receives a great deal of feedback—both during and after a game—and can improve both immediate and later performance. Programmed instruction is based on the demonstrated principle that learning is most efficient, and improvement most rapid when precise feedback is given immediately (Skinner, 1958). In general, immediate and complete feedback is followed by both improved performance and increased confidence—except, of course, where feedback is highly divergent and the individual sees no way of improving his or her course of action.

Unlike its inanimate counterpart, the human "computer" uses feedback not only to monitor its progress in carrying out a course of action but also to check on the validity of its goal and the wisdom of its current "program." If the situation changes or if feedback tells us that our goal is going to be too expensive or not worth achieving, we can abandon one course of action in midstream and embark on another. For this reason, human beings are self-correcting systems.

# COPING WITH THE PERCEPTION OF STRESS

*"Man is disturbed not by things but the views he takes of them."*
**(EPICTETUS, THE ENCHIRIDION)**

In the previous section, we focused on the skills and competencies needed to cope successfully with stressors. Learning how to use these techniques is an important part of a stress management program.

Another important aspect of the stress response is our personal experience and interpretation of stress. While it is possible to know the appropriate course of action to deal with a stressor, we must also develop the cognitive skills to enhance our coping responses. For example, a student who is terrified of speaking in front of a class not only needs to develop public speaking skills but also needs skills to deal with the unpleasant thoughts and feelings that accompany both the act and thought of public speaking.

In this section, we shall focus primarily on the cognitively oriented approach of **stress inoculation** (Meichenbaum, 1977). Stress inoculation training has been employed to help people cope with a variety of stress reactions, including severe fear, anger, and pain. Although it is analogous to the techniques we have described for coping with stressors, its focus is on the cognitive and perceptual components of the stress response.

**stress inoculation: cognitively oriented approach to dealing with stress, consisting of educational, rehearsal, and application phases**

As we shall see, stress inoculation is a three-part process involving *(1)* an educational phase, *(2)* a rehearsal phase, and *(3)* an application phase:

1. *Educational phase.* In the first phase of stress inoculation training, an individual is given a framework for understanding his or her response to stressful events (Meichenbaum, 1977). For example, a person who has difficulty controlling her angry outbursts under conditions of stress might be given information on how emotional responses develop (see Chapter 6). Similarly, the person who panicked at the sight of snakes and rats might be asked to pay greater attention to the "internal dialogue" that accompanied his responses. Some of these internal responses might include thoughts of disgust related to the snakes and rats, thoughts of panic, thoughts of being overwhelmed by anxiety, a desire to flee the situation, fears of social embarrassment, or fears of "going crazy."

This phase of stress inoculation training is similar to the early phases of the procedure for dealing with stressors. As you recall, some of the first steps in dealing with stressors involve defining the situation accurately and categorizing the experience. In stress inoculation training, however, the emphasis is on the personal reactions and experiences that are occurring during a stress response. In other words, the individual is receiving "education" and awareness about his or her internal responses.

2. *Rehearsal phase.* During the rehearsal phase, the person develops and rehearses a variety of coping responses. This phase of the training incorporates many of the suggestions we have already made for coping with stressors and developing effective plans of action. In the stress inoculation approach, however, cognitive coping skills are emphasized.

The cognitive training and rehearsal focuses on five major areas: *(a)* an assessment of the reality of the situation, *(b)* control of negative thoughts and images, *(c)* acknowledgment and relabeling of unpleasant arousal, *(d)* preparation to confront the stress-inducing situation, and *(e)* reflection on performance and reinforcement for having tried.

In the case of the person whose anger is uncontrolled during stress situations, the training might involve a variety of self-statements. In assessing the reality of the situation, the individual might learn and practice saying to herself, "This could be a difficult situation, but I can handle it," or "Try not to take this too seriously. Keep your sense of humor." To control negative thoughts and feelings, the individual might say to herself, "There is no point in getting mad. Just stay calm." Or, she might think, "I'm not going to let him get to me."

The acknowledgment and relabeling of unpleasant arousal can also help control stress. For the angry individual, the cognitive statements that she would rehearse might include, "I'm getting angry. Time to relax," or "Don't let anger lead to more anger. Anger is a signal to try a new approach." Confronting the stress situation can also be helped through cognitive rehearsal: "One step at a time. Don't get overwhelmed."

Finally, cognitive statements can be employed to help control feelings of disappointment (when things do not turn out well) or to reinforce trying and success: "Aggravating situations do not last forever." "I handled that pretty well" (Novaco, 1975).

3. *Application phase.* In the application phase, the attitudes and skills learned in the education and rehearsal phases are put to good use. During this time, the individual tries out his or her new skills in increasingly stressful situations. It is not necessary that the person show mastery of the skills. Rather, the individual need only use his or her new skills in the situation, evaluate the outcome of the new approach, and modify the action responses and cognitive statements where necessary.

## COPING EFFECTIVELY WITH THE RESPONSES TO STRESS

In coping effectively with stressors and with the perception of stress, we do not suddenly stop experiencing the effects of stress on our physiological and psychological functioning. For example, in working out a solution to a difficult interpersonal problem at home, we must solve both the problem and our current reaction to the problem. Similarly, in the case of an individual whose self-esteem is threatened by failure to meet unrealistic goals, application of some of the principles we have discussed may help him or her develop more realistic goals, eventually lessening the effects of stress.

In some cases, we may find it difficult to leave the stress-inducing situation. For example, we may find it difficult to leave an unpleasant job when the alternatives are even less satisfying than the current situation. We may decide to continue a previously satisfactory relationship in the hope that more positive times

# Psychology in Action

## COPING SELF-STATEMENTS USED IN STRESS-INOCULATION TRAINING

**Preparing for a stressor**

"What is it I have to do?"
"I can develop a plan to deal with it."
"Just think about what I can do about it. That's better than getting worried."
"No negative self-statements: just think rationally."
"Don't worry: worry won't help anything."
"Maybe what I think is anxiety is actually eagerness to confront the stressor."

**Confronting and handling a stressor**

"Just 'psych' myself up—I can meet this challenge."
"I can convince myself to do it. I can reason my discomfort away."
"One step at a time: I can handle the situation."
"Don't focus on feelings; just think about what I have to do. Stay relevant."
"This anxiety is a reminder to use my coping exercises."
"This tenseness can be an ally; a cue to cope."
"Relax; I'm in control. Take a slow, deep breath."

**Coping with the feeling of being overwhelmed**

"When worry comes, just pause."
"Keep the focus on the present; what is it I have to do?"
"I expect my fear to rise."
"Don't try to eliminate discomfort entirely; just keep it manageable."

**Reinforcing self-statements**

"It worked, I did it."
"It wasn't as bad as I expected."
"I made more out of my worries than it was worth."
"When I control my thoughts, I control my fear."
"It's getting better each time I use the procedures."
"I can be pleased with the progress I'm making."
"I did it!"

(Adapted from Meichenbaum, 1974, 1977, p. 155)

lie ahead. In each situation, we may decide not to leave the stress-inducing circumstances, but rather try to deal with the demands as well as we can. At the same time, we can take steps to cope with our physiological and psychological responses to these circumstances.

While the choice to remain in a stress-inducing situation may be the best possible alternative we have, the choice nonetheless leads to some physiological and psychological responses to stress. And, while many of the techniques we have presented thus far can be quite helpful in providing good and lasting solutions, they may take some time to reach their maximum effectiveness, exposing us to needlessly high levels of stress.

Our task in this section is to describe a variety of techniques that can be of assistance in coping with the physiological and psychological responses to stress. We shall discuss three approaches in particular: relaxation and meditation, exercise, and involvement in alternative activities.

## Relaxation and Meditation

Each of us has probably heard the familiar refrain, "You're tense and uptight. Relax." The instruction seems simple enough, "Relax," as though there were nothing to this particular skill. And, it would be convenient if we could simply and easily throw an internal switch from the position marked "Tense" to the "Relaxed" position. However, our naive attitudes about **relaxation** help *prevent* us from learning how to relax. Instead, we too often turn to alcohol, marijuana, or pills to help us achieve a desired relaxed state.

**relaxation: a pleasant state characterized by the absence of tension**

Interest in relaxation has taken several forms since the beginning of this century. Early in his career, physiologist Edmund Jacobson noticed that shortened or contracted muscle fibers were often associated with subjective reports of tension (Jacobson, 1934). He assumed that if an individual's muscles were totally relaxed (that is, no muscle contractions at all), he or she would report feeling relaxed as well.

**relaxation training: techniques used to help an individual attain a relaxed state**

Jacobson was perhaps the first to develop a specific, nonpharmacological approach to **relaxation training.** Through his research, Jacobson (1938) found that systematically tensing and relaxing various muscle groups aided people in achieving muscle relaxation. Jacobson did not simply have individuals tense and relax muscles, however. He also instructed participants to pay attention to the various sensations produced by the tensing and relaxing of these muscles. In this way, the relaxation achieved by his procedures would be aided and supplemented by an internal awareness of the feelings of tension and relaxation, and the participants could eventually learn to develop deep levels of relaxation. Unfortunately, Jacobson's procedures never achieved great popularity, primarily because the procedures that he advocated were very long and time-consuming, requiring over fifty sessions of training.

Wolpe's work in systematic desensitization (see Chapter 11) led to a renewed interest in relaxation training. Wolpe (1958) found that he could shorten Jacobson's procedures considerably and achieve virtually the same results. Wolpe found that six twenty-minute sessions supplemented by twice-daily home practice could help clients achieve the deep relaxation levels useful in carrying out systematic desensitization.

Wolpe's rediscovery of Jacobson's procedures spurred psychologists to try to learn more about relaxation. Their findings suggested that relaxation training typically resulted in lowered levels of physiological arousal and decreased subjective anxiety (e.g., Paul, 1969).

Several aspects of relaxation training appear to be important. First, achieving a deep state of relaxation is a learned skill, not an ability that you either have or don't have. All individuals can, with practice, learn the skill of relaxation. As with any other skill, consistent practice will increase a person's proficiency at initiating or maintaining relaxation when needed.

Second, as a self-control skill, relaxation training may be more beneficial than the drugs commonly used to achieve relaxation. When we use alcohol, marijuana, or tranquilizers to achieve a state of relaxation, we also recognize that our relaxed state is brought on by the drug, not by our own efforts. On the other hand, relaxation that we can attribute to our own efforts, rather than to some pharmacological agent, appears to be longer lasting and more beneficial to the individual in aiding him or her to deal successfully with various problems (Davison, Tsujimoto, & Glaros, 1973).

Finally, relaxation training can aid in the identification of the factors that produce stress. Through training, an individual can become more sensitive to various levels of tension and relaxation and can use his or her heightened awareness to identify and deal with the factors that bring on discomfort.

Research studies have reported that during relaxation and meditation, respiratory rate, oxygen consumption, heart rate, and muscle tension decrease—physiological effects directly opposite those that occur in the response to stress.

# Psychology in Action

### LEARNING HOW TO RELAX

Relaxation is a skill that anyone can learn. And like other skills, relaxation is best learned in the proper setting using the proper techniques.

First, prepare a relaxing setting. Find a comfortable chair (preferably a recliner), a wide couch, chaise lounge, or bed in which to practice relaxation. Second, remove all distractions. Make sure that you will not be bothered by phone calls, visitors, television, stereo, radios, etc. A darkened, quiet room is ideal. Loosen all tight clothing. Since you will probably want to close your eyes during relaxation training, remove contact lenses if you wear them.

The relaxation instructions we have presented here assume that you will record them on a tape recorder. If you do not have access to a tape recorder, someone can read them to you. Or, you can memorize the sequence and practice relaxation alone. While it does not matter whether the instructions are tape-recorded or memorized, it is important to take your time while going through the exercises. It should take you about twenty minutes to complete this relaxation program.

A final rule for relaxing: Make time to practice relaxation. Don't let old ways and worn phrases such as "I just don't have the time" stand in the way of learning this useful skill.

Now settle back as comfortably as you can in the chair and listen to what I'm going to be telling you. If you listen closely, you'll be able with enough practice to learn to relax the various muscles of your body and to enjoy the accompanying feelings of relaxation, pleasantness, and calm.

Clench your left hand into a fist. Just clench your fist tighter and tighter, and study the tension as you do so. *(Five-second pause.)* And now, let go. Try to let go entirely of the tensions in your left hand. Let your fingers become loose. Notice the contrast between the degree of relaxation in your hand now and the degree of tension that you created in your left hand just a moment ago. *(Ten-second pause.)* As we go through these various procedures and I ask you to let go of a given muscle group, see if you can let go all at once rather than gradually releasing the tension. Almost throw the tension out of your muscles as well as you can. This is something you'll get more of a feel for as we proceed.

Now clench your right hand into a fist, study the tension, and pay close attention to what that feels like. *(Five-second pause.)* Now let go. Let go and see if you can keep letting go a little bit more, even though it seems as if you've let go as much as you possibly can. There always seems to be that extra bit of relaxation. Just keep letting go of your right hand and your left hand as well, just relaxing as best you can. *(Ten-second pause.)*

Now, bend both hands back at the wrists so that you tense the muscles in the back of your hand and in your forearm, pointing your fingers at the ceiling. Study the tension. *(Five-second pause.)* And now let it go. Let it go and keep letting go to the best of your ability, becoming more and more relaxed. *(Ten-second pause.)* Once again, bend both hands back at the wrists, fingers pointing toward the ceiling. Study the tension, notice what it feels like, pay close attention to it. *(Five-second pause.)* And now let go. Notice and enjoy the contrast between tension and relaxation. *(Ten-second pause.)* Now clench both your hands into fists and bring them toward your shoulders so as to tighten your bicep muscles, the large muscle in the upper part of your arm. Study that tension. *(Five-second pause.)* And now let go, letting your arms drop down again to the chair, relaxing once again. Even as you think of letting go, you can feel the tensions leaving your muscles. *(Ten-second pause.)*

Now concentrate on your forehead. I would like you to wrinkle up your forehead. Wrinkle the muscles in your forehead and study the tension. *(Five-second pause.)* And now smooth it out; relax those muscles. Don't tense them any more. Smooth out and relax your forehead as best you can, noticing the difference between tension and relaxation. *(Ten-second pause.)* I would like you now to close your eyes tightly so that you feel tension around your eyes. Notice what that feels like. *(Five-second pause.)* And now relax. Relax, allowing your eyes to remain lightly closed if that's comfortable for you. And notice once again the difference between the tension you created before and the relaxation that you are creating now. *(Ten-second pause.)* Now I would like you to press your lips together. Press your lips together so that you feel tension around the mouth and the chin and the cheeks. *(Five-second pause.)* And now let go. Let go of the tension as best you can. Let go all at once, and enjoy the contrast between tension and relaxation. *(Ten-second pause.)*

Now I would like you to shrug your shoulders. Bring both your shoulders up as if to touch your ears. Feel the tension in your upper back and your neck. *(Five-second pause.)* And now let go. Let your shoulders drop down. Feel that relaxation. Just let go of those tense muscles. *(Ten-second pause.)* Perhaps you are feeling some different sensations at this time—a tingling feeling or sensations of warmth. Whatever it is you're experiencing, just enjoy it; go along with it. Let yourself enjoy the feelings that accompany relaxation.

And now press your head back against the couch. Study the tension; pay close attention to it. *(Five-second pause.)* And now let go. Let your head come back to a resting position and relax the muscles in your neck. *(Ten-second pause.)* Now bring your head forward and try to bury your chin into your chest. Notice the feeling. *(Five-second pause.)* Now relax. *(Ten-second pause.)*

Now I would like you to take a deep breath and hold it. A deep breath and hold it. Study that tension; feel the growing discomfort. *(Five-second pause.)* And now exhale and breathe normally once again. *(Ten-second pause.)* Let each exhalation become a signal to let go generally, to let your muscles become more and more relaxed. *(Ten-second pause.)*

I would now like you to arch your back so that you're sticking your chest out and the arch of your back is leaving the chair somewhat. Study the tension. *(Five-second pause.)* Now let go. Let your back drop down once again. And relax once again. *(Ten-second pause.)* Now I'd like you to tense your stomach muscles as if someone were going to punch you in the stomach. *(Five-second pause.)* Now relax them. Let your stomach become softer once again. Relax those muscles. *(Ten-second pause.)* And now I'd like you to tense the muscles in your buttocks by trying to lift yourself out of your chair. Tense those muscles. Study the tension. *(Five-second pause.)* And now let go; relax those muscles. *(Ten-second pause.)* Notice once again the contrast between the tension and the relative relaxation you experience when you're no longer tensing those muscles, when you're letting go and trying to let go even further.

And now I'd like you to extend your legs and lift your feet so that your thighs are tensed. Feel the tension in your thighs; notice it, study it. *(Five-second pause.)* And now let your feet drop down. Let your legs become looser and more relaxed. *(Ten-second pause.)* I would like you now to bend both feet back at the ankles in the same fashion as you did with your wrists before. Your toes are pointing back toward your face. *(Five-second pause.)* And now let go; let go of that tension. *(Ten-second pause.)*

I'm going to review with you briefly the various muscle groups that we've covered. As I call out the name of each group, just think of releasing the tension in those muscles. Think of letting go a little bit more if you can. Relax your hands. *(Five-second pause.)* And your forearms. *(Five-second pause.)* Your upper arms: the biceps, the triceps. Your entire arms down to your fingertips. Let them become more relaxed. *(Five-second pause.)* Relax your shoulders, the muscles of your face, your forehead, your cheeks, your mouth, your jaws, and your neck. *(Five-second pause.)* A wave of relaxation spreading downward from your head, coming now into your chest and down into your stomach. *(Five-second pause.)* And relax your calves, your thighs, and your feet. *(Five-second pause.)* Let your entire body become more relaxed. *(Five-second pause.)*

Let yourself relax like that for a while, and in a moment I will have you open your eyes once again. *(Two-minute pause.)* I'm going to count from five to one, and as I count, you'll begin to stretch and gradually arouse yourself. At the count of one, let your eyes open, be wide awake and refreshed, alert, and probably a little more relaxed than when you started. Five . . . four, stretching . . . three . . . two, take a deep breath . . . and one . . . eyes open, wide awake, refreshed, and relaxed.

The relaxation technique described on pages 240–42 is only one of many possible relaxation procedures (Shapiro, 1982). In a relaxation exercise, an individual can focus on mental images and relaxing thoughts. For example, he or she could imagine seeing a flower in the distance or imagine floating in warm water (Davison et al., 1973).

Similarly, a variety of meditative techniques could be employed. In **meditation,** a person could regulate his or her breathing, focus on a mental image, or silently repeat a word or phrase. As Shapiro has pointed out:

> *. . . meditation has been found to influence an impressive number of different outcome criteria in a positive direction. For example, meditation has been shown to be effective for clinical concerns such as stress, substance abuse, fears and phobia, psychosomatic complaints, reduction of neuroticism and depression, increasing congruence between a person's real and ideal self, [and] fostering self-actualization. (1980, pp. 1–2)*

Of course, relaxation and meditation are not cure-alls to harmful stress, but they can be useful, beneficial additions to a stress-management program.

**meditation: set of techniques in which attention is focused in a non-analytical way, often used in assisting individuals to learn to relax**

### Exercise

Exercise is another useful technique for controlling and reducing the physiological and psychological responses to stress. Whether our activity is with others, as in group sports, or by ourselves, exercise can provide release from the stresses and tensions that develop day after day.

Exercise helps release tensions in several ways. First, some of the physiological changes associated with stress, described earlier in Chapter 8, are significantly reduced or eliminated after vigorous exercise. Secondly, the time that we spend exercising tends to reduce the time we spend in stressful situations. The time away from the demands placed upon us also gives us time to think of potentially useful strategies to solve the problematic situation. Finally, exercise helps by increasing our levels of fitness. As our levels of fitness increase, our physical resources for dealing with demands increase as well.

Obviously, exercise must be tailored to our interests, age, and fitness levels. For example, the three sets of tennis or five miles of jogging for the adolescent or young adult may have to give way to vigorous walking or swimming for older adults.

As with relaxation, exercise is only useful when we continue our involvement. Many experts advise exercising three times per week as an aid to maintaining health. This type of schedule is best maintained when we deliberately set aside time for exercising. The participation of a friend in an exercise program also increases the chances that we will continue in the program and may make exercising significantly more enjoyable.

## Involvement in Alternative Activities

Since stress situations are typically negative and aversive, we may find that immersing ourselves in some alternative activities can help relieve the pressures and demands placed upon us. Some of the more common alternatives involve hob-

Many people who exercise regularly report not only an increase in their physical well-being but also a reduction of tension in their lives.

bies. The man who takes time out for practice on a musical instrument or who engages in some "creative cookery" may find that the interlude away from adjustive demands is both refreshing and renewing. Similarly, the woman who enjoys the company of friends or who participates in dance lessons may find that her ability to cope with stress is enhanced.

Alternative activities need not involve hobbies alone, but involvement in hobbies is one of the more accessible alternatives to remaining in a stressful situation. Everyone can develop a hobby, and hobbies can range from needlepoint stitching to painting and to beer can and matchbox collecting. Hobbies take us away from the stress situation for brief times, and these respites from stress can allow us to renew our resources.

Involvement in social activity can also be an alternative to a stressful situation. Social activity can involve dating, spending time with neighbors or family, or going out with friends. Social activity can also serve communities as well. People can become involved with their churches, synagogues, and temples; community activity involving clean-ups and beautification, for example, can serve stress-reducing functions.

Finally, volunteer work can be a satisfying and useful alternative. Many people donate their time to help the hospitalized sick. Others assist those who, through physical or mental disabilities, cannot provide for themselves. Individuals also volunteer their skills and energies in child and youth groups, such as Big Brothers, scouting, and athletic teams.

These are but a few of the many alternatives to stress. Not only can these alternatives renew our resources and remove us from stress situations, they are enjoyable activites in themselves. Our involvement in these positive alternatives can be a source of satisfaction and a means for us to increase our sense of self-worth and self-esteem.

**Some older adults find that participation in volunteer programs such as Foster Grandparents is one way to cope successfully with the stresses that accompany aging.**

# GUARDING AGAINST COMMON ERRORS

Present-day computer studies which simulate the functioning of the human brain in dealing with adjustive demands support the notion that the brain is an elaborate communication and control center where incoming information is continuously evaluated, alternative responses are formulated and weighed, decisions are made and implemented, and feedback is checked and used to make needed corrections.

Our self-aware "human computer" is both more efficient and less efficient at handling problems than is the electronic computer. It is more inventive and creative, but it is also slower and more subject to error. We often come up with "wrong" definitions of and answers to stress situations not only because we lack accurate information or needed competencies but also because of time pressures, emotional involvement in the stress situation, and other conditions that seem peculiarly human.

For our immediate purposes we shall discuss seven of the more common sources of error in the processing of stress situations: inadequate information and faulty assumptions, time pressure, oversimplification, emotions, defensive orientation, self-pity, and social influences.

1. *Inadequate information and faulty assumptions.* As Shubik (1967) has pointed out:

*Man lives in an environment about which his information is highly incomplete. Not only does he not know how to evaluate many of the alternatives facing him, he is not even aware of a considerable percentage of them. His perceptions are relatively limited; his powers of calculation and accuracy are less than those of a computer in many situations; his searching, data processing, and memory capabilities are erratic. As the speed of transmission of stimuli and the volume of new stimuli increase, the limitations of the individual become more marked relative to society as a whole. (p. 772)*

And often we fail to acquire needed information about problems we are likely to encounter in life even when such information is available.

2. *Time pressure.* In some stress situations, we can take our time, get more information if we need it, weigh and balance all factors carefully, and emerge with a course of action in which we have considerable confidence. And, of course, problems tend to be processed more effectively when we deal with them thoughtfully and when we are not feeling intensive time pressure.

In other situations we may feel we are under so much time pressure that we decide on a course of action even though we have serious doubts that it will be a satisfactory solution to the problem. In studying the job stress of police administrators, Kroes, Hurrell, and Margolis (1974) found that the pressure to make decisions without adequate information was a major source of stress.

When we feel that we must take action but do not have time to obtain needed information or to formulate an adequate course of action, we tend to act on impulse or hunches. The result, of course, is likely to be ineffective coping. As Seyle (1976) has expressed it, avoid the "Hurry-Flurry-Worry Syndrome."

3. *Oversimplification.* We have noted the importance of accurately evaluating the stress situation, and our tendency to fit a new stressor into some familiar

category on the basis of our coding patterns. This tends to simplify the problem and to make it more understandable.

Unfortunately, however, in categorizing and defining a problem, there is the danger of oversimplifying and failing to perceive key aspects of the problem. Even though a problem may fit into a given category, it may have unique characteristics which must be considered if we are to cope with it effectively. For example, an obstetrician may have delivered hundreds of babies. However, an obstetrician must always be alert, for each new birth is a unique event which may be accompanied by unexpected problems.

4. *Emotions.* We often tend to perceive what we want to perceive and to believe what we want to believe rather than face the realities of given situations. For example, many people make financial investments and other important decisions based on wishful thinking rather than on cold hard facts concerning the risks and possible costs involved. Our emotions can thus influence our coping responses.

Intense emotions—such as anxiety, fear, and anger—often distort our perception and thought processes and lead to ineffective coping behavior. Fear may exaggerate the severity of the problem and generate an attitude of apprehension which paralyzes effective action. An action taken when we are angry and wish to get even with someone is likely to be an unwise one.

Even positive emotions may lead to costly errors. Many people who feel that they are in love may get married when they are in fact only infatuated. In many obvious as well as subtle ways, our emotions may lead to errors in coping.

5. *Defensive orientation.* The person whose behavior is directed primarily toward enhancing feelings of adequacy and worth or toward protecting an inaccurate self-concept shows considerable resistance to accepting new information or to facing unpleasant problems. The problem-solving ability of such persons is also likely to be impaired by a tendency to rationalize away errors, which, in turn, makes it difficult to learn from mistakes.

The handling of problems is often complicated by such a defensive orientation. For example, a supervisor at work may feel threatened by co-workers and insist that his way of dealing with work issues is correct, despite evidence to the contrary. Emotional involvement in the situation prevents him from approaching the problem with the needed objectivity.

6. *Self-pity.* While it is easy to detect self-pity in the behavior of others, it is often less easy to detect it in our own behavior. And undetected and uncorrected self-pity can be a particularly pernicious form of self-defeating behavior. In permitting ourselves the luxury of self-pity, we alienate others and neglect constructive action.

Often, of course, it is difficult to avoid self-pity. After some painful loss or setback, each of us has probably asked "Why did this have to happen to me?" or speculated about "If *only* . . ." Both of these responses offer possible means of detecting self-pity in ourselves and of taking possible measures to deal with it. But the more we indulge in self-pity and permit past hurts and traumas to dominate our behavior, the more immobilized we become in taking effective action in coping with present realities.

7. *Social influences.* We often fail to see the dimensions of stressful situations because our perspective is limited by the cultural setting in which we live.

We learn certain approved ways of perceiving and dealing with problems and are prone to think of these as the only "right" ways. If we are aware of other approaches at all, we consider them inferior or ridiculous. There is an old story of an American who ridiculed his Chinese friend for putting food upon the graves of his loved ones—a foolish custom, he pointed out, since the dead could not eat. The Chinese friend replied that what the American said was true but that the custom was no more foolish than the American one of putting flowers on the graves of loved ones—for neither could the dead see or smell. In essence, while we tend to attribute irrational and ineffective coping behavior to limitations of the individual, such behavior may also reflect cultural limitations and irrationality which are widely shared and usually considered normal.

## USING STRESS FOR PERSONAL GROWTH

Stress is an inevitable fact of life. Faced with this inevitability, we can respond in one of two ways: we can simply *react* to stress, allowing the events of life to push us willy-nilly from one difficult situation to another. Or, we can take advantage of stress and make it work for us. While stress can exact a high toll in lowering adaptive resources and in wear and tear on the human system, it can also produce stronger and more mature persons forged by the demands and challenges of severe stress situations.

Our task in this section is to show how stress situations can be utilized for personal growth. We shall assume that stress is an inevitable part of normal life and that individuals can plan for and utilize stress situations for personal growth. Specifically, we shall focus on: *(a)* increasing our understanding of ourselves and our world, *(b)* working out more realistic goals and values, and *(c)* developing increased competence and stress tolerance.

### Increasing Our Understanding

At the age of fifty-seven, a woman of world renown looked back at her life and wrote: "Somewhere along the line of development we discover what we really are and then we make our real decision for which we are responsible. Make this decision primarily for yourself because you can never really live anyone else's life, not even your own child's. The influence you exert is through your own life and what you become yourself" (Lash, 1971).

The woman was Eleanor Roosevelt. A crucial decision point in her life was apparently precipitated by a painful event during her mid-thirties—her husband's infidelity. It led her to the realization that we cannot aspire to self-fulfillment through someone else—that we must shape our own lives. As a result, she left an indelible imprint on over four of the most significant decades in our country's history.

# Insight
## PERSONALITY CHARACTERISTICS ASSOCIATED WITH EFFECTIVE COPING

Another approach to assessing coping and adjustment is in terms of those personality characteristics that appear to foster personal effectiveness (Jahoda, 1958).

**Attitudes toward self**
- Emphasizing self-acceptance, adequate self-identity, realistic appraisal of one's assets and liabilities

**Perception of reality**
- A realistic view of oneself and the surrounding world of people and things

**Integration**
- Unity of personality, freedom from disabling inner conflicts, good stress tolerance

**Competencies**
- Development of essential physical, intellectual, emotional, and social competencies for coping with life problems

**Autonomy**
- Adequate self-reliance, responsibility, and self-direction—together with sufficient independence of social influences

**Growth, self-actualization**
- Emphasizing trends toward increasing maturity, development of potentialities, and self-fulfillment as a person

Through our experiences in stressful situations, we often gain a clearer view of who and what we are. For example, successfully completing a difficult course is not only a source of satisfaction in its own right, but also evidence that our abilities and competencies are much greater than we had assumed them to be.

Similarly, a traumatic experience may help us to learn more about the nature of our world. In a divorce, for example, we may for the first time gain a realistic view of the person we married. And we may also learn to better understand the hurtful experiences that other people undergo. Unless we have "been there" ourselves, it is often impossible to understand and empathize with another person's experiences or even to help, even though we sincerely desire to do so. It is perhaps for this reason that people who have undergone highly stressful experiences are often effective in helping others with similar problems. Members of Alcoholics Anonymous, former heroin addicts, and exconvicts may be more effective therapists than trained mental health workers who have never undergone such experiences themselves.

In this general context, Bovet (1973) has summarized the improved understanding of self and others that may stem from our reactions to stress—even highly negative experiences—as follows: "It is a curious fact . . . that such loss and such pain frequently enlarge a person's vision and feeling. It can lead to an enlargement of the understanding of the suffering of others . . ." (p. 6). Such experiences are not without their costs, of course. But, when they are used constructively, they can be a "creative suffering" whose outcome can be personal growth.

## Working Out More Realistic Goals and Values

*"God grant me the serenity to accept the things I cannot change,*
*Courage to change the things I can*
*And wisdom to know the difference."*
*SERENITY PRAYER (ATTRIBUTED TO REINHOLD NIEBUHR)*

If we fail to achieve difficult goals which are unrealistic in terms of our coping resources, we may utilize feedback constructively and lower our aspirations to a more realistic level. Or, our successes may encourage us to raise our aspirations and bring them in line with our abilities. In essence, the problem is not to avoid challenge and stress, but to pick the right kind.

Unfortunately, this is not always an easy task. Because of parental and self-expectations and pressures, for example, some students pursue educational and career goals which are inappropriate to their own interests and resources. In one instance, a mother and father—both of whom were physicians—had high hopes that their only son would also become a physician. As a result, the son dutifully embarked on a premedical major at a large university. The results were failing

A realistic assessment of our abilities and talents will help us meet life's challenges.

grades, feelings that he had let himself and his parents down, and depression. Three weeks before final exams, he attempted suicide.

Later, he obtained professional counseling concerning his interests and capabilities and changed his college major. Had he received such assistance earlier, he could have avoided a highly traumatic situation. When we are emotionally involved in stress situations, however, we often fail to see the alternatives available to us. But awareness that we can usually exercise some measure of control over the stresses to which we expose ourselves can be helpful.

In another situation, the student involved had set her aspirations too low. Taught from birth that females from her ethnic and racial background were expected to become little more than educated homemakers and mothers, the student was surprised to find that she was challenged and stimulated by her college courses. Responding to the challenge, she studied hard and received excellent grades. Perhaps more importantly, she learned that her skills and abilities were greater than she had been taught to believe or imagined them to be, and her self-esteem improved as well. For this student, working out more realistic goals and values involved *raising* her aspirations.

When our goals prove unrewarding and unsatisfying, we must take a hard look at our aspirations and values and, perhaps, modify our assumptions and goals. If our aspirations are unrealistically high, we may need to modify them. And, if we are unstimulated, bored, and unchallenged, our values and goals may also need modification.

## Improving Our Competence and Stress Tolerance

In the process of dealing with life's problems, we usually learn through experience to deal more effectively with various stress situations. And when we fail in these situations, we need not see the failure as unmitigated disaster but as a cue to alert us to the need for improving our competencies in given areas.

Severe stress may "sensitize" us to certain types of stressful situations or it may "immunize" us and increase our feelings of self-confidence and our coping ability. As West (1958) has pointed out: ". . . an experience may be both frightening and painful, yet its repetition may be less stressful because it is now familiar, because its limits have been perceived, because the memory and imagination of the individual enable him to equate it with other known experiences, and because defenses have been developed through fantasied reexperiences during the interval" (p. 332). He might have added that we may also go about improving our competence systematically if we feel we are likely to encounter the same type of stress situation in the future.

Improving our competence and stress tolerance appears to involve two basic tasks: *(1)* the acquisition of essential knowledge and *(2)* the inner control over such knowledge (Anderson, 1982; Hammond & Summers, 1972). In a study of parachutists, for example, Fenz and Epstein (1969) found that while all were anxious, the anxiety of trained parachutists peaked some time before the actual jump. For the untrained parachutists, intense anxiety continued right up to the jump and interfered with performance. A number of other investigators have made comparable findings with trained astronauts and concluded that they had learned some method of controlling anxiety during stressful situations. In essence, as an individual becomes increasingly capable of functioning in a stressful situation, any emotional distress he or she may experience tends to occur before or after the stress is over—thus permitting the adaptive capabilities to work best when they are most needed.

This section on utilizing stress for personal growth goes beyond the problem of learning to cope with simple adjustive demands to the problem of learning to cope constructively with severe and sustained stress situations. This is a never ending process for most of us whereby we learn to understand more about ourselves and others, to modify our goals and expectations in keeping with our skills and with reality, and to increase our competence and stress tolerance. Thus while adaptation to severe stress can be unpleasant, it can also serve as a constructive experience in which we become wiser, stronger, and more mature persons.

## SUMMARY

1. Psychologists and others have developed a variety of techniques that an individual can use to cope effectively with stress.

2. Using a general problem-solving strategy, we can describe a four-step process for dealing with stress. First, we must evaluate the stress situation. Second, we must work out an appropriate course of action. This part of the problem-solving strategy involves a number of procedures, including formulating alternatives, weighing benefits, and balancing probabilities of success and costs. In the third step, we take positive action. Finally, we use feedback to help assess the quality of our stress-coping mechanisms and to guide our future actions.

3. Cognitive techniques, including those of stress inoculation, can be used to deal with the perception of stress. Stress inoculation typically involves three stages: an educational phase, a rehearsal phase, and an application phase.

4. Relaxation, exercise, and involvement in alternative activities are methods that can be used to help control the physiological and psychological responses to stress.

5. Assuming that we guard against errors in our stress-coping strategies, we may find that stress situations can lead to personal growth by increasing our understanding of ourselves and our world, by establishing more realistic goals, and by improving our competence and stress tolerance.

# Chapter 10

# Maladaptive Behavior

Behavior becomes maladaptive when it no longer meets the adjustive demand, when it no longer meets the needs of the individual, or when it disturbs the well-being of society. In applying these criteria, it becomes apparent that we are dealing with a continuum of effective-ineffective coping behavior. Most people cluster around the central point of the continuum and show an average level of adjustment. At one end of the continuum, we find a few people who lead unusually effective lives and achieve a superior level of adjustment. And, at the other end of the continuum, we find a minority with severe maladjustment.

Specific individuals may fall anywhere on this continuum, and their position on the continuum may change with time. Under sustained exposure to severe stress, an individual's level of adjustment may show a marked decline, improving when the person's life situation becomes less stressful or when more effective coping methods are learned.

Our organization in this chapter reflects this continuum. First, we shall discuss some potentially maladaptive behaviors that are very common but whose effect on the general functioning of the individual is very mild. Next, our discussion turns to some traditional, but relatively common maladaptive disorders. Finally, we shall discuss some maladaptive patterns whose effects on the individual can be very severe. The diagnostic labels we shall employ come primarily from the third edition of the Diagnostic and Statistical Manual **(DSM-III)** of the American Psychiatric Association (1980).

**DSM-III: third edition of the Diagnostic and Statistical Manual of the American Psychiatric Association, used in diagnosing mental disorders**

Within each subsection, evidence of the adaptive-maladaptive continuum may be present. For example, our discussion of depression, a relatively common though usually mild maladaptive behavior, will also touch on the less frequent but more serious problem of suicide.

As you read through this material, keep in mind the "medical students' disease syndrome." As medical students learn about the various diseases and disorders that people are prey to, they worry whether they too have the disease. Each twinge and pain that they experience is overinterpreted by the students as unambiguous evidence that they are suffering from the disease being studied.

The same can happen to readers of psychology texts. While reading about maladaptive behavior, some students may overinterpret every minor idiosyncrasy and creative thought as undeniable evidence of severe psychopathology. Having one or more characteristics of the maladaptive problems described in this chapter may *not* be evidence that you have a maladaptive behavior.

## LIFE-STYLE PROBLEMS

Some behavior patterns are so common that we often do not think of them as maladaptive. Because they are so prevalent, they are often considered part of an individual's life-style. However, a person who engages in these behaviors may eventually find him- or herself experiencing psychological and physical difficulties.

Our focus in this section will be on three areas in which problems frequently occur: smoking, drinking, and eating. Of necessity, our coverage of each area will be relatively brief.

# Insight

It is not easy to make a distinction between adaptive and maladaptive behaviors. Since our behavior has mixtures of both adaptive and maladaptive aspects, we cannot easily decide whether our behavior is best considered adaptive or maladaptive, normal or abnormal.

Consider Figure 10-1; this curve represents the adaptive-maladaptive continuum. Extremely adaptive individuals would be located on the left side of the graph, while the behavior of individuals on the right side would be very maladaptive. As you can see, most individuals fall in the middle of the adaptive-maladaptive continuum.

At what point in this graph should we consider behavior to be maladaptive or in need of therapeutic intervention? Should the upper 1 percent (represented by those individuals to the right of point A), 5 percent (represented by individuals to the right of point B), 10 percent (represented by

## WHAT IS MALADAPTIVE?

point C), 25 percent (point D), or 50 percent (point E) be considered maladaptive? How is the selection of one point justified over the selection of another point?

As you might guess, these decisions are generally difficult to make. One factor, however, seems to be quite important in helping make this subtle distinction: a behavior is considered maladaptive when the individual or society at large labels it as maladaptive. The decision whether a behavior is adaptive or maladaptive essentially rests on a *personal* or *social labeling process* (Lahey & Ciminero, 1980). That is, when an individual is sufficiently distressed, he or she will seek assistance. In some cases, the individual does not feel distress, but the behaviors involved are sufficiently distressing that the individual's family or society at large labels the behavior as maladaptive. This second process can occur in cases of schizophrenia or antisocial behavior.

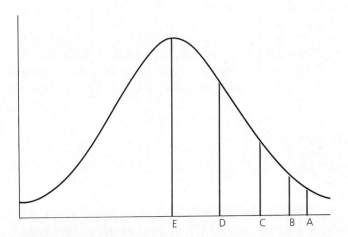

**FIGURE 10.1 The Adaptive-Maladaptive Continuum**

## Problems with Smoking

The two common life-style problems associated with smoking are the use of tobacco and the use of marijuana. About 30 percent of females and 38 percent of males over twenty years of age used cigarettes regularly in 1979—smoking over 600 billion cigarettes (United States Public Health Service, 1980). Similarly, it was estimated that more than 60 percent of young adults have used marijuana, and 20 percent or more use it regularly. As we shall see, however, both tobacco and marijuana use are associated with significant risks for the individual.

**nicotine: central nervous system stimulant and the active ingredient in tobacco**

**Tobacco and nicotine.**   The active ingredient in tobacco is **nicotine,** a central nervous system stimulant. Nicotine is an addictive drug, and withdrawal from nicotine (smoking cessation) is, for many, a frustrating experience.

Most people begin smoking because of peer pressure. They think that smoking makes them more "mature." They think that smoking makes them more alluring and sophisticated, or that smoking gives them a mean, tough image. Whatever the initial reasons, most smokers believe they can quit anytime. Unfortunately, the evidence on this point is not encouraging: of all smokers who enter smoking cessation programs, only about 33 percent remain exsmokers one year after the end of the program (Lichtenstein & Penner, 1977; Pomerleau, Adkins, & Pertschuk, 1978). However, many smokers do quit without treatment (Schachter, 1982).

The side effects of nicotine use are many and severe. It is estimated that an individual's life is shortened by fourteen minutes for each cigarette smoked (Julien, 1981). Cigarette smokers have an increased likelihood of dying from cancers of the lung, voice box, mouth, and throat, from heart attacks and coronary artery disease, and from chronic lung diseases. Although many of these diseases historically were concentrated among men, the increased incidence of cigarette smoking among women has caused cigarette-related death rates for women to increase as well. And, pregnant women who smoke have more difficult pregnancies, more still-births, and lower-weight babies as compared with women who do not smoke.

Many smokers deny that these negative effects could happen to them. However, there is no denying the stained fingers and teeth of smokers, the innumerable ashes, cigarette butts, and unpleasant odors cigarette smokers leave behind. Despite these many negatives, many smokers are unwilling to give up their habit. Graham Lee Hemminger (1915) has summarized the paradox of smoking in his poem, "Tobacco":

*Tobacco is a dirty weed. I like it.*
*It satisfies no normal need. I like it.*
*It makes you thin, it makes you lean,*
*It takes the hair right off your bean.*
*It's the worst darn stuff I've ever seen.*
*    I like it.*

**marijuana: dried leaves and tops of a hemp plant that produce a tranquilizing or psychoactive effect when smoked or eaten**

**Marijuana.**   **Marijuana,** also known as grass, pot, and weed, has been used since ancient times. It comes from the plant *cannabis sativa* whose resin can be dried to form *hashish*. The active ingredient in both marijuana and hashish is *tetrahydrocannabinol,* also known as *THC.* THC has a mild tranquilizing effect at low doses, while at higher doses it can have a hallucinogenic effect. Marijuana is not an addicting drug, but users may develop psychological dependence upon it. As with tobacco, initial use of marijuana typically occurs in association with peer models.

The short-term effects of marijuana can include a sense of well-being, relaxation, and relief from anxiety. Users may find that their perception of time is altered. They may report an increased sensitivity to stimuli and an increased appetite. Because marijuana affects judgment and motor skills, those who are intoxicated by this drug should not drive or use dangerous equipment.

The long-term effects of marijuana are a matter of controversy, but evidence is mounting that its long-term use may be associated with some risks to the individual. Two such risks are the suppression of immune responses in males and females and a lowering of testosterone levels in males.

Current evidence on marijuana suggests that it is not the "killer weed" it was once thought to be, but neither is it a totally harmless substance. Users should be aware of the potential risks that marijuana poses to both their physical and psychological functioning.

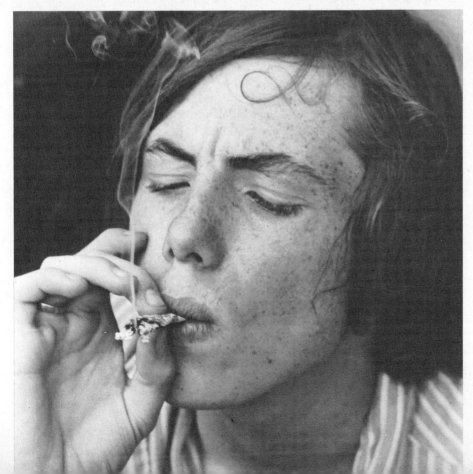

Some people smoke marijuana to experience the heightened sensitivity to sensory stimuli associated with use of the drug. Negative side effects may include depression, loss of energy, coughing, and, occasionally, nausea and vomiting.

## Problems with Drinking

Another area in which life-style problems occur is in the area of drinking. In this section we shall discuss problems associated with two substances: caffeine and alcohol. Because alcohol use and abuse can have serious effects, both for the individual and for society, our coverage of this substance will be somewhat more comprehensive.

**caffeine: central nervous system stimulant found in coffee, tea, and many soft drinks**

**Caffeine.** **Caffeine** is probably the most commonly used drug in the United States. It is found in coffee, tea, cola drinks, chocolate candy, and cocoa. Approximately 15 million pounds of caffeine are consumed every year in the United States (Julien, 1981).

Caffeine is a central nervous stimulant, and its stimulating properties are well-known by students who use this substance to stay awake and maintain mental alertness during study sessions that last long into the night. When high levels of caffeine are ingested, however, the individual may become restless, irritable, and have difficulty sleeping. Pregnant women should avoid caffeine, particularly during the first three months of pregnancy.

Unfortunately, avoiding caffeine may be difficult. Not only is caffeine present in many nonalcoholic social beverages such as coffee, tea, and cola drinks, it can also be found in a variety of carbonated citrus-flavored drinks and aspirin compounds. However, the risks to the individual from moderate caffeine use are fairly small, and most people can sip their favorite beverages without needless worry about its effects upon them.

**alcoholism: excessive use of and dependence on alcohol, impairing important life adjustments**

**Alcohol.** An estimated 100 million or more Americans use alcoholic beverages. The majority of their drinking is moderate, responsible, and socially approved. However, an estimated 12 to 15 million Americans use alcohol excessively and are labeled alcoholics—individuals whose drinking seriously impairs their life adjustment in terms of health, personal relationships, and occupational functioning. In recent years, alcohol has become the "drug of choice" among teen-agers, and the incidence of alcoholism in this age group has risen dramatically. Among college students, alcohol is one of the most commonly abused drugs. **Alcoholism** has also increased among women and now approaches that of men.

The potentially detrimental effects of alcoholism for the individual and his or her loved ones—as well as society—are legion. As Bengelsdorf (1970) has written, "its abuse has killed more people, sent more victims to hospitals, generated more police arrests, broken up more marriages and homes, and cost industry more money than has the abuse of heroin, amphetamines, barbiturates, and marijuana combined" (p. 7).

It might be added that alcohol has been implicated in more than half the deaths resulting from automobile accidents, 50 percent of all murders, 35 percent of rapes, and 30 percent of the suicides that occur each year in our society. The life span of the average alcoholic is about twelve years shorter than that of the nonalcoholic. Alcoholism and its complications now rank as the third leading cause of death in the United States, behind only heart disease and cancer.

Although alcohol is a drug widely used by American youths to-day, many of them fail to recognize the seri-ous health hazards as-sociated with alcohol abuse.

Contrary to popular belief, alcohol is not a stimulant but a depressant that numbs the higher brain centers and thus lessens their inhibiting control. This release may lead people to say or do things they would normally inhibit. Drinkers may also find that alcohol provides a sense of well-being in which unpleasant realities are minimized and their sense of adequacy is increased. When the alcohol content of the blood reaches 0.1 percent, visual-motor and thought processes are seriously impaired and the individual is assumed to be in a state of **alcoholic intoxication.** When the alcoholic content reaches 0.5 percent, the neurophysi-ological balance is severely disturbed and the drinker passes out.

alcoholic intoxication: disruption of inhibi-tions, visual-motor pro-cesses, and cognitive functions produced by alcohol ingestion

Because alcoholism often progresses slowly and by subtle degrees in its po-tential victim, the line that separates social drinking from alcoholism is not always readily observable. According to the Japanese proverb, ''First the man takes a drink, then the drink takes a drink and then the drink takes the man.'' A general view of the stages which are commonly involved in the development may be outlined as follows (Jellinek, 1971):

1. *Prodomal phase.* The social drinker turns increasingly to alcohol for relief of tension, present or anticipated. Toward the end of this period a number of warning signs, including morning drinking, point to approaching alcoholism.

2. *Crucial phase.* People lose control over their drinking in this phase. One drink seems to start a chain reaction, although they can still partially control the occasions when they will or will not take the first drink. In this phase, people frequently begin to rationalize and make alibis for their drinking. Often they en-counter criticism from family and friends.

3. *Chronic phase.* Here the drinkers' control over drinking completely breaks down and alcohol plays an increasingly dominant role in everyday activities. At the same time, the drinkers' physiological tolerance for alcohol decreases, and they now become intoxicated on far less alcohol than previously. They may also begin to experience tremors and other symptoms while sober—leading to further

# Insight

1. *Frequent desire.* An early warning sign of potential alcoholism is an increase in desire, often evidenced by eager anticipation of drinking after work and careful attention to maintaining a supply of alcohol.

2. *Increased consumption.* Another early warning sign is increasing consumption of alcohol. This increase may seem gradual, but a marked change takes place from month to month. Often the individual will begin to worry about his or her drinking at this point and begin to lie about the amount actually consumed.

3. *Extreme behavior.* When the individual, under the influence of alcohol, commits various acts that cause guilt and embarrassment the next day, it is an indication that the person's drinking is getting out of control.

4. *Blackouts.* When the individual cannot remember what happened during an alcoholic bout, his or her indulgence is becoming excessive.

5. *Morning drinking.* An important sign that a frequent drinker may be becoming an alcoholic appears when he or she begins to drink in the morning—either as a means of reducing a hangover or as a "bracer" to help start the day.

A person who exhibits the preceding pattern of behavior is well on the road to becoming an alcoholic. Often an additional indication is persistent absenteeism from work, especially on Mondays.

drinking to control such symptoms. During this period, the alcoholic's life situation usually undergoes serious deterioration.

The causal patterns in alcoholism are not fully understood, but several biological, psychological, and sociocultural factors have been emphasized. One biological possibility is that some individuals—perhaps as a result of genetic factors—develop a physiological addiction to and craving for alcohol more readily than others (Miller, 1976). Psychologically, alcoholism has been viewed as stemming from excessive stress, and the learned use of alcohol has been seen as a crutch in trying to cope with life's problems. In fact, many investigators view alcoholism as a learned maladaptive response which is reinforced and maintained by the brief release of tensions that accompany intoxication. Still other studies have emphasized parental models and broader sociocultural conditions that encourage or discourage the excessive use of alcohol. For example, alcoholism is rare among Mormons, whose religious values prohibit the use of alcohol. As with many other life-style problems, alcohol use is often initially associated with peer pressure.

Researchers are now working on methods to help the alcoholic individual quit drinking and to maintain new sober habits for long periods of time. Very often, the alcoholic individual finds his or her drinking so disruptive that he or she must enter an alcohol detoxification program in a hospital. Once the individual is thoroughly withdrawn from alcohol and any medical problems have been treated, the focus of treatment shifts to learning how to handle daily stresses without reaching for the bottle. Some of the more promising programs teach individuals how to recognize situations that are "high-risk" for drinking and how to deal with these troublesome situations (Marlatt & Gordon, 1980).

Among the traditional programs for treating alcoholism are the well-known self-help groups such as **Alcoholics Anonymous** (AA). AA, for example, teaches that for an alcoholic to be helped, he or she must "hit bottom" and admit his or her alcoholism. Then the group supports available within AA are used to help the alcoholic through crisis periods or difficult times. Although statistics on their effectiveness are not available, AA chapters and affiliated groups such as Al-Anon and Al-Ateen are probably the most readily accessible and available programs for the alcoholic and his or her family.

**Alcoholics Anonymous (AA): organization composed of alcoholics for treatment of alcoholism and maintaining of abstinence via personal, religious, and social reinforcement**

## Problems with Eating

For many Americans, the major problem associated with eating is obesity. Some people eat in binges and become bulimic. And, a small but apparently growing proportion of the population voluntarily chooses not to eat in anorexia nervosa.

**Obesity.**   Depending on the measure used, between 40 and 80 million Americans are obese (Lahey & Ciminero, 1980). **Obesity** occurs in both young and old alike, and it is caused by an imbalance between caloric intake and energy expenditure.

**obesity: excessive weight**

The major physical risk of obesity is cardiovascular disease. Additionally, poor weight control can increase the severity of disorders such as diabetes and hyper-

**In a society like ours, which associates attractiveness and social desirability with thinness, the obese individual may suffer from social isolation and loss of self-esteem.**

tension. On a more individual level, obesity may produce depression, social withdrawal, and anxiety.

Because obesity is socially and individually disapproved, many individuals undertake a variety of diets to help them get their weight under control. Some of these diets emphasize protein intake or carbohydrate intake. Some suggest fasting to help control weight. However, all these exotic diets (many of which can be found in books on best-seller lists) fail in an important way. That is, most diets do not change the individual's eating habits and life-style sufficiently to help ensure permanent weight control. The most effective approaches (Abramson, 1977) combine diet control with increases in exercise and a general alteration of obese life-styles.

**anorexia nervosa: disorder characterized by excessive weight loss**

**Anorexia nervosa.**    Unlike the obese individual, the person suffering from **anorexia nervosa** eats far too little. In essence, anorexia nervosa produces self-starvation. Although rare, this disorder appears to be increasing in frequency.

Most anorexic individuals are females in their teens or twenties. Part of the reason for the predominance of this disorder among females is the cultural ideal for females to be "model thin." Often the anorexic individual is highly achievement-oriented, conscientious, and somewhat shy and introverted. Anorexics are frequently good students. However, their self-image is of someone who is too fat (Bemis, 1978). There is also some suggestion that anorexic females turn to dieting as a means of trying to resolve emotional problems.

**bulimia: disorder characterized by abnormal, uncontrolled eating**

Many anorexics are obsessed with food and go on periodic binges during which huge amounts of food are consumed—a behavior pattern characteristic of **bulimia**. To prevent this food from adding weight, the anorexic often deliberately induces vomiting or abuses laxatives.

## Life-Style Problems and Adjustment

The life-style problems we have discussed range from the easily controllable use of caffeine to the almost obsessional nature of anorexia and bulimia. In each case, however, the adjustment issue is not simply that of altering the maladaptive behavior. Rather, each life-style problem is uniquely and deeply related to other aspects of our lives. And, the solution for these problems must be multifaceted as well. For example, if we overuse caffeine, we could, of course, switch to decaffeinated beverages. However, it might be better to examine our lives and see whether improvements in other areas might eliminate our need for caffeine. If our overuse of caffeine is related to inefficient study habits or failure to get enough sleep, we might be better off improving our study habits or finding ways to get the rest we need.

Life-style problems are, for the most part, cues that our efforts to cope with the stresses and demands of life are not meeting with entirely adequate success. Our task, when we are faced with life-style problems, is to use our personal resources, skills, and competencies (or professional assistance if necessary) to develop more adequate coping strategies.

In our next section, we examine some issues that have traditionally been defined as maladaptive problems.

## COMMON MALADAPTIVE PROBLEMS

The three maladaptive problems discussed in this section, anxiety, depression, and psychophysiological disorders, are relatively common. Each of us has, at some time, felt anxiety, experienced the "blues," or had a stomachache before an important school, work, or social event. For most of us, the experience was relatively mild or we were not overly upset by the experience or the episode quickly passed. However, about 5 percent of the population experiences maladaptive levels of these problems (Lahey & Ciminero, 1980). Our discussion begins with anxiety, an experience that is virtually universal.

### Anxiety

*"During the time when Richard Benson, age 38, was experiencing intense anxiety, it often seemed as if he were having a heart seizure. He experienced chest pains and heart palpitations, numbness, shortness of breath, and he felt a strong need to breathe in air. He reported that in the midst of the anxiety attack, he developed a feeling of tightness over his eyes and he could only see objects directly in front of him. He further stated that he feared that he would not be able to swallow. The intensity of the anxiety symptoms was very frightening to him and on two occasions his wife had rushed him to a local hospital because he was in a state of panic, sure that his heart was going to stop beating and he would die."*

*(LEON, 1977, P. 113)*

Richard Benson experienced a high degree of anxiety during a **panic** attack. His panic attack contains most of the elements of **anxiety.** In anxious individuals, a sense of apprehension or dread occurs. The experience is highly aversive, and individuals seek to reduce or eliminate the experience altogether. Anxiety is often accompanied by biological changes, including increased heart rate, perspiration, and blood pressure. Normal activities, such as eating, sleeping, and sex, may be disrupted. The individual may fidget or look upset and preoccupied. Finally, the experience may last only a matter of minutes or may extend for days and weeks at a time.

In Richard Benson's case, the cause of the anxiety attack was not obvious. When the individual cannot identify or does not know the factors that bring on the anxiety, we speak of **free-floating anxiety.** Anxiety of this type is often

**panic: intense anxiety accompanied by signs of physiological arousal and a sense of impending doom**

**anxiety: generalized feelings of fear and apprehension**

**free-floating anxiety: anxiety that is apparently unrelated to specific causes**

associated with troublesome interpersonal relationships. Those who have free-floating anxiety may avoid everyday situations.

In contrast, anxiety may be related to a specific object, person, or situation. In these situations, we speak of a **phobia.** In a phobia, the individual has a grossly exaggerated fear of a situation or object. Although phobics realize that their fear is irrational, their recognition of the irrational nature of their fears does not prevent them from experiencing intense anxiety when in the presence of the object.

**phobia: irrational fear related to a specific situation or object**

Many phobias have been identified. Some of the more common ones are:
- Acrophobia        high places
- Agoraphobia       open places
- Claustrophobia    closed places
- Nyctophobia       darkness
- Zoophobia         animals

Agoraphobia is particularly interesting, since individuals with this disorder rarely leave the safety of their homes. In a case seen by one of the authors, a woman with agoraphobia left her home only three times in seventeen years. Each of the three occasions involved a trip to the hospital where she gave birth to one of her children.

Severe phobic disorders rarely occur in isolation. Often the individual with agoraphobia also reports feelings of depression, abuse of alcohol and other anxiety-reducing drugs, and other fears, frequently involving social situations.

Mild anxiety is a common event. New and unfamiliar work and social situations often produce mild anxiety. Demands placed upon us to perform can produce anxiety as well. We may, for example, feel anxious in a social situation in which we know few people. Giving a speech in front of a large group can also produce anxiety. And failing to meet our own or other people's expectations can be anxiety-evoking as well. Often the anticipation of an event causes significantly more anxiety than the event itself. Our fears prior to giving a speech may be greater than our fears while giving the speech. In these situations, it is important that this anticipatory anxiety not prevent us from accomplishing the task at hand.

**Obsessive-compulsive disorders.**   In some people, anxiety is expressed as an **obsession**—a persistent, often irrational, thought. Often the thought involves issues such as dying, becoming ill, or becoming contaminated. Occasionally, the thoughts involve harming others. Thus, a young mother might be concerned with her child's becoming ill or dying. Or, she may have the horrifying thought of killing her baby.

**obsession: persistent idea or thought**

In contrast, **compulsions** refer to irrational, repetitive, ritualistic acts the individual feels compelled to perform. Just as obsessions are associated with unpleasant thoughts, compulsions are experienced as unpleasant, almost foreign activities. Compulsions can have many forms. A woman may wash her hands every fifteen minutes. Or, a man may check and recheck windows, doors, gas flames, and so forth, prior to retiring for the evening.

**compulsion: irrational and repetitive impulse to perform some act**

Obsessions and compulsions often appear at times of stress. In their mild, nonpathological form, compulsions can be seen in an increased rigidity of behavior. Under heavy pressure, people may set up strict and unvarying procedures for maintaining order and predictability. They may constantly remind themselves of the things that need to be accomplished. Maladaptive obsessions and compulsions are marked exaggerations of these normal patterns.

**Somatoform and dissociative disorders.** **Somatoform disorders** involve the complaint of a physical disorder in the absence of any physical causes of the disorder, while **dissociative disorders** involve a sudden loss of memory or alteration of personal identity.

In somatoform disorders, the complaint can be quite striking: a soldier complains of blindness just prior to entering battle; a woman experiences complete loss of feeling in her arm from the elbow to the fingertips. No physical reasons for the complaints are identifiable in either case. Less dramatically, the **hypochondriac** may have multiple but vague aches, pains, and symptoms.

Somatoform disorders tend to occur during periods when a person is under severe stress. In these individuals, the only acceptable expression of anxiety may be through physical complaints. In Freudian terms, the person "converts" anxiety into physical complaints. Although the complaint is without any physical cause, the symptom is very real to the individual. Surprisingly, many people with these **conversion disorders** show little outward anxiety or concern about their symptoms; indeed, the indifference of these patients toward their symptoms may be striking.

Dissociative disorders, on the other hand, are characterized by a marked alteration of consciousness. People may forget significant parts of their lives. They may wander from familiar surroundings, occasionally developing a new identity in a setting far removed from their homes. In the most severe cases, individuals may take on different personalities.

Dissociative disorders are a dramatic reaction to stress. Often the stress is very severe and sudden and the individual has no adaptive resources with which to handle the demands placed upon him or her. Fortunately, dissociative disorders do not last a long time and are among the least common of the anxiety disorders.

# Depression

At one time or another, we may experience the "blues." Usually, these spells pass fairly quickly, and we can put aside our doubts and worries. At other times, however, depression may linger and become a serious problem. For some persons, depression can be so severe that the individual attempts suicide.

**Mild depression.** **Depression** is a disorder of *affect* (emotion) and occurs so frequently that it has been termed "the common cold of psychopathology" (Seligman, 1975, p. 76). There are literally millions of Americans—some estimates go as high as one person in seven—who each day show mild depression. These individuals usually experience loss of appetite, markedly lowered sex drive, difficulty

**somatoform disorder:** unsubstantiated physical complaint

**dissociative disorder:** alteration of consciousness or identity, associated with severe stress

**hypochondriasis:** disorder in which individuals have many vague physical complaints

**conversion disorder:** loss of motor or sensory functioning without corresponding organic pathology

**depression:** emotional state characterized by feelings of dejection, worthlessness, and gloomy ruminations

# Insight SUICIDE AMONG COLLEGE STUDENTS

**Incidence and methods**

● Ten thousand students in the United States attempt suicide each year, and more than 1000 succeed. The incidence of suicide is twice as high among college students as it is among young people in the same age range who are not in college. The greatest incidence of suicidal behavior occurs at the beginning and the end of the school quarter or semester. Approximately three times more female than male students attempt suicide, but the incidence of fatal attempts is considerably higher among males. More than half of those attempting suicide take pills, about one third cut themselves, and the remainder—mostly males—use other methods, such as hanging or gunshot.

**Warning signs and threats**

● A change in a student's mood and behavior is a most significant warning that he or she may be planning suicide. Characteristically, the student becomes depressed and withdrawn, undergoes a marked decline in self-esteem, and shows deterioration in habits of personal hygiene. This is accompanied by a profound loss of interest in his or her studies. Often the student stops attending classes and remains in his or her room most of the day. Usually the student communicates his or her distress to at least one other person, often in the form of a veiled suicide warning. A significant number of students who attempt suicide leave suicide notes.

**Precipitating factors**

● When a college student attempts suicide, one of the first explanations to occur to friends and family is that he or she may have been doing poorly in school. However, students

in concentrating and making decisions, and impaired personal effectiveness. Tasks that could ordinarily be handled with ease require Herculean effort or seem impossible. Sharing leisure-time pursuits or other activities with loved ones and friends is no longer rewarding. In essence, the joy has gone out of living, to be replaced by an uncomplimentary and unflattering view of oneself and one's world.

The causal factors in depressive episodes may vary, but a relatively common factor seems to be *learned helplessness* (Seligman, 1975). Research studies have shown that when individuals encounter a traumatic situation they cannot control—or *believe* they cannot control—they tend to experience feelings of helplessness and self-devaluation and to become depressed. Action seems futile, and the person stops trying to cope and gives up. Such traumatic experiences include loss of loved ones, educational and occupational failures, chronic illness, and accelerating social change that makes it increasingly difficult for people to sort things out and find meaning in their lives. From an existential perspective, individuals who do not make choices and actualize their potentials may experience a sense of emptiness

who manifest suicidal behavior are, as a group, superior students; they tend to expect a great deal of themselves in terms of academic achievement and to exhibit scholastic anxieties. Grades, academic competition, and pressure over examinations are not significant precipitating stresses. Also, while many lose interest in their studies and their grades get lower prior to the onset of suicidal behavior, the loss of interest appears to be associated with depression and withdrawal caused by problems other than academic ones. Often, the problems are loss of self-esteem and failure to live up to parental expectations, rather than the academic failure itself.

For most suicidal students, both male and female, the major precipitating stress appears to be either the failure to establish, or the loss of, a close interpersonal relationship. The breakup of a romance can be a key precipitating factor. There are also significantly more suicide attempts and suicides by students from families where there has been separation, divorce, or the death of a parent. A particularly important precipitating factor among male college students appears to involve close emotional involvement with his parents, which is threatened when the student becomes involved with another person in college and tries to break this "parental knot."

**Need for assistance**

● Although most colleges and universities have mental health facilities to assist distressed students, few suicidal students seek professional help. Thus, it is of vital importance for those around a suicidal student to notice the warning signs and to try to obtain assistance.

and purposelessness in their lives. Additionally, depressed persons may develop an overly negative view of themselves and their abilities and may interpret their experience in consistently negative ways (Beck, 1972; Weingartner, Cohen, Murphy, Martello, & Gerdt, 1981).

Such episodes of depression are affecting an increasing number of people, including teen-agers and young adults. College students, in particular, seem to be subject to depression—possibly due to the stress of leaving their families, establishing a sense of identity, deciding on life goals, and competing for grades. Sexual adjustments such as "intimacy without emotion" may increase this stress.

Therapy for such mild depressive episodes focuses on changing the individual's feelings of helplessness to the realization that his or her actions can make a difference—that there is hope (Lewinsohn, 1974). Therapy also focuses on replacing the person's negative self-perception with more realistic thoughts and self-concepts (Beck, Rush, Shaw, & Emery, 1979). Most depressive episodes last only a short time; virtually all individuals with mild depression recover fully.

**Suicide.**

*Dear Jim:*
*I've just emptied forty capsules and put the powder in a glass of water.*
*I'm about to take it. I'm scared and I want to talk to someone but I just*
*don't have anybody to talk to. I feel like I'm completely alone and nobody*
*cares. I know our breakup was my fault but it hurts so bad. Nothing I do*
*seems to turn out right, but nothing. My whole life has fallen apart.*
*Maybe if, but I know.*

*I've thought about all of the trite phrases about how it will get*
*brighter tomorrow and how suicide is copping out and really isn't a*
*solution and maybe it isn't but I hurt so bad. I just want it to stop. I feel*
*like my back is up against the wall and there is no other way out.*

*It's getting harder to think and my life is about to end. Tears are*
*rolling down my face and I feel so scared and alone. Oh Jim . . . if you*
*could put your arms around me and hold me close . . . just one last time*
*. . . . . . . . . . . .*

*J . . . m*

suicide: taking one's own life

This note was written by a nineteen-year-old college girl who committed **suicide.**

According to official statistics, more than 200,000 people attempt suicide each year in the United States, and over 25,000 succeed. Of these "successes," 1000 will be college students. The preceding figures indicate that someone in our society attempts suicide every twenty minutes, and that well over 7 million living Americans have attempted to take their lives. In addition, the number of suicides among teen-agers and young adults has more than doubled during the last decade. Since many self-inflicted deaths are officially attributed to other, more "respectable" causes than suicide, experts have estimated that the actual number of suicides in our society is two to five times as high as the number officially reported. And these statistics do not begin to convey the tragedy of suicide in human terms.

Many people go through periods of severe stress during which they contemplate suicide as an answer to their problems. Most do not accept this answer, and even those who do are usually ambivalent about taking their lives. Research studies indicate that the great majority of people who attempt suicide—80 percent or more—are suffering from feelings of hopelessness and depression related to aversive stress. Depression and suicide are distinct but closely related patterns. Depressed persons are a high-risk group with respect to suicide. And the majority of individuals who attempt or commit suicide do so when they are depressed.

In essence, they have a negative view of themselves and their life situation and feel that nothing can be done to improve matters. While the stress factors in suicide may be diverse, they tend to focus around crises in interpersonal relations, failure and self-devaluation, and inability to find—or loss of—meaning in life. Here one is reminded of the haunting lines that open Camus' *Myth of Sisyphus*

# Insight

In assessing "suicide potential," or the probability that a person might carry out a threat to take his or her life, the Los Angeles Suicide Prevention Center uses a "lethality scale" consisting of ten categories:

1. *Age and sex.* The potential is greater if the individual is male rather than female, and is over fifty years of age.

2. *Symptoms.* The potential is greater if the individual manifests such symptoms as sleep disturbances, depression, feelings of hopelessness, or alcoholism.

3. *Stress.* The potential is greater if the individual is subject to such stress as the loss of a loved one through death or divorce, the loss of employment, increased responsibilities, or serious illness.

4. *Acute vs. chronic aspects.* The potential is greater when there is a sudden onset of specific symptoms, a recurrent outbreak of similar symptoms, or a recent increase in long-standing maladaptive traits.

5. *Suicidal plan.* The potential is greater when the lethality of the proposed method, and the organizational clarity and detail of the plan are increased.

## "LETHALITY SCALE" TO ASSESS SUICIDE POTENTIAL

6. *Resources.* The potential is greater if the person has no family or friends, or if his family and friends are unwilling to help.

7. *Prior suicidal behavior.* The potential is greater if the individual has attempted suicide in the past or has a history of repeated threats and depression.

8. *Medical status.* The potential is greater when there is chronic, debilitating illness or the individual has had many unsuccessful experiences with physicians.

9. *Communication aspects.* The potential is greater if communication between the individual and his or her relatives has been broken off, and they reject efforts to reestablish communication.

10. *Reaction of significant others.* The potential is greater if a significant other such as the husband or wife, has a defensive, rejecting, or punishing attitude, and denies that the individual needs help.

The final suicide potential rating is a composite score based on the weighting of each of the ten individual items.

*Based on information supplied by the Los Angeles Suicide Prevention Center

---

(1942/1955): "There is but one truly philosophical problem and that is suicide. Judging whether life is or is not worth living amounts to answering the fundamental question of philosophy" (p. 3).

Suicide prevention is an extremely difficult problem. This is in part due to the diversity of reasons for committing suicide as well as the fact that most people contemplating suicide do not fully realize how badly they need help. However, if the person's "cry for help" can be heard in time, successful intervention is often possible. This is the goal of the over 200 professionally operated suicide-prevention centers in the United States. Such centers ordinarily provide help twenty-four hours a day, usually through telephone services and "outreach teams" aimed at immediate **crisis intervention.**

**crisis intervention:** immediate, short-term assistance provided during a life crisis

## Psychophysiological Reactions

As we have seen in Chapter 8, environmental and perceived stressors produce a number of physiological effects, including changes in the cardiovascular system, respiratory system, and other physical systems. In most people, these changes disappear when the stressors are reduced or eliminated. In some individuals, however, stress produces a pathological change in an organ system. These people suffer from **psychophysiological disorders,** physical disorders produced by psychological stress. Psychophysiological disorders are *not* like the somatoform disorders discussed earlier. In somatoform disorders, the complaint has no physical basis. In contrast, psychophysiological disorders are accompanied by pathological changes. For example, gastric ulcers, which are commonly related to stress, occur when stomach acids destroy part of the stomach lining.

**psychophysiological disorder: physical disorder produced by stress**

Psychophysiological disorders used to be called *psychosomatic* disorders. The term psychosomatic was employed to show that mind ("psyche") and body ("soma") were intimately connected and that each influenced the other. Unfortunately, some individuals have used the term to imply that a patient's sufferings were "all in your mind." That, of course, is not the case. People with psychophysiological disorders have a clearly defined physical problem, one that is related to stress. To eliminate the negative connotations associated with "psychosomatic," workers in this field have adopted the term "psychophysiological."

Psychophysiological disorders comprise a painful and costly group of disorders. These disorders produce significant discomfort, and they may be life-threatening as well. The cost of these disorders is also high. Approximately 50 percent of patient visits to general practitioners involve a psychophysiological stress-related disorder, and these visits clearly place a significant burden on the health care system, as well as on the finances of the patient.

Psychophysiological reactions are classified according to the organ system affected, and no organ system appears to be immune. Among the more common psychophysiological reactions are the following:

1. *Gastrointestinal reactions,* including peptic ulcers, ulcerative colitis, and irritable bowel syndrome.

2. *Respiratory reactions,* including asthma, bronchial spasms, and hyperventilation.

3. *Musculoskeletal reactions,* including backache, muscle cramps, and bruxism (teeth-grinding).

4. *Skin reactions,* including hives, pruritus (itching), and hyperhydrosis (excessive sweating).

5. *Cardiovascular reactions,* including migraine headaches, hypertension (high blood pressure), and tachycardia (rapid heart beat).

6. *Immune reactions,* including rheumatoid arthritis, systemic lupus erythematosus, and chronic active hepatitis.

One question whose answer has eluded researchers in psychophysiological disorders is that of *organ specificity*--why one individual develops peptic ulcers, another high blood pressure, and still another backaches. It may be that the organ system affected is especially vulnerable as a result of prior injury, illness, or other conditions. Or it may be that psychophysiological reactions have been learned through selective reinforcement. For example, a child who has been allowed to avoid school because of a stomachache may learn to manifest gastrointestinal upsets to avoid stress-producing situations as an adult.

A third possibility is that there exist certain "personality types" prone to react to stress with specific emotions that are more likely to affect one organ system than another. For example, we have already noted (Chapter 7) the role that Type A behavior may play in cardiovascular disease.

A more recent and more comprehensive model of psychophysiological disorders focuses on the interaction of the sympathetic and parasympathetic branches of the nervous system with other parts of the body. According to this *disregulation model,* information or feedback about the functioning of the body is not properly utilized (Schwartz, 1977). An individual may deliberately ignore the subtle indicators of an oncoming physical problem, as when a headache sufferer ignores the warning signs of a migraine. Or the person may suffer from some subtle or gross damage to the body that prevents feedback information from being generated or used, as when blood pressure receptors in the circulatory system are damaged through exposure to chronic hypertension.

Although controversy exists regarding the exact causes of psychophysiological disorders, such disorders are relatively common. Peptic or gastric ulcers will affect an estimated 10 percent of the population, and at least 15 percent of the population suffers from hypertension. We will review three of the most common types of psychophysiological reactions: peptic ulcers, migraine and tension headaches, and hypertension.

**Peptic ulcers.**   It is estimated that one in every ten Americans now living will at some time develop a **peptic** (or gastric) **ulcer.** The incidence of such ulcers is some two to three times higher among men than women.

peptic ulcer: also known as *gastric ulcer;* a pathological condition of the stomach brought about by excessive stress

The ulcer itself results from an excessive flow of the stomach's acid-containing digestive juices which eat away the lining of the stomach, leaving a craterlike wound. Although diet, disease, and other organic conditions may lead to peptic ulcers, negative emotional states—such as anxiety, anger, and resentment—can stimulate the flow of stomach acids beyond what is needed for digestion.

Some of our most useful knowledge of ulcers comes from a historic study reported by Wolf and Wolff (1947). In this study, the researchers reported on the case of Tom, an individual whose surgery left him with a "window" to his stomach. When Tom was subjected to interview experiences designed to elicit strong negative emotions, his stomach became engorged with blood and increased its production of acids. When the emotional experiences stopped, his stomach gradually returned to normal. If, however, his stomach lining was continually exposed to increased acid production, an ulcer occurred.

It is likely that similar events occur in daily living. That is, we may become upset and angry and our stomachs may respond in an equally negative manner. If we can manage the stress, our stomachs will produce less acid. If, however, we cannot control the stresses, our stomachs, like Tom's, will be continually bathed in strong acids, and an ulcer may occur.

**Migraine and tension headaches.** Although headaches can result from a wide range of organic conditions, most headaches—about nine out of ten—seem to be related to emotional tension. An estimated 20 million Americans suffer from recurrent migraine and tension headaches, with the incidence apparently being higher among women than men.

**Migraine headaches** are caused when the cranial arteries overdilate and become inflamed. Occasionally, migraine sufferers are warned that a migraine attack is about to occur. These warnings, called the **aura,** may consist of unusual sensitivity to light and sound; occasionally, the onset of a migraine attack may be signaled by the presence of spots of light in the visual field. If the individual takes certain drugs, particularly those containing ergot derivatives, the migraine attack may be prevented. If not, the person not only suffers from intense head pain, but also may report dizziness, nausea, and vomiting. Migraines can appear on just one side of the head or may appear on both sides. These dramatic symptoms may be caused by hormonal changes, allergies, and other organic conditions, but the majority of migraine attacks are related to psychological stress.

In contrast, **muscle contraction** or **tension headaches** occur as "bands" of pain around the head. Less dramatic than migraines, tension headaches occur more frequently and may last significantly longer than the six to twenty-four hours of a migraine attack. Although the phrase *tension headache* implies that muscle tension is involved in tension headaches, the data on this point are surprising. The research that is available suggests that people with tension headaches have, in fact, *less* muscle tension in the forehead and neck than non-headache sufferers (Bakal & Kaganov, 1977). However, the possibility exists that tension headache sufferers are more likely to respond to psychological stress with muscle tension, and researchers are exploring this possibility.

Treatment for both types of headaches often focuses on identifying and coping with the events that precipitate stress. If, for example, it is discovered that a headache follows an unpleasant encounter with a loved one, the therapist might teach the headache sufferer how to deal more effectively with the relationship issues that appear to cause the individual so much pain.

Another interesting avenue of treatment involves helping people directly control the physiological events producing the headache. For example, a treatment procedure called **biofeedback** may be used to help people control the cranial arteries that dilate during a migraine attack. Through biofeedback, the individual receives information about physiological processes that occur, such as the dilation of cranial arteries, and then uses this information to control the activity of these cranial arteries. Studies using this procedure have been remarkably successful in reducing both the incidence and intensity of migraines (Bild & Adams, 1980).

**Hypertension.** Of the various organ systems, the circulatory system is perhaps the most sensitive to emotional stress. As stress mounts, the heart beats faster and with greater force, and blood pressure mounts. Usually, when the stress or crisis passes, the body resumes normal functioning and blood pressure returns to normal. But under sustained exposure to emotional stress, high blood pressure

---

migraine headache: severe, intense headache, often accompanied by nausea and vomiting

aura: warning symptoms of an oncoming migraine headache

muscle contraction (tension) headache: most common form of headaches, characterized by "bands" of pain around the head

biofeedback: self-control procedure in which feedback of biological activity is used to control bodily processes

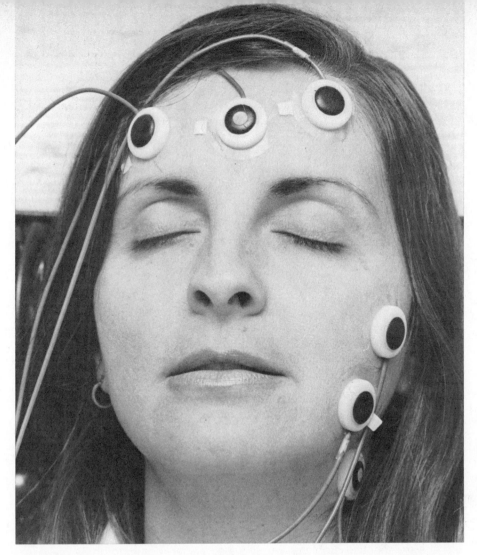

Through biofeedback, an individual can learn to control certain bodily processes which were once considered automatic. For example, a person can learn to raise or lower skin temperature or blood pressure and to control certain brain waves.

may become chronic. Only 10 percent of high blood pressure cases can be attributed to organic factors, such as diseases of the kidney (Benson, 1975). In the remaining cases, dietary factors, obesity, and emotional stress play a key role.

Over 25 million persons in the United States suffer from chronically high blood pressure or **hypertension.** It is a primary cause of more than 60,000 deaths each year and a major underlying factor in another million or more deaths from strokes and heart attacks. The incidence of hypertension ranges from 15 percent of whites to 30 percent of blacks (Freis, 1973). The increased rate of hypertension among blacks may be due to both dietary factors and environmental stressors.

hypertension: chronically high blood pressure

Unlike most other psychophysiological disorders, there are usually no symptoms to signal high blood pressure. The individual usually experiences no personal distress, although in severe cases some persons complain of headaches, tiredness, insomnia, or occasional dizzy spells—symptoms often easy to ignore. As Mays (1974) has described the situation: "In most instances . . . the disease comes as silently as a serpent stalking its prey. Someone with high blood pressure may be unaware of his affliction for many years and then, out of the blue, develop blindness or be stricken by a stroke, cardiac arrest, or kidney failure'' (p. 7).

There is no such thing as ''benign hypertension.'' High blood pressure is an insidious and life-threatening disorder. Fortunately, it is both simple and painless to detect and can usually be controlled by changes in diet, weight loss, medication, and stress-reduction techniques.

In general, psychophysiological reactions appear to involve three aspects: *(a)* sustained exposure to stress which arouses emotional tension; *(b)* the individual's failure to cope adequately with the stress, resulting in the continuation of emotional arousal on a chronic basis; and *(c)* organ specificity, in which the effects of chronic emotional arousal are concentrated in a specific organ system, presumably as a result of the vulnerability of the system due to such factors as prior illness or conditioning.

As Hull (1977) has pointed out, a wide range of physical and mental disorders can be influenced in their onset, course, and outcome by life stress. And while psychophysiological reactions do not always seriously impair the individual's coping ability, they tend to be costly reactions to stress in terms of personal discomfort and/or tissue damage.

## MORE SERIOUS MALADAPTIVE PROBLEMS

In this section we shall deal with behavior patterns which are seriously maladaptive. These patterns are highly detrimental to the individual and often to those around him or her. The specific patterns we shall discuss include: *(a)* drug abuse, *(b)* antisocial behavior, and *(c)* schizophrenia and the other psychoses. Of necessity our coverage will be limited, but we shall try to cover the key factors involved in each of these maladaptive patterns. Keep in mind that these maladaptive patterns, like the maladaptive problems we discussed earlier, occur on an adaptive-maladaptive continuum.

### Drug Abuse

One way we can cope with stress is to escape by chemical means—through alcohol and other drugs. Although problems of drug abuse are by no means new, scientific attention has only recently focused upon them.

In our discussion, we will be identifying some commonly abused drugs and describing the effects of drug abuse and dependence. But first, we need to define some of the terms we will be using in our discussion.

In traditional usage, the term *dependence* has signified psychological dependence on a particular drug, while *addiction* has signified physiological dependence, as indicated by *withdrawal symptoms* if the drug is discontinued. Recently, however, the term **drug dependence** has come to include both physiological and psychological dependence on the drug. **Drug abuse** refers to the excessive use of a drug whether or not the individual is dependent on it. For example, an individual

**drug dependence: psychological or physiological need for a drug**

**drug abuse: use of drugs to the extent that it interferes with health or adjustment**

# Insight

## HOMOSEXUALITY: A MALADAPTIVE BEHAVIOR?

Homosexuality has been widely misunderstood throughout history. The Judeo-Christian tradition in Western thought has consistently maintained that homosexuality is unnatural and sinful (Katchadourian & Lunde, 1980). Laws and traditions have imposed severe sanctions on homosexual behavior, including imprisonment and burning at the stake. Even today, the general population of the United States does not approve of homosexuality (Katchadourian & Lunde, 1980).

Given these negative feelings, it is no surprise that homosexuality was, until recent times, a little-known and little-understood phenomenon. While much has been said and written about homosexuality throughout history, little that was known about homosexuality had a scientific basis. Some of the earliest and most reliable information about homosexuality came from the famous Kinsey studies (Kinsey et al., 1948, 1953). As part of the survey of sexual behaviors, Kinsey et al. reported that 37 percent of men and 13 percent of women had had some homosexual encounter at some point in their lives. These numbers, suggesting that homosexual behavior was a relatively common occurrence, were considered shocking and scandalous when they were first published.

Later studies continued to suggest that the differences between heterosexuals and homosexuals were not as great as had been originally thought. The sexual responses of homosexuals are no different from those of heterosexuals (Masters & Johnson, 1979). And homosexuals are, as a group, no more and no less psychologically disturbed than their heterosexual counterparts (Bell & Weinberg, 1978). As research continues to be carried out, the stereotype of the homosexual as a sad and lonely individual is being replaced with the more accurate portrait that suggests that homosexuals are no different from heterosexuals, except, of course, for their sexual preference.

The American Psychiatric Association recognized this altered portrait of homosexuals by voting in 1974 to abolish homosexuality as a mental disorder. They noted that *some* homosexuals might be disturbed and unhappy with their sexual orientation, and this "ego-dystonic homosexuality" was put in place of the broader, more inclusive category.

Our current information thus suggests that homosexuals are very much like heterosexuals. Just as some heterosexuals can exhibit maladaptive characteristics, so, too, can homosexuals exhibit maladaptive characteristics. It is probably incorrect, therefore, to label *all* homosexuals as maladaptive simply because of their sexual orientation.

---

may need to be hospitalized for drug abuse even though a given drug, such as LSD, has been used only once.

**Tolerance** refers to the need to increase the dosage of a drug to produce the effects previously produced by a smaller dose. **Psychoactive drugs** are those that have a marked effect on mental processes. *Psychedelic* is a more specific term referring to drugs, like LSD or mescaline, that can produce hallucinations.

**Commonly abused drugs.** In this section we will briefly describe five psychoactive drugs—heroin, barbiturates, amphetamines, cocaine, and LSD.

**drug tolerance:** increased dosage of a drug needed to obtain effects previously produced by smaller doses

**psychoactive drug:** drug having marked, extensive effects on mental or sensory processes

**heroin: addicting cortical depressant derived from opium**

● **Heroin.** This drug is a derivative of opium and produces a feeling of euphoria and contentment together with pleasant reverie or daydreaming. It is highly addictive, and there are an estimated 300,000 to 400,000 persons who use heroin daily.

The use of heroin, its derivatives, and their synthetic counterparts (such as methadone) leads to physiological craving for and dependence on the drug. In addition, users of heroin gradually build up a tolerance to the drug so that ever larger amounts are needed to achieve the desired effect. This in turn increases the cost of the habit, and addicts often turn to criminal activities such as theft, burglary, or prostitution, to finance their habit.

When persons addicted to heroin do not get a dose of the drug within approximately eight hours, they start to experience withdrawal symptoms. Contrary to popular opinion, these symptoms are not always painful or even dangerous. For individuals who use heavy dosages and have neglected their health, however, withdrawal can be a perilous experience. Withdrawal symptoms usually reach a peak in about forty hours and are on the decline by the third or fourth day.

Since heroin addicts retain their craving for the drug long after their withdrawal symptoms are over, the danger of relapse is great. Many treatment programs are unsuccessful because they fail to deal with this craving for the drug. Newer methadone treatment programs have been advanced as an alternative to the "revolving door" programs of the past in which addicts were withdrawn from heroin only to be returned to the streets. As a long-acting narcotic, methadone can, in proper doses, satisfy the craving for heroin without producing the drowsy symptoms associated with heroin. Methadone programs, whose aim is to return the addicts to their jobs, families, and communities, have come under heavy

Many heroin users "mainline" the drug by injecting it directly into the bloodstream. Repeated injections into the main veins, such as those in the arm, can make these veins inaccessible; the addict then injects the drug into minor veins in the legs, the hands, or other parts of the body.

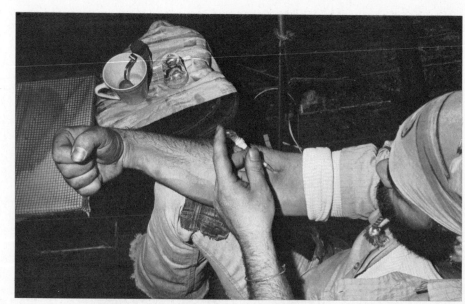

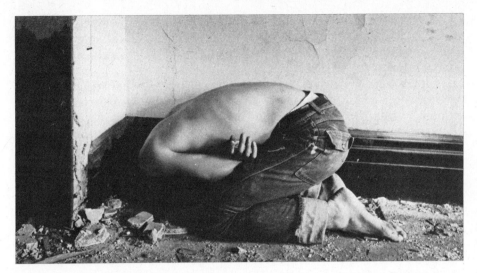

The risks associated with barbiturate abuse include overdosing, addiction, and severe, long-lasting withdrawal symptoms should the person decide to quit using the drug. Some of these withdrawal symptoms are weakness, shaking, nausea, vomiting, seizures, delirium, hallucinations, convulsions, and cardiovascular collapse.

criticism. Much of the criticism involves the fact that methadone is highly addictive and that some methadone programs are poorly supervised. Many critics are worried that methadone, developed as a substitute for heroin, will have the same unfortunate history as heroin, which was developed as a substitute for morphine and opium. However, Dole (1982) makes a strong case for methadone treatment.

● **Barbiturates.** Medically, these drugs are used to calm patients and induce sleep. They act as cortical depressants, much like alcohol.

barbiturates: addicting central nervous system depressants

Barbiturates are highly dangerous drugs, and their excessive use over a period of time leads to a building up of tolerance and to physiological dependence. Especially prone to abuse are the short-acting barbiturates, such as Seconal ("red devils") and Tuinal ("rainbows"). There are an estimated 1 million or more barbiturate addicts in the United States, most of them between thirty and fifty years of age.

Excessive use of barbiturates results in a number of undesirable effects, including general sluggishness, poor comprehension, impaired memory, confusion, irritability, and depression. Barbiturates are often prescribed as sleep medications, but their continued use paradoxically *increases* sleep disturbances (Julien, 1981). The barbiturates are also associated with more suicides than any other drug.

While an overdose of barbiturates can be lethal, the withdrawal symptoms are also very dangerous. In fact, they are more severe and last longer than those in heroin addiction. In severe cases, an acute, delirious psychosis develops.

● **Amphetamines.** The amphetamines are "pep pills"—cortical stimulants— and are often used by truck drivers and students to stay awake and continue to function. At one time, they were commonly used as an appetite suppressant to aid in weight control. Currently, some 5 billion amphetamine pills are manufactured each year in the United States—enough to supply every man, woman, and child with about twenty doses each.

amphetamines: cortical stimulants

The most potent and dangerous of the amphetamines is methedrine or "speed." To get high on amphetamines, habitual users may ingest very large doses, or they may go on sprees lasting for several days. As with other amphetamines, excessive use of methedrine over time leads to the building up of tolerance but not to physiological dependence.

For the person who uses large doses of methedrine, the results can be highly detrimental; psychosis, suicide, homicide, and other acts of violence may be associated with the abuse of this drug. Since there is no physiological addiction, withdrawal from the drug is relatively uncomplicated, but psychological dependence may still have to be conquered.

**cocaine: central nervous system stimulant**

● **Cocaine.** Cocaine is a plant product discovered and used in ancient times. According to Jarvik (1967): "The Indians of Peru have chewed cocoa leaves for centuries and still do, to relieve hunger, fatigue, and the general burdens of a miserable life" (p. 52). Cocaine has been endorsed by such diverse figures as Sigmund Freud and the legendary Sherlock Holmes. The use of cocaine has increased markedly. An estimated one third of American youth have used cocaine (National Institute on Drug Abuse, 1982). Fortunately, its expense limits the number of people who use this drug on a regular basis.

Cocaine is usually sniffed or injected. Like heroin, cocaine leads to a euphoric state which may last from a few minutes to as long as four to six hours. Unlike heroin, cocaine is a cortical stimulant inducing sleeplessness and excitement. Dependence on cocaine also differs from that of the opiates, in that tolerance is not increased appreciably with its use, nor is there any physiological dependence. However, psychological dependence on cocaine, like addiction to opiates, often leads users to center their behavior around getting cocaine at the expense of other life activities.

For some people, cocaine's effect occurs in two phases—an initial period of mild euphoria followed by a period of mild anxiety and depression, often referred

Sniffing or snorting cocaine through a rolled-up $100 bill projects the image of the drug as the fashionable recreational drug of the wealthy.

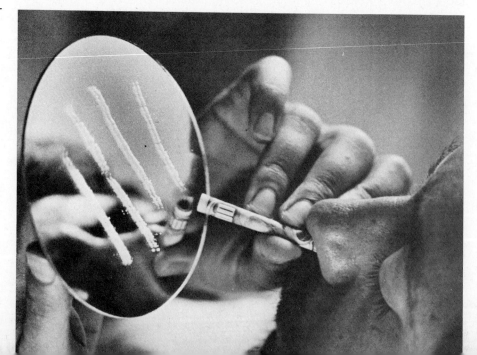

to as the "post-coke blues" (Resnick, Kestenbaum, & Schwartz, 1977). And when cocaine is chronically abused, it can lead to a state of acute intoxication in which the individual experiences frightening visual, auditory, and tactual hallucinations, such as the "cocaine bug."

● **LSD.** Lysergic acid diethylamide (LSD), a chemically synthesized substance, was first discovered in 1938. Although odorless, colorless, and tasteless, it is an extremely potent hallucinogen. In fact, a dosage of LSD smaller than a grain of salt can produce intoxication.

**LSD: lysergic acid diethylamide, hallucinogenic drug that produces potent effects in extremely small doses**

A major effect of taking LSD is a tremendous intensification of sensory perception. Objects seem to become brighter, more colorful, and endowed with dimensions the individual has never noticed before. Thus, the individual may become absorbed in the contemplation of a flower or some other object. Often he or she has the feeling of somehow being tuned in to all humankind in experiencing such universal emotions as love, loneliness, or grief.

The LSD trip, however, is not always pleasant. It can be an extremely traumatic experience in which everyday objects take on a bizarre and terrifying appearance, or in which the individual sees monsters which seem to be after him or her. It has been estimated that about one in twenty LSD users experience "flashbacks," recurring, intrusive thoughts of a negative or frightening nature. It has also been estimated that about 3 percent of LSD users experience psychosis, a break with reality, sometimes on their first trip.

**Drug use and abuse.** Although drug use has always been a part of the youth culture, dimensions of the problem have become increasingly greater in recent years. Prior to the 1960s the drug of choice for most teen-agers and young adults was alcohol. However, from the 1960s to the present, the scope of drug use has increased.

Starting in the 1960s, drug use expanded to include psychedelics, marijuana, amphetamines, barbiturates, heroin, cocaine, and a host of "street drugs." As might be expected, many young people used such drugs at the expense of their health and life adjustment. Many were treated for drug intoxication and dependence. Some died of drug overdose. Many combined drugs in a haphazard fashion in the pursuit of different, presumably thrilling sensations.

Drug abuse is an extremely complex topic. Some of the drugs which seem to pose serious problems in our society are highly dangerous, such as heroin and the barbiturates. Others, such as marijuana and cocaine, fall in the controversial category, since we have little information on their long-term effects. And some drugs which were frequently abused in the past—such as LSD—have now fallen into disrepute.

The reasons behind drug abuse are varied. The majority of young people probably use drugs because of peer group pressure, for thrill seeking, or to find relief from stressful situations. Since psychoactive drugs tend to result in lowered anxiety and tension, their use is reinforced on a psychological level. In addition, we live in a pill-oriented society in which we learn to believe that almost any problem can be eased or solved simply by taking a pill. And the young can often observe parental and other models who act on this conviction.

## Antisocial Behavior

*"Donald S., 30 years old, has just completed a three-year prison term for fraud, bigamy, false pretenses, and escaping lawful custody. The circumstances leading up to these offenses are interesting and consistent with his past behavior. With less than a month left to serve on an earlier 18-month term for fraud, he faked illness and escaped from the prison hospital. During the ten months of freedom that followed he engaged in a variety of illegal enterprises; the activity that resulted in his recapture was typical of his method of operation. By passing himself off as the "field executive" of an international philanthropic foundation, he was able to enlist the aid of several religious organizations in a fund-raising campaign. The campaign moved slowly at first, and in an attempt to speed things up, he arranged an interview with the local TV station. His performance during the interview was so impressive that funds started to pour in. However, unfortunately for Donald, the interview was also carried on a national news network. He was recognized and quickly arrested. During the ensuing trial it became evident that he experienced no sense of wrongdoing for his activities."*
(HARE, 1970, PP. 1–2)

**antisocial behavior:** disorder characterized by lack of moral development and inability to feel guilt or anxiety

**Antisocial behavior** involves a pattern of "acting out" with little or no sense of personal distress and little regard for the rights of others. In the past, this problem was labeled as *psychopathy* and *sociopathy*.

Individuals labeled as antisocial personalities are not mentally retarded, neurotic, or psychotic. Rather, their most outstanding characteristic is a lack of ethical or moral development and an inability to follow desirable models of behavior. Their callous disregard for the rights of others leads to serious difficulties with interpersonal relationships and usually brings them into conflict with society.

Included in this category are a sizable number of unprincipled business executives, shyster lawyers, crooked politicians, compulsive gamblers, prostitutes, drug pushers, and assorted delinquents and criminals. Despite the tendency for their behavior to lead to problems with constituted authority, the great majority of these people manage to stay out of jails and prisons. The incidence of antisocial personalities is approximately 1 percent of the population—greater than 2.5 million people.

The following traits are indicative of an antisocial personality and will help us to gain a clearer overall perspective of this behavior pattern. Of course, not all of these traits will be found in every case.

1. *Amoral, unreliable, irresponsible.* May deceive others by verbal endorsement of high standards, but does not understand or adhere to accepted moral values. Pathological lying, deceitfulness, and a callous disregard for the rights of others. Often a marked discrepancy between intellectual level and conscience development.

2. *Impulsive, hedonistic, unrealistic goals.* Prone to thrill seeking, deviant sexual patterns, and unconventional behavior. Lives in present with primary concern for immediate pleasures and no long-range goals. Shows poor judgment and often

engages in impulsive acts detrimental to personal well-being and that of others. Dislikes routine work and frequently changes jobs, moves from place to place, lives by his or her wits, or depends on others for support. Abusive of alcohol and other drugs.

3. *Ability to impress and exploit others.* Often a charming individual with a good sense of humor and a generally optimistic outlook. Easily wins the liking and friendship of others but ruthlessly exploits these interpersonal relationships. Often shows contempt for those taken advantage of—the "marks." Unable to give or receive love.

4. *Lack of anxiety and guilt.* Little or no sense of guilt. Lack of anxiety combined with seeming sincerity often enables them to lie their way out of difficulties. Undeterred by punishment.

5. *Early onset.* Maladaptive patterns emerge in adolescence and continue throughout most of adult life. Violence and aggressive behavior easily provoked.

The causal factors underlying antisocial behavior are not fully understood and probably differ considerably from case to case. Antisocial personalities are more likely to be identified in individuals from lower socioeconomic levels and more likely to be male than female (Lahey & Ciminero, 1980). There is evidence to suggest that antisocial personalities come from families that had at least one antisocial parent (Robins, 1966). There is also evidence to suggest that antisocial personalities show a lower level of physiological arousal than normal individuals (Hare, 1970). Presumably, this lowered level of arousal accounts for the failure of the antisocial personality to learn from punishment. It is likely that these cultural, genetic, and learning effects interact to produce antisocial behaviors.

Unfortunately, the impact that antisocial personalities have on society at large is in excess of their relatively small representation in the population. Crimes of violence, including homicide and rape, as well as crimes against property, including breaking and entering, have nearly doubled in the past decade. As a result, many Americans feel apprehensive and insecure even in their own homes. Of course, not all crimes are committed by antisocial personalities, but the lack of guilt and remorse shown by these antisocial individuals is frightening and disheartening to many Americans.

Treatment for this maladaptive behavior is generally unsuccessful. Antisocial personalities are not distressed by their behavior, and their motivations for change are, therefore, virtually absent.

## Schizophrenia and the Other Psychoses

Schizophrenia and the other **psychoses** are characterized by marked disturbances in thinking, feeling, and acting. The individual's contact with reality and coping ability are seriously impaired. The term *insanity* is sometimes used in referring to psychotic disorders, but this is a legal term rather than a clinical one, indicating that the individual is unable to manage his or her affairs or function as a responsible member of society.

Several distinctive psychotic patterns have been delineated, including schizo-

**psychosis: loss of contact with reality**

**organic psychosis: psychosis associated with brain pathology**

**functional psychosis: psychosis that is not associated with brain pathology**

phrenia, affective (mood) disorders, and the organic psychoses associated with brain pathology. Psychoses associated with demonstrable brain pathology are called **organic psychoses;** those with no known brain pathology are called **functional psychoses.**

We begin our discussion with an examination of schizophrenia, the psychotic disorder that occurs most frequently among adolescents and young adults.

### Schizophrenia.

*To Dr. H. G.*
*If you have the time I would appreciate some information concerning mind reading. I believe its possible for a person to be able to read another persons mind and be able to let that person communicate with him. Can a person with these extraordinary powers be capable of doing the following things below, I have read somewhere before where this can happen. (The X's before the numbers are of great importance to me."*
*X 1.  Burning sensations. Are these feelings a generation of some kind, an electromanatic energy.*
*2.  headaches, feeling of an energy, wave of some kind in brain, head.*
*X 3.  When writing something down or speaking you write something else down you did not intend on writing down or saying? How?*
*X 4.  Sex.*
*5.  crying—emotional stress*
*6.  stirring into mirror and seeing an hallucination of your face changing*
*7.  vibrations of hands, face, other parts of body*
*X 8.  Loss of concentration*
*a. when a person is talking out loud you can't concentrate on what they are saying.*
*I read a book once about these strange happenings and found them interesting, but I wanted to know more information of the subject of mind reading. These things above can happen, quickly, very frequently, seldom, come fast and be over with quickly. This I know. I hope you will be able to help me in my research concerning this type of communication between two people. Thank you for your time.*

*Sincerly,*
*D. S.*

This letter, with its patterns of disorganized and confused thoughts, was written by a schizophrenic woman.

**schizophrenia: psychosis characterized primarily by disturbances in thought and emotion**

The term **schizophrenia** refers to a split between thought and emotion accompanied by a loss of contact with reality. The schizophrenic does not have a dual or "split personality." Rather, the schizophrenic is characterized by severe disturbances in thought and emotion. Schizophrenia is a worldwide problem affecting approximately 1 percent of the population. It accounts for about 50 percent of all hospitalized mental patients in the United States.

The clinical picture of the schizophrenic differs from one person to another but is typically characterized by:

1. *Thought disturbances.* Changes in the cognitive processes of schizophrenics are so marked that schizophrenia is often termed a *thought disorder.* Schizophrenic thought processes and language are typically bizarre and disorganized. Schizophrenics will make up words and jumble ideas around in a confusing, unfathomable pattern.

2. *Delusions.* These are false beliefs that the individual defends despite their logical absurdity and despite all other contrary evidence. The most common types of **delusions** are *(a) delusions of grandeur,* in which individuals believe they are exalted and important beings, *(b) delusions of reference,* in which individuals interpret chance happenings as having special meaning for them, and *(c) delusions of persecution,* in which individuals feel that "enemies" are plotting against them.

3. *Hallucinations.* Schizophrenics may have **hallucinations.** They may hear voices, see things, smell peculiar odors, or report other false sensory phenomena.

4. *Affective changes.* These alterations of mood may take many forms. In some cases, the individual is apathetic and emotionally unresponsive. Some may be violently active; others may appear to be depressed. Still others may have inappropriate emotional states, such as laughing when informed that a spouse or a child has been killed.

5. *Withdrawal, isolation, and disorganization.* Many schizophrenics withdraw from reality and lose interest in people and events. Their social skills may be limited, and they may be unable to provide even the simplest information about the current time, where they are, or even their names and identities. Often they neglect personal hygiene.

6. *Motor disturbances.* Schizophrenics may engage in a variety of repetitious, stereotyped muscular activities. In some cases, the schizophrenic engages in virtually no motor activity, and the individual may allow his or her arms, legs, and other parts of the body to be placed into unusual positions. The schizophrenic with this **waxy flexibility** will hold these seemingly uncomfortable positions for hours at a time.

Four distinctive patterns of schizophrenia have been identified in the diagnostic system currently in use in the DSM-III: paranoid schizophrenia, disorganized (or hebephrenic) schizophrenia, catatonic schizophrenia, and undifferentiated schizophrenia. Identifying the particular pattern is a skillful task requiring an accurate assessment and understanding of each individual's clinical picture.

1. *Paranoid schizophrenia.* The **paranoid schizophrenic** is characterized by delusions, typically those of persecution and grandeur. This type of schizophrenia is the most commonly diagnosed, accounting for about half of all cases (Lahey & Ciminero, 1980). The typical paranoid schizophrenic is an individual, often male, in his late twenties. Prior to his (or her) hospitalization, there were no markedly unusual aspects to his or her behavior. Often the individual has functioned effectively up to the point of hospitalization and may have had an adequate work and personal history.

---

**delusions:** false beliefs an individual defends against logical evidence

**hallucinations:** perceptual or sensory processes that are not based in reality

**waxy flexibility:** characteristic of schizophrenics in which they will remain in any position in which they are placed for extended periods of time

**paranoid schizophrenia:** type of schizophrenia characterized by delusions of grandeur or persecution

Issues of control and sexual identity and activity are common in this group of schizophrenics. The paranoid schizophrenic may believe that impure sexual thoughts are being "placed" in their brains by electronic devices.

**catatonic schizophrenia:**
**type of schizophrenia**
**predominantly marked**
**by periods of inactivity**
**and waxy flexibility, al-**
**though outbursts of ex-**
**cited activity may occur**

2. *Catatonic schizophrenia.* Disturbances in motor activity are the characteristic feature of the **catatonic schizophrenic.** This individual is typically inactive and passive, although bursts of hyperactivity may occur. Stereotyped movements and waxy flexibility are also found in this type. Catatonic schizophrenia is relatively uncommon and is diagnosed in fewer than 10 percent of all cases.

**hebephrenic (disorga-**
**nized) schizophrenia:**
**type of schizophrenia**
**characterized by inap-**
**propriate affect**

3. *Disorganized or hebephrenic schizophrenia.* Inappropriate affect and disorganization are the hallmarks of this diagnostic category. The **hebephrenic schizophrenic's** day is punctuated with episodes of laughter and silliness with no apparent cause. Emotional blunting, bizarre and obscene behavior, and peculiar mannerisms may typify those with the diagnosis of disorganized schizophrenia. The patterns of maladjustment in this individual usually begin early in life. The course of the disorder is gradual, often ending with long-term hospitalization. Like catatonic schizophrenia, disorganized schizophrenia is uncommon, accounting for about 5 percent of diagnoses.

4. *Undifferentiated schizophrenia.* This is the second largest category of diagnoses of schizophrenia. Many psychotic individuals do not present clear-cut symptoms of the three types discussed above. In these cases, the symptoms overlap, and the diagnostician is unable to say with certainty that a particular diagnostic category is applicable. For these "mixed" cases, a diagnosis of **undifferentiated schizophrenia** is assigned.

**undifferentiated schizo-**
**phrenia: type of schizo-**
**phrenia with mixed**
**symptoms**

A fifth group of maladaptive individuals were, in the past, given a diagnosis of *simple schizophrenia.* These individuals lead only a marginal existence; they exhibit curious behavior patterns, and they appear to be somewhat odd and eccentric. They often make up the "bag ladies" and hoboes of our larger cities and countryside. However, since they do *not* have hallucinations, or other signs of schizophrenia, they are no longer given the label of simple schizophrenic. Rather their maladaptive behavior is considered to be a reflection of a long-standing personality disorder.

Despite a great deal of research, the causal patterns in schizophrenic reactions remain largely an enigma. A good deal of recent research evidence points to the role of genetic and biochemical factors in schizophrenia. For example, numerous studies have provided strong evidence that children of schizophrenic parents are more likely than the general population to be diagnosed as schizophrenic at some point in their lives, even when these children are adopted shortly after birth and raised by normal parents (Wender, Rosenthal, Kety, Schulsinger, & Welner, 1974).

However, genetic predisposition is not the whole story. Psychological, interpersonal, and family interaction patterns have also been associated with schizophrenia (Harrow, Grossman, Silverstein, & Meltzer, 1982; Parnas, Schulsinger, Schulsinger, Mednick, & Teasdale, 1982). Schizophrenics show alterations of thinking, feeling, and relating to the external world which are unique to this disorder. In fact, the schizophrenic may behave in apparently bizarre ways as a "special sort of strategy that a person invents in order to live in an unlivable world" (Laing, 1967, p. 56). Disturbed communication patterns in the family may also account for schizophrenia. Bateson and his associates, for example, pro-

# Momma

By Mell Lazarus

posed that the families of schizophrenics engage in **double-bind communication** in which conflicting messages are received (Bateson, Jackson, Haley, Weakland, 1956).

Both genetic predisposition and psychological and interpersonal factors probably interact to produce a schizophrenic reaction. In some individuals, the genetic predisposition is probably very strong, and only a little stress is sufficient to set off the reaction. In others, the genetic predisposition may be extremely small, but the stress that an individual experiences might be so extraordinarily severe that a schizophrenic reaction begins (Zubin & Spring, 1977).

Treatment of schizophrenic reactions is primarily dependent on drugs, particularly the major **tranquilizers** such as Thorazine. The introduction of these drugs in the 1950s produced a revolution in the care of the schizophrenic individual and changed the mental hospital from a custodial warehouse to a treatment-oriented facility whose goal was to return the individual to as normal functioning as possible. The major psychological approaches have involved community programs such as community mental health centers, day hospitals, and the like. These programs attempt to ease the transition from the hospital to the community in a nonstressful way. Care within the hospital has also undergone marked changes in recent years. More and more hospitals are adopting programs that more or less explicitly aid the schizophrenic in learning the skills and behaviors that are expected of "normal" people (Paul & Lentz, 1977).

**Affective psychoses: Manic-depressive reactions.** The affective psychoses primarily involve disturbances of mood or emotion. They seem to represent an exaggeration of normal mood fluctuations—elation and euphoria, agitation, discouragement and depression—which most of us experience. The most distinctive of these disorders are **manic-depressive reactions**—characterized by exaggerated gaiety and elation or dejection and depression.

During the initial phase of a manic reaction, the person may feel elated, express feelings of well-being and optimism, and make exciting plans for the future. It soon becomes apparent, however, that the individual is highly distractible, overly talkative, and incapable of following through on proposed projects. As the disorder progresses, the clinical picture becomes increasingly exaggerated and such individuals show: *(a)* psychomotor overactivity in which they are constantly

**double-bind communication: communication containing conflicting messages**

**tranquilizers: drugs that produce a sense of calm and release from anxiety or other disturbing mental processes**

**manic-depressive reaction: psychotic reaction characterized by prolonged periods of excitement and overactivity (mania) or by periods of dejection and underactivity (depression) or by alternation of the two**

talking and moving about under a "pressure of activity," (b) flight of ideas involving extreme distractibility and rapid shifts of thought, (c) delusions and hallucinations, usually of a transient and grandiose nature in keeping with the elated mood, and (d) impaired judgment and lowered ethical restraints—which may lead to unwise financial investments, promiscuous sexual acts, and other behavior indicative of lowered inner controls. In extreme form, the manic reaction progresses to delirious ideation and disorientation.

In the depressive reaction, the clinical picture is essentially reversed. These persons become discouraged and dejected, and there is a slowing down of thought and activity. Feelings of failure, unworthiness, and often guilt dominate their thinking. Apprehensiveness and anxiety are also common, and such individuals often contemplate and may attempt to commit suicide. In extreme form they may lapse into a depressive stupor with an almost complete lack of response.

As in schizophrenia, the causal factors in manic-depressive reactions are unclear. A biological basis is suggested by the fact that such reactions tend to be associated with changes in the levels of brain chemicals and their metabolites. Other investigators who have studied manic-depressive reactions have been impressed with the key role of life stress, pointing to a general excess of aversive life events prior to the onset of the disorder (Hirschfeld & Cross, 1982).

In concluding our discussion of the functional psychoses, it may be emphasized that: (a) psychotics often show mixed symptoms that do not fit well into any category, (b) the clinical picture may shift rapidly over short periods of time, and (c) persons in a given category, such as schizophrenia, differ markedly in personality makeup. And while the causal picture is unclear, varying combinations of biological, psychological, and sociocultural factors appear to be involved.

**Disorders associated with brain pathology.**    There are a number of conditions—such as injuries, tumors, infectious diseases, drugs, and the deteriorative changes of old age—which interfere with brain functioning and result in mental disorders. An estimated 20 million people in the United States suffer from such disorders. Fortunately the great majority of cases do not involve seriously maladaptive behavior. Even so, mental disorders associated with brain pathology—particularly psychoses associated with old age—constitute more than a fourth of all first admissions to mental hospitals and clinics.

These organic psychoses are often classified as *acute* or *chronic.* An acute disorder—as in drug intoxication—is likely to be temporary and reversible. Here the individual may show such symptoms as coma and stupor or disorientation and delirium, which clear up over a period of hours or days. A chronic disorder—as in syphilis of the brain—involves permanent damage to the nervous system; here the brain pathology is not reversible or only partially so. Some individuals are able to compensate better than others for brain damage, but there are limits. Where brain damage is severe, symptoms may include:

1. *Impairment of orientation*—especially for time but often also for place and person.

2. *Impairment of memory*—notably for recent events and less so for events of remote past, with a tendency to confabulate, or "invent" memories to fill in gaps.

3. *Impairment of learning, comprehension, and judgment*—with ideation tending to be concrete and impoverished—and with inability to think on higher conceptual levels and to plan.

4. *Emotional impairment*—with emotional overreactivity and easy arousal to laughter or tears, or with a blunting of affect.

5. *Impairment of inner reality and ethical controls*—with lowering of behavioral standards and carelessness in personal hygiene and appearance.

## SUMMARY

1. Behavior is maladaptive when it no longer meets the adjustive demand, when it no longer meets the needs of the individual, or when it disturbs the well-being of society. Behavior can be described as occurring on a continuum. At one end are behaviors that are considered very effective and adaptive; at the other end are behaviors that are considered seriously maladaptive.

2. Some behavior patterns are so common that we often do not think of them as maladaptive. These common life-style problems, which can become seriously maladaptive, include problems associated with smoking, drinking, and eating.

3. Three common maladaptive problems are anxiety, depression, and psychophysiological disorders. Anxiety is an unpleasant experience associated with cognitive, behavioral, and physiological events. Some uncommon forms of anxiety include obsessive-compulsive, somatoform, and dissociative disorders.

4. Depression, another common maladaptive behavior, also has cognitive, behavioral, and physiological components. Although the "blues" are relatively mild, they can become very severe and increase the possibility of suicide.

5. Psychophysiological disorders, sometimes known as psychosomatic disorders, involve physical disruption of the body's functioning. Ulcers, headaches, and hypertension, for example, involve changes in normal physical function and are related to stress. Psychophysiological disorders are quite real and are not "made up" illnesses.

6. The more serious maladaptive problems include drug abuse, antisocial behavior, and the psychoses. These problems not only present difficulties for the individual, but they also are costly to society. Drug abuse, for example, is dangerous for the individual. Additionally, abuse of drugs such as the barbiturates, amphetamines, and cocaine produces a modeling effect in which young people also abuse drugs and perpetuate a self-destructive cycle.

7. Antisocial personalities feel no remorse for their violent and antisocial acts. Although the number of people who can be diagnosed as having antisocial personalities is small, the fear of crime and violence that these and other individuals produce in society at large is considerable.

8. The psychoses involve breaks with reality. Some, like schizophrenia and the affective disorders, do not appear to involve clear-cut damage to the brain. Other psychoses clearly involve some damage or structural change in the brain and are therefore known as organic psychoses. The most common psychotic condition is schizophrenia which is *not* a "split personality" but descriptive of a condition in which thought and emotion are separated.

# Chapter 11

# Psychotherapy and Counseling

*"To be listened to*
*& to be heard . . .*
*to be supported*
*while you gather your*
*forces & get your bearings.*

*A fresh look at alternatives*
*& some new insights;*
*learning some needed skills.*

*To face your lion—your fears.*
*To come to a decision—*
*& the courage to act on it.*
*& to take the risks*
*that living demands."*

**(DAVID PALMER, THE STUDENT COUNSELING CENTER, UNIVERSITY OF CALIFORNIA,
LOS ANGELES)**

Seeking professional assistance for personal problems is always a difficult task. Much of our training and experience has taught us to be as self-reliant as possible. And despite our enlightened views about behavior disorders, there is nonetheless a stigma attached to consulting a mental health professional. While we do not hesitate to consult a physician about a health problem and we do not hesitate to discuss a troublesome issue with a close friend or family member, we feel uncomfortable about seeing a counselor or psychotherapist.

This hesitancy is unfortunate. Counselors and psychotherapists are well trained and have many skills to offer people seeking assistance. Problems ranging from career planning, marital and family relationships, and personal maladjustment can be competently handled by mental health professionals (Landman & Dawes, 1982; Smith, 1982; Wright, 1982).

In this chapter we will introduce you to some of the techniques and procedures used by professionals trained in assisting those who have problems in daily living. After we have described the therapeutic setting and process, we will focus on two aspects of the therapeutic process: assessment and therapy. In the assessment section, we will cover the general strategies and resources that a therapist invokes in assessing problems. In the therapy section, we will discuss the three major approaches to individual psychological therapy and some approaches that attempt to solve interpersonal relationship or family problems.

We begin with a discussion of therapeutic settings and processes.

## THE THERAPEUTIC SETTING AND PROCESS

Entering into a therapeutic or counseling setting for the first time can be an anxiety-evoking experience. To the first-time client, the setting poses many questions: "What will the therapist or counselor be like?" "Will I like him or her?" "What will she or he think of me?" "Can he or she help me?" These are, of

# Insight

### PERSONNEL IN COUNSELING AND PSYCHOTHERAPY

|  | **Professional Requirements** | **Type of Therapy** |
|---|---|---|
| **Clinical psychologist** | Ph.D. in clinical psychology plus internship training in psychological assessment and therapy | Wide range of individual and group procedures including behavior therapy |
| **Counseling psychologist** | Essentially same as for clinical psychologist but with emphasis on assisting less maladaptive individuals and relationships | Counseling with personal, educational, marital, and family problems |
| **Psychiatrist** | M.D. degree plus specialized training in mental hospitals or clinics | Medical therapy (drugs, shock, etc.) and/or psychotherapy |
| **Psychoanalyst** | M.D. degree plus extensive training in theory and practice of psychoanalysis | Intensive system of psychotherapy based largely upon Freudian theory |
| **Social worker** | M.A. degree in social work plus supervised experience in clinics or social service agencies | May work with spouses or other family members of clients, with groups in community, and with individuals |
| **Guidance counselor** | M.A. or Ph.D. in counseling psychology | Counseling with educational and career problems |
| **Occupational therapist** | B.S. plus clinical internship | Therapy with children and adults suffering from physical handicaps, helping them to make the most of their resources |
| **Speech therapist** | M.A. in speech pathology plus internship training | Procedures appropriate to treatment of stuttering and other speech disorders |
| **Paraprofessional** | Limited but intensive training in helping approaches with supervised field experience | May utilize wide range of procedures under supervision of professional in field |
| **Interdisciplinary team** | Often programs in psychotherapy include personnel from several disciplines including clinical psychologists, psychiatrists, social workers, and other professional or paraprofessional personnel. This approach is more likely to take place in a clinic setting than in private practice. | |

course, important questions, and they are generally answered within the first few meetings.

Nonetheless, the therapeutic setting remains a mystery to many people. Without direct experience, we rely on the few sources of information available to us. Some of these include our impressions of psychologists, counselors, and other therapists from television, from "media psychologists," and from friends and acquaintances who have participated in the experience. While these pieces of information are valuable, they are not fully representative of the range of settings in which psychotherapists work, and they are not fully representative of the range of activities that psychologists and counselors engage in.

## The Therapeutic Setting

Typically, psychotherapists and counselors work in one of two general settings— within an institution or within a private office. The institutions can vary from a community mental health center to schools and universities to a general medical center to industrial settings, to a psychiatric hospital. Private offices can also vary as well. Some private offices might be located within large medical buildings, within general office buildings, or within private homes.

In the institutional setting, the individual psychotherapist generally is part of a psychology or counseling center or clinic. Members of the staff are generally individuals who have completed their training, although a portion of the staff may consist of individuals who are still in training. These latter individuals are generally advanced graduate students who are completing their training under the supervision of the more experienced members of the staff.

In a private setting, the therapist may work totally independently or may be part of a private practice. Just as physicians often combine their resources and talents to operate a multiperson clinic, so too do psychologists share office space and secretarial staff.

Most settings consist of a reception area, and one or more individual or group meeting rooms. Most settings also have a receptionist/secretary to schedule appointments, answer phones, type letters, fill out forms, and carry out other clerical duties. Sitting in a waiting room of a clinic can be worrisome and embarrassing. Often, the first-time visitor examines the other people waiting in the room: "Maybe he thinks I'm crazy." "I wonder what her problem is." "I'm only waiting for my friends; I don't really belong here." Many of these fears disappear rapidly, since the people in the waiting rooms of psychologists are as ordinary and unremarkable as people in the waiting rooms of other professionals.

## The Therapeutic Process

Once ushered into a consulting room, the first-time visitor can expect that the room will contain the same furniture as other offices. That is, the office will contain a desk, some books and pictures, degrees and citations on the walls, and perhaps a filing cabinet. The first-time visitor may be looking for the stereotypical couch but is more likely to find a comfortable chair or recliner instead.

**rapport: feelings of empathy, understanding, and trust developed in a therapeutic relationship**

Invited to sit down, the therapist will first attempt to establish **rapport** with the visitor. The feelings of trust, confidence, respect, and understanding that comprise rapport are an important part of the assessment and therapeutic process. Clients must feel free to respond honestly and completely during any therapeutic process. The therapist is aware of the initial feelings of anxiety and mistrust that a client has and attempts to present him- or herself as a friendly, competent, trustful, and warm individual. It is important here for clients to feel that they have come to the right place for assistance and that they will be understood, accepted, and helped.

**Stages in the therapeutic process.**     Not only is rapport established in the first part of the therapy process, but the problem to be examined is identified as well. During the **assessment phase** problems are identified and the individual's personal history, likes and dislikes, attitudes toward significant people and situations, skills and liabilities, and the like are also described. While the assessment is underway, the client will probably find that his or her anxieties about discussing these personal matters will decrease somewhat. The client may also find it easier to discuss those feelings and attitudes that are not always socially acceptable. For example, a woman may find that her strong negative feelings about her husband and children are easier to discuss in a therapeutic situation. Also, a skillful therapist may discover problem areas and attitudes that the client may not be aware of. A man may find, for example, that he has aesthetic and artistic interests that he has repressed and ignored because a "real man" would not admit interests in these non-"macho" activities.

assessment phase: first phase of the therapeutic process in which an individual's current concerns, history, and present circumstances are identified

Once the assessment is completed, the second or **feedback phase** begins. In this stage, the therapist provides feedback on the assessment. Essentially the therapist acts as a mirror for the client, discussing and evaluating the information that the client has provided in the first stage. This process allows the client to gain a different perspective on his or her problems.

feedback phase: second phase of the therapeutic process in which assessment information is used to help establish therapeutic goals

After seeing his or her problems in a somewhat newer and more accurate light, the client must then decide upon the goals of therapy and counseling: "Given current trends and expectations, is it reasonable for me to seek work, training, and education in this particular field?" "Are my feelings about my partner so negative that terminating the relationship is the most reasonable answer, or do I feel that the relationship should be salvaged?" "Can the therapist help me with my feelings of guilt, anxiety, or depression?"

Establishing rapport and making the client feel comfortable about discussing his or her problems openly and honestly are important aspects of the therapeutic process.

The third and final stage involves the implementation of these decisions. This **implementation phase** is the part of the process that we normally think of when we discuss ''psychotherapy'' or ''counseling.'' Like the first two parts, the third part can run for various lengths of time. The client works with the therapist in resolving the problems identified earlier in such a way that the client minimizes his or her discomfort and maximizes progress toward the final goal. Although progress is not always steady and clients can experience occasional setbacks, the overall trend is toward more and more effective functioning.

**Action- vs. insight-oriented approaches.** The overall style and involvement of the therapist at this and earlier states can take one of two forms: an action- or insight-oriented approach. In the **action-oriented approach**, the therapist and client work actively and purposively to solve the client's problems. In the action-oriented approach, the emphasis is on activity and on accomplishing tasks.

In contrast, the **insight-oriented approach** focuses on generating an understanding of the client's problem. In this approach, the therapist and client try to understand the reasons for the client's complaints and problems. Insight-oriented practitioners believe that a thorough appreciation of the background and development of a problem is the most important step toward resolving the problem.

Action-oriented therapists tend to be relatively **directive**. In the extreme form, the therapist assesses the client's problems, works out an acceptable solution to the problem, and then concentrates on implementing the solution. Insight-oriented therapists tend to be relatively **nondirective**. These therapists believe that the relationship between the therapist and the client should be the predominant focus of therapy. As a result, nondirective therapists do not provide as many specific suggestions and comments to the client. Rather, the nondirective therapist feels that the client has the resources within him- or herself to solve the problems and that the therapist's task is to provide the proper circumstances for allowing this natural healing process to occur.

Both types of approaches have been the subject of criticism. Critics of the action-oriented approaches maintain that the characteristically directive style of these approaches does not help clients to organize their own resources or make their own decisions. Critics also maintain that the directive approach deprives clients of a sense of responsibility and adequacy in making decisions and in guiding their own lives. Critics of the insight-oriented, nondirective approaches note that it is difficult to justify spending money and other resources on a therapist who offers little to no obvious guidance. Indeed, say the critics, the client comes to the therapist for assistance and guidance, and anything less than active involvement on the part of the therapist is unethical.

In actual practice, of course, few therapists are entirely directive or nondirective, action- or insight-oriented. Some therapists will take a more active role with some of their clients while taking a more insight-oriented role with other clients. And therapists will often use both directive and nondirective techniques with the same client. For example, a therapist might use directive techniques with a client who ''freezes up'' during an exam while using nondirective methods with a client who is uncertain whether he or she should remain in school. Similarly, a therapist might use nondirective methods to help establish rapport and to assess the client and use more directive techniques during the implementation phase.

In general, the most effective therapists are those who, regardless of their general orientation, use their clients' resources to the fullest extent. Effective therapists also modify their own approach to ensure that the therapeutic contact will be maximally beneficial to the client and structure the therapeutic process so that the clients will feel more competent and more self-reliant and will experience personal growth.

Once the therapeutic goals have been achieved, the therapy is terminated, at least for the time being. Often the therapist will ask the client to report back to the therapist on a more or less regular schedule. This intermittent contact allows the therapist to assess his or her own success (or failure) and also allows the therapist to offer suggestions and further assistance if necessary.

While the assessment-decision-therapy process is normally carried out on a one-to-one basis, it is also possible for couples and families to enter therapy as well. Finally , it should be noted that conversations between a client and a therapist are private and confidential; people who have fears that a therapist will ''tell all'' to strangers should be reassured that such behavior on the part of the therapist is very strongly disapproved and is considered extremely unethical.

## Initiating and Terminating a Therapeutic Relationship

Although the settings and procedures that a psychotherapist or counselor uses are not mysterious, many people do not know when to seek the assistance of these professionals. Many people deny themselves competent professional help because of their unfounded fears and concerns about consulting a psychologist. And a small number of people seek assistance for each minor problem or stumbling block that crosses their lives.

Many people find that consulting friends, family, or religious leaders is a useful and inexpensive way to deal with some problems. Of course, most friends and relatives do not have professional expertise, and the ways in which they can help may be correspondingly limited. Also, asking the advice of friends, relatives, and religious leaders may sometimes be more difficult than seeing a psychologist; family members may be too close to the problem to give impartial advice.

When confiding in close friends and relatives is not possible or desirable, seeking a counselor or a therapist is the next appropriate step. Individuals who have received professional help before may be invaluable sources of information. People who have already participated in counseling or psychotherapy are often good sources of information on professionals whose assistance was particularly helpful (or not helpful at all). Other good sources of information include college and university counseling centers and psychology clinics, hospital programs, and independent referral sources. This latter source can be found in the yellow pages of many telephone directories.

The potential client should be a good "consumer" of counseling and therapeutic services (Watson & Tharp, 1977). The length of treatment, cost, insurance matters, day and time of appointments, and similar issues should be discussed and settled before or during the first meeting. The therapist should be asked to describe his or her approach to dealing with clients, experience in dealing with similar problems, training and education, and so forth.

If the potential client finds him- or herself reasonably confident that the counselor or therapist can help with the problem, then a therapeutic relationship can be established. If not, he or she should seek another therapist. And, if the client loses confidence in the ability of the therapist during the assessment or treatment program, the client should seek other professional assistance. It is important to keep in mind that the client is paying for a service and should feel that he or she is receiving something of value for the money and time that is spent.

Naturally, therapy is not always a smooth process, and difficulties will occur from time to time. A single disagreement or disenchantment is not sufficient reason to terminate therapy. However, if the difficulties persist after a reasonable length of time, the client should discuss the difficulties with the therapist and make an appropriate decision.

Therapy also ends when the client is reasonably satisfied with the outcome. Some clients continue to see a therapist for minor or trivial issues, but most therapists see their function as helping their clients develop more effective strategies for living happier, more useful lives. Ending a therapeutic relationship can be, of course, a sad and painful experience, but it can also be a joyous one, signaling the new-found abilities and skills of the client to lead a personally meaningful life.

## PSYCHOLOGICAL ASSESSMENT

psychological assessment: use of psychological tests and other methods for the diagnosis of maladaptive behavior

**Psychological assessment** represents a systematic attempt to collect, organize, and interpret relevant information about a person and his or her life situation. This information is then used as a starting point in planning whatever help is needed.

### Types of Assessment Information

Although the information obtained in psychological assessment may vary considerably depending upon the specific goals in a particular case, the assessment usually covers most or all of the following areas:

1. *Major complaint:* Information concerning the problem or problems that bring the individual to a counselor or psychotherapist.

2. *Medical and psychiatric information:* Information concerning current and past medical illnesses and injuries and information concerning current or past encounters with psychotherapists.

3. *Personal and family history information:* Information concerning individual history, interpersonal relationships and group memberships, educational and occupational experiences, and family relationships.

4. *Current social stresses:* Information concerning stresses in the client's life situation that may exacerbate or alleviate the problems described in the major complaint.

5. *Strengths and resources:* Information concerning environmental and personal resources and supports, skills and abilities, and prior successes at coping.

6. *Frame of reference:* Information concerning reality and value assumptions, including the way clients view themselves and their world.

Naturally, the emphasis placed on these six areas will differ from individual to individual and from problem to problem. For example, an individual whose major complaint is social unease will be assessed more thoroughly in those areas concerned with interpersonal history and skills than an individual whose major complaint concerns stress-related headaches. Similarly, an individual who complains of test anxiety will be assessed more carefully in those areas dealing with prior educational experiences and study skills than an individual who fears that she is unable to control her use of drugs.

## Methods of Assessment

In gathering information about clients and their life situations, psychologists may select from a wide range of assessment methods. We may divide these various procedures into three general categories: interviews, tests, and direct observation (Bernstein & Nietzel, 1980):

**Interviewing.**   This is probably the oldest and most widely used method for gathering information and making judgments about others. The **interview** is usually defined as a conversation with a specific purpose, conducted so that one person can obtain information from or evaluate another. This definition, however, belies the wide range and complexity of interview situations. For example, the interview may vary from the *simple interview* in which a specific set of questions is asked (as in a job interview); to the *stress interview,* designed to see how an individual functions intellectually and emotionally in a difficult situation; to the technically complex *therapeutic interview,* which may involve both assessment and therapy.

**interview: conversation with a purpose, conducted so that one person can obtain information from or evaluate another person**

Although the interview is of undoubted value for obtaining certain kinds of information, it is not always a wholly reliable technique. The biases, values, motives, and limited range of experience of interviewers (and interviewees) may distort the process. Factors such as age, sex, race, socioeconomic status, and language variables can reduce the quality and usefulness of information gathered during an interview (Pope, 1979).

**Psychological tests.**   Although the assessment goals of interviews and psychological tests may be similar, a **psychological test** differs from an interview in its *systematic and standardized observation and collection of information about*

**psychological test: standardized procedure designed to measure a person's performance on a specific task**

Some intelligence tests attempt to measure a person's intellectual functioning by proposing certain tasks and then asking the subject to make the best response.

*an individual* (Cronbach, 1970). While interviews may deal with virtually any issue, the purposes to which psychological tests are put are typically more limited. Nonetheless, there are a wide range of psychological tests designed to yield information about virtually any aspect of an individual. Some of the more common psychological tests include intelligence tests, personality inventories, projective tests, aptitude and ability tests, and tests of attitudes and values.

**intelligence test:** psychological test used to help assess complex mental abilities, involving both verbal and nonverbal components

● The **intelligence test** is the oldest type of psychological test. In the typical intelligence test, an individual is asked to answer questions and complete tasks designed to assess complex intellectual functions. For example, an individual's short-term memory can be assessed by asking him or her to repeat increasingly longer strings of numbers. Or in a test of abstract abilities, an individual may be asked to describe the attributes an apple and an orange have in common. Other tasks that are typically found on intelligence tests involve defining the meaning of certain words, using colored blocks to reproduce a printed pattern, and successfully solving simple arithmetic problems. While intelligence tests are easily scored, the proper interpretation of the results depends on the full cooperation and motivation of the subject.

**personality inventory:** psychological test used to assess specific aspects of an individual's personality

● The **personality inventory** is usually made up of a series of direct questions to which the individual is asked to respond "true" or "false" (or "yes" or "no"). (Some inventories allow for intermediate "don't know" or "cannot say" responses.) Examples of possible inventory items are:

| | | |
|---|---|---|
| I often feel as if things were unreal. | Yes | No |
| When I am disappointed, I like to talk with someone else. | Yes | No |
| I have engaged in deviant sexual behavior about which I feel guilty. | Yes | No |

Personality inventories may be designed to assess severe psychopathology, or they may assess normal interests, attitudes, abilities, and the like.

Perhaps the best known personality inventory is the Minnesota Multiphasic Personality Inventory, the MMPI. The MMPI is typically used to assess the extent to which an individual has psychological problems. In contrast, the California Psychological Inventory (CPI), another widely employed inventory, is used to assess *normal* psychological functioning.

The MMPI is particularly interesting because of its four validity scales. These validity scales are used to determine the extent to which the subject approached the test in an honest and open fashion and to determine the extent of "faking bad" or "faking good" on the test. When the validity scales are used in conjunction with the ten "clinical" scales, hundreds of *MMPI profiles* can be constructed, each describing a unique personality pattern.

● The **projective test** consists of an unstructured or ambiguous stimulus to which the subject is asked to respond. For example, in the well-known Rorschach technique, an individual is shown an inkblot and asked to tell what he or she sees in it. In other types of projective tests, an individual may be shown a picture and asked to make up a story about it or be given an incomplete sentence and asked to complete it. Since the stimulus is ambiguous, the creators of projective tests felt that the individual's cognitive patterns, conflicts, and self-defenses would be revealed in their responses (Exner, 1974).

**projective test: psychological assessment technique using relatively unstructured stimuli**

Although widely used, projective tests are much more difficult to administer and score than intelligence tests and personality inventories, and highly trained psychologists may offer strikingly different interpretations of a subject's responses. Projective tests are often used to confirm the findings of other personality tests and to help uncover aspects of an individual's personality that were not revealed by other assessment procedures.

● **Aptitude and ability tests** are typically used to assess specific potentials and skills. An example you may be familiar with is the Scholastic Aptitude Test (SAT) or the American College Test (ACT); both of these tests are often employed in admissions decisions at colleges and universities. Individuals seeking information about occupations may be asked to take the Strong-Campbell Interest Inventory or the Career Assessment Inventory. More specialized skills can also be assessed.

**ability and aptitude tests: psychological tests used to assess specific potentials and skills**

In the Rorschach test, the subject describes what he or she sees in inkblots like these and from the subject's response, the Rorschach expert identifies clues to personality functioning.

Reprinted courtesy *Omni Magazine* © 1982.

The Minnesota Clerical Test might be used to assess office skills prior to employ-ment, and musical aptitude can be assessed with the Seashore Measures of Musical Talents.

**tests of attitudes and values:** psychological tests used to assess an individual's beliefs and attitudes

- **Tests of attitudes and values** are also available. These devices can be used to measure political orientation, honesty, anxiety, and other traits that are diffi-cult to measure by performance on set tasks. These tests often use **rating scales,** and a rating scale item for aggressiveness, for example, might be as follows:

**rating scale:** psychologi-cal assessment technique for evaluating an indi-vidual on a specific trait

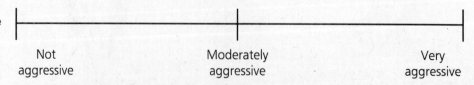

| Not aggressive | Moderately aggressive | Very aggressive |

Although these scales are easy to complete and easy to score, they are subject to many sources of error. One important source of error, **social desirability,** deals with the tendency of people to respond in an expected or socially correct manner. However, tests of attitudes and values are rarely used alone, and the information received from multiple sources helps yield accurate and useful assessment data.

**social desirability: tendency of a person to respond in socially correct manner**

**Direct observation.**   Most psychological tests attempt to identify consistencies in individuals. However, clinicians are also aware that situational factors can markedly affect the ways in which people behave (Hancock, 1982). If a child behaves poorly in school but behaves well at home, we would want to know more about the school setting and the home setting. A psychologist would, with the permission of those involved, observe the child in the classroom (and, perhaps, at home as well) to try to identify the factors that seem to encourage the poor behavior in school.

**Direct observation** also occurs when a psychologist sets up a simulated situation. A young man, for example, who complains that he has difficulty talking to women might be asked to act as though he were calling a female acquaintance. The psychologist would then observe the young man's performance and later suggest some ways the man might decrease his anxiety and improve his conversational skills.

**direct observation: assessment technique focusing on situations and their effect on behavior**

Finally, direct observation occurs whenever a psychologist interacts with another person. In talking with someone during an interview, the psychologist may notice subtle nonverbal signs that are clues to the person's emotional state. During an individually administered psychological test, the psychologist may observe the individual's problem-solving strategies and thereby gain further insight into the person.

## Evaluation and Integration of Assessment Data

In evaluating the significance of assessment data, psychologists are vitally concerned with the **validity, reliability,** and **standardization** of their tools. An intelligence test, for example, is *valid* if it actually measures intelligence and *reliable* if it gives consistent results at different times. If it has been *standardized,* the individual's score can be compared with the scores of a representative group of subjects, and the psychologist can say whether it is a high, low, or intermediate score.

**validity: extent to which a measuring instrument actually measures what it is designed to measure**

It is risky to draw conclusions from single items of information. The psychologist feels more confident if there is interlocking evidence from independent sources. Even when the reliability of single scores is limited, as in the case of projective test scores, the probability that a conclusion is accurate is increased if several independent sources of information point in the same direction. Since the overall goal of psychological assessment is to formulate an accurate "working model" of the client in relation to his or her life situation, it is essential that the assessment data not only be carefully evaluated but also be integrated into a coherent picture.

**reliability: degree to which a psychological test produces the same result each time it is used on the same person**

**standardization: characteristics of a psychological test allowing comparison of an individual score with a reference group**

# PSYCHOTHERAPY

Once an assessment is completed, the therapist and client may decide that a continuing relationship is necessary to help deal with the problems that were described in the assessment. This continuing contact forms the basis for **counseling** and **psychotherapy.** Originally, the word psychotherapy meant treatment ("therapy") of the mind ("psyche"). In the early days of Freudian psychoanalysis, psychotherapy practitioners literally believed that the mind was ill and that only extended treatment could bring the mind back to a semblance of normal and healthy functioning.

counseling and psychotherapy: use of psychological methods to assist or treat an individual

More recently, however, these terms have taken on a broader meaning. People may seek counseling or psychotherapy for a variety of reasons: an individual feels guilty, anxious, or depressed; a relationship is troubled; a child may be difficult to manage; people may feel vaguely dissatisfied with their lives. In other words, people may seek assistance for virtually any type of behavioral or emotional difficulty.

The abilities and skills of counselors and psychotherapists have broadened as well. Psychologists used to be trained almost exclusively as test-givers. Now, psychologists are trained to offer assistance in a variety of ways to deal with a variety of problems. Indeed, the plethora of approaches makes the field complicated and confusing to the average person.

Fortunately, psychotherapies generally fall into one of three major categories (see Chapter 2): psychoanalytic, social-learning, and humanistic-existential. Within each of the major categories there are subareas as well. Our coverage will concentrate on the major areas, and our coverage will, of necessity, be relatively brief. We begin our discussion with the first of the psychotherapies to be developed, psychoanalytic psychotherapy.

## Psychoanalytic Therapy

As developed by Sigmund Freud, psychoanalytic therapy emphasizes three basic ideas. First is the important role of irrational and unconscious processes—such as repressed memories, motives, and conflicts—in self-defeating and maladaptive behavior. Second is that such difficulties originate in early childhood experiences and in the conflict between social prohibitions and basic instinctual drives. Third is the importance of bringing these unconscious and irrational processes to consciousness so that the individual does not squander his or her energies on repression and other defense mechanisms.

Psychoanalytic therapy is a complex and long-term procedure. Perhaps the simplest way to describe it is to note the four basic techniques utilized in this approach.

1. *Free association.* The technique of **free association** is the "basic rule" of psychoanalytic therapy. The client tells the therapist whatever comes into his or her mind, regardless of how personal, painful, or seemingly irrelevant it may be.

free association: psychoanalytic procedure in which an individual gives a running account of every thought and feeling

2. *Dream interpretation.* Presumably when an individual is asleep, repressive defenses are lowered and forbidden desires and feelings find an outlet in dreams.

# Insight

**MYTHS AND REALITIES IN HYPNOSIS**

One of the earliest therapeutic tools used by Sigmund Freud was hypnosis. In working with patients who today would receive a diagnosis of conversion disorder (see Chapter 10), Freud found that he could reduce or eliminate the physical complaints presented by a substantial proportion of his patients. Freud eventually abandoned hypnosis, finding it less reliable and satisfactory than free association.

Today, hypnosis is used in a variety of settings for a variety of purposes. Probably most common is the use of hypnosis in psychotherapy to instill a sense of relaxation, to control pain, or to allow repressed memories to enter conscious awareness.

Unfortunately, many people's beliefs about hypnosis are based on incorrect impressions and stereotypes. In movies, hypnotists are often portrayed as distinctly evil characters, while hypnotists who perform on stage reinforce the impression that hypnosis is nothing more than an amusing parlor game.

Below are listed some myths and realities concerning hypnosis. In reviewing this list, you may wish to see how well your conceptualization of hypnosis corresponds to current research findings.

**Myths**

1. *A hypnotized person is under the control of the hypnotist.* In fact, a hypnotized person remains under his or her own control at all times.

2. *A hypnotized person can be made to do things he or she normally wouldn't do.* In fact, a person's values are no different under hypnosis than at any other time.

3. *A hypnotized person can perform superhuman acts.* In fact, physical strength is not altered under hypnosis.

4. *A person can learn more rapidly and retain more of what is learned under hypnosis.* In fact, mental abilities are unaffected by hypnosis.

5. *The characteristics of a hypnotized person are easy to spot.* In fact, most trained observers cannot tell the difference between a hypnotized person and a nonhypnotized person asked to fake being hypnotized.

**Realities**

1. *No physiological measures, including brain wave patterns, can distinguish a hypnotized from a nonhypnotized person.* The only reliable cue to whether a person is hypnotized is the individual's self-report.

2. *Hypnosis can be induced by a variety of means.* Virtually any stimulus, including suggestions of falling asleep, pedaling an exercise bike, or watching a pendulum swing back and forth, can be used to induce hypnosis.

3. *Hypnosis can be used to induce anesthesia.* Some hypnotic subjects can control surgical pain to such a degree that anesthetics are unnecessary during surgery.

4. *Expectations are important.* Some of the earliest hypnotic subjects believed they would and did have convulsions while hypnotized. Today, we expect that hypnotic subjects will appear limply relaxed.

5. *The ability to be hypnotized is unrelated to an individual's "willpower."* People easily hypnotized are no different in willpower than people who have difficulty becoming hypnotized.

(Barber, 1969; Hilgard, 1973; Hilgard & Hilgard, 1975; Wadden & Anderton, 1982)

**dream interpretation:** analysis of dreams for hidden meanings, used predominately by psychoanalytic therapists

For this reason, dreams have been referred to as the "royal road to the unconscious." In **dream interpretation,** the client relates his or her dreams and the therapist interprets their symbolism to the client.

3. *Analysis of resistance.* As psychoanalysis proceeds, certain painful memories or forbidden wishes become increasingly likely to enter the client's consciousness. In an attempt to prevent this material from entering conscious experience, the client may begin to miss appointments, argue with the therapist, and question the value of the therapy. If the therapy is to proceed successfully, however, this **resistance** to treatment must be reduced. Through the therapist's skillful interpretation of the client's behavior, the client becomes increasingly aware of and accepts these formerly threatening ideas and wishes, and resistance is reduced.

**resistance:** opposition of a client to uncovering repressed thoughts and feelings

4. *Analysis of transference.* During the course of psychoanalysis, clients usually "transfer" their feelings about some significant individual from the past, such as their mother or father, to their therapists. An important part of therapy is helping clients deal with this irrational **transference** and see past relationships as well as their present life situations in a more realistic light.

**transference:** process whereby the patient projects attitudes and emotions applicable to another significant person onto the therapist

Classical psychoanalysis is a very lengthy and expensive process. As proposed by Freud, psychoanalysis involves three to five therapy sessions per week over the course of three to five (or more) years. These requirements obviously place severe restrictions on the number of individuals who might benefit from psychoanalysis.

To deal with these limitations, contemporary analysts have worked out modifications of Freud's original approach. These modifications have reduced the time and expense involved in analytic therapy. A second modification adopted by many contemporary psychoanalysts involves a reassessment of the roles of unconscious and conscious experience. These **neo-Freudians** have placed more emphasis on the importance of conscious experience and the role of social and cultural variables. The neo-Freudians emphasize the day-to-day coping and striving of individuals over instinctual and unconscious processes.

**neo-Freudians:** analytically oriented therapists who emphasize the role of the ego and interpersonal processes in personality development and therapy

An early neo-Freudian, Robert White (1960), placed emphasis on the ego's desire to achieve competence and mastery—in contrast to the typical Freudian view of the ego defending against the awareness of unpleasant thoughts. More recent neo-Freudians, such as Judd Marmor (1980), emphasize a flexible approach to psychotherapy utilizing elements of psychoanalytic, behavioristic, and humanistic therapy as the needs of the patient dictate.

## The Social-Learning Approach

As we noted in Chapter 2, the social learning model views maladjusted individuals as differing from other people only in that *(a)* they have learned faulty coping patterns that are being maintained by some kind of reinforcement or *(b)* they have failed to acquire needed competencies for coping with the problems of living. The predominantly directive approaches used in social-learning therapy (sometimes called **behavioral therapy**) specify both the maladaptive behaviors to be modified and the adaptive behaviors to be learned.

**behavior therapy:** form of psychotherapy emphasizing learning of adaptive patterns and modification of maladaptive patterns of behavior

Social-learning approaches tend to be more specifically oriented to particular problems than psychoanalytic approaches. It is therefore impossible to discuss social-learning approaches as though they were comprised of a single, unified set of techniques. Instead, we will concentrate on a small number of techniques that appear to be highly effective for particular problems.

**Anxiety management.**    Anxiety management has focused largely upon the elimination of irrational fears or phobias. The procedure which has been particularly prominent here is **systematic desensitization.** Systematic desensitization was developed by Joseph Wolpe (1958, 1969, 1981) as a means to eliminate fears and phobias. Wolpe believed that phobic reactions could be decreased and eliminated if a response antagonistic to anxiety could be produced in the presence of the anxiety-eliciting stimulus. In other words, an individual who was relaxed while in the presence of the fear-producing stimulus, such as an elevator car, would find the fear gradually going away.

**systematic desensitization: technique used mainly by social-learning therapists to eliminate clients' fears and phobias**

Wolpe structured his technique so that it had three parts: In the first part, the client and therapist put together a graded list of fear-producing stimuli. This list of anxiety-evoking stimuli was called a **hierarchy.** If, for example, the client had a fear of speaking in front of a class, the hierarchy might be as follows:

**hierarchy: list of fear-producing situations, used in systematic desensitization**

Step  1. *I am reading about speeches alone in my room. It is about a week or two before the time I have to give the speech.*
Step  2. *It is one week before the speech. I am discussing the speech with someone after class.*
Step  3. *It is one week before my speech, and I am sitting in class listening to another person give a speech.*
Step  4. *I am writing my speech in a study area.*
Step  5. *I am practicing the speech while alone in my room.*
Step  6. *I am getting dressed on the morning of the speech.*
Step  7. *I am carrying out some activities prior to leaving to give the speech.*
Step  8. *It is the day of the speech, and I am walking to class.*
Step  9. *I am entering the classroom.*
Step 10. *I am waiting while another person gives the speech.*
Step 11. *It is time for me to give the speech. I am walking up before the audience.*
Step 12. *I am giving the speech, and I am noticing the faces in the audience and seeing their reactions. (Adapted from Paul, 1966)*

Through the technique of systematic desensitization, the client who fears speaking in front of a group can learn to overcome that anxiety by pairing the relaxation response with each of the fear-producing situations of the hierarchy.

In the second part of desensitization, the client learns relaxation techniques similar to those presented in Chapter 9. In the third part, portions of the hierarchy are paired with relaxation. The client is asked to imagine the least anxiety-evoking situation while attempting to remain relaxed. If thinking of the scene disturbs relaxation, the client is asked to stop and to concentrate fully on relaxation. When the client can imagine the scene with no disruption, the next hierarchy item is presented. This process continues until the client can imagine the most anxiety-evoking situation without disturbance.

The ability to imagine these scenes without anxiety typically generalizes to the client's day-to-day experience. That is, if the client is able to *imagine* a scene without anxiety, it is also likely that the client will respond with little or no anxiety in the actual situation.

An alternative form of desensitization, called *in-vivo desensitization,* employs hierarchy items that can readily be found in real-world situations. For example, an individual who fears entering an elevator may be able to construct a hierarchy in which he or she actually enters a building with an elevator, approaches the elevator, enters the car, takes the car up one floor, and so forth.

**Assertiveness training.**     Social-learning approaches have focused upon helping clients develop the social skills essential for dealing with a variety of real-life problems. A business executive, for example, might be highly competent in dealing with peers but encounter serious difficulties in communicating and interacting with spouse and children. Similarly, a college student may express thoughts and feelings freely to other students but feel seriously inhibited in communicating with professors.

Two social skills areas that have received special attention are heterosexual interactions, such as dating and marital communication, and assertive behavior. We shall focus on **assertiveness training.** Assertiveness training is particularly useful in helping individuals who have difficulties in interpersonal situations because learned anxiety responses prevent them from speaking up for what they consider to be appropriate and right. Such inhibition may lead to continual inner turmoil, particularly if he or she feels strongly about the situation. Assertiveness training may also be useful for individuals who consistently allow other people to take advantage of them or maneuver them into uncomfortable situations.

**assertiveness training: social-learning technique for helping individuals express their feelings and gain their rights without being uncooperative or overbearing**

Social-learning therapists believe that assertive skills lie on a continuum. At one end of the continuum, the individual is *nonassertive.* This person has difficulty demanding correct change from a salesperson in a department store, refuses to comment when others crowd ahead in a long line, or has difficulty expressing positive emotions toward others.

At the other end of the continuum is the *aggressive* individual whose only concern is for him- or herself. The aggressive individual might be unreasonable, demanding, and uncooperative. Between these two extremes is the *assertive* individual. This person does not allow others to take advantage of him or her. The assertive individual is expressive and attempts to fulfill needs and desires without abusing the rights and privileges of others.

The expression of assertive behaviors—first by role-playing and obervational learning (modeling) in the therapy setting and then by practice in real-life situations—is guided by the therapist. The client learns to identify the situations in which he or she is unduly aggressive or nonassertive and to identify options to current behavior. Clients are also shown how to "think ahead" about the consequences of their acts. Often attention is focused on developing more effective interpersonal skills, and clients may devise an "assertion hierarchy" to help them structure their therapeutic endeavors.

**Contingency management and behavioral contracting.** Our society is oriented toward punishment. Our laws and customs operate under the thesis that "In order to avoid punishment, you must behave in such and such a way." Social-learning therapists feel that a punishment-oriented approach is ineffective in teaching appropriate ways to behave. Punishment, they feel, only teaches the individual what *not* to do; it does not teach desirable alternatives.

To help individuals reach positive goals, social-learning therapists have developed the techniques of contingency management and behavioral contracting. **Contingency management** uses positive reinforcement; desired behavior is reinforced as soon as possible. This reward-oriented approach operates under the rule that "In order to receive a reward, you must behave in such and such a way." The reinforcer can be material, as in money or food, access to desired behaviors (child is allowed to play when homework is completed), "tokens" that can be exchanged for desired objects or activities; or the reinforcer can be intangible, as in praise, a smile, or a pat on the back.

> contingency management: social-learning technique used to help individuals reach positive goals

When attempts are made to deal with a broad spectrum of behaviors, or when the program becomes complex, social-learning therapists speak of **behavioral contracting.** In behavioral contracting, a written or oral agreement is made between individuals. This agreement specifies the rules, behaviors, and changes that must occur before reinforcers can be earned. In marital therapy, for example, a couple may, with the assistance of the therapist, set up a behavioral contract. The husband may agree to baby-sit with the children in exchange for an afternoon of watching sports on television. At the same time, the wife may agree to manage the family finances in exchange for two evenings of dance exercises at the local high school or college.

> behavioral contracting: complex program for changing many behaviors, used primarily by social-learning therapists

**Cognitive change.** Cognitive events, such as thought and emotion, play an interesting role in the social-learning approach. Social-learning theorists have traditionally been more interested in easily measured overt behaviors than in those aspects of the individual that are difficult to observe. Improvements in measurement instruments and acceptance of a client's self-report as a reliable and valid measure of cognitive events have led social-learning therapists to attempt to teach clients how to change maladaptive cognitive patterns.

One approach to cognitive change has been termed **Rational-Emotive Therapy** (RET). RET stems from the work of Albert Ellis (1973) who theorized that ineffective and self-defeating behaviors stemmed from irrational, maladaptive thought patterns. Some of the irrational beliefs identified by Ellis are:

> Rational-Emotive Therapy: form of psychotherapy which encourages the client to substitute rational for irrational assumptions in his or her inner dialogues

1. One should be loved or approved by everyone.
2. One should be competent and adequate in all possible respects.
3. It is catastrophic when things are not as they should be.

4. One's present behavior is irreversibly dependent on significant past events.

5. One should get upset over the problems of others.

Such faulty assumptions are presumably maintained by a process of "self-talk," a sort of internal dialogue in which the client continually reaffirms his or her own faulty assumptions. For example, the client may continually remind him- or herself that it is essential to be approved by everyone, or that it is tragic not to be highly successful.

*Take the case of an individual who believes that he is unattractive and unappealing to the opposite sex. If he seeks out an attractive female, he might say out loud,*

"Hi. My name's Pat."

*while thinking to himself,*

I don't know why I'm even bothering to talk with her. She's only going to turn me down.

*Although he might appear to be talking to another person, he is, in fact, holding a conversation with himself:*

"We're in the same psychology of adjustment class."
How wonderfully creative. Why don't you also say that the sky is blue?
"How do you like it so far?"
The all-time champ of the one-liners strikes again!
"Say, some friends and I are going to see a movie this weekend. Would you like to join us?"
Brace yourself. Here it comes.
"Oh, that's too bad. Well, maybe some other time."
Congratulations. You really out-did yourself this time. Did you seriously believe that she would go out with you?

*Negative self-statements are often constructed so that we cannot allow ourselves or others to win. If this luckless fellow had succeeded in winning a date, he might have said to himself:*

Oh-oh. There must be something wrong with her to want to go out with me. Only a loser would want to go out with me.

*Ellis has suggested a number of ways in which problems such as these could be treated. In the first step, the individual would be asked to become aware of his thought patterns. Next, he would challenge the validity of his beliefs. Is it necessary for him to succeed at all things, including getting a date for a weekend movie? Does rejection for a date imply that he is an utterly worthless individual? Is it a catastrophe if he goes to a movie alone? Finally, he would be asked to replace these irrational beliefs with more logical, rational ones. For example, he might say to himself:*

I'd like to have a date for this weekend. If I don't, it won't be the end of the world. It would be nice to go with someone, but it's not a necessity. Not everything can turn out the way I would like it to be. I can still have fun this weekend and enjoy the movie.
*(Glaros, 1980, p. 27)*

Thus, the primary goal of therapy becomes that of helping the client identify and change inaccurate assumptions. This is largely achieved by helping the client to see that beliefs, like actions, have consequences, and that irrational beliefs, like irrational actions, usually lead to frustration, disappointment, and emotional hurt. With the help of the therapist, the client is then in a position to identify and change irrational beliefs and adopt more appropriate ones.

**Self-control.**  Most of the social-learning procedures we have reviewed lend themselves to self-administration. Thus, they can also be used as **self-control** procedures.

As in other forms of social-learning therapy, the focus is on eliminating mal-adaptive behaviors and replacing them with needed adaptive ones. Thus, a student may wish to spend less time watching television and more time studying for his or her classes. Or a person may wish to eliminate unrealistic feelings of inadequacy and helplessness and replace them with a more positive self-image. And again, it becomes essential to specify target behaviors, establish baselines, specify the procedures to be used, and assess results.

We shall briefly review two procedures that are commonly used in the self-regulation and control of behavior: biofeedback and environmental planning.

● *Biofeedback.*  The concept of the self-regulation and self-control of behavior received a strong boost during the last decade following intensive research on biofeedback.

The concept of biofeedback is relatively simple. It is based on using sensitive recording devices to record brain waves, blood pressure, and other bodily functions and feeding this information back to the subject by means of auditory signals or visual displays so that the subject knows what a given part of his or her body is doing. Although the precise process is not understood, this procedure enables the individual to gain some measure of self-control over bodily functions that were once thought automatic and hence not subject to learned control. As yet the full potentials of biofeedback are not known, but it has been used to enable patients to control brain waves associated with epileptic seizures and to reduce the number of attacks, to reduce the frequency and duration of migraine head-aches, to lower heart rate and blood pressure, and to exercise some measure of control over a wide range of other bodily functions (Blanchard & Epstein, 1978). In a similar fashion, dedicated Zen and Yoga masters are capable of not only raising and lowering their blood pressure, body temperature, and related functions but also of controlling their brain waves (Shapiro, 1980).

Despite initial successes in dealing with a number of stress-related disorders, many questions remain concerning the range of use and long-range effectiveness of biofeedback training. Certainly it is no "miracle cure" (Andrasik & Holroyd, 1980). But, when used in comprehensive treatment programs for dealing with maladaptive behaviors, it can be highly beneficial.

● *Environmental planning.*  The self-control procedure of **environmental planning** focuses on changing the environmental cues that precede and elicit specific maladaptive behaviors. For example, overeating is often influenced by a variety of physical and social cues that prompt eating even when the person is not hungry (see Chapter 5). Many people overeat to avoid wasting food. In social situations, they often eat high calorie desserts because other people are eating and enjoying them. Or an individual may develop a habit of eating and/or drinking

**self-control: process in which an individual guides and directs his or her behavior to achieve positive goals**

**environmental planning: self-control procedure in which an individual structures his or her environment to achieve positive goals**

while watching television. Stuart and Davis (1972) have shown that people trained to detect and avoid or alter maladaptive eating "cues" can reduce unnecessary food intake and weight gain.

Using a similar approach, Upper and Meredith (1970) reduced the smoking behavior of excessive smokers. Initially, clients were asked to record their daily smoking rate. They then computed the average time between cigarettes—about fifteen minutes—and asked the clients to wear a small portable timer. The timer was set to buzz when the smoker's average time between cigarettes had elapsed, and the clients were instructed to smoke only after the timer had buzzed. With use, the buzzer replaced previous cues that had elicited smoking, such as the conclusion of a meal, conversation with a friend, or some tension-arousing experience. The interval on the timer was then gradually increased until smoking behavior was markedly reduced.

By environmental planning we can play an active role in influencing the environmental contingencies that infringe upon us and hence control our behavior. Thus, it is important not only to assess the role of environmental conditions in shaping behavior but also to analyze how we can change environmental conditions in order to foster adaptive behavior.

Although far-reaching conclusions are premature, it appears that self-control is part of "the wave of the future." These methods may provide for improving personal effectiveness and balancing the environmental control of behavior with inner self-control. As Bandura (1977b) has expressed it: "Within the process of reciprocal determinism lies the opportunity for people to influence their own destiny as well as the limits of self-direction. . . . Both people and their environments are reciprocal determinants of each other" (p. vii).

In closing our discussion of the social-learning approaches, we should note that combinations of these techniques are often used in therapy. It is a rare individual whose only problem is a phobic reaction or unassertive behavior. Sensitive assessment helps pinpoint the areas of maladaptive functioning; and the social-learning therapist uses the techniques that are best suited to the treatment of these various problems.

## The Humanistic-Existential Therapies

*"A person-centered approach is based on the premise that the human being is basically a trustworthy organism, capable of evaluating the outer and inner situation, understanding herself in its context, making constructive choices as to the next steps in life, and acting on those choices."*
*(ROGERS, 1977, P. 15)*

The *humanistic-existential* therapies (often termed the *phenomenological* therapies) focus on creating a "psychological climate" or relationship that releases the client's capacity for understanding and managing his or her life. We shall confine ourselves to a brief review of the most prominent of these therapies.

**Person-centered therapy.**    Most closely associated with the name of Carl Rogers (1951, 1961), this therapeutic approach emphasizes an attitude of caring and of positive acceptance on the part of the therapist. In such a psychological climate, individuals are able to discover and be themselves.

In **person-centered therapy** (also known as *client-centered therapy*) the primary responsibility rests upon the client. The therapist plays a relatively passive role, since it is assumed that the client is inherently able to solve his or her problems. The therapist approaches the person with as few preconceived notions as possible and works with the material presented by the individual, repeating or reflecting the client's feelings and thoughts and helping to clarify them. In this process, the therapist avoids interpreting what the person is saying or attempting to force insight on the individual.

**person-centered therapy: nondirective approach to psychotherapy developed primarily by Carl Rogers; also called** *client-centered therapy*

The following excerpt from a therapy session demonstrates the person-centered approach.

ALICE. *I was thinking about this business of standards. I somehow developed a sort of a knack, I guess, of—well—habit—of trying to make people feel at ease around me, or to make things go along smoothly. . . .*

COUNSELOR. *In other words, what you did was always in the direction of trying to keep things smooth and to make other people feel better and to smooth the situation.*

ALICE. *Yes. I think that's what it was. Now the reason why I did it probably was—I mean, not that I was a good little Samaritan going around making other people happy, but that was probably the role that felt easiest for me to play. I'd been doing it around home so much. I just didn't stand up for my own convictions, until I don't know whether I have any convictions to stand up for.*

COUNSELOR. *You feel that for a long time you've been playing the role of kind of smoothing out the frictions or differences or what not. . . .*

ALICE. *M-hm.*

COUNSELOR. *Rather than having any opinion or reaction of your own in the situation. Is that it?*

ALICE. *That's it. Or that I haven't been really honestly being myself, or actually knowing what my real self is, and that I've been just playing a sort of false role. Whatever role no one else was playing, and that needed to be played at the time, I'd try to fill it in. (Rogers, 1951, pp. 152–53)*

Rogers has found that person-centered therapy follows an orderly and predictable sequence: *(a)* the creation of the therapeutic climate, *(b)* the client's expression of feelings and thoughts that had formerly been denied or distorted, including many negative feelings, *(c)* insight and increased self-understanding, *(d)* positive steps toward resolving conflicts and achieving more positive feelings about one's self and others, and *(e)* termination of therapy. The last step is initiated by the client who arrives at a point where he or she no longer needs the support of the therapeutic relationship.

**Existential therapy.**    As we noted in our review of the existential model, existential psychologists are very much concerned about the predicament of humankind today. They emphasize the breakdown of traditional faith, the alienation and depersonalization of the individual in our mass society, and the loss of meaning in human existence. Despite their predicament, however, humans are viewed as essentially free. Unlike other living creatures, humans have the ability to be self-aware, to reflect on their own existence, and to do something about their problems through their choices and actions.

existential therapy: form of psychotherapy that attempts to develop a sense of self-direction and meaning in one's existence

Thus, the primary concern of **existential therapy** is helping the client to clarify his or her values and to work out a meaningful way of "being-in-the-world." Since each individual is unique, each must find the pattern of values capable of giving meaning to his or her life. As Nietzsche has expressed it, "He who has a *why* to live can bear with almost any *how*." But to find values and meaning, the individual must have the courage to break away from old views and defenses, to make choices, to face existential anxiety, and to take responsibility for his or her life.

confrontation: situation in which one's positive and negative feelings about another person are presented directly to that person

Existential therapists do not follow any prescribed procedures but believe that a flexible approach is necessary in therapy (Havens, 1974; Frankl, 1971; May 1969). However, they do stress the importance of the **confrontation**—challenging the individual directly with questions concerning the meaning and purpose of his or her existence—and the encounter—the relationship established between two interacting human beings in a therapeutic situation. The focus is on the here and now—on what the individual is choosing to do, and therefore be, at this moment. This sense of immediacy, of the urgency of experience, is the touchstone of existential therapy and sets the stage for clarifying and choosing among alternative ways of being. Existential therapists also emphasize the individual's responsibility to others. One's life can only be meaningful and fulfilling if it involves socially constructive values and choices.

logotherapy: form of therapy developed by Viktor Frankl that attempts to instill a sense of meaning and purpose in life

Viktor Frankl's (1971) logotherapy is a representative example of the existential therapies. **Logotherapy** means a "therapy of meaning," and it was developed out of Frankl's experiences as an inmate in a concentration camp during World War II. As a physician in the camp, Frankl saw much suffering and death, and he also noted that those who succumbed to the horrors of these camps were also those who gave up hope (an observation which has since been confirmed through the experiences of the Vietnam War). According to Frankl, survival is enhanced when individuals have a "will-to-meaning"—a purpose or goal in life. Logotherapy

One of the goals of logotherapy is helping the client find something that gives meaning and significance to living.

thus hopes to instill in individuals a sense of meaning and purpose in life through the tools of choice and responsibility.

While existential psychotherapy is similar in many ways to person-centered psychotherapy—both approaches view psychotherapy as growth of the self—the existential approach places less emphasis on discovering the true self behind the façade and more emphasis on taking the responsibility for one human life—for shaping one's self into the kind of person one wants to be and living in a socially constructive and meaningful way. The Greek oracle said "Know thyself"; the poet Emerson said "Trust thyself"; and, to paraphrase Kierkegaard, the existentialists have said "Choose thyself."

**Gestalt therapy: Becoming a "whole" person.**   As developed by Fritz Perls (1969), **Gestalt therapy** is typically used in a group setting, but the emphasis is on the individual. Working intensively with one client at a time, the therapist helps clients perceive those aspects of themselves and their world that are "blocked out," correct inaccuracies in their views, and achieve greater competence in coping with the problems of living.

Gestalt therapy utilizes a number of specific techniques including "awareness training," the "hot seat," and dream interpretation. Awareness training focuses on helping clients become more perceptive and enrich their experiencing. The "hot seat" is utilized in helping clients perceive themselves more clearly. Here one person occupies the "hot seat" while the others provide feedback about their reactions to the client and his or her behavior—with the proviso that the feedback be sincere. This results in clients achieving somewhat different impressions of themselves than they had before. In "dreamwork," the therapist helps the client interpret the meaning of given dreams and perceive their application to real-life situations.

These various techniques are referred to as "taking care of unfinished business." According to Perls, we all go through life with blind spots and unresolved conflicts and traumas. This unfinished business can be carried over into new situations and relationships, often with detrimental results. Consequently, completing this unfinished business should help clients achieve a more realistic awareness of themselves and their world, reduce their level of anxiety and tension, and achieve greater effectiveness in coping.

**Transactional analysis.**   Eric Berne (1964, 1972) developed an innovative technique of interpersonal therapy based on the notion that our personalities are composed of three "ego states"—Child, Adult, and Parent—which correspond very roughly to Freud's id, ego, and superego. In **transactional analysis**, the therapist analyzes the interactions among individuals and helps the participants understand the ego states in which they are communicating with each other. As long as each participant reacts to the other in the way that he or she is being addressed, for example, as a Child to a Parent, the transactions may continue indefinitely. However, when one party decides to stop playing Child to the other's Parent, the game ceases, and conflicts develop that must be worked out.

**Gestalt therapy: type of psychotherapy emphasizing the wholeness of the patient and the integration of thoughts, feelings, and action**

**transactional analysis: humanistic-existential approach to psychotherapy based upon understanding the interaction of "Child," "Parent," and "Adult" ego states**

# Insight

A confusing variety of terms may be encountered in discussing intensive group experiences. A few of the more common of these are described below.

1. *Sensitivity training groups* or *T-groups* initially focused on the development of human relations skills and on understanding and increasing the effectiveness of group functioning but have since become much broader in scope.

2. *Encounter groups* may focus either on the treatment of maladaptive behavior or on fostering the personal growth and effectiveness, including improved interpersonal relationships, of essentially normal persons.

3. *Awareness groups* usually focus on sensory awareness, body awareness, and body movement, utilizing awareness train-

## FORMS OF INTENSIVE GROUP EXPERIENCE

ing, nonverbal expression, spontaneous dance, and related activities.

4. *Creativity groups or workshops* focus on individual spontaneity, expression, and creativity, often through painting and other artistic media.

There are also a number of other forms of intensive group experience including *team building groups,* which are widely used in industry to facilitate the attainment of production and related goals as well as providing opportunities for improved human relations and personal growth. The *Synanon group* or "game," developed originally for the treatment of drug addiction, may also be considered a type of encounter group, as may groups engaged in Gestalt therapy or transactional analysis.

---

By analyzing the games we play, transactional analysis makes us aware of our basic coping patterns and their consequences in terms of our interpersonal relationships and life adjustment. In holding up a mirror so that we can see our behavior for what it really is, transactional analysis reveals how we often unthinkingly manipulate and harm other people as well as ourselves. And as a form of therapy, it holds out the possibility of eliminating the subterfuge and deceit with which we deal with one another and of achieving more authentic, meaningful, and satisfying interpersonal relationships and life-styles.

**encounter group: small group designed to provide an intensive interpersonal experience focusing on feelings and group interactions**

**Encounter groups.**   **Encounter groups** are intensive group experiences. These groups are of two distinct types, depending on their focus: *(a)* treating maladaptive behavior, such as encounter groups for juvenile delinquents, and *(b)* helping normal persons learn more about themselves, develop more satisfying interpersonal relationships, and open pathways to personal growth.

● *Group format and climate.*   Usually the encounter group consists of six to twelve members, including the group leader who is also a participant. The physical setting is usually relatively bare, permitting maximum freedom of movement by group members. Group leaders are usually responsible for screening members for admission to the group and for scheduling group meetings. Leaders also serve as models by expressing their own feelings openly and honestly and accepting

# Insight

Just what is it that goes on in an encounter group? On the basis of his work with such groups, Rogers (1970) has delineated a typical pattern of events:

1. *Milling around.* As the group leader makes it clear that group members have unusual freedom but also responsibility for the direction of the group, there tends to be an initial period of confusion, frustration, awkward silences, and "cocktail-party talk"—polite talk intermixed with questions about the group.

2. *Resistance to personal expression or exploration.* Initially, members tend to portray only their "public selves"; only fearfully and gradually do they begin to reveal aspects of the private self.

3. *Description of negative feelings.* The first expression of feelings concerning the here-and-now interaction in the group tends to involve negative feelings directed toward the group leader or other group members.

4. *Expression and exploration of personally meaningful material.* The event most likely to occur next is for some member to take the gamble of revealing some intimate information—perhaps a seemingly hopeless problem of communication with a spouse. Apparently this member has come to realize that this is "his" or "her" group, and he or she can help shape its direction; apparently also the fact that negative feelings have been expressed without catastrophic results tends to foster a climate of trust.

5. *The expression of immediate interpersonal feelings in the group.* This may occur at any point. It involves the explicit expression of feelings, positive or negative, experienced at the moment by one member toward another. Each of these immediate expressions of feeling is usually explored in

## EVENTS IN ENCOUNTER GROUPS

the increasing climate of trust which is developing in the group.

6. *Development of a healing capacity in the group and the beginning of change.* Some group members show a spontaneous capability for responding to the pain and suffering of others in a therapeutic way—thus paving the way for change. This healing capacity may extend beyond the regular group sessions, as when a few members remain after the session to offer support and therapeutic aid to a member they sense is experiencing serious difficulties.

7. *Dropping of façades, confrontations, and feedback.* As time goes on, the group finds it increasingly unacceptable for any member to hide behind a mask or façade, refusing to reveal the self to the group. In a general sense, the group *demands* that each individual be his or her true self. This may result in a direct confrontation, often negative in tone, between two group members. In this type of basic encounter, individuals come into more direct, honest, and closer contact than is customary in ordinary life. This is likely to provide individuals with a good deal of totally new feedback concerning themselves and their effects on others.

8. *Expression of positive feelings and behavior change.* Rogers states that "an inevitable part of the group process seems to be that when feelings are expressed and can be accepted in a relationship, then a great deal of closeness and positive feeling results. Thus as the sessions proceed, an increasing feeling of warmth and group spirit and trust is built up, not out of positive attitudes only but out of a realness which includes both positive and negative feeling" (pp. 34–35). He concludes that, while there are certain risks, there is also great therapeutic potential.

hostility or other negative feelings directed toward them without becoming defensive. It is their responsibility to see that confrontations among group members are resolved in a constructive way. In general, the group leader serves as a resource person when the group needs guidance or comes to an impasse.

The most important function of the group leader is that of establishing a climate of "psychological safety" in which the members feel free to lower their defenses, to express their feelings, and to try out new ways of interacting with others. When such a psychological climate is coupled with the intensive give-and-take of group interaction, the possibilities for increased awareness, understanding, and personal growth are greatly enhanced.

● *Group process.* The emphasis in encounter groups is on the open and honest communication of feelings and the constructive resolution of confrontations. This in turn requires prompt and sincere feedback from other group members. In order to foster a climate of psychological safety the group leader encourages members to give descriptive rather than evaluative feedback. An example of a descriptive response would be "When you said that, it made me feel uncomfortable" rather than the evaluative response "Only a real jerk would make a statement like that." In group interaction the emphasis is upon present feelings and interactions—not on the past or future.

The actual sequence of events which typically occur in encounter groups has been well described by Rogers (1970) and is summarized on page 315. One aspect of encounter groups that is not included in Rogers' description is the **reentry problem** (Yalom & Lieberman, 1971). This refers to the return of the group members from the climate of psychological safety and the openness of the encounter group to the everyday world where new understandings and ways of interacting may not be readily accepted. Obviously there is considerable risk in being completely open in one's interactions with family, work, or social groups—if one does not wish to endanger the relationship. As yet there is no simple solution to the reentry problem, although some group leaders utilize the final session of the group for "reflections" in which members share their feelings about the group experience and how it may carry over into their everyday lives.

**reentry problem:** difficulties faced by members of encounter groups when leaving the group and returning to the everyday world

## Sex, Marital, and Family Therapy

Therapeutic approaches to maladaptive behavior are not limited to particular theoretical points of view. Some therapeutic approaches draw from a number of theoretical orientations in their attempts to solve or ameliorate problems within a relationship. In this section, we will concentrate on three areas in which troubled relationships are at the center of maladaptive problems: sex therapy, marital therapy, and family therapy.

**Sex therapy.** Masters and Johnson (1975) have concluded from their extensive research that some 50 percent of American marriages suffer from sexual dysfunctions. And they consider such problems largely responsible for our high rates

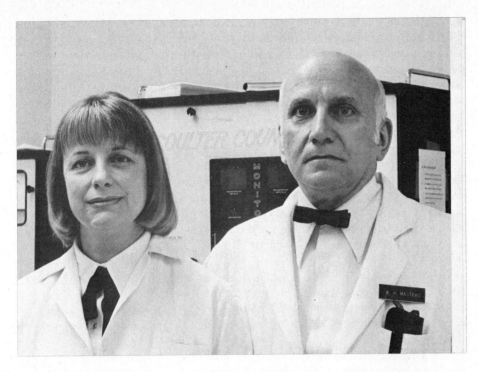

The sex therapy techniques developed by Virginia E. Johnson and William H. Masters focus on the reduction of anxiety, learning of sexual skills, and improved communication between the partners.

of marital dissatisfaction and divorce. **Sex therapy** refers to treatment for various forms of sexual dysfunction, such as impotence, orgasmic dysfunction, and premature ejaculation.

**sex therapy:** therapy focusing on the treatment of sexual dysfunction

Although there are various approaches to sex therapy, the best known and most widely used is based on the pioneering work of Masters and Johnson (1970, 1975, 1976). Fundamental to this approach are the assumptions that: *(a)* the sexual response is a natural function, *(b)* it is ordinarily possible to identify and remove the obstacles that are interfering with effective sexual functioning, and *(c)* the sexual partners should work together to eliminate the dysfunction. A thorough medical examination is required to rule out the possibility that the dysfunction is the result of organic causes.

In actual therapy, the preceding assumptions can be roughly translated into the following steps and procedures. (1) An initial period focuses on an analysis of the problem, an understanding of the therapy goals of the partners, and on basic sex education, including information concerning the anatomy, physiology, and psychology of the sexual response. (2) This initial period blends into a second stage focusing on sensual pleasure and improved communication between the partners. Prominent here is the use of *sensate focus.* This involves learning to experience sensual pleasure in caressing each other's bodies and genitals while temporarily refraining from intercourse. Sensate focus serves to remove stereotypes of what sexual interaction "should be," to foster nonverbal communication and natural sexual responsiveness, and to alleviate anxiety. Emphasis is also placed on techniques for improving verbal communication between the partners, which leads to better understanding and more intimate feelings between the couple. This, in turn, helps to release their sexual feelings toward one another. (3) This second period overlaps with and blends into the final period of therapy, which focuses on maintaining and improving open communication between the partners and utilizes a series of sexual exercises that emphasize pleasure and intimacy. In this last part of therapy, specific techniques may be used to deal with the sexual dysfunction. A "squeeze technique" is often suggested for premature ejaculation, for example.

The data reported by Masters and Johnson suggest that their treatment of sexual dysfunctions is highly effective. Success rates appear to be very high for problems such as vaginismus and premature ejaculation and somewhat lower for problems such as primary orgasmic dysfunction. Of course, sexual dysfunctions may reflect relationship difficulties, and the therapist must deal with these issues as well as with the sexual dysfunctions.

**marital therapy: therapy focusing on the marital relationship**

**Marital therapy.** The large numbers of people seeking assistance with problems centering around their marriage have made **marital therapy** an important field of counseling. Typically the marital partners are seen together, and therapy focuses on clarifying and improving the interactions and relationships between them.

Attempts to achieve this goal include a wide range of concepts and procedures. Most therapists emphasize mutual need gratification, social role expectations, communication patterns, and similar interpersonal factors. Not surprisingly, happily married couples tend to differ from unhappily married couples in that they talk more to each other, keep channels of communication open, make more use of nonverbal techniques of communication, and show more sensitivity to each other's feelings, expectations, and needs.

Often faulty communication and role problems play havoc with marital relationships. The following example is instructive:

HUSBAND. *She never comes up to me and kisses me. I am always the one to make the overtures.*

THERAPIST. *Is this the way you see yourself behaving with your husband?*

WIFE. *Yes, I would say he is the demonstrative one. I didn't know he wanted me to make the overtures.*

T. *Have you told your wife that you would like this from her—more open demonstration of affection?*

H. *Well, no, you'd think she'd know.*

W. *No, how would I know? You always said you didn't like aggressive women.*

H. *I don't, I don't like dominating women.*

W. *Well, I thought you meant women who make the overtures. How am I to know what you want?*

T. *You'd have a better idea if he had been able to tell you. (Satir, 1967, pp. 72–73)*

One of the difficulties in marital therapy is the intense emotional involvement of the marital partners, which makes it difficult for them to perceive and accept the realities of their relationship. Often, wives can see clearly what is "wrong"

# Insight

In recent years many have questioned the value of psychotherapy. Despite the fact that hundreds of thousands of people undergo some form of psychotherapy each year, we have surprisingly little scientific data to show how often such therapeutic intervention is successful. While attempts have been made to assess and compare the outcomes of various forms of therapy, the wide variations among therapists, patients, goals, procedures, and definitions of success have made it virtually impossible to reach any valid conclusions.

Attempts at evaluation have usually depended on one or more of the following sources of information: *(a)* the therapist's impression of changes that have occurred, *(b)* the patient's report of change, *(c)* comparison of pre- and posttreatment personality test scores, and *(d)* measures of change in selected overt behaviors. Unfortunately, each source has serious limitations.

Since a therapist usually wants to see himself or herself as competent, therapists are not the best judges of their own effectiveness. They can also inflate their improvement rate by encouraging difficult patients to discontinue therapy. It has also been facetiously remarked that the therapist often thinks the patient is getting better, just because the therapist is getting used to the patient's symptoms. Patients are another unreliable source concerning the outcome of therapy, since they too may want to think they are improving. Psychological tests may show change but are not necessarily valid indicators of how the client will behave in real-life situations. And neither psychological tests nor measures of change in overt behaviors indicate whether such change is likely to be enduring. Finally, many emotionally disturbed people show improvement over time without psychotherapy. Thus, the question is often raised whether the patient improved because of or despite psychotherapy.

Nonetheless, the evidence that is available suggests that psychotherapy is generally better than no treatment at all. One "metanalysis" of psychotherapy outcome studies (Smith & Glass, 1977) found that the typical therapy client is better off than 75 percent of untreated control patients. At this point, there is no evidence to suggest that one particular type of therapy is better than another. However, as our knowledge and understanding of the complex process of psychotherapy improves, it is likely that psychotherapists will become increasingly selective in their use of psychological treatment techniques. Rather than give all clients the same treatment, psychotherapists in the future will use a particular set of techniques for one unique person/problem combination and an entirely different set of techniques for another person/problem combination.

with their husbands but not with themselves, while husbands usually have remarkable "insight" into their wives' flaws but not their own. To help correct this problem, videotape recordings have been used increasingly to recapture crucial moments of intense interaction between the marital partners. Watching these tapes helps the couple become more aware of the nature of their interactions. Thus, the husband may realize for the first time that he tries to dominate rather than listen to his wife and consider her needs and expectations. A wife may realize that she is continually nagging and undermining her husband's feelings of worth and esteem.

family therapy: form of
therapy focusing in rela-
tionships within the
family

**Family therapy.**  **Family therapy** closely parallels the pattern of marital therapy but involves a larger and more complex group system. A pioneer in the field of family therapy has described the problem as follows:

*Psychopathology in the individual is a product of the way he deals with his intimate rela-*
*tions, the way they deal with him, and the way other family members involve him in*
*their relations with each other. Further, the appearance of symptomatic behavior in*
*an individual is necessary for the continued function of a particular family system.*
*Therefore changes in the individual can occur only if the family system changes. (Haley,*
*1962, p. 70)*

This viewpoint led to an important concept in the field of psychotherapy, namely, that the problem of the "identified patient" is often only a symptom of a larger family problem. A careful study of the family of a disturbed child may reveal that the child is merely reflecting the pathology of the family. If the child is seen alone in therapy, he or she may be able to work out some of the problems. But when the child goes back home, it will be to the same pathological circumstances that led to the problems in the first place. As a result, most family therapists share the view that the family—and not simply the designated person—should be directly involved in therapy.

Perhaps the most widely used approach to family therapy is the *conjoint family therapy* of Virginia Satir (1967, 1972). In conjoint family therapy, treatment involves all family members as a group. The emphasis here is on improving faulty communications, interactions, and relationships among family members and fostering a family system that better meets the needs of family members.

## SUMMARY

1. The decision to seek psychological assistance is a courageous one, reflecting the individual's limitations in solving a particular problem and the individual's maturity in acknowledging the need for assistance.

2. Psychologists and counselors work in a variety of settings using a variety of techniques. Therapists can generally be classified as action-oriented or insight-oriented, directive or nondirective, depending on the approach they use in assisting others.

3. The general process of psychotherapy can be described as a three-step process of assessment, decision, and implementation. The major assessment techniques that psychologists and counselors use are interviews, psychological tests, and direct observation. Within each major category of assessment techniques, there are a variety of more specialized techniques. For example, psychological tests can range from intelligence tests, personality inventories, and projective tests to aptitude and ability tests and tests of attitudes and values.

4. Psychoanalytic therapy is one of the major approaches to psychotherapy. Psychoanalysis derives primarily from the theories of Sigmund Freud and utilizes

the techniques of free association, dream interpretation, analysis of resistance, and analysis of transference.

5. In the social-learning approach, the emphasis is on the observation of overt behavior, the learning of adaptive behaviors, and the elimination of maladaptive patterns. Some of the techniques used in this approach are systematic desensitization, assertiveness training, and contingency management and behavioral contracting. The social-learning approach is also placing increasing emphasis on cognitive events and self-control in its approach to treatment.

6. The humanistic-existential therapies (sometimes called the phenomenological therapies) focus on the individual's perception of the world and experience. Roger's person-centered therapy, existential therapy, Gestalt therapy, and group techniques are some commonly used humanistic-existential approaches.

7. The focus of therapy need not be limited to an individual; some treatment approaches deal with more than one person. In this category are sex therapy, marital therapy, and family therapy. These three approaches focus on problem areas rather than theoretical orientations; the techniques used in these therapies come from a variety of sources.

# Part Four

# Interpersonal and Social Aspects of Adjustment

Interpersonal Patterns and Relationships

Human Sexuality

Marriage and Intimate Relationships

Work and Leisure

The Individual and the Group

# Chapter 12

# Interpersonal Patterns and Relationships

*"Selves can only exist in definite relationships to other selves."*
*(MEAD, 1934, P. 164)*

Probably no aspect of our experience is more loaded with emotions or has a greater impact on our lives than our one-to-one relationships with significant others. Our success in making friends, in attracting a desired mate, in raising children, and in performing our chosen occupation depends heavily upon the ways in which we relate to significant others.

**interpersonal relationship: relationship established between two or more people**

We can easily agree on the importance of **interpersonal relationships** in our lives. But, it is another matter to understand them, since each of us approaches an interpersonal relationship from our unique perspective. Our perceptions, needs, goals, feelings, and assumptions about ourselves and our world enter into an interpersonal relationship, and when we add another unique individual to the mixture, it is apparent that the interaction that follows is likely to be a very complex one. To understand what happens, we need to understand the nature of the interactions involved, the type of relationship which develops, and the effects of the relationship on each person involved.

In our discussion of interpersonal relationships, we shall focus on four topics that seem particularly important: *(a)* ways of viewing interpersonal relationships, *(b)* relating to significant others, *(c)* maladaptive interpersonal patterns, and *(d)* the foundations for building satisfying interpersonal relationships. While we shall deal with these topics separately, we shall see that they are closely interwoven.

## WAYS OF VIEWING INTERPERSONAL RELATIONSHIPS

At one time or another, most of us will probably examine our past and present interpersonal relationships and ask such questions as: "What do we really *want* in our relationships?" "What can we realistically *expect* to receive from our relationships?" "What do satisfying interpersonal relationships *require* of us?"

In attempting to answer such questions, we shall find it helpful to examine three models of interpersonal relationships and note their implications for our behavior and lives. Specifically, we shall focus on: *(a)* the social exchange model, *(b)* the role model, and *(c)* the "games people play" model.

### Social Exchange Model

**social exchange model: view that interpersonal relationships are governed by exchanges that meet the needs of the persons involved**

The **social exchange model** is based on the view that interpersonal relationships are formed for the purpose of meeting our needs. Each person in the relationship wants something from the other, and the resulting exchange is governed by economic principles. Thibaut and Kelley (1959), who have been influential in the development of this model, have stated the matter this way: "The basic assumption running throughout our analysis is that every individual volun-

# Insight

## THE "PRISONER'S DILEMMA"

A variety of two-person games for studying interpersonal relationships have been devised. One such game is called the "Prisoner's Dilemma." In this game, the two players are accomplices in a crime who have been arrested and placed in separate cells. Each is urged by the "District Attorney" to confess and testify against the other, with the promise that he or she will receive only a light sentence in return. If the player refuses, he or she is threatened with a trumped-up conviction on some minor charge.

The dilemma is this: If neither prisoner confesses, both will get off with relatively light sentences due to the lack of evidence. If one remains silent but the other does not, the "silent" one is likely to receive the maximum sentence. If both confess, both will probably receive fairly severe sentences. If you were one of the prisoners, would you confess to avoid the maximum sentence, or

remain silent and trust that your accomplice would do the same?

This simple situation can be used in a laboratory setting to explore many aspects of interpersonal interactions. In the prisoner's dilemma game, for example, we can manipulate several parts of the game. The investigator can change the possible outcomes of the game, specifying the payoffs, losses, and outcomes preferred by a player. Similarly, the investigator can manipulate the level of risk or uncertainty involved and can attempt to identify the strategy employed by the players or see whether the strategy changes during the course of the game. Through these laboratory analogues, originally designed to explore aspects of international relations, we can learn about caution, suspicion, trust, vengefulness, and other characteristics of behavior relevant to interpersonal reltionships.

---

tarily enters and stays in a relationship only as long as it is adequately satisfactory in terms of his rewards and costs" (p. 37).

From a slightly broader perspective, the social exchange model can be summarized in terms of three key concepts:

1. *Rewards and costs.* Any positively valued consequence which a person gains from the relationship is a **reward.** Rewards may vary from money to affection to social approval.

A **cost** is any negatively valued consequence incurred by a person in the relationship. Costs may take a variety of forms, including time, effort, conflict, anxiety, self-devaluation, or any other conditions that deplete the individual's adaptive resources or have aversive consequences. Of course, what may be highly rewarding for one person may have little or no reward value for another, and what one person may consider a high cost may be viewed differently by another.

2. *Outcomes and profit.* A key factor in the social exchange model is **outcome** or **profit,** which is calculated as rewards minus costs. The participants in a relationship expect to receive something of a value that is roughly equal to what is given. Normally, the participants do not enter the relationship to make the largest possible profit or to incur the least possible loss. Presumably, in a

**reward: positively valued consequence gained from an interpersonal relationship**

**cost: negatively valued consequence incurred in an interpersonal relationship**

**outcome: also known as a *profit;* the difference between rewards and costs in an interpersonal relationship**

"just" exchange, the participants receive about what they give. In other words, they should just about "balance their books."

In one unique example of the application of the social exchange model, the owner of an appliance store allowed his employees to decide their pay:

*Delivery truck driver Charles Ryan . . . demanded a $100 [a week] raise. In most companies, Ryan would have been laughed out of the office. His work had not been particularly distinguished. His truck usually left in the morning and returned at 5 in the afternoon religiously, just in time for him to punch out. He dragged around the shop, complained constantly and was almost always late for work. . . . [According to owner Arthur Friedman], "The raise made him a fabulous employee. He started showing up early in the morning and would be back by 3, asking what else had to be done." (Koughan, 1975)*

Some employees balanced their "profits" in a different manner:

*One service man who was receiving considerably less than his co-workers was asked why he did not insist on equal pay. "I don't want to work that hard," was the obvious answer. (Koughan, 1975)*

When the costs in a relationship outweigh the rewards, the outcome is a loss. And when the loss seems excessive, a person will ordinarily look for another relationship that promises a more favorable outcome.

**comparison level: standards based on experience or potential alternatives against which interpersonal relationships are evaluated**

3. *Comparison level.* The **comparison level** refers to the standard or standards against which we evaluate our present relationship. Essentially there are two kinds of standards: *(a)* those based on experience, in which we evaluate our present relationship in terms of the outcomes of prior relationships of a similar type, and *(b)* those based on other alternatives we perceive as open to us. If the outcome of our present relationship is favorable, presumably we will be satisfied with it. If the outcome is unfavorable, then we will probably be dissatisfied with the relationship, particularly if similar relationships in the past have been favorable or if potentially available relationships seem more rewarding. As might be expected, comparison level is also influenced by our observation of the payoffs that other people seem to be obtaining in comparable relationships.

Finally, comparison level may vary depending upon the way we view our resources and our ability to control our choices. If we feel that we have a great deal to offer and have control over our choices, we may expect a highly favorable outcome. On the other hand, if we feel that we have little to offer and little control over our choices, we are likely to have a low comparison level and settle for a much less favorable outcome.

In the social exchange model, the exchange of anything of value between two people is the foundation of an interpersonal relationship. What emerges in the relationship is a compromise involving mutual concessions as well as mutual giving (Blau, 1967; Rand, 1965). In a sense it is a compromise between what we might like to have (fantasy) and what we have to settle for (reality). As a consequence, each of us will presumably end up with the person and the relationship which we "deserve," in terms of what we have to offer and what we are willing (or forced) to accept as a compromise.

According to the social exchange model, interpersonal relationships are based on the exchange of something of value. A satisfying relationship is one in which the rewards obtained from the exchange balance or outweigh the costs.

The social exchange model may seem somewhat cynical in its emphasis on the individual's "value" on the "open market" of interpersonal relationships. But it also emphasizes the conditions that constitute an equitable exchange—one that is likely to prove satisfying and enduring.

## Role Model

*"All the world's a stage*
*And all the men and women merely players."*
*(SHAKESPEARE)*

A second way of looking at what goes on between people is the **role model.** The term **role** was borrowed from the theater and refers to a specified part in a play. The words and actions of a role are designated by the script and remain essentially the same regardless of who plays the role.

Society also prescribes roles for its members that are designed to facilitate the functioning of the group. While each individual lends his or her own interpretation to the role, there are usually limits to the "script" beyond which the individual is not expected to go. As Biddle and Thomas (1966) have summarized it: "The role perspective assumes, as does the theater, that performances result from the social prescriptions and behavior of others, and that variations in performance, to the extent that they do occur, are expressed within the framework created by these factors" (p. 4).

**role model:** view that partners perform certain agreed-upon roles in interpersonal relationships

**role:** socially expected behavior pattern

Interpersonal relationships also involve role expectations and demands on each person. We expect others to act in a certain way, and gross violations of these expectations and demands are likely to lead to conflict and possibly to the termination of the relationship.

1. *Role expectations.* Certain obligations, duties, and rights go with any given position and role in the group. For example, there are **role expectations** associated with the roles of nurse, student, and general. A general who tells people that he has a phobia of guns would not be living up to his role expectations.

On a more intimate level, we can point to the complications that arise when a person fails to live up to the role expectations of his or her spouse. For example, the husband who expects his wife to do all cooking and housework may be sorely disappointed when it becomes clear that she has no intention of assuming total responsibility for these duties. Similarly, a woman who expects men to always be strong and supportive may be shaken and dissatisfied if a man expresses doubt or fear or solicits her support.

2. *Role demands.* **Role demands** refer to the social pressures that are exerted to force the individual to live up to role expectations. When a major breach in role behavior occurs—as when a priest reveals information given to him in the confessional—social sanctions will be brought to bear.

3. *Role conflict.* **Role conflict** occurs when a person feels uncomfortable in playing a particular role or seems unable to reconcile apparently contradictory role demands. For example, a man may feel uncomfortable playing a dominant role in relationships with women. Or a woman may try to play the roles of wife, lawyer, and mother at the same time and feel that she is not doing justice to any of them.

Some aspects of role expectations, role demands, and role conflict can be seen in these responses to a questionnaire sent to ministers' wives:

*All of [the congregations] expected a lead from the minister's wife and in each I have been president of the Woman's Guild during the time of my husband's ministry. When we were married over twenty years ago that was expected, though nowadays I think there is greater resistance among ministers' wives. (Banton, 1965, p. 159)*

Another woman noted how the role of minister's wife could negatively affect her interpersonal relationships:

*Do not be distressed if you are treated as "different" because you are married to a minister. A roomful of . . . women may fall silent as you enter, but do not take it as personal, it is really respect for your position. (Banton, 1965, p. 159)*

While the social exchange model may seem "materialistic," the role model seems to carry a connotation of "phoniness," of "not being one's true self." However, we should note that when people really believe in their roles and are committed to playing them, they are acting sincerely and are not phonies. The real "phonies" are the people who play a role in which they do not believe and to which they are not committed, or who play a role that arouses expectations in others that they have no intention of meeting, as in the case of a con artist.

---

**role expectations:** obligations associated with a particular interpersonal role

**role demands:** social pressures exerted upon an individual to live up to role expectations

**role conflict:** condition arising when an individual must play incompatible roles

## "Games People Play"

*"Oh, the games people play now,*
*Ev'ry night and ev'ry day now,*
*Never meanin' what they say now'*
*Never sayin' what they mean."*
*(SOUTH, 1968)*

Another way of viewing interpersonal relationships is in terms of a **games model.** We shall deal here with psychiatrist Eric Berne's concept of games, which is described in his book *Games People Play* (1964). To understand interpersonal transactions in terms of this model, it is useful to review several underlying concepts.

**games model: view of interpersonal relationships as controlled or heavily influenced by games or strategies for interacting with others**

1. *Child, Parent, Adult.* Berne (1964, 1972) believes that an individual's personality is comprised of three parts or ego states: the Child—innocent, spontaneous, and fun-loving; the Parent—authoritative and conditioned to behave in "correct" ways; and the Adult—mature and reality oriented.

Berne then analyzes interpersonal relationships in terms of the ego states that are actually in use when two people are interacting. For example, we may observe a woman berating her husband for failing to take out the garbage. However, says Berne, the ego states that may be operating in this example are the Parent state of the woman ("How many times have I asked you to take out the garbage, you bad boy?") and the Child state of the man ("Aw, mom."). Thus, while we see an interaction between two adults, the underlying process is better understood through reference to the Parent and Child ego states of the woman and man. Berne hypothesizes that all interpersonal relationships can be analyzed in terms of these three ego states.

2. *Games.* Berne suggests that most people are constantly playing **games** in their relationships with others—that is, they utilize strategies which have a payoff.

**game: interpersonal strategy used to exert influence over another**

Berne has labeled the most common game played by spouses as "If It Weren't For You." We may use this game to illustrate the general characteristics of games and the purposes they serve.

*Mrs. White complained that her husband severely restricted her social activities, so that she had never learned to dance. Due to changes brought about by psychiatric treatment . . . her husband became more indulgent. Mrs. White was then free to enlarge the scope of her activities. She signed up for dancing classes, and then discovered to her despair that she had a morbid fear of dance floors and had to abandon this project.*

*This unfortunate adventure, along with similar ones, laid bare some important aspects of the structure of her marriage. Out of her many suitors she had picked a domineering man for a husband. She was then in a position to complain that she could do all sorts of things "if it weren't for you." (Berne, 1964, p. 50)*

The "payoff" for Mrs. White was that her husband was protecting her from doing something she was deeply afraid of and permitting her to take the stance "It's not that I'm afraid, it's that he won't let me," or "I'm trying, but he holds

# Insight

## SOME GAMES PEOPLE PLAY

Here are a few of the more common games delineated by Berne (1964).

*TAC (Try and Collect).* I go into debt to you. You try to collect and I keep putting off repaying. Finally, you take stern measures and I point out how greedy and ruthless you are.

*WAHM (Why Does This Always Happen to Me?).* I continually provoke people into mistreating and rejecting me; then I whine, "Why does this always happen to me?" This is the game of those who are perennially the jilted, the fired, the scorned.

*NIGYSOB (Now I've Got You, You Son of a Bitch).* I allow you to take advantage of me until you are quite vulnerable; then I rise in righteous indignation.

*AIA (Ain't It Awful?).* I constantly invite mistreatment, then complain to others that I am mistreated.

*SWYMD (See What You Made Me Do).* I am nervous or upset and drop or break something. I turn angrily to whoever is closest and say, "See what you made me do."

*YDYB (Why Don't You—Yes But).* I invite you to give me advice, then find a good reason for rejecting everything you suggest—thus putting you down.

*Wooden Leg.* What do you expect of a man with a "wooden leg"? Here I use any weaknesses I have to keep people from expecting things of me.

*GYWP (Gee, You're Wonderful, Professor!).* This is a way of getting the professor to act the way I want, and, if he or she doesn't, I can be disappointed in my fallen idol. It works especially well if the professor responds with *YUP, "You're uncommonly perceptive."*

me back." The payoff for the husband was presumably the boost he received from playing a domineering role.

3. *Function of games.* Games are played because they serve two functions. First, they are substitutes for true intimacy in daily life—intimacy for which there is presumably little opportunity and for which many people are unprepared. Second, they serve as homeostatic mechanisms in maintaining interpersonal relationships, as in the "If it weren't for you" game played by the Whites. It is important to note that these games are not consciously planned. Rather, the participants may be only partially aware or even entirely unaware of the games they are playing.

Games can be both constructive and destructive. Some games, for example, may add a touch of excitement and romance to an intimate relationship. However, most of the games described by Berne are rarely played for fun. In fact, many of them are serious and highly destructive in their effects. While games may help maintain a relationship, they may exact a high cost in terms of blocked personal growth. In our discussion of maladaptive interpersonal patterns, we shall see how truly destructive some games can become.

In the remainder of this chapter, as well as in the chapters that follow, we shall have occasion to see the importance of these three models for understanding interpersonal relationships.

## RELATING TO SIGNIFICANT OTHERS

**Significant others** are people who are important to us and to our lives. In childhood, significant others can include parents, teachers, and friends. In adulthood, significant others may be spouses, friends, children, and co-workers. Our discussion will focus on four key steps and processes involved in the development and course of intimate relationships: *(a)* the encounter, *(b)* interpersonal attraction, *(c)* interpersonal accommodation, and *(d)* the special question of self-disclosure. As we shall see, our level of involvement increases and our commitment to the other deepens as we move from the superficial level of the encounter to the more intimate level of self-disclosure.

**significant other: any person who is very important to an individual**

### The Encounter

The first step in relating to others is the initial **encounter** or interaction with another person. Many people find such encounters exciting and rewarding, particularly if the other person is perceived as attractive and nonthreatening. If, on the other hand, we perceive others as unattractive and threatening, we may avoid these encounters. Similarly, our fears of rejection may cause us to avoid others. Despite the potential risks in encounters, however, we usually make ourselves accessible to selected people.

**encounter: interaction between two persons**

**Initiating the encounter.**   The encounter begins with some sort of communicative act that invites a response from another person. Such an act may involve a smile, a gaze, or a pleasant remark. It the other person responds positively, the encounter is underway.

Initially there tends to be a good deal of uncertainty, and the parties usually engage in rather tentative and safe interactions until respective roles become clear. Lalljee and Cook (1973), for example, found uncertainty in verbal expressions during the initial phase of the encounter. This gradually decreased as the encounter progressed and each person received feedback from the other person.

To facilitate interpersonal interactions, many societies provide guidelines for structuring the initial encounter. In Japan, for example, when two strangers meet they usually first exchange name cards so that the appropriate roles (style of language, depth of bowing, and so on) may be enacted. In the United States, most encounters are initiated on a much less formal basis. Structuring usually develops as the encounter progresses and each person learns more about the position, status, and other relevant characteristics of the other. Nevertheless, there are often unwritten "rules" for encounters, even though such rules may be vague and subject to different interpretations.

### "Rules" for encounters.

Encounters may take many different forms and involve diverse roles, interactions, and settings. A formally arranged date may involve quite different roles and interactions than a pick-up in a bar, while giving a hitchhiker a ride may involve quite different roles and interactions than meeting and talking to one's instructor after class.

In general, the setting in which the encounter occurs tends to establish certain guidelines. For example, an encounter that begins in a church will normally be different from an encounter that begins at a race track. Similarly, we may use the actions of others as a means of guiding our own behavior. If we are uncertain how to behave at a party, we can use the principles of observational learning and watch others as a way to structure our own behavior.

Once an encounter is underway, an unwritten agreement usually develops about the expected roles and interactions. If one person suddenly changed roles or otherwise broke the agreement, the individual is likely to be resented. An example would be the person who encourages another person to reveal intimate and potentially embarrassing confidences, only to ridicule that person when he or she does "open up."

### Termination of the encounter.

Most encounters end with a ritualistic role enactment in which each participant is assured that the encounter will be resumed. Telephone numbers may be exchanged and promises made to "get together as soon as possible." This enactment occurs when both parties are satisfied with the encounter and when only one person wishes to continue the encounter. For the second person, the hope that the encounter will be resumed will eventually be replaced by the realization that it has actually been terminated. This realization may cause temporary feelings of disappointment.

It is likely that most encounters do not progress past this stage. Although these encounters can be satisfying, they are also superficial. Those that progress and deepen beyond the initial phase often involve interpersonal attraction.

The setting in which an encounter takes place often establishes certain guidelines and expected forms of behavior. If the parties disagree about these expectations or violate the guidelines, the encounter may be terminated.

# Interpersonal Attraction

"What does she see in him?" or "What does he see in her?" are questions commonly asked about relationships that seem to work out for reasons that are unclear. Of course, we are usually ready with some "common-sense" explanation. When two people are very different in background and personality makeup, we may point out that "Opposites attract." When two people who are very much alike get along well together, we may decide, "Birds of a feather flock together."

In this section we shall examine the factors that influence our perception of others and our attraction to them.

**How we perceive others.**   Our **interpersonal perceptions** are strongly affected by our use of stereotypes and by our first impressions. For example, we may believe that all college instructors are preoccupied idealists and that all hunters are gun-happy fanatics. These *stereotypes* strongly influence the ways in which we will initially respond to these people. To the forgetful professor, our initial response may be one of bemused appreciation, while our response to the hunter may be one of outright hostility.

We then use our initial interactions with others as a means to confirm our stereotypes. If the instructor mentions misplacing his or her keys, we use this information to uphold our beliefs that professors are forgetful. And if a hunter describes the pleasures associated with hunting, we take this as continuing evidence of blood lust. It is important to note that information contradictory to the stereotype may be considered less important than information consistent with the stereotype. For example, the college instructor may describe prodigious feats of memory, but because of the stereotype, we may be more likely to remember the keys that were misplaced.

**First impressions** often help determine whether we are attracted to another individual. Our first impressions of a person have a great impact on our perception of him or her, even though the initial encounter may be very brief. Thus, the effort that we expend to make a good impression has a worthwhile "payoff."

Our perceptions of others are subject to several sources of error. Although we are interested in positive traits, we attach particular importance to negative information (Hamilton & Zanna, 1972), often overruling all the positive information that we have received. We may find ourselves initially attracted to another individual and find him or her both pleasant and charming. However, when we find that he or she holds political beliefs that are directly opposite our strongly held beliefs, the overall perception of the individual may be negative.

The **halo effect** (Nisbett & Wilson, 1977a) can also influence our perceptions of others. In the halo effect, our overall impression of a person may carry over to the evaluation of specific attributes. Consider the case of a woman who is regarded positively by one individual and negatively by another. When asked to comment upon a specific attribute, her speech accent for example, the first person may find it appealing, while the second may judge it irritating instead.

Finally, a person may mislead us by putting on a "good front." As we get

interpersonal perception: way in which we perceive another person

first impressions: relatively enduring judgments made about another person within the earliest moments of an encounter

halo effect: tendency to assess a person on the basis of one or two easily perceived traits, such as seeing attractive persons as being friendly

to know a person better, we may have an opportunity to observe many additional characteristics that were not apparent during the initial encounter. This enables us to make corrections in our original perceptions and assessment.

**interpersonal attraction: extent to which another person attracts or repels us**

**What makes the other person attractive to us?**  Researchers have identified four factors that are important in **interpersonal attraction.** These are: physical attractiveness, proximity, availability, and similarity and complementarity of interest and beliefs.

1. *Physical attractiveness. Physical attractiveness* is probably the most important factor in interpersonal attraction, at least in the early stages of the relationship. As Krebs and Adinolfi (1975) have pointed out "there is a growing body of evidence which shows that the average person drastically underestimates the influence of physical attractiveness. . ." (p. 245). In general, people prefer to interact with people who are physically attractive. Although this factor is highly important in affecting initial attraction, the importance of physical attractiveness may diminish over time and be replaced by other personality characteristics.

**proximity: nearness in place; principle that people located near each other are more likely to become attracted to one another**

2. *Proximity.* Physical closeness or **proximity** is another important factor in interpersonal attraction. Although the process may seem quite obvious, its effects on our behavior can be significant. In one study reported by Festinger, Schachter, and Back (1950), residents of a housing complex reported the greatest number of friendships with the next-door neighbors and almost no friendships with neighbors who lived four or five doors away. In a more experimental vein, Saegert, Swap, and Zajonc (1973) found that as the number of contacts between strangers increased, their evaluations of each other became more positive as well.

These findings suggest that initial attraction is most likely to develop between individuals who have frequent contact with one another. Although proximity need not be limited to the "boy or girl next door," other sources of physical closeness and social contact may prove important in initial attraction. Thus, students who take the same classes, workers in an office or factory, members of the same club, or people who routinely take the same bus together may find themselves attracted to one another.

3. *Availability.* A third factor in initial attraction is the accessibility or *availability* of the partner. Although we may enjoy the fantasy of a tumultuous love affair with a famous television, sports, or music personality, we are most likely to turn our attentions to the individual who is available for a date on the weekend.

Interestingly, too much availability may have negative effects. Research reported by Walster and Walster (1978), for example, found that men were most strongly attracted to women who were accessible to them, but only on an exclusive basis.

4. *Similarity and complementarity.* We are most attracted to individuals who share similar backgrounds, educational levels, beliefs, values, and purposes. We are most likely to become deeply involved with someone who shares a similar socioeconomic background, educational experiences, and values. For example, college students are most likely to become involved with someone who also has had some college experiences than with someone who has only completed the eighth grade.

The most satisfying interpersonal relationships are likely to be those between individuals who have similar backgrounds, experiences, beliefs, and values.

**Similarity,** however, does not extend to all aspects of a relationship. Some aspects seem to operate best on the principle that "opposites attract." This is the principle of **complementarity**, and it is best illustrated by the frequently reported observation that very sociable and outgoing individuals are often attracted to people who are somewhat shy and more reserved.

Complementarity seems to operate in the early stages of a relationship when it seems exciting to meet and relate to someone "different." But it appears much more likely that, over the long range, "birds of a feather flock together," particularly when mutual needs can be satisfied in a deepening relationship.

In general, it appears that we are attracted to others who are physically attractive, who are physically accessible and socially available, and who have similar purposes, backgrounds, beliefs, and needs. However, the qualities that attract one person to another on first acquaintance are not necessarily the ones that account for the continuation and progression of the relationship. This requires interpersonal accommodation as well as interpersonal attraction.

**similarity: principle that interpersonal attraction is strongest between people who share like interests, goals, and values**

**complementarity: principle that attraction between individuals occurs because each person has traits or abilities that supplement areas of weakness in the other or that contrast with the other's traits**

## Interpersonal Accommodation

*"Persons are decidedly the hardest things we have to deal with."*
*(SULLIVAN, 1962, P. 246)*

**Interpersonal accommodation** is the process by which two people evolve patterns of interaction that enable them to attain common goals, meet mutual needs, and build a satisfying relationship. As the relationship grows and develops, the

**interpersonal accommodation: process of adjusting to problems that arise in interpersonal relationships**

partners will encounter a variety of problems that require mutual adjustments. Some of these problems will arise from within the relationship; others will arise from external or environmental sources. An example of the latter would be an elderly couple whose retirement income is ravaged by inflation or a homosexual couple whose relationship is socially disapproved.

Our focus will be on the adjustive demands that arise within the relationship itself, and we shall focus on three key areas: *(a)* communication, *(b)* the structure of the relationship, and *(c)* resolving disagreements and conflicts.

> *"We are living in a world saturated with communication, on the verge of perishing for lack of it; a world smothered with words, hungry for one meaningful word; a world bombarded with data, rarely capable of sorting out the truth; and a world in which we can flash messages across the ocean by way of space, but one in which we find it difficult to get through to each other face to face."*
> **(SCHINN, 1976, P. 2)**

**The key role of communication.**   In order for an interpersonal relationship to grow and move forward toward mutual goals, it is essential that the people communicate with each other. This **communication** involves two kinds of information: *(a)* **cognitive information,** which is concerned primarily with facts about each other and the surrounding world, and *(b)* **affective information,** which is concerned with feelings and emotions. When we tell another person our college major, our address, and our experiences as children, we are conveying cognitive information. On the other hand, when we express feelings of tenderness toward others, we are providing affective information.

There are many ways of communicating information—spoken words, voice inflection, facial expression, gestures, body movements, and even moments of silence. Communication can therefore take place on *nonverbal* as well as *verbal* levels. It appears that verbal communication is used primarily to communicate cognitive information, while **nonverbal communication** is used primarily to communicate information about feelings and emotions. Obviously, we must pay attention to both the verbal and nonverbal components if communication is to be interpreted accurately. For example, the phrase "How exciting" accompanied by rolled, upturned eyes conveys a sardonic quality very different from the message conveyed when the same phrase is accompanied by a bright smile.

Effective communication is not synonymous with verbosity. People can spend hours talking to one another and not communicate any information. Whether the partners in a relationship spend twenty minutes or twenty hours speaking to each other, it seems crucial that they understand one another, feel understood, and be able to express clearly their feelings on important issues.

Clarity of communication accompanied by a sensitivity to the other person's feelings and point of view is probably an effective method of communication. For example, when we are dissatisfied with some aspect of the relationship, it is probably better to express our feelings directly than to express them indirectly

**communication: the sending or receiving of information**

**cognitive information: information concerned primarily with facts**

**affective information: information concerned primarily with feelings, emotions, and attitudes**

**nonverbal communication: communication through gesture, eye contact, and body posture**

# Insight

## INFORMATION DERIVED FROM NONVERBAL COMMUNICATION

Nonverbal communication, by means of gestures or inflections, can impart various kinds of information that supplement whatever is being communicated on a verbal level (Ekman & Friesen, 1968; Mahl, 1968).

1. The nonverbal can express the same meaning as the verbal message. (I say I don't like you and my voice, gestures, and facial expression say so too.)

2. The nonverbal can anticipate future amplification of the concurrent verbal context. (Even before I tell the punch line, I start to laugh.)

3. The nonverbal can be contradictory to the verbal message. (I say I like you, but I'm backing away.)

4. The nonverbal can be delayed, undermining what has already been expressed. (I tell you something in all seriousness, then after a moment's delay I explode with laughter.)

5. The nonverbal can be related to the more global aspects of the interaction. (I call you a bad name, but I am smiling.)

6. The nonverbal can be a substitute for a word or a phrase in a verbal message. (I shrug my shoulders, meaning "Who cares!)

7. The nonverbal can fill or explain silences. (I stop talking and indicate with my eyes that the person we've been gossiping about is approaching.)

---

through shortened tempers and bad moods or by picking a fight on an unrelated topic. Thus, if we are distressed by our partner's abuse of alcohol in social situations, we can more effectively communicate our feelings by saying so directly than by acting in a distant fashion or by complaining about our partner's taste in clothes.

Similarly, interpersonal sensitivity and tact are also useful skills for improving communication. In the example described above, we could express our concern by saying, "You're a drunk and a lush" or we can express our feelings in an equally clear but less destructive fashion, "I get very upset when you drink too much at parties."

**Structuring the relationship.**   Once the encounter is underway and channels of communication have been opened, the partners begin the process of **structuring the relationship**—defining roles, responsibilities, norms, and the other dimensions of the emerging relationship.

1. *Roles and responsibilities.* For a relationship to be successful, it is important that each individual know what is expected and in turn make it clear what he or she expects of the other person.

In our discussion of the role model, we noted the emphasis placed upon role expectations and demands in interpersonal relationships. Suppose a couple are contemplating marriage, and the man expects that his partner will be affectionate, be an interesting companion, and earn a reasonable income. The woman may also expect that her partner will be affectionate, be an interesting compan-

**structuring a relationship: negotiating the terms of desirable behavior in an interpersonal relationship**

In the game of chess, each of the pieces may be moved only in certain prescribed ways. Our interpersonal relationships are similarly structured by the expectations and demands of the various roles we play.

ion, and earn a reasonable income. If each person is able to enact the expected role to the satisfaction of the other, the relationship is likely to flourish.

Where role expectations and responsibilities are not mutually satisfactory, some adjustments must be made in order to arrive at an agreed-upon structure. If such adjustment measures are not taken, the relationship is likely to be plagued with misunderstandings and conflict—and may even end.

2. *Standards of satisfaction.* When attending a movie we expect it to meet certain standards of plot, character portrayal, and photography, and we usually avoid movies that seem unlikely to meet our standards. Similarly, we establish *standards of satisfaction* in interpersonal relationships. For example, standards are established with respect to honesty, dependability, faithfulness, and other aspects of the relationship. And these standards are used in evaluating the overall relationship in terms of its reward-cost value.

**Resolving disagreements and conflicts.**   This process may take a variety of forms. It may involve one-sided compromise and concession or an exchange of some kind. Through barter, compromise, and concession, there may be a continual structuring and restructuring of the relationship as the partners attempt to deal with problems and work out agreements.

Although bargaining and compromise are basic methods of resolving disagreements and conflicts, other patterns may also be involved. A person who does not like his in-laws may simply have to accept them as part of the "package deal." A woman who dislikes her husband's occupation because it is hazardous or keeps him away from home a great deal may force herself to adapt to it. Finally, in those cases when bargaining and compromise are not successful, mediation by counselors may prove successful.

**Some unpredictable outcomes.**   Some relationships continue despite a lack of affection or the obvious presence of hostility. In such relationships certain basic needs are apparently being met. Or perhaps neither partner sees the possibility of finding a better relationship with anyone else, so they simply let matters drift along.

Conversely, there is no guarantee that a stable and mutually fulfilling relationship will endure. Demands on interpersonal relationships change over time. Thus, the problems faced by a young married couple will be quite different from those they will face twenty years later. While they may have accommodated to the original demands, they may not be able to cope with the new demands, and the relationship may end.

Similarly, friends must adapt to the changes that occur as both the friendship grows and as the individuals in the friendship develop as well. Sometimes we "outgrow" friendships in the course of our personal development. Attending college, for example, may ultimately result in the end of friendships with people who do not share our experiences. Although the end of a relationship can be a sad event, it can also serve as a sign that our needs and requirements in an interpersonal relationship are undergoing a normal process of change.

# Self-Disclosure

*". . . obviously, all relations which people have to one another are based on their knowing something about one another."*
**(SIMMEL, 1964, P. 307)**

While it is difficult to argue with this statement, it does not resolve the problem in interpersonal relationships of what is best kept secret and what is best disclosed. While the answer to this question depends in part on the type and intimacy of the relationship and the persons involved, we can at best only consider certain aspects of the problem that may help the individual make decisions about self-disclosure in his or her relationships.

**The nature and course of self-disclosure.**   **Self-disclosure** may be defined as any information we communicate about ourselves to another person. The basic dimensions of self-disclosure include: *(a)* the amount and breadth of information disclosed, *(b)* the intimacy and depth of information disclosed, *(c)* the positive or negative nature of the information disclosed, and *(d)* the timing of the information disclosed (Cozby, 1973; Gilbert, 1976). Timing refers primarily to whether information is disclosed during initial or later phases of a relationship.

**self-disclosure: disclosure of information about one's self to another person**

As the partners in an interpersonal relationship learn to trust each other, they may feel encouraged to disclose information about their inner selves, their feelings, and, perhaps, their deepest secrets.

During the initial stage of a relationship, medium amounts of self-disclosure tend to be interpreted as indications of a person's trustfulness and desire for a closer relationship. Low self-disclosers who reveal little or nothing about themselves are likely to experience difficulty in establishing a relationship. High self-disclosers, on the other hand, are often perceived as overly preoccupied with themselves and maladjusted (Strassberg, Robak, D'Antonio, & Gabel, 1977; Wortman, Adesman, Herman, & Greenberg, 1976).

As a relationship progresses, the amount and intimacy of self-disclosure usually increases. Each person tends to reveal about the same amount of information as he or she receives. However, the eventual amount and intimacy of self-disclosure may vary greatly, depending on the characteristics of the persons involved, the nature of the relationship, and the specific information involved. Interestingly enough, low disclosers as compared with high disclosers tend to mask or "gild" information they do not wish to reveal and sometimes to resort to outright falsification (Gitter & Black, 1976).

**Secrets: To tell or not to tell?**   Unfortunately, the decision to tell or not tell "secrets" about oneself is not always simple, and even deciding how much information to disclose can pose a conflict.

Often, as a relationship progresses, one or both partners wish to know about the other's past. The question of whether to tell or not to tell may then become an important one. Does a person owe it to a prospective spouse to reveal past sexual experiences? An abortion? A criminal record? Should the person be governed by honesty and openness and reveal all? Or should one consider the possible cost in damage to the relationship? And how does one realistically weigh the risk of self-disclosure against that of later exposure by a third party?

Here it is interesting to note the findings of Cozby (1973) that highly intimate levels of self-disclosure tend to be rewarding at first. Eventually, however, the costs outweigh the rewards. The most apparent cost is anxiety about upsetting the other person, demeaning oneself in the other person's eyes, and damaging the relationship. This conclusion applied both to "past" and "now" secrets. In fact, "now" secrets—such as dissatisfaction with some aspect of the relationship or confessions of infidelity—are often more difficult to reveal than "past" secrets.

Although we may be convinced and proud that we are making an effort to be more open and honest in our interpersonal relationships, we should also consider the consequences of unrestrained self-disclosure. In fact, Altman and Taylor (1973) have expressed concern about a "tyranny of openness" in which persons are denied privacy and perhaps even mystery because others demand full self-disclosure in interpersonal encounters and relationships. At this point, it seems most sensible to view self-disclosure as a problem which can best be resolved by the individual in relation to his or her beliefs, feelings, perception of the other person in the relationship, and the nature of the relationship itself.

## MALADAPTIVE INTERPERSONAL PATTERNS

GEORGE. *I warned you not to go too far.*

MARTHA. *I'm just beginning.*

GEORGE. *I'm numbed enough . . . and I don't mean by liquor, though maybe that's been part of the process—a gradual, over-the-years going to sleep of the brain cells—I'm numbed enough now, to be able to take you when we're alone. I don't listen to you, I sift everything, I bring everything down to reflex response, so I don't really hear you, which is the only way to manage it. But you've taken a new tack, Martha, over the past couple of centuries—or however long it's been I've lived in this house with you—that makes it just too much . . . too much.*

**(ALBEE, 1962, P. 155)**

The preceding excerpt from the play *Who's Afraid of Virginia Woolf?* dramatically illustrates the point that the partners in an interpersonal relationship create their own unique patterns of interaction and determine the climate and quality of the relationship. The outcome—as in the marriage of George and Martha—may be destructive and maladaptive for one or both partners.

At one time or another, all of us have probably been involved in a maladaptive interpersonal relationship. And we have probably all wondered what went wrong and whose fault it was. Unfortunately, it is often difficult or impossible to ascertain exactly what did go wrong, but in many instances we may have a good idea. It may be helpful to examine some of the ways in which interpersonal relationships can go seriously wrong.

Here our focus will be on three types of maladaptive interpersonal patterns: *(a)* fraudulent interpersonal contracts, *(b)* collusion in interpersonal contracts, and *(c)* discordant interpersonal patterns.

## Fraudulent Interpersonal Contracts

We have noted that, as a relationship progresses beyond the initial encounter, the partners enter into an arrangement, usually of informal nature, in which the "terms" of the relationship are agreed upon. In this "contract," the partners stipulate the type of relationship they hope to achieve and what each expects to contribute and to receive from the relationship. Mutual acceptance of the contract usually indicates that each partner believes he or she is receiving a fair return on the investment. Here we are, of course, using the social exchange model.

In a **fraudulent interpersonal contract,** the terms of the contract are violated by one partner in a way that exploits the other. Such fraudulent patterns may take a variety of forms, but Carson (1969) has delineated a common underlying sequence which may be summarized as follows:

1. *A* implicitly offers *B* a type of relationship in which *B* has a high degree of interest because it seems to offer favorable possibilities for satisfaction.

2. *B* indicates acceptance of the contract and proceeds with activities appropriate to the terms of the contract.

3. *A* then assumes a stance that makes it seem "justified" to alter the terms of the contract.

4. *B* is forced to accept the new terms, thus enabling *A* to achieve the type of relationship that *A* wanted to begin with.

Such an approach is fraudulent in that *A* presumably could not have achieved his or her objectives by an honest and straightforward approach, but only by deceit and fraud. An example of this type of interpersonal contract might involve a man who proposed marriage to a woman, promising the woman a very traditional marital relationship. However, several years into the marriage, it becomes clear that the man is no longer interested in the original contract and justifies his insistence that the woman take a job outside the home by referring to the family's economic conditions. The woman, correctly inferring that the relationship will last only if she accedes to her husband's wishes, reluctantly begins to seek work.

*B,* however, is likely to sense that he or she has been "had," and the new contractual terms are likely to prove highly frustrating to *B* and may damage the relationship. Over time *B* may feel so dissatisfied that he or she will terminate the relationship. In this case *A* is also the loser providing he or she really did want to make the relationship work, albeit on selfish terms. Nevertheless, it is surprising to note how many fraudulent interpersonal contracts seem to endure, in marriage and in other interpersonal settings.

## Collusion

In **collusion,** an interpersonal relationship is established and maintained only because the partners agree that their deviant rules and norms will be substituted for established social rules and norms. Of course there are many permissible life-

---

**fraudulent interpersonal contract: violation of the rules or norms governing a satisfying interpersonal relationship through the use of deceit or other unethical means**

**collusion: agreement of partners to substitute deviant rules and norms of their own choosing for established norms**

styles and types of interpersonal relationships in our society, and many of these do not conform strictly with established social rules and norms. Here, however, we are referring to the use of collusion which is maladaptive and destructive, usually for both partners.

One person usually takes the initiative in laying down the terms of the contract that the other must meet. Typically these terms call for the partners to jointly deny or falsify some aspect of reality. For example, *A*, who drinks excessively, may agree to an intimate relationship with *B* only if *B* accepts the excessive drinking as normal. While *B* may not wish to do so, he or she may be forced to do this to complete the contract. Of course, *B* may anticipate rewards from the relationship that will outweigh this particular cost.

However, the ensuing relationship is maladaptive because the rewards do not in fact justify the costs. The excessive drinking of *A*, for example, may seriously interfere with his or her occupational adjustment, the couple's social life, their sexual relationship, and many other aspects of their relationship. If the excessive drinking increases and hospitalization is required for treatment, tremendous stress may then be placed on the other partner—particularly in marital relationships. In nonmarital as well as marital relationships, the result is likely to be highly detrimental to the relationship as well as to the persons involved, and it may well lead to termination of the relationship.

## Discordant Interpersonal Patterns

Some degree of friction seems inevitable in interpersonal relationships, but serious and continued disagreements and conflicts hurt both the people involved as well as the quality of their relationship. These **discordant interpersonal patterns** may involve a number of areas in the relationship, or they may center on some enduring conflict. Nye (1973) has delineated five common sources of conflict, which include:

**discordant interpersonal patterns:** relationships involving serious and continuous disagreements and conflicts detrimental to the quality of the relationship

1. *Competition,* in which one partner gains something at the expense of the other. For example, one person may establish superiority in some area in such a way that the other feels put down.

2. *Domination,* in which one partner attempts to control the other person, who then feels that his or her rights and integrity are being violated.

3. *Failure,* in which both partners resort to blaming each other when things go wrong in their efforts to achieve agreed-upon goals.

4. *Provocation,* in which one partner consistently and knowingly does things to annoy the other, and in the process, receives satisfaction from keeping things stirred up.

5. *Value differences,* which may lead to serious disagreement about a variety of topics from spending money to sexual behavior to the use of leisure time.

Closely related to the preceding sources of discordance are the problems produced by *conflicting communications* in which the sender codes a message in such a way that it has two opposite meanings. For example, a woman may be very seductive on her first date with a man. But when he makes physical overtures, she reacts with surprise, shock, and rejection. Such a conflict between verbal and nonverbal components of a message is likely to leave the other person baffled. It may, of course, also leave a person feeling foolish and hostile.

A variation on this theme is the double-bind, those cases where we are "damned if we do and damned if we don't." For example, a husband may complain that his wife never takes the initiative in matters of affection, but when she does, he finds some excuse to reject her advances. In short, she cannot win in such a double-bind situation and is likely to end up feeling confused, devaluated, and discouraged.

Despite the wide variety of maladaptive patterns, many people do build satisfying interpersonal relationships. It is to these types of relationships that we now turn our attention.

## FOUNDATIONS FOR BUILDING SATISFYING INTERPERSONAL RELATIONSHIPS

Despite the importance of achieving constructive and satisfying interpersonal relationships, little research effort has focused on this problem. Most of the popular literature on interpersonal relationships tends to oversimplify. The emphasis is on influencing and exploiting others. The well-publicized tactic of praising others, for example, is likely to backfire if the praise is insincere. Many people who adopt such techniques are shocked to find that they have reaped a harvest of suspicion, dislike, and hostility.

In this section, we shall attempt to avoid oversimplification. Our discussion will be based on available research findings as well as conclusions that follow logically from the general principles we have reviewed.

### Recognition of Mutual Rights and Purposes

In beginning our discussion, it seems appropriate to emphasize the importance of mutual rights in building healthy interpersonal relationships. This principle is illustrated in the Golden Rule—"Do unto others as you would have them do unto you."

Respect for the rights of others is essential not only from an ethical standpoint but from a practical one as well. We have noted, for example, the destructive effects on a relationship when one person attempts to infringe on the rights and integrity of the other. Violating these rights almost always destroys any common ground for mutually satisfying interaction.

Through our relationships with others, we try to meet certain basic needs—perhaps for love and affection, self-esteem and worth, social approval, or maybe just feeling related to a significant other. But when the relationship meets one person's needs but fails to meet those of the other person, it is likely to be difficult or impossible to maintain. Even the most generous and devoted friend may become tired of a relationship in which he or she is continually giving and never receiving in return. In essence, to have a friend, you must be a friend.

A common interest is often the basis of an interpersonal relationship. The close relationship between a high-school athlete and his coach, for example, may end when the student graduates.

To meet the needs of both persons, a relationship must have a common purpose. Without a shared purpose, the individuals may no longer need each other in the relationship. Two members of a college swimming team, for example, may become close friends. But after graduation, when they pursue different careers and ways of life, the bonds that once held them together will dissolve. Similarly, a romantic relationship may be ended when one person wishes to get married and the other does not.

It seems then that a common purpose and mutual need gratification are basic essentials for establishing and maintaining a lasting interpersonal relationship. Again we come face to face with the social exchange model and the relation of cost to satisfaction in an enduring relationship.

## Adequate Structure and Communication

In some cases, structure and communication patterns are specified by social norms. For example, there is general agreement about the type of structure and communication between teacher and student, employer and employee, bishop and parish priest, general and lieutenant. But in most of our more personal relationships—such as those involving husband and wife, parent and child, or friend and friend—the structure and communication patterns are determined by the parties involved. This places considerable responsibility on each person in the relationship, if he or she wishes to make it a satisfying one.

**Adequate structure.**   All interpersonal relationships become structured with time, whether or not the individuals involved take it upon themselves to establish a particular type of structure. To take a simple example, we may examine the behavior of a young married couple. Unless they take active measures to structure their relationship in terms of behavior with others, of mutual effort in maintaining their relationship, of courtesy and honesty in dealing with each other, such limits will eventually become established simply by what actually takes place—whether or not these limits are satisfactory to the individuals involved. Moreover, once certain patterns have been established, it becomes increasingly difficult to change the structuring.

**Effective communication.**   It is apparent that meaningful communication does not take place automatically in interpersonal relationships. But there are a number of factors which appear to foster effective communication. Here we shall mention three interrelated factors which seem to be of importance.

1. *Be a good sender.* As a sender, each of us has to know *what* we are trying to communicate and *how* to code the message in such a way that the receiver can interpret it accurately. If we are unclear about the message we are trying to convey or fail to code the message appropriately, the message will

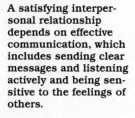

A satisfying interpersonal relationship depends on effective communication, which includes sending clear messages and listening actively and being sensitive to the feelings of others.

# Insight

## COMMON ERRORS IN INTERPERSONAL COMMUNICATION

There are a number of factors that may lead to communication problems in interpersonal relations, even though the persons involved want to understand each other and make their relationship work. Among the more important of these are:

1. *Differences in background and experience.* Differences in educational, ethnic, and other background factors can create difficulties in communication. Words may mean different things to different people, depending upon their past experiences.

2. *Selective attention.* Here the receiver only processes part of the information that is communicated by the other person and ignores the remainder. As a result he or she receives a fragmented rather than a complete message.

3. *Motivation.* As we have noted, we tend to perceive what we want to perceive. Often this means interpreting a message in terms of what we would like it to mean rather than what the sender intended it to mean.

4. *Feelings and emotions.* A wide range of feelings and emotions, including insecurity, fear, or anger, can be elicited by the other person or by situational factors and these can lead to misinterpretation by the receiver.

5. *Insensitivity.* There are many situations in which the feelings behind the words are more important than the words. If the receiver fails to perceive the feelings of the sender, it can be a potent source of misunderstanding.

---

probably not be received accurately. The high incidence of failure here is exemplified by the frequent complaint, "You misunderstood what I was trying to say."

2. *Be a good receiver: Listen actively.* To be good receivers, we must listen actively and make a sincere effort to understand what the other person is trying to communicate to us. We have probably all had the experience of feeling that the other person was not really listening—not really tuning us in. Perhaps the person was too busy to take time to listen, did not want to hear what we had to say, or was busy thinking about what to say next.

We can improve our listening skills in three ways: *(a)* Be alert to the facial expression, posture, and vocal intonation of the other person. This can help you detect the feeling behind the words. Try to understand what the other person *wants* to say rather than what he or she *is* saying. *(b)* Ask questions involving the word *feeling* rather than *thinking*. This gives the other person an opportunity to express his or her feelings and may help that person realize that his or her feelings do matter. *(c)* Mirror or reflect the feelings that the other person seems to be expressing. In this way, you help the other person bring his or her feelings into the open where you both can examine them for what they are.

3. *Examine metacommunication.* One approach to fostering better communication involves the concept of **metacommunication**—examining the ways in which we typically communicate with another person in a relationship.

This might entail an analysis of such factors as *(a)* who does most of the

**metacommunication: communication about the way in which two people typically communicate**

talking and who does most of the listening, *(b)* what areas or problems seem to elicit particular difficulties in communicating and understanding, *(c)* the amount of relevant information communicated vs. uninformative "noise," and *(d)* the typical emotional climate created by talking about problems. Such information can be used as a basis for making needed corrections in communication patterns.

In dealing with these various aspects of communication we are also dealing with coping behaviors and styles in interpersonal relationships. For better or worse, our interpersonal style affects our ability to transmit and receive information, and hence, it will affect the quality of relationships we are able to achieve.

## Awareness

Carl Rogers (1968, 1977) and a number of other psychologists have emphasized the importance of being aware of the key ingredients in our significant interpersonal relationships. At first glance this may seem like belaboring the obvious, but the processes involved are considerably more subtle than one might initially think. **Awareness** comes in many forms, but three are particularly relevant: a realistic view of one's self, a realistic view of the other person, and an accurate view of the relationship.

1. *A realistic view of one's self.* As a starting point, this involves an accurate view of our own "stimulus value"—of how the other person sees us. We may view ourself as generous, while the other person sees us as stingy; we may view ourself as flexible, while the other person views us as rigid; we may view ourself as cooperative and undemanding, while the other person views us as competitive and highly demanding. While the other person's view of us may be inaccurate, it is an important source of feedback about how we are perceived.

**awareness: accurate perception and understanding of one's self and one's relationships**

Through the phenomenon known as the halo effect, we generalize a person's positive qualities in one area to cover all aspects of the individual's personality.

2. *An accurate view of the other person.* An accurate view of the other person is equally important if we are to establish a satisfying interpersonal relationship. One common error we can avoid, particularly during the period of getting acquainted, is the "halo effect" described earlier. For example, when we know a person is superior in some important respect, we may tend to put a "halo" over his or her head and, through a process of generalization, overrate his or her qualities in other areas. And as we have noted, we often tend to see others as we would like them to be rather than as they really are—a tendency which is readily apparent in romantic infatuations.

3. *An accurate view of the relationship.* When one is emotionally involved in an intimate relationship, it is often difficult to perceive the situation objectively. It is not only important to understand our own needs and motives in the relationship but also those of the other person—and this is not always an easy task. Drawing from social exchange theory, we can ask ourselves what we are "paying" for the satisfactions we are receiving. Are we deceiving ourselves about what we are receiving from the relationship? Is the cost greater than the reward?

Furthermore, if we consider the relationship a satisfying one, then it is important that we be alert for possible indications of trouble, such as signs of dissatisfaction from the other person. Building a satisfying interpersonal relationship requires effort on the part of both persons and the early detection and correction of misunderstandings, communication problems, conflicting purposes, or other possible difficulties. Unfortunately, many relationships that were once satisfying are allowed to deteriorate eventually and to end, simply because one or both partners failed to realize that vigilance and effort are costs involved in ensuring the continuation of a rewarding relationship.

## Helping Each Other Grow as Persons

*I love you,*
*Not only for what you are,*
*But for what I am*
*When I am with you.*

. . . . . . . . . . .

*I love you*
*For the part of me*
*That you bring out.*
*(ROY CROFT)*

As we have seen, our closest interpersonal relationships have a profound influence upon us—whether for better or for worse. Our relationships with others can diminish us or they can help us to grow as persons. In our discussion of maladaptive interpersonal relationships, we focused on the former. In the final section of this chapter, we shall focus on those conditions in interpersonal relationships which help us to grow as persons—to actualize our potentials as human beings.

While avoidance of maladaptive patterns and pursuit of the conditions that foster satisfying interpersonal relationships can help us to grow as persons, three additional factors merit consideration. These are *(a)* openness and empathy, *(b)* acceptance, and *(c)* caring.

**Openness and empathy.** **Openness** refers to more than a lowering of defenses and a dropping of masks by each person. It also includes a willingness to share beliefs, hopes, feelings, defeats, achievements, and despair with another. As we noted in our discussion of self-disclosure, however, openness does not necessarily mean completely baring one's soul to the other person. But it does mean being open and willing to exchange information that will contribute to better understanding and greater security in the relationship. As Rogers (1968) has expressed it, "We shall discover that security resides not in hiding oneself but in being more fully known, and consequently in coming to know the other more fully" (p. 269).

The other side of the coin is **empathy**, the ability to put oneself in the other's place. In interpersonal relationships, empathy means that each person knows what the other has experienced, is experiencing, and is trying to communicate.

**Acceptance.** In an interpersonal context, **acceptance** means that neither person takes a judgmental attitude toward the other. This does not mean that one has to agree with everything the other person believes in or does. And when people do disagree, it is important that they do not reject each other as persons. In some instances, acceptance means "agreeing to disagree"—accepting the other person's right to entertain his or her own convictions while retaining the same freedom for one's self. Finally, acceptance is also essential if each person in a relationship is to feel free to share his or her private world with the other. This kind of sharing enhances mutual understanding and personal growth.

**Caring.** **Caring** is an elusive concept that means many things, but perhaps its central theme is concern about and commitment to the well-being of the other person. Caring may be expressed in words, as when we tell the other person "I love you"; or it may be expressed in actions ranging from simple courtesy to support in times of severe stress or crisis.

Caring may take the form of expressing sincere appreciation of the good qualities of the other person, thus confirming his or her worth as a human being. Each of us has good qualities which merit appreciation, but all too often these qualities are taken for granted. Instead of appreciation, we are subjected to nagging criticism for real or alleged shortcomings or mistakes.

## Putting It All Together

In this chapter, a number of recurring themes have emerged that are directly relevant to building satisfying interpersonal relationships: *(a)* the concept of balancing satisfaction and cost, *(b)* the central importance of communication, *(c)* the

---

**openness:** willingness to share information about one's self without a high degree of defensiveness

**empathy:** ability to share or participate in another person's feelings

**acceptance:** lack of judgmental attitudes toward another person

**caring:** concern for and commitment to the well-being of another person

need for adequate structure, *(d)* the necessity of interpersonal accommodation, and *(e)* conditions that appear to be constructive and destructive in building satisfying interpersonal relationships.

These themes form part of a total pattern which characterizes the **interpersonal style** of each person. For example, some of us are open and honest in our relationships, while others may wear a mask and be manipulative. Although we are likely to relate to different people in different ways, it seems useful to become aware of our characteristic interpersonal style, the motives, assumptions, and coping patterns on which our interpersonal style is based, and the type of relationship it will probably lead to.

Carl Rogers (1968) has attempted to extend this perspective by projecting the potential for change and enrichment in the interpersonal world by the year 2000: "There can be more of intimacy, less of loneliness, an infusion of emotional and intellectual learning in our relationships, better ways of resolving conflicts openly, man-woman relationships which are enriching, family relationships which are real, a sense of community which enables us to face the unknown. All this is possible if as a people we choose to move into the new mode of living openly as a continually changing process" (pp. 279–80).

**interpersonal style:** characteristic manner in which an individual interacts with others

## SUMMARY

1. Several models of interpersonal relationships have been developed. One model, the social exchange model, emphasizes the "economic" nature of an interpersonal relationship. In contrast, the role model emphasizes the demands and expectations that we and others place on our behavior. Finally, the "games people play" model examines interpersonal relationships in terms of ego states and gamelike strategies for dealing with others.

2. There are a variety of processes involved in relating to significant others. Among these are the encounter, interpersonal attraction, interpersonal accommodation, and self-disclosure. The encounter is the first step in relating to others. Although the outcome of the encounter is unpredictable, our perceptions, physical attractiveness, proximity, availability, and compatibility of purposes, beliefs, and values can enhance our attraction to another.

3. Once a relationship develops, interpersonal accommodation must occur so that the relationship can continue to grow and develop. Among the factors that are important in accommodation are communication, structure, and the resolution of disagreements and conflicts. And as a relationship continues, self-disclosure increases, as do the advantages and potential dangers of revealing intimate information about ourselves.

4. Three common maladaptive interpersonal patterns are fraudulent interpersonal contracts, collusion, and discordant interpersonal relationships.

5. Building a satisfying interpersonal relationship involves a recognition of mutual purposes and rights, adequate structure and communication, awareness, and helping each other grow as persons.

# Chapter 13

# Human Sexuality

*"Sex lies at the root of life, and we can never learn to reverence life until we know how to understand sex."*
*(HAVELOCK ELLIS)*

Human sexuality is one of the most discussed, most pleasurable, and most feared aspects of human life. Human sexuality is both a private and a shared, interpersonal activity. It can be used to help maintain and solidify a relationship with another. It can be used in a manipulative fashion, in which the sharing aspects of sexuality are forgotten in a selfish quest for personal satisfaction. Human sexuality thus exemplifies all the positive aspects of the human experience, and all the negative, destructive ones as well.

In this chapter, we shall discuss several aspects of human sexuality. After a brief review of the anatomy of the human sexual system, we will discuss the nature of the sexual response. We will also address issues in sexual dysfunction, contraception, and sexually transmitted diseases, and end with a consideration of sexuality and values.

## THE SEXUAL SYSTEM

*"The omnipresent process of sex . . . as it is woven into the whole texture of our man's or woman's body, is the pattern of all the process of our life."*
*(HAVELOCK ELLIS, 1921, P. 124)*

### The Female Sexual System

external genitals: portion of the sexual system that is easily visible

internal genitals: portion of the sexual system that can be found within the body

labia majora: large, fleshy folds of tissue appearing on both sides of the vaginal opening

labia minora: smaller folds of erectile tissue found on both sides of the vaginal opening

clitoris: organ whose function is the transmission of sexual pleasure in women

The female sexual system can be divided into two parts: the *internal* and *external* genitals. The **external genitals** are comprised of those portions of a woman's sexual system that are easily visible, while the **internal genitals** are comprised of those portions of the sexual system that cannot normally be seen.

**The external genitals.**   The external genitals of the female are comprised of the *labia majora, labia minora,* and the *clitoris.* The **labia majora** ("major lips") are comprised of soft, fleshy folds of tissue that normally cover the entrance to the vagina and help protect the urethral opening. Beneath the labia majora are the **labia minora** ("minor lips"), which are comprised of tissue that becomes engorged with blood during sexual arousal.

Portions of the labia minora form a hood which covers the **clitoris,** the most sexually sensitive part of a woman's body. The clitoris is comprised of erectile tissue that becomes enlarged with blood during sexual arousal. And, the clitoris is well supplied with nerve receptors to transmit sexual sensations to the nervous system. Among all of the organs in the human body, including both males and females, the clitoris is unique in that its sole function appears to be the transmission of sexual stimulation and the production of pleasure.

**The internal genitals.**   The internal genitals of the female are comprised of a variety of organs. Among them are the *vagina, cervix, uterus, fallopian tubes,* and *ovaries.*

The **vagina** is a muscular tube lined internally with mucous membranes that help keep the vaginal walls moist and lubricated. During sexual intercourse, the vagina acts as a passageway for the male penis, and during pregnancy, the vagina becomes the birth canal.

The **uterus** is a pear-shaped organ comprised primarily of muscular tissue. The uterus, of course, plays a major role in pregnancy and childbirth and is also responsive to sexual arousal. The **cervix,** the neck of the uterus, protrudes slightly into the vagina, and an opening in the cervix, called the *os,* acts as a passageway for menstrual fluids and sperm.

The inner lining of the uterus changes with each menstrual cycle, preparing for the possibility of a pregnancy. Should a pregnancy occur, the uterus (also called the *womb*) enlarges dramatically to accommodate the growing fetus. At childbirth, the muscles of the uterus contract to help push the fetus through the vaginal canal.

Most menstrual cycles do not result in pregnancy, and the inner lining of the uterus sheds itself during **menstruation.** After menstruation, the lining of the uterus begins growing and thickening again in preparation for a pregnancy.

Attached to the top part of the uterus are two tubes that play a major role in reproduction. These are the **fallopian tubes,** named for Gabriel Fallopio, the Italian anatomist who first discovered them. The fallopian tubes bring the unfertilized egg toward the uterus and aid the transport of sperm to meet and fertilize the egg. Contrary to popular belief, conception, the beginning of life, occurs in the fallopian tubes, not in the uterus.

The **ovaries** produce both *ova* (eggs) and the female sex hormones. At birth, the ovaries contain many thousands of immature *follicles,* structures containing the cells that eventually become ova. During a woman's reproductive years, one of the follicles matures and releases an ovum each month. In *menopause,* the ovaries stop releasing ova and also cease their cyclic production of hormones.

**The extragenital system.**   A number of structures that are not directly related to the genitals and reproduction can also produce sexual pleasure. For example, the lips and mouth can be powerful sources of arousal, and stroking the skin can be highly pleasurable.

Our society, however, has emphasized the female breasts as a primary site of **extragenital** activity and pleasure. The breasts are comprised primarily of fat tissue and milk glands. Differences between the size and shape of the left and right breasts are present in virtually all women, and breast size is determined primarily by heredity. No amounts of creams, massages, or lotions can influence breast size. While the muscles underlying the breast can be enlarged somewhat through exercise, only pregnancy and breast implants can alter breast size. (After pregnancy, the breasts typically return to their prepregnancy dimensions.) Reductions of breast size are similarly difficult, although the obese woman may find that her breasts decrease in size as she loses weight.

---

**vagina:** muscular tube providing a passage for the penis in sexual intercourse and the fetus during childbirth

**uterus:** muscular organ in which the fetus develops

**cervix:** portion of the uterus that protrudes into the vagina

**menstruation:** periodic shedding of the uterine lining in a nonpregnant woman

**fallopian tube:** tube that transfers eggs from the ovaries to the uterus

**ovaries:** pair of glands producing both eggs (ova) and female sex hormones

**extragenital system:** nongenital organs that can produce sexual pleasure

The primary biological function of breasts is to provide milk for young infants, and a woman with large breasts has no advantage in breastfeeding over the woman with small breasts. The breasts can also be a source of sexual pleasure to both a woman and her partner. However, some women report receiving no pleasure from breast stimulation. In other women, the breasts are quite sensitive to the touch, and any stimulation may be perceived as painful rather than pleasurable.

Unfortunately, our society has placed undue emphasis on women's breasts. Faced with men's magazines that feature women with prominent breast development, a typical woman may feel inadequate and unworthy. She may then attempt to augment her breasts with padded bras or silicone implants. These may be temporary solutions, however, since a woman needs to develop a sense of satisfaction and pride in her body, whatever its contours. Fortunately, the woman's movement, with its emphasis on intellectual, social, and occupational achievement, has helped women to see that male preoccupation with breast size need not have any implications for a woman's self-esteem.

**The popular media and a society that determines and rewards certain standards of beauty can help shape our feelings about ourselves and our bodies.**

**Women's reactions toward their genitals.**   Women's response to their bodies and their sexual systems can range from basically positive to thoroughly negative. One woman who regarded her genitals negatively wrote:

*Somewhere around the age of 10 or 12 I wanted to see what I looked like "DOWN THERE." . . .When the house was empty I got my mother's big ivory hand mirror from her dresser and went into my bedroom, closed the door, and went over by the window with sunlight pouring in. I looked . . . and was instantly horrified! I was obviously deformed. . . .When I saw [my inner lips] hanging out the only association I could make visually was that they looked like those things that hang down from a chicken's neck, a wattle. I thought I had stretched them like that from masturbating . . . . I swore off masturbation on the spot, asking God to get rid of those things that hung down, in exchange for my promise to be a good girl, stop swearing, love my little brothers, and to keep my room clean. (Dodson, 1974, p. 23)*

On the other hand, some women respond to their bodies in a more positive light:

*I used to be very modest in dress and no one ever saw me naked. I guess I never really saw myself in the nude either until one day I took a good look at myself in the mirror. And you know what? I'm not bad. I'm not any beauty from a model's magazine, but I'm not repulsive either. (Morrison, Starks, Hyndman, & Ronzio, 1980, p. 165)*

A second woman expressed her feelings in this way:

*I like me. I like my body. The more I learn about my body the better I feel, the happier I am, and the more I love myself and others. (Morrison et al., 1980, p. 165)*

As the quotations suggest, our reactions to our bodies and our genitals can involve a whole range of feelings and emotions.

## The Male Sexual System

As in the female sexual system, both internal and external genital structures can be described.

**The external genitals.**   The external genitals of the male are the *penis* and the *scrotum.*

The **penis** is the primary sexual organ of the male. It is comprised of three spongy cylinders of tissue surrounding the **urethra.** The urethra is the muscular tube that carries both semen and urine from the internal organs to the end of the penis. One of the spongy cylinders flares at the end to form the rounded head of the penis, the **glans.** The underside of the glans is particularly well-supplied with nerve endings and is the most sensitive part of the penis.

The adult penis in the unaroused state is typically less than four inches long and less than one inch in diameter. With sexual stimulation, the spongy bodies of the penis fill with blood, and the penis becomes enlarged and erect. In this state, the penis is slightly more than six inches in length.

There is substantial variation in the size of the nonerect or flaccid penis,

**penis: sexually responsive cylindrical organ in the male, comprised of erectile tissue**

**urethra: muscular tube that provides passage for sperm in males and urine in both males and females**

**glans: the head of the penis**

causing many men to be concerned about the size of their penis. However, research by Masters and Johnson (1966) has suggested that differences in flaccid penises may disappear in the erect state. That is, a smaller flaccid penis shows a greater increase in size during erection than the larger flaccid penis. Thus, during erection, penis sizes are somewhat comparable.

**scrotum: saclike external genital in males containing the testes**

The other external genital of males is the **scrotum.** The scrotum is the sac located behind the penis which contains the testes or testicles. The testes are sensitive to heat and need a temperature slightly lower than normal body temperature to insure sperm production. The scrotum helps perform this temperature-regulating function. When the testes need cooler temperatures, the skin and muscles of the scrotum relax, moving the testes away from the heat of the body. And, when warmth is needed, the scrotum contracts to raise the testes and reduce heat loss.

**The internal genitals.**    The internal genitals of the male include the *testicles, epididymis, vas deferens, seminal vesicles, prostate gland,* and the *urethra.*

**testicles (testes): pair of glands producing both sperm and male sex hormones**

**spermatozoa (sperm): male reproductive cells capable of fertilizing an ovum**

The **testicles** or **testes** are the male equivalent to the ovaries. The testes produce **spermatozoa** or **sperm** necessary for fertilization. Additionally, the testes produce male sex hormones. The testes produce sperm from puberty until death, thus allowing males the ability to retain their reproductive capabilities well into old age.

It is estimated that several hundred million sperm are produced daily in the *seminiferous tubules* of the testes. The sperm travel from the testes, to the *epididymis,* the coiled tubular structure atop the testes, and to the *vas deferens,* part of the cord that arises from the epididymis and travels into the body, where some maturation takes place. The sperm are then stored in the *seminal vesicles* above the *prostate gland.* During sexual arousal, fluids from the prostate gland are mixed with sperm to form **semen,** which is forced out of the urethra in rhythmic contractions.

**semen: sperm—containing fluid produced during ejaculation**

**The extragenital structures.**    The extragenital structures of males are, of course, virtually identical with those of females. While males do not normally have the breast development characteristic of women, male breasts are just as sensitive to stimulation as are female breasts. Similarly, certain areas of the skin, the mouth, and the lips, areas behind the external genitals, and the area around the anus have the same sensitivity in males as in females.

**Men's reactions to their genitals.**    The area of greatest concern to men is the size of their penis and their general muscular development. As noted above, penis size in the erect state is more similar than might be guessed from the nonerect state. However, this knowledge is small consolation to the man who constantly wonders if his penis can "measure up" to those he has furtively glimpsed inside a locker room.

Men, as well as women, seem to be excessively concerned with defining the "perfect" penis. Since men normally do not have the opportunity to see other erections, they rely on overworked imaginations and on exaggerated descriptions in magazines and novels to help them decide what an average penis is like.

Our attitudes toward the human body and sexual activity can be influenced by our early experiences.

However, the "average" penis in written works and in imaginations is typically huge. As Bernie Zilbergeld, author of *Male Sexuality,* has suggested, the imaginary penis comes in three sizes: "large, gigantic, and so big you can barely get them through the doorway" (Zilbergeld, 1978, p. 23). As long as men (and their partners) search for the "perfect penis," men's acceptance of their bodies in all of their good and "bad" aspects will be significantly slowed.

Similarly, men tend to be overly concerned with muscular and bodily development. The cultural ideal for men involves muscular development and strength. As with women, the man who does not meet the ideal may feel inadequate and devalued. One man wrote:

*If there was ever a rite of passage to male adulthood for me, it was shaving. Large biceps, muscular shoulders and broad chest were things I hoped to see in the mirror but did not. Gradually I accepted bumps and pimples, knobs, and moles as myself—it was a slow, painful process. (Morrison et al., 1980, p. 153)*

This concern can involve other aspects of physical development and sexual responding. Consider the following written by a thirty-eight-year-old man:

*We were all bathing in the pool naked. I hated to do it, because my peter looked so small—men's get so small in the cold water. So when I got out, I quickly wrapped a towel around me. (Delora, Warren, & Ellison, 1981, p. 81)*

It thus appears that men are no less anxious than women where their sexual systems are concerned.

## THE NATURE OF THE SEXUAL RESPONSE

Until recently, little was known about the nature of the sexual response. In 1966, this lack of understanding was dramatically altered with the publication of *Human Sexual Response* by researchers William Masters and Virginia E. Johnson.

While earlier studies had focused primarily on self-report, Masters and Johnson took the daring step of measuring sexual responses in a laboratory setting.

The work of Masters and Johnson is important because it provided us with the first detailed, reliable knowledge about the nature of the sexual response. Additionally, their research cleared up many areas of uncertainty and effectively ended a number of myths about sexual responding. For example, Masters and Johnson found that, contrary to psychoanalytic theory, a woman does not experience two different types of orgasm, the "vaginal" and the "clitoral." Rather, said Masters and Johnson, orgasm is physiologically the same whether a woman experiences this pleasant and enjoyable sensation from sexual intercourse or through masturbation.

In this section, we will review the findings from Masters and Johnson (1966), and we shall examine the personal experience of orgasm, looking especially at the question whether the experience of orgasm is similar or different for men and women.

## The Sexual Response Cycle

The sexual response cycle can be broken into two, three, or four stages. One of the earliest sex researchers, Havelock Ellis (1906), felt that the sexual response cycle could be broken into two stages—tumescence (the building up of sexual tension) and detumescence (the release of sexual tension). Helen Singer Kaplan (1979), on the other hand, has suggested that a three-stage model is more appropriate. In her model, sexual response begins with *desire,* builds during an *excitement* phase, and reaches a peak at *orgasm.* Masters and Johnson (1966) propose four stages: *excitement, plateau, orgasmic,* and *resolution* phases.

Each of the models is relatively arbitrary in nature. However, Masters and Johnson's fourfold model and their discussion of the physiological changes that accompany sexual stimulation are well known. We shall therefore adopt their perspective for our discussion, recognizing the somewhat arbitrary nature of their approach.

**The excitement phase.** In the female, the first sign of response to sexual stimulation is vaginal lubrication. In younger women, this lubrication can occur within ten seconds of stimulation. The lubrication comes directly from a "sweating" action of the vaginal walls.

The external genitals of the woman also show some changes. The major labia thin somewhat in women who have never born children, while in women who have given birth, the labia majora increase in size. The labia minora also increase in size for both groups of women, as does the clitoris.

In men, a somewhat similar pattern of responses emerges. The first response of the male to sexual stimulation is penile erection. Erection can occur within a few seconds after the onset of sexual stimulation. In older men, erection may take longer to develop. Externally, the scrotum thickens during the excitement phase, and the testes are drawn closer to the body.

In both sexes, the extragenital responses show marked similarity. In both women and men, nipple erection may occur. Muscle tension increases, as do heart rate and blood pressure. In women, some increase in breast size may be noted during this period.

An interesting phenomenon, termed the *sex tension flush,* can also occur during the **excitement phase.** This flush appears as a measleslike rash, first appearing in the mid-chest region. It tends to appear more often in women than in men.

Subjectively, the excitement phase is experienced as a period of waxing and waning interest. Interruptions during the excitement phase typically lower sexual arousal, but the pleasant, though mild, stimulation occurring during this phase are sufficiently rewarding to encourage continued activity, leading to the plateau phase.

**excitement phase:** first stage of sexual response cycle in which physical signs of sexual arousal become evident

**The plateau phase.** During the **plateau phase,** the changes that were initiated during the excitement phase continue and intensify. In women, vaginal lubrication continues, as does the enlargement of the vagina. The outer one third of the vagina shows marked engorgement with blood during the plateau phase. This *orgasmic platform,* as it was termed by Masters and Johnson, marks the achievement of the plateau phase in women.

The external genitals of women also continue to show changes. The labia minora, in particular, develop a much deeper color (the *sex skin*) during this phase. In women who developed this "sex skin," orgasm invariably followed continued sexual stimulation. The clitoris appears to retract from its normal body position during the plateau phase. Although somewhat retracted, the clitoris continues to respond to sexual stimulation.

In men, some changes that were initiated during the excitement phase con-

**plateau phase:** second stage of the sexual response cycle in which physical changes initiated in the excitement phase are intensified

tinue during the plateau phase. In the penis, the ridge at the base of the glans (the *coronal ridge*) increases in size and may deepen in color. Similarly, the testes continue their elevation and become enlarged by as much as 50 percent.

In both sexes, extragenital changes continue. The sex tension flush appears in increasing proportions of people and covers a larger part of the chest, shoulders, and back. In both sexes, muscle tension continues to increase, as do blood pressure, heart rate, and respiration.

The experience of the plateau phase is not markedly different in kind from the excitement phase, but it is more intense in nature. During the plateau phase, the participant is less willing to discontinue stimulation. The individual's involvement in sexual arousal increases, pressing for the release of the orgasmic phase. Should stimulation cease at this point without the experience of orgasm, both males and females may experience discomfort and pain in the genitals resulting from the slow reduction of accumulated physical tension and arousal.

**orgasmic phase: third stage of sexual response cycle in which a peak of sexual pleasure is experienced**

**The orgasmic phase.**    In the **orgasmic phase,** the accumulated sexual tensions are discharged in a brief, but extremely pleasurable set of sensations.

In women, the orgasmic phase is marked by contractions of the orgasmic platform. These contractions typically number from three to fifteen and the first few contractions are typically spaced 0.8 seconds apart.

**ejaculation: expulsion of semen from the penis, indicating orgasm in the male**

In men, orgasm is accompanied by **ejaculation,** the process by which semen is forced out of the body. Orgasm is initiated by contractions of seminal vesicles, ejaculatory duct, and prostate gland. During these contractions, the male experiences a sense of "inevitability" in which no amount of self-control could prevent an orgasm from reaching completion. Following the contractions of these internal structures, the penile urethra contracts at 0.8 second intervals for three or four times, followed by several more contractions at irregular intervals.

In both sexes, the extragenital responses reach a peak. Muscular tension is at its highest, and orgasm is often accompanied by specific contractions of muscles in the pelvic area. Heart rate and blood pressure also reach a peak, as does the sex tension flush.

Since male orgasm is typically marked by the ejaculation of semen, males have little difficulty learning when an orgasm occurs and what it feels like. On the other hand, women do not have physical evidence that an orgasm has occurred. Some women may mistake intense arousal for orgasm. And some women, thinking that all orgasms should be earth-shattering experiences, may not label a less intense orgasm in the proper manner.

There is little doubt, however, that both sexes report that orgasm is extremely pleasurable. During an orgasm, consciousness dims and perception is clouded. Awareness is typically focused on physical sensations during orgasm. Surprisingly, the facial expressions of individuals experiencing orgasm do not suggest pleasure but instead suggest pain or discomfort. No matter what the facial expressions may suggest, many people feel that the pleasure is well worth the price.

**resolution phase: fourth stage of sexual response cycle in which signs of sexual arousal disappear**

**The resolution phase.**    During the **resolution phase,** many of the physiological changes rapidly disappear, often in the reverse order of their appearance.

For example, the orgasmic platform rapidly dissipates following orgasm, followed by a return to the normal size of the vagina within a few minutes. Similarly, changes in the labia are rapidly reversed, as are changes in the clitoris and uterus.

In males, erection is lost in two stages. In the first stage, erection is reduced by about 50 percent within a few minutes. The remainder of the erection is reduced more slowly. These changes are accelerated in the older male. Both the testes and scrotum return to their normal positions.

In both sexes, the extragenital changes disappear. The sex tension flush disappears rapidly, and muscle tension, blood pressure, and respiration also return to normal. A *sweating reaction* may also occur. This sweating is unrelated to the amount of physical activity that preceded the resolution phase.

Continued stimulation may result in *multiple orgasms* for some women. That is, if she desires it and the stimulation is effective, a woman can go from orgasm to orgasm without entering the resolution phase. In men a related process, *sequential orgasm,* may occur. Following ejaculation, men typically enter a **refractory period** in which no type or degree of stimulation is effective in producing an erection. In younger men, the refractory period may last for only a matter of minutes, while in older men, the refractory period may be considerably longer. Interestingly, some recent investigations by Robbins and Jensen (1978) have suggested that men may also have the capability to experience multiple orgasms.

**refractory period:** period in which no amount, variety, or intensity of stimulation can produce sexual arousal

## The Experience of Sexual Arousal and Orgasm

It is, of course, impossible to know precisely what another individual's experience is like. People can look at the same sunset, eat the same apples, and look at the same paintings. But their experience while viewing the sunset, while eating the apple, and while looking at the painting is a very private and personal experience.

The same can be said of an orgasm. Although people use the same verbal label "orgasm," we have no way of knowing whether the experience of an orgasm is basically similar or intrinsically different between men and women. Some investigators have come to the conclusion that men's orgasms are more sudden and explosive, while women's orgasms are more prolonged but much less violent (Vance & Wagner, 1976). And, as we have noted, some theorists have assumed that a woman's orgasm can differ from a "vaginal" to a "clitoral" type.

Two researchers have attempted to resolve the question of whether orgasms are essentially similar or different between the sexes (Vance & Wagner, 1976). Vance and Wagner asked some psychology students to write a description of an orgasm and a description of a non-sexually oriented event. These latter descriptions were then examined by a group of judges who attempted to determine whether the description had been written by a male or a female. If the judges could reliably ascertain the sex of the writer, the description of orgasm prepared by the same student was eliminated from consideration. This procedure reduced the possibility that the sex of the writer of the orgasm experience could be identified by writing style alone.

# Psychology in Action
## THE SEX OF ORGASM QUESTIONNAIRE

Here are some of the descriptions used in the Sex of Orgasm Questionnaire developed by Vance and Wagner (1976). For each item, decide whether the item was written by a male (M) or a female (F). A helpful hint: there are unequal numbers of males and females in this group of experiences. Match your answers against the correct answers which can be found at the end of the questionnaire.

1. _____ An orgasm feels like heaven in the heat of hell; a tremendous build-up within of pleasure that makes the tremendous work of releasing that pleasure worthwhile.

2. _____ There is a building up of "tension" (poor description) to a very high stage. There is then a surging release which is exhilarating, leaving me in a totally relaxed, exhausted state.

3. _____ Spasm of the abdominal and groin area, tingling sensation in limbs, and throbbing at the temples on each side of my head.

4. _____ Experience of a build-up of tension, uncoordination of movement—to a few seconds of amazing feeling, to a release of tension and a period of satisfaction and relaxation.

5. _____ Often loss of contact with reality. All senses acute. Sight becomes patterns of color, but often very difficult to explain because words were made to fit in the real world.

6. _____ A feeling where nothing much else enters the mind other than that which relates to the present, oh sooo enjoyable and fulfilling sensation. It's like jumping into a cool swimming pool after hours of sweating turmoil. "Ahh Relief!" What a great feeling it was, so ecstatically wild and alright.

7. _____ A feeling of intense physical and mental satisfaction. The height of a sexual encounter. Words can hardly describe a feeling so great.

8. _____ Stomach muscles get "nervous" causing a thrusting movement with hips or pelvis. Muscular contraction all over the body.

From the remaining descriptions, twenty-four written by females and twenty-four written by males were randomly selected. These descriptions were then given to groups of medical students, clinical psychologists (both graduate students and faculty), and obstetrician-gynecologists. All the groups were asked to judge whether a given item was written by a male or a female. Since forty-eight items were used, a score of twenty-four would be expected by chance alone.

9. _____ Building of tenseness to a peak where it seems as if everything is going to drain out of you. It's almost like a complete physical drain.

10. _____ Starts with hot-cold tingles up in the back of the thighs. What happens from there depends on the strength of the stimulation. Usually, shuddery contractions and the same sort of hot-cold feeling only in the genital area. Sometimes, with a really strong stimulation, there's more of a blackout of complete mental awareness of what's happening, then a gradual letting down.

11. _____ An orgasm is a heightening relief of tension wherein the muscles are flexing and a great deal of tension is relieved in an extremely short period. It's a feeling of incurring climax and enjoyment due to the acute sensual nerve feelings and consciousness (kind of two opposing dialectics).

12. _____ Building up of a good type of tension. With the release of all this build-up in one great rush that makes your whole body tingle and feel very pleasurable. Feeling is weakening and is great. Just want to stay still for a long time.

13. _____ Has a build-up of pressure in genitals with involuntary thrusting of hips and twitching of thigh muscles. Also contracting and releasing of the genital muscles. The pressure becomes quite intense—like there is something underneath the skin of the genitals pushing out. Then there is a sudden release of the tension with contraction of genitals with a feeling of release and relaxation.

14. _____ I have had orgasm at times under certain conditions. I also have had it during intercourse. It is more relaxing with less mental duress during intercourse. It is a tensing of the whole body and a bright sensual feeling of release after.

15. _____ Orgasm amounts to a build-up of muscle tension accompanied by an increase in respiration rate. A sudden release of the build-up constitutes an orgasm. All in all, a highly pleasurable physical sensation.

16. _____ A complete relief of all tensions. Very powerful and filled with ecstasy. Contraction of stomach and back muscles.

Answers for the Sex of Orgasm Questionnaire: 1–M, 2–M, 3–M, 4–F, 5–M, 6–M, 7–F, 8–M, 9–M, 10–F, 11–M, 12–M, 13–F, 14–M, 15–F, 16–M

The results were surprising. No group performed at a level significantly better than chance. The medical students' score was 25.96, the obstetrician-gynecologists' score was 25.03, and the psychologists' score was 24.92.

It appears that the experience of an orgasm is relatively similar for both sexes. These researchers found no "male orgasm" nor any "female orgasm." In essence, they conclude that, "all orgasms are created equal."

## SEXUAL DYSFUNCTION

*When I was overseas I was having problems with my wife—but a lot of the guys were having problems with their wives. As soon as I got back to the states I called her and first thing she said she wanted a divorce. . . . The next week I met a girl at a pool party, and it did not take much before we were in bed together. She was really a doll and really built. But when I got ready to go in her, I lost my hard. I tried again later in a little while, but the same thing happened. It happened about three more times after that. It really shook me up. . . . I had been through Vietnam and everything over there and people were getting killed all around me and I was never afraid of death. But this was something else, and it shook me up more than anything I had been through. Maybe it was the stress of Vietnam and getting out, or maybe it was guilt because I knew I was still married then, or maybe it was just everything at once like the divorce and my brother on drugs and finding out my best friend was a homosexual. But it really cracked me up when it happened.*

*(DELORA ET AL., 1981, PP. 139—40)*

**sexual dysfunction: sexual difficulty occurring in a relationship**

The occurrence of a **sexual dysfunction** can be among the most devastating of life experiences. For those who have experienced satisfactory and pleasurable sexual activities, the dysfunction is a frightening, worrisome event. For those who have never enjoyed satisfactory sexual activities, questions of their adequacy and concerns about self-esteem become increased.

Sexual dysfunction may arise from a variety of sources. Among the most important factors that produce sexual dysfunctions are fears and anxiety, poor communication, anger and hostility (particularly toward one's partner), and an upbringing that emphasized control, lack of physical and emotional closeness, and other negative emotions regarding sex and sexual activity. Traumatic experiences can also produce sexual dysfunction, as can poor or incorrect information regarding sex. Finally, cultural variables that emphasize passivity in women and aggressiveness and "macho" characteristics in men contribute in subtle ways to sexual dysfunction.

In this section we shall focus on four types of sexual dysfunction: orgasmic dysfunction, vaginismus, impotence, and premature ejaculation. Although there is a temptation to say that orgasmic dysfunction and vaginismus are "female" problems and premature ejaculation and impotence are "male" problems, we should recognize that sexual difficulties do not "belong" to an individual. Rather, these are problems that are shared by the couple. As Masters and Johnson (1970) have pointed out, it is the relationship that suffers when a sexual dysfunction occurs.

**orgasmic dysfunction: persistent difficulty achieving orgasm**

● **Orgasmic dysfunction.** Orgasmic dysfunction refers to a long- or short-term difficulty of a woman to achieve sexual satisfaction through orgasm. When the problem is long-standing and the woman has never achieved orgasm or when the woman has never experienced sexual arousal, we speak of *primary sexual dysfunction.* In some cases, women are capable of achieving orgasm, but only under specific conditions. In these cases of *situational orgasmic dysfunction,* a woman may be capable of achieving orgasm with, for example, her lover but not with her husband.

Orgasmic dysfunction or *anorgasmia* is probably the most common sexual problem reported by women. A woman who has never experienced orgasm may have to be taught how to relax, how to be stimulated, how to enjoy stimulation, and how to communicate her needs to her partner. In the woman with situational dysfunction, the relationship between the partners comes under closer scrutiny, and other aspects of the woman's feelings about sexual activity and her sexual history are explored.

● **Vaginismus.** The involuntary spasm of the muscles surrounding the entrance to the vagina is called vaginismus. This relatively uncommon disorder prevents any object from being introduced into the vagina. Women with this disorder may have had some traumatic experience such as rape, have undergone painful pelvic examinations, or they may have fears regarding men, penetration, pregnancy, or childbirth. Fortunately, treatment of this dysfunction is generally neither complicated nor expensive.

**vaginismus: strong contraction of the vaginal muscles, making intercourse painful or impossible**

● **Impotence.** This sexual dysfunction involves the inability to achieve or maintain an erection long enough to have successful sexual relations. Although men with this disorder can frequently masturbate to orgasm, the dysfunction most often occurs in the context of a sexual encounter. As with orgasmic dysfunction, males can experience both primary and situational forms of impotence. With primary impotence, the male has never had an erection sufficient for sexual intercourse. In situational impotence, the man has had at least one successful sexual encounter.

**impotence: inability to achieve or maintain an erection sufficient for sexual intercourse**

The primary forms of this disorder are probably due to the same types of factors that are related to primary orgasmic dysfunction. Upbringing, relationship issues, and cultural variables serve to produce the primary form of impotence; only a small proportion of these disorders are due to medical conditions (Masters & Johnson, 1970).

In secondary or situational impotence, occasional failure and its associated worries may breed additional failure. The majority of men will experience at least occasional episodes of impotence throughout their lives. Many of these occasional problems are due to excessive alcohol consumption or other drug use, fatigue, or temporary relationship difficulties. If the man were to regard his situation as only temporary, he would, in all likelihood, not experience the difficulty on a second, later occasion. If, however, the man were to worry about a single episode and adopt a **spectatoring** attitude in which he "views" himself in the sexual encounter, the dysfunction would be likely to occur again. This negative process feeds upon itself and produces a self-perpetuating cycle of worry-dysfunction-worry. Therapy for this difficulty involves the elimination of worry and the reestablishment of nondemanding pleasurable activity.

**spectatoring: detached participation in sexual activity, often signifying anxiety about sexual performance**

● **Premature ejaculation.** In premature ejaculation, the male is unable to delay his orgasm sufficiently to allow his partner to achieve orgasm at least 50 percent of the time. Obviously, this definition is a complex one, involving both the man and the satisfaction of his partner. This definition was chosen by Masters and Johnson over other definitions that emphasized rigid time limits.

**premature ejaculation: inability of a male to delay orgasm long enough to allow his partner an opportunity to achieve orgasm**

# Insight

ACHIEVING SEXUAL SATISFACTION

Masters, Johnson, and Kolodny have offered a number of suggestions to help people achieve sexual satisfaction:

1. Approach sex as an opportunity for exploration and intimacy instead of as a job to be done. Goal-oriented sex creates performance demands, which can lead to improper and inappropriate self-observation and impaired responsivity. Remember that there's no "right" way of having sex; it's a matter of personal interest and comfort.

2. Try to develop open, effective lines of communication with your partner. Guessing about what your partner wants is difficult at best; making your partner guess about your needs is equally problematic. Effective communications includes being able to say "no" just as well as "yes."

3. Don't believe everything you read or hear about sex. Many books and articles about how people "should" respond are oversimplified and may be inaccurate and misleading. It's easy to talk yourself into a problem by comparing yourself to what "others" say.

4. If you're having a sexual problem of any sort, discuss it with your partner instead of pretending it doesn't exist. Through the use of some self-help techniques, a solution can often be found. However, if the problem doesn't go away fairly quickly, seek professional help. It's usually much easier to treat recent problems than problems that have solidified over a long time.

(Adapted from Masters, Johnson, & Kolodny, 1982)

Premature ejaculation can occur for a variety of reasons. A male may be involved with an exciting new partner, or he may express his hostility toward his partner through premature ejaculation. Perhaps the most important factor, though, is learning. As a young man, the individual may have learned to hurry sexual activity, perhaps to prevent detection and embarrassment by parents who returned home too quickly. Or, the man (and his partner) may not be aware that voluntary control is possible and potentially desirable. Fortunately, nonmedical treatment techniques to increase the time that a man can be highly sexually excited without orgasm are available and quite effective.

## CONTRACEPTION AND SEXUALITY

The reasons that people have for using **contraceptives** can range from the personal to the societal. For example, people may use birth control techniques to prevent pregnancy from occurring, as might be the case with an individual who is not emotionally, physically, or financially ready to assume the responsibility for children, or to control fertility in a planned way. An example of the latter would be a couple who wish to plan for and space their children.

**contraceptive:** device or technique used to allow sexual intercourse while preventing pregnancy in fertile individuals; also known as *birth control*

Birth control can also be used to express a social ideal. Many people, for example, are quite concerned about overpopulation and the straining of world resources. They are concerned that the ability of the world to care for, house, and feed the millions who are born every year is becoming increasingly taxed. By using contraception, these individuals are acting in a very personal way to help solve a worldwide problem of overpopulation.

In this section, we shall briefly review a number of the more widely used contraceptive techniques and examine some of the psychological factors that appear to influence contraceptive use.

### Contraceptive Techniques

For many people, engaging in sexual relations also involves a consideration of the risks of pregnancy. Of the sexually active, premenopausal women who do not use contraceptive techniques, approximately 60 percent will become pregnant within three months. In more personal terms, approximately one of every five women will become pregnant each month unless they or their partners use some type of contraceptive method.

The perfect contraceptive would be easy to use, inexpensive, extremely effective, produce no side effects, not interfere with sexual intercourse, and be easily reversible. Unfortunately, the perfect contraceptive does not exist. Individuals must choose from a variety of contraceptives, each with its own mixture of positive and negative qualities. Of course, conscientious, careful, and consistent use of a contraceptive will reduce the risks of pregnancy, since most failures are due to poor use.

No one contraceptive technique is best for all people. Given personal preferences, evaluations of risks, side effects, and effectiveness, each person must choose the contraceptive that is most appropriate to his or her needs and desires.

We have briefly summarized the effectiveness (both theoretical and actual), advantages, and disadvantages for a number of contraceptive techniques on pages 374–75. Our presentation should not be considered comprehensive, and the reader who wishes more detailed information can consult a number of sources, including *Birth Control Handbook* published by the Montreal Health Press (1975) and *Contraceptive Technology,* published periodically by Irvington Publishers. Information can also be obtained in college and community health centers as well as through Planned Parenthood offices.

## Psychological Factors Affecting Contraceptive Use

The number of teen-agers and young adults who engage in sexual activity prior to marriage is probably higher than at any time in our nation's history. Teenagers and adults are enjoying sexual activity more frequently and at an earlier age than ever before. And part of the reason for this dramatic increase in premarital sexual activity is the availability of effective contraceptive methods.

Given the ready availability of many effective contraceptives, why do so many teen-aged women become pregnant? As reported by Byrne (1977), 700,000 unwanted pregnancies occur among teen-aged girls each year. And it is now estimated that one out of every six teen-aged girls becomes pregnant prior to graduation from high school.

These statistics are startling. Despite all parental and societal efforts to explain and control teen-aged sexuality, our efforts seem to be failing. And, this failure is not due to widespread ignorance of contraceptive techniques.

In his survey of some sexually active undergraduate women, Byrne (1977) found that less than a third of the women *always* used contraceptives, and more than a third *never* did. These behavior patterns persisted even though half of the women had had the frightening experience of thinking they had become pregnant. Bryne felt that the decision of these women not to use contraceptives reliably was in part related to their feelings about sex.

**erotophiles: individuals who are comfortable with sexual materials and their sexual feelings and behaviors**

Based on their reactions toward sexually explicit materials, Byrne found that people could be placed into one of two groups. One group, the **erotophiles,** tended to rate sexually explicit materials as pleasant and arousing. Additionally, they were fairly open and accepting about sexual matters. They noted that sex was discussed in their homes, and felt that they had few problems in their sexual adjustment.

**erotophobes: people who have difficulty dealing with sexual materials and their sexual feelings and behaviors**

In contrast, the **erotophobes** reported much more negative attitudes toward sexual materials, rating sexually explicit materials as shocking and pornographic. Additionally, they reported that sexual matters were not often discussed in their homes. They disapproved of premarital sex and tended to be less well informed about sexual matters. Despite their strongly negative attitudes, erotophobes did not refrain from premarital sex, although the frequency of their premarital sexual activity tended to be less than that of erotophiles.

However, when it came to contraceptive use, it was the erotophobes who tended *not* to use contraceptives. Despite their worries, concerns, and anxieties about sex, and despite their negative feelings about sex, the erotophobes appeared to be more willing to risk an unwanted pregnancy through their refusal to use contraceptives.

Byrne felt that four reasons accounted for this seemingly paradoxical outcome. First, the decision to use contraceptives is also an admission that sexual intercourse is likely to occur. Although erotophobes have negative feelings about premarital sex, their negative feelings are not strong enough to totally prevent sexual desires and activities. One way to deal with these sexual feelings, however anxiety-provoking they might be, is to regard sexual activity as a spontaneous event. Thus, says Byrne, the erotophobe is likely to say that "It just happened," rather than admit that sexual activity had been planned.

Second, once an individual decides that sex is likely to occur, he or she must consult a physician or clinic or purchase the necessary contraceptive supplies in a drug store. This is a difficult task initially for many people, but it is especially difficult for erotophobes. For example, Byrne sent groups of men to a drug store to purchase condoms. For the man who has never done so, the purchase of condoms for the first time can be an acutely embarrassing experience, especially if the pharmacist or salesclerk is a woman. Erotophobes who completed this task felt that the druggist was judging them as immoral persons, an evaluation they found particularly troublesome. In a real-world situation, this discomfort might reduce the probability that contraceptive devices would be procured.

The third factor involves communication. Using contraception implies at least some level of communication between the partners. Erotophiles seem to be able to discuss sex matters, including contraceptive use, more easily than eroto-

Responsible sexuality involves communication between the partners, including a consideration of the possibility of pregnancy, a decision about whether to use contraceptives, and an agreement about what type of contraception is most appropriate for the couple.

# Insight

## RESPONSIBLE SEXUALITY

Too many people often rely on hopes to prevent pregnancy. For example, some people believe that certain periods in a woman's menstrual cycle are "infertile" times. This is incorrect, as is the assumption that a woman cannot become pregnant if she does not have an orgasm or if she douches immediately after intercourse.

People may also avoid the use of contraceptives because they feel some residual guilt about their sexual activity, maintaining that the use of contraception would spoil the "spontaneity" of the moment. This is a poor reason for avoiding the use of contraceptives. People who engage in sexual intercourse must also make a decision about a

### COMPARISON TABLE OF CONTRACEPTIVE METHODS

| Method | Theoretical Pregnancy Rate | Actual Pregnancy Rate | How it Works |
|---|---|---|---|
| Birth control pills (Combination pills) | 0.34 | 4–10 | prevents ovulation |
| Intrauterine device (IUD) | 1–3 | 5 | prevents implantation of fertilized ovum |
| Condom | 3 | 10 | barrier to sperm |
| Diaphragm and cream or jelly | 3 | 17 | barrier to and chemical destruction of sperm |
| Spermicides | 3 | 17–22 | immobilization and destruction of sperm |
| Rhythm (cervical mucus, basal body temperature, calendar) | 2–13 | 20–25 | periodic abstinence |
| Withdrawal | 9 | 20–25 | external ejaculation |
| Douching | ? | 40 | mechanical removal of sperm |
| Lactation (breast-feeding) | 15 | 40 | inhibition of ovulation |
| Vasectomy | 0.15 | 0.15+ | mechanical barrier to sperm |
| Tubal ligation | 0.04 | 0.04 | mechanical barrier to sperm |
| Abortion | 0 | 0+ | removal of fetal tissue |
| Abstinence | 0 | ? | prohibit intercourse |
| No method of contraception used | 90 | 90 | |

possible pregnancy. Refusing to deal with the biological connection between sexual activity and reproduction is not acting in a responsible fashion, particularly when contraceptives can "take the worry out of being close."

The following table lists a variety of contraceptive techniques, along with their theoretical and actual effectiveness rates, as well as the advantages and disadvantages associated with each method. Proper use of a technique reduces the risk of failure, as does the use of multiple techniques.

The pregnancy rate is expressed as the number of pregnancies per 100 women per year. Pregnancy rate data from *Contraceptive Technology 1980–1981*.

## COMPARISON TABLE OF CONTRACEPTIVE METHODS

| Advantages | Disadvantages |
| --- | --- |
| extremely effective; coitus independent; reduced menstrual flow and cramping | continual cost; daily use; side effects |
| effective; coitus independent; no memory or motivation required for use | increased cramping and bleeding; expulsion |
| effective; only major technique available to males; protects against STD | coitus dependent; reduced sensation |
| effective; inexpensive; few side effects | coitus dependent; aesthetic objections |
| easily available; no prescription required | unreliable when used improperly |
| low cost; acceptable to Catholic Church | requires periods of abstinence; best suited for women with regular cycles |
| no cost | reduces sexual pleasure; produces spectatoring attitude; unreliable |
| inexpensive | unreliable |
| no cost | unreliable |
| permanent; extremely reliable | substantial one-time expense; should be considered irreversible |
| permanent; extremely reliable | substantial one-time expense; should be considered irreversible |
| extremely effective | risk of miscarriage increases with repeated abortions |
| extremely effective | prohibits sexual intercourse |

phobes. The increased difficulty that erotophobes have with discussing sexual matters and their unwillingness to raise the subject of sexual activity and contraceptive use also decreases the chances that contraceptives will be effectively employed.

Finally, contraceptives must be used. Pills must be swallowed, diaphragms inserted, and condoms unrolled onto an erect penis. In contrast to erotophiles, erotophobes reported greater difficulty with contraceptive methods that require them to touch their genitals.

Other reasons for the failure to use contraceptives can be described. For example, contraceptive use has traditionally been defined as part of the woman's role. Some men have argued that it is the woman who gets pregnant, not the man. However, this argument ignores the implied partnership and shared responsibility that is an integral aspect of an intimate relationship. Biologically, of course, women do become pregnant, but they do not become pregnant without assistance from their partners.

Failure to use contraceptives can also be a deliberate act. Women who are trying to become pregnant will obviously not use contraceptives. However, the decision to become pregnant may not involve a shared decision between the woman and her partner. For example, a teen-aged girl may decide to become pregnant to prove to herself and to her parents that she is a "woman." Or, she may become pregnant as a way of getting back at real or imagined hurts and disappointments she has received at home or in school.

The failure to use contraceptives and the resulting pregnancy may be used by some people to help bolster a faltering relationship or as a way to help prevent a relationship from dissolving. The cost of contraceptives may be a deterrent to some.

Finally, some individuals hold strong religious beliefs in which the use of contraceptives is considered unnatural or improper. For these individuals, pregnancy is something to be desired and valued.

In essence, it appears that contraceptive use can be an integral part of responsible sexuality. Contraceptive use appears to be highest in those who readily acknowledge their sexual desires and activities, while it appears to be lowest in those who feel the greatest degree of anxiety and uncertainty regarding their sexuality. Engaging in sexual activity without the willingness to either use contraceptives or accept a probable pregnancy incurs a great price to the individual's sense of him- or herself as a thoughtful, competent individual.

## SEXUALLY TRANSMITTED DISEASES

**sexually transmitted diseases: diseases that are typically transmitted by sexual activity**

**Sexually transmitted diseases** are diseases that are transmitted primarily by sexual contact. They are also known as *venereal diseases*. We have chosen the phrase "sexually transmitted diseases" (STD) because it is a term gaining favor with researchers in sexual health and because the term does not have the negative connotations associated with "V.D."

# Types of Sexually Transmitted Diseases

In this section, we shall discuss five of the most common and most troublesome sexually transmitted diseases: gonorrhea, syphilis, genital herpes, nonspecific urethritis, and pubic lice.

- **Gonorrhea.** Gonorrhea is probably second only to the common cold in frequency (Masters, Johnson, & Kolodny, 1982). Its symptoms in men include a yellowish discharge from the penis, and a burning sensation during urination. In women, symptoms may include increased vaginal discharge.

gonorrhea: common sexually transmitted disease with few symptoms in women

Unfortunately, 10 percent of men and 80 percent of women show no symptoms whatsoever. And, untreated gonorrhea may spread to other parts of the body, causing arthriticlike inflammations of the joints and other symptoms. When the infection spreads in women, *pelvic inflammatory disease* may develop. PID, as it is sometimes known, is an infection of the uterus, fallopian tubes, and ovaries. The unfortunate outcome of PID in women and untreated gonorrhea in men can be sterility.

Not only do women show fewer symptoms, they are also more likely to contract the disease. Men who are exposed to an infected partner are likely to develop the disease about 25 percent of the time, while women who are exposed to infected partners may develop gonorrhea up to 90 percent of the time. If a woman is taking oral contraceptives, her chances of developing gonorrhea are virtually 100 percent (Masters, Johnson, & Kolodny, 1982).

The detection of gonorrhea requires examination of the discharge or the examination of cultures. Treatment typically involves injection of large doses of penicillin. Some recent reports have, however, suggested that some strains of gonorrhea may be resistant to penicillin. In these cases, other antibiotics may be used.

- **Syphilis.** Syphilis is caused by a corkscrewlike organism that invades the body. The first symptom of syphilis is the appearance of a **chancre,** a painless, round, ulcerated sore about the size of a dime, surrounded by a red rim. It usually appears two to four weeks after exposure, and heals within three to six weeks. The chancre may appear in the vagina or on the cervix in women and may therefore not be noticed.

syphilis: sexually transmitted disease whose course may extend over many years

chancre (pronounced SHAN-ker): painless ulcerated sore that is the first sign of syphilis

Once the chancre has disappeared, the disease enters the secondary phase. In this phase, which can last from three to six months, an individual may suffer from a rash, fever, sore throat, headache, and other symptoms. These symptoms may come and go and not be particularly severe. However, the infected individual can still pass the disease on to sexual partners.

After the secondary phase, the disease enters the latent phase in which no obvious symptoms are present. Somewhat less than half of these untreated individuals will enter the last, tertiary phase, in which a variety of neurological and cardiovascular problems develop, including psychosis and death.

Syphilis may be diagnosed through a blood test, and the usual treatment is injections of penicillin.

- **Genital herpes.** Genital herpes is a viral infection that is similar to the herpes infections that cause cold sores or fever blisters around the mouth. The first sign

genital herpes: painful viral infection of the genitals

of herpes is the appearance of small, fluid-filled blisters in the genital area. These blisters then ulcerate, producing severe pain. In from one to three weeks, the ulcers heal, leaving no visible damage. However, the herpes virus remains in the body, and herpes attacks can occur again at unpredictable intervals. There is no cure for genital herpes and no specific treatment for this disease. Pregnant women may have a higher risk of miscarriage if a herpes attack occurs during pregnancy. And, because of the seriousness of the effects of genital herpes on newborns, a woman who has an attack of genital herpes at the time of delivery is strongly urged to deliver by cesarean section. Also, women with genital herpes seem to have a higher risk of cervical cancer (Katchadourian & Lunde, 1980; Wallis, Redman, & Thompson, 1982).

**NSU (nonspecific urethritis): infection of the urethra that is not caused by gonorrhea**

- **Nonspecific urethritis (NSU).** Most infections of the male urethra are not caused by gonorrhea, but by a variety of organisms that are sexually transmitted. Like gonorrhea, NSU causes a penile discharge and a burning sensation during urination. And as with gonorrhea, treatment is through antibiotics. In women, untreated NSU can cause pelvic inflammatory disease. However, NSU infections are more difficult to identify than gonorrhea.

**pubic lice: parasites that attach themselves to pubic hairs and cause intense itching**

- **Pubic lice.** Pubic lice or *crabs* are parasites that attach themselves to pubic hairs and feed on fresh blood. The major symptom of pubic lice is intense itching. A variety of creams, lotions, and shampoos is available to kill the lice. However, the eggs of the lice can fall into sheets and clothing and reinfest the individual. Thus, it is necessary to use fresh bed linens and clothing during treatment.

## Avoiding Sexually Transmitted Diseases

Since the discomfort, danger, and embarrassment of sexually transmitted diseases is fairly high, people may wish to take a variety of steps to avoid contracting these diseases. The most useful tactic that an individual can take to avoid these diseases is to avoid sexual contact with an infected person. If you are unsure about your partner, the use of a condom can help reduce the chances of becoming infected. If you become infected, inform your partner or partners promptly so that they too can seek treatment. Finally, be aware that one exposure to the sexually transmitted diseases we have discussed does not confer immunity to the disease. It is possible to be infected, treated, and reinfected unless every individual takes steps to prevent the spread of these diseases.

## SEXUALITY AND VALUES

Sexuality is intimately related to our values. Our sense of right and wrong help guide our behavior and attitudes in sexual matters.

In this section, we shall discuss several issues related to sexuality and values. We shall discuss premarital sexual activity, the emphasis on sex vs. intimacy, and

# Insight

## THE "EVILS" OF MASTURBATION

In the past, **masturbation** was viewed with considerably less tolerance than today. Indulgence in masturbation was considered a sign of disease or moral laxness, and parents were urged by a variety of sources to prevent masturbation at all costs.

Below, we have printed a segment of a text by H. R. Stout. The text, *Our Family Physician*, was printed in 1885 and vividly illustrates how far we have come in our views of masturbation in the past hundred years:

*This is a very degrading and destructive habit, indulged in by young people of both sexes. There is probably no vice which is more injurious to both mind and body, and produces more fearful consequences than this. It is generally commenced early in life before the patient is aware of its evil influence, and it finally becomes so fastened upon him, that it is with great difficulty that he can break off the habit.*

*The symptoms produced by this vice are numerous. When the habit begins in early life, it retards the growth, impairs the mental faculties and reduces the victim to a lamentable state. The person afflicted seeks solitude, and does not wish to enjoy the society of his friends; he is troubled with* headaches, wakefulness and restlessness at night, pain in various parts of the body, indolence, melancholy, loss of memory, weakness in the back and generative organs, variable appetite, cowardice, inability to look a person in the face, lack of confidence in his own abilities.

*When the evil has been pursued for several years, there will be an irritable condition of the system; sudden flushes of heat over the face; the countenance becomes pale and clammy; the eyes have a dull, sheepish look; the hair becomes dry and split at the ends; sometimes there is pain over the region of the heart; shortness of breath; palpitation of the heart . . .; the sleep is disturbed; there is constipation; cough; irritation of the throat; finally the whole man becomes a wreck, physically, morally and mentally.*

*Some of the consequences of masturbation are epilepsy, apoplexy, paralysis, premature old age, involuntary discharge of seminal fluid, which generally occurs during sleep, or after urinating, or when evacuating the bowels. Among females, besides these other consequences, we have hysteria, menstrual derangement, catilepsy and strange nervous symptoms.*

**masturbation:** deliberate stimulation of one's body to produce sexual arousal and satisfaction

---

abortion. Our hope in this section is not to give specific directions, but to show the ways in which personal values can be employed in making some important decisions in the sexual sphere.

## Premarital Sexuality

A pressing problem for the adolescent and young adult prior to marriage is how to gratify his or her sexual needs. Traditional standards for sexual behavior in our society have emphasized abstinence from sexual relations prior to marriage, par-

**premarital sex:** sexual intercourse occurring prior to marriage

ticularly for women. However, both attitudes and behavior toward **premarital sex** have changed dramatically. A study of college students reported in 1940 showed that 6 percent of women and 15 percent of men approved of premarital sex for both men and women. In a similar survey reported in 1971 the percentages approving jumped to 59 percent and 70 percent for women and men respectively (Landis & Landis, 1973). Population surveys done in the 1970s showed that 80 percent of women and 90 percent of men had engaged in premarital sex (Hunt, 1974). It thus appears that the **double standard** that approved premarital sex for men but disapproved it for women is fast disappearing.

**double standard:** unequal standard stating that premarital intercourse is acceptable for men but unacceptable for women

While we do not know the full extent of change in attitudes or behaviors, we cannot deny that a veritable revolution has occurred in our views of sex. There is increased acceptance of sexual expression and experimentation, and more open discussion and expectation of enjoyment among all ages. But "free" sexual expression does not come naturally and painlessly to all. Whether or not to engage in a premarital or nonmarital sexual relationship remains a source of conflict for many people.

In the rush to engage in premarital intercourse, many individuals have acted in response to peer pressure rather than to their internal values:

*My older sister says she used to lie to her friends and say she was a virgin to protect her reputation. It is just the opposite for me. I lie to my friends claiming I'm not a virgin. (Crooks & Baur, 1980, p. 397)*

While premarital intercourse can be a positive experience, it is important that people make this decision in terms of their readiness for sexual activity, not the taunts of their friends.

The sexual revolution and sexual liberation have created new problems for many people. Some may feel pressured to enter a sexual relationship before they are ready; others may feel uneasy about permitting sexual activity in a casual relationship.

## Sex vs. Intimacy

The growing emphasis on sexual expression in relationships offers the opportunity to move away from arbitrary restriction and toward personal choice and responsibility. But there is another side to the new freedom. Many contend that we have entered a phase of overt preoccupation with sex—mass-produced, slickly marketed, dehumanizing, performance-oriented sex. Some social commentators suggest that we are "doing it more and enjoying it less," that, in fact, the new freedom causes anxiety. This viewpoint has been well expressed by the existential psychotherapist and author, Rollo May (1969): "By anesthetizing feeling in order to perform better, by employing sex as a tool to prove prowess and identity, by using sensuality to hide sensitivity, we have emasculated sex, and left it vapid and empty. The banalization of sex is well-aided and abetted by our mass communication. For the plethora of books on sex and love which flood the market have one thing in common—they oversimplify love and sex, treating the topic like a combination of learning to play tennis and buying life insurance. In this process, we have robbed sex of its power by sidestepping eros; and we have ended by dehumanizing both" (pp. 64–65).

A further difficulty is that both men and women, in an atmosphere of free sexual experimentation, expect themselves to act without inhibition and perform with great competence and variety, and make sexual excitement a high priority. As Lydon (1971) expresses it:

*Rather than being revolutionary, the present sexual situation is tragic. Appearances notwithstanding, the age-old taboos against conversation about personal sexual experience still haven't broken down. This reticence has allowed the mind-manipulators of the media to create myths of sexual supermen and superwomen. So the bed becomes a competitive arena, where men and women measure themselves against these mythical rivals, while simultaneously trying to live up to the ecstasies promised them by the marriage manuals and the fantasies of the media. ("if the earth doesn't move for me, I must be missing something," the reasoning goes.) Our society treats sex as a sport, with its record-breakers, its judges, its rules, and its spectators. (p. 66)*

Obviously, all the expectations surrounding sexual behavior in our era of "sexual freedom" can be a painful burden. Perhaps more than ever before, people must evaluate the meaning of sexual relations to them and choose for themselves how to satisfy their sexual needs without doing violence to other needs and values (Robinson & Jedlicka, 1982). Like all freedoms, sexual freedom exacts the heavy cost of personal choice and responsibility.

## The Issue of Abortion

Of the many issues that are involved in human sexuality, few are as emotionally laden as the issue of **abortion.** On the one side are a substantial number of people, both men and women, who believe that abortion is wrong and morally repugnant. On the other side are people who feel that an abortion is a woman's right and an important aspect of her ability to control her body and her fate.

**abortion: premature termination of a pregnancy**

Between these two positions are a large group of people whose feelings about abortion are quite mixed. These people can understand reasons for making abortion generally available but have a sense of uneasiness about this procedure nonetheless.

In this section, we shall present the two opposing perspectives on abortion and illustrate some personal reactions that women can have to abortion. We will focus on induced abortion, not spontaneous abortion or miscarriage.

**The pro-life position.** The opposition groups to liberalized abortion are collectively known as the **pro-life** groups. The term "pro-life" was chosen to reflect this group's advocacy for the unborn, not their opposition to abortion.

The basic thesis of the pro-life position is that life begins at conception, that the fetus is a person from the moment of conception, and that abortion is, therefore, a form of murder.

Other sources of opposition to abortion can also be identified in the pro-life position. For example, many people believe that children should be accorded rights because of their special vulnerabilities. The pro-life position maintains that these rights should be extended to the time prior to birth as well as to the times after birth. The rights of children prior to birth, say the pro-life groups, are affirmed in the United Nations Declaration of the Rights of the Child, a document supported by the United States. Additionally, note the pro-life groups, "genocide" in all forms should be opposed. That is, if we feel that the extermination of millions of Jews and Eastern Europeans by the Nazis was a morally repugnant act, we should feel the same repugnance toward abortion.

**The pro-choice position.** In contrast to the pro-life groups, advocates of the **pro-choice** positions offer a very different set of arguments in favor of continued availability of abortions. As the pro-choice groups note, laws against abortion do not prevent abortions but increase both the economic costs and health risks to the woman. Additionally, restrictive abortion laws discriminate against the poor. A wealthy woman, it is argued, will have the option to seek an abortion, an option that will not be safely available to the poor woman.

One major argument used by pro-choice groups is that not all contraceptive techniques are perfect. Thus, these groups maintain that abortion should be available as a "back-up" in case contraceptives fail.

Also, the pro-choice groups note that the circumstances of some pregnancies may not warrant continuation of the pregnancy. For example, a woman who is pregnant as a result of rape, incest, or other sexual molestation may not have been a willing participant in the act that resulted in the pregnancy. Also, some pregnancies can harm both the physical and mental health of the woman. A woman with kidney disease, for example, might die as a result of the pregnancy.

Finally, pro-choice groups argue that only the woman should be allowed to control what happens to her body. Her womb and her body are not the "property" of the state, her parents, or her partner. If a woman wishes to bear a child, it is because she feels emotionally, financially, or physically ready to have children. And, she should not be forced to bear an unwanted child. Her body is hers alone, and only she should be allowed to decide what should happen to her.

**pro-life: groups and opinions upholding the rights of the fetus**

**pro-choice: groups and opinions upholding the rights of women to have abortions**

The issue of abortion generates strong feelings among those in favor and those opposed. On the one side are those who say that a woman should have the right to decide for herself what to do about a pregnancy. Those opposed to abortion argue in favor of the rights of the unborn.

**Deciding for yourself.**   The arguments in the abortion controversy ultimately rely on some indisputable facts: Contraceptives, even when used conscientiously, occasionally fail. Not all pregnant women and their partners look forward to the emotional, physical, and financial burdens of caring for a child. And, given reasonable care and nutrition, an embryo and fetus will develop into a healthy infant. The abortion controversy thus raises a seemingly unresolvable conflict.

It is clear from public surveys that neither perspective on abortion is strongly represented in the population at large. A Gallup survey reported in 1980 showed that 25 percent of the population felt that abortion should be legal under any circumstances, while 18 percent of the population felt that it should be illegal under all circumstances. In contrast, a majority of the population, 53 percent, felt that abortion should be legal, but only under certain circumstances. Unfortunately, we do not know what these circumstances are. The conditions might be very narrow—"Abortion is okay only if the woman became pregnant as a result of rape or incest"—or they might be relatively broad—"It's okay for other women to have an abortion, but it's not for me."

**Personal reactions to abortion.**   We have been dealing with abortion in a fairly abstract manner. However, abortion is clearly and intensely a personal and emotional experience. The woman who decides to have an abortion tends to be relatively young (typically under age twenty-five), typically unmarried (approximately 75 percent are not married), and equally likely to already have children as to be childless (about 50 percent are already mothers). Many of the women who undergo an abortion do so with a mixture of fear, depression, and anxiety. Although many are relieved that they are no longer pregnant, an abortion is typically not experienced in a light-hearted fashion:

*I was so relieved not to be pregnant any more that I didn't think I had any sad feelings at all. Then a few days later, on my way to a friend's house, I saw a young couple walking a new baby and I burst out crying right there on the street.*

*Even though my husband was very supportive, I felt angry—not so much because he put the sperm in me as because he in no way could understand what I had experienced.*

*I left the clinic with my friend, feeling two ways about the whole experience: One, that I'd had as good and supportive an abortion experience as a woman could have; and two, I would never put myself in the position of having to go through it again. (Boston Women's Health Book Collective, 1976, pp. 234–235)*

Clearly, the issue of abortion is a complicated one, and one that may not be easily resolved. However, it is a decision that tests our ability to address the issues clearly and make judgments in accord with our own value systems.

In the future, other issues involving sexuality and values will need to be addressed. Among these are the issue of "test-tube" babies, surrogate mothers, and genetic manipulation. Again, our values will play an important role in helping us come to decisions on these important issues.

## Sexuality as a Source of Pleasure and Meaning

Our sexuality can be used to express our values and to find joy and meaning in life. Our beliefs and attitudes about ourselves and others help influence the ways in which we express and experience our sexuality.

Knox (1979) has suggested that our motives for sexual activity can vary widely:

1. *Intimacy.* In an impersonal society, sexuality can be used to experience emotional and physical closeness with another person.

2. *Love.* Our deeper feelings of love and caring can be expressed in sexual activity.

3. *Fun.* In addition to love, sexual activity with another person can be a highly enjoyable, delightful experience.

4. *Ego enhancement.* Sexual activity can be a means to build up one's sense of self-esteem, sometimes at the expense of another person.

5. *Improve or maintain a relationship.* In some relationships, sexual activity is a "next step" in the course of the relationship. In others, sexual activity can be used to maintain the relationship. And in still others, sexual activity can be used to prevent the relationship from faltering or dissolving.

6. *Rebellion, revenge, or pressure.* Sexual activity can be used to rebel against parents, established authority, or previous partners. Or, sexual activity can occur in response to pressure from a partner.

This list is not exhaustive and could also include factors such as relief from boredom and tension, duty, and reconciliation. However, our list clearly illustrates that sexual activity can occur for a variety of reasons, ranging from the positive to the negative. And it is likely that a mixture of these motives prevails during any particular sexual act.

These motives illustrate the importance of our values in sexual relationships. We can engage in sexual activity for a variety of positive, enhancing reasons or for a variety of manipulative, interpersonally destructive reasons.

A second, related point is that the same sexual act can have a variety of meanings depending on the attitudes and values that we bring to the situation.

Thus, in making decisions about our sexuality, it is not enough to make a judgment about a particular activity but also about the feelings we bring to the activity. For example, we may have generally positive attitudes toward premarital intercourse. However, our positive attitudes about premarital sexual activity can have a variety of meanings, depending on our motivations for engaging (or not engaging) in this behavior.

Finally, we should note that the largest sexual organ for both the male and the female is the organ that lies between the ears. We are, of course, speaking of the brain. A substantial portion of our sexual inclinations and feelings are located in the brain, not the genitals. Thus, it is important that we do not confuse smooth sexual technique with loving concern and involvement with others. Sex is not a mechanized "touch here, stroke that" endeavor. Rather, it is a means by which loving partners can give and receive pleasure. In our society with its numerous sex manuals, "experts" on sex, and sexual symbols in various media, it may be easy to forget that the most important variables are still the human ones.

As Kirkendall and Anderson (1973) have put it, "The most intimate and meaningful experiences come when [sexuality] is . . . an integral part of a relationship in which people are trying to express care and love for one another. Sex is not simply an end, but is a part of a more encompassing relationship" (p. 420).

## SUMMARY

1. The sexual system can be divided into the internal and external genitals. People can also respond sexually to stimulation in other areas of the body. However, the reactions that we have to our bodies and to our genitals can vary from the negative to the positive.

2. The sexual response cycle can be arbitrarily broken into four phases: excitement, plateau, orgasmic, and resolution. In each of the phases, a coordinated series of genital and extragenital reactions occurs. These physical changes are similar in both sexes, and the personal experience of orgasm is also similar in both sexes.

3. Sexual dysfunction is not a problem that an individual has, but a problem shared by partners. Some common types of sexual dysfunction include impotence, orgasmic dysfunction, premature ejaculation, and vaginismus.

4. Biologically, intercourse in fertile individuals can lead to pregnancy. However, not all people wish to assume responsibility for child rearing or wish to postpone child rearing. For these individuals, contraceptive techniques will help prevent pregnancy. Psychological factors can also affect contraceptive use.

5. One of the risks of sexual activity is contracting a sexually transmitted disease. Five common disorders are gonorrhea, syphilis, genital herpes, nonspecific urethritis, and pubic lice.

6. Sexuality and values are closely related. Issues such as intimacy, premarital sexuality, and abortion are some of the areas in which sexual values can have a significant impact on our behavior and on our sense of self-esteem.

# Chapter 14
# Marriage and Intimate Relationships

intimate relationship: personally meaningful, emotionally deep relationship with another person

intimacy: feelings characteristic of a very close contact with, knowledge of, or familiarity with another person

Of all the endeavors that exert their influence on people's lives, the quest for **intimate relationships** must be the most sought after, longed for, dreamed about, sung about, joked about, and cursed at. Few human experiences inspire the pangs, joys, ecstasies, fears, cheers, and tears that accompany the growth and development of intimacy. Such relationships are a major source of need fulfillment, stress, and challenge in our lives.

For most people, achieving **intimacy** with an individual of the opposite sex is a major goal of life, marking maturity and adulthood as well as personal fulfillment and achievement. Only a small percentage of Americans will not marry at some point in their lives. Most will marry at least once in the hope of experiencing the benefits, challenge, and excitement of intimacy and companionship.

For many people, the decision to marry will be the most important decision of their lives.

Intimate relationships vary considerably from one society to another and within subgroups of a given society. In our culture, both the typical form and the expected content of intimate man-woman relationships have changed significantly in recent years. The reasons for making long-term commitments and for entering legally sanctioned relationships, and the behavior of both men and women within such relationships, have changed and continue to change. In this chapter we shall describe and attempt to define love, explore the impact of these changing attitudes and behavior, describe the factors involved in choosing a mate, describe the obstacles to "living happily ever after," discuss the causes and effects of divorce and remarriage, and describe some alternatives to marriage.

## LOVE

*'That he sings, and he sings; and for ever sings he—*
*'I love my Love, and my Love loves me!'*
*(SAMUEL TAYLOR COLERIDGE, ANSWER TO A CHILD'S QUESTION)*

*"Heigh-ho! sing, heigh-ho! unto the green holly:*
*Most friendship is feigning, most loving mere folly."*
*(SHAKESPEARE, AS YOU LIKE IT)*

*"He loves me, he loves me not.*
*He loves me, he loves me not."*
*(CHILDREN'S RHYME)*

The issues of liking and loving have occupied poets, playwrights, and people in all walks of life for generations. As our quotations suggest, the answers that they have developed to the problem of **love** have differed greatly. Fortunately, psychological research has begun to shed some light on this most interesting of subjects. Although our understanding of love is incomplete, we shall explore several topics: Are there different types of love? Is love different from other intense emotions? How can you tell when you are in love? Our focus in this section will be on Westernized views of love, and it is important to note that love in non-Western societies may be experienced somewhat differently.

**love: mental and physical attraction to another person; strong or passionate attachment**

## Types of Love

Throughout our lives, we may have experienced many different types of love. For example, we can love our parents and they in turn can love us. As children, we can love our siblings and friends. Similarly, we can find ourselves sexually attracted to and in love with others.

Normally, we distinguish between three different types of love. The first is termed **agape**. Agape describes a love of humanity, a concern and affection for others. For example, when we send food and clothing to victims of a disaster,

**agape (pronounced ah-GAH-pay): selfless, nonsexual form of love**

we are exhibiting agape. In its ideal, agape is a selfless and nonsexual type of love.

**philia: nonsexual form of love that is reciprocated**

**Philia**, or brotherly love, refers to the affection that we feel for our families and close friends. Like agape, philia is a nonsexual type of love; unlike agape, philia involves **reciprocity** between people. Thus, in philia we expect that acts of friendship and affection toward our family members or close friends will be returned in kind.

**reciprocity: mutual give and take**

**eros: reciprocal, sexual form of love**

Finally, **eros** describes erotic love. Normally, those who share the love of eros (named for the Greek god of love) are unrelated to one another and sexually attracted to each other as well. Eros is the type of love that we normally think of when we use the phrase "love" or when we say "I love you" in a moment of passion.

Psychologists and sociologists have further explored eros and discovered that it often changes and varies with age. For example, in adolescence and early adulthood, eros is often expressed in *romantic* love, while love in the later years of life may be seen in *companionate* love.

**romantic love: type of love characterized by intense, passionate feelings**

The concept of **romantic love** developed in the Middle Ages. During this time, knights would idealize their ladies and perform many difficult tasks to "prove" or test their love. For example, these knights would demonstrate the purity of their love by sleeping in the same bed as the woman and making sexual advances toward her, but stopping short of sexual intercourse (McCary, 1980).

Today, romantic or passionate love is the type of love depicted in books, magazines, and movies. In passionate love, men are strong and tender and women develop a radiant bloom that they and their friends notice.

This clearly stereotypical description of passionate love hints at the ecstasies and agonies of this type of love. People in the throes of romantic love have strong feelings of attraction and affection for their partners. They feel concern for the other's well-being and are eager to make more of themselves for the sake of the loved one. They want to contribute to their partner's happiness and personal growth. Romantic love may have an exclusive and possessive nature. Finally, romantic love can express itself as a sexual attraction to the other person.

A couple who share a deep romantic love may, indeed, have "eyes only for each other."

Although the person with romantic love "only has eyes" for his or her partner, romantic love has its negative side as well. People in romantic love may feel fear and anxiety when they are near the loved one. Often, their desire to make a good impression results in so much anxiety that their fantasies of acting in a suave, sophisticated fashion dissolve into cold sweats, social ineptness, and tongue-tied fear. People in romantic love may also develop intense jealousy of their loved one's thoughts and actions. They may become jealous of the Other Man or the Other Woman, even if they exist as only a theoretical possibility. These feelings of jealousy may turn into anger and hostility and may result in physical violence. Finally, people in romantic love may be unsure of their feelings. While their positive feelings toward the partner may be strong, they may also experience some negative feelings (Walster & Walster, 1978).

The fires of passionate love eventually become less intense, and many partners discover **companionate love**. Where passionate love is intense and unpredictable, companionate love is friendlier and more stable. The partners feel affectionate toward and attached to each other. In many ways, companionate love has the characteristics of an excellent friendship.

companionate love: love for one's partner accompanied by strong feelings of liking for the partner

Many couples start out with passionate love. For example, one study measured the passionate love scores of couples married up to three years and found that they averaged over ninety-eight points. However, couples who had been married more than ten years reported passionate love scores of eighty-four. Interestingly, there were no differences in the liking scores between newly married and long-married couples. For both kinds of couples, liking scores remained uniformly high (Cimbalo, Faling, & Mousaw, 1976).

These data suggest that both liking and passionate love are important in a long-term relationship. Passionate love may be strong in the early phases of the relationship, but it by no means disappears in marriage only to be replaced by companionate love. As one woman noted,

*When I fell in love I felt fantastic! I glowed, people said they never saw me look prettier or happier. I felt this way, I think, because of the new self-confidence Ted gave me, and because of the feeling of just being needed and desired. . . . As it turned out, I married Ted. We're still very happy and very much in love, but there is a definite difference between the first passionate feelings of love and the now-mellowed-out feelings.*

*Don't get me wrong, though, there are still plenty of passionate times. It's just that when you live together, the passion is not as urgent a thing. You're more loving friends. (Walster & Walster, 1978, p. 4)*

## Love and Emotions

To the individual in the middle of a passionate and romantic love affair, the feelings of love are as special and unique as any in human existence. However, research in emotions suggests that feelings of love share a number of features with other intense emotions.

Earlier in Chapter 6, we discussed Schachter and Singer's theory of emotions. In our discussion, we noted that emotions may consist of physiological arousal accompanied by emotional and cognitive labels. Thus, a rapidly beating heart can be interpreted as a sign of anger or euphoria, depending on environmental circumstances.

As described by Walster and Walster (1978), love, like other strong emotions, may consist of physiological arousal accompanied by the appropriate cognitive label. In other words, a rapid heart beat and other signs of general physiological arousal can be labeled as signs of love when the circumstances are correct. Thus, when we are with another individual in a setting that we define as romantic, we have virtually no choice but to label our feelings of excitement as indicators of love.

In one interesting examination of this hypothesis, Dutton and Aron (1974) told one group of college-aged males that they would have to undergo a series of painful shocks as part of a "learning" experiment. The other group of males were also to receive shock, but the shocks would be barely perceptible. For both groups, the "partner" in the experiment was a very attractive woman. After the experiment, the men who received the intense shocks reported greater attraction to the woman than the men who received minimal shock. As predicted by the Walsters' hypothesis, the men who received the high levels of shock apparently attributed their heightened arousal to their lab partner rather than to the experimental conditions. Assuming that these studies are valid, they imply that we may just as easily fall in love with the person who accompanies us on an amusement park roller coaster as with the person sharing a candlelit dinner with us.

Despite these similarities, the feelings of love also differ from other emotions. The primary difference is that love is almost universally regarded as a positive and desirable emotion. In contrast, other strong emotions, such as fear or anger, are generally considered to be negative and undesirable. In the same vein, love, under the right circumstances, can lead to personal happiness and growth, while the negative emotions produce unhappiness and place substantial adjustive demands upon us.

## Being in Love

Although we see romantic love depicted virtually every day on television or in magazines, few people are able to express the feelings that constitute love. For example, our parents or friends often respond to our inquiries of how to know when we are in love with "You'll know when it happens." In some cases, descriptions of love may be indistinguishable from some rare and presumably fatal disorder: "You get butterflies in your stomach, and you can't sleep well at night."

Fortunately, we can estimate the attraction between two people by examining their nonverbal behavior. People who are in love with one another spend more time gazing into each other's eyes, and they tend to be physically closer to one another than is socially common. Additionally, loving partners tend to orient their bodies toward and "lean in" to each other.

**liking: deep sense of affection and companionship for another**

Interestingly, the sexes tend to respond to **liking** and loving differently. For example, men make sharper distinctions between liking and loving their partners

Nonverbal behavior is often a cue to the attraction between two people. A couple who are in love may demonstrate their attraction for each other through physical closeness and "leaning in" to one another.

than do women. Contrary to stereotypes, men fall in love more quickly than women, and men take longer to fall *out* of love than women. While women may be more cautious in their initial commitment to loving their partners, their feelings are stronger than those of men when they decide that they are in love (Rubin, 1970; Walster & Walster, 1978).

In summary, our findings suggest that there are many different types of love, ranging from the nonsexual to the passionate. Our feelings for our partners can be both passionate and companionate in nature, and the degree to which we experience these different types of love is often related to the length of the relationship. While love is an emotion that can develop like other emotions, the experiences of men and women "in love" and "in like" may be quite different.

## ATTITUDES AND BEHAVIORS IN INTIMATE RELATIONSHIPS

More than 95 percent of all American men and women will marry at some time in their lives. Couples still take the traditional vows to love and honor each other. And most individuals who marry do so with certain expectations about fidelity, security, permanence, and prescribed roles for both husband and wife.

Although these things have remained the same, our traditional assumptions and practices have not. There are many indications that the intimate relationships men and women establish today are significantly different from the relationships their parents established. In this section we shall point out some of these trends and their possible causes.

## Goals in Intimate Relationships

*With all the variations among American families, it is apparent that they are all in greater or lesser degree in a process of change toward an emerging type of family that is perhaps most aptly described as the "companionship form". . . . The essential bonds in the family are now found more and more in the interpersonal relationships of its members, as compared with those of law, custom, public opinion, and duty in the older institutional forms of the family.*
**(BURGESS, 1964, P. 196)**

**marriage: a socially sanctioned intimate relationship**

Many people today see **marriage** as a way of meeting their needs and achieving psychological satisfactions in our society. Marriage is a means of gaining companionship, mutual emotional support, a secure "home base," and most of all an intimate relationship in which to share all aspects of one's life and achieve happiness. For many, an intimate relationship is also expected to serve as a medium for personal growth.

Another goal of intimate relationships appears to be an effort by couples to know each other fully and without façade. Many couples feel that dating and courting rituals are an artificial and limited means of obtaining information necessary to make decisions about future relations. While formal dating may serve some useful functions, particularly during the early stages of a relationship, many couples seek to expand their knowledge and understanding of each other through shared experiences.

One common outcome of this goal is the practice of *cohabitation,* or living together before marriage. Premarital sexual relations are also a means by which couples attempt to achieve full sharing and knowledge of each other in their quest for authenticity in their relationship.

## Challenges to Old Patterns and Assumptions

Today's goals in intimate relationships challenge traditional patterns and assumptions. Instead of marrying, rearing children, and dying within a thirty-year period, today's couples can expect as long as fifty years together, less than half of which may be taken up with child rearing. The mobility of our population and the enormous variety of models and life-styles we come into contact with can also serve as disruptive elements. These and other factors inevitably affect the relationships we build. And they have given rise to three important challenges to our traditional patterns of marriage:

1. *The challenge to the permanence of marriage.* Most people who marry today do so with the expectation that their relationship will be permanent. Nevertheless, a marriage that lasts a lifetime is difficult to attain. One factor is the rate and multiplicity of change—in jobs, sexual patterns, leisure-time pursuits, values, and life-styles—all of which make it more difficult for a husband and wife to grow together over the years.

Some investigators have suggested that a commitment to permanence should

*"More or less."*

© William Hamilton

not be made at all. As sociologist Jessie Bernard (1973) has noted, the advocates of **renewable marriage** argue that couples who depend upon the law or other institutional props to support their marriage are likely to let the conscious, voluntary supports decay. If the marriage were subject to optional renewal, the couple would presumably make the relationship stronger and happier.

An alternative perspective has been presented by Toffler (1971), who argues that the goal of permanence will gradually shift to a more temporary marital arrangement. In essence, Toffler (and others) are predicting that people will shift to the one-after-another pattern of **serial marriage.** Toffler's position receives support from statistics showing that 80 percent of widowed and divorced people eventually remarry.

Renewable marriages, trial marriages, cohabitation, serial marriage, and other patterns that recognize the strong possibility of impermanence from the start may yield benefits in terms of freedom and choice, but they are likely to exact a high price in insecurity and anxiety about continuation of the relationship.

2. *The challenge to fidelity.* Statistics indicate that about 40 to 70 percent of married persons have engaged in extramarital sexual activities (Hite, 1981; Wolfe, 1981). Shere Hite (1981) reported that the majority of men in her study were not monogamous. In fact, 72 percent of ''men married two years or more

**renewable marriage: marriage contract that is extended only when the partners specifically agree to continue the marriage**

**serial marriage: two or more marriages for an individual in which one marriage follows the termination of the preceding one**

had had sex outside of marriage; the overwhelming majority did not tell their wives, at least at the time'' (p. 142).

One response to these data has been the suggestion that marital partners enter an **open marriage** (O'Neill & O'Neill, 1972). In an open marriage, the partners agree beforehand that extramarital sexual activity may occur, and they agree to respond to extramarital activity in a permissive, nonpossessive fashion. In its ideal form, open marriage would allow for extramarital activity without feelings of jealousy, resentment, or competition. Presumably, an open marriage would ultimately produce a stronger, more growth-oriented relationship between the partners. However, even as its advocates have noted (O'Neill, 1978), it is difficult to give a spouse permission for extramarital activity and not feel jealousy or discomfort at the same time. It thus appears that marital fidelity still remains a cherished goal for many, but it is a goal that many will find difficult to attain.

3. *The challenge of changing sex roles.* Our training to become masculine and feminine begins early and continues throughout much of our lives. The toys we play with as children, our first awkward encounters in adolescence with the opposite sex, and our social and occupational roles as adults force us into rigid **sex roles**. We train males to be independent, unemotional, aggressive, and physically active, while we train females to be dependent, emotional, socially aware, and nurturant.

These training experiences were reflected in traditional marriages. Females were expected to provide for household and child care needs, and males were expected to provide economic security for their families. As many observers have noted, however, there are no compelling reasons why women should be the primary child care providers or why men should be the primary economic providers. Except for reproduction, most of the observed differences between the sexes in terms of dress, habits, behavior, and opportunity are to a large extent related to our learning experiences and to cultural stereotypes and models.

As couples have begun to grapple with the recognition that men and women are potentially equal in aptitudes, abilities, and skills, they have also begun to restructure their goals and expectations in the relationship. Women are demanding that men take a more active role in child care and housekeeping, and men are demanding that women take a more active role in economic support of the family. In turn, men are allowing their emotional lives to become more complex, and women are allowing their independent aspects an opportunity for growth. Although these changes have not occurred without some difficulties, the challenge to traditional sex roles may ultimately result in relationships in which assigned tasks and roles are based on skill and knowledge, not on genital structure.

## CHOOSING A MATE

Romantic myth is that ''marriages are made in heaven,'' that couples are ''destined to marry.'' The fact is, however, that the origins of most partnerships are more mundane than heavenly, and they are often influenced more by social expectations than by romantic ideals or rational decision making.

---

**open marriage: marriage in which both partners are free to take other sexual partners**

**sex roles: expected behavior patterns based solely on gender**

In our discussion, we will consider some of the reasons why people marry at all and examine some factors that influence mate selection.

## Reasons for Marrying

For many, marriage is assumed to be such an integral part of their life that they cannot verbalize their reasons for marrying. Others, if asked, may cite a variety of reasons ranging from love and companionship to financial security and pregnancy. Here we shall comment on four reasons which are commonly given for marrying: love; companionship, fulfillment, and escape from loneliness; sexuality, reproduction, and child rearing; and economic security.

**Love.**    The most common reason given by both men and women for marrying is love. In an analysis of the replies of 75,000 wives to a *Redbook* questionnaire on marriage, for example, psychologist Carol Tavris and researcher Toby Jayaratne (1976) reported that love is "the key word—in the decision to marry, in marriage itself, in an evaluation of the success of marriage. . . . Eight out of ten women rated love more important than any other consideration in their marriage" (p. 90). In addition, women who married primarily for love reported themselves as more satisfied with their marriages than women who married primarily for other reasons—such as sex, to avoid loneliness, or for financial security.

While love may be rather "romantic," it is by no means "impractical." As Tavris and Jayaratne (1976) expressed it: "Perhaps the reason love turns out to be a sound foundation for marrying, rather than the shaky one the experts fear it to be, is that among these respondents love means more than sunshine and champagne. The women who are most satisfied with their marriages describe a relationship that is not the starry-eyed, adolescent, heaven-made version of marriage. In fact, couples who have the best relationships do admit to hacking over problems and worries and disagreeing with each other—but they disagree more or less agreeably" (p. 92). In essence, available research points to a marked tendency among Americans to put love at the center of the "marital stage."

**Companionship, fulfillment, and escape from loneliness.**    Regardless of the type of partnership they choose, most people seek **companionship** and fulfillment in their marriage. The *Redbook* survey found that companionship and fulfillment as a person ranked just behind love as main reasons for marrying. Companionship and fulfillment involve a mutual sharing of thoughts, feelings, interests, tasks, decision making, and personal growth. They also require the couple to have a high number of shared interests in which they actively participate together. Mutual love and giving are other important aspects of companionship and fulfillment.

companionship: harmonious relationship in which partners keep company with each other

Intimate relationships offer a buffer as well—especially in times of trouble—against the fear that accompanies the awareness of one's separateness from everyone else. Thus, it is not surprising that more than half of the women in the *Redbook* survey said that avoiding loneliness was a matter of some, if not pri-

# Insight

## HOW IMPORTANT TO YOUR MARRIAGE IS EACH ITEM?

When the *Redbook* survey asked 75,000 married women, "How important to your marriage is each of the following items?" They answered as shown in the figure below. Their answers led the researchers to conclude: "A large majority of wives felt that love, respect, and friendship were the most important elements in their relationship. They rated sexual compatability desirable but not essential" (Tavris & Jayaratne, 1976, p. 91).

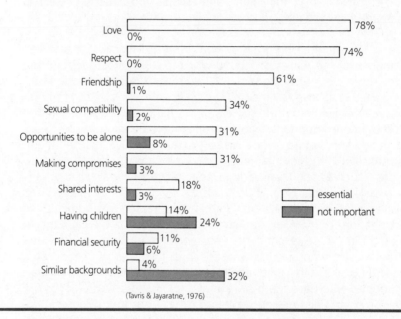

(Tavris & Jayaratne, 1976)

mary, importance in their marrying. Unfortunately, however, many marriages are entered with the hope of eliminating or avoiding loneliness as a major, if unspoken, goal—only to discover that this is usually an unsatisfactory and inadequate basis for marriage.

**Sexuality, reproduction, and child rearing.** For many people, marriage provides the only legal and moral basis for engaging in sexual relations. For example, in the past, it was generally expected the couples (particularly the women) would remain virgins until their marriage. Although this requirement is not as strongly upheld in our society today, many people find that marriage provides a highly stable and satisfying outlet for sexual urges.

Although single people of all ages can and do engage in sexual activities, the stereotype of the "swinging single" as a sexually licentious person bouncing from bed to bed is highly inaccurate. Statistics indicate that the frequency of and the satisfaction associated with sexual activity is significantly higher among married couples than among single people (Hunt, 1974). As is clear, most marriages have a highly sexual component.

Marriage also provides a legally sanctioned structure for bearing and rearing children. Until recent times, marriage was the only acceptable means through which children could be conceived, born, and reared. In fact, a woman who bore a child out of wedlock was likely to be stigmatized by society. Today, the situation has changed dramatically, with a substantial proportion of pregnancies occurring among unmarried teen-agers. Nonetheless, the majority of children are the product of a marriage.

Marriage also provides a means to rear children and guide their development. Children need food, shelter, and clothing. Adults must also take time to guide the social and emotional development of a child. Finally, adults must find a means to educate their children both in academic areas and in ethical and moral areas as well. All of these activities require a tremendous amount of energy. Not only are these tasks difficult for one parent to accomplish, but they are also adjustive demands that tax the financial and emotional resources of the parent. The presence of a partner can help lighten these responsibilities and can also provide some "time out" so that one parent can attend to his or her own needs for growth and development.

**Economic security.**    In earlier times, marriage provided a way to ensure the economic survival of the individual and the family. Women were not expected to be financially independent; marriage or spinsterhood were their only options.

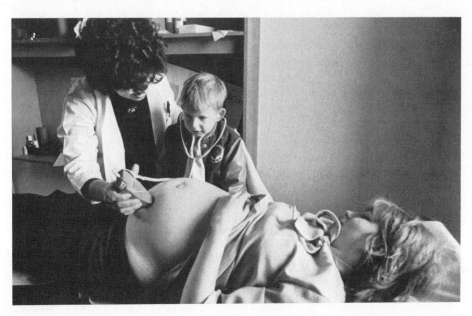

Although a couple may look forward to the birth of a baby, the arrival of children calls for enormous adjustments in marriage. No longer are the couple husband and wife only; now they must learn to combine these roles with their new roles as parents.

Similarly, the lack of retirement programs for the elderly often meant utter poverty for the couple as they grew older and became less able to work. For these couples, the only solution was to bear many children who could then help support them.

Nowadays, the increasing independence of women and the presence of social welfare programs such as Social Security make economic security a less important reason for marriage. Although "golddiggers" who marry primarily to gain the financial resources of their spouses still exist, most people can live independently. Two cannot live "as cheaply as one," but the sharing of financial resources can help couples attain economic goals—such as the purchase of a house—that each individually would find very difficult.

## Mate Selection

Each of us probably has some mental image of an ideal mate. This is not to say, however, that we hold back from marriage until we find our ideal. Environmental factors and characteristics of one's partner other than ideal qualities influence mate selection.

**What do people look for?**  Most people have definite ideas about what they are looking for in a mate and about what categories of persons are eligible or ineligible. Some individuals may be excluded automatically on the basis of age, education, race, body type, and social orientation. In addition, a whole array of personal and social factors—such as special personality needs and social pressures—may enter into the selection process. A woman may consistently look for a man who is strong and masterful or socially facile or sensitive and introspective.

**How do they select?**  Mate selection is essentially a *filtering process* in which the field of "acceptable" candidates is successively narrowed until a choice is made. In some non-Western societies, the filtering may be made by family members, as in arranged marriages. In contrast, members of Western societies normally select mates in an individual fashion and without the direct intervention of families.

One filtering model of mate selection has been described by Janda and Klenke-Hamel (1980). At first a very large field of potential candidates is available for marriage. Availability and proximity initially limit the choices that can be made (see Chapter 12). The similarity factor further limits the number of candidates.

At this point, those who are not interpersonally attracted to one another are filtered out of the process. As relationships begin to form, the couples begin evaluating each other as potential partners. The factors on which they judge their compatibility can range from the sexual to the interpersonal. Assuming that the partners assess each other as compatible, they must then decide whether the role demands and expectations that each has for the other can be met. If they can agree on their hopes and plans for the structure of a marriage, they may take the final step and marry.

# Insight

**FILTERING MODEL OF
MATE SELECTION**

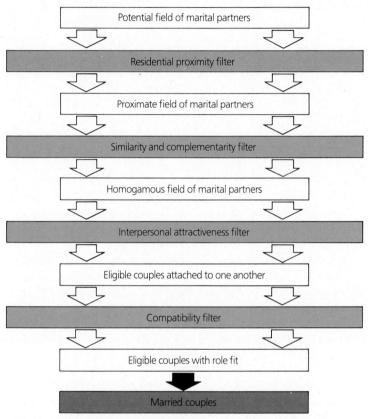

Potential field of marital partners

Residential proximity filter

Proximate field of marital partners

Similarity and complementarity filter

Homogamous field of marital partners

Interpersonal attractiveness filter

Eligible couples attached to one another

Compatibility filter

Eligible couples with role fit

Married couples

(Adapted from Janda & Klenke-Hamel, 1980)

## "LIVING HAPPILY EVER AFTER"

Once two people have made a commitment to each other, many factors come to bear upon the success of their relationship, some quite apart from all the influences that brought them together. What they make of their marriage depends upon things that enter into the daily pattern of living—their activities, their decision-making procedures, their ability to encourage each other's growth, and their ways of adjusting and accommodating to each other's needs, habits, and personalities.

In this section, we shall examine the factors that can influence the happiness of a marriage, including the adjustive demands that normally develop during the course of a marriage. Specifically, we shall examine the early years of marriage, marital conflict, sexual compatibility in marriage, and children and child rearing.

## The Early Years of Marriage

Most relationships begin with some form of courtship, in which the individuals present themselves in the most favorable light possible. With most couples, extra attention is given to behaviors and appearances that might impress or delight the other in the hope of winning love and approval. Undesirable qualities are hidden, ignored, or simply diminished in the warm glow of romance and the promise of a beautiful future. In the excitement that often accompanies the establishment of a partnership, the couple is likely to experience optimism about any possible future problems, and to expect the dramatic and tingling qualities of the relationship to continue evermore.

Unfortunately, this rosy bloom does not last forever and disappointment may set in. As we noted earlier, most successful marriages experience a lessening of romantic love but the maintenance of the less passionate but satisfying companionate form of love. Friendship, mutual respect, tolerance, and acceptance must be developed in the posthoneymoon phase of the marriage. Without the compromise and accommodation that accompany companionate love, the relationship may founder. Given the numbers of marriages that end within a few years, it is clear that many couples either fail to make such adjustments or decide that their expectations and hopes for the relationship cannot be met.

In this early phase, couples must also come to grips with some potential problem areas. Here we shall consider jealousy and possessiveness, power and control, and communication.

*"In a world where we are so at the mercy of rapid change and capricious chance, it is little wonder that we seek stability and certainty in intimate relationships, especially with the one we love most. Anything that seems likely to upset or interfere with that becomes a threat. Jealousy, most psychologists agree, is one understandable response to this situation."*
*(LOBSENZ, 1975, P. 77)*

**jealousy: hostility toward another person based on suspicions, rivalry, or other insecurities in the relationship**

**possessiveness: domination and control exerted by one individual over another**

**Jealousy and possessiveness.** The related problems of **jealousy** and **possessiveness** are common sources of conflict in marriage. Whatever draws the partner's attentions and energies away—whether it be attraction to another person, an absorbing hobby, the person's job, or even the children—may arouse jealousy. Since jealousy and possessiveness are commonly based on feelings of insecurity in the relationship, they may both indicate and complicate an already troubled marriage.

In some instances such feelings of insecurity arise suddenly in a seemingly stable relationship and catch the person off guard.

*Wendy's marital breakup affected me very deeply. I've been married for almost seven years to a man I adore. I'd never allowed myself to consider the possibility of our ever breaking up. We were so perfectly matched. Divorce was as unreal to me as the planet earth shifting out of its orbit around the sun.*

*Then, during dinner one evening, my husband in a rather whimsical way and with an enigmatic grin asked me whether I thought I could survive "if something happened to us." Sheer whimsy—sure, how sure? It got me thinking and it was disturbing. What upset me most was my emotional instability at just the thought of parting from him. It dawned on me that my entire world revolved around my marriage. If it fell to pieces, I would crumble along with it. (Butler, 1976, p. 23)*

Intense feelings of jealousy may lead to various reactions. For example, we may become possessive of our marital partners. We may deliberately break our deep emotional dependency on the relationship. Or we may attempt to strengthen the marital bonds. As might be expected, the first two alternatives are likely to lead to a less intimate and satisfying marriage, and may lead to divorce. Conversely, efforts to improve the quality and stability of the relationship, which may entail an analysis of the basis for our feelings of jealousy, may lead to constructive results and a more satisfying marriage.

**Power and control.**    A related source of potential conflict concerns the distribution of **power** within the partnership. Jay Haley (1963), psychotherapist and theorist in family relations, remarked that ". . . the major conflicts in a marriage center in the problem of who is to tell whom what to do under what circumstances. . . ."

**power: control, authority, or influence over another**

Traditionally, our society has assumed that the best marriages are those in which the husband is dominant and the wife **submissive.** Interestingly enough, however, Tavris and Jayaratne (1976) found that the happiest marriages were those in which power was shared more or less equally, while the least likely to be successful were marriages in which one spouse was dominant and the other submissive.

**submission: giving in to the authority or control of another; the condition of being humble and compliant**

Nevertheless, when two people enter an intimate relationship, some difficulties are likely to be encountered in making decisions about the roles and functions of each—and about who makes the decisions about what. And unfortunately, some couples do engage in power struggles, sometimes open and sometimes hidden. The couple who fight over whose turn it is to empty the trash may actually be battling about a more fundamental issue in their relationship.

**Ineffective communication.**    Accommodation in marriage depends heavily upon effective communication—open communication lines and the ability and willingness to use them. Without good communication, information cannot be exchanged, efforts cannot be coordinated, and the other person's feelings and reactions may not be understood. Minor misunderstandings can become major sources of resentment, and accommodation will not take place.

In a study of communication patterns in marriage, Navran (1967) found that happily married couples, as compared with unhappily married couples: *(a)* talk to each other more; *(b)* convey the feeling that they understand what is being said

Conflicts in a marriage can arise over financial problems, sexual difficulties, or disagreements about the children. Often, one of the requirements for resolving conflicts is establishing effective communication. Professional counseling can help a couple learn how to communicate effectively and thus resolve some of the problems that are threatening the relationship.

to them; *(c)* communicate about a wider range of subjects; *(d)* preserve communication channels and keep them open; *(e)* show more sensitivity to each other's feelings; *(f)* personalize their language symbols; and *(g)* make more use of supplementary nonverbal techniques of communication. The feeling that it is safe to be open and honest about one's feelings, both positive and negative, seems essential if such open communication is to take place between marital partners (Honeycutt, Wilson, & Parker, 1982; Montgomery, 1981).

Here it is of interest to allude again to the findings of Tavris and Jayaratne (1976): "The most happily married wives are those who say that *both* they and their husbands tell each other when they are displeased and thus try to work out their displeasure together by communicating in a calm and rational way. They also say that they and their husbands rarely or never fight in any of the different ways we listed; that is, they seldom resort either to the active-aggressive fighting (swearing, shouting, hitting out, crying or breaking things) or to passive-aggressive fighting (leaving the room, sulking or staying silent)" (p. 92). Conversely, it was found that the most unhappily married wives felt that they could not talk to their husbands about what was bothering them without it ending up in a fight or other misunderstanding. In short, they were caught in a vicious circle of misunderstanding.

## Marital Conflict

During courtship, partners may find that there is nothing to disagree about. In the glow of romantic love, any minor disputes that may occur are rapidly and lovingly resolved, and the partners may assume that the ease with which they now deal with problems will characterize their married life as well.

This soft-focused view of conflict resolution during courtship often gives way to the hard-edged realities of married life. In their day-to-day accommodations to each other, the partners may find that they are in disagreement on both minor issues, such as who takes out the garbage, and on major issues, such as how many children they should have. And, they will also learn that conflict resolution is not always as easy a task as it was during courtship.

**Areas of conflict.**     Although researchers disagree on which areas are the most common sources of conflict, the following eight issues are frequently mentioned areas of conflict (Knox, 1979): *(1)* Money—too little, who spends it, how it is spent, debt; *(2)* Sex—how much, when, contraceptive use, dysfunctions; *(3)* In-laws—meddling, when to visit or have visit, rejection by in-laws; *(4)* Recreation—what kind, solitary vs. family, how much time, cost; *(5)* Friends—shared vs. individual friends, resentment of time spent with friends; *(6)* Drug use—who drinks or smokes what, how much, concern over health; *(7)* Religion—little vs. major involvement, role in children's lives; and *(8)* Children—how many, when to have, type of discipline.

In each of these areas, our backgrounds and values will influence the position we take on these issues. To the highly religious person, it may seem self-evident that children should be taught strong religious values. If, however, our partner belongs to a different faith or is opposed to formal religious training, significant conflict can occur. The areas in which conflicts are likely to occur will depend heavily on individual differences and perspectives, and it is likely that the areas of conflict will change as the spouses change.

**Resolving conflict.**     Effective conflict resolution depends heavily upon effective communication. Some of the skills that have been suggested (Bach & Wyden, 1968; Knox, 1979) for resolving conflicts include:

1. *Listening effectively.* Although we may feel threatened by our partner's complaints, the first step in resolving conflicts is to listen to the complaint and acknowledge its existence. If our partner complains that we do not share in managing the family finances, our first response should not be, "I do too help with the finances!" but, "Apparently, we disagree about our finances."

2. *Giving nondefensive feedback.* Rogers (1951) has shown that rephrasing the content of our partner's complaints can indicate that we are listening and paying attention. Additionally, our feedback can clarify and limit the area of conflict. Knox (1979) gives the following example of nondefensive feedback:

*A wife told her husband, "I get upset when you go out with Ben." Her husband's feedback (what he heard) was, "You don't want me to see Ben anymore." And the wife replied, "No, I didn't say that. Saturday night is our time, and I would like you two to play handball sometime other than Saturday night." (p. 327)*

Not only can the facts of the conflict be clarified with nondefensive feedback, but the emotional tone of the conflict can be acknowledged as well. In the example above, the husband might have said, "You got angry when I went out with Ben on Saturday night." (Knox, 1979, p. 327). Using nondefensive feedback can thus define and limit the area of conflict.

3. *Staying on target.* Once an area of conflict has been identified, it is helpful for the partners to keep their focus on the conflict area and not drift into

other areas. If a husband, for example, remarks that he dislikes his wife's best friend and wishes that she would not see her friend anymore, it is more likely that this conflict can be successfully resolved if the partners focus on the wife's friendship than if the husband adds, ''And, by the way, I also don't like the way you're wearing your hair these days.'' Straying from the topic invites retaliation from the partner and lessens the chances that the immediate conflict can be resolved.

4. *Specifying behaviors to change.* Providing a partner with specific, clear suggestions for behavioral change is very helpful in resolving conflicts. Vague, ambiguous, or general requests are difficult to fulfill. For example, the request to ''be more considerate'' is subject to a number of interpretations. However, if the partner makes the request specific—''When you fix yourself a snack at night, I want you to ask me if I would like a snack, too.'' (Knox, 1979)—the request can be fulfilled.

Some marital partners feel that their spouses should be mind readers. ''I shouldn't have to tell her. She should be able to figure it out.'' This belief places the partner in the awkward position of knowing that the other is unhappy, of knowing that change is desired, but not knowing what areas to change. Again, specific suggestions can allow the individual to carry out the desired acts.

5. *Not expecting immediate solutions or immediate results.* Some difficult problems will need more than a few minutes to resolve, and some solutions will need a long time to become effective. If we insist on immediate resolution of problems and equally rapid implementation of the solution, we will likely be disappointed. Often, issues of values and goals will be among those that are most difficult to resolve.

As we have suggested, there is a middle ground between the brooding, destructive effects of excessive niceness and the outbursts of uncontrolled anger. However, we should note that not all conflicts will be resolved. Depending on the depth of conflict, these unresolved issues can produce very little disturbance to the relationship or they can ultimately lead to a breakup of the relationship through separation and divorce.

## Sexual Compatibility in Marriage

It is commonly assumed that both partners in a marriage will find satisfaction in their sexual relationship. However, the partners may disagree about their preferences for certain sexual behaviors. And, sexual difficulties in marriage may be a source of distress, recrimination, and self-blame.

**sexual compatibility: degree to which sexual activity is mutually satisfying to both partners**

The importance of **sexual compatibility**, however, may vary considerably from one couple to another. Tavris and Jayaratne (1976) found that sexual compatibility ranked fourth behind love, respect, and friendship as the most important element in the marital relationships of the wives they studied. Nevertheless, in this age of the ''obligatory orgasm,'' sexual compatibility plays an important role in marriage. For example, Fisher (1973) found that women who reported

# Insight

As might be expected, there are a number of common misconceptions concerning the emotionally involved topic of marriage. Listed here are some popularly held myths about marriage.

1. Love can guarantee a happy marriage.

2. Children tend to stabilize an unhappy marriage.

3. Marriages among younger people are likely to be happier than those among older people.

4. Wives who are strongly religious usually experience less sexual satisfaction and happiness in marriage.

5. Arranged marriages are much less happy than those based on love.

6. People who seek counseling or psychotherapy rarely do so for marital problems.

happier marriages were more consistent in attaining orgasms than women who reported less happy marriages.

We should also be careful to note that sexual compatibility and satisfaction cannot be divorced from other aspects of a couple's relationship. Satisfying marital relationships may both foster and be enhanced by sexual satisfaction, while unsatisfying marital relationships may decrease both the frequency and enjoyment of sexual activity (Edwards & Booth, 1976).

## Children and Child Rearing

It has become popular to write articles proclaiming that the family is on its way out, dying, or dead. Like Mark Twain's statement that reports of his death had been "greatly exaggerated," those of us who were raised in families and plan families of our own may find such claims excessive. Giving birth and raising children to be competent, healthy persons is a notable achievement and can be a source of pride and fulfillment. And a majority of married couples today appear to want and do have children.

The advent of a child launches the married couple on a new career—parenthood—that may last for some twenty years. This new career brings changes in living routines, social roles, and the husband-and-wife relationship.

**Role changes.**   For the mother in particular, the advent of the baby is likely to lead to a drastic change in everyday activities. She may feel that she has suddenly undertaken a new twenty-four-hour-a-day job. If she had expected to fit the baby into an already full schedule, she may find that caring for a baby is far more time consuming than she realized and that she has little time or energy for anything else.

The woman's transition from the role of "wife" to that of "mother" has

Grandparents, as well as other members of the extended family, can supplement the nurturing that parents provide for their children.

numerous implications for the marital relationship. The husband must often face the difficult adjustment of recognizing that his wife now has less time and energy to devote to meeting his needs. He must recognize that he must now share her love and attention while attempting to respond to her need for extra emotional support and physical help. When the husband feels that he is being neglected and left out, considerable strain may be placed on the marriage. Similarly, when the wife feels that her husband does not help with household duties or child care or does not fully appreciate the fatigue that accompanies the care of an infant, an additional source of strain on the relationship can develop.

In some societies, certain factors help to bolster the stability of individual marriages and ease child rearing. One of these factors is the **extended family**—a family who maintains contact with a wide circle of relatives. Aunts and uncles, cousins, and grandparents—all can supplement the physical and emotional resources of the **nuclear family**—a husband, a wife, and their children. Other environmental supports may include a stable social structure and clear, consistent expectations for both husbands and wives. But in our complex and rapidly changing society, married couples have few such external supports and are largely on their own. And easier divorce laws, the decreasing influence of religion, and an abundance of adult models—often including both friends and parents—who have been divorced make it easier for people to consider divorce a solution to the problems of adjusting to marriage and child rearing.

**extended family:** relatives other than parents and their children, all of whom maintain contact with one another

**nuclear family:** parents and their children

**The empty nest.** Studies indicate that even in good marriages, the level of marital satisfaction tends to decrease during child-rearing years and to improve when the children are grown (Glenn & McLanahan, 1982; Waldron & Routh, 1981). It appears that it is less fun to be raising a family than to have it done.

Once the children have left the family home, the couple faces a new series of adjustive demands. Some couples will examine their relationship and rediscover in each other the reasons for which they originally married. For example, one couple may find that they still share a love for classical music and jazz, a love that was often submerged in the insistent beat of the music preferred by their children. Similarly, a couple may find that their desires for travel can now be fulfilled.

On the other hand, some couples will find that the children's leaving home also results in the disappearance of the reason for continuing the relationship. In these situations, the couple remained together solely "for the children's sake." Once the children have left, the couple finds the relationship untenable, and it may dissolve.

Many couples use their new-found time and financial resources to revitalize their relationship and to increase their opportunities for individual personal growth. Like any other relationship, the husband-wife relationship is subject to constant change—both short-term and long-term. Periods of closeness may be followed by periods of emotional distance, excitement by calm, and growth by stagnation. These short-term changes take place in the context of long-term change and its effects on the nature and stability of the marriage.

A crucial problem here is the challenge both partners face in adjusting to change and growth in the other. Since one partner does not ordinarily change and grow at the same time or in the same areas as the other, this poses a difficult challenge—that of being supportive and maintaining closeness while experiencing change both in one's self and one's partner.

In our complex and rapidly changing world, marital happiness is not something that, once achieved, can be counted on to continue indefinitely. Rather couples must be willing to work to continue achieving happiness.

# DIVORCE AND REMARRIAGE

*"For every two couples who will take the big step to the altar this year, there will be a man and woman somewhere else in the U.S. who have found marriage to be one of life's most painful and wrenching experiences. They will be getting divorced."*
*("TODAY'S MARRIAGES," 1975, P. 35)*

The divorce rate in the United States has shown a dramatic increase in the past half century. One in seven marriages ended in divorce in 1920, compared with one in four in 1960 and one in three in 1974. The ratio is now approaching one

**divorce: legal end or dissolution of a marriage**

**separation: agreement between spouses to cease living together; often a prelude to divorce**

in two. Moreover, these figures do not include the substantial number of married couples who separate without bothering to get a divorce.

Of course, **divorce** and **separation** statistics do not tell the whole story about the incidence of unhappiness and maladjustment in marriages. Many unhappily married couples stay together because of religious or financial considerations, reluctance to disrupt the lives of their children, fear of not being able to do any better on a second try, or simply habit or lethargy. Thus, many of the marriages that end in divorce may have been as happy as or even happier than some of those that endure.

## Causes of Divorce

Many factors undoubtedly combine to account for our high divorce rate. These factors include characteristics of the two people involved and of the pattern of interaction between them and the conditions in the social setting.

**Reasons given for divorce.**   In one of the few large-scale studies available, Levinger (1966) examined the counseling records of 600 couples applying for divorce and compared the complaints of husbands and wives of middle-class and lower-class couples. Husbands complained of mental cruelty, neglect of home and children, infidelity, and sexual incompatibility. Complaints most often made by the wives were of physical and mental cruelty, financial problems, and drinking. In general, the middle-class couples were more concerned with psychological and emotional satisfactions while the lower-class couples were more concerned with financial problems and the physical actions of their partners.

The reasons for divorce today have probably changed somewhat as a result of changing roles and expectations in marriage. Thus, we might expect that lack of compatibility, intimacy, and love would loom large, followed by the usual assortment of financial, sexual, and in-law problems, as well as interpersonal conflict. Delving more deeply, we might find that unrealistic expectations and failure to invest the effort necessary to make the marriage work were basic underlying factors leading to divorce.

**General social change.**   As we have seen, most of our traditional values and social structures have been challenged in recent years. Mobility, instability, and change appear to be both commonplace and expected—both in our society and in our personal lives. And our high standard of living has raised our expectations for satisfactions of all kinds, including those by which we measure the acceptability of a marital relationship. It is also possible that marriages based on love and emotional need fulfillment are inherently more hazardous than those based on economic and other pragmatic considerations, where the conditions that give rise to the marriage help to maintain it.

Modern urbanization and the rise of the nuclear family have removed many of the supports and the help that tend to be available to the extended family living in a less hurried, less impersonal, more stable social network. At the same

# Insight

## SUMMARY OF BACKGROUND FACTORS RELATED TO DIVORCE

**Educational level**

The lower the educational level, the higher the divorce rate.

**Occupational status**

Divorce more common among lower socio-economic groups than among professional groups.

**Family background**

Higher divorce rate among couples raised in unhappy homes and/or by divorced parents.

**Racial background**

Nonwhite marriages more divorce-prone than white marriages at all educational and occupational levels.

**Religion**

Higher divorce rates among nonchurchgoers.

**Length of courtship**

Divorce rates higher for those with brief courtships.

**Age at time of marriage**

Divorce rates very high for those marrying in their teens.

**Factors not related to divorce rate**

Interracial, mixed religion, sexual experience prior to marriage, age difference between spouses.

---

time, occupational opportunities for women have given wives caught in unhappy marriages an alternative to continuing the marriage. Better opportunities for remarriage may also influence their decision. And with less stringent divorce laws and less stigma attached to divorced people, there is wider acceptance of divorce as a means to resolve an unsatisfactory marital situation. All these factors make stable, satisfying marriages more difficult and separation more attractive when expectations are not met.

Unfortunately, the rate and complexity of social change, with all its implications for mate selection and marital happiness, have not been matched by preparation of young people in realistic expectations or in the attitudes and skills needed for a stable and satisfying marriage in this kind of society. A great deal of misery and many wasted years might be avoided by more adequately preparing young people for both choosing and living with a mate.

In any case, American marriages today are undertaken against a cultural background which places an increasingly heavy burden on the marital partners for establishing stability and meeting each other's psychological needs. And as society's stake in stable families has come to be regarded as secondary to the individuals' happiness—in marked contrast to the priorities established in many other cultural groups—the way appears to be paved for a continued high incidence of marital failure.

## Effects of Divorce

*"Divorce is a disorganizing and reorganizing process in a family with children. The process extends over time, often several years. Although it has, like most life events and crises, the potential for growth and new integrations, the road is often rocky and tortuous and many people underestimate the vicissitudes and difficulties of the transition."*
**(WALLERSTEIN & KELLY, 1977, P. 5)**

The specific effects of divorce upon the married couple depend upon many factors, such as the emotional involvement of the partners, the happiness and duration of the marriage prior to divorce, the opportunities for remarriage, and the stress tolerance and other personality characteristics of both partners.

Divorce is often interpreted as a sign of failure, and divorced persons often feel that they have failed in one of life's most important tasks. Following a divorce, many people experience a sense of personal inadequacy, disillusionment, and depression. Often they are torn by self-recrimination and thoughts of what they might have done that would have made their marriage a success.

Divorced persons are likely to face difficult adjustments brought about by changes in their life situations. They may have to cope with loss of security, guilt and self-recrimination, the cessation or disruption of sexual satisfactions, and financial problems. Feelings of alienation and loneliness may add to the stress. Where the divorce was sought by the other partner, a sense of having been rejected usually leads to feelings of hurt and self-devaluation. Even for the partner who sought the divorce, the stress of divorce and readjustment may bring more severe problems than those from which he or she was trying to escape.

Bohannan (1972) has analyzed the enormously complex and overlapping experiences which divorce brings; he terms them the "six stations of divorce":

1. *The emotional divorce.* This occurs when spouses withhold emotion from their relationship because they dislike the intensity or ambivalence of their feelings. The couple grows mutually antagonistic. The natural response to the loss of a meaningful relationship is grief. Yet, Bohannan notes, the grief has to be worked out alone.

2. *The legal divorce.* The couple makes a public declaration that their marriage has ended. Although "no fault" divorces and marital dissolution have made this step simpler, the parties normally consult lawyers and must often appear in court—often an emotional, humiliating, and anxiety-provoking experience.

3. *The economic divorce.* This aspect of divorce involves the settling of property and the division of assets and may involve many painful aspects including loss of wealth and support.

4. *The coparental divorce.* This aspect of divorce centers around the children—custody and visitation rights—and affects not only the children (who often feel that they have been divorced by one parent or the other), but also the spouses, since the family unit changes unalterably. The loss of the relationship with the children, or the prospect of raising the children alone may, of course, be very painful experiences for the parents.

The dissolution of a marriage can be stressful for both parents and children. The parents often have to learn how to function not only as single persons but as single parents as well. Children may have to learn to adjust to a new style of family life—the single-parent home.

5. *The community divorce.* The spouses experience the loss of friends and, often, of community ties, in addition to the other losses occasioned by divorce.

6. *The psychic divorce.* "Psychic divorce means the separation of self from the personality and the influence of the ex-spouse. . . . " The issue of gaining new autonomy and becoming once again whole and complete may be one of the most difficult of the six aspects, but also potentially the most personally constructive.

In their five-year study of sixty divorced families, Wallerstein and Kelly (1976) not only found that divorce is an extremely disorganizing process in a family but that: ". . . we may reasonably expect a period of several years of disequilibrium before new, more gratifying job, social, and sexual relationships can become stable enough to provide comfort and a renewed sense of continuity. . . . It is important to keep in mind that two or three years of disequilibrium in the life of a child may represent a significant proportion of his entire life experience. . . . Therefore, the parent's functioning following the divorce, especially in the instance of the young child, is of crucial importance in the child's continued development. . ." (p. 5). Although older children and adolescents were found to be less dependent on the custodial parent, it was found that the youth's capacity to maintain his or her developmental stride was "related inversely to the (custodial) parent's need to lean heavily on the child for emotional and social sustenance and to involve the child in continuing battles and recriminations with the divorced spouse" (p. 5).

In essence, divorce typically involves difficult adjustments for children as well as parents. The magnitude of this problem is indicated by the finding that in the United States, one child in six under the age of eighteen lives in a one-parent home. Usually the custodial parent is the mother, due to her traditional role in childbearing. The short-term effects upon children may vary considerably depending upon age, the effectiveness of the custodial parent, and success in alleviating feelings of rejection and insecurity—the fear of "what will happen to me?" The long-term effects may also vary markedly, even being favorable in some instances when compared to remaining in a home torn by marital conflict and dissension.

## Remarriage

*"But one lives and loves, suffers and forgets, and begins again—perhaps even thinking that this time, this new time, is to be permanent."*
**(CLARK E. MOUSTAKAS)**

In colonial times nearly all remarriages were of widowed persons, but in recent decades there has been a gradually swelling tide of remarriages of those who have been divorced. Overall about 75 percent of divorced women and 80 percent of divorced men remarry within two to five years. Remarriages occur, on the average, about two and a half years after the divorce.

**Reasons for remarriage.**    Both societal pressures and individual needs steer divorced persons toward remarriage. A divorced mother may be encouraged to remarry because, she is told, the children need two parents in the home. Divorced persons often feel awkward in the company of married friends. Both divorced men and women may find themselves incapable of handling all the responsibilities of maintaining a household for themselves and their children. Factors such as these, together with the need for affection, adult companionship, and sexual intimacy lead many divorced persons to seek new marital partners.

In considering remarriage, there are often new factors to be weighed: a woman who has children from a previous marriage may be concerned about how her children will accept their prospective stepfather and how he will relate to them. A man considering remarriage may have financial responsibility for children of a former marriage. If he pays alimony and child support, he may not be in a position to assume the financial responsibilities of another family. The individual may also be strongly motivated by a need to overcome the emotional hurt and self-devaluation from the prior divorce. The possibility that one may be marrying "on the rebound" is a factor to be considered carefully.

**How successful are remarriages?**    Do second marriages have a better chance of success than first marriages? Has the divorced person's past experience taught him or her how to avoid the common pitfalls in marriage, or should earlier failure be taken as a sign that the person is a poor marital risk? The research evidence is both scanty and contradictory. In general, however, it appears "that remarriages of divorced persons which do not quickly end in divorce probably are, as a whole, almost as successful as intact first marriages" (Glenn & Weaver, 1977, p. 331). Marriages in which one or both of the spouses have had multiple prior marriages are probably least stable. But there are many exceptions, and each marriage has to be evaluated on its own merits.

Although more remarriages than first marriages end in divorce, many remarried persons find that their second marriages are much happier than their first. Udry (1966) has suggested several possible reasons:

*There are many factors which contribute to the satisfaction which people find in second marriages after divorce. The divorced person has probably learned something about marriage from the first failure. If age contributes anything to maturity, he should be able to make a more mature choice the second time. The significance of sex is transformed, since it can be more taken for granted in the approach to second marriage. Second marriages have the advantage of being compared with a marriage which recently ended in bitterness and conflict. The second time around, the first-time loser has probably readjusted his expectations of marriage and is simply easier to please than those without previous marital experience. (p. 521)*

Whether or not divorced persons learn from their failure, and regardless of the odds against them, the potential rewards of the marital relationship appear to lead most divorced persons to try again. Apparently we do not easily abandon our romantic dream of "living happily ever after."

## ALTERNATIVES TO MARRIAGE

Although culturally desirable and individually popular, marriage is not the only means by which people can develop satisfying interpersonal or intimate relationships. Perhaps two of the most popular alternatives to marriage are cohabitation and singlehood.

### Cohabitation

**Cohabitation,** or living together without marriage, is the fastest growing alternative to traditional marriage in the United States. In the mid-1960s a woman student made the front page of the *New York Times* because she shared her living quarters and bed with a man. More recent studies, however, have suggested that the incidence of cohabitation ranges from about 20 percent to 35 percent of college students (Cole, 1977).

Much of the impetus for living together stems from a number of sources (Knox, 1979). One major factor is changing sexual norms. In the past, a couple who lived together without marriage were likely to be lower-class, uneducated individuals who were "shacking up," and the woman who engaged in these activities was looked upon with disfavor. However, the replacement of the dou-

**cohabitation:** process involving emotional commitments and living arrangements similar to marriage but without a formal or legal announcement of marriage

# Insight

### "WILL YOU BE MY POSSLQ?"

When the U.S. Census Bureau developed the acronym POSSLQ, or Persons of the Opposite Sex Sharing Living Quarters, to describe people who cohabitated, newsman Charles Osgood penned this whimsical poem:

*Come live with me and be my love,*
*And we will some new pleasures prove*
*Of golden sands and crystal brooks*
*With silken lines and silver hooks.*

*There's nothing that I wouldn't do*
*If you would be my POSSLQ.*
*You live with me, and I with you,*
*And you will be my POSSLQ.*
*I'll be your friend and so much more;*
*That's what a POSSLQ is for.*

*And everything we will confess;*
*Yes, even to the IRS.*
*Someday, on what we both may earn,*
*Perhaps we'll file a joint return.*
*You'll share my pad, my taxes joint.*
*You'll share my life—up to a point!*
*And that you'll be so glad to do,*
*Because you'll be my POSSLQ.*

*Come live with me and be my love,*
*And share the pain and pleasure of*
*The blessed continuity,*
*Official POSSLQuity.*
*And I will whisper in your ear*
*That word you love so much to hear.*
*And love will stay forever new,*
*If you will be my POSSLQ.*

---

**permissiveness with affection: standard allowing sexual activity to occur between individuals only if each feels a deep sense of affection for the other**

ble standard with a standard of **permissiveness with affection** (Reiss, 1976) and the availability of effective contraceptive methods has removed much of the worry and stigma of living together.

There is also a growing number of elderly people who are cohabiting as well. While a sexual element is typically very strong in young cohabiting couples, the major reason for cohabiting among the elderly appears to be companionship. Although many cohabiting elderly would like to marry their partners, the couple may suffer a financial loss if they do so, since some retirement plans reduce benefits to an individual if he or she marries.

Despite their aversion to official marriage, cohabiting partners share a relationship strikingly similar to that of married partners. People who live together are as affectionate toward, concerned about, and supportive of their partners as are married couples. Cohabiting couples, on the other hand, are not as sure of the future of the relationship as are married couples. And while cohabiting couples believe that ending their relationship would be easier and less troublesome than dissolving a marriage, the breakup of a cohabiting relationship is probably as difficult and stressful as is divorce for married couples.

Not surprisingly, the personal characteristics of cohabiting individuals differ significantly from those of noncohabiting individuals. Cohabiting persons tend to be less involved in organized religion, have a liberal life-style, and be friends of other cohabitants. On the other hand, those who live together do not differ from noncohabitants in terms of grades, the perceived happiness of their parents' marriages, the educational or occupational status of their parents, or whether they

Some couples participate in a wedding ceremony to give public affirmation to their commitment to marriage. Other couples may choose not to have such a ceremony, although they may still share a warm, caring, intimate relationship with each other.

came from urban or rural backgrounds. Although cohabitation is often seen by the couple as preparation for marriage, studies reveal that cohabitants who eventually married are not different from couples who did not live together prior to marriage (Hanna & Knaub, 1981; Risman, Hill, Rubin, & Peplau, 1981).

Like other aspects of intimate interpersonal relationships, the decision to live together can have both positive and negative effects. On the positive side, people can get to know their partners well and can share in their lives. On the other hand, cohabiting partners can use their relationships as a means to shock their parents and other family members. Additionally, cohabiting individuals may use the relationship to avoid long-term emotional commitments to their partners. In essence, an individual can use the relationship to satisfy his or her own needs while manipulating the feelings and emotions of the partner.

Although cohabitation is increasingly popular, the differences between married and cohabiting partners are becoming smaller. As we have seen, the personal and emotional factors in most cohabiting relationships are similar to those in marriage. And the successful prosecution of "palimony" suits suggests that even the legal distinctions between living together and marriage are disappearing as well. Regardless of legal status, the relationship between the partners remains a key factor in determining the quality of an intimate relationship.

## Singlehood

**singlehood: life-style stressing the positive aspects of being unmarried**

At any one time, about one-third of adult Americans are single (Libby, 1977). The largest proportion of these are the never-married, followed by separated and divorced singles, and by widowed singles. Of the never-married, the large majority eventually become married. But an increasing number of people see **singlehood** as a life-style in its own right, not as just a way station to matrimony.

For those who see singlehood as a positive alternative to marriage, singlehood offers many advantages. Some of the ones that are most commonly mentioned include freedom to travel, to come and go as the individual pleases, to seek friendships and sexual experiences, and to have no responsibilities to anyone else (Nadelson & Notman, 1981).

Of course, some people use singlehood as a means to avoid marriage. Perhaps they or their parents had a bad marriage. Perhaps they do not want to be answerable to a spouse or children. Or, perhaps, they simply do not feel ready to marry and need more time to develop their interests and careers. Finally, there may not be suitable partners available for marriage. This is especially true of elderly widows.

Many people use singlehood as a way to develop their sense of autonomy and self-worth. For these individuals the ability to "make it" on their own can be a tremendous source of pride and can lead to personal growth.

## SUMMARY

1. There are many different types of love, and they range from the nonsexual *agape* to the sexual *eros*. We can also distinguish between romantic (passionate) love and companionate love. The types of love between people change as the relationship changes. Love, like other emotions, seems to consist of physiological arousal and a cognitive label. Although it is hard to describe the feelings of love, there are some nonverbal cues that we can look for. Finally, women and men experience love and liking in somewhat different ways.

2. Marriage and intimate relationships are changing, as psychological need fulfillment becomes increasingly important to the growth and maintenance of a long-term relationship. The challenges that are being made in our assumptions about these relationships are many: permanence, fidelity, and sex roles are all being called into question.

3. People have many reasons for marrying, but the most important is love. They select their mates based on the principles of interpersonal attraction discussed in Chapter 12 and on a filtering process in which potential candidates are eliminated.

4. Once married, people must adapt to the changing demands of the relationship. In the early years of marriage, issues of jealousy, power, and communication must be dealt with. The couple must work out conflicts and achieve a satisfying sexual relationship. Couples must also deal with issues of children and child rearing and prepare for the time when children leave home.

5. A very substantial proportion of marriages are not successful and end in divorce, and the reasons for divorce range from personal dissatisfactions to general social change. For most people, divorce is a painful process, but the large majority of divorced people eventually remarry, many successfully.

6. Finally, marriage is not the only means through which people develop intimate relationships. Some people choose cohabitation or singlehood as alternatives to marriage.

# Chapter 15

# Work and Leisure

*"Without work all life goes rotten. But when work is soulless, life stifles and dies."*
*(ALBERT CAMUS)*

Work is one of the most basic of all human institutions. Its importance stems not only from its necessity to survival, but also from the philosophical, moral, religious, political, and psychological significance attributed to it over the centuries.

An adequate definition of work must include more than the idea of "paid employment," for this concept ignores many of work's social and psychological aspects. Moreover, the woman who spends eight or ten hours a day in cooking, cleaning, laundering, marketing, and child care does not receive a salary for her labors but works nonetheless. Therefore, we will define **work** in agreement with the Special Task Force on Work in America (1972) as "an activity that produces something of value for other people." Similarly, the use of leisure time is becoming increasingly important. A historic transition is taking place in the workplace which will profoundly affect both work and leisure—quite possibly leading to greater leisure and closer ties between work and leisure (Brown, 1982).

In modern America, work is an activity that takes a major portion of the time of most adults. And while the types of work and the hours per week devoted to it may change, most people can anticipate spending some forty years of their lives working with an increasing amount of time available for leisure. Thus, it seems important to consider: *(a)* the function of work and its changing significance in our lives, *(b)* occupational choice and adjustment, and *(c)* issues related to leisure.

**work: any activity that produces something of value for other people**

## THE FUNCTION OF WORK

The word *work* conjures up odious images of toil, effort, energy-sapping activity that one *must* do. It is usually assumed that work is something few people do willingly, that everyone would prefer other activities if it weren't for financial necessity. This viewpoint, however widespread, neglects many crucial psychological aspects of work. Moreover, our views of work have changed considerably over the past decades. Today, people expect more from work than economic reward.

### The Puritan Work Ethic

The Puritan concept that work was both necessary for survival and a duty and virtue in and of itself has dominated our culture since Captain John Smith presumably told the early settlers those "who will not work shall not eat." In those times, work, thrift, and self-denial were considered basic virtues.

But much as we have come to view marriage as far more than a simple economic necessity and basis for raising children, so too have we come to demand more of work than simply "doing a job" and "making a living." The questioning of the **Puritan work ethic** has been vividly described by Studs Terkel (1974) in his book *Working:* "For the many, there is a hardly concealed discontent. The blue-collar blues is more bitterly sung than the white-collar moan. 'I'm a machine,' says the spot welder. 'I'm caged,' says the bank teller, and echoes the hotel clerk. 'I'm a mule,' says the steelworker. 'A monkey can do what I do,' says the receptionist. 'I'm less than a farm implement,' says the migrant worker. 'I'm an object,' says the high-fashion model. Blue collar and white call upon the identical phrase 'I'm a robot' " (p. xiv).

We are again reminded here of the concept of a hierarchy of needs. As basic needs are met in one's work—such as an adequate wage, job security, and working safety—higher needs emerge. Thus, people are increasingly seeking jobs that are interesting and meaningful and that provide opportunities for responsible participation, creativity, and fulfillment. As we shall see, these needs are important not only to white-collar and professional individuals, but to blue-collar workers as well.

## Work and Self-Expression

The economic functions of work are obvious: people work to support themselves and their families. As important as this function is, however, there are also enormously significant personal and social functions of work.

1. *Personal identity.* To a large extent, people become what they do. Asking someone, "Who are you?" almost invariably elicits occupational responses, such as "I am a lawyer," or "I work for Lockheed," or "I am a homemaker." In view of the vast amounts of time and energy devoted to one's job, this is not surprising, and is certainly one of the more salient means of identifying one's self in our society.

> Puritan work ethic: historically, a Christian concept of work as a duty and a virtue in itself; hard work as a sign of righteousness

> Economic rewards are not the only satisfactions people seek in work. Many people also look upon their work as an opportunity for challenge, growth, creativity, and fulfillment.

2. *Self-esteem.* Closely related to personal identity is the function of work for self-evaluation. Work has the capacity to assure the individual of his or her ability to master self and environment. Most work situations provide continual feedback about one's ability to perform satisfactorily. Work can also provide a sense that one is valued by society, that one is doing something which needs to be done, and that the product, whether material or service, is valued by others. To the degree that we take pride in the quality and significance of our work, self-esteem may be enhanced.

3. *Social role.* Sociologists note that one of the major determinants of status in our society is occupation. Indeed, the entire family typically takes on the status of the job held by the head of the household. Additionally, the social role helps regulate our interpersonal contacts and life experiences.

Since work is an important source of personal identity, self-esteem, and social position, several implications follow. People who cannot find employment or who are forced to retire at an arbitrary age are denied an important source of identity and worth. And the people who work in low-status jobs may experience severe self-devaluation. The poor and unemployed—regardless of race or sex— identify their self-esteem and adequacy with work to the same extent as the nonpoor and employed.

Research evidence supports the importance of these noneconomic functions of work. In one study, a cross section of workers were asked if they would continue working if they received an inheritance that would permit them to live comfortably without working. Fully 80 percent of the respondents replied that they would continue working (Morse & Weiss, 1955). And, as we noted in Chapter 4, retirement is one of the predictable crises of adult life (Sheehy, 1976).

Many people believe that they would not only feel lost and useless but would go "crazy" if they didn't have a job. As a woman in her thirties remarked: "Everyone needs to feel they have a place in the world. It would be unbearable not to. I don't like to feel superfluous. One needs to be needed. I'm saying being idle and leisured, doing nothing, is tragic and disgraceful. Everyone must have an occupation" (Terkel, 1974, p. 554). Research has also revealed many suggestive links between occupational satisfaction and mental and physical health—in addition to broader areas such as family stability and useful community participation (Hornung & McCullough, 1981; Terkel, 1980).

## Occupational Roles for the Sexes

Work is a reality for both sexes. Over 44 million women and over 62 million men in the United States hold jobs. The search for self-fulfillment and the increasing pressures of inflation have led many women to combine a paid job with the roles of wife, mother, and homemaker. In fact, one of the most remarkable changes in our society has been the marked increase in the number of married women who work outside the home. In 1960, for example, 30 percent of all wives were in the labor force. By 1980, the number had grown to about 50 percent. Of that number, 14 million were working mothers.

# Insight

### FACTS ABOUT WOMEN AND WORK

| | |
|---|---|
| Number of workers in U.S. labor force | Over 106 million |
| Number of women in U.S. labor force | Over 44 million |
| Number of wives who work outside home | About 50 percent |
| Number of mothers of school-age children who work outside home | Over 60 percent |
| Number of women living alone, most of whom work to support themselves | Over 9 million |
| Number of different types of jobs | Over 40 thousand |
| Number of jobs that do *not* require a higher degree | Over 85 percent |
| Number of so-called prestige jobs held by women, e.g., in law, medicine, engineering | About 1 in 6 |
| Number of women in service jobs, nurturing tasks (e.g., nursing), assistance roles | About 9 out of 10 |
| Women entering college who plan a career in business, engineering, law, or medicine | About 1 in 6 |

(Department of Labor & Census Bureau)

Additional data: The main marital problem for working wives: to get husbands to help with household duties

The number of women who work in fields once dominated by men has also grown. Women now successfully work as welders, construction workers, and professional athletes. By the same token, men are now working in fields that were once almost exclusively the domain of women. Men are employed as elementary school teachers, telephone operators, and nurses. Choice of **occupation** is increasingly a matter of choice and aptitude, not sex. As the traditional divisions between man's work and woman's work continue to crumble, it will probably become apparent that self-direction is a crucial factor in occupational choice and adjustment for both sexes.

**occupation: work activity for which one may receive wages or salary**

## CHOOSING AN OCCUPATION

As we have noted, people seek a great deal from their jobs in terms of good psychological conditions as well as good physical working conditions. Hence, the issue of occupational choice is a critical one, which most young people take very seriously. In this section we shall consider factors affecting job choice as well as factors affecting the individual's satisfaction and success in his or her chosen work.

## Choosing the "Right" Occupation

**career: work activity in which continuous personal or professional advancement and growth is expected; a profession**

**Career** choice is something relatively new. In earlier times—and in many other societies today—most people had their choices made for them or were at best severely limited in what they could choose. Of necessity, most males followed what their fathers had done or entered whatever apprenticeship training was available to them in their communities. Women remained in the home. Today, people have a choice of careers, within the range of their abilities and preparations. Thus, we need to examine both the characteristics of the individual and the characteristics of the occupation as they relate to career choice.

**Characteristics of the individual.** Three issues appear to be of particular significance from the standpoint of personal characteristics:

1. *What does the individual want to do?* The answer to this question involves interests, motives, and values. Does the individual like to work with people? With ideas? With things? Does the person prefer a leisurely pace or thrive on pressures and deadlines? Another relevant question concerns what the individual would like the occupational experience to help him or her become.

2. *What can the individual do—or learn to do?* The answer to this question involves abilities and aptitudes. What knowledge and skills does the person possess? What is the individual's potential for acquiring further competence in particular areas? What special abilities, such as artistic, athletic, or mechanical skills, does he or she possess? Does the individual have any special physical or mental limitations that might rule out a particular occupational area?

3. *What economic pressures does the individual face?* Economic issues can have an effect on career choice. For example, the cost of a college education is often a significant burden for many families, and many students must work during their college years. As a result, these economic pressures may cause the student to prematurely foreclose occupational opportunities and seek safe, available, but possibly uninteresting or unchallenging careers.

**Characteristics of the occupation.** Here, three general questions appear to be relevant:

1. *What are the requirements and working conditions?* What training and skills are needed? What general personal qualities—such as initiative, social competence, a particular temperament, or physical endurance—are required? What would the individual be doing? In what kind of setting? Equally important, how do these requirements fit what the individual has to offer and what he or she enjoys doing?

Here it may be emphasized that work activities and conditions within a broad occupational category may vary greatly. For example, a farmer may need special-

To make a wise career decision, we must know both what we can bring to a particular occupation and what the occupation offers us. Our career decisions may also be affected by the economic realities and pressures facing us.

ized agricultural skills for planting and may also need mechanical skills for repairing tractors and other farm equipment.

2. *What does the occupation have to offer?* What rewards and satisfactions can be expected in terms of income, social status, and opportunities for advancement and personal growth? Are the rewards and satisfactions the kind the person wants? Will the individual find the work interesting and personally fulfilling? What can he or she expect to contribute?

3. *What changes are likely to occur in the field?* Since today's college students will be working well into the twenty-first century, the question of future trends in one's chosen occupational area is a relevant one. With the accelerating rate of technological and social change, major shifts in many occupations are taking place even in relatively short periods of time. Thus, it is important that the individual not only gain a clear view of given occupations as they now exist but also know about probable changes in the near and distant future that might affect his or her work.

**Stages in the selection of an occupation.** An occupational choice may not be made until the individual reaches late adolescence or early adulthood. But prior to this time, many decisions have been made that have lead toward or away from given occupations. Long before the first job, he or she has developed ideas about the function of work and attitudes toward different kinds of work. Similarly, early work experiences, exposure to positive (or negative) models, and the training and education the individual has received help point the way to some field of work. Thus, career choice is a developmental process: the groundwork for it has been laid in many kinds of experiences long before the final, explicit choice is made. Investigators have pointed to three stages in career choice (Ginzberg, 1966):

**fantasy period:** first stage of occupational selection in which choices are based on fantasy, not fact or ability

- *Stage I. Fantasy period.* For most children, this period extends until about age eleven. In the **fantasy period,** children do not relate occupational choice to their intellectual and personal qualifications or to realistic opportunities. Rather, they tend to assume that they can become whatever they want to become— whether it be a police officer, a model, an astronaut, or a nurse. Children try out many occupational roles in their play, often identifying with the occupation of their father or mother or other adults they know or have seen on television.

**tentative period:** second stage of occupational choice in which occupational preferences begin to be based on the person's strengths and weaknesses

- *Stage II. Tentative period.* From about eleven to seventeen years of age, young people recognize the need to decide sometime on a future occupation. In the **tentative period,** they make tentative choices based on whatever awareness they have of their interests, abilities, and opportunities. At first, compatible interests appear to be a primary consideration in career choice. Later they begin to consider ability and training prerequisites, and still later personal values become an important consideration. By the end of this period, they recognize that it is necessary to integrate these aspects to allow for the realities of environmental limitations and opportunities in making a tentative vocational choice.

**realistic choice stage:** third stage of occupational choice in which preferences are tested in the world of work

- *Stage III. Realistic choice stage.* From about the age of seventeen, young people try to work out a suitable occupational plan by translating their own desires into a real-life occupation. In the **realistic choice stage,** people often realize that it is necessary to compromise their hopes and desires with reality. This in turn, involves *exploration,* as young people acquire information and possibly work experience; *crystallization,* as they narrow their range of alternatives and prepare to make a career choice; and finally, *specification* with commitment to a given occupational goal.

**negative choice:** process of choosing among alternatives by systematically eliminating undesirable options

For many people, occupational selection involves **negative choices.** Often people are sure about what they do *not* want to do, while they are unclear about what they *do* want to do. Besides limiting occupational possibilities, negative choices also form points of reference against which new possibilities are evaluated. Thus, in a general sense, we narrow our field of choice over time. Again, however, caution is desirable since we may inadvertently rule out career possibilities on the basis of inadequate or inaccurate information.

## Interests and Occupations

Researchers have found that work is centrally related to other aspects of our lives. We do not choose jobs; rather, we choose life-styles. For example, if an individual is interested in entering the restaurant business, he or she must also be willing to work during the evening hours. If people are interested in sales, they must also be sociable and outgoing. Our abilities and patterns of interests can help us to choose the "right" occupation.

One way in which we can help select an appropriate occupation is to examine the similarity of our likes and dislikes on six general occupational themes.

The themes, identified through research (Holland, 1966, 1973), are Realistic, Investigative, Artistic, Social, Enterprising, and Conventional. Each theme represents a "pure" interest type. For example, if a person's interests were extremely "social" in nature, he or she would likely be sociable and concerned with the welfare of others. Typically, the social person prefers working in groups or on a one-to-one basis rather than working alone. The social person also dislikes physical activity or working with machinery.

Most people do not show such an extreme pattern of interests, instead exhibiting a mixture of interests. For example, a person whose interests are highest on the realistic theme may also have relatively high interests in conventional and investigative themes, while showing little social interests. Based on the responses of many individuals, Holland (1966, 1973) was able to construct a **hexagonal model of interests.** This model, illustrated in Figure 15-1, suggests that occupational themes closest to any one theme will be highly intercorrelated, while the theme opposite on the hexagon will be poorly correlated.

This hexagon can be used to predict which jobs will be satisfying to us. If our interests are primarily realistic, we are most likely to enjoy jobs emphasizing the outdoors, use of machinery, and things rather than people. Or we may enjoy jobs with strong conventional or investigative components. As the figure illustrates, investigative and conventional occupational themes are closest to the realistic theme. At the same time, we are least likely to enjoy jobs with a strong social component. Thus, we may find greatest occupational satisfaction in realistic areas such as construction work, wildlife management, or agriculture. We may also enjoy "investigative" jobs in engineering or "conventional" jobs such as bookkeeping and financial analysis. On the other hand, we may find "social" occupations such as marriage counselor or clinical psychologist least satisfying.

One practical implication of this research has been the development of **interest inventories** that can be used to help people select occupations. Although

**hexagonal model of interests:** model of occupational interests stating that an individual who shows high interest on one theme will show low interest on the theme directly opposite on the hexagon

**interest inventories:** psychological tests used to help an individual make an appropriate occupational selection

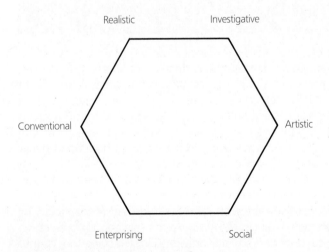

**FIGURE 15.1 Holland's Hexagonal Model of Interests**

According to Holland's hexagonal model of interests, themes that are nearest to each other on the hexagon are highly correlated. Thus, a person whose interests are mainly artistic in nature may also derive satisfaction from the social activity of teaching his or her skill to others.

it might be possible to ask people directly about their occupational preferences, an individual's lack of knowledge about an occupation might result in a poor choice. Similarly, an individual's stereotypes about an occupation might mislead the individual (Anastasi, 1982). For example, many people believe that physicians are all-knowing, calm people who diagnose rare diseases and save lives with ease. Unfortunately, this stereotype does not disclose the long hours and heavy record-keeping that are important parts of a physician's life.

A better approach to occupational selection involves an *indirect* approach. Through instruments such as the Strong-Campbell Interest Inventory, an individual's interests are compared to the interests of workers in an occupation. The degree of similarity is then noted. Since interest patterns successfully predict occupational happiness, these tests can aid an individual in selecting the "right" occupation.

Several resources are available to the person who is unsure about occupational plans. One very useful method of learning more about the match between an individual's needs and goals and the potential offered by a job is working part-time or summers in a setting that closely matches career plans. If, for example, an individual is interested in pursuing a law career, he or she might find it helpful to work in a law office as a clerk. Although this experience is not, strictly speaking, equivalent to being a lawyer, it can give the individual an opportunity to match personal expectations against the realities of the chosen field.

People can volunteer their time as a means of learning more about a profession. Volunteer work in psychology and other health-related fields can provide much useful information about the chosen field. Some occupations, such as engineering and food service, provide apprenticeships or work-study programs—both of which can be helpful.

In those situations where paid or volunteer work is not possible, contact with a representative of an occupation may provide useful insights. Similarly, information available from professional organizations and libraries can also fill in the gaps.

And, of course, career counseling programs are available at most colleges and universities. These programs usually offer psychological testing to help match the individual and an occupation. Such programs can often be found in college and university psychology clinics, counseling centers, or offices that provide student services.

## CHANGING OCCUPATIONS

Career choice, like development, is not a finite process. People may be constantly reevaluating their work experiences or they may suddenly find that they are bored and unfulfilled, disheartened and saddened by a career that once gave them pleasure and excitement. Or perhaps a change in health may force a worker to seek another career, as when a surgeon develops arthritis, a dancer is crippled by bad knees, or a construction worker develops heart disease. Or a change in the economy or technology may eliminate jobs and force even successful and satisfied workers into other fields. Like everything else in our lives, career choice is subject to change.

### Multiple Careers

Many people work in a single field for all of their lives. For example, a person trained as a hairdresser or engineer might always work in his or her respective field, even if he or she changed employers. However, some people take risks and decide to switch their occupations. Although this act is a difficult one and takes great courage, the outcome can be, for some people, highly beneficial. Studs Terkel (1974) describes a number of those who have switched careers:

*[Fred Ringley] is forty years old. Until a year ago he had lived all his life in the environs of Chicago. He was born in one of its North Shore suburbs; he was raised, reached adult-hood, and became . . . a "typical suburbanite." He had worked in advertising as a copy-writer and salesman.*

*[As Ringley put it,] We were caught up in the American Dream. You've gotta have a house. You've gotta have a country club. You've gotta have two cars. . . . I doubled my salary. I also doubled my grief. . . . We got a house in the suburbs and we got a coun-try club membership and we got two cars and we got higher taxes. We got nervous and we started drinking more and smoking more. Finally, one day we sat down. We have everything and we are poor. (pp. 688–89)*

To deal with the accumulating stresses that he had as a salesman, Ringley moved to a small farm in Arkansas. Since the family's savings were being depleted and the farm was not yet productive, Ringley also borrowed money to purchase a small restaurant/dairy fountain. Although he was satisfied with his new life, many of his former associates were taken aback:

*People say, "You're wasting your college education." My ex-employer said to my father, "You didn't raise your son to be a hash slinger." I've lost status in the eyes of my big city friends. But where I am now I have more status than I would in the city . . . I can be a hash slinger [in Arkansas] and be just as fine as the vice president of the Continen-tal Bank [in Chicago]. My personal status with somebody else may have gone down. My personal status with myself has gone up a hundred percent. (p. 693)*

Another individual interviewed by Terkel avoided some of the traps associ-ated with staying in a job that is too stressful by leaving her job as a television producer and becoming a librarian. She discusses the costs of staying in an un-pleasant job:

*My father was a mechanical engineer, hated every day of it. He couldn't wait forty-six years, or whatever it was, until he retired. When we were little, we knew he loathed his job. . . . He went through the motions and did it very well. But he dreaded every min-ute of it.*

*I have a sister who can't wait until December, 'cause she's going to retire at a bank. She's just hanging on. How terrible.*

*I don't think I could ever really retire. There's not enough time. (p. 702)*

As these examples point out, some people benefit from changing occupa-tions. Other people make career choices that are ill-considered or impulsive. Of-ten they simply "drift" into an occupation. Or they may follow a family tradition of entering a specific occupation. For example, the children of a physician may be expected to enter medicine to satisfy their parents' wishes. Unless these choices are based on realistic desires and a rational analysis of personal interests, strengths, and weaknesses, the choice of a particular occupation may end in dissatisfaction.

Interestingly, many of the "second chancers" interviewed by Terkel switched occupations after some life crisis, often of a philosophical nature. As we dis-cussed earlier in Chapter 4, issues of what we want to do with our lives are a major part of the transitions that we undergo during adulthood. For some peo-ple, the resolution to a life crisis was to change jobs.

## Reentering the Work Force

A substantial proportion of adults leave the work force for extended periods of time. The majority of these individuals are women who quit their jobs to raise children but who have decided to return to work. The motivations for returning to work can be varied: both spouses may have to work to help pay for expenses incurred in raising children; economic circumstances, such as inflation or the loss of a spouse, may force the person to seek employment; individuals may decide to work to enhance their self-esteem.

Whatever the motivation, people who have been outside the labor force for a long time may find that the work environment they were familiar with before has changed dramatically. For example, the woman who was a secretary prior to her marriage may find that a similar job today requires skills in managing word processors and other computer-based equipment.

Many people find that the skills they developed outside the work situation are not appreciated. For example, an individual who has successfully run a home, reared children, and managed the family finances may find that his or her qualifications may not be satisfactory for the job. In other words, a person who gains

Many changes in the work place have come about as the result of technological change and advances. A person reentering the work force often has to learn new skills to cope with these changes.

meaningful experience in an employed situation may have an advantage over the individual who has similar (or superior) skills which were developed in a volunteer or home situation.

A final issue that those reentering the work force must face is the difficulty involved in restarting a career. Most careers require virtually full-time employment for advancement and promotion. It may thus be frustrating to a talented but less experienced older worker to find that he or she does not garner the recognition that younger but more experienced workers receive. Nonetheless, if the person who reenters the work force does not seek to compress many years of work experience into a few short months, he or she is likely to rediscover the potential pleasures that can accompany meaningful employment.

## WORK ADJUSTMENT AND JOB SATISFACTION

*"The confrontation of the young person with the world of work is a major change in the environment. The world of work is a new world of meanings."*
*(TIEDEMAN & O'HARA, 1963, P. 49)*

The complete transition from school to work not only represents a major milestone in a person's life but often poses a difficult stage of transition. In moving from the competitive but relatively protected setting of school to the more demanding and often less supportive job setting, young people may feel that they have entered an unknown new world full of dangers and pitfalls they do not know how to anticipate. Thus, it is not surprising that many young people are somewhat fearful about their ability to make the transition successfully.

One common fear is of failing, not being able to do the work satisfactorily. Even when people have adequate ability, they may still fear being confronted with tasks for which they have not been adequately prepared. A second common fear is of not being accepted or not getting along well with colleagues and superiors. Other fears may center around whether they have made the right choice and whether the new endeavor will live up to their hopes and expectations. Of course, people who are unsure about their abilities and motives as well as the demands of the job may feel doubly insecure in their new setting.

The first job can also be a source of disappointment. The new employee is often ambitious and enthusiastic. However, the realities of work often cause the employee to lose motivation. Ready to become company president within a few short years, the employee instead finds that he or she is in a boring or routine job. Or workers discover that they are overtrained for their jobs and their skills are not being utilized.

If the individual has indeed made a poor job choice, he or she can probably find more suitable employment. However, for both the dissatisfied and satisfied worker, the first job can be a learning experience in which the individual can analyze his or her fitness for a certain type of job and can emerge as a more self-knowledgeable person in the process.

## Achieving Job Satisfaction

Two areas are important to achieving job satisfaction. One area concerns personal characteristics. The other concerns the types of satisfactions found in work—whether intrinsic or extrinsic.

**Personal characteristics.**   Among the personal characteristics related to satisfactory work adjustment are a realistic view of one's self, tolerance for delayed gratification, and a willingness to make realistic compromises.

In an occupation, as in any other life task, a person often must endure hardships and wait for rewards that may be forthcoming only after long periods of concentrated effort. Beginning jobs, which are usually low in the organizational hierarchy, are especially likely to bring frustration and dissatisfaction unless the individual realizes that they are necessary stages to be gone through and that promotions come as more skill, maturity, and judgment are acquired.

Some people are able to establish themselves in an occupation with apparent ease. Although they may change jobs, they show an orderly progression of advancement in their chosen field. Other persons have a great deal of difficulty in finding a job that satisfies them and in "taking hold."

It is unlikely that all the individual's needs and expectations will be satisfied in any occupation, even at more authoritative and responsible levels. The young person looking for the "ideal job" may well find that it does not exist.

**Intrinsic vs. extrinsic satisfactions.**   The satisfactions found in work can be either *intrinsic* or *extrinsic*. **Intrinsic satisfactions** are found in the work itself—in its ability to satisfy one's needs for self-esteem, relatedness, meaning, and personal growth and fulfillment. Many workers find their jobs so interesting and meaningful that they work at them longer and harder than is required. **Extrinsic satisfactions** are extraneous to the work itself and involve rewards such as money, fringe benefits, and working conditions.

**intrinsic satisfactions:** satisfactions found in a work situation itself

**extrinsic satisfactions:** satisfactions found outside a work situation

Some theories of management state that intrinsic satisfactions including opportunities for responsibility, recognition, challenge, achievement, and personal growth and development motivate workers to perform well. An organizational atmosphere that encourages communication and a group orientation are thought to increase both job performance and worker satisfaction.

Traditionally it has been assumed that work is unpleasant and that people will try to avoid it. Thus, emphasis has been placed on pay and other extrinsic incentives and on strict supervision. Another view, however, holds that constructive effort is natural and that there are ways—in addition to money—to motivate people to work. Thus, people can be expected to perform better if their work is made interesting and if they are involved in decision-making processes concerning it. While salary and working conditions are still considered important, strong emphasis is also placed on intrinsic satisfactions.

These two ways of viewing the satisfactions that an individual can receive from an occupation are also reflected in the ways that companies view and structure jobs. One view, termed the **Theory X** approach, argues that workers are motivated only by extrinsic factors. In this view, workers are lazy, disinterested, and unmotivated in their jobs. Since workers must be closely monitored, a fairly rigid, authoritarian supervisory system must be established to insure worker productivity (McGregor, 1960; O'Toole, 1982).

The second view suggests that people are, in fact, quite interested in their jobs and wish to participate in and be involved with the people and the processes that comprise their jobs. This approach, termed **Theory Y**, suggests that intrinsic satisfactions are an important part of all jobs.

It has long been assumed that professional and executive people are highly attracted to the intrinsic satisfactions of their work while blue-collar and unskilled workers are more attracted by the extrinsic satisfactions of work. However, research suggests that both white-collar and blue-collar workers benefit from a Theory Y approach, particularly when extrinsic satisfactions are at a reasonable level. In one study, for example, janitorial personnel in an office building were split into two groups. One group was asked to develop a plan to help curb absenteeism. In discussions with management, a bonus plan for reducing absenteeism was developed. This plan was put into effect for both groups of janitors, but it was successful only for the group that helped develop the plan (Lawler & Hackman, 1969). This result, predictable from the Theory Y approach, suggests that both workers and management can benefit when workers have some control and autonomy over their work situations.

**Theory X:** theory which states that workers are motivated solely by extrinsic satisfactions

**Theory Y:** theory which states that high worker motivation can be achieved in jobs with intrinsic satisfactions

## Job Dissatisfaction and Job Discrimination

Many fortunate individuals are contented with their jobs—pay, status, working conditions, and the like. There are a substantial number of other workers, however, who are dissatisfied with their work. In this section, we shall examine the reasons workers are dissatisfied with their work and also explore the issue of job discrimination, including the special problems faced by women.

**Job dissatisfaction.** The measurement of job satisfaction or discontent is a complex task. We cannot simply rely on public opinion polls for reports of attitudes toward work. Indeed, when measured in this fashion, most workers report that they are satisfied with their jobs. To be "satisfied" usually means only that the pay is acceptable and environmental conditions adequate. Also, workers tend

# Insight

## THEORY Z

An alternative to the Theory X and Theory Y approaches to organizational structure and management has been developed by William G. Ouchi (1981). His approach, which has been termed **Theory Z**, is a variant of the Theory Y approach.

Ouchi, drawing from the successes of Japanese business, feels that a Theory Z organization has several characteristic features. Primary among these features is the "corporate culture" of a Theory Z company. Far from being a place where people work "nine to five," the Theory Z organization is, in a sense, part of an employee's "family." One company noted by Ouchi helped develop the friendly, easy going atmosphere of a family by holding "beer busts" once a month. These beer busts were not meant solely for production-line employees but for all members of the organization, including executive and managerial personnel.

A party for employees, however, is only an outward sign of a Theory Z company. More important than parties is a company philosophy in which each person is made to feel as though he or she were important to the company and had something to contribute to the overall success of the organization. Trust and friendship are an integral part of a Theory Z company, as are an emphasis on working together and decision by consensus. Often the outcome of such a corporate culture is the production of products in which each worker takes pride and in which quality is uniformly high.

Although Theory Z organizations are characteristic of Japanese organizations, they may not be easily transplanted to an American culture. For one thing, workers in Japan typically spend their entire working lives with a single organization. In contrast, many Americans expect to change jobs when conditions warrant. Similarly, promotions and advancement are quite slow in Japan, even for people with recognized talent and ability. In contrast, Americans expect that rapid promotion will accompany personal success. Finally, the Japanese emphasis on group consensus and long-term results contrasts markedly with the American emphasis on the "maverick" style and short-term performance.

Several American companies have adopted a Theory Z approach. Among them are the electronics giant Hewlett-Packard and the retailing company of Dayton-Hudson (probably best known for its Waldenbooks stores). Several other companies have also experimented with various aspects of the Theory Z approach, including General Motors. Although it may not be possible to adopt fully the characteristics of successful Japanese companies, the Theory Z approach emphasizes again the importance of work to the individual and shows how an individual's sense of involvement in a group setting can aid American business.

**Theory Z: variant of Theory Y approach, emphasizing group processes and decision making**

---

to answer this question the way they think they should. Measures that are more sensitive, such as absenteeism, turnover rates, inferior work, and accidents on the job, reveal considerable dissatisfaction at all occupational levels.

One source of **job dissatisfaction** is the job itself. Many jobs are boring, repetitive, and meaningless. Many do not allow for creativity or initiative. The very size of many organizations also helps produce job dissatisfaction. In many of today's factories and offices, a worker may have little appreciation of how his or her efforts contribute to the overall functioning and production of the orga-

**job dissatisfaction: dislike or displeasure with current job**

nization. In comparison, a craftsperson, such as a silversmith, starts with a piece of raw material and transforms it into a useful, often beautiful, finished piece that he or she can take pride in.

A second reason for job dissatisfaction deals with **overeducation** and rising expectations. In the past, a college education practically guaranteed the degree holder a better job, higher status, and better pay. Today, college educations are more common, but the payoff is not as great. Indeed, some of the highest levels of job dissatisfaction can be found among educated young people who hold low-paying, low-status, and generally unrewarding jobs ("Education and Job Satisfaction," 1976).

Fortunately, the human and financial costs of worker dissatisfaction have become evident and many organizations are making an effort to humanize jobs. Some of the methods that these organizations are using to increase job satisfaction are "quality of work life" and "job enrichment" programs (Landy & Trumbo, 1980; Lawler, 1982). Interestingly, many of these programs derive from the Theory Y approach.

**Job discrimination.** In spite of continuing efforts to end discrimination, race and sex still limit career choices and occupational opportunities for many people. It has been estimated that one in three minority workers is employed irregularly or is unemployed. And the annual salary of employed minority males is far below that of the average salary of white workers.

Relatively slow progress is being made to undo the damage of decades of persistent **job discrimination** and closed-off opportunity. Unfortunately, discrimination tends to be a two-way street. Jobs have been denied to people because of their race or ethnic background. At the same time, those discriminated against have lowered their educational and occupational sights. Thus, members of ethnic minorities may limit their career choices to occupations with low pay and status.

The black American has been subjected to the greatest discrimination in education, career choice, and occupational opportunity. However, varying degrees of discrimination have also been directed—and continue to be directed—toward Americans of Spanish-speaking, Indian, and Asian ancestry. Additionally, discrimination against the handicapped has also occurred. In an attempt to deal with these problems, antidiscrimination laws, including the Civil Rights Act of 1964 and the Rehabilitation Act of 1973, have been enacted. Furthermore, many organizations have established training and recruitment programs specifically designed to aid members of those groups who have been discriminated against in the past.

**Women and work.** Husband's occupation, family, and home were formerly the key determinants of a woman's status and identity. But, as we have noted, an increasing number of women have entered the work force and are seeking the same sort of financial and psychological rewards as their male co-workers. About half of all women between the ages of eighteen and sixty-four are in the work force and studies suggest that more than 90 percent of women will work outside of the home at some time in their lives. Thus, issues such as job dissat-

**overeducation:** education, training, knowledge, or skills possessed by the individual that are in excess of that required by a particular job

**job discrimination:** systematic exclusion of members of particular groups from employment or job advancement

Women who are employed outside the home often face a number of problems stemming from job discrimination. Despite the increasing number of women in the work force, women are disproportionately represented in lower-income and lower-status jobs. Disparity in pay is another problem. Even in the highly skilled professions, women typically earn less than men.

isfaction and discrimination in employment apply not to a minority of females but to millions of women workers.

Although there is a trend toward converging sex roles in occupations, women are still overrepresented in low-paying and low-status jobs. Nine out of ten women work in service jobs, nurturing tasks, and assistance roles—as waitresses, clerical workers, secretaries, phone operators, lab technicians, nurses, and teachers. Only a very small percentage of women—as compared with men—enter so-called high-status fields, such as engineering, law, and medicine. And until recently women have also been underrepresented in such "male" trades as law enforcement, construction, welding, carpentry, and auto mechanics.

In spite of laws forbidding discrimination in employment, the average income for women who work full time is less than 60 percent of that of men in this category. In part, this may be explained by the fact that women are more heavily represented in lower paying occupations, such as secretaries, food-service workers, and clerical workers. Even when women work in the same occupations as men, they may receive less pay. For example, the average income of women in technical and professional occupations in 1979 was less than 65 percent of the average income of men in the same occupations. Only part of this difference can be explained by the presumably greater seniority of men in the same jobs.

Many of the obstacles women face in the world of work stem from such sources as occupational stereotypes and various discriminatory practices in hiring and salaries. However, some researchers have suggested that many women also erect barriers for themselves. Based on early socialization experiences that do not prepare them for success-oriented roles and that teach them not to compete with men for fear of losing their femininity, some women may avoid success in a career.

This was reflected in the findings of a study conducted by Matina Horner (1970). Horner asked both male and female subjects to write a story based on a single sentence. For women, the sentence read, "After first-term finals, Anne finds herself at the top of her medical school class." Men were asked to write about "John." Ninety percent of the men's stories reflected pride in John's accomplishments, while 65 percent of the women wrote stories that expressed fears of social rejection, loss of femininity, or denied that a woman could be so successful. Horner's findings were widely publicized and the trait she identified as "the motive to avoid success" became known as the "fear of success."

However, later studies have come to a somewhat different conclusion. In their review of studies on fear of success in women, psychologists Miron Zuckerman and Ladd Wheeler (1975) concluded that the evidence for fear of success in women was not as common or pervasive as Horner's results first suggested. Indeed, many studies suggested no differences between the sexes in this regard.

Although women are as motivated to succeed as men, job discrimination still exists, and women, along with other minorities, face a variety of problems in the workplace. As more and more women enter occupations formerly dominated by men, the success of these women will be forceful models to other women, their daughters, and men who doubt that women (like men) have "what it takes" to succeed in the world of work.

## Occupational Stress and Unemployment

Since work is an important source of self-identity, esteem, and fulfillment, it could be predicted that job satisfaction and related sources of stress would have many consequences for the physical and psychological well-being of the worker and for his or her interpersonal, family, and community adjustment. Among the conditions that have been associated with physical and mental disorders among workers are stressful conditions on the job and the even greater stress of being out of work.

**Stress on the job.** A number of job-related factors are considered highly stressful. These include:

1. Dissatisfaction resulting from demeaning and boring work, lack of recognition, and poor working conditions.

2. Incongruity between job status and other aspects of life, such as educational achievement.

3. Excessively rapid and continuous change in employment, often involving changes from one type of work to another.

4. Lack of stability, security, and support in the job environment.

5. Work overloads, responsibility without authority, time pressures, and conflict or ambiguity in work rules.

6. Interpersonal conflicts and competition with coworkers.

7. Lowering of self-esteem caused by failure to achieve internal (or external) standards of achievement.

The costs of such **occupational stress** are high. Among the most common are anxiety, tension headaches, depression, abuse of alcohol and drugs, and peptic ulcers, heart attacks, and other psychophysiological reactions. And this says nothing of the cost in terms of marital and other interpersonal problems.

**occupational stress: adjustive demands on an individual in a work setting**

**Unemployment.**   Social scientists have studied the effects of unemployment on lower socioeconomic workers and found that unemployment generally leads to financial hardship, self-devaluation, and apathy.

One of the first studies on the effects of unemployment on middle-class men was made by Powell and Driscoll (1973). These investigators found that when joblessness was prolonged, their subjects progressed through four well-defined stages:

● *Stage I. A period of relaxation and relief.* Most of the men in this study had seen their companies failing and had anticipated a layoff. The mood following the layoff was one of relief and relaxation and they viewed this initial period as sort of a vacation at home, a time to be with family, read, and catch up on hobbies. There was a sense of being between jobs, and the men were confident that they could obtain another job as soon as they were ready to return to work.

● *Stage II. A period of concerted effort.* After about twenty-five days, the men began to feel bored and edgy and started to make systematic attempts to find work. During this second stage, the period of concerted effort, they typically relied on job-finding strategies they had used in the past, such as calling friends, going back to the university placement center, and sending resumés to potential employers. They were still optimistic and did not become anxious or depressed when they received letters of rejection or no response at all.

● *Stage III. A period of vascillation and doubt.* In the third stage, most of the men had been out of work longer than ever before and realized that their job-seeking efforts were not succeeding. Job-seeking behavior became sporadic and alternated between intense activity and none at all. Extreme moodiness characterized the men during this stage, and family and other interpersonal relationships began to deteriorate. After three to nine weeks, the men stopped trying and job-hunting came to a virtual halt.

● *Stage IV. A period of malaise and cynicism.* If the men continued to look for a job during the fourth stage, they tended to use job-seeking strategies that were oriented more toward protecting their self-esteem than obtaining employment. For example, the men would not seek a job unless it matched their training and experience exactly. The men now lost hope and became listless and apathetic. Eventually they simply gave up. Some even stopped thinking about work and returning to the world of work. They were defeated.

The researchers did not consider these reactions unique to the scientists and engineers in this study, but felt that these stages were typical of prolonged unemployment. As they concluded: ''The image of competent and energetic men reduced to listless discouragement highlights the personal tragedy and the loss of valuable resources when there is substantial unemployment. . . . Perhaps more significantly, the situation of these middle-class unemployed further dramatizes the plight of the larger number of unemployed nonskilled workers whose fate is

Loss of income is only one of the problems suffered by the unemployed. Being out of work can also threaten a person's self-esteem and sense of personal and social worth and can upset family and social relationships.

to deal with unemployment often during their lifetime'' (1973, p. 26). Finally, available evidence indicates that the loss of employment is equally or more trying for women and often represents a family as well as individual crisis (Derr, 1977).

Loss of employment leads to more than loss of wages. Earlier, in Chapter 7, we noted that losing a job and changes in economic status were high-stress life changes. Based on the hypothesis that such major life changes lead to emotional and physical disorders, we would predict an increase in emotional disorders following unemployment. The research on this point is clear: economic hard times lead to an increased incidence of emotional disorders, perhaps due to the psychological stress of lowered self-esteem. Admissions to mental hospitals and suicide rates increase during economically troubled times. These studies suggest that the highest associations between economic distress and mental anguish are strongest soon after the individual loses a job and after approximately one year of unemployment (Dooley & Catalano, 1980).

Businesses and communities can help reduce the effects of unemployment in several ways. For example, losing a job is frequently an abrupt experience, and it may help people to adapt to unemployment if they can be forewarned that they are about to lose their jobs and can begin to seek alternative employment. Communities can help by making treatment facilities known and available to the unemployed and their families. A well-functioning social support network of family and friends can reduce the stress associated with unemployment. And, the person most directly affected can take steps to cope effectively with the stresses of losing a job. Through the utilization of all of the available resources, the individual can greatly increase his or her chances of adaptive adjustment to this major life change (Dooley & Catalano, 1980).

## LEISURE

If work has the connotation of drudgery, leisure invokes images of lounging around a beach or swimming pool on a warm, sunny day, sipping cool drinks brought by an attentive waiter or waitress. However, as we shall see, leisure is a more complex phenomenon. In this section, we shall discuss several issues related to

# Insight

The experience of being fired can be shattering, even when one has nothing to lose. To illustrate this, Studs Terkel offers the following excerpt from a story printed in the *New York Times* (June 10, 1973):

*Dr. John R. Coleman, president of Haverford College, took an unusual sabbatical during the early months of 1973. He worked at menial jobs. In one instance, he was fired as a porter-dishwasher. 'I'd never been fired and I'd never been unemployed. For three days I walked the streets. Though I had a bank account, though my children's tuition was paid, though I had a salary and a job waiting for me back in Haverford, I was demoralized. I had an inkling of how professionals my age feel when they lose their job*

*and their confidence begins to sink.'' Dr. Coleman is 51.*

*Perhaps it is this specter that most haunts working men and women: the planned obsolescence of people that is of a piece with the planned obsolescence of the things they make. Or sell. It is perhaps this fear of no longer being needed in a world of needless things that most clearly spells out the unnaturalness, the surreality of much that is called work today.*

*Since Dr. Coleman happens to be chairman of the Federal Reserve Bank of Philadelphia, he quit his ditchdigging job to preside over the bank's monthly meeting. When he looked at the other members of the board, he could not keep from feeling that there was something unreal about them all. (Terkel, 1974, pp. xxi–xxii)*

---

leisure and its appropriate use. In particular, we shall *(a)* define leisure, *(b)* describe the relationship between leisure and work, and *(c)* discuss some ways in which leisure can be used for personal growth.

## Nonwork, Leisure, and Maintenance

Washing cars, brushing teeth, watching a movie, and taking a vacation are all examples of activities that people can do in their nonwork time. But as these examples suggest, not all nonwork activities are also leisure activities. Some of our nonwork time is spent in **maintenance activities,** such as cleaning up after dinner, buying food, and sleeping.

**maintenance activities: nonwork activities important for normal daily functioning**

Maintenance activities can be distinguished from leisure activities in the degree of *constraint* upon the individual (Kabanoff, 1980). Preparing food is a necessity of life, as are sleeping and physical care activities. Similarly, social conventions require that people clean dishes after a meal, wash clothes, and take baths and showers.

The line between leisure activities and maintenance activities is not always so easy to make. For example, people can satisfy their need for food by going to a fast-food outlet, or they can accomplish the same goal by preparing an elaborate gourmet meal. Both activities contain elements of maintenance activities, but the preparation time involved in the gourmet meal is not necessary to the activity of eating. Similarly, physical activity is a necessity for health. We can accomplish this goal through normal, everyday activity, through organized sports, or through two or more hours of jogging and running per day.

In contrast, **leisure** is "a set of activities that individuals perform outside of their work context and excludes essential maintenance functions" (Kabanoff, 1980, p. 69). As explained by Kabanoff, this definition of leisure contains six points:

1. *Nonwork context.* In general, leisure activities occur outside work situations. According to this definition, a business lunch or golf date with customers of a firm would not be considered leisure.

2. *Nonmaintenance activities.* Maintenance activities are also excluded from the definition of leisure.

3. *Element of choice.* People who engage in leisure activities do so because they choose to—they have an option to engage in the activity.

4. *Prescribed tasks or operations.* Leisure activities are not free-form or undefined. Planning and participating in a vacation involves prescribed tasks and processes, as does participating in a team sport. On the other hand, staying at home and watching television has very few of the prescribed tasks associated with leisure activities.

**leisure: nonwork, non-maintenance activities involving prescribed tasks that people choose for their intrinsic motivating qualities**

There are a number of ways of looking at leisure. Some people regard leisure as the time left over after work and the performance of maintenance activities are completed. Others see leisure as the time for learning and contemplation. Finally, many consider leisure the time to play and engage in recreational activities. All three views are probably represented among the people enjoying the sun and socializing on this beach.

# Insight

**RECREATION AND LEISURE
FACT SHEET**

| | |
|---|---|
| Amount spent on recreation | Over $100 billion |
| Percentage of total income spent on recreation and leisure | 6.7 percent |
| Common recreation and leisure expenditures: | |
| • radios, TVs, records, and musical instruments | Over $21 billion |
| • sport supplies | Over $13 billion |
| • admissions to theaters, sport events, concerts | Over $4 billion |
| Percentage of population participating in outdoor activities: | |
| • camping | 51 percent |
| • fishing | 53 percent |
| • walking and jogging | 68 percent |
| • bicycling | 46 percent |
| • golf | 15 percent |
| • tennis | 32 percent |
| • observer at outdoor sports events | 61 percent |
| • picnicking | 72 percent |
| • snowmobiling | 8 percent |
| • skate-boarding | Less than 1 percent |

(U.S. Bureau of the Census, *Statistical Abstract of the United States 1980*.)

5. *Intrinsic motivation.* The motivation for engaging in leisure activities is primarily personal and individual. People engage in leisure activities because the activity is personally meaningful.

6. *Absence of monetary reward as a motivator.* People engage in leisure activities because they are enjoyable in their own right, not because they get paid for their activities. This part of the definition excludes professional athletes and other sports individuals whose activities may seem to involve leisure but which are work activities instead.

As this definition suggests, leisure is often a personally defined and personally meaningful activity. In the next section, we shall examine how leisure and work are related.

## The Relationship of Work and Leisure

Psychologists and sociologists have developed a number of theories to help explain the relationship between work and leisure. In this section, we shall discuss three approaches that have been developed to help understand this relationship: (1) the compensatory hypothesis; (2) the alienation hypothesis; and (3) the segmentalist hypothesis.

**compensatory hypothesis: theory stating that leisure provides a release from accumulated work tensions**

**The compensatory hypothesis.**   The **compensatory hypothesis** of leisure suggests that people use leisure as a way to release tensions and deprivations accumulated at work. In essence, leisure provides a way to "blow off steam."

Some studies have provided support for this hypothesis. In one such study (Mansfield & Evans, 1975), the management and personnel of a bank were asked to rate their satisfactions at work and leisure. The findings of this study suggested that workers who reported deprivation at work attempted to compensate for this deprivation through leisure activities. The compensation hypothesis may also account for the large numbers of bars in areas near factories.

**alienation hypothesis: theory stating that work satisfaction and involvement in leisure activities are highly correlated**

**The alienation hypothesis.**   The **alienation hypothesis** suggests that qualities of the job "spill over" into leisure activities. According to this hypothesis, people who are satisfied with their jobs will report more involvement in satisfying leisure activities, while those who are dissatisfied at work will also report reduced participation in leisure activities.

In one examination of this hypothesis, Meissner (1971) reported that work involving a high degree of personal involvement and social interaction was positively associated with leisure activities. Similarly, work with little or no personal involvement, such as an unskilled job at an assembly line, was associated with little participation in voluntary social and leisure activities.

These findings have also been extended to the personal adjustment of workers. Workers with jobs that require individual responsibility and that have higher wages and status also tend to have better mental health.

**segmentalist hypothesis: theory stating that work satisfactions and involvement in leisure activities are not correlated**

**The segmentalist hypothesis.**   Unlike the compensatory and alienation hypotheses which propose a relationship between work and leisure, the **segmentalist hypothesis** suggests that work and leisure are psychologically independent (Dubin, 1958; Kabanoff, 1980). If the segmentalist hypothesis is correct, there should be no relationship between work and leisure satisfaction.

In one examination of this hypothesis (London, Crandall, & Seals, 1977), a representative sample of 1297 American workers were interviewed about aspects of their leisure, work, and quality of life. The results indicated that job satisfaction was related to overall quality of life and that satisfaction with leisure activities was also related to overall quality of life. However, job satisfaction and leisure satisfaction showed very little relationship to one another. In fact, the average correlation between leisure satisfaction and job satisfaction was a very low 0.14. Thus, most American workers view work and leisure activities as separate and unrelated.

## Personal Characteristics in Work and Leisure

Given the difficulties involved in defining work and its attributes and the even greater difficulties involved in defining leisure and its characteristics, it should come as no surprise that none of the three hypotheses clearly predominates over the others. Just as people work for money, security, and personal development, so too can people engage in leisure for a variety of reasons. It thus appears that these work and leisure patterns may be related to personal characteristics.

A number of work and leisure interactions have been identified, along with the personal characteristics of the individuals who fit these patterns (Kabanoff & O'Brien, 1980; Kando & Summers, 1971):

1. *Passive generalization.* This pattern involves low levels of satisfactions in both work and leisure. People who showed this pattern tended to be males with low education and low income. Additionally, the work motivation for these individuals was primarily extrinsic rather than intrinsic in nature.

2. *Supplemental compensation.* This pattern describes low involvement in work but high involvement in leisure. People in this category tended to have low income and low extrinsic work motivation. While a large percentage were older women, a substantial proportion were fairly young men and women whose work and leisure patterns seemed to fit the compensatory pattern described above.

3. *Active generalization.* People in this category reported high involvement in both work and leisure. Those individuals who best fit this pattern tended to be well-educated and well-paid. The satisfactions they derived from work were primarily intrinsic. The high level of activity, however, suggests that they used leisure to fulfill self-actualization needs that were not met at work (Parker, 1971).

4. *Reactive compensation.* In this category, people reported high involvement in work and low involvement in leisure. People in this category tended to be males who were primarily extrinsically motivated in their work. These are "job-centered" individuals for whom work satisfactions are primarily economic.

These patterns clearly indicate that work and leisure are related to one another. However, the relationship between leisure and work is a complex one that is highly dependent on personal characteristics and satisfactions.

## Leisure and Personal Growth

In earlier times, life was well-integrated, and leisure activities were not distinctly different from other aspects of life. However, the Industrial Revolution and its subsequent sharp differentiation of work and nonwork times (Wilensky, 1960)

As people have more time to pursue leisure activities, leisure becomes an important part of self-expression and a path to fulfillment and self-realization.

have led psychologists to consider the question of how leisure can be used for personal growth.

Numerous studies, summarized by Kabanoff (1980), have shown that a decrease in work time does not automatically result in an equivalent increase in leisure. Although the historical trend is toward a shorter work week, many people find that the increasing amounts of time available for leisure are not used in a personally productive fashion. For example, many people who are placed on a four-day work week initially report substantial satisfaction with their new working hours. However, a significant proportion of people on this shortened work week find that their satisfaction decreases over time, primarily because much of the newly available time is taken up with maintenance activities such as chauffeuring children.

In essence, there is a danger that the time available for leisure will be taken up by maintenance activities rather than by leisure activities. In cases such as these, little personal growth can occur (Linder, 1970).

In order for individuals to gain the advantage of leisure time, they must *plan* for personally beneficial leisure activities. Nonwork time is unstructured time, and an individual can choose how that time will be allocated. While a certain amount of time must be allocated to maintenance activities, we have great leeway in deciding how the remaining portion of time can be spent. We can, on the one hand, use the time to get together with friends, to engage in physical activities, or to work on a favorite hobby. We can use our leisure time for personal growth and fulfillment. On the other hand, we can also choose to sit around and watch television and become mesmerized by the ''boob tube.''

The need to choose and plan for leisure becomes especially important during the retirement years. Retirees, more than any other adult group, are subject to the adjustive demands of unlimited nonwork time. As we noted earlier, the freedom from work that retirement brings is often experienced by retirees with a pleasurable sense of relief. However, only those who have well-developed social and familial contacts and who have personally rewarding activities to engage their time will find that the opportunity for leisure that retirement brings is also an occasion for personal growth (O'Brien, 1981).

In summary, we can choose how to use nonwork time. With care and planning, nonwork time can become a growth-inducing leisure experience.

Families who share leisure activities may experience an improvement in their family relationships.

# Psychology in Action

## LEISURE PREFERENCE QUESTIONNAIRE

What do you prefer doing during your free time? Do you prefer helping others or would you rather enjoy viewing or listening to the arts? Do you prefer forming or enhancing sexual relationships or would you rather be "on the go?"

Listed below are nine paragraphs, each describing a particular kind of free-time activity. After reading the paragraphs, rank the paragraphs from 1 to 9, that is, from most to least desirable. Place a *1* next to the activity you like most; then place a *9* next to the one you like least. Next, place a *2* next to the activity you like second best, and an *8* next to the activity you like second least. Continue in this manner until you have ranked all the paragraphs.

When you have completed the questionnaire, you should have a better idea of the types of activities you most and least prefer.

1. _____ This activity gives you a chance to organize and arrange things. It demands precision and neatness. It requires a sense of planning, order and forethought.

2. _____ This activity allows you to do as you please regardless of rules or conventions. It provides for adventure, change and independence, involving a minimum of rules.

## SUMMARY

1. Work produces things of value for other people. In the past, people worked primarily for economic reasons. Now, people work for additional reasons, including personal identity and self-esteem.

2. Differences in occupational goals and tasks are narrowing for both sexes, and the large and growing number of occupational roles increase the difficulty involved in selecting the "right" occupation. In making this selection, the characteristics of the individual, the job, and the individual's interests must be considered.

3. As in other aspects of an individual's life, occupational selection is a developmental process that changes with time. Mistakes in occupational selection are possible, however, and people can change occupations. Similarly, those who have not worked in a great while can reenter the work force.

4. Work adjustment and satisfaction depend on patience and other personal characteristics. The job itself can also contribute to work adjustment, particularly

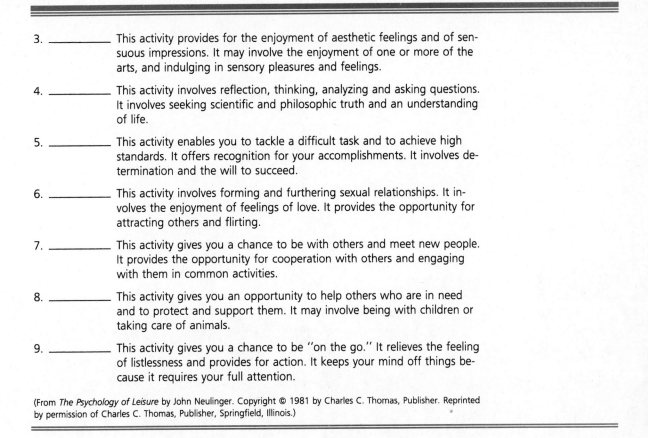

3. _____ This activity provides for the enjoyment of aesthetic feelings and of sensuous impressions. It may involve the enjoyment of one or more of the arts, and indulging in sensory pleasures and feelings.

4. _____ This activity involves reflection, thinking, analyzing and asking questions. It involves seeking scientific and philosophic truth and an understanding of life.

5. _____ This activity enables you to tackle a difficult task and to achieve high standards. It offers recognition for your accomplishments. It involves determination and the will to succeed.

6. _____ This activity involves forming and furthering sexual relationships. It involves the enjoyment of feelings of love. It provides the opportunity for attracting others and flirting.

7. _____ This activity gives you a chance to be with others and meet new people. It provides the opportunity for cooperation with others and engaging with them in common activities.

8. _____ This activity gives you an opportunity to help others who are in need and to protect and support them. It may involve being with children or taking care of animals.

9. _____ This activity gives you a chance to be "on the go." It relieves the feeling of listlessness and provides for action. It keeps your mind off things because it requires your full attention.

(From *The Psychology of Leisure* by John Neulinger. Copyright © 1981 by Charles C. Thomas, Publisher. Reprinted by permission of Charles C. Thomas, Publisher, Springfield, Illinois.)

if the satisfactions that the individual derives from the job are intrinsic in nature. Boring jobs and overeducation, on the other hand, can lead to job dissatisfaction.

5. Although against the law, job discrimination continues to be a major problem for a substantial proportion of the population. Unfortunately, job discrimination can lead to lowered expectations in those who are the victims of discrimination.

6. Several factors contribute to stress on the job: dissatisfaction, lack of security, work overloads, and interpersonal conflicts with co-workers. One of the most stressful life changes, unemployment, not only causes financial difficulty but also may have serious consequences in terms of self-devaluation and loss of self-esteem.

7. Leisure is a set of activities, excluding maintenance activities, that are performed outside of work. The relationship between work and leisure is a complex one that is better described by a number of approaches than by a single, general theory. Leisure time, planned for and appropriately used, can contribute to personal growth and development.

# Chapter 16

# The Individual and the Group

*"If it were possible for the overworked hypothetical man from Mars to take a fresh view of the people of Earth, he would probably be impressed by the amount of time they spend doing things together in groups. He would note that most people cluster into relatively small groups, with the members residing together in the same dwelling, satisfying their basic biological needs within the group, depending upon the same source for economic support, rearing children, and mutually caring for the health of one another. He would observe that the education and socialization of children tend to occur in other, usually larger, groups in churches, schools, and other social institutions. He would see that much of the work of the world is carried out by people who perform their activities in close interdependence within relatively enduring associations. He would perhaps be saddened to find groups of men engaged in warfare, gaining courage and moral from pride in their unit and a knowledge that they can depend on their buddies. He might be gladdened to see groups of people enjoying themselves in recreations and sports of various kinds. Finally he might be puzzled why so many people spend so much time in little groups talking, planning, and being 'in conference.' Surely he would conclude that if he wanted to understand much about what is happening on Earth he would have to examine rather carefully the ways in which groups form, function, and dissolve."*

*(CARTWRIGHT & ZANDER, 1968, P. 3)*

**group: any collection of people who share some characteristic or goal and who meet either by chance or design**

In our discussion of interpersonal relations, sexuality, marriage, work, and leisure, we have seen the extent to which we interact with others, the degree to which we are group creatures. Only recently, however, have psychologists systematically studied the structure and behavior of groups and the ways in which individuals and groups mutually influence each other. As we probe into the interactions between a **group** and its members, we add indispensable information to our understanding of human behavior.

In this chapter, then, we shall concern ourselves with the social setting of behavior. Specifically, we shall study: *(a)* why we have groups, *(b)* how groups affect us, and *(c)* the interaction of the individual and the group, including leadership and prejudice.

## WHY WE HAVE GROUPS

To observe people even casually is to see that much of their time is spent in groups. And if we take a closer look at any individual, we will find that he or she is a member of a large number of groups.

Let us take a fictitious man named Mr. Smith. In describing him, those who know him will tell us he is a human being (species identification), he is a man (sexual identification), he is a Smith (family identification), he is a teacher (occupational identification), he is a Christian (religious identification), he is an American (national identification), he is Irish (ethnic identification), and he is a Democrat (political identification). Besides being all these, we might be told he is a golfer, a beer drinker, a lover of popular music and impressionist art, a football fan, and a devotee of old movies. All these adjectives indicate his membership in groups.

During the course of the day, Mr. Smith will engage in numerous activities, many of which will demonstrate his membership in the groups we have named. And at times during the day, he will be part of groups so transient that they have little meaning for him: the group eating in a restaurant at one time, the group in the elevator, the group on the bus, or the group stuck in a traffic jam.

## The Variety of Groups to Which We Belong

In seeking to understand the impact of groups on the behavior of individuals, we must take into account the variety of groups to which people belong. In looking more closely at these groups, we can see several different kinds:

1. We are involuntary members of some groups. It is difficult, if not impossible, to get out of these. For example, we are born into our family, our race, and our ethnic group. Involuntary membership due to birth can be a source of pride or can be experienced as a burden; it can confer great privilege (as it does for members of high-status families) or it can saddle us with substantial difficulties (as many members of ethnic and racial minorities know).

2. We must, of necessity, belong to *some* groups, though we may have some choice about which particular group we will belong to. For example, most of us must live in *some* community, work in *some* group, go to *some* school, and associate with *some* people. If we want to work, we may have to join unions or other work-related associations; if we want to practice our religious faith, we will probably have to be part of some religious community; if we want to participate in political processes, we will have to be part of some political party or organization.

3. There are many groups to which we belong where membership is strictly voluntary. We join these groups in order to enjoy sharing interests with others of like mind, to work with others for common goals, to increase our social status,

The groups that we belong to involuntarily can offer us benefits and impose demands upon us. Our families, for example, provide us with love and companionship and satisfy many of our material needs. In exchange for these benefits, we are often expected to follow some rules and conform to certain standards of behavior.

or because joining promises to be profitable in some other way. For example, we can join neighborhood associations to help better our communities.

4. We belong to other groups because we have a particular trait or characteristic. Mr. Smith is forty years old, so he is in the forty-year-old age group. He watches old movies on television, so he is in the group of old-movie fans, and so on. These groups usually have little influence on the individuals who comprise them and cause them few problems. Occasionally, outside factors may make this type of group membership important. If a movement develops to make everyone retire at age sixty, then all in this group would likely be far more conscious of their group membership. The same would be true if there should develop a movement to outlaw the reading of *Playgirl* or the playing of tennis and basketball on Sunday or the televising of football games. Then all the people who belong to the group characterized by the interest or activity in question would likely become more aware of their membership in this group, and we might see this group become organized.

5. We also belong to many transient groups, which form and dissolve leaving no traces that they ever existed. We mentioned Mr. Smith's elevator companions and the group in the restaurant. While ordinarily these groups have little importance in themselves, they constitute one of the important arenas of social action. They make up what we call the **public,** and, as Goffman (1967, 1972) has pointed out, our behavior in these situations is as carefully regulated as our behavior in the most tightly controlled groups.

**public: nonpersonal, nonintimate group or setting**

Thus, like it or not, we are involved in groups. What are the rewards and costs of this involvement? How do the rewards and costs balance out?

Even within a group as transitory and nonpersonal as the crowd of spectators at a football game, certain forms of behavior, such as cheering for the teams and yelling at the officials, are considered appropriate.

## The Rewards of Group Membership

Groups evolve and exist because important needs of individuals are best met in this way. Among the benefits of group membership are mutual help and identity.

**Mutual help and security.** We belong to most groups in order to benefit from various kinds of mutual help. Group membership helps provide for food, shelter, and companionship. While it is not impossible for individual people to provide their own food and shelter and care for themselves in other respects, it is not easy even in reasonably favorable circumstances. For most residents of large cities, this kind of self-sufficiency is virtually impossible.

Our needs for companionship are just as strong. While some can learn to live alone and others seek solitude, the presence of others is normally a great comfort to us. For some people, the threat of social ostracism can be a very powerful persuader.

Finally, the protection of the group is vital, due to our long period of helplessness after birth and because we are defenseless against many kinds of attack. Because it is easier to see this need for group protection in primitive societies, we may be tempted to think that we are no longer so dependent on the group for security. A little thought, however, may make us aware that life in our "advanced" civilization is, if anything, even more group dependent. It is simply that the group's methods for protecting us generally work so well that we are not aware of them. But when the systems break down, as in the inability to control violence, runaway inflation, or mob rule, we recognize how important groups are for mutual help and security.

**Identity and fulfillment.** Group membership can also satisfy our needs for identity and self-esteem. For example, we noted in Chapter 15 that work is an important source of identity and self-esteem for the individual. As we participate in other group settings, our identity and self-esteem can become even stronger.

Many of our finest possibilities as human beings can be fulfilled only in a group. A sense of achievement, the joys of loving and being loved, the feeling of being needed, and some of the greatest opportunities for growth are found only in a group setting.

Without the group there is no opportunity for leadership and there is no fellowship. Without the community there is no continuity of values that we call **heritage,** no shared vision to live and die for, no sowing of seeds that only others can harvest. Without ties to certain special others, there is no enlargement of the self to include a family, a nation, a people. All of these supraindividual identities may become—and at times have become—destructive. Yet it is through such communities that people have often fulfilled their greatest potentials.

heritage: legacy passed on from generation to generation

## The Costs of Group Membership

Even as we have described the rewards of group membership we have hinted at some of the costs.

**Limitations.**    The first cost of group membership is the experience of limitations. As children, we learned that those who protected and cared for us also restricted us. As adults, we continue to find that membership in a group brings limitations with it. To be a member of a particular church we must limit our behavior. If we are active in a political party, beliefs we hold contrary to the party cannot be easily expressed. Even informal groups have limits. Though they may not be so clearly defined, we know when we have gone too far.

**Demands.**    Not only does the group set limits; it also makes demands of us, and sometimes these demands can be very heavy. There is, first of all, and perhaps most important, the demand that we be loyal to the group: "Are you with us or against us?" Much deviant behavior will be tolerated if there is no question about loyalty, while scrupulous conformity will be of no avail if there is a strong suspicion that one's loyalties are with the "other side."

There are also demands for conformity, especially in public. The demand to conform or take the "correct" stand on issues can be one of the most unpleasant costs of group membership. This is the theme of *A Man for All Seasons,* a powerful story of Sir Thomas More's conflict with England's King Henry VIII. There are times when those with integrity and conscience (like Sir Thomas More) are sacrificed in the name of group ideals, while unethical and opportunistic people ride high.

Finally, there are the demands for responsible participation—for assuming specified roles, paying dues and taxes, voting, or backing leadership. Few groups will allow members to benefit from the rewards of group membership without sharing in the cost of group maintenance. For example, a neighborhood association may form to build a park for the community. However, to reap the benefits of the park, community residents may have to join the organization or pay fees to use the park. Sometimes the demand for responsible participation involves fighting in battles the group is involved in. In war, this demand can cost group members their lives. Less dramatically, membership in an organization fighting a public works project that will destroy many homes or irreparably damage the natural environment may require the individual to participate in the group's struggle against the project. For some, responsible participation may involve writing letters to public officials, while others may speak out against the project in public hearings or community meetings.

**Threats to integrity.**    The real issue in meeting both the limitations and the demands of the group is the threat these can pose to an individual's integrity. All group life calls for compromise. But how far can a person compromise before losing his or her soul? When is silence discreet and when is it cowardly? When is dissent irresponsible and when is it courageous? There are no easy answers here, and the struggle for integrity by people who love the group but have misgivings about its actions can be intensely painful. It is this price of group membership that makes many people reluctant to join groups and commit themselves to group goals.

# Insight

After analyzing a number of high-level decisions that led to historic fiascoes and blunders, such as the lack of preparedness at Pearl Harbor, the Bay of Pigs invasion, and the Vietnam War, Janis and Mann (1977) identified eight common characteristics that can lead to **groupthink,** the tendency to preserve group unity at the cost of ignoring danger signals. These are:

*1. an illusion of invulnerability, shared by most or all of the members, which creates excessive optimism and encourages taking extreme risks;*

*2. collective efforts to rationalize in order to discount warnings which might lead the members to reconsider their assumptions before they recommit themselves to their past policy decisions;*

*3. an unquestioned belief in the group's inherent morality, inclining the members to ignore the ethical or moral consequences of their decisions;*

*4. stereotyped views of rivals and enemies as too evil to warrant genuine attempts to negotiate, or as too weak or stupid to counter whatever risky attempts are made to defeat their purposes;*

## THE CHARACTERISTICS OF GROUPTHINK

*5. direct pressure on any member who expresses strong arguments against any of the group's stereotypes, illusions, or commitments, making clear that such dissent is contrary to what is expected of all loyal members;*

*6. self-censorship of deviations from the apparent group consensus, reflecting each member's inclination to minimize to himself the importance of his doubts and counterarguments;*

*7. a shared illusion of unanimity, partly resulting from this self-censorship and augmented by the false assumption that silence implies consent;*

*8. the emergence of self-appointed "mindguards"—members who protect the group from adverse information that might shatter their shared complacency about the effectiveness and morality of their decisions. (pp. 130–31)*

If group members are to minimize the influence of these irrational factors, it seems important that they be aware of these characteristics—especially if their group decisions will have serious effects on the lives of others.

**groupthink: tendency to make decisions in a group that will preserve group unity at the cost of ignoring other important issues or data**

## The Balance Sheet

We have noted some of the rewards and some of the costs of group membership. If we weigh one against the other, how do they balance? Undoubtedly each individual will find a different answer. For some, the costs are greater than the rewards, and for others the rewards are greater than the costs. And the balance may be different for each group to which we belong.

But once we have balanced costs against rewards, what can we do? The social exchange model described in Chapter 12 suggests a solution: If the costs are greater than the rewards, we can get out of the group.

However, we cannot withdraw or resign from the many groups in which we have involuntary membership. Thus, when our life in these groups is unrewarding there may be no easy solution. Sometimes we can learn skills with which to change the group or improve our position in it. Or, we can seek as much satisfaction as possible outside the group.

## HOW GROUPS AFFECT US

Although we bring our selves, energies, and skills to a group setting, the group can in turn influence us. The level of influence can range from the subtle and delicate to the powerful and obvious. In this section, we shall consider the ways in which an individual can be affected by the group. In particular, we shall discuss social facilitation, social contagion, conformity, obedience, and helping.

### Social Facilitation

**social facilitation: effects of presence or observation of others upon the behavior of an individual**

One of the earliest topics of research in social psychology was the study of **social facilitation**—how the presence of others can influence individual behavior. Consider the following situation: an athlete whose specialty is sprinting has a choice of two ways in which to train. In one type of training, the athlete can train alone against his or her own best performance. In the second type of training, the athlete can train with other sprinters. Which of these two situations is most likely to improve the runner's performance (Morgan, King, & Robinson, 1979)?

Some research in social facilitation suggests that the mere presence of others can improve performance. The beneficial impact of the presence of others has been demonstrated in both human and nonhuman species. For example, in the presence of "co-actors" performing the same behavior, chickens and rats eat more, ants work harder in building nests, and cyclists ride faster (Zajonc, 1968).

However, another group of studies has suggested that the presence of others can have a detrimental effect on individual performance. Humans in a motor-learning task made more errors in the presence of others, and cockroaches performed more poorly in maze learning while in the presence of other cockroaches.

Psychologist Robert Zajonc (1968) has proposed a solution that reconciles these apparently contradictory results. Zajonc notes that the presence of others has a general arousing effect on the person. Depending on the nature of the task that the individual must perform, however, this arousal can have either positive (facilitative) or negative effects. When the task to be performed is a set of behaviors or activities in which the individual is highly skilled, the presence of others is likely to facilitate performance. On the other hand, when the task to be performed has not been well learned, the presence of others will adversely affect performance.

These findings are well known to many parents. For example, a parent may unobtrusively note that a young child has learned how to throw a basketball through a hoop. The child, thrilled by his or her new-found skill, delightedly asks

Research into the phenomenon of social facilitation has suggested that the presence of others can enhance performance when the task is a well-learned response. If the task requires mastery of a new skill, the presence of others may have a detrimental effect.

the parent to watch. While the parent watches, the child's performance slips badly. However, as soon as the parent turns his or her attention to other matters, the child is again successful and implores the parent to "Watch me!" On the other hand, the more skillful older child or adolescent finds that his or her performance improves when others (especially peers) watch. For the more experienced individual, the presence of others gives the individual the opportunity to "show off."

Thus, individual performance is enhanced in the presence of others when our confidence and skills are relatively high. However, when skills and confidence are low, performance is often better when we are alone. In the case of the runner noted earlier, the better choice would be to train with others.

## Social Contagion

The presence of others can also influence the degree to which individual behaviors and beliefs can be influenced. In **social contagion,** a generally inaccurate belief or idea spreads rapidly through a population or group of people, and this idea can significantly influence an individual's behavior.

social contagion: type of social facilitation in which being in a crowd can stimulate activity

Social contagion can be seen in many ways, including rumors and panics. For example, one recent rumor held that a well-known fast-food chain was placing horsemeat into its hamburgers. This rumor became so prevalent in some parts of the country that the firm began to lose business. Only an intensive advertising campaign stressing the "100 percent beef" content of the hamburgers prevented serious and continuing damage to the firm. Similarly, a rumor that continues in many parts of the country is that the collection of many thousands of tax stamps from cigarette packages and their delivery to some (unknown) firm will result in the donation of a kidney dialysis machine to the National Kidney Foundation.

As we can see from these examples, rumors can involve positive and negative behaviors. Whether the rumor is positive or negative, however, the source of the rumors cannot be identified. Despite repeated denials by the various firms and agencies noted above, those rumors continued and people's behaviors were affected.

In large cities, the effects of a rumor can be devastating, leading to civil disobedience and violence. In an attempt to limit the effects of rumors, many cities have established rumor control "hot lines" in which residents of a city can call a central office and receive current and correct information. Presumably, this correct information limits the degree to which a rumor is taken seriously.

**panic: unfounded or ir-rational fear producing mass flight**

**Panic** is another, more dramatic example of the social contagion of crowd behavior. The flavor of such social contagion has been well captured by humorist James Thurber (1933):

Suddenly somebody began to run. It may be that he had simply remembered, all of a moment, an engagement to meet his wife, for which he was now frightfully late. Whatever it was, he ran east on Broad Street (probably toward the Maramor Restaurant, a favorite place for a man to meet his wife). Somebody else began to run, perhaps a newsboy in high spirits. Another man, a portly gentleman of affairs, broke into a trot. Inside of ten minutes, everybody on High Street, from the Union Depot to the Courthouse was running. A loud mumble gradually crystallized into the dread word "dam." "The dam has broke!" Two thousand people were abruptly in full flight. "Go east!" was the cry that arose—east away from the river, east to safety. "Go east! Go east!" . . .

A tall spare woman with grim eyes and a determined chin ran past me down the middle of the street. I was still uncertain as to what was the matter, in spite of all the shouting. I drew up alongside the woman with some effort, for although she was in her late fifties, she had a beautiful easy running form and seemed to be in excellent condition. "What is it?" I puffed. She gave me a quick glance and then looked ahead again, stepping up her pace a trifle. "Don't ask me, ask God!" she said. (pp. 41–42, 47)

Unfortunately, the social contagion of crowd behavior is not usually as comical as in the preceding passage. A more serious example of social contagion has been presented by Kerckhoff and Back (1968). These researchers reported on an outbreak of "hysterical contagion" in a clothing factory. In this incident, 62 workers from a total of 965 reported an illness that they presumed was caused by a bug bite. Almost all the affected workers were women, most of whom worked in the dressmaking department. One woman reported on her experience:

I was bit by the bug and it was such a sudden and sharp bite, you really didn't know what happened. It felt like a pin sticking me. Then the pain went down and up my arm and into my neck. I walked about six steps, and my legs started getting weak, and I just passed out. (p. 8)

Some of those affected were hospitalized; some vomited; some had seizures. Although health officials could not find any insects in the factory that could cause such an extreme reaction, the building was "debugged." After one week, the "epidemic" was over.

These researchers also reported that the outbreak occurred during a peak production time in a new factory in which personnel policies were not yet well formed. Prior to the outbreak, rumors had circulated around the factory that the

Sometimes being in a group can make it easier to express our feelings.

building was infested. And there were many more "cases" than were reported to the factory officials and medical authorities.

These findings, as well as others, give credence to the suggestion that social diffusion and contagion, rumors and panic, are group phenomena whose roots go much deeper than their visible manifestations. That is, the undercurrents of rumor and belief must be present in the group and accepted by the group for a considerable period of time. Under these circumstances, only a minor incident may be necessary to set off a much larger group response.

There are several practical implications of these findings. Group concerns and beliefs, whether accurate or inaccurate, must be taken seriously. If these concerns can be seriously addressed, some action can be taken to alleviate the concerns. Secondly, group concerns, such as those illustrated by the Kerckhoff and Back study, can also be an expression of some underlying problem. That is, the group concerns can be used as a cue to those in charge that some problem needs solving. In the examples noted above, the group belief that bugs were infesting the factory might have been used by a perceptive manager to determine that the women in the dressmaking department were under great stress and anxiety.

# Conformity

*"To most of us, conformity is a dirty word evoking images of robot-like acceptance of the attitudes, opinions, and beliefs of others."*
**(MCNEIL, 1974, P. 410)**

conformity: acceptance of and abidance by established social norms and rules of a group

While we often resent them, group pressures toward **conformity** help serve the group's basic needs for maintenance and task performance. For example, the conformity demanded and needed in a work organization helps define the roles that individuals are assigned and the tasks they must complete. Conformity also occurs in leisure situations, such as group sports, and in family situations as well. Without some measure of conformity and obedience, individual behavior would be chaotic and unpredictable, and group tasks would never be coordinated and completed.

There is also a negative side to conformity and obedience. Pressures toward conformity may produce a stifling and unproductive uniformity that violates individual autonomy. In this section, we shall attempt to note some of the reasons people conform, as well as some of conformity's consequences, both positive and negative.

**Why do people conform?** Both in the laboratory and in natural settings, researchers and others have been intrigued with the relative ease with which people can be induced to behave similarly to others. A rather dramatic example is provided in the early conformity studies by Asch (1952, 1955).

In this classic experiment, groups of seven to nine male college students were asked to say which of three lines on a card (Figure 16-1a) matched the length of a standard line on a second card (Figure 16-1b). One of the three lines they could choose from was the same length as the standard line; the others differed from the standard by anywhere from three fourths of an inch to an inch and three fourths. It had been determined in advance that these differences were clearly distinguishable.

In each group all but one of the "subjects" were actually stooges, previously instructed to make a *unanimous wrong* choice on most of the trials after the

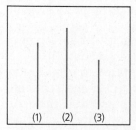

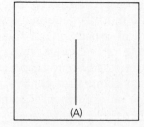

**FIGURE 16.1a Comparison Lines**    **FIGURE 16.1b Standard Line**

first two. The actual subject could not announce his own judgment until after most or all of the others had announced theirs. Thus, after hearing the false judgment given by the planted majority, the minority subject had to choose between denying the evidence of his senses and contradicting the judgment of the group.

Under such pressure, subjects accepted the majority's wrong selections in 36.8 percent of the trials. About a fourth of the 123 naïve subjects clung consistently to their minority judgments, while a few subjects yielded to the majority decision on almost every trial.

When the test subjects were interviewed after the experiment, it was found that some had yielded out of fear of "seeming different," even though they continued to believe in the correctness of their own judgments. Others assumed that, although their own perceptions clearly *seemed* correct, the majority could not be wrong. In a few cases, the perception was distorted, and the subject was unaware of having yielded to group pressure.

Even subjects who consistently maintained their independent judgments were considerably disturbed by their disagreement with the majority and reported that they had been seriously tempted to go along with the group in order to avoid seeming inferior or absurd. In fact, a later study by Bogdonoff, Klein, Estis, Shaw, and Back (1961) found that students who "called them as they saw them" suffered more anxiety, as seen by physiological changes. One subject who consistently disagreed with the group was dripping with perspiration by the end of the session, even though his judgments were right in each instance.

These and other studies in conformity suggest that conformity may be related to four factors:

1. *Personality factors.* Two personal characteristics of the individual seem to be important in conformity. Individuals who have a low opinion of themselves appear more likely to yield to group pressure than persons with high self-esteem. A related factor is the individual's feeling of competence in the situation. People who perceive their competence as high conform less than those who perceive their competence as low. On the other hand, personality characteristics unrelated to conformity include sex and intelligence.

2. *Situational factors.* The nature of the situation is a potent determinant of whether or not conformity occurs. The more ambiguous or confusing the situation, the more likely people are to conform. Apparently when people have little objective evidence to go on, they look to others for guidelines.

Aronson (1972) has illustrated this point: "Suppose that you need to use the toilet in an unfamiliar classroom building. Under the sign 'Rest Rooms' there are two doors, but, unfortunately, a vandal has removed the specific designations from the doors—that is, you cannot be certain which is the Men's room and which is the Women's room. Quite a dilemma—you are afraid to open either door for fear of being embarrassed or embarrassing others. As you stand there in dismay and discomfort, hopping from one foot to the other, the door on the left opens and out strolls a distinguished-looking gentleman. With a sigh of relief, you are now willing to forge ahead, reasonably secure in the knowledge that left is for men and right is for women" (p. 24).

3. *Group factors.* These include various characteristics and behaviors of the group, such as qualifications of group members, unanimity of opinion, and the importance of the group to the individual. Additionally, when group members are perceived as competent, conformity is increased.

4. *Social pressure.* Social pressure can be used in a variety of ways to induce conformity. For example, group-determined role definitions, involvement in group decision making, manipulation of rewards and punishments, recognition and approval, advancement and honors, and fear of expulsion are some of the ways in which conformity can be induced. Sometimes, social pressure is more subtle, as when certain information is used to convince individuals of the validity of group goals and values. In some situations, the pressures can be quite structured and formal, as in codes of law.

In summary, conformity can be influenced by the personality characteristics of group members, particularly those who have low self-esteem and a low sense of competence; by the characteristics of the task, particularly when the task is ambiguous; by the characteristics of the group, especially when the group is important to the individual and the group members are seen as competent; and by social pressure, through subtle or obvious, structured or informal ways that the group rewards conformity or punishes nonconformity.

**The group's need for nonconformists.**    Groups have needs of their own that may differ from the needs of individual members. Paradoxically, one of these needs is for members who have integrity and commitment to values beyond the group to challenge the group when it makes mistakes.

**nonconformity:** tendency to believe in or put forth goals or methods for achieving goals different from the group or society at large

Although some measure of conformity appears essential for coordinating group effort, some measure of **nonconformity** is needed to maintain the group's adaptability. If a group is to adapt effectively to changing conditions, it must be capable of making needed changes within its structure and functioning. This means that someone in the group must recognize the new conditions, propose new approaches, and make other group members aware of the need for change. It also means that the group itself must be open to and accepting of some nonconformity. Without adaptability and change, alternative ideas and behaviors are not possible; the group's thinking and structure become rigid, and the group ceases to function effectively (Buckley, 1968; Miller, 1977).

For some people, nonconformity implies automatic disapproval of the group's decision, despite the quality or reasonableness of the ideas that the group developed. These are the "nay sayers" of groups. For some individuals, nonconformity stems from a vision of the world and humankind radically different from what others believe. Individuals like Jesus, Galileo, Sigmund Freud, and Albert Einstein produced enormous and lasting changes in our perception of our world, our selves, and our society, often at great personal sacrifice. As Einstein (1949) wrote: " . . . in the face of all ties, I have never lost an obstinate sense of detachment, of the need for solitude—a feeling which increases with the years" (p. 3). Thus, while nonconformity can alter large and small groups, it often involves a cost that the individual must pay in a sense of difference and separateness from the group.

# Obedience

The classic studies in **obedience** were conducted by psychologist Stanley Milgram (1963, 1968). The basic structure of Milgram's studies involved three individuals—the experimenter and two subjects. However, one of the "subjects" was in fact an accomplice of the experimenter. The subjects were told that they would be involved in a study concerning learning. One of the subjects would be the learner, and one would be the teacher. The experimenter rigged the situation so that the accomplice was always the learner, and the real subject was the teacher.

The teacher was seated in front of an impressive-looking machine with a large number of switches and labels, giving the impression that the machine would deliver shocks ranging from 15 to 450 volts. The teacher was instructed to shock the learner each time that the learner made a mistake, and to increase the voltage level with each mistake. While the learner was *never* shocked, the teacher was made to believe that the learner was being shocked through the learner's orchestrated series of grunts, cries, and screams.

Although many people outside of the experiment felt that virtually no one would give the 450-volt "shock," Milgram found that in fact 65 percent of the subjects administered the 450-volt "shock," even though they showed signs of nervousness and anxiety, such as nervous laughter.

These studies are a powerful statement regarding the degree to which the commands of people in authority are obeyed. Although we cannot generalize from this experiment to all of human behavior, the experiment shows that under the proper conditions, people can behave in ways contrary to their beliefs and values if they are pressed forcibly enough by someone in authority.

**obedience: tendency to follow instructions from those in authority**

# Helping

On March 13, 1964, on Austin Street in the borough of Queens in New York City, a woman was attacked by a man wielding a knife. The woman's name was Kitty Genovese, and the attack began at 3:20 A.M. Kitty Genovese was first attacked on the street. After fighting off her attacker, she ran to a street corner where she screamed for help, "He stabbed me! Please help me!" However, her attacker soon cornered her again, and she was fatally stabbed. She again screamed for help, "I'm dying! I'm dying!" but to no avail.

A particularly upsetting aspect of Kitty Genovese's experience was reported by the *New York Times:* thirty-eight people viewed the attack on Kitty Genovese, and not one aided her by even so much as a telephone call to the police. Even more extraordinary, the attack lasted nearly forty-five minutes, and in that time, not one person on Austin Street helped save a dying woman.

Ten years later, at exactly 3:20 A.M. Sandra Zahler was attacked on Austin Street, and again, no one helped her. In January 1973, a woman was attacked and raped on a bridge in Trenton, New Jersey. At least twenty-five people viewed the attack, and no one helped her. In 1974, a woman was sexually molested in a crowded food shop, and no one helped her (Worchel & Cooper, 1979).

# Insight

## SOCIOBIOLOGY: THE BIOLOGY OF HELPING

sociobiology: theory stating that social behavior has a biological basis in both animals and human beings

Do helping and altruism have a biological basis? Edward O. Wilson, author of *Sociobiology: The New Synthesis* (1975), feels that the answer is yes.

According to Wilson, the premise underlying **sociobiology** is that the sole purpose of an individual's life is to pass on his or her genetic material to the next generation. Sociobiologists maintain that evolutionary changes help make the individual's adaptation to the environment better and increase the chances that the individual will survive long enough to pass on his or her genes so as to ensure the survival of the species.

Wilson and other sociobiologists (Dawkins, 1976; Leak & Christopher, 1982) are especially interested in social organization. As they point out, social organizations seem to follow the evolutionary pattern of diversity and complexity apparent in genetic structures. That is, the social organizations of species tend to become more complex as we move from single-celled organisms to the enormous complexity of human life. If biological development can be explained in evolutionary terms, argue the sociobiologists, it may also be possible to describe social development and organization in evolutionary, biological terms.

Using sociobiological concepts may help explain some interesting aspects of human and animal life. For example, worker ants will fight fiercely and die in an attempt to protect the colony and its nesting areas and fertilized eggs. Similarly, it has been reported (Wilson, 1975) that some elderly, disabled Eskimos will choose to stay behind and die rather than undertake a long and arduous journey on which their physical infirmities would only slow down and endanger the group as a whole. And, as we have

seen in our discussion of helping, some people heroically risk their lives so that others, unrelated by blood or marriage, may live.

In these cases, we may praise the incredible and heroic self-sacrifice that these individuals make. On the other hand, these acts may also be extraordinarily self-destructive. How can we explain and understand behavior that is clearly not adaptive for the individual?

The answer, claim the sociobiologists, is that human beings have genes for altruistic behavior. These genes are shared with other members of our species. And when one member of the group engages in altruistic acts, the group as a whole is spared, along with the altruistic genes. Thus, altruism is part of the adaptive evolution of the human species.

Of course, there is no way that the sociobiologists' hypothesis can be tested directly with human beings. Nonetheless, the sociobiologists raise a significant challenge to psychologists and other social scientists. Most social scientists believe that learning, society, and other cultural forces explain most of human behavior. But, this is primarily an assumption, not a proven fact.

We noted in Chapter 2 that there were several conflicting views of human behavior. The sociobiology controversy reminds us that even when we feel we are certain about the nature of one small aspect of human beings, there may be other interesting and potentially valid approaches to the same issue. In essence, the sociobiology controversy teaches us to be aware of the great vastness of our ignorance and to be open to new ideas and discoveries that can help us understand the complexities of human behavior.

These horrifying reports stand in marked contrast to the generous and helping acts that also occur. For example, when an airline jet crashed into the bitterly cold Potomac River in January 1982, a man refused a lifeline five times so that other people could be saved. His sacrifice cost him his life. And, warm summer weather reliably brings stories of how people have jumped into lakes, streams, and rivers to save a foundering swimmer or the victim of a capsized boat.

**Factors influencing helping.**    How can we reconcile these apparently contradictory aspects of human behavior? What are the factors that increase or decrease the probability of helping others?

Part of the answer lies in the number of people involved in the situation calling for help. Researchers J. M. Darley and B. Latane (1968) hypothesized that as the number of people involved in a situation increased, the sense of responsibility for helping another would decrease. In a test of their hypothesis, Darley and Latane asked college students to discuss the problems they were having adjusting to college life. So that they would be more likely to discuss their thoughts freely and without embarrassment, the two students who participated in the study were escorted to separate, isolated booths. In fact, one of the two students was an accomplice of the experimenter.

After the students were placed in the booths, the accomplice began "speaking" of the stress he was under and how he was susceptible to epileptic seizures under times of stress. Because the booths did not allow for face-to-face communication, the true subject was unable to detect that the conversation he was hearing had in fact been tape-recorded earlier.

When it came time for the experimental accomplice to "speak" again, an "emergency" began. The true subject heard the accomplice saying, "I-er-um-I think I-I need-er-if-if- could-er somebody er-er-er-er-er-er- give me a little-er give me a little-er give me a little help here because I-er-I'm . . . " (chokes, then quiet) (Darley & Latane, 1968, p. 379).

The experimenters then measured the number of people who responded and the time it took for the subject to seek assistance. In one experimental condition, the subject was led to believe that the discussion group consisted of two people (the subject and the victim); in another condition, the subject believed that the group consisted of three people (the subject, the victim, and another tape-recorded voice); in the third condition, the subjects were led to believe that they were part of a six-person group.

The results of this study were striking: as the group size increased from two to three to six people, the percent of subjects who responded to the victim's cries for help by the end of the seizure *decreased* from 85 percent, to 62 percent, to 31 percent. Similarly, the time that it took for subjects to respond to the victim increased as the group size increased: when the group consisted of two people, the response time was 52 seconds; when the group contained three people, response time was 93 seconds; and when the group was six people, response time was 166 seconds. In essence, this study found that helping was inversely proportional to the size of the group and that the delay in offering help increased as the group size increased.

Helping, however, is not dependent only on the numbers of bystanders. First, the bystanders must notice the event and they must interpret the event as an emergency. For example, many children play in a park, and many fall down and begin to cry. However, people might not even notice the children's behavior, and few would interpret crying as a sign of emergency.

**diffusion of responsibility: inhibition of individual action while in a group setting**

Next, bystanders must assume responsibility for acting. It is at this point that **diffusion of responsibility** occurs. When other people are present, we assume (or hope) that the "other guy" will act. Diffusion of responsibility is not limited to situations calling for assistance; it occurs in self-help situations as well. In a study conducted by Petty, Williams, Harkins, and Latane (1977), coupons for free hamburgers at McDonald's were placed in an elevator. When only one person was riding the elevator, 81 percent helped themselves to the coupons. However, when the number of riders increased to two or more, the number of riders who took coupons dropped to 14 percent.

Assuming that people take responsibility for others, they must know what to do in an emergency. If they do not know how to provide appropriate assistance, they will, of course, not act (Brickman, Rabinowitz, Karuza, Coates, Cohn, & Kidder, 1982). Finally, bystanders must implement their decisions. If the cost of helping is perceived as too great, no assistance may be provided. For example, many people might refuse to intervene in an attack, fearful that they themselves might become victims as well. In these cases, indirect help, such as calling the police, may be the outcome.

Some additional situational factors influence helping. We help others when

We often find that we are more likely to help people we know, people who are like us, and people who truly need help. All these factors probably influenced these residents of Idaho Falls, Idaho, to work together filling sandbags to contain the flood waters threatening their town after the collapse of the Teton Dam in 1976.

we are rewarded, when we feel good, when helping is modeled for us, when social norms permit helping, when we have time to act, and when we recipro- cate help given to us (Worchel & Cooper, 1979). For example, giving to the Salvation Army at Christmastime is increased by the models of giving that we see and because it is particularly appropriate to help others during the holidays.

There are also types of people that we consistently help. For example, we are more likely to help those whom we like, those who are similar to us, and those who are truly in need. Thus, we are more likely to help our friends than strangers, more likely to help those who are similar to us in dress, and more likely to help those who clearly need assistance.

If we return to the examples presented in the beginning of this section, we can see that helping is not a general trait inherent in human nature, but a com- plex interaction between ourselves, our skills, our experiences; the size, compo- sition, and action of the groups to which we belong; the situation; and the needs and characteristics of those who need our help.

**Urban density, crowding, and environmental design.**   Our discussion of helping and the findings of the Darley and Latane (1968) study lead us indirectly to the issue of how the mass of people in our urban areas affects us.

Although it is generally thought that high urban density leads to increased amount of mental stress, alienation, and social violence, research into this area has failed to confirm these theories in a general fashion. For example, areas of Hong Kong are five times more dense than the densest areas of New York, but the levels of sickness, crime, and mental disorders are significantly higher in New York. When researchers *have* found a connection between density and crime, it often relates to the number of individuals who share the same living space, not the number of people per square block (Galle, Gove, & McPherson, 1972).

Perhaps more important than density is the concept of crowding. Density relates to the number of people per unit of space. **Crowding,** on the other hand, describes the psychological interpretation of the presence and effects of other people. For example, we may feel crowded in an elevator that is half full, while we may not feel so crowded in an overflowing theater or concert hall.

Part of the reason for the experience of crowding lies in the violation of **territoriality** and **personal space** by others. We try to "protect" our territory and personal space. When they are violated, we feel uncomfortable. These ef- fects were noted in a study by Felipe and Sommer (1966–67). In this experiment, researchers went to a library to see how students reacted to the violation of personal space. When the researcher sat in a chair next to the student, 70 per- cent of the students got up and left within thirty minutes. In contrast, 25 percent of the students left if the experimenter sat further away or across from the stu- dents, and only 15 percent left if no one sat next to them.

It is possible to minimize the sensation of crowding through effective envi- ronmental design. In one interesting study, Baum and Valins (1977) studied the residents of a hall-type dormitory and a suite-type dormitory. In the hall-type design, bedrooms were aligned along a long hall, with bathrooms generally in the middle of the hall. In the suite-type dormitory, a smaller number of students

**crowding: psychological discomfort produced by the presence of other people**

**territoriality: psychologi- cal attachment to a spe- cific area**

**personal space: psycho- logical boundaries sur- rounding an individual's body: violation of these boundaries produces personal discomfort**

We are likely to feel crowded when the presence of many people threatens our privacy, violates our personal space, and frustrates our attainment of some goal, such as finding a seat on the subway.

shared a common bathroom and lounge area. Access to the bedrooms in the suite arrangement was only through the lounge. Although the density was similar in the two dormitories, students in the suite arrangement reported less crowding than students in the hall-type dormitory, probably because the residents of the suite felt they had more control over those with whom they would come into contact.

These findings have implications for urban planning. As seen in the disastrous Pruitt-Igoe public housing project in St. Louis, Missouri, poor environmental design, characterized by huge, massive buildings in which people feel defenseless, can lead to significant dissatisfaction and crime. These buildings did not allow residents to develop close relationships with their neighbors, and residents reported that it was difficult to supervise children at play. In contrast, smaller scale, more intimate design fosters interaction and gives people a sense that they belong, that they have a neighborhood that all can care for.

# INTERACTION OF THE INDIVIDUAL AND THE GROUP

In previous sections, we have considered the necessity for groups, types of groups, and rewards and costs of group membership. We have also discussed a number of topics in which group processes influence individuals. In this section, we will consider some ways in which groups and individuals interact.

Group interaction is not a one-way street, and the individual may exert a major influence on the group. Group characteristics can also markedly influence our behavior. That is, our assumptions about group membership can influence the ways in which we interact with other people on a one-to-one basis.

In this section, we will discuss two topics related to the interaction of the individual and the group. First, we will focus on leaders and examine the factors both within the situation and within the person that are conducive to leadership behavior. Next we will discuss prejudice, examining the many sources of prejudice and some theories of why prejudice develops.

*"The final test of a leader is that he leaves behind him in other men the conviction and the will to carry on."*
*(WALTER LIPPMANN, ROOSEVELT HAS GONE)*

*"The people have always some champion whom they set over them and nurse them into greatness."*
*(PLATO, THE REPUBLIC)*

*"A leader is best*
*When people barely know that he exists."*
*(WITTER BYNNER, THE WAY OF LIFE ACCORDING TO LAOTZU)*

## Leadership: The Influence of the Individual on the Group

A **leader** is an individual who has a greater than average amount of influence in the group. Groups differ greatly in their leadership structure. In informal or loosely organized groups, leadership may be virtually nonexistent or constantly shifting, especially where there is unanimity of purpose. In highly organized groups, on the other hand, leadership becomes an important characteristic of group structure. As we shall see, leadership is a highly complex phenomenon and is strongly influenced by many aspects of the group.

**leader: group member who is able to direct group behavior toward goals and maintain functional harmony of the group**

**Leadership as a personal quality.** One controversy about leadership asks the question whether leaders make history or history makes leaders. Early concepts of leadership invariably stressed characteristics of individuals that made them unique and successful in their prominent and influential roles. These early views emphasized the "Born Leader" or trait approaches to leadership.

But the search for unique qualities within the person that distinguish him or her as a leader has been hampered by methodological problems such as difficulty in identifying "good" leaders and measuring personality traits. An additional problem is the belief that good leadership inevitably results in a high level of group effectiveness. According to the trait approach to leadership, a poorly functioning group will improve its performance when a strong leader is placed in charge. These beliefs have not been confirmed, and support for the concept of leadership as a unique personal quality has been mixed.

A slight preponderance of evidence suggests that successful leaders are brighter but not too much brighter, show greater knowledge and skills related to the task to be accomplished, display sociability factors such as greater activity and participation, popularity, and cooperativeness, have higher initiative and persistence, and are older than other members of the group.

**Leadership as a function of the situation.**     A more fruitful approach to leadership comes from the study of the needs and characteristics of the group and their effect upon the emergence of certain leaders. This more contemporary perspective stresses the emergence of leaders according to situational factors operating in a given group at a given time. Among them are the complexity of decisions that have to be made or goals to be reached, the size of a group, and the urgency of a situation or the importance of taking decisive and effective action. Given certain of these elements, several factors may influence the rise to prominence of particular people:

1. *Chance.* Jones and Gerard (1967) have noted that: " . . . it is important to recognize the potential role of chance in the emergence of particular leaders. In the early stages of group formation it may happen that a particular person quite accidentally makes a correct suggestion or two and as a consequence finds himself thenceforth in the leadership role" (p. 670).

Chance may determine that the first person who speaks up at a meeting is assumed by the others to have leadership qualities. Or, the oldest member of a group may be thought to have greater knowledge or skill, and members may react to that person as if he or she is the group leader. In situations like these, the actual personality and skill characteristics of the individual may have little to do with his or her selection as leader.

2. *Participation rate.* The rate of participation among members is positively related to members' evaluation of contributions to the group, especially in the earlier stages of group formation. A high contributor is very likely to be selected as leader. In one interesting study (Riecken, 1958), rate of participation appeared to influence members' judgments of each other more than did actual skill. Following two problem-solving discussions in four-person groups, high and low participators were identified by the researcher. For the third problem-solving task, the solution was subtle and not likely to appear freely in the discussion. For half of the groups, a hint about the solution was given to a high participator. For the other half of the groups, the hint was given to a low participator. If the solution was offered by the high participator, it was much more likely to be accepted by the group (eleven of sixteen acceptances) than if offered by the low participator (five of sixteen acceptances). However, the maturity of the group may influence

A strong leader can lead a group in any of several directions, but the group's effectiveness ultimately depends on the abilities, attitudes, actions, and commitment of the group's individual members.

their perception of participation rate (Wheeler & Csoka, 1975). For example, the more mature the members of the group, the more likely they are to evaluate the quality of participation rather than just participation rate only.

3. *Other factors conducive to leadership.* Other situational factors include the question of who selects the leader—whether, for example, the leader is selected by his or her superior or by the members of the group. Communication networks also affect leadership. Studies have shown that central persons in the communication network, through whom a great deal of information is passed, are frequently identified as leaders. Additionally, time, feedback, and actual competence are also important factors. Over time, and if there is feedback about the adequacy of the leader's decisions, then actual competence is likely to emerge as the key ingredient in leadership.

**Types or styles of leadership.**    The methods used by leaders in exerting their influence and control appear to depend upon the characteristics of the leader, the group, and the situation. Some leaders are prone to **autocratic,** others to **democractic,** and still others to **laissez-faire** methods of **leadership.** Similarly, some groups will respond favorably to one kind of leadership and not another, often depending upon what they are used to or what the larger culture expects. For example, individuals in a military setting may accept autocratic leadership that they would not countenance in a civilian setting. Or they may accept laissez-faire leadership in a neighborhood group but reject it in a business organization.

The general nature and effects of autocratic, democratic, and laissez-faire methods of leadership were demonstrated in the classic study by Lewin, Lippitt, and White (1939). In this study, clubs were formed of ten-year-old boys matched for age, intelligence, economic background, and so on. Three different types of adult leadership were practiced in the various groups. In the autocratic groups the leader set the group goals, controlled all activity with step-by-step directions,

**autocratic leadership:** form of leadership in which the leader sets the goals and controls the activity of the group

**democratic leadership:** form of leadership in which the leader and members of the group jointly discuss and determine policies and activities

**laissez-faire (pronounced leh-zhay-FAIR) leadership:** leadership in which the leader exerts no influence and group members determine policies and activities

# Insight

In situations in which the labor is divided and the achievement of the final goal requires the coordination of many people, groups are essential. Examples include playing a Beethoven string quartet, mass-producing automobiles, or providing mental-health services for a large community. In such instances, the group clearly represents an improvement over the individual.

When the task involves problem solving, research suggests that groups produce more and better solutions to some problems than do individuals. There are many factors that may account for this, including the summation or coordination of individual strengths; rejection of incorrect suggestions and the checking of errors; and social stimulation and the arousal of greater interest in the task. On the other hand, when time is a factor, the number of person-hours per solution is lower for the individual than for the group. Although groups may provide superior solutions in many instances, efficiency is the price that must be paid. Shaw (1971) has summarized his finding:

*Groups are more effective than individuals on tasks which require a variety of information, which can be solved by adding individual contributions, and which require a number of steps that must be correctly completed in a definite order; individuals are*

*better on tasks that call for centralized organization of parts. Groups perform better than individuals when the process is learning or problem solving, but not necessarily when the process investigated is judgment. These conclusions are based upon measures of outcome; when the measure of effectiveness is the amount of investment per man, individuals are generally shown to be more efficient. (pp. 70–71)*

In decision-making, group participation can have a number of interesting effects. At one time, it was assumed that group interaction would eliminate radical or risky alternatives, resulting in a conservative decision that was acceptable to all members (Whyte, 1956). Researchers have since found that some people are willing to make a riskier decision after they have discussed the decision in a group than if they had decided alone (Wallach, Kogan, & Bem, 1962). This phenomenon is called the **risky shift.**

Further research has suggested that group interaction can shift decisions either way, toward greater risk or greater caution (Fraser, 1971; Moscovici & Zavalloni, 1969). Social psychologists now believe that this is part of a more general effect called the **shift toward polarization.** Following a group discussion, an individual's views will become more extreme, in either the risky or cautious direction.

**risky shift: group phenomenon in which members make riskier decisions following group discussion than they would make singly**

**shift toward polarization: tendency for an individual's attitudes to become more extreme following group discussion**

and evaluated the boys' work. In the laissez-faire groups the leader simply stood by and answered when spoken to. These groups were entirely on their own in planning and assigning work. In the democratic groups members and leader discussed and determined policies and assignments together. The factor of possible personality differences was controlled by having each leader and all the boys operate in at least two different climates.

Differences in performance and other reactions were striking. In the autocratic groups performance was fairly good, but motivation was low and the boys worked only when the leader was present to direct them. The laissez-faire groups did less work and their work was of a poorer quality. The boys in the democratic groups, however, showed more originality and interest in their work and kept on working whether the leader was present or not.

There was more destruction of property, aggressiveness, and hostility in the autocratic groups, but the hostility was channeled toward a scapegoat member or toward the working materials rather than toward the leader. Members of autocratic groups were also more dependent and submissive, showed less individuality, and gave less friendly praise to each other. Morale and cohesiveness were lowest in the laissez-faire groups and highest in the democratic groups. The democratic leaders were liked best by the boys.

Past socialization experiences and other cultural learning also play an important role in leadership, and individuals with different past social experience may respond differently to the same kind of leadership. For example, Americans and western Europeans are reared under conditions which lead to a preference for democratic methods of leadership—whether in the family or in a larger group setting. But in a society in which leaders are expected to be autocratic, a democratic leader may be perceived as weak and inept and may elicit noncooperation instead of better member participation. Thus, it is risky to predict the effects of a method of leadership without knowing something about the particular group.

Autocratic leadership may be efficient for meeting immediate and temporary crisis situations. But, if maintained over a long period of time or used in situations that do not require it, autocratic leadership tends to defeat its own purposes, for it usually reduces the initiative and creativity of individual group members, thus eventually reducing the adaptive potential of the group.

On the other hand, democratic leadership appears to have greater long-range survival value for a group because it elicits member involvement and places minimum restraints on their initiative and creativity. This tends to promote the adaptability necessary for meeting changing conditions and demands. Democratic leadership is often more difficult to achieve, however, because it demands more of the leader as well as of the group members.

## Prejudice

In the early part of the 1930s a researcher named LaPiere (1934) traveled with a Chinese couple across the United States. In more than 10,000 miles of travel with stops at 66 hotels and other lodging places and 194 restaurants and cafés, they were refused accommodations only once. Six months after their visits, LaPiere sent the establishments they had visited a questionnaire asking, "Will you accept members of the Chinese race as guests in your establishment?" The letters were sent during a time when anti-Chinese feelings were running quite high, and it is not surprising that the overwhelming majority of responses he received were emphatically negative. Not one establishment indicated a positive willingness to accept a Chinese couple as guests.

During the 1950s and 1960s, the civil rights movement generated unforgettable images of blacks denied service at restaurant counters, of black children requiring the National Guard to escort them to school, and civil rights marchers hosed down and jolted with cattle prods during nonviolent protests.

**prejudice: prejudgment based solely on group characteristics**

All of these examples touch upon the complex issue of **prejudice,** the tendency for an individual to hold unjustified beliefs about another individual primarily on the basis of the groups to which the individuals belong. For example, a person may hold the unjustified belief that another is not capable of performing adequately in a particular job because of the second individual's membership in the group of women. Similarly, we may dismiss opinions offered by older adults solely on the basis of their membership in the group of older adults.

Most of the time, we interpret prejudice as a bias against an individual. In many large cities, for example, gangs are immediately hostile toward members of other gangs, even though they may have no other knowledge about the members of the other gangs except their group membership. However, prejudice can also be a bias in *favor* of an individual, particularly when the individual is a member of our own group or when they share some important group memberships with us. We thus protect the members of our family group. And we may be positively inclined toward others if they share our religious beliefs, race, or ethnic background.

**discrimination: prejudiced outlook, action, or treatment**

Prejudice thus works in two ways. Prejudice unjustifiably aids those who share our group characteristics. Prejudice also unjustifiably discriminates against those who are not members of our groups or who are members of groups we disparage. In either case, we form some opinion about a person solely on the basis of group memberships, not on our knowledge and understanding of that individual. Our prejudiced beliefs can also produce **discrimination,** in which our negative attitudes and actions have effects in areas such as housing, employment, and education.

Of course, prejudice can take many forms. Prejudice can be expressed as an attitude and as a behavior. It can be expressed as *racism*—bias regarding members of a racial or ethnic group. It can be expressed as *sexism*—bias regarding males or females as a group. It can be expressed as *ageism*—bias about an individual based on the individual's age. It can be expressed as a bias regarding members of religious groups, as in *anti-Semitism.* Our task in this section is not to try to explain one form of prejudice, such as racism, but to try to understand the factors that contribute to prejudice generally.

**Foundations of prejudice.** Psychologist Gordon Allport (1954) has described several facets of prejudice. First, he notes that prejudice has a *historical* basis. Early modes of prejudice probably developed out of a sincerely held belief in the superiority of group members over members of other groups. For example, a belief in the superiority of males over females has a long historical basis. Similarly, those who were engaged in the slave trade of the seventeenth, eighteenth, and early nineteenth centuries often had deeply held convictions that whites were superior to all other races. Even today, we may see the historical beginnings of prejudice in the sincerely held belief that women should not compete with men in the work force and that women deserve special legal protection afforded by a variety of state laws.

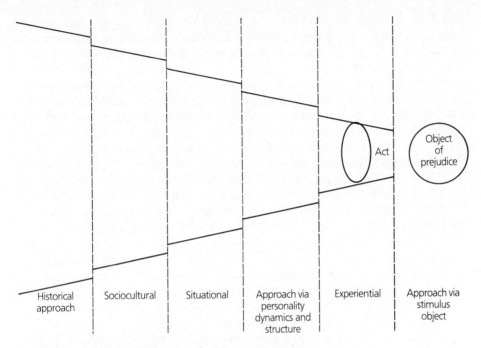

Historical approach | Sociocultural | Situational | Approach via personality dynamics and structure | Experiential | Approach via stimulus object

Act

Object of prejudice

**FIGURE 16.2 Allport's Theoretical Approach to the Study of Prejudice**
(Adapted from G. Allport, *The Nature of Prejudice.* Reading, Mass.: Addison-Wesley, 1954.)

Prejudice also has a *sociocultural* facet. The impersonal nature of many urban and suburban areas often forces people to seek group identification wherever possible. Often, groups are formed out of racial and ethnic identities, and groups representing different people often come into conflict. The areas of conflict typically center over opportunities for education, jobs, housing, and city services—vital but increasingly scarce commodities. Thus, one group may wish for additional housing, while others may argue for increased police protection. In the financially strapped urban areas of the United States, both demands may be difficult, if not impossible, to satisfy fully.

*Situational* factors play a role in prejudice. For example, the racially segregated housing patterns characteristic of many parts of the United States deprive individuals of contact with members of other groups. Children of a predominately white suburb may be exposed to very few black, Oriental, or Hispanic children in their neighborhoods, churches, and schools. And, the black children of the inner cities are equally deprived of one-to-one contact with a heterogeneous mixture of white children.

*Personality dynamics* play a role in prejudice as well. Typically, the prejudiced individual bases an evaluation of another solely upon group characteristics of the individual, not upon an intimate knowledge of the person. In essence, the prejudiced individual has limited his or her **cognitive complexity.** By keeping ideas and attitudes simple and uncomplicated, the individual may have increased his or her resources for dealing with other aspects of his or her life.

One method for measuring the type of thinking characteristic of prejudiced

**cognitive complexity:**
**degree to which ideas or attitudes are simple or complex**

individuals was developed by Adorno, Frenkel-Brunswik, Levinson, and Sanford (1950). Although Adorno was initially interested in studying anti-Semitism, he found that some of the characteristics of anti-Semites could be found in other prejudiced individuals.

**F scale: psychological scale used to measure prejudice**

Using his newly developed **F scale,** Adorno found that the prejudiced person was also likely to identify strongly with his or her ethnic group. Interestingly, the backgrounds of those who scored high on the F scale suggested that their upbringing as children was fairly severe and demanding. Punishment was frequently used in the homes of prejudiced individuals, and parents of these prejudiced individuals often held very high goals and aspirations for their children.

The work of Rokeach (1960) extended these findings to show that prejudice cannot be explained simply through racial or ethnic identification or through mechanisms such as scapegoating. A major factor identified by Rokeach was the **congruity of belief.** Rokeach's research suggested that prejudice occurs primarily because we dislike those whose beliefs are different from our own.

**congruity of belief: degree to which another person's ideas are similar to or different from our own**

Thus, the research in personality factors suggests that a variety of personal beliefs, cognitive and perceptual processes, and personality styles may contribute significantly to the development and maintenance of prejudice. Of course, personality factors build upon the historical, sociocultural, and situational factors already present in the individual's environment.

The *experiential* emphasis considers the experience of prejudice and the feelings and emotions that accompany an act of prejudice. For each individual, the personal consequences of prejudice directed toward others is unique. While we cannot always enter the person's experiencing during the act of prejudice, we can surmise that the prejudiced person feels a variety of emotions, including anger and hostility, retribution, and perhaps, guilt and remorse.

**Levels of prejudice.**     Jones (1972) has identified three levels of prejudice. The first level deals with *individual prejudice.* Individual prejudice is concerned with our attitudes and behaviors and with our socialization and self-interest. Prejudice on the individual level is the type of prejudice we can alter in a most direct and personal way. Through examination of our attitudes and beliefs, our behavior toward others, and our self-interest with respect to other groups, we may be able to alter our prejudicial beliefs. For example, if we find that we treat members of a group in an offhand or demeaning manner, we can recognize this tendency in ourselves and alter our attitudes and behaviors appropriately. And, while we can do little to change the patterns of our socialization, we can raise our children to recognize and accept the complexity in others.

**apartheid: legal policy of prejudice, discrimination, and segregation practiced against non-white people in the Republic of South Africa**

A more difficult level of prejudice to change is the *institutional* level. Here, patterns of housing, education, and occupation contribute obviously and subtly to prejudice. Legal structures, such as **apartheid** in South Africa, can contribute to prejudice. Limited access to health care systems and to political systems can encourage prejudice. The suffrage movement of the late 1800s and early 1900s, for example, removed a very significant legal barrier to women's full access to and participation in our political system.

Removal of institutional prejudice is somewhat more difficult than elimina-

# Psychology in Action
## GHETTO FOR BLUE-EYES IN THE CLASSROOM

The development of prejudice is a complex phenomenon. Whether prejudice is a central aspect or value in our lives or whether it is a specific attitude, it is clear that prejudice is learned in both subtle and obvious ways.

The following excerpt (Leonard, 1970) demonstrates the learned nature of prejudice. As the excerpt shows, prejudice not only has negative effects on those who are "one-down" but positive effects for those who are "one-up." In addition, any difference between individuals can be used as a pretext for prejudice. Finally, the excerpt implies that altering prejudice is not just an individual matter. Rather, the social and institutional supports for prejudice must be altered as well:

*For the third year in a row, Jane Elliott has introduced a little terror into the classroom where she teaches at the Riceville, Iowa elementary school. She conducted a simple experiment. She divided her class according to the color of each child's eyes. One day the blue-eyed children were declared to be superior. They sat where they preferred, went early to lunch, stayed late at recess, and were mightily encouraged in their work. The brown-eyed children wore collars, and were not permitted to eat with or play with the blue-eyed children. The next day Mrs. Elliott reversed the situation; brown eyes were now on top.*

*It began with giggles, but presently became serious. Mrs. Elliott knew her children and exploited their various vulnerabilities. Had a brown-eyed child been struck by his father for misbehaving? Brown-eyed children deserved it. Had a blue-eyed child forgotten his glasses? Dimwitted, typical. And the favored children did some exploiting of their own, proposing ingenious discriminations, affecting a lofty contempt, immensely enjoying their top-dog role, behaving in some instances viciously.*

*One significant result of the experiment was its effect on performance. On their day of inferiority, the brown-eyed children fared poorly on card-recognition tests; the blue-eyed ones surpassed themselves. The following day, the opposite occurred, with the "inferior" blue-eyed children admitting that they couldn't stop thinking about the collars around their necks or the taunts of their classmates.*

*When Mrs. Elliott ended the experiment, the whole class joined in song. But, one little girl was in tears and one little boy was wholly absorbed in ripping apart his collar before flinging it into the wastepaper basket.*

*This experiment teaches us that children aren't innocent, any more than adults are; that decency, justice and morality are abstractions that must be communicated and sustained; that our condition is poor and solitary indeed, perhaps even "nasty, brutish and short," without a community to provide the mechanisms of interdependence and the means to protect individuality, otherness.*

tion of individual prejudice. While laws can officially ban discrimination against members of certain groups, the implementation of the laws must be done at the individual level. For example, elimination of segregated schools was essentially accomplished in the landmark 1954 decision of the Supreme Court, *Brown* v.

*Board of Education* that declared unconstitutional "separate but equal" educational facilities. But the actual implementation of integrated education remains an elusive goal for a large number of school districts around the country.

Finally, *cultural* prejudice can have an impact on us. Religious and philosophical beliefs, expression of prejudice in music and the arts, and our values, needs, and beliefs can all contribute to prejudice. If, for example, our cultural system teaches us that youth is more valuable than old age, we may find it difficult to respond in an even-handed fashion to older individuals.

**Effects of prejudice.**     In an interesting experiment reported in 1972, psychologist Philip Zimbardo reported on the effects of a "prison" experiment. Zimbardo set up a mock prison in the basement of the psychology building at Stanford University. He recruited a number of student volunteers for this experiment. To be a part of this study, the volunteers had to be emotionally stable, physically healthy, and law-abiding.

The volunteers were randomly assigned to be either "prisoners" or "guards." At the start of the experiment, the "guards" and "prisoners" were essentially similar, but as the experiment progressed, some important differences began to emerge. The guards, dressed in khaki uniforms that emphasized their group identity, began to order the "prisoners" around and generally asserted their authority. The "prisoners" on the other hand, became increasingly passive in the face of the aggressiveness of the guards. Some prisoners became confused and disoriented; some cried and showed other signs of depression, and some developed "psychosomatic" rashes. Because these adverse reactions developed quite rapidly, the experiment had to be terminated short of its two-week goal.

This particular study suggests that prejudice is not a one-way street, in which the individuals remain relatively unscathed by the experience. As this study shows, those who are "one-up" inflict prejudicial acts upon those who are "one-down," and those who are "one-down" begin to behave in the ways expected by those in power. In essence, prejudice breeds negative emotional and behavioral change. Those who are the objects of prejudice may alter their actions, attitudes, and self-esteem to conform to the expectations of those in power. For example, if we have a prejudicial belief that old people are incapable of meaningful participation in the life of the community, our beliefs may produce prejudicial changes in the individual, institutional, and cultural levels. And, the aged, upon experiencing the prejudice against their involvement in the community will withdraw and make the prejudice a self-fulfilling prophecy.

Eliminating prejudice is neither a simple nor an easy task. No one aspect of prejudice is the sole cause of prejudice, nor can the effects of one level of prejudice be easily separated from the effects of another level. Prejudice cannot be eliminated simply by a change in situational factors, for example. Individual change unaccompanied by institutional or cultural change may not succeed. All the various aspects and the various levels of prejudice must be identified, examined, and altered before prejudice can be eliminated from American society.

In closing our discussion of prejudice, we note the importance of accurate perceptions and flexibility in dealing with the various aspects of our lives. Individ-

Although eliminating prejudice is a difficult, if not impossible, task, some theorists have proposed methods for reducing prejudice. Among their suggestions are increasing opportunities for social contact between individuals of equal status and having the individuals work together to achieve some common goal.

uals and groups interact on a variety of levels, in profound and subtle ways, and in ways which either detract from our functioning as human beings or which enhance our full and active participation in and enjoyment of life.

## SUMMARY

1. Groups are an integral part of the human experience, and the types of groups and their functions are many and varied. Groups can range in importance from those which are an essential part of an individual's identity to those that are fleeting and unimportant. Similarly, groups can aid in identity and fulfillment and in providing security and belongingness. Participation in groups involves a number of rewards as well as a number of costs.

2. Groups affect us in several ways. Groups can facilitate performance, help spread ideas and attitudes, produce conformity and obedience, and help alter the chances that we will assist others in need. It is important to note, however, that the effects of groups occur in the context of individual perception and environmental variables. For example, crowding and other environmental factors may influence our tendency to aid others.

3. Individuals and groups can also interact in a variety of ways. In leadership, the individual affects the group. Prejudice, on the other hand, occurs when group characteristics are unfairly applied to the individual. Prejudice has a number of bases, ranging from the historical to the situational and experiential. Prejudice has effects at the individual, institutional, and cultural levels, and it may be destructive in its self-fulfilling prophecy.

# Epilogue

# The Quest for Values

*"Psychology cannot tell people how they ought to live their lives. It can, however, provide them with the means for effecting personal and social change. And it can aid them in making value choices by assessing the consequences of alternative life-styles and institutional arrangements."*
(BANDURA, 1977b, P. 213)

In this book we have taken a long journey into the world of human nature and behavior. Now as we approach the end of this journey, it is fitting that we come to grips with the issue of values and the role that values can play in our lives.

Throughout this book, we have suggested that the recognition of and the selection among options help facilitate adjustment. Our discussion of stress, for example, illustrated some options we can employ to control these adjustive demands. And our discussion of interpersonal relationships, marriage, divorce, and alternatives to marriage illustrated the variety and choices available to us in our relationships with others.

The availability of choices, however, presents a dilemma—which of the options should we choose? Which options are better? What is the "good" or "right" choice? Answering these questions involves values.

Since values help inform and influence our choices, we need to understand and examine our values. The formulation of an adequate and personally meaningful value system can help us guide our lives and achieve better adjustment. While we cannot solve the problem of finding adequate values for each individual, we can attempt to clarify the dimensions of the problem and point to some of the directions a solution may take.

As a starting point, we shall note some differences in people's value orientations. Then we shall look at the sources of our values and some criteria for a sound value system. Finally, we shall examine the significance of values for personal becoming—for personal growth and fulfillment—and for determining the kind of world for which we should strive.

Through scientific investigation, we discover facts and information, but how we use what we learn—whether we use our knowledge for the growth and improvement of society or its destruction—is a judgment that is based on values.

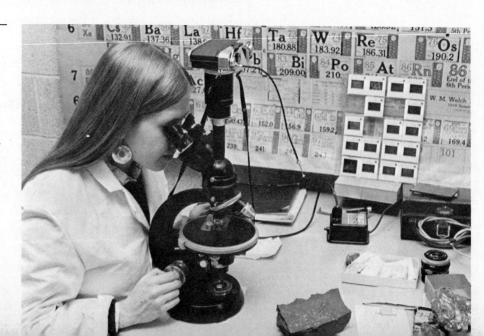

# ABOUT VALUES

**Values** are the implicit or explicit judgments we have about things, goals, and actions we consider desirable or undesirable. In selecting goals, in choosing means for reaching them, and in resolving conflicts, we are influenced at every turn by our conception of the preferable, the good, and the desirable. Values thus help determine our behavior, but they are not the only determinants of behavior. As we have seen, any act reflects the interplay of a wide range of inner and outer determinants, including our needs, goals, and various situational factors. However, our key choices and decisions are based upon our values. They shape the kind of person we become and the type of life we build for ourselves.

**values: assumptions or beliefs concerning good and bad, desirable and undesirable**

## Value Orientations

There are various ways of describing value orientations. We could describe several world views, such as communism or democracy. We could delineate the characteristic value patterns of various ethnic groups in our society. Or we could compare individuals in terms of their specific value orientations.

For our immediate purposes, the most useful way of viewing value orientations seems to be in terms of: *(a)* value types, *(b)* conceived and operative values, and *(c)* the distinction between values relating to goals or ends and values relating to the means for achieving these goals.

**Value types.** Some years ago Spranger (1923/1928) contended that each person can be regarded as approaching—but rarely fitting perfectly within—one of six value types. According to Spranger, there are six main types of values that appeal to people in varying degrees and around which they build the unity of their lives.

1. *The theoretical.* The primary value of the theoretical person is the discovery of *truth.* Since this involves the use of rational, critical, and empirical processes, the theoretical type is an intellectual—often a philosopher or scientist.

2. *The economic.* The economic person values what is *useful* and is concerned with the business world or other practical affairs involving the production, marketing, or consumption of goods. Tangible wealth and material possessions are of central importance.

3. *The esthetic.* The esthetic person values *form* and *harmony.* People of this type may or may not be creative artists, but their chief interest is the artistic or esthetic experiences in life.

4. *The social.* The social person places great value on *affiliation* and *love.* The social person values other persons as individuals and tends to be kind and sympathetic.

5. *The political.* The political person places great value on *power.* Activities of persons of this value type need not be restricted to politics alone, but may involve power, influence, and active competition to maintain and expand power in personal relationships.

6. *The religious.* The highest value for the religious person may be called

*unity.* Religious people are mystical and seek to comprehend and relate to the cosmos and to find higher value experiences through their religious philosophy.

This classification of value types is necessarily limited. Few individuals approach the ideals described above, and many people appear to have few, if any, strong values beyond those of hedonism and sensual pleasure. Despite such limitations, however, these value orientations can help us understand the general directions in which our values may lead us, as well as their influence upon the careers we choose, the quality of interpersonal relationships we achieve, and the life-styles we develop.

**Conceived and operative values.**   People who have studied values systematically often distinguish between conceived and operative values. **Conceived values** are conceptions of the ideal. For the most part, these are the values that the culture teaches and the ones most likely to be talked about in any discussion of morality or ethics. But conceived values, even though held with a good deal of conviction, sometimes have little practical influence on behavior. For example, people who espouse human equality, nonviolence, service to humanity, and complete honesty may not be guided by these values in their actions—even when circumstances make it fairly easy for them to do so. **Operative values,** on the other hand, are the actual value assumptions we use in making decisions and taking action.

In trying to identify a person's real values, then, we must analyze not only what he or she *says* but what they *do* in situations that involve an element of choice. Sometimes the discrepancy between a person's conceived and operative values is alarming. The husband or wife who extols selfless love but contributes little to the relationship, and the politician who praises freedom but votes for measures that curtail the freedom of fellow citizens are examples of an all too common phenomenon. In essence, we become and are what we do—not what we say we believe in or want to be.

It is rarely if ever possible, of course, to bring conceived and operative values into complete harmony. The person who places a high value on nonviolence will usually fight rather than be killed, and the person who values complete honesty may lie to protect a friend. The complexities of human nature and human society make Utopia an ideal against which to measure our progress rather than a goal we can realistically hope to achieve. But this does not invalidate conceptions of the ideal or strip them of their practical value. Salvador de Madariaga, a Spanish diplomat and political essayist, made this point well: ''Our eyes must be idealistic and our feet realistic. We must walk in the right direction but we must walk step by step'' (In Smith & Lindeman, 1951, p. 123).

**Instrumental and terminal values.**   In his extensive studies of values, Rokeach (1973) has made the following distinction between instrumental and terminal values: ''When we say that a person has a value, we may have in mind either his beliefs concerning desirable *modes of conduct* or desirable *end-states of existence.* We will refer to these two kinds of values as *instrumental* and *terminal* values'' (p. 7).

conceived values: values an individual feels are valid and ideal, but not necessarily the values he or she actually lives by

operative values: values which actually guide the behavior of an individual, as opposed to the values he or she may profess to believe in

# Psychology in Action

## PERSONAL VALUES

What are the most important values in your life? What are the least important values?
The scale presented below, containing the eighteen terminal values identified in Rokeach's research, will give you an opportunity to learn which values are most (and least)
important as guiding principles in your life.

The values are arranged in alphabetical order. After studying the list, place a "1"
next to the value which is most important for you, place a "2" next to the value which is
second most important to you, etc. The value you consider least important, relative to
the others, should be ranked "18."

In completing this scale, it is best to think carefully and work slowly. If you change
your mind, feel free to change your answer. While there are no right or wrong answers,
the end result should help show which values are important in your life.

_____ A COMFORTABLE LIFE (a prosperous life)

_____ AN EXCITING LIFE (a stimulating, active life)

_____ A SENSE OF ACCOMPLISHMENT (lasting contribution)

_____ A WORLD AT PEACE (free of war and conflict)

_____ A WORLD OF BEAUTY (beauty of nature and the arts)

_____ EQUALITY (brotherhood, equal opportunity for all)

_____ FAMILY SECURITY (taking care of loved ones)

_____ FREEDOM (independence, free choice)

_____ HAPPINESS (contentedness)

_____ INNER HARMONY (freedom from inner conflict)

_____ MATURE LOVE (sexual and spiritual intimacy)

_____ NATIONAL SECURITY (protection from attack)

_____ PLEASURE (an enjoyable, leisurely life)

_____ SALVATION (saved, eternal life)

_____ SELF-RESPECT (self-esteem)

_____ SOCIAL RECOGNITION (respect, admiration)

_____ TRUE FRIENDSHIP (close companionship)

_____ WISDOM (a mature understanding of life)

**instrumental values: values used in achieving goals**

**terminal values: values representing desirable end-states or goals**

In essence, **instrumental values** represent *means* for achieving goals, such as being honest or dishonest, while **terminal values** represent *ends* or *goals,* such as personal security or a world of beauty. This distinction is a thought-provoking one since many people feel that "the end justifies the means." Thus, in the pursuit of goals that most people would consider desirable, such as social order and security, political leaders might resort to means most people would consider undesirable or unethical, such as repression and torture. Similarly, some people resort to dishonesty and deceit in the pursuit of goals, such as professional achievement, that most people would consider desirable. But on both group and individual levels, the use of unethical means often defeats the achievement of ethically desirable goals.

## Sources of Values

When Neil Armstrong set foot on the moon and declared his first small step to be "one giant step for mankind," it may have forced many of us to realize that we are barely on the threshold of understanding the physical, spiritual, mental, and moral forces in our universe. Even though we have made remarkable progress in many areas, where can we find sound values? How can we arrive at a system of values that is both stable and flexible enough to survive change? The complexity of this problem has been well summarized by Sinnott (1955):

*One of man's chief problems is to determine what the basis of a moral code should be, to find out what he ought to do. Is the right that which is the word of God given to man in the Ten Commandments? Is it what is revealed to us by conscience and intuition? Is it whatever will increase the sum of human happiness? Is it that which is the most reasonable thing to do? Is it whatever makes for the fullness and perfection of life? Above all, is there any absolute right, anything embedded, so to speak, in the nature of the universe, which should guide our actions? Or are right and wrong simply relative, dependent on time and place and culture pattern, and changing with environment and circumstance? What, in short, is the basis of our moral values? These questions are of vital importance in a day when intellectual power threatens to outrun moral control and thus destroy us. (p. 147)*

While we cannot fully answer the questions raised by Sinnott, there are four key sources of values that we can use in formulating a workable value system: *(a)* culture, *(b)* science, *(c)* religion, and *(d)* experience, including our own and others' life experiences.

**Culture.**   To some extent, our values are determined by our culture. What might be considered normal and moral in one culture might seem strange or even bizarre in another culture. The extent to which this is true is shown in the following analysis by Robertson (1977): "Americans eat oysters but not snails. The French eat snails but not locusts. The Zulus eat locusts but not fish. The Jews eat fish but not pork. The Hindus eat pork but not beef. The Russians eat beef but not snakes. The Chinese eat snakes but not people. The Jalé of New Guinea find people delicious" (p. 61).

In a pioneering attempt to show the systematic nature of such cultural similarities and differences in values, Kluckhohn and Strodtbeck (1961) suggested that the core values of a society reflect its orientation to five basic problems:

1. *Orientation toward human nature.* Is human nature basically good, bad, or neutral?

2. *Orientation toward the environment.* Is the environment to be preserved as crucial to our life support system or is it a resource to be conquered in the interest of our material comfort and convenience?

3. *Time orientation.* Should a person live for the present or for the future? Should customs and traditions be preserved or should they be replaced by new standards and patterns?

4. *Activity orientation.* What kind of activity is most valued? Making money? Service to others? Getting things done?

5. *Interpersonal orientation.* What is the dominant or desired relationship among members of the group? Is it competitive or cooperative, hostile or friendly? Are warm and loving relationships valued?

The answers given to these questions in our society determine the background against which we develop our personal system of values. Depending on our concept of what is good and bad in human life, we tend to select certain goals over others and to pattern our behavior according to standards of what we believe to be desirable and worthwhile.

**Science.**    Psychology and other sciences have the advantage of providing us with information that has been checked and rechecked by objective methods. But facts are impersonal and provide the basis for values only to the extent that we use them as a basis for deciding what is desirable or what ought to be. Albert Einstein, perhaps the greatest scientist of our age, acknowledged that "the scientific method can teach us nothing beyond how facts are related to, and conditioned by, each other."

*One can have the clearest knowledge of what* is, *and yet not be able to deduce from that what should be the goal of our human aspirations. Objective knowledge provides us with powerful instruments for the achievement of certain ends, but the ultimate goal itself and the longing to reach it must come from another source. . . . The knowledge of truth as such is wonderful, but it is so little capable of acting as a guide that it cannot prove even the justification and the value of the aspiration toward that very knowledge of truth. Here we face, therefore, the limits of the purely rational conception of our existence. (1950, pp. 21–22)*

In short, science can provide us with information about what is good or bad for our physical, psychological, and social well-being, but it cannot make the value judgments needed to decide how to use this information. For example, we have ample scientific evidence that atomic bombs can be hazardous to health—as seen by the results of the bombs dropped on Hiroshima and Nagasaki—but yet we continue to build ever more powerful and deadly thermonuclear weapons. And we can choose whether they will be used at some future date in a nuclear holocaust. These are actions and choices based on value judgments.

Fortunately, modern science is increasingly concerned not only with acquiring dependable information about human beings and their world but also with how this information is actually used. The old dictum that "Science deals only with facts, not values" is being increasingly questioned. Bandura (1977b) has expressed the situation in this way: "As a science concerned with the social consequences of its applications, psychology must promote understanding of psychological issues that bear on social policies to ensure that its findings are used in the service of human betterment" (p. 213). And this statement applies to the physical and biological as well as the behavioral sciences.

**Religion.**    Religion, as we customarily think of it in its institutionalized form, is based on revelation believed to be from God as recorded in tradition and sacred literature. Typically religion involves a formal system of values that can be passed on from generation to generation, as well as a theology, a system of worship, and prescriptions for social relationships. Many of the basic values familiar to us in Christianity are found also in other great religions of the world such as Confucianism, Judaism, Islam, and Buddhism. For example, the mandate "Do unto others as ye would have them do unto you" appears in one form or another in most religions.

For many people, their religious faith is the source and the expression of their values.

# Insight

## THE GOLDEN RULE

The "Golden Rule" represents one of our highest value aspirations and is found in its essential form in all the great religions of the world.

*Hinduism.* "Good people proceed while considering that what is best for others is best for themselves." (Hitopadesa)

*Judaism.* "Thou shalt love thy neighbor as thyself." (Leviticus 19:18)

*Christianity.* "Therefore all things whatsoever ye would that men should do to you, do ye even so to them." (Matthew 7:12)

*Buddhism.* "Hurt not others with that which pains yourself." (Udanavarga 5:18)

*Confucianism.* "What you do not want done to yourself, do not do to others." (Analects 15:23)

*Islam.* "No one of you is a believer until he loves for his brother what he loves for himself." (Traditions)

Although theologians have used logic, reasoning, and historical arguments to help prove the existence of God and the validity of their beliefs, the proof of religious truth must rest finally on faith. People who have received strength and comfort from their religion may have an unshakable belief in the reality of God, but the correctness of their belief can never, by argument alone, be made convincing to anyone who has not shared a similar experience. In the well-known words of Pascal, "The heart has its reasons which reason knows nothing of."

Unfortunately, for a substantial number of people, religion consists of repeating religious beliefs but not practicing them. Thus, the religious beliefs espoused by many people often seem hypocritical. As someone has put it, "They pray in church on Sunday and they prey on their fellow human beings the rest of the week."

It has become increasingly apparent, however, that religion has not lost its essential relevance to our existential problems, particularly for those who have rediscovered and reinforced religious values in their lives.

*" 'I am not the same man,' Rusty Schweickart says, 'none of us are.' The Apollo veterans have become poets, seers, preachers, all of them evangelists for the privileged vision from space."*
*(MAHS, 1973, P. 50)*

**History and experience.** In the life of the group and of the individual, many values originate from experience. Each of us experiences success or failure, satisfaction or dissatisfaction in different situations. We are constantly making judgments about what is good and bad, more desirable and less desirable, more meaningful and less meaningful. And as we make these judgments about our experiences, we modify our value system accordingly.

Through the study of history, we can examine events that led to the rise and downfall of past civilizations. As we learn the effects of values held by people in the past, we can begin to choose our values and shape our value systems.

We can also draw on the experience of others. Through our libraries and our museums, we can refer to the experience of individuals and nations throughout the world since the beginning of human history. We can observe the effects that the values of various civilizations have had on the well-being of their citizens. We can observe the effects of greed, selfishness, and ignorance in causing general human misery and warfare. And we can note the ultimate futility of war in solving basic problems. In the long run, most of the values that actually influence our behavior are validated by the satisfaction we have experienced in pursuing them. Hence, experience becomes a key factor in determining the values we follow and the ones we discard.

## Criteria of a Sound Value System

Although values are an individual matter based largely on our experiences, the following three standards appear to be useful criteria of a sound value system: integration and faith, realism and flexibility, and meaning and satisfaction.

**Integration and faith.** An adequate value system is both internally consistent and integrated with our reality. It is also something in which we can have a good deal of faith. An integrated value system implies a hierarchy of values that enables us to choose confidently between things of greater and lesser importance and to be relatively undisturbed by frustrations that temporarily interfere with the attainment of short-range goals.

Values come alive in direct proportion to how much faith we have in them. Faith helps to close the gap between conceived and operative values and enables us to achieve a sense of wholeness in everything we feel, say, and do. This is the kind of faith illustrated in the lives of the "self-actualizing" persons studied by Maslow (1954, 1971). The kind of faith that encourages personal growth and self-actualization is quite different, however, from the type of dogmatic faith that seems to reflect fear and uncertainty more than positive understanding and conviction.

It is important to note that the integration of our value system is primarily related to our self-esteem. As Rokeach (1968) put it: "consistency with self-esteem is probably a more compelling consideration than consistency with logic or reality" (p. 164) in maintaining a value system.

Of course, our value systems undergo change as we go through life. Typically this change is related to one of three factors: *(a)* we engage in some acts that are not consistent with our value systems; *(b)* we are exposed to new information that may be inconsistent with other information; and *(c)* we perceive an inconsistency or contradiction in our values. Like other cognitive inconsistencies, inconsistencies in our value systems motivate us to change our values and to reestablish a new, more appropriate, more integrated system.

**Realism and flexibility.** An adequate value system requires accurate assumptions concerning reality. This implies, first of all, the individual's need to be informed—to have adequate information. Socrates believed that no person knowingly chooses falsehood over truth. In a similar vein, Jefferson's concept of democracy is based on the belief that full information leads to right action and that right action is not possible without it. The feeling that each of us is fully informed about a given situation makes the matter of choice or value judgment much easier and more decisive.

A realistic value system also implies the need for a certain amount of flexibility. Fundamental values may remain relatively stable, but they must be refined and their compass extended as the individual's understanding broadens. This is essentially the attitude expressed by Mahatma Gandhi (1948) in his autobiography: "I am far from claiming any finality or infallibility about my conclusions. One claim I do indeed make and it is this. For me they appear to be absolutely correct, and seem for the time being to be final. For if they were not, I should base no action on them" (p. 5).

If values are to prove adequate, they must keep pace with changes in the individual's understanding and knowledge, in his or her life situation, and in the physical and sociocultural environment. Such an attitude enables the individual to take forthright action based on conviction while at the same time maintaining an openness to new or fuller truth.

**Meaning and satisfaction.** A final consideration in judging the adequacy of our value system is the amount of satisfaction that we derive from living by it—whether it gives meaning to our lives and a sense that we are fulfilling the purposes of our existence. Dorothy Lee, an anthropologist who has made intensive studies of value in other cultures, has emphasized the experience of satisfaction as a universal criterion of value: " . . . we experience value when our activity is permeated with satisfaction, when we find meaning in our life, when we feel good, when we act not out of calculating choice and not for extraneous purpose but rather because this is the only way that we, as ourselves, deeply want to act" (1959, p. 165). Similarly, John Dewey (1939) has suggested that we derive a sense of meaning and satisfaction from our values when we carefully choose from alternative values and repeatedly act upon and prize our choice.

We often find that the greater our faith in our values, the greater will be our efforts to pursue goals based on them.

In short, values are subject to the pragmatic test of their consequences for the individual and for the group. As Janis and Mann (1977) put it: "Gaining utilitarian and social rewards is not enough; the person has to live with himself" (p. 9). And as the existentialists have pointed out, one's life can be meaningful and fulfilling only if it involves socially as well as personally constructive values and choices.

## VALUES AND BECOMING

**becoming: referring to personal growth**

**Becoming** refers to personal change over time. We all are in the process of becoming throughout our lives, for every experience of life leaves us changed. And we would all like to expect that this continuing change is in positive directions and that we are becoming more proficient, more capable, and more attractive. But sometimes change is in a negative direction, as in the case of people who become chronic alcoholics or who become cynical and embittered and feel that their lives have been wasted.

Opportunities, chance factors, personal resources, and many other conditions enter into our lives. But it is largely through our choices and our actions that we shape the kind of person we will become as well as the kind of personal world that we will make to live in.

In this context, three aspects of becoming merit special consideration: becoming an authentic person, building a favorable life for ourselves, and building a favorable life for others.

## Becoming an Authentic Person

The authentic person is an individual who lives a truthful, insightful existence. They are people who have integrity, have thought through their values, and live by them. The alternative to seeking and living the truth is to be a phony, to be unauthentic, to lead a wasted life, and to be the architect of one's destruction.

One of the first requirements for becoming an authentic person is trusting our own values. As we have seen, we derive some of our values from external sources, such as science, religion, culture, and the experience of others, and some from our own direct experiences of values. Ideally, we are selective in what we accept from external sources, enriching our insights by adding those of other people, weighing the value experiences of others for relevance to us, and choosing the particular values which have validity for *us*.

When our own experiences of value contradict the value judgments of our culture or the prescriptions of science or religion, we must decide which we trust most—our experience or that of others. Rogers (1969, 1977) has found that many of those who seek therapy have, knowingly or not, chosen to follow external value judgments, ignoring or denying their own perceptions of value. These persons have blindly accepted the values of others and find them unsatisfactory.

Assuming that people are not estranged and alienated from their inner selves and that they understand the consequences of various alternatives, they can become true to themselves—both in terms of being what they are and in

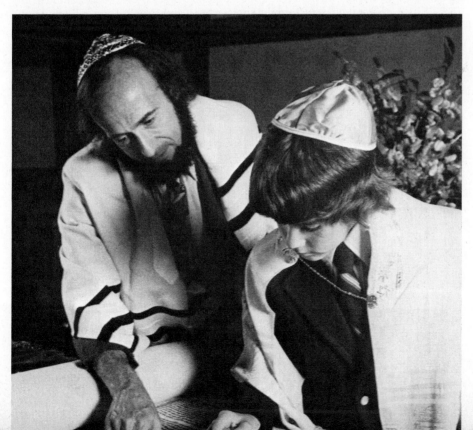

Although many personal values come from external sources, if a person is to achieve authenticity, the locus of valuing must be the inner self.

# Psychology in Action

## THE QUALITY OF LIFE FOR AMERICANS

In a large-scale survey Flanagan (1978) asked thirty-, fifty-, and seventy-year-old Americans to rate fifteen components that had been defined as important or very important to Americans' quality of life. Health and personal safety, having and raising children, and understanding one's self were typically rated as important to quality of life. Surprisingly, the differences among the various age groups and between men and women were fairly small. Some differences that emerged from the data were relatively obvious. Older Americans, for example, rated work as less important to their quality of life than did young and middle-aged Americans.

You may identify some values in your life by completing Flanagan's questionnaire. Rate each of the components from 0 to 4, where 0 = not at all important, 1 = slightly important, 2 = moderately important, 3 = important, and 4 = very important to you.

### Physical and Material Well-Being

_____ A. *Material comforts*—things like a desirable home, good food, possessions, conveniences, an increasing income, and security for the future.

_____ B. *Health and personal safety*—to be physically fit and vigorous, to be free from anxiety and distress, and to avoid bodily harm.

### Relations with Other People

_____ C. *Relationships with your parents, brothers, sisters, and other relatives*—things like communicating, visiting, understanding, doing things, and helping and being helped by them.

_____ D. *Having and raising children*—this involves being a parent and helping, teaching, and caring for your children.

_____ E. *Close relationship with a husband/wife/a person of the opposite sex.*

**authenticity:** human quality of being spontaneous and genuine, of being one's true self without a false front or façade

terms of shaping their self through their choices and actions. This is a basic theme underlying **authenticity.** A second and equally important theme is concern for and commitment to others. In the humanistic-existential model, commitment to others follows almost automatically from commitment to one's self. Humanistic-existential theorists believe there is a basic unity of humanity, and the task of learning to live constructively leads automatically to involvement, obligation, and commitment to one's fellow human beings. Rogers (1964) has dealt with this point succinctly: "I believe that when the human being is inwardly free to choose whatever he deeply values, he tends to value those objects, experiences, and goals which make for his own survival, growth, and development, and for the survival and development of others" (p. 166). Thus, the authentic person's life leads to self-fulfillment and to the well-being of others.

_____ F. *Close friends*—sharing activities, interests, and views; being accepted, visiting, giving and receiving help, love, trust, support, guidance.

## Social, Community, and Civic Activities

_____ G. *Helping and encouraging others*—this includes adults or children other than relatives or close friends. These can be your own efforts or efforts as a member of some church, club, or volunteer group.

_____ H. *Participation in activities relating to local and national government and public affairs.*

## Personal Development and Fulfillment

_____ I. *Learning,* attending school, improving your understanding, or getting additional knowledge.

_____ J. *Understanding yourself* and knowing your assets and limitations, knowing what life is all about and making decisions on major life activities. For some people, this includes religious or spiritual experiences. For others, it is an attitude toward life or a philosophy.

_____ K. *Work* in a job or at home that is interesting, rewarding, worthwhile.

_____ L. *Expressing yourself* in a creative manner in music, art, writing, photography, practical activities, or in leisure-time activities.

## Recreation

_____ M. *Socializing*—meeting other people, doing things with them, and giving or attending parties.

_____ N. *Reading, listening to music, or observing* sporting events or entertainment.

_____ O. *Participation in active recreation*—such as sports, traveling and sightseeing, playing games or cards, singing, dancing, playing an instrument, acting, and other such activities.

## Building a Favorable Life for Ourselves

The structure of our lives will usually have elements common to many people. Most of us will, in the course of our lives, build friendships, undertake specific occupations, get married, and raise families. We will see our values coming into play in our decision to marry, in describing the type of person that we might marry, and in the emphasis that we will place on material possessions and interpersonal relationships.

Our reactions to stress and to the changes that occur throughout life are other ways that we can help build a favorable life for ourselves. Even the way we approach the end of life reflects our values and can become the final stage of personal growth and development.

In essence, we hold the potential for both a growth-inducing or growth-retarding type of life within our grasp. Our choice will determine whether we achieve this potential (Bandura, 1982b; Furlong, 1981).

## Building a Favorable Life for Others

Positive becoming is not entirely a matter of change and growth in one's self. Of crucial importance, too, is the type of world we construct for ourselves and others to live in. Our choices for a constructive or destructive life-style affect others as well as ourselves. For example, our determination to speed down a highway while intoxicated has consequences for ourselves and for other people.

The choices we make today will also affect future generations. Our decision to pollute the air and water and to desecrate the land leaves a legacy for our descendants that will take many lifetimes to restore. For example, the radioactivity that is generated in a nuclear reactor container vessel will remain dangerous for at least 80,000 years (Norman, 1982). Similarly, our polluted environment, our self-centered concerns, and the world, the history, and the values that we give to our children will not be easy to change.

Becoming an authentic person obviously involves our personal growth and development, but it is not limited to ourselves. Our acts have consequences for ourselves and for others as well. If our hope is to become authentic, we must not forget others in the process. As John Donne has expressed it, "No man is an island, entire of itself; every man is a piece of the continent, a part of the main."

## VALUES AND THE WORLD OF THE FUTURE

While "Spaceship Earth" has an efficient life-support system, it is limited. Yet the number of its inhabitants is increasing with frightening rapidity and overburdening its decreasing resources. At the same time we see people divided into conflicting groups who often fight and kill each other, and we note that several nations have developed thermonuclear weapons capable of killing every human being several times over.

It seems apparent that in the last decades of the twentieth century, the world's peoples are faced with three herculean tasks: (1) to eliminate poverty and discrimination and provide equal opportunity for all; (2) to cope with new problems produced by our technological advances—pollution, the population explosion, and accelerating and largely uncontrolled technological and social change; and (3) to plan and achieve a good future for all of us on earth.

## Exploring Alternative Futures

*"The future is not a result of choices among alternative paths offered by the present, but a place that is created—created first in mind and will, created next in activity. The future is not some place we are going to, but one we are creating. The paths to it are not found but made, and the activity of making them changes both the maker and the destination."*
**(SCHAAR, 1974, P. 1)**

We are confronted today with the problem of how we shall survive—the quality of life that we will be able to achieve. Saving the human race for a future world of insanity or for a dehumanizing, lock-step regimentation in a world of bare subsistence is hardly sufficient. But a good future will not come automatically.

In recent years a growing number of organizations and scientists have become directly involved in delineating various possible futures for our country and for the world as a whole. These groups have been set up by the federal government, by major universities, and by private foundations and organizations. They are composed of interdisciplinary teams of scientists, historians, philosophers, and specialists from a diversity of fields. They devote their time to considering the range of alternatives open to us in planning a good future and the probable consequences of given alternatives.

The "futurists" point to the fact that throughout history, those organisms unable to adapt to the demands of a changing environment have perished. The dinosaur, thought to have a low level of intelligence survived for some 150 million years. In contrast, the human race threatens itself with extinction after a mere 2 million years on this planet. Unlike the dinosaur, however, human beings have options. Thus, it becomes essential that we carefully explore and evaluate the options open to us.

We are not trapped by some absurd fate like the dinosaur but can and must choose our own future. Through the advances in psychology and technology, we are no longer limited by the "givens" in ourselves and our surroundings but are increasingly capable of directing the destiny of ourselves and our world. But it is our choices that will determine our destiny. The only question is whether these choices will be made by default or with imagination and the use of all the information potentially at our disposal.

Many behavioral scientists—and others—are seriously worried about the possibility that some elite minority may someday plan and exercise control over the rest of us, utilizing behavioral scientists primarily as tools in achieving their goals. This is the warning in such prophetic and frightening "utopias" as Aldous Huxley's *Brave New World,* and George Orwell's *1984.*

To safeguard ourselves against the possibility of science being used to restrict rather than enrich our lives, many psychologists and other investigators are becoming increasingly concerned not only with the alternative futures science and technology are making possible but also with the value orientations on which a choice among these futures may be based (Fishman & Neigher, 1982).

## The Crucial Role of Values in Shaping the Future

*"Human values, in addition to their commonly recognized significance from a personal, religious, or philosophic standpoint, can also be viewed objectively as universal determinants in all human decision making . . . More than any other causal system with which science now concerns itself, it is variables in human value systems that will determine the future."*
**(SPERRY, 1977, P. 237)**

# Insight

### HOW CAN WE CONTRIBUTE TO A GOOD FUTURE WORLD?

Our society has frequently been accused of being a dehumanizing mass bureaucracy in which individuals are becoming increasingly alienated and feel they have little or no control over their destiny, let alone that of society. In a sense, the "average citizen" has become an alienated observer rather than an active and enthusiastic participant in the American Dream.

When citizens become aware of the problems facing society, most of them realize that their future as well as that of their children directly involved. And they ask "What can I do?"

Perhaps the starting point is to become familiar with the special needs and problems of one's community. Whatever his or her occupation—student, homemaker, teacher, lawyer, executive, trade-unionist—an interested person can find ways to contribute, such as participating in various civic organizations, serving as a part-time volunteer in a hospital or community mental health center, working for the election of particular political candidates, taking an active and responsible role as a citizen. Often, over time, many persons find themselves in leadership positions where their individual influence can be more strongly exerted. In any event, if we are to survive as a society it seems essential that we each not only "do our thing" but also "do our part."

As science and technology steadily increase our power not only to shape our future environment but also to control our development and behavior, most scientists consider it inevitable that such controls will be used. This has given rise to several serious questions: *(a)* What type of controls will be used? *(b)* Who will exercise these controls? and *(c)* What values will they be based on?

The models of human nature and behavior that we discussed in Chapter 2 are value laden and contain differing guides to the type of future we should try to construct for humankind. In an attempt to resolve such differences, Collier (1968) has suggested a basic value orientation with which most scientists and nonscientists alike would probably agree: "the constructive concern for whatever capacity the individual has for self-regulation and self-determination" (p. 5).

Implicit in this value orientation is the concept of "a participatory and anticipatory democracy in which the people are directly involved in establishing priorities and guiding social change—a society in which each individual has maximal opportunities for fulfilling his potentialities and living a meaningful and fulfilling life, a society in which human freedom and dignity are truly established" (Coleman, 1973, p. 178).

In any event, we can, if we choose to, create a future society that will provide our descendants with richer lives and greater opportunities for self-direction and self-actualization than has ever been known. In fact, humans of the future may well be as different from us as we are from our Neanderthal ancestors.

As we embark upon the great adventure of shaping our own future, let us hope that we will find new solutions that will change what needs to be changed while preserving essential values that are still valid. For it has taken the human race many thousands of years to achieve the imperfect level of freedom and opportunity for self-determination that we have reached. If these crucial achievements and other time-tested values are carelessly discarded, the change can bring us more loss than gain, and it may take long effort and suffering just to regain our present position. The warning that "the price of freedom is eternal vigilance" is not one to be dismissed lightly in our age of turmoil and rapid change.

In accepting the Nobel Prize for Literature in 1950, William Faulkner (1961) made this prophetic statement, which seems equally relevant today and a fitting conclusion for our discussion:

*I decline to accept the end of man. It is easy enough to say that man is immortal simply because he will endure: that when the last ding-dong of doom has clanged and faded from the last worthless rock hanging tideless in the last red and dying evening, that even then there will still be one more sound: that of his puny inexhaustible voice, still talking. I refuse to accept this. I believe that man will not merely endure: he will prevail. He is immortal, not because he alone among creatures has an inexhaustible voice, but because he has a soul, a spirit capable of compassion and sacrifice and endurance. (p. 4)*

## SUMMARY

1. There continues to be a great need for values that can withstand the impact of scientific and technological advances. As an initial attempt, we can describe six general value types, and we can distinguish between conceived and operative values and between instrumental and terminal values.

2. Culture, science, religion, and experience all contribute to the formation of values, but they cannot inform us whether the values are sound. To help determine the soundness of values, we must look to the three criteria of integration and faith, realism and flexibility, and meaning and satisfaction.

3. In becoming or developing an authentic person, we must also look to the type of world we make for ourselves and for others. Much of what we do now will affect both our future and the future of our descendants. We need values to help us adequately shape the future.

4. Throughout this book, we have examined the many facets of our existence and the many ways that we can cope with the adjustive demands of life. We have used the resources of modern psychology to provide guidelines that can help us find answers to the questions we posed in the first chapter of this book: *Who am I? Where am I going? How do I get there?* We hope that the people and ideas you have met on this journey have become a valued part of your experience, one that will help you as you continue your quest for a meaningful and fulfilling life.

# Contemporary Psychology and Effective Behavior

**Fifth Edition**

References

Acknowledgments

Name Index

Subject Index

# References

The reference list includes not only the sources from which the authors have drawn material, but also the acknowledgments of the permission granted by authors and publishers to quote directly from their works.

**Abelson, H. L., Fishburne, P. M., & Cisin, I.** *National survey on drug abuse: 1977.* (DHEW Publication No. ADM, 78–618). Washington, D.C.: U.S. Government Printing Office, 1977.

**Abramson, E. E.** Behavioral approaches to weight control: An updated review. *Behaviour Research and Therapy,* 1977, *15,* 355–63.

**Adorno, T. W., Frenkel-Brunswik, E., Levinson, D. J., & Sanford, R. N.** *The authoritarian personality.* New York: Harper, 1950.

**Albee, E.** *Who's afraid of Virginia Woolf?* New York: Atheneum, 1962.

**Alberti, R. E., & Emmons, M. L.** *Your perfect right: A guide to assertive behavior.* San Luis Obispo, Calif.: Impact Press, 1974.

**Allport, G. W.** ''Theoretical and methodological approaches to the study of the causes of prejudice'' adapted from Prejudice: A problem in psychological and social causation by Gordon W. Allport in *Journal of Social Issues,* Supplement Series, No. 4, 1950. Reprinted by permission of the Journal of Social Issues.

**Allport, G. W.** *The nature of prejudice.* Copyright 1954 by Addison-Wesley Publishing Co., Reading, Massachusetts, p. xiv. Reprinted with permission.

**Allport, G. W.** *Becoming: Basic considerations for a psychology of personality.* New Haven, Conn.: Yale University Press, 1955.

**Altman, I., & Taylor, D. A.** *Social penetration: The development of interpersonal relationships.* New York: Holt, 1973.

**American Psychiatric Association.** *Diagnostic and statistical manual of mental disorders* (3rd ed.). Washington, D.C.: American Psychiatric Association, 1980.

**Anastasi, A.** *Psychological testing* (5th ed.). New York: Macmillan, 1982.

**Anderson, J. R.** Acquisition of cognitive skill. *Psychological Review,* 1982, *89*(4), 369–406.

**Andrasik, F., & Holroyd, K. A.** A test of specific and nonspecific effects in the biofeedback treatment of tension headache. *Journal of Consulting and Clinical Psychology,* 1980, *48*(5), 575–86.

**Ardrey, R.** *African genesis.* New York: Atheneum, 1961.

**Arlin, P. K.** Cognitive development in adulthood: A fifth stage? *Developmental Psychology,* 1975, *11,* 602–6.

**Aronson, E.** *The social animal.* San Francisco: W. H. Freeman, 1972.

**Asch, S. E.** *Social psychology.* New York: Prentice-Hall, 1952.

**Asch, S. E.** Opinions and social pressure. *Scientific American,* 1955, *193*(5), 31–35.

**Atkinson, J. W.** *An introduction to motivation.* Princeton, N.J.: Van Nostrand, 1964.

**Atkinson, J. W.** Studying personality in the context of an advanced motivational psychology. *American Psychologist,* 1981, *36*(2), 117–28.

**Ax, A. F.** The physiological differentiation between fear and anger in humans. *Psychosomatic Medicine,* 1953, *15,* 433–42.

**Bach, G., & Wyden, P.** *The intimate enemy: How to fight fair in love and marriage.* New York: Avon, 1968.

**Bakal, D. A., & Kaganov, J. A.** Muscle contraction and migraine headache: Psychophysiologic comparison. *Headache,* 1977, *17,* 208–15.

**Baltes, P. B., & Schaie, K. W.** On the plasticity of intelligence in adulthood and old age. *American Psychologist,* 1976, *31,* 720–25.

**Bandura, A.** A social learning interpretation of psychological dysfunctions. In P. London & D. Rosenhan (Eds.), *Foundations of abnormal psychology.* New York: Holt, Rinehart and Winston, 1968.

**Bandura, A.** *Principles of behavior modification.* New York: Holt, 1969.

**Bandura, A.** Behavior theory and the models of man. *American Psychologist,* 1974, *29,* 859–69.

**Bandura, A.** Self-efficacy: Toward a unifying theory of behavioral change. *Psychological Review,* 1977, *84,* 191–215. (a)

**Bandura, A.** *Social learning theory.* Englewood Cliffs, N.J.: Prentice-Hall, 1977. (b)

**Bandura, A.** Reflections on self-efficacy. In S. Rachman (Ed.), *Advances in behaviour research and therapy* (Vol. 1). Oxford: Pergamon Press, 1978.

**Bandura, A.** The psychology of chance encounters and life paths. *American Psychologist,* 1982, *37*(7), 747–55. (a)

**Bandura, A.** Self-efficacy mechanism in human agency. *American Psychologist,* 1982, *37*(2), 122–47. (b)

**Banton, M.** *Roles: An introduction to the study of social relations.* New York: Basic Books, 1965.

**Barber, T. X.** *Hypnosis: A scientific approach.* New York: Van Nostrand Reinhold, 1969.

**Bateson, G., Jackson, D. D., Haley, J., & Weakland, J.** Toward a theory of schizophrenia. *Behavioral Science,* 1956, *1,* 251–64.

**Baum, A., & Valins, S.** *Architecture and social behavior: Psychological studies in social density.* Hillsdale, N.J.: Lawrence Erlbaum, 1977.

**Beck, A. T.** *Depression: Causes and treatment.* Philadelphia: University of Pennsylvania Press, 1972.

**Beck, A. T., Rush, A. J., Shaw, B. F., & Emery, G.** *Cognitive therapy of depression.* New York: Guilford, 1979.

**Bell, A. P., & Weinberg, M. S.** *Homosexualities: A study of diversity among men and women.* New York: Simon & Schuster, 1978.

**Bemis, K. M.** Current approaches to the etiology and treatment of anorexia nervosa. *Psychological Bulletin,* 1978, *85,* 593–617.

**Bengelsdorf, I. S.** Alcohol, morphine addictions believed chemically similar. *Los Angeles Times,* March 5, 1970, Part II, p. 7.

**Benson, H.** *The relaxation response.* New York: Morrow, 1975.

**Berger, K. S.** *The developing person.* New York: Worth, 1980.

**Bernard, J.** *The future of marriage.* New York: Bantam Books, 1973.

**Berne, E.** *Games people play.* New York: Grove Press, 1964.

**Berne, E.** *What do you say after you say hello?* New York: Grove Press, 1972.

**Bernstein, D. A., & Nietzel, M. T.** *Introduction to clinical psychology.* New York: McGraw-Hill, 1980.

**Berrill, N. J.** *Man's emerging mind.* New York: Dodd, Mead, 1955.

**Bettelheim, B.** Individual and mass behavior in extreme situations. *Journal of Abnormal and Social Psychology,* 1943, *38,* 417–52.

**Biddle, B. J., & Thomas, E. J.** *Role theory, concepts, and research.* New York: Wiley, 1966.

**Bierman, E., & Hazzard, W.** Biology of aging. In D. Smith & E. Bierman (Eds.), *The biologic ages of man.* Philadelphia: W. B. Saunders, 1973.

**Bild, R., & Adams, H. E.** Modification of migraine headaches by cephalic blood volume pulse and EMG biofeedback. *Journal of Consulting and Clinical Psychology,* 1980, *48,* 51–57.

**Blanchard, E. B., & Epstein, L. H.** *A biofeedback primer.* Reading, Mass.: Addison-Wesley, 1978.

**Blanchard, E. B., & Young, L. D.** Self-control of cardiac functioning: A promise as yet unfulfilled. *Psychological Bulletin,* 1973, *79,* 145–63.

**Blau, P. M.** *Exchange and power in social life.* New York: Wiley, 1967.

**Bluestone, H., & McGahee, C. L.** Reaction to extreme stress: Impending death by execution. *American Journal of Psychiatry,* 1962, *119,* 393–96.

**Bogdonoff, M. D., Klein, R. F., Estis, E. H., Shaw, D. M., Jr., & Back, K. W.** The modifying effect of conforming behavior upon lipid responses accompanying CNS arousal. *Clinical Research,* 1961, *9,* 135.

**Bohannan, P.** The six stations of divorce. In J. Bardwick (Ed.), *Readings on the psychology of women.* New York: Harper & Row, 1972.

**Boston Women's Health Book Collective.** *Our bodies, ourselves: A book by and for women* (2nd ed.). New York: Simon & Schuster, 1976.

**Bovet, T.** Human attitudes toward suffering. *Humanitas,* 1973, *9*(1), 5–20.

**Bradburn, N. M., & Berlew, D. E.** Need for achievement and English economic growth. *Economic Development and Cultural Change,* 1961, *10,* 8–20.

**Branden, N.** *Psychotherapy and the objectivist ethics.* New York: Nathaniel Branden Institute, 1965.

**Branden, N.** *The psychology of romantic love.* Los Angeles: J. P. Tarcher, 1980.

**Brecher, E. M., & the Editors of Consumer Reports.** *Licit and illicit drugs: The Consumers Union report on narcotics, stimulants, depressants, inhalants, hallucinogens, and marijuana—including caffeine, nicotine, and alcohol.* Mount Vernon, N.Y.: Consumers Union, 1972.

**Brickman, P., Rabinowitz, V. C., Karuza, J., Coates, D., Cohn, E., & Kidder, L.** Models of helping and coping. *American Psychologist,* 1982, *37*(4), 368–84.

**Brown, L. R.** Living and working in a sustainable society. *The Futurist,* 1982, *16*(2), 66–74.

**Browning, R.** "Rabbi Ben Ezra" from *Dramatis personae,* 1864.

**Bruner, J. S., Goodnow, J. J., & Austin, G. A.** *A study of thinking.* New York: Wiley, 1956.

**Buckley, W.** Society as a complex adaptive system. In W. Buckley (Ed.), *Modern systems research for the behavioral scientist.* Chicago: Aldine, 1968.

**Burgess, E. W.** The family in a changing society. In A. Etzioni & E. Etzioni (Eds.), *Social changes: Sources, patterns, and consequences.* New York: Basic Books, 1964.

**Burke, C., & Cummins, R.** (Eds.). *Searching for meaning.* Winona, Minn.: St. Mary's College Press, 1970. Copyright © 1970, St. Mary's College Press. Used by permission.

**Burns, R.** "To a mouse," 1785.

**Butler, R. A.** Discrimination learning by rhesus monkeys to visual-exploration motivation. *Journal of Comparative and Physiological Psychology,* 1953, *46,* 95–98.

**Butler, R. A.** Incentive conditions which influence visual exploration. *Journal of Experimental Psychology,* 1954, *48,* 19–23.

**Butler, R. N.** *Why survive? Being old in America.* New York: Harper & Row, 1975.

**Butler, S.** Breaking dependency in marriage. *Marriage and Family Living,* August 1976, *58*(8), 23–25.

**Bynner, W.** *The way of life according to LaoTzu.* New York: John Day Co., 1944.

**Byrne, D.** A pregnant pause in the sexual revolution. *Psychology Today,* 1977, *11*(2), 67–68.

**Campbell, D. P.** Adapted with permission of the publisher from the *Manual for the Strong-Campbell Interest Inventory,* Form T325 of the Strong Vocational Interest Blank, Third Edition, by David P. Campbell and J-Ida C. Hansen. Stanford: Stanford University Press, 1981.

**Camus, A.** [*The myth of Sisyphus and other essays*] (J. O'Brien, Trans.). New York: Knopf, 1955. (Originally published, 1942.)

**Cantril, H.** *The politics of despair.* New York: Basic Books, 1958.

**Caplan, G.** Mastery of stress: Psychosocial aspects. *American Journal of Psychiatry,* 1981, *138*(4), 413–20.

**Carson, R.** *Interaction concepts of personality.* Chicago: Aldine, 1969.

**Cartwright, D., & Zander, A.** (Eds.) *Group dynamics: Research and theory* (3rd ed.). New York: Harper & Row, 1968.

**Cattell, R. B.** *Abilities: Their structure, growth, and action.* Boston: Houghton Mifflin, 1971.

**Chandler, R.** Global problems: Isolation, anxiety top crisis survey. *Los Angeles Times,* May 17, 1976, Part II, p. 3.

**Chapman, L. J., & McGhie, A.** A comparative study of disordered attention in schizophrenia. *Journal of Mental Science,* 1962, *108,* 487–500.

**Cholden, L.** Some psychiatric problems in the rehabilitation of the blind. *Menninger Clinic Bulletin,* 1954, *18,* 107–12.

**Cimbalo, R. S., Faling, V., & Mousaw, P.** The course of love: A cross-sectional design. *Psychological Reports,* 1976, *38,* 1292–94.

**Cohen, A. R.** An experiment on small rewards for discrepant compliance and attitude change. In J. W. Brehm & A. R. Cohen, *Explorations in cognitive dissonance.* New York: Wiley, 1962.

**Cole, C. L.** Cohabitation in social context. In R. Libby & R. Whitehurst (Eds.), *Marriage and alternatives: Exploring intimate relationships.* Glenview, Ill.: Scott, Foresman and Co., 1977.

**Coleman, J. C.** Life stress and maladaptive behavior. *The American Journal of Occupational Therapy,* 1973, *27*(4), 169–78.

**Coleridge, S. T.** "Answer to a child's question," 1802.

**Collier, R. M.** A biologically derived basic value as an initial context for behavioral science. *Journal of Humanistic Psychology,* 1968, *8*(1),1–15.

**Comfort, A.** Maturation, autoimmunity, and aging. *Lancet,* 1963, *2,* 138.

**Coopersmith, S.** *The antecedents of self-esteem.* San Francisco: Freeman, 1967.

**Cozby, P. C.** Self-disclosure: A literature review. *Psychological Bulletin,* 1973, *79,* 73–91.

**Craighead, W. E., Kazdin, A. E., & Mahoney, M. J.** *Behavior modification: Principles, issues, and applications* (2nd ed.). Boston: Houghton Mifflin, 1981.

**Croft, R.** From "Love" by Roy Croft. Reprinted from *The family book of best loved poems,* copyright 1952 by Doubleday & Co., Inc. by permission of Copeland & Lamm, Inc.

**Cronbach, L. J.** *Essentials of psychological testing* (3rd ed.). New York: Harper & Row, 1970.

**Crooks, R., & Baur, K.** *Our sexuality.* Menlo Park, Calif.: Benjamin/Cummings Publishing Co., 1980.

**Cumming, E., & Henry, W.** *Growing old.* New York: Basic Books, 1961.

**Darley, J. M., & Latane, B.** Bystander intervention in emergencies: Diffusion of responsibility. *Journal of Personality and Social Psychology,* 1968, *8,* 377–83.

**Davison, G. C., Tsujimoto, R. N., & Glaros, A. G.** Attribution and the maintenance of behavior change in falling asleep. *Journal of Abnormal Psychology,* 1973, *82,* 124–33.

**Dawkins, R.** *The selfish gene.* New York: Oxford University Press, 1976.

**Decke, E.** Effects of taste on the eating behavior of obese and normal persons. In S. Schachter, *Emotion, obesity, and crime.* New York: Academic Press, 1971.

**DeLora, J. S., Warren, C. A. B., & Ellison, C. R.** *Understanding sexual interaction,* second edition, by Joann S. DeLora, Carol A. B. Warren and Carol Rinkleib Ellison. Copyright © 1981 by Houghton Mifflin Company. Reprinted by permission.

**Dembar, W.** Motivation and the cognitive revolution. *American Psychologist,* 1974, *29*(3), 161–68.

**Dement, W.** Effects of dream deprivation. *Science,* 1960, *113,* 1705–7.

**Derr, M.** Unemployment: The family crisis. *Marriage and Family Living,* January 1977, *59*(1), 18–20.

**Dewey, J.** *Theory of valuation.* Chicago: University of Chicago Press, 1939.

**Dickens, C.** *A tale of two cities.* New York: Dutton, 1958. (Originally published, 1859.)

**Dodson, B.** *Liberating masturbation: A meditation on self-love.* 1974, p. 23.

**Dole, V. P.** Addictive behavior. *Scientific American,* 1980, *243*(6), 138–57.

**Dollard, J., & Miller, N. E.** *Personality and psychotherapy: An analysis in terms of learning, thinking, and culture.* New York: McGraw-Hill, 1950.

**Dooley, D., & Catalano, R.** Economic change as a cause of behavioral disorder. *Psychological Bulletin,* 1980, *87,* 450–68.

**Dubin, R.** *The world of work: Industrial society and human relations.* Englewood Cliffs, N.J.: Prentice-Hall, 1958.

**Durant, W., & Durant, A.** *Rousseau and revolution.* New York: Simon & Schuster, 1967.

**Dutton, D., & Aron, A.** Some evidence of heightened sexual attraction under conditions of high anxiety. *Journal of Personality and Social Psychology,* 1974, *30,* 510–17.

**D'Zurilla, T. J., & Goldfried, M. R.** Problem solving and behavior modification. *Journal of Abnormal Psychology,* 1971, *78,* 107–26.

**Education and job satisfaction.** *Science News,* May 8, 1976, *109*(19), 297.

**Edwards, A. L.** *The social desirability variable in personality assessment and research.* New York: Dryden, 1957.

**Edwards, J. N., & Booth, A.** Sexual behavior in and out of marriage: An assessment of correlates. *Journal of Marriage and the Family,* 1976, *38*(1), 73–81.

**Einstein, A.** *The world as I see it.* New York: Philosophical Library, 1949.

**Einstein, A.** *Out of my later years.* New York: Philosophical Library, 1950.

**Ekman, P.** Face muscles talk every language. *Psychology Today,* September 1975, pp. 35–36; 38–39.

**Ekman, P., & Friesen, W. V.** Nonverbal behavior in psychotherapy research. In J. M. Schlien (Ed.), *Research in psychotherapy.* Washington, D.C.: American Psychological Association, 1968.

**Ekman, P., Friesen, W., & Ellsworth, P.** *Emotion in the human face: Guidelines for research and an integration of findings.* New York: Pergamon Press, 1973.

**Elliott, J.** Feeling: The key to personal growth. *Personal Growth,* 1976, No. 25, 9–16.

**Ellis, A.** *Reason and emotion in psychotherapy.* Secaucus, N.J.: Lyle Stuart, 1962.

**Ellis, A.** Rational-emotive therapy. In R. Corsini (Ed.), *Current psychotherapies.* Itasca, Ill.: F. E. Peacock, 1973.

**Ellis, A., & Harper, R. A.** *A guide to rational living.* Hollywood, Calif.: Wilshire, 1961.

**Ellis, H.** *Studies in the psychology of sex.* New York: Random House, 1906.

**Ellis, H.** *The new spirit.* New York: Boni and Liveright, 1921.

**Erickson, M. H.** Experimental demonstration of the psychopathology of everyday life. *Psychoanalytic Quarterly,* 1939, *8,* 338–53. Reprinted by permission.

**Erikson, E. H.** *Childhood and society* (Rev. ed.). New York: Norton, 1963.

**Erikson, E. H.** *Identity, youth, and crisis.* New York: Norton, 1968.

**Ethical standards of psychologists** (Rev. ed.). *APA Monitor,* March 1977, *8*(3), 22–23.

**Evans, P., & Bartolomé, F.** *Must success cost so much?* New York: Basic Books, 1980.

**Exner, J. E.** *The Rorschach: A comprehensive system.* New York: Wiley, 1974.

**Eysenck, H. J.** *The biological basis of personality.* Springfield, Ill.: Charles C. Thomas, 1967.

**Faberow, N. L., & Litman, R. E.** *A comprehensive suicide prevention program.* Suicide Prevention Center of Los Angeles, 1958–1969. (Unpublished final report DHEW NIMH Grants No. MH 14946 and MH 00128). Los Angeles, 1970.

**Fairbank, D., & Hough, R.** Life event classification and the event-illness relationship. *Journal of Human Stress,* 1979, *5,* 41–47.

**Farnsworth, D. L.** Motivation for learning: Community responsibility. In E. P. Torrance & R. D. Strom (Eds.), *Mental health and achievement.* New York: Wiley, 1966.

**Faulkner, W.** "Acceptance Speech Upon Receipt of the Nobel Prize for Literature" from *The Faulkner reader.* New York: Random House, 1961.

**Felipe, N. J., & Sommer, R.** Invasion of personal space. *Social Problems,* 1966–1967, *14,* 206–14.

**Fenz, W. D., & Epstein, S.** Stress: In the air. *Psychology Today,* September 1969, pp. 27–28; 58–59.

**Feshbach, S., & Weiner, B.** *Personality.* Lexington, Mass.: D. C. Heath, 1982.

**Festinger, L., Schachter, S., & Back, K.** *Social pressures in informal groups: A study of human factors in housing.* New York: Harper & Row, 1950.

**Fidler, J.** Loneliness—the problems of the elderly and retired. *Royal Society of Health Journal,* 1976, *96*(1), 39–41.

**Fisher, S.** *The female orgasm.* New York: Basic Books, 1973.

**Fishman, D. B., & Neigher, W. D.** American psychology in the eighties: Who will buy? *American Psychologist,* 1982, *37*(5), 533–46.

**Fitch, G.** Effects of self-esteem, perceived performance, and choice on causal attribution. *Journal of Personality and Social Psychology,* 1970, *16,* 311–15.

**Flanagan, J. C.** From "A research approach to improving our quality of life" by John C. Flanagan in *American Psychologist,* February 1978. Copyright © 1978 by the American Psychological Association. Reprinted by permission of the author.

**Flavell, J. H.** Changes in adulthood. In L. R. Goulet & P. B. Baltes (Eds.), *Life-span developmental psychology: Research and theory.* New York: Academic Press, 1970.

**Flavell, J. H.** *Cognitive development.* Englewood Cliffs, N.J.: Prentice-Hall, 1977.

**Fordyce, W. E.** *Behavioral methods for chronic pain and illness.* St. Louis: C. V. Mosby, 1976.

**Frankl, V.** *Man's search for meaning.* New York: Simon & Schuster, 1971.

**Fraser, C.** Group risk-taking and group polarization. *European Journal of Social Psychology,* 1971, *1,* 493–510.

**Freeman, N. H.** *Strategies of representation in young children: Analysis of spatial skills and drawing processes.* London: Academic Press, 1980.

**Freis, E. D.** Age, race, sex, and other indices of risk in hypertension. *American Journal of Medicine,* 1973, *55,* 275–80.

**Freud, S.** *Psychopathology of everyday life* (2nd ed.). London: Ernest Benn, Ltd., 1954. (Originally published, 1901.)

**Freud, S.** *Civilization and its discontents.* Westport, Conn.: Associated Booksellers, 1955. (Originally published, 1930.)

**Freud, S.** Female sexuality. In S. Freud, *The standard edition of the complete psychological works of Sigmund Freud. Vol. XXI. The future of an illusion, civilization and its discontents, and other works.* London: Hogarth Press, 1961. (Originally published, 1931.)

**Friedman, M., & Rosenman, R. H.** *Type A behavior and your heart.* New York: Knopf, 1974.

**Fromm, E.** *The sane society.* New York: Holt, 1955.

**Fromm, E.** *The art of loving.* New York: Harper & Row, 1956.

**Furlong, F. W.** Determinism and free will: Review of the literature. *American Journal of Psychiatry,* 1981, *134*(4), 435–39.

**Fyans, L. J., Jr.** (Ed.). *Achievement motivation: Recent trends in theory and research.* New York: Plenum Press, 1980.

**Galle, O. R., Gove, W. R., & McPherson, J. M.** Population density and pathology: What are the relationships for man? *Science,* 1972, *176,* 23–30.

**Gandhi, M.** *An autobiography: The story of my experiments with truth* (M. Desai, Trans.). Boston: Beacon Press, 1957.

**Garmezy, N.** Vulnerable and invulnerable: Theory, research, and intervention. *Master Lectures in Developmental Psychology,* American Psychological Association, 1976. (Ms. No. 1337)

**Gazzaniga, M. S.** *The bisected brain.* New York: Appleton-Century-Croft, 1970.

**Geer, J. H., Davison, G. C., & Gatchel, R. I.** Reduction of stress in humans through nonveridical perceived control of aversive stimulation. *Journal of Personality and Social Psychology,* 1970, *16,* 731–38.

**Geiwitz, P. J.** *Non-Freudian personality theories.* Belmont, Calif.: Brooks/Cole, 1969.

**Gelven, M.** Guilt and human meaning. *Humanitas,* 1973, *9*(1), 69–81.

**Gesell, A.** *Youth: The years from ten to sixteen.* New York: Harper & Row, 1956.

**Ghiselin, M. T.** *The economy of nature and the evolution of sex.* Berkeley: University of California Press, 1974.

**Gilbert, S. J.** Self-disclosure, intimacy, and communication in families. *The Family Coordinator,* 1976, *25*(3), 221–31.

**Ginott, H. G.** *Between parent and child: New solutions to old problems.* New York: Avon, 1965.

**Ginzberg, E.** *The development of human resources.* New York: McGraw-Hill, 1966.

**Gitter, A. G., & Black, H.** Is self-disclosure self-revealing? *Journal of Counseling Psychology,* 1976, *23,* 327–32.

**Glaros, A. G.** From *Student study guide* to accompany *Maladaptive behavior: An introduction to abnormal psychology* by Alan G. Glaros. Copyright © 1980 by Scott, Foresman and Company.

**Glenn, N. D., & McLanahan, S.** Children and marital happiness: A further specification of the relationship. *Journal of Marriage and the Family,* 1982, *44*(1), 63–72.

**Glenn, N. D., & Weaver, C. N.** The marital happiness of remarried divorced persons. *Journal of Marriage and the Family,* 1977, *39*(2), 331–37.

**Goertzel, V., & Goertzel, M.** *Cradles of eminence.* Boston: Little, Brown, 1966.

**Goffman, E.** *Interaction ritual: Essays on face-to-face behavior.* Garden City, N.Y.: Doubleday, 1967.

**Goffman, E.** *Relations in public.* New York: Harper & Row, 1972.

**Goldfried, M. R., & Sobocinski, D.** Effects of irrational beliefs on emotional arousal. *Journal of Counseling and Clinical Psychology,* 1975, *43,* 504–10.

**Gonzales, P.** *Tennis.* New York: Cornerstone Library, 1972.

**Gough, H. G.** *California Psychological Inventory: Manual.* Palo Alto, Calif.: Consulting Psychologists Press, 1957.

**Gould, R. L.** The phases of adult life: A study in developmental psychology. *American Journal of Psychiatry,* 1972, *129,* 521–31.

**Grant, I., Sweetwood, H., Yager, J., & Gerst, M.** Quality of life events in relation to psychiatric symptoms. *Archives of General Psychiatry,* 1981, *38*(3), 335–39.

**Grinker, R. R., & Spiegel, J. P.** *War neuroses.* Philadelphia: Blakiston, 1945.

**Haley, J.** Whither family therapy. *Family Process,* 1962, *1,* 69–100.

**Haley, J.** *Strategies of psychotherapy.* New York: Grune & Stratton, 1963.

**Hamilton, D. L., & Zanna, M. P.** Differential weighting of favorable and unfavorable attributes in impressions of personality. *Journal of Experimental Research in Personality,* 1972, *6,* 204–12.

**Hammarskjöld, D.** [*Markings*] (L. Sjoberg and W. H. Auden, Trans.). New York: Knopf, 1974. Copyright © 1964 by Alfred A. Knopf, Inc. and Faber & Faber, Ltd. Reprinted by permission of Alfred A. Knopf, Inc., and Faber & Faber, Ltd.

**Hammond, K. R., & Summers, D. A.** Cognitive control. *Psychological Review,* 1972, *79,* 58–67.

**Hancock, T.** Beyond health care: Creating a healthy future. *The Futurist,* 1982, *16*(4), 4–18.

**Hanna, S. L., & Knaub, P. K.** Cohabitation before marriage: Its relationship to family strengths. *Alternative Lifestyles,* 1981, *4*(4), 507–22.

**Hare, R. D.** From *Psychopathy: Theory and research* by Robert D. Hare. New York: Wiley, 1970. Copyright © 1970 by John Wiley & Sons, Inc. Reprinted by permission of John Wiley & Sons, Inc.

**Harlow, H. F., & Harlow, M. K.** Learning to love. *American Scientist,* 1966, *54,* 244–72.

**Harman, W. W.** *An incomplete guide to the future.* San Francisco: San Francisco Book Company, 1976.

**Harman, W. W.** The coming transformation. *The Futurist,* February 1977, *11*(1), 4–12.

**Harrow, M., Grossman, L. S., Silverstein, M. L., & Meltzer, H. Y.** Thought pathology in manic and schizophrenic patients. *Archives of General Psychiatry,* 1982, *39,* 665–71.

**Haskins, C. P.** *Report of the president, 1966–1967.* Washington, D.C.: Carnegie Institute of Washington, 1968.

**Hatcher, R. A., Stewart, G. K., Stewart, F., Guest, F., Schwartz, D. W., & Jones, S. A.** *Contraceptive technology 1980–1981* (10th rev. ed.). New York: Irvington Publishers, 1980.

**Hathaway, S. R., & Meehl, P. E.** *An atlas for the clinical use of the MMPI.* Minneapolis: University of Minnesota Press, 1951.

**Havens, L. I.** The existential use of the self. *American Journal of Psychiatry,* 1974, *131*(1) 1–10.

**Havighurst, R. J.** Research and development in social gerontology: A report of a special committee of the Gerontological Society. *The Gerontologist,* 1969, *9,* 1–90.

**Haythorn, W. W., & Altman, I.** Together in isolation. *Trans-action,* 1967, *4*(3), 18–22.

**Hemingway, E.** *The short stories of. . . .* New York: Scribner's, 1955.

**Hemminger, G.** "Tobacco" by Graham Hemminger from the *Penn State Froth,* November, 1915. Reprinted by permission.

**Hershey, D.** *Life span and factors affecting it.* Springfield, Ill.: Charles C. Thomas, 1974.

**Hess, E. H., & Polt, J. M.** Pupil size as related to interest value of visual stimuli. *Science,* 1960, *132,* 349–50.

**Hilgard, E. R.** *Hypnotic susceptibility.* New York: Harcourt Brace Jovanovich, 1965.

**Hilgard, E. R.** The domain of hypnosis: With some comments on alternative paradigms. *American Psychologist,* 1973, *28*(11), 972–82.

**Hilgard, E. R., & Hilgard, J. R.** *Hypnosis in the relief of pain.* Los Angeles: Kaufman, 1975.

**Hirschfeld, R. M. A., & Cross, C.** Epidemiology of affective disorders. *Archives of General Psychiatry,* 1982, *39*(1), 35–46.

**Hite, S.** *The Hite report on male sexuality.* New York: Alfred A. Knopf, 1981.

**Holland, J. L.** *The psychology of vocational choice.* Waltham, Mass.: Blaisdell, 1966.

**Holland, J. L.** *Making vocational choices: A theory of careers.* Englewood Cliffs, N.J.: Prentice-Hall, 1973.

**Holmes, T. H., & Rahe, R. H.** The social readjustment rating scale. *Journal of Psychosomatic Research,* 1967, *11,* 213–18.

**Holmes, T. S., & Holmes, T. H.** Short-term intrusions into the life-style routine. *Journal of Psychosomatic Research,* 1970, *14*(2), 121–32. Copyright © 1970 by Pergamon Press Ltd. Reprinted by permission.

**Honeycutt, J. M., Wilson, C., & Parker, C.** Effects of sex and degrees of happiness on perceived styles of communicating in and out of the marital relationship. *Journal of Marriage and the Family,* 1982, *44*(2), 395–406.

**Horner, M.** Femininity and successful achievement: A basic inconsistency. In J. Bardwick, E. Douvan, M. Horner, & D. Guttman (Eds.), *Feminine personality and conflict.* Belmont, Calif.: Wadsworth, 1970.

**Hornung, C. A., & McCullough, B. C.** Status relationships in dual-employment marriages: Consequences for psychological well-being. *Journal of Marriage and the Family,* 1981, *43*(1), 125–41.

**Howe, E. E., Jr.** (Series Ed.), **& Flowers, J. H.** (Vol. Ed.). *Nebraska symposium on motivation, 1981: Cognitive processes* (Vol. 28). Lincoln: University of Nebraska Press, 1981.

**Howe, H. E., Jr.** (Series Ed.), **& Page, M.** (Vol. Ed.). *Nebraska symposium on motivation, 1979: Beliefs, attitudes, and values* (Vol. 27). Lincoln: University of Nebraska Press, 1979.

**Hubbard, B. M.** Critical paths to an all-win world. *The Futurist,* 1981, *15*(3), 31–37.

**Hulicka, I. M.** Age differences in retention as a function of interference. *Journal of Gerontology,* 1967, *22,* 180–84.

**Hull, D.** Life circumstances and physical illness: A cross-disciplinary survey of research content and method for the decade 1965–1975. *Journal of Psychosomatic Research,* 1977, *21*(2), 115–39.

**Hunt, J. McV.** *Intelligence and experience.* New York: Ronald Press, 1961.

**Hunt, M.** *Sexual behavior in the 1970s.* Chicago: Playboy Press, 1974.

**Huxley, A.** Human potentialities. In R. E. Farson (Ed.), *Science and human affairs.* Palo Alto, Calif.: Science and Behavior Books, 1965.

**Huxley, J.** *Evolution in action.* New York: Harper & Row, 1953.

**Ivanhoe, A. J.** Overcoming loneliness. *Elysium,* January/February/March 1977, pp. 18–19.

**Jacobson, E.** *You must relax.* New York: McGraw-Hill, 1934.

**Jacobson, E.** *Progressive relaxation.* Chicago: University of Chicago Press, 1938.

**Jahoda, M.** *Current concepts of positive mental health.* Joint Commission on Mental Illness and Health. New York: Basic Books, 1958, No. 1.

**James, W.** *The principles of psychology.* New York: Holt, 1890.

**Janda, L. H., & Klenke-Hamel, K. E.** *Human sexuality.* New York: D. Van Nostrand, 1980. Copyright © 1980 by Litton Educational Publishing, Inc. Reprinted by permission of the publisher, Brooks/Cole Publishing Company, Monterey, California.

**Janis, I. L., & Mann, I.** *Decision making.* New York: The Free Press, 1977. Copyright © 1977 by The Free

Press, a division of Macmillan Publishing Co., Inc. Reprinted by permission of Macmillan Publishing Co., Inc.

**Jarvik, M. E.** The psychopharmacological revolution. *Psychology Today,* May 1967, *1*(1), 51–58.

**Jellinek, E. M.** Phases of alcohol addiction. In G. D. Shead (Ed.), *Studies in abnormal behavior.* Chicago: Rand McNally, 1971.

**Jones, E. E., & Gerard, H. B.** *Foundations of social psychology.* New York: Wiley, 1967.

**Jones, J. M.** *Prejudice and racism.* Reading, Mass.: Addison-Wesley, 1972.

**Jouvet, M.** The sleeping brain. *Science Journal,* 1967, *3*(5), 105–11.

**Julien, R. M.** *A primer of drug action* (3rd ed.). San Francisco: W. H. Freeman, 1981.

**Kabanoff, B.** Work and nonwork: A review of models, methods, and findings. *Psychological Bulletin,* 1980, *88,* 60–77.

**Kabanoff, B., & O'Brien, G. E.** Work and leisure: A task attributes analysis. *Journal of Applied Psychology,* 1980, *65,* 596–609.

**Kando, T., & Summers, W.** The impact of work on leisure. *Pacific Sociological Review,* 1971, *14,* 310–27.

**Kaplan, H. S.** *Disorders of sexual desire.* New York: Brunner/Mazel, 1979.

**Kastenbaum, R.** *Death, society, and human experience.* St. Louis: C. V. Mosby, 1977.

**Kastenbaum, R.** *Growing old: Years of fulfillment.* New York: Harper & Row, 1979.

**Katchadourian, H. A., & Lunde, D. T.** *Fundamentals of human sexuality* (3rd ed.). New York: Holt, Rinehart & Winston, 1980.

**Kaufman, W.** *Without guilt and justice: From decidophobia to autonomy.* New York: Wyden, 1973.

**Kelly, G. A.** *The psychology of personal constructs* (Vols. 1 and 2). New York: Norton, 1955.

**Kerckhoff, A. C., & Back, K. W.** *The June Bug: A study of hysterical contagion.* New York: Appleton-Century-Crofts, 1968. Copyright © 1968 by Meredith Corporation. Reprinted by permission of Prentice-Hall, Inc., Englewood Cliffs, New Jersey.

**Kinsey, A. C., Pomeroy, W. B., & Martin, C. E.** *Sexual behavior in the human male.* Philadelphia: W. B. Saunders, 1948.

**Kinsey, A. C., Pomeroy, W. B., Martin, C. E., & Gebhard, P. H.** *Sexual behavior in the human female.* Philadelphia: W. B. Saunders, 1953.

**Kirkendall, L. A., & Anderson, P. B.** Authentic selfhood: Basis for tomorrow's sexuality. In E. S. Morrison & V. Borosage (Eds.), *Human sexuality: Contemporary perspectives.* Palo Alto, Calif.: National Press Books, 1973.

**Kluckhohn, F. R., & Strodtbeck, F. L.** *Variations in value orientation.* New York: Harper & Row, 1961.

**Knobloch, H., & Pasamanick, B.** (Eds.) *Gesell and Amatruda's developmental diagnosis: The evaluation and management of normal and abnormal neuropsychologic development in infancy and early childhood* (3rd ed., revised and enlarged). Hagerstown, Md.: Harper & Row, 1974.

**Knox, D.** *Exploring marriage and the family.* Glenview, Ill.: Scott, Foresman and Co., 1979.

**Kohlberg, L.** Moral stages and moralization: The cognitive-developmental approach. In T. Lickona (Ed.), *Moral development and behavior: Theory, research, and social issues.* New York: Holt, Rinehart & Winston, 1976.

**Kohut, H.** *The restoration of the self.* New York: International Universities Press, 1977.

**Kornhauser, A. W.** *Mental health of the industrial worker.* New York: Wiley, 1965.

**Koughan, M.** Arthur Friedman's outrage: Employees decide their pay. *Washington Post,* February 23, 1975. Copyright © 1975 by the Washington Post. Reprinted by permission.

**Krebs, D., & Adinolfi, A. A.** Physical attractiveness, social relations, and personality style. *Journal of Personality and Social Psychology,* 1975, *31,* 245–253.

**Kroes, W. M., Hurrell, J. J., & Margolis, B.** Job stress in police administrators. *Journal of Police Science and Administration,* 1974, *2*(4), 381–87.

**Kübler-Ross, E.** *On death and dying.* New York: Macmillan, 1969.

**Lahey, B. B., & Ciminero, A. R.** *Maladaptive behavior: An introduction to abnormal behavior.* Glenview, Ill.: Scott, Foresman and Co., 1980.

**Laing, R. D.** *The politics of experience.* New York: Pantheon, 1967.

**Lalljee, M., & Cook, M.** Uncertainty in first encounters. *Journal of Personality and Social Psychology,* 1973, *26,* 137–41.

**Lamott, K.** *Escape from stress.* New York: G. P. Putnam's Sons, 1975.

**Landis, J. T., & Landis, M. G.** *Building a successful marriage* (6th ed.). Englewood Cliffs, N.J.: Prentice-Hall, 1973.

**Landman, J. T., & Dawes, R. M.** Psychotherapy outcome: Smith and Glass' conclusions stand up under scrutiny. *American Psychologist,* 1982, *37*(5), 504–16.

**Landy, F. J., & Trumbo, D. A.** *Psychology of work behavior.* Homewood, Ill.: Dorsey Press, 1980.

**LaPiere, R. T.** Attitudes vs. actions. *Social Forces,* 1934, *13,* 230–37.

**Lash, J. P.** *Eleanor and Franklin.* New York: Norton, 1971.

**Laszlo, E.** *The systems view of the world.* New York: Braziller, 1972.

**Latane, B., & Darley, J. M.** *The unresponsive bystander: Why doesn't he help?* Englewood Cliffs, N.J.: Prentice-Hall, 1970.

**Lawler, E. E.** Strategies for improving the quality of work life. *American Psychologist,* 1982, *37*(5), 486–93.

**Lawler, E. E., & Hackman, J. R.** The impact of employee participation in the development of pay incentive plans: A field experiment. *Journal of Applied Psychology,* 1969, *53,* 467–71.

**Leak, G. K., & Christopher, S. B.** Freudian psychoanalysis and sociobiology: A synthesis. *American Psychologist,* 1982, *37*(3), 313–22.

**Lee, D.** Culture and the experience of value. In A. H. Maslow (Ed.), *New knowledge in human values.* New York: Harper & Row, 1959.

**Leon, G. R.** *Case histories of deviant behavior: An interactional perspective.* Boston: Allyn & Bacon, 1977.

**Leonard, J.** Ghetto for blue-eyes in the classroom. *Life,* May 8, 1970, p. 16.

**Levine, J., & Zigler, E.** Denial and self-image in stroke, lung cancer, and heart disease patients. *Journal of Consulting and Clinical Psychology,* 1975, *43,* 751–57.

**Levinger, G.** Sources of marital dissatisfaction among applicants for divorce. *American Journal of Orthopsychiatry,* 1966, *36,* 803–7.

**Levinson, D., & Malone, M. J.** *Toward explaining human culture: A critical review of the findings of worldwide cross-cultural research.* New Haven, Conn.: Human Relations Area File Press, 1980.

**Levinson, D. J., Darrow, C. N., Klein, E. B., Levinson, M. H., & McKee, B.** *The seasons of a man's life.* New York: Ballantine Books, 1978.

**Lewin, K., Lippitt, R., & White, R. K.** Patterns of aggressive behavior in experimentally created "social climates." *Journal of Social Psychology,* 1939, *10,* 271–99.

**Lewinsohn, P. M.** Clinical and theoretical aspects of depression. In K. S. Calhoun, H. E. Adams, & K. M.

Mitchell (Eds.), *Innovative treatment methods in psychopathology.* New York: Wiley-Interscience, 1974.

**Libby, R. W.** Creative singlehood as a sexual life-style. In R. W. Libby & R. N. Whitehurst (Eds.), *Marriage and alternatives: Exploring intimate relationships.* Glenview, Ill.: Scott, Foresman and Co., 1977.

**Lichtenstein, E., & Penner, M.** Long-term effects of rapid smoking treatment. *Addictive Behaviors,* 1977, *2,* 109–12.

**Linder, S. B.** *The harried leisure class.* New York: Columbia University Press, 1970.

**Lipton, R. J.** *The broken connection: On death and the continuity of life.* New York: Simon & Schuster, 1979.

**Lobsenz, N. T.** Taming the green-eyed monster. *Redbook,* March 1975, pp. 74; 76–77; 188; 190.

**London, M., Crandall, R., & Seals, G. W.** The contribution of job and leisure satisfaction to the quality of life. *Journal of Applied Psychology,* 1977, *62,* 328–34.

**London, P.** *The modes and morals of psychotherapy.* New York: Holt, Rinehart and Winston, 1964.

**LoPiccolo, J., & Lobitz, C.** The role of masturbation in the treatment of sexual dysfunction. *Archives of Sexual Behavior,* 1972, *2,* 163–71.

**Lorenz, K.** [On aggression] (M. K. Wilson, Trans.). New York: Harcourt, Brace and World, 1963.

**Lydon, S.** The politics of orgasm. In M. Garskof (Ed.), *Roles women play: Readings toward women's liberation.* Belmont, Calif.: Brooks/Cole, 1971.

**Lynch, J. J.** *The broken heart: The medical consequences of loneliness.* New York: Basic Books, 1977.

**Maehr, M., & Kleiber, D. A.** The graying of achievement motivation. *American Psychologist,* 1981, *36*(7), 787–93.

**Mahl, G. H.** Gestures and body movements in interviews. In J. M. Schlien (Ed.), *Research in psychotherapy,* Washington, D.C.: American Psychological Association, 1968.

**Mahoney, M. J.** The sensitive scientist in empirical humanism. *American Psychologist,* 1975, *30,* 864–67.

**Mahoney, M. J., & Arnkoff, D. B.** Cognitive and self-control therapies. In S. L. Garfield & A. E. Bergin (Eds.), *Handbook of psychotherapy and behavior change* (2nd ed.). New York: Wiley, 1978, 689–722.

**Mahoney, M. J., & Thoresen, C. E.** *Self-control.* Monterey, Calif.: Brooks/Cole, 1974.

**Mahs, M.** God, man, and Apollo. *Time,* January 1, 1973. pp. 50–51.

**Mansfield, R., & Evans, M. G.** Work and non-work in two occupational groups. *Industrial Relations*, 1975, *6*, 48–54.

**Marcia, J. E.** Development and validation of ego-identity status. *Journal of Personality and Social Psychology*, 1966, *3*, 551–58.

**Marks, I. M.** *Fears and phobias*. New York: Academic Press, 1969.

**Marlatt, G. A., & Gordon, J. R.** Determinants of relapse: Implications for the maintenance of behavior change. In P. O. Davidson & S. M. Davidson (Eds.), *Behavioral medicine: Changing health lifestyles*. New York: Brunner/Mazel, 1980.

**Marmor, J.** Recent trends in psychotherapy. *American Journal of Psychiatry*, 1980, *137*(4), 409–16.

**Marx, M. B., Garrity, T. F., & Bowers, F. R.** The influence of recent life experience on the health of college freshmen. *Journal of Psychosomatic Research*, 1975, *19*, 87–98. Copyright © 1975 by Pergamon Press, Ltd. Reprinted by permission.

**Maslow, A. H.** *Motivation and personality*. New York: Harper & Row, 1954.

**Maslow, A. H.** *Toward a psychology of being* (2nd ed.). New York: D. Van Nostrand, 1968.

**Maslow, A. H.** Toward a humanistic biology. *American Psychologist*, 1969, *24*, 734–35.

**Maslow, A. H.** *The farther reaches of human nature*. New York: Viking, 1971.

**Masters, W. H., & Johnson, V. E.** *Human sexual response*. Boston: Little, Brown, 1966.

**Masters, W. H., & Johnson, V. E.** *Human sexual inadequacy*. Boston: Little, Brown, 1970.

**Masters, W. H., & Johnson, V. E.** *The pleasure bond*. Boston: Little, Brown, 1975.

**Masters, W. H., & Johnson, V. E.** Principles of the new sex therapy. *American Journal of Psychiatry*, 1976, *133*, 548–54.

**Masters, W. H., & Johnson, V. E.** *Homosexuality in perspective*. Boston: Little, Brown, 1979.

**Masters, W. H., Johnson, V. E., & Kolodny, R. C.** *Human sexuality*. Boston: Little, Brown, 1982.

**Matarazzo, J. D.** The interview. In B. B. Wolman (Ed.), *Handbook of clinical psychology*. New York: McGraw-Hill, 1965, 403–50.

**Matarazzo, J. D.** *Wechsler's measurement and appraisal of adult intelligence*. Baltimore: Williams & Wilkins, 1972.

**Mathes, E.** Nine "colours" or types of romantic love. *Psychological Reports*, 1980, *47*(2), 371–76.

**May, R.** *Love and will*. New York: Norton, 1969.

**Mays, J. A.** High blood pressure, soul food. *Los Angeles Times*, January 16, 1974, Part II, p. 7.

**McCall, G. C., & Simmons, J. L.** *Identity and interaction*. New York: The Free Press, 1966.

**McCann, R.** "Inconsistency." From *Complete Cheerful Cherub* by Rebecca McCann. Copyright, 1932, by Covici, Friede, Inc. Copyright renewed 1960 by Crown Publishers, Inc. Used by permission of Crown Publishers, Inc.

**McCary, J. L.** Historic development of romantic love. In C. Gordon & G. Johnson (Eds.), *Readings in human sexuality: Contemporary perspectives* (2nd ed.). New York: Harper & Row, 1980.

**McClelland, D. C., Atkinson, J. W., Clark, R. A., & Lowell, E. L.** *The achievement motive*. New York: Appleton-Century-Crofts, 1953.

**McGregor, D.** *The human side of enterprise*. New York: McGraw-Hill, 1960.

**McNeil, E. B.** *The psychology of being human*. New York: Canfield Press, 1974.

**Mead, G. H.** *Mind, self, and society*. Chicago: University of Chicago Press, 1934.

**Mead, M.** *From the South Seas: Studies of adolescence and sex in primitive societies*. New York: Morrow, 1939.

**Mechanic, D.** *Students under stress*. New York: The Free Press, 1962.

**Meichenbaum, D.** *Cognitive behavior modification*. Morristown, N.J.: General Learning Press, 1974.

**Meichenbaum, D.** *Cognitive-behavior modification: An integrative approach*. New York: Plenum, 1977.

**Meissner, M.** The long arm of the job: A study of work and leisure. *Industrial Relations*, 1971, *10*, 239–60.

**Michener, J. A.** *The fires of spring*. New York: Random House, 1949.

**Milgram, S.** Behavioral study of obedience. *Journal of Abnormal and Social Psychology*, 1963, *67*, 371–78.

**Milgram, S.** Some conditions of obedience and disobedience to authority. *International Journal of Psychiatry*, 1968, *6*, 259–76.

**Miller, G. A.** *Psychology: The science of mental life*. New York: Harper & Row, 1962.

**Miller, J. G.** Living systems: Basic concepts. *Behavioral Scientist*, 1965, *10*, 193–237. (a)

**Miller, J. G.** Living systems: Structure and process. *Behavioral Scientist*, 1965, *10*, 337–79. (b)

**Miller, J. G.** *Living systems*. New York: McGraw-Hill, 1977.

**Miller, N. E.** Experimental studies of conflict. In J. McV. Hunt (Ed.). *Personality and the Behavior Disorders I*. New York: Ronald Press, 1944, pp. 431–65.

**Miller, P. M.** *Behavioral treatment of alcoholism.* New York: Pergamon Press, 1976.

**Mischel, W.** *Personality and assessment.* New York: Wiley, 1968.

**Mischel, W.** *Introduction to personality* (3rd ed.). New York: Holt, Rinehart & Winston, 1981.

**Mischel, W., & Ebbesen, E.** Attention in delay of gratification. *Journal of Personality and Social Psychology,* 1970, *16,* 329–37.

**Montgomery, B. M.** The form and function of quality communication in marriage. *Family Relations,* 1981, *30*(1), 21–30.

**Montreal Health Press.** *Birth control handbook* (12th ed.). Montreal: Author, 1975.

**Morgan, C. T., King, R. A., & Robinson, N. M.** *Introduction to psychology* (6th ed.). New York: McGraw-Hill, 1979.

**Morrison, E. S., Starks, K., Hyndman, C., & Ronzio, N.** *Growing up sexual* by Eleanor S. Morrison et al. Copyright © 1980 by Litton Educational Publishing, Inc. Reprinted by permission of Wadsworth Publishing Company.

**Morse, R., & Weiss, N.** The function and meaning of work and the job. *American Sociological Review,* 1955, *20,* 191–98.

**Moscovici, S., & Zavalloni, M.** The group as a polarizer of attitudes. *Journal of Personality and Social Psychology,* 1969, *12,* 125–35.

**Moustakas, C. E.** *Loneliness.* Englewood Cliffs, N.J.: Prentice-Hall, 1961.

**Murphy, H. B. M.** The advent of guilt feelings as a common depressive symptom: A historical comparison of two continents. *Psychiatry,* 1978, *41,* 229–42.

**Murphy, L. B.** *The widening world of childhood.* New York: Basic Books, 1962.

**Murphy, L. B., & Moriarty, A. E.** *From infancy to adolescence.* New Haven, Conn.: Yale University Press, 1976.

**Nadelson, C. C. & Notman, M. T.** To marry or not to marry: A choice. *American Journal of Psychiatry,* 1981, *138*(10), 1352–56.

**Nardini, J. E.** Survival factors in American prisoners of war of the Japanese. *American Journal of Psychiatry,* 1952, *109,* 242–43.

**National Institute on Drug Abuse.** (*Special report on cocaine,* Mar. 9, 1981.) Reported by Lang, J. S. Cocaine spreads its deadly net. *U.S. News & World Report,* Mar. 22, 1982, pp. 27–29.

**Navran, L.** Communication and adjustment in marriage. *Family Process,* 1967, *6*(2), 173–84.

**Neugarten, B. L.** Adult personality: Toward a psychology of the life cycle. In B. L. Neugarten (Ed.), *Middle age and aging.* Chicago: University of Chicago Press, 1968.

**Neugarten, B. L., & Hagestad, G. O.** Age and the life course. In R. H. Binstock & E. Shanas (Eds.), *Handbook of aging and the social sciences.* New York: Van Nostrand Reinhold, 1977.

**Neugarten, B. L., Wood, V., Kraines, R. J., & Loomis, B.** Women's attitudes toward the menopause. *Vita Humana,* 1963, *6,* 140–51.

**Neulinger, J.** *The psychology of leisure* (2nd ed.). Springfield, Ill.: Charles C. Thomas, 1981.

**Nisbett, R. E., & Wilson, T. D.** The halo effect: Evidence for unconscious alteration of judgments. *Journal of Personality and Social Psychology,* 1977, *35,* 250–56.

**Norman, C.** A long-term problem for the nuclear industry. *Science,* 1982, *215,* 376–79.

**Novaco, R.** *Anger control: The development and evaluation of an experimental treatment.* Lexington, Mass.: D. C. Heath, 1975.

**Nye, R. D.** *Conflict among humans.* New York: Springer, 1973.

**O'Brien, G. E.** Leisure attributes and retirement satisfaction. *Journal of Applied Psychology,* 1981, *66,* 371–84.

**O'Neill, N.** *The marriage premise.* New York: Bantam Books, 1978.

**O'Neill, N., & O'Neill, G.** *Open marriage: A new lifestyle for couples.* New York: M. Evans and Co., 1972.

**Orlofsky, J. L., Marcia, J. E., & Lesser, I. M.** Ego identity status and the intimacy versus isolation crisis of young adulthood. *Journal of Personality and Social Psychology,* 1973, *27,* 211–29.

**Orne, M. T.** The nature of hypnosis: Artifact and essence. *Journal of Abnormal and Social Psychology,* 1959, *58,* 277–99.

**Osborn, A. F.** *Applied imagination: Principles and procedures of creative thinking.* New York: Charles Scribner's Sons, 1953.

**Osgood, C.** "POSSLQ" from *There's nothing that I wouldn't do if you would be my POSSLQ* by Charles Osgood. Copyright © 1981 by CBS, Inc. Reprinted by permission of Holt, Rinehart and Winston, Publishers.

**O'Toole, J.** How to forecast your own working future. *The Futurist,* 1982, *16*(1), 5–11.

**Ouchi, W. G.** *Theory Z: How American business can meet the Japanese challenge.* New York: Avon Books, 1981.

**Overstreet, H., & Overstreet, B.** *The mind goes forth.* New York: Norton, 1956.

**Parker, S. R.** *The future of work and leisure.* London: MacGibbon & Kee, 1971.

**Parkes, C. M.** Components of the reaction to loss of limb, spouse, or home. *Journal of Psychosomatic Research,* 1972, *16,* 343–49.

**Parnas, J., Schulsinger, F., Schulsinger, H., Mednick, S. A., & Teasdale, T. W.** Behavioral precursors of schizophrenia spectrum. *Archives of General Psychiatry,* 1982, *39,* 658–64.

**Paul, G. L.** *Insight vs. desensitization in psychotherapy.* Stanford, Calif.: Stanford University Press, 1966.

**Paul, G. L.** Physiological effects of relaxation training and hypnotic suggestion. *Journal of Abnormal Psychology,* 1969, *74,* 425–37.

**Paul, G. L., & Lentz, R. J.** *Psychosocial treatment of chronic mental patients: Milieu versus social-learning programs.* Cambridge, Mass.: Harvard University Press, 1977.

**Peel, E. A.** *The nature of adolescent judgment.* New York: Wiley, 1971.

**Perls, F. S.** *Gestalt therapy verbatim.* Lafayette, Calif.: Real People Press, 1969.

**Peterson, C. R., & Beach, L. R.** Man as an intuitive statistician. *Psychological Bulletin,* 1967, *68,* 29–46.

**Petty, R. E., Williams, K. D., Harkins, S. G., & Latane, B.** Social inhibition of helping yourself: Bystander response to a cheeseburger. *Personality and Social Psychology Bulletin,* 1977, *3,* 571–74.

**Piaget, J.** *The origins of intelligence in children.* New York: International Universities Press, 1952.

**Piaget, J.** *Genetic epistemology.* New York: Columbia University Press, 1970.

**Platt, J.** A fearful and wonderful world for living. In College of Home Economics, *Families of the future.* Ames, Iowa: The Iowa State University Press, 1972. Excerpt reprinted by permission, © 1972 by the Iowa State University Press, Ames, Iowa.

**Pomerleau, O. F., Adkins, D., & Pertschuk, M.** Predictors of outcome and recidivism in smoking cessation treatment. *Addictive Behaviors,* 1978, *3,* 65–70.

**Pope, B.** *The mental health interview: Research and application.* New York: Pergamon Press, 1979.

**Posner, M. J.** Cumulative development of attentional theory. *American Psychologist,* 1982, *37*(2), 168–79.

**Powell, D. H., & Driscoll, P. F.** Middle class professionals face unemployment. *Society,* 1973, *10*(2), 18–26.

**Rabkin, J. G., & Struening, E. L.** Life events, stress, and illness. *Science,* 1976, *194,* 1013–19.

**Rahe, R. H., & Lind, E.** Psychosocial factors and sudden cardiac death: A pilot study. *Journal of Psychosomatic Research,* 1971, *15,* 19–24.

**Ramsay, R. W.** Behavioral approaches to bereavement. *Behaviour Research and Therapy,* 1977, *15,* 131–35.

**Rand, A.** *The virtue of selfishness.* New York: The New American Library, 1965.

**Reiss, I. L.** The effect of changing trends, attitudes, and values on premarital sexual behavior in the United States. In S. Gordon & R. Libby (Eds.), *Sexuality today and tomorrow.* North Scituate, Mass.: Duxbury, 1976.

**Resnick, R. B., Kestenbaum, R. S., & Schwartz, L. K.** Acute systemic effects of cocaine in man. *Science,* 1977, *195,* 696–98.

**Rich, L. D.** *Happy the land.* Philadelphia: Lippincott, 1946.

**Richter, C. P.** On the phenomenon of sudden death in animals and man. *Psychosomatic Medicine,* 1957, *19,* 191–98.

**Riecken, H. W.** The effect of talkativeness on ability to influence group solution of problems. *Sociometry,* 1958, *21,* 309–21.

**Riegel, K. F.** The dialectics of human development. *American Psychologist,* 1976, *31,* 689–700.

**Rinder, W.** *Love is an attitude.* San Francisco: Celestial Arts Publishing, 1970. Copyright © 1970 by Celestial Arts, 231 Adrian Road, Millbrae, California 94030. Reprinted with permission of the publisher.

**Risman, B. J., Hill, C. T., Rubin, Z., & Peplau, L. A.** Living together in college: Implications for courtship. *Journal of Marriage and the Family,* 1981, *43*(2), 77–83.

**Robbins, M., & Jensen, G. D.** Multiple orgasm in males. *Journal of Sex Research,* 1978, *14,* 21–26.

**Robertson, I.** *Sociology* (2nd ed.). New York: Worth, 1981.

**Robins, L. N.** *Deviant children grown up: A sociological and psychiatric study of sociopathic personality.* Baltimore: Williams and Wilkins, 1966.

**Robinson, E. A.** "Richard Cory," in *The children of the night.* Copyright under the Berne Convention. Reprinted with the permission of Charles Scribner's Sons.

**Robinson, I. E., & Jedlicka, D.** Change in sexual attitudes and behavior of college students from 1965 to 1980: A research note. *Journal of Marriage and the Family*, 1982, *44*(1), 237–40.

**Rogers, C. R.** *Client-centered therapy.* Boston: Houghton Mifflin, 1951. Copyright © 1951 by Carl R. Rogers. Reprinted by permission of Houghton Mifflin Company.

**Rogers, C. R.** *On becoming a person.* Austin: University of Texas Press, 1958.

**Rogers, C. R.** A theory of therapy, personality, and interpersonal relationships, as developed in the client-centered framework. In S. Koch (Ed.), *Psychology: A study of a science* (Vol. 3). New York: McGraw-Hill, 1959.

**Rogers, C. R.** *On becoming a person: A therapist's view of psychotherapy.* Boston: Houghton Mifflin, 1961.

**Rogers, C. R.** Toward a modern approach to values: The valuing process in the mature person. *Journal of Abnormal and Social Psychology*, 1964, *68*(2), 160–67.

**Rogers, C. R.** Interpersonal relationships: U.S.A. 2000. *Journal of Applied Behavioral Science*, 1968, *4*(3), 265–80.

**Rogers, C. R.** *Freedom to learn.* Columbus, Ohio: Charles E. Merrill, 1969.

**Rogers, C. R.** *Carl Rogers on encounter groups.* New York: Harper & Row, 1970.

**Rogers, C. R.** *Carl Rogers on personal power.* New York: Delacorte Press, 1977.

**Rokeach, M.** *The open and closed mind.* New York: Basic Books, 1960.

**Rokeach, M.** *Beliefs, attitudes, and values: A theory of organization and change.* San Francisco: Jossey-Bass, 1968.

**Rokeach, M.** *The nature of human values.* New York: The Free Press, 1973. Reprinted with permission of Macmillan Publishing Co., Inc. from *The nature of human values* by Milton Rokeach. Copyright © 1973 by The Free Press, a Division of Macmillan Publishing Co., Inc.

**Rollins, B. C., & Feldman, H.** Marital satisfaction over the family cycle. *Journal of Marriage and the Family*, 1970, *32*, 20–28.

**Rosenman, R., Friedman, M., Strauss, R., Wurm, M., Jenkins, D., & Messinger, H.** Coronary heart disease in the Western Collaborative Group Study: A follow-up experience of two years. *Journal of the American Medical Association*, 1966, *195*, 86–92.

**Rotter, J. B.** Generalized expectancies for internal versus external control of reinforcement. *Psychological Monographs*, 1966, *80*(1, Whole No. 609).

**Rubin, Z.** Measurement of romantic love. *Journal of Personality and Social Psychology*, 1970, *16*, 265–73.

**Rychlak, J. F.** *Introduction to personality and psychotherapy: A theory-construction approach* (2nd ed.). Boston: Houghton Mifflin, 1981.

**Sackheim, H.** Emotions are expressed more intensely on the left side of the face. *Science*, 1978, *202*, 434–36.

**Saegert, S., Swap, W., & Zajonc, R. B.** Exposure, context, and interpersonal attraction. *Journal of Personality and Social Psychology*, 1973, *25*, 234–42.

**Satir, V. M.** *Conjoint family therapy* (Rev. ed.). Palo Alto, Calif.: Science and Behavior Books, 1967.

**Satir, V. M.** *Peoplemaking.* Palo Alto, Calif.: Science and Behavior Books, 1972.

**Sattler, J. M.** *Assessment of children's intelligence.* Philadelphia: W. B. Saunders, 1974.

**Schaar, J.** In *Footnotes to the future*, 1974, *4*(3), 1.

**Schachter, S.** Recidivism and self-cure of smoking and obesity. *American Psychologist*, 1982, *37*(4), 436–44.

**Schachter, S., & Gross, L. P.** Manipulated time and eating behavior. *Journal of Personality and Social Psychology*, 1968, *10*, 98–106.

**Schachter, S., & Singer, J. E.** Cognitive, social, and physiological determinants of emotional state. *Psychological Review*, 1962, *69*, 379–99.

**Schaie, K. W., Labouvie, G. F., & Buech, B. U.** Generational and cohort-specific differences in adult cognitive functioning: A fourteen-year study of independent samples. *Developmental Psychology*, 1973, *9*, 151–66.

**Schinn, R.** Telecommunication policy and the information society. *Footnotes to the Future*, 1976, *6*(2), 2.

**Schoenberg, B., Carr, S. C., Pereta, D., & Kutscher, A. K.** *Loss and grief: Psychological management in medical practice.* New York: Columbia University Press, 1970.

**Schwartz, G. E.** Psychosomatic disorders and biofeedback: A psychobiological model of disregulation. In J. D. Maser & M. E. P. Seligman (Eds.). *Psychopathology: Experimental models.* San Francisco: W. H. Freeman, 1977.

**Sears, R. R., Maccoby, E. E., & Levin, H.** *Patterns of child rearing.* New York: Harper & Row, 1957.

**Seligman, M. E. P.** *Helplessness: On depression, development, and death.* San Francisco: W. H. Freeman, 1975.

**Selye, H.** *The stress of life* (Rev. ed.). New York: McGraw-Hill, 1976.

**Selye, H.** On the real benefits of eustress. *Psychology Today,* 1978, *11*(10), 60–64.

**Selye, H.** The stress concept today. In I. L. Kutash, L. B. Schlesinger, & Associates (Eds.), *Handbook on stress and anxiety.* San Francisco: Jossey-Bass, 1980.

**Severin, F. T.** *Discovering man in psychology: A humanistic approach.* New York: McGraw-Hill, 1973.

**Shane, H. G.** America's educational future. *The Futurist,* October 1976, *10*(5), 252–57.

**Shapiro, D. H., Jr.** *Meditation: Self-regulation strategy and altered state of consciousness. A scientific/personal exploration.* New York: Aldine, 1980.

**Shapiro, D. H.** Overview: Clinical and physiological comparison of meditation with other self-control strategies. *American Journal of Psychiatry,* 1982, *139*(3), 267–74.

**Shaw, M. E.** *Group dynamics.* New York: McGraw-Hill, 1971.

**Sheehy, G.** *Passages: Predictable crises of adult life.* New York: Dutton, 1976.

**Sherbin, J.** Why older marriages work. *Modern Maturity,* February-March 1977, *20*(1), 53–54.

**Sherwood, G. G.** Self-serving biases in person perception: A reexamination of projection as a mechanism of defense. *Psychological Bulletin,* 1981, *90*(4), 445–66.

**Sherwood, G. G.** Consciousness and stress reduction in defensive projection: A reply to Holmes. *Psychological Bulletin,* 1982, *91*(2), 372–75.

**Shibutani, T.** The structure of personal identity. In E. E. Sampson (Ed.), *Approaches, contexts, and problems of social psychology.* Englewood Cliffs, N.J.: Prentice-Hall, 1964.

**Shubik, M.** Information, rationality, and free choice in a future democratic society. *Daedalus,* 1967, *96,* 771–78.

**Simmel, G.** The secret and the secret society. In K. Wolff (Ed.), *The sociology of Georg Simmel.* New York: The Free Press, 1964.

**Simos, B. G.** Grief therapy to facilitate healthy restitution. *Social Casework,* June 1977, *195*(4283), 337–42.

**Sinclair, D.** *Human growth after birth.* London: Oxford University Press, 1969.

**Singer, J. L.** Fantasy: The foundation of serenity. *Psychology Today,* July 1976, pp. 32–34; 37.

**Sinnott, E. W.** *The biology of the spirit.* New York: Viking Press, 1955.

**Skinner, B. F.** *Science and human behavior.* New York: Macmillan, 1953.

**Skinner, B. F.** Teaching machines. *Science,* 1958, *128,* 969–77.

**Skinner, B. F.** *Beyond freedom and dignity.* New York: Knopf, 1971.

**Skinner, B. F.** *About behaviorism.* New York: Knopf, 1974.

**Skinner, B. F.** The force of coincidence. *The Humanist,* May/June 1977, *37*(3), 10–11.

**Smith, D.** Trends in counseling and psychotherapy. *American Psychologist,* 1982, *37*(2), 802–9.

**Smith, M. L., & Glass, G. V.** Meta-analysis of psychotherapy outcome studies. *American Psychologist,* 1977, *32,* 752–60.

**Smith, T. V., & Lindeman, E. C.** *The democratic way of life.* New York: New American Library, 1951.

**South, J.** "Games people play." Atlanta: Lowery Music Co., 1968. Copyright © 1968 by Lowery Music Co., Inc., Atlanta, Ga. International Copyright Secured. All Rights Reserved. Used by permission.

**Southgate, M. T.** Remembrance of things (hopefully) past. *Journal of the American Medical Association,* 1975, *232,* 1331–32.

**Special Task Force, to the Secretary of Health, Education, and Welfare.** *Work in America.* Cambridge, Mass.: MIT Press, 1972.

**Sperry, R. W.** Bridging science and values. *American Psychologist,* 1977, *32,* 237–45.

**Spranger, E.** [*Types of men,* 3rd ed.] (P. Pigors, Trans.). New York: Steckert, 1928. (Originally published, 1923.)

**Springer, S. P., & Deutsch, G.** *Left brain, right brain.* San Francisco: W. H. Freeman, 1981.

**Stevens-Long, J.** *Adult life: Developmental processes.* Palo Alto, Calif.: Mayfield, 1979.

**Stout, H. R.** *Our family physician.* Peoria: Henderson and Smith, 1885.

**Strassberg, D., Robak, H., D'Antonio, M., & Gabel, H.** Self-disclosure: A critical and selective review of the clinical literature. *Comprehensive Psychiatry,* 1977, *18*(1), 31–40.

**Stuart, R. B.** Operant-interpersonal treatment for marital discord. *Journal of Consulting and Clinical Psychology,* 1969, *33,* 675–82.

**Stuart, R. B., & Davis, B.** *Slim chance in a fat world: Behavioral control of obesity.* Champaign, Ill.: Research Press, 1972.

**Student Counseling Center at the University of California at Los Angeles.** Poem by David Palmer published in *Counsel,* a publication of the Student

Counseling Center at the University of California at Los Angeles. Reprinted by permission of the author.

**Sullivan, H. S.** *Schizophrenia as a human process.* New York: Norton, 1962.

**Suls, J.** (Ed.). *Psychological perspectives on the self* (Vol. 1). Hillsdale, N.J.: Erlbaum, 1982.

**Super, D. E.** Vocational development theory: Persons, positions, and processes. *The Counseling Psychologist,* 1969, *1,* 2–8.

**Tavris, C., & Jayaratne, T. E.** How happy is your marriage? What 75,000 wives say about their most intimate relationship. *Redbook,* June 1976, pp. 90–92; 132; 134. Copyright © 1976 The Redbook Publishing Company. Reprinted by permission.

**Teilhard de Chardin, P.** *The phenomenon of man.* New York: Harper & Row, 1961.

**Terkel, S.** *Working.* New York: Pantheon, 1974. Copyright © 1972, 1974 Studs Terkel. Reprinted by permission of Pantheon Books, a division of Random House, Inc., and Wildwood House, Ltd. Excerpt from *The New York Times,* June 10, 1973 copyright © 1973 by The New York Times Company. Reprinted by permission.

**Terkel, S.** *American dreams: Lost and found.* New York: Pantheon Books, 1980.

**Thibaut, J. W., & Kelley, H. H.** *The social psychology of groups.* New York: Wiley, 1959.

**Thorndike, E. L.** Animal intelligence. An experimental study of the associative processes in animals. *Psychological Monographs,* 1898, *2*(No. 8).

**Thurber, J.** The day the dam broke. In *My life and hard times.* New York: Harper & Row, 1933. Copyright 1933, 1961 James Thurber. From *My Life and Hard Times,* published by Harper & Row, New York. (British title: *Vintage Thurber* by James Thurber. The collection Copyright © 1963 Hamish Hamilton Ltd., London.) Originally printed in *The New Yorker.*

**Tiedeman, D. V., & O'Hara, R. P.** *Career development: Choice and adjustment.* New York: College Entrance Examination Board, 1963.

**Timiras, P. S.** *Developmental physiology and aging.* New York: Macmillan, 1972.

**Today's Marriages: Wrenching experience or key to happiness.** *U.S. News & World Report,* October 27, 1975, pp. 35–38.

**Toffler, A.** *Future shock.* New York: Random House, 1970.

**Toffler, A.** In Kronenberger, J. Is the family obsolete? *Look,* January 26, 1971, pp. 35–36.

**Toffler, A.** *The third wave.* New York: William Morrow, 1980.

**Toynbee, A.** *Human savagery cracks thin veneer. Los Angeles Times,* September 6, 1970, Section C, p. 3.

**Trivers, R. L.** Parental investment and sexual selection. In B. Campbell (Ed.), *Sexual selection and the descent of man.* Chicago: Aldine, 1972.

**Tucker, D. M.** Lateral brain function, emotion, and conceptualization. *Psychological Bulletin,* 1981, *89,* 19–46.

**Udry, J. R.** *The social context of marriage.* Philadelphia: Lippincott, 1966.

**U.S., Department of Commerce, Bureau of the Census.** *Statistical abstract of the United States: 1980* (101st ed.). Washington, D.C.: U.S. Government Printing Office, 1980.

**United States Public Health Service.** *Public health reports.* Washington, D.C.: U.S. Government Printing Office, 1980.

**Upper, D., & Meredith, L.** *A stimulus control approach to the modification of smoking behavior.* Paper presented at the meeting of the American Psychological Association, Miami, August 1970.

**Vaillant, G. E., & McArthur, C. C.** Natural history of male psychologic health: I, The adult life cycle from 18–50. *Seminars in Psychiatry,* 1972, *4,* 415–27.

**Vaillant, G. E., & Milofsky, E.** Natural history of male psychological health: IX, Empirical evidence for Erikson's model of the life cycle. *American Journal of Psychiatry,* 1980, *137*(11), 1348–59.

**Vance, E. B., & Wagner, N. N.** From ''The Sex of Orgasm'' questionnaire by Nathaniel N. Wagner and Ellen Bell Vance in *Archives of Sexual Behavior,* Volume 5, 1976. Copyright © 1976 by Plenum Publishing Company. Reprinted by permission.

**Van Maanen, J., & Schein, E. H.** Career development. In J. R. Hackman & J. L. Suttle (Eds.), *Improving life at work.* Santa Monica, Calif.: Goodyear Publishing Co., 1977.

**Viscott, D.** *The language of feelings.* New York: Arbor House, 1976. Copyright © 1976 by David Viscott, M.D. Reprinted by permission of Arbor House Publishing Company.

**von Bertalanffy, L.** General systems theory. In W.

Buckley (Ed.), *Modern systems research for the behavioral scientist.* Chicago: Aldine, 1968.

**Wadden, T. A., & Anderton, C. H.** The clinical use of hypnosis. *Psychological Bulletin,* 1982, *91*(2), 215–43.

**Waldron, H., & Routh, D. K.** The effect of the first child on the marital relationship. *Journal of Marriage and the Family,* 1981, *43*(4), 785–98.

**Wallach, M. S., Kogan, N., & Bem, D. J.** Group influence on individual risk taking. *Journal of Abnormal and Social Psychology,* 1962, *65,* 75–86.

**Wallerstein, J. S., & Kelly, J. B.** Divorce counseling. *American Journal of Orthopsychiatry,* 1977, *47*(1), 4–22.

**Wallis, C., Redman, C., & Thompson, D.** Battling an elusive invader. *Time,* Aug. 2, 1982, pp. 68–69.

**Walster, E., & Walster, G. W.** *A new look at love.* Reading, Mass.: Addison-Wesley, 1978. Reprinted from *A new look at love* by Elaine Hatfield and G. William Walster, copyright © 1978 by Elaine Hatfield and G. William Walster, by permission of Addison-Wesley Publishing Co., Reading, Massachusetts.

**Watson, D. L., & Tharp, R. G.** *Self-directed behavior: Self-modification for personal adjustment* (2nd ed.). Monterey, Calif.: Brooks/Cole, 1977.

**Watson, J. B.** *Psychology from the standpoint of a behaviorist.* Philadelphia: Lippincott, 1919.

**Watson, J. B., & Rayner, R.** Conditioned emotional reactions. *Journal of Experimental Psychology,* 1920, *3,* 1–14.

**Weingartner, H., Cohen, R. M., Murphy, D. L., Martello, J., & Gerdt, C.** Cognitive processes in depression. *Archives of General Psychiatry,* 1981, *38,* 42–47.

**Wender, P. H., Rosenthal, R., Kety, S. S., Schulsinger, S., & Welner, J.** Cross fostering: A research strategy for clarifying the role of genetic and experimental factors in the etiology of schizophrenia. *Archives of General Psychiatry,* 1974, *30,* 121–28.

**West, L. J.** Psychiatric aspects of training for honorable survival as a prisoner of war. *American Journal of Psychiatry,* 1958, *115,* 329–36.

**Westberg, G. E.** *Good grief.* Philadelphia: Fortress Press, 1962.

**Wheeler, W. R., & Csoka, L. S.** Leader behavior: Theory and study. In Associates in Military Leadership (Ed.), *A study of organizational leadership.* West Point, N.Y.: United States Military Academy, 1975.

**Whitbourne, S. K., & Weinstock, C. S.** *Adult development: The differentiation of experience.* New York: Holt, Rinehart & Winston, 1979.

**White, R. W.** Competence and the psychosexual stages of development. In M. R. Jones (Ed.), *Nebraska symposium on motivation* (Vol. 8). Lincoln: University of Nebraska Press, 1960.

**Whitman, R. D.** *Adjustment: The development and organization of human behavior.* New York: Oxford University Press, 1980.

**Whyte, W. H.** *The organization man.* New York: Simon & Schuster, 1956.

**Wilensky, H. L.** Work, careers, and social integration. *International Social Science Journal,* 1960, *12,* 543–60.

**Wilson, E. O.** *Sociobiology: The new synthesis.* Cambridge, Mass.: Harvard University Press, 1975.

**Winterbottom, M. R.** The relation of need for achievement to learning experience in independence and mastery. In J. W. Atkinson (Ed.), *Motives in fantasy, action, and society.* Princeton, N.J.: Van Nostrand Reinhold, 1958.

**Wolf, S., & Wolff, H. G.** *Human gastric functions.* New York: Oxford University Press, 1947.

**Wolfe, L.** *The Cosmo report.* New York: Arbor House, 1981.

**Wolpe, J.** *Psychotherapy by reciprocal inhibition.* Stanford, Calif.: Stanford University Press, 1958.

**Wolpe, J.** *The practice of behavior therapy.* New York: Pergamon Press, 1969.

**Wolpe, J.** Behavior therapy versus psychoanalysis. *American Psychologist,* 1981, *36*(2), 159–64.

**Woodward, W. B.** The "discovery" of social behaviorism and social learning theory, 1870–1980. *American Psychologist,* 1982, *37*(4), 396–410.

**Worchel, S., & Cooper, J.** *Understanding social psychology* (Rev. ed.). Homewood, Ill.: Dorsey, 1979.

**Wortman, C. M., Adesman, P., Herman, E., & Greenberg, R.** Self-disclosure: An attributional perspective. *Journal of Personality and Social Psychology,* 1976, *33,* 184–91.

**Wright, L.** Rethinking clinical psychology's turf. *The Clinical Psychologist,* 1982, *35*(2), 3–4.

**Wylie, E.** When a widow remarries. *Marriage and Family Living,* April 1977, *59*(4), 18–19.

**Yalom, I. D., & Lieberman, M. A.** A study of encounter group casualties. *Archives of General Psychiatry,* 1971, *25,* 16–30.

**Yarnold, P. R., & Grimm, L. G.** Time urgency among coronary-prone individuals. *Journal of Abnormal Psychology,* 1982, *91*(3), 175–77.

**Zajonc, R. B.** Social facilitation. In D. Cartwright & A. Zander (Eds.), *Group dynamics: Research and theory* (3rd ed.). New York: Harper & Row, 1968.

**Zilbergeld, B.** *Male sexuality: A guide to sexual fulfillment.* Boston: Little, Brown, 1978.

**Zimbardo, P. G.** Pathology of imprisonment. *Society,* April 1972, *9,* 4–8.

**Zubin, J., & Spring, B.** Vulnerability: A new view of schizophrenia. *Journal of Abnormal Psychology,* 1977, *86,* 103–26.

**Zuckerman, M., Albright, R., Marks, C., & Miller, G.** Stress and hallucinatory effects of perceptual isolation and confinement. *Psychological Monographs,* 1962, *76.*

**Zuckerman, M., Persky, H., Link, K., & Basu, G.** Experimental and subject factors determining responses to sensory deprivation, social isolation and confinement. *Journal of Abnormal Psychology,* 1968, *73,* 184–94.

**Zuckerman, M., & Wheeler, L.** To dispel fantasies about the fantasy-based measure of fear of success. *Psychological Bulletin,* 1975, *82,* 932–46.

# Acknowledgments

Credits for the illustrations and photographs not given on the page where they appear are listed below. Credits for quoted material will be found in the References. All photographs not credited are the property of Scott, Foresman.

**Cover**
H. Armstrong Roberts

**Part Opener, Part 1**
xxiv–1 Rod Kahaian/The Picture Cube

**Chapter 1**
2   Algimantas Kezys
7   Suzanne Szasz
8   Peter Arnold
12   Dave Repp/DPI
15   Paul Conklin
17   Mimi Forsyth/Monkmeyer
18   Sybil Shelton/Peter Arnold, Inc.

**Chapter 2**
20   Frank Siteman/The Picture Cube
25   Wide World Photos
33   left, Joel Gordon
33   right, Lisa Ebright
39   Richard Kalvar/Magnum

**Part Opener, Part 2**
48–49 Carolyn McKeone

**Chapter 3**
55   Suzanne Szasz
58   Reprinted with permission from the *Minneapolis Star and Tribune*
60   Joel Gordon

64   Suzanne Szasz
67   Paul Conklin
70   Brent Jones
78   Joanne Meldrum
80   Photograph by Arnold J. Saxe

**Chapter 4**
82   Peter Menzel/Stock, Boston, Inc.
87   Wide World Photos
91   Arnold Hinton/Nancy Palmer Photo Agency, Inc.
101   Donald Dietz/Stock, Boston, Inc.
103   left, Photograph by Ken Heyman
103   right, David S. Strickler/The Picture Cube
106   Photograph by Ken Heyman
108   Elizabeth Crews
114   Linda Bartlett/Woodfin Camp and Associates

**Chapter 5**
120   Dal Bayles
124   United Press International, Inc.
125   Dal Bayles
133   Joel Gordon
135   Norma Holt/DPI
139   Ann Hagen Griffiths/DPI
143   Phiz Mezey/DPI
147   Ann Hagen Griffiths/Omni-Photo Communications, Inc.
148   Joel Gordon

## Chapter 6

150  Jean-Claude LeJeune
153  Joel Gordon
155  Michael D. Sullivan
164  Reprinted by permission of *Science Magazine* from "Emotions are Expressed More Intensely on the Left Side of the Face"
166  Charles Harbutt/Archive
171  Jean-Claude LeJeune
174  top, Susan Lapides 1981/Design Conceptions
174  left, Joel Gordon
174  right, Joel Gordon

## Part Opener, Part 3

176–77  David Frazier

## Chapter 7

182  Burk Uzzle/Magnum
186  Suzanne Szasz
188  United Press International, Inc.
192  David E. Kennedy/Sullivan Associates
195  Paul Conklin

## Chapter 8

200  David Frazier
206  Suzanne Szasz
208  Brent Jones
209  Charles Gatewood
210  George W. Gardner/Stock, Boston, Inc.
216  Elizabeth Crews
219  Lisa Ebright

## Chapter 9

222  Jim Anderson/Woodfin Camp and Associates
225  United Press International, Inc.
229  Photograph by Ken Heyman
233  Judith D. Sedgewick/The Picture Cube
239  Joel Gordon
243  Dal Bayles
244  Erika Stone/Peter Arnold, Inc.
249  Chris Reeberg/DPI

## Chapter 10

252  Carolyn McKeone
257  Paul Conklin
259  Bill Owens/Archive
261  David S. Strickler/Monkmeyer
273  Peter Southwick/Stock, Boston, Inc.
276  Charles Gatewood
277  Joel Gordon

278  Joel Gordon
285  Courtesy of Mell Lazarus and Field Newspaper Syndicate

## Chapter 11

288  Freda Leinwald/Monkmeyer
298  Cary Wolinsky/Stock, Boston, Inc.
305  Sybil Shelton/Peter Arnold, Inc.
312  Inge Morath/Magnum
317  Reproductive Biology Research Foundation, St. Louis

## Part Opener, Part 4

322–23  Sybil Shelton/Peter Arnold, Inc.

## Chapter 12

324  Carolyn McKeone
329  Joel Gordon
334  Ellis Herwig/Stock, Boston, Inc.
337  Elizabeth Hamlin/Stock, Boston, Inc.
340  Charlotte Livingstone
342  Peter Vandermark/Stock, Boston, Inc.
347  Phyllis Graber Jensen/Stock, Boston, Inc.
348  Cary Wolinsky/Stock, Boston, Inc.
350  Owen Franken/Stock, Boston, Inc.

## Chapter 13

354  Jeff Albertson/Stock, Boston, Inc.
358  Bobbi Carrey/The Picture Cube
361  Joel Gordon
363  Jerry Howard/Positive Images
370  Joel Gordon
373  Joel Gordon
380  Barbara Pfeffer/Peter Arnold, Inc.
383  left, Martin Alder Levick/Black Star
383  right, Jean-Claude LeJeune

## Chapter 14

386  Phoebe Dunn/DPI
390  Jean-Claude LeJeune
393  Joel Gordon
399  Ken Love
404  Sybil Shelton/Peter Arnold, Inc.
408  Les Mahon/Monkmeyer
413  Charles Gatewood
417  Jerry Howard/Positive Images

## Chapter 15

420  General Electric Company
423  Mimi Forsyth/Monkmeyer

427 Carolyn McKeone
430 Elizabeth Crews
433 Photo by Shar Feldheim
435 Hazel Hankin/Stock, Boston, Inc.
439 Abigail Heyman/Archive
442 Ed Hof/The Picture Cube
444 Rick Smolan/Stock, Boston, Inc.
448 Fredrick D. Bodin/Stock, Boston, Inc.
449 Jean-Claude LeJeune/Stock, Boston, Inc.

**Chapter 16**
452 Jean-Claude LeJeune
455 Joanne Meldrum
456 Jean-Claude LeJeune

461 left, Gregg Mancuso/Stock, Boston, Inc.
461 right, Jean-Claude LeJeune
463 Joel Gordon/DPI
470 David Frazier
472 Donald Dietz/Stock, Boston, Inc.
483 Elizabeth Crews

**Epilogue**
484 Carolyn McKeone
486 Fredrick D. Bodin/Stock, Boston, Inc.
492 Peter Menzel/Stock, Boston, Inc.
494 Rick Smolan/Stock, Boston, Inc.
496 Jean-Claude LeJeune
497 Peter Southwick/Stock, Boston, Inc.

# Name Index

# Subject Index

Items printed in **boldface** type are terms which are defined in the margins. The page number of the page on which the definition appears is also printed in **boldface**.